EUROPEAN UNION LAW
VOLUME I

To Vee and the memory of Chris

European Union Law
Volume I

Law and EU Government

DAMIAN CHALMERS

Ashgate

DARTMOUTH

Aldershot • Brookfield USA • Singapore • Sydney

Published by
Dartmouth Publishing Company Limited
Ashgate Publishing Limited
Gower House
Croft Road
Aldershot
Hants GU11 3HR
England

Ashgate Publishing Company
Old Post Road
Brookfield
Vermont 05036
USA

British Library Cataloguing in Publication Data
Chalmers, Damian
European Union law
Vol. 1: Law and EU government
1.Law - European Union countries
I.Title
341.2'422

Library of Congress Catalog Card Number: 98-73151

ISBN 1 85521 680 9 (Hbk)
ISBN 1 85521 693 0 (Pbk)

Printed and bound in Great Britain by
Biddles Ltd, Guildford and King's Lynn

Contents

Chapter 1.
The Origins and Structure of the Treaty on European Union

Chapter 2.
The Institutions of the European Union

Chapter 3.
Law-Making by the European Community

Chapter 4.
The Competences of the Union

Chapter 5.
Constitutionalism and the European Communities

Chapter 6.
Member States and The Court of Justice

Chapter 7.
Enforcement of EC Law Through National Courts

Chapter 8.
Relations Between the Court of Justice and National Courts

Chapter 9.
Conditions of Legality

Chapter 10.
Judicial Control of the EC Institutions

Table of Cases

National Cases

England and Wales

France

Germany

Ireland

Northern Ireland

Spain

Table of Treaties and Legislation

Treaty on European Union

Treaty on European Union
(following ratification of the Treaty of Amsterdam)

EC Treaty

EC Treaty
(Following ratification of the Treaty of Amsterdam)

Secondary Legislation

Regulations

Directives

Decisions

Note on Treaty Article Numbering and the Treaty of Amsterdam

The EC Treaty and the Treaty on European Union are to be renumbered upon the coming into force of the Treaty of Amsterdam. For existing provisions present numbering is used with the numbering anticipated by Amsterdam italicised and placed in square brackets after it, where appropriate. Where the Treaty of Amsterdam has introduced new Treaty provisions or ones that are substantially different from existing ones, only the anticipated numbering is used. All amendments introduced by the Treaty of Amsterdam have been italicised for the purposes of clarity.

Preface

The achievements of early writers on EC law was monumental. For, without their suggesting new doctrines and probing existing ones, the monument that is EC law could not have been created. There has, however, been a symbiosis between the integration process and writing on EC law. As the social and political importance of EU law has magnified, not only were many writers from related fields attracted to the area but it became increasingly clear that formal explanations were becoming ever less satisfactory in explaining the dynamic and evolution of the subject. It can be taken almost as a sign of maturity that EU law became increasingly subject to the same critical pathologies as those to which domestic law has been subjected for the last 20 year. By the early 1990s much of the richest literature in the area has been of an interdisciplinary nature. This book would claim to be part of that tradition.

It is becoming increasingly unsatisfactory, however, to make the bald claim that one is interdisciplinary. To assert this, questions as to which other discipline is chosen, why that other discipline was chosen and the relationship between EC law and that discipline. There is, moreover, the danger with interdisciplinary work that if one squashes the law through a particular conceptual prism, one is likely to see merely the reflection of that prism. Questions are framed purely in terms of the conceptualisation used and inconvenient phenomena that do not fit the theory are marginalised or ignored.

In this regard, this book does not set out to set out a single theory or pathology for EU law. Such a view both oversimplifies and over-objectivises the process. This book does take, however, a number of starting points. The first is that the influence of EU law is felt in any arena in which there is an interest in it. The fora in which this is occurring are now so diverse that it is becoming increasingly impossible to talk of even supranational and infranational influences. How does one explain, for example, the use of Court of Justice jurisprudence by the

Argentinean Supreme Court in October 1994 in considering the legality of commercial relations between Argentina and Brazil. This increasing diversity and complexity is undoubtedly changing the nature of EU law. That said, a student text must start somewhere. The institutional arrangements in Brussels and Luxembourg still play a central part in determining the way EU law is used and developed. At the risk of creating an artificial cut-off point, this book focuses on these arrangements, pointing to other arena and influences where appropriate.

The second feature is that whilst it is right to state that law can only ever frame a question in legal terms, such a statement trivialises the richness, complexity and importance of law. A legal system both affects and is conditioned by its environment and all the influences therein - be they historical, social, political or economic. The excitement of EU law lies in the rich diversity of these influences and the interaction between them and EU law. In this respect, the sheer diversity of these sources has resulted in a central mantra of EU law being a tension between assimilative and counter-assimilative pressures. Whilst different accounts gauge this in different manners, a feature of all the best writing in the field is, in the author's view, a consideration of this tension.

The central aim of this book is not to give a comprehensive account of EU law or these influences, but to convey to students the intellectual excitement and diversity of EU law. If it begins to do that, in the author's terms at least, it will have succeeded. As any writer on EU law will tell you, writing a book on EU law is attempting to hit a moving target. Publication of this book was initially postponed to take account of the Treaty of Amsterdam. It was written to take account both of the eventuality that the Treaty of Amsterdam may be ratified and the eventuality that it may not. That said, it states the law as of 15 October 1997.

There are a number of debts that I must also acknowledge in writing this book. It owes much to the support of Professor Trevor Hartley and of Professor Carol Harlow. It also owes much to the excellent research assistance of Anne Santos, Liz Start,Kartik Varma, Stefan Weiser, Stuart Woodley and, particularly, Stuart Brittenden.

There are three people without whom this book could not have been written, however. The first is Dr Erika Szyszczak, my co-author on the second Volume, who has been a source of constant support and advice during my time at the London School of Economics and Political Science. The second is Rhian Whitehead. Her administrative efficiency and attention to detail has been amazing. I owe a bigger debt to her, however, for her great sense of humour and for just keeping me going (and putting up with me!) during this long process. The biggest debt I owe, however, is to Flàvia Neves Martins. Academia can be a self-indulgent and self-obsessive profession. Research is probably the most self-indulgent and self-obsessive part of it. She has not only put up with all this but has greatly enriched my life during the writing of this book.

Acknowledgements

The author and publishers wish to thank the following for permission to use copyright material.

American Political Science Association for the extract: George Tsebelis (1994), 'The Power of the European Parliament as a Conditional Agenda Setter', *American Political Science Review,* **88**, pp. 128-131.

Blackwell Publishers for the extracts: D. Obradovic (1996), 'Policy Legitimacy and the European Union', *Journal of Common Market Studies,* **34**, pp. 191, 208-15; M. Shapiro (1996), 'Codification of Administrative Law: The US and the union', *European Law Journal,* **2**, pp. 26, 43; J. Lodge (1994), 'Transparency and Democratic Legitimacy', *Journal of Common Market Studies,* **32**, pp. 343, 350-51; J. Habermas (1995), 'Comment on the Paper by Dieter Grimm: "Does Europe Need a Constitution?"', *European Law Journal,* **1**, pp. 303, 305-307; D. Chalmers (1997), 'Judicial Preferences and the Community Legal Order', *Modern Law Review,* **60**, pp. 164, 170, 176-77; N. Mccormick (1995), 'The Maastricht Treaty Sovereignty Now', *European Law Journal,* **1**, pp. 259, 264-65; G. De Bùrca (1992), 'Giving Effect To European Community Directives', *Modern Law Review,* 55, pp. 215, 230-31; C. Harlow (1996), 'Francovich and the Problem of the Dishonest State', *European Law Journal,* **2**, pp. 199, 210-11; J. Weiler (1995), 'Does Europe Need a Constitution? Reflections on Demos, Telos and the German Maastricht Decision', *European Law Journal,* **1**, pp. 219, 225-26.

Brookings Institution for the extract: D. Cameron (1992), 'The 1992 Initiative: Causes and Consequences', in A. Sbragia (ed.), *Euro-Politics,* Brookings Institution, Washington D.C., pp. 23, 53.

Canadian Council for European Affairs for the extract: I. Ward (1993),

Community System: The Duel Character of Supranationalism', *Yearbook of European Law*, 1, pp. 267, 291-292. By permission of Oxford University Press; M. Waelbroeck (1982), 'The Emergent Doctrine of Community Pre-emption -Consent and Re-delegation', in Sandalow and Stein (eds.), *Courts and Free Markets: Perspectives in the United States and Europe: Volume II,* Clarendon, Oxford, pp. 548,551. By permission of Oxford University Press; A. Clapham (1990), 'Human Rights Policy for the European Community', *Yearbook of European Law,* 10, pp. 309, 311. By permission of Oxford University Press; T. Hartley (1994), 'The Foundations of European Community Law', 3rd Edition, Clarendon, Oxford, pp. 281. By permission of Oxford University Press; R. Cotterell (1994), 'Judicial Review and Legal Theory', in Richardson & Genn (eds.) *Administrative Law and Government Action,* Clarendon, Oxford, pp. 13,17-19. By permission of Oxford University Press; Harlow (1992), 'Towards a Theory of Access for the European Court of Justice', *Yearbook of European Law,* 12, pp.213, 247-48. By permission of Oxford University Press; R. Baldwin (1995), 'Rules and Government', *OUP*, Oxford, pp. 62-63. By permission of Oxford University Press; D. Galligan (1996)' 'Due Process and Fair Procedures', Clarendon, Oxford, pp. 29-30. By permission of Oxford University Press.

Routledge for the extracts: A. Milward (1992), 'The European Rescue of the Nation State', Routledge: London, pp. 4-5; F. Scharpf (1994)' 'Community and Autonomy: Multi-Level Policy-Making in the European Union', *Journal of European Public Policy,* 1, pp.219,225; T. Christiansen (1997), 'Tensions of European Governance: Politicised Bureaucracy and Multiple Accountability in the European Commission', *Journal of European Public Policy,* 4, pp.73, 82-83; M. Shapiro (1997), 'The Problems of Independent Agencies in the United States and in the European Union', *Journal of European Public Policy,* 4, pp.276, 281-82.

SLS Legal Publications (NJ) for the extract: R.Harmsen (1994), 'A European Union of Variable Geometry: Problems and Perspectives', *Northern Ireland Law Quarterly,* 109, pp.109, 129-31.

Sweet & Maxwell Limited for the extracts: J. Weiler (1989), 'Pride and

Prejudice - Parliament v Council', *European Law Review,* **14,** pp.334, 338-339 & 342-343; J.C. Piris (1994), 'After Maastricht, are the Community Institutions more Efficacious, More Democratic, More Transparent?', *European Law Review,* **19,** pp.449-, 462-63; Court of First Instance (1991), 'Reflections on the Future Development of the Community Judicial System', *European Law Review,* **16,** pp. 175, 176-77; J. Schwarze (1992)' 'European Administrative Law', Sweet & Maxwell: London, pp. 552-53; N. Walker (1996), 'European Constitutionalism and European Integration', *Public Law,* pp.266, 272-75.

The University of Chicago Press for the extract: N. Fligstein and I. Mara-Drita (1996), 'How to make a Market: Reflections on the Attempt to Create a Single Market in the European Union', *American Journal of Sociology,* **102,** pp. l, l 1-13.

Walter de Gruyter for the extract: European Union of Federalists: Resolutions of the Montreux Conference 31 August 1947, W. Lipges & W. Loth (eds.), *Documents* on *the History of European Integration: Volume 4* (1991, De Gruyter, Berlin), pp. 35-36.

John Wiley & Sons, Ltd for the extract: J. Steiner (1994), 'Subsidiarity Under the Maastricht Treaty', pp. 49, 51 & S. Weatherill 'Beyond Pre-emption? Shared Competence and Constitutional Change in the European Community', pp. 13, 18-19 & 31-32 in D. O'Keeffe and P. Twomey, *Legal Issues of the Maastricht Treaty,* Wiley Chancery Law: London.

Yale Law Journal for the extracts: J. Weiler (1991), 'The Transformation of Europe', *Yale Law Journal,* **l00,** pp. 2403, 2460-61, 2476-77. Reprinted by permission of The Yale Law Journal Company and Fred B. Rothman & Company from The Yale Law Journal, Vol. 100, pages 2403-2483; P. Allot (1991), 'The European Community is Not the True European Community', *Yale Law Journal,* 100, pp. 2485, 2498. Reprinted by permission of The Yale Law Journal Company and Fred B. Rothman & Company from The Yale Law Journal, Vol. 100, pages 2485-2498.

Yale University Press for the extract: G. Majone (1989), 'Evidence, Argument and Persuasion in the Policy Process', *Yale University Press,* pp. 17-18.

Abbreviations

AJCL	American Journal of Comparative Law
BYIL	British Yearbook of International Law
CAP	Common Agricultural Policy
CDE	Cahiers de Droit Européen
CFI	Court of First Instance
CFSP	Common Foreign and Security Policy
CLJ	Cambridge Law Journal
CMLR	Common Market Law Reports
CMLRev	Common Market Law Review
COREPER	Committee of Permanent Representatives
DG	Directorate General
ECB	European Central Banks
ECJ	European Court of Justice
ECHR	European Convention on Human Rights and Freedoms
ECLR	European Competition Law Review
ECSC	European Coal and Steel Community
EC	European Community
EC Bull	European Communities Bulletin
ECR	European Court Reports
EDC	European Defence Community
EEA	European Economic Area
EEC	European Economic Community
EFTA	European Free Trade Association
EIOP	European Integration Online Papers
EIPR	European Intellectual Property Review
EJIL	European Journal of International Law
ELJ	European Law Journal
ELRev	European Law Review
EMS	European Monetary System
EMU	Economic and Monetary Union

EPC	European Political Cooperation
ERM	Exchange Rate Mechanism
ERT	European Round Table of Industrialists
ESCB	European System of Central Banks
EU	European Union
EU Bull	European Union Bulletin
EuR	Europa Recht
Euratom	European Atomic Energy Community
GATT	General Agreement on Tariffs and Trade
GNP	Gross National Product
ICLQ	International and Comparative Law Quarterly
IGC	Inter-Governmental Conference
ILJ	Industrial Law Journal
JBL	Journal of Business Law
JCMS	Journal of Common Market Studies
JEL	Journal of Environmental Law
JEPP	Journal of European Public Policy
JHA	Justice and Home Affairs
LIEI	Legal Issues of European Integration
LQR	Law Quarterly Review
MLR	Modern Law Review
NATO	North Atlantic Treaty Organisation
NILQ	Northern Ireland Law Quarterly
OJ	Official Journal
OJLS	Oxford Journal of Legal Studies
PL	Public Law
QB	Queen's Bench Reports
RTDE	Revue Trimestrielle de Droit Européen
SEA	Single European Act
TEU	Treaty on European Union
WEP	West European Politics

1. The Origins and Structure of the Treaty on European Union

I. Introduction: The Early Searches for European Unity?

What is Europe? One of the earliest and probably less problematic views was that found in Greek mythology. Europa, in Greek mythology, was a Phoenician woman who was seduced by the Greek god, Zeus, to come from Lebanon to Crete.[1] A school textbook answer to the question, however, would be the more prosaic one suggested by Mikhail Gorbachev of a territorial entity which stretches from the Atlantic in the West to the Urals in the East.[2] Others have seen it in cultural terms. Milan Kundera, the Czech writer, for example, considered it in a celebrated article to be a spiritual unity rooted in Roman Christianity.[3]

Basing European identity upon territorial or cultural exclusivity is doubly problematic. It suggests a distinction between Europeans and non-Europeans which is distasteful for some,[4] and bestows upon the concept monolithic, homogenising qualities which are anathema to others.[5] Others, by contrast, therefore see European identity, as, historically, little more than a discursive strategy to legitimate the actions

---

[1]   De Rougemont, D. *The Idea of Europe* (1965, Macmillan, New York) 6-19.

[2]   Gorbachev, M. *Perestroika* (1987, Harper Collins, London) 197-198.

[3]   Kundera, M. 'The Tragedy of Central Europe' *New York Review of Books* 26 April 1984, 33.

[4]   Arendt, H. 'Dream and Nightmare. Europe and America' (1957) 60 *Commonwealth* 551; Neumann, I. & Welsh, J. 'The Other in European Self-Definition: An Addendum to the Literature on International Society' (1991) 17 *Review of International Studies* 327; Delanty, G. 'The Frontier and Identities of Exclusion in European History' (1996) 22 *History of European Ideas* 2.

[5]   Derrida, J. *The Other Heading: Reflections on Today's Europe* (1992, Bloomington, Indiana). See also Ward. I, 'In Search of a European Identity' (1994) 57 *MLR* 315.

of those invoking it. Appeals to the European idea have thus been used to bolster the Byzantine Empire, Christendom, the colonisation of the Americas, as a conservative counterweight against nationalism in the system set up by the Congress of Vienna in 1815, and as an arm in the West's fight against Soviet Communism.[6] Indeed, recent interpretations of the history of the European Union perceive it primarily as an attempt to rescue the nation-state from its own contradictions and limitations.[7] The absence of a central meaning to the European idea might suggest a hollowness and irrelevance to it. Its importance, however, lies in its very persistence and the constant referral to it. It provides, after all, much of the cultural context from which the process of integration cannot be separated.

Christiansen, T. 'Reconstructing European Space: From Territorial Politics to Multilevel Governance' 51, 58-59 in Jørgensen, K. (ed.) Reflective Approaches to European Governance (1997, Macmillan, Basingstoke)

It is important, in this context, to examine the construction of 'Europe'. This includes, but goes beyond, the debate about whether there is a 'European identity' able to compete with established national identities. At stake is also the more general discourse about 'Europe' - the way in which the region has come to be seen as a natural space for politics (even if these are adversarial).

The building-blocks for a constructivist perspective on 'Europe' are there: in literature and the arts, in general, the presence of a specifically 'European' dimension is long recognised. Yet this 'Europe' clearly is a social and political construct: there is no 'natural' boundary - indeed current attempts at constructing such a boundary to the Euro-polity are fraught with difficulty and contradiction. The acceptance of a specifically European perspective to politics in this region was, indeed is, contingent and competing with alternative visions such as 'the Atlantic' or 'the West'.

At the same time, the construction of this 'Europe' has depended on the parallel construction of an 'Other' against which a separate identity could be established. There are also diverse national interpretations of what 'Europe' actually constitutes. Indeed, the

---

[6]   See, generally, Delanty, G. *Inventing Europe: idea, identity, reality* (1995, Macmillan, Basingstoke).

[7]   Milward, A. *The European Rescue of the Nation-State* (1992, Routledge, London); Milward, A. (et al.) *The Frontiers of National Sovereignty* (1993, Routledge, London); Dunn, J. (ed.), *The Contemporary Crisis of the Nation State?* (1995, Blackwell, Oxford).

success of the European project might well depend on the distinctive to interpretation each nation can extract from the discourse on 'Europe'.

This approach indicates that the political meaning of 'Europe' has a structuring impact on the present which is, to a large extent, independent of any current rationalisation that is preoccupied with 'facts' or 'interests'. A constructivist perspective on the presence of 'Europe' is bound to show the elements of structure that are, respectively, underpinning and weakening the significance of that space.

Notwithstanding its chimeric qualities, the idea of European unity has therefore always had certain mobilising qualities. The quest for European unity can be traced back to 1306 and a French lawyer, Pierre Dubois, who in a *Treatise on the Way to Shorten Wars* suggested that, in order to prevent an outbreak of hostilities, a Council should oversee all the monarchies and cities in Europe and that a panel of judges should be established to arbitrate on any dispute.

There were two other significant proposals during the Middle Ages. The proposal of 1465 of Podebrad, the King of Bohemia, suggested a Confederation based around a Council of Kings and Princes. The second was the Grand Design of Henry IV of France. This envisaged the division of Europe into fifteen States of equal size all of whom were to send representatives to a common senate. Crucially, this senate was to have ultimate sovereign legislative authority.

All these visions were hatched to serve local interests. The proposal of Dubois envisaged a scheme which would have extended French hegemony within Europe. Podebrad was eager to secure protection against the existing Turkish threat without succumbing to Papal hegemony and the Grand Design has been seen as an attempt to counter Habsburg influence within Europe.[8] Significant independent proposals did not emerge until the end of the seventeenth century. In 1693 the English Quaker, William Penn, wrote *An Essay Towards the Present and Future Peace of Europe*. Penn suggested that a European Parliament should be established consisting of representatives of the Member States. The primary purposes of this Parliament were to

---

[8]   Heater, D. *The Idea of European Unity* (1992, Leicester University Press, Leicester) 7-38. On the origins of the idea of European unity see also De Rougemont, D. *The Meaning of Europe* (1965, Sidgwick & Jackson, Liverpool) esp. 63-85.

prevent wars breaking out between States and to promote justice. Crucially, its decisions should be binding upon States. A more far-reaching proposal was put forward by Penn's friend, John Bellers, in 1710. Bellers proposed a cantonal system based upon the Swiss model whereby Europe would be divided into 100 cantons, each of which would be required to contribute to a European army and each of which should contribute to a European Senate.

All the schemes up until this point were confederal in nature. They envisaged ultimate authority vesting with the State, with the pan-European structures acting as predominantly little more than a fetter upon the autonomy of the States. A possible exception was the Grand Design which envisaged ultimate authority being vested in the central body but, as has been said, doubts have been expressed about the motives behind the proposal. The first proposal which in any way suggested a federal Europe where the state system was replaced by a system within which there was a central body with sovereign powers was the pamphlet published by the Frenchman, Saint-Simon, in 1814 entitled *'Plan for the Reorganisation of the European Society'*. Saint-Simon took a romanticised view of the Middle Ages which he considered had been disrupted by the religious wars. He also approved of the British parliamentary model. He therefore considered that all European States should be governed by national parliaments but that a European Parliament should be created to decide on common interests. This Parliament would consist of a House of Commons peopled by representatives of local associations and a House of Lords consisting of peers appointed by a European monarch.

Saint-Simon's views enjoyed considerable attention during the first part of the nineteenth century. The *eminence grise* of Italian nationalism, Mazzini, and the Frenchmen, Proudhon and Victor Hugo all declared themselves in favour of a United Europe. Yet the nineteenth century represented the age of the nation-State and the relationship between that structure and that of a united Europe was never fully explored. The balance was only altered by the shock of the First World War. The recognition in the Wilson Plan and the 1919 Treaty of Versailles to the right to national self-determination seems at first to contradict this, emphasising as it does the centrality of the nation-State within Europe. Yet the First World War also acted as a stimulus for an increase in intellectual and non-governmental activity by those who saw European union as the only means both to prevent war breaking out again between the nation-States and as a means of responding to increased competition from the United States, Argentina and Japan. Most prominently, the Pan-European movement was set up in the 1920s by the Czech, Count Coudenhove-Kalergi.[9] This movement not only enjoyed considerable support amongst many of Europe's intellectuals and some politicians but was genuinely transnational, having 'Economic Councils' both in Berlin and in Paris. Secondly, the idea of European union received governmental support for the first time since the Industrial Revolution in the shape of the 1929 Briand Memorandum. This Memorandum, submitted by the French Foreign Minister to 26 other European States, considered the League of Nations to be too weak a body to regulate international relations, and therefore proposed a European Federal Union which would still not 'in any way affect the sovereign rights of the States which are members of such an association'. This proposal was ahead of its time, however, and received only a lukewarm response from the other States. It needed a further shock in the form of the Second World War for greater governmental interest in the idea to be aroused.

II. The Steps Towards the European Coal and Steel Community

The Second World War had a cathartic effect on existing political structures and ideologies.[10] Its aftermath left a set of circumstances which both contributed to the putting in place of the integration process which has resulted in the current Treaty of European Union and which,

---

[9] Coudenhove-Kalergi's plans for a unified Europe can be found in Coudenhove-Kalergi, N. *Pan-Europe* (1926, Knopf, New York). An excellent discussion of the evolution of the European idea during this period can be found in Pegg, C. *Evolution of the European Idea 1914-1932* (1983, University of North Carolina Press, Chapel Hill).

[10] An excellent collection of essays on this can be found in Stirk, P. & Willis, D (eds.) *Shaping Postwar Europe: European Unity and Disunity 1945-1957* (1991, Pinter, London).

arguably, have still left their mark on that process. These can be placed into four categories.

The first was that National Socialism represented a particularly virulent and hateful form of nationalism. For many it represented the bankruptcy of the nineteenth century nationalist ideal. In rejecting nationalism, European federalism derived therefore a considerable part of its strength from the former's associations with fascism. In 1941 the Italians, Spinelli and Rossi, drew up the Ventotene Manifesto, named after the island where opponents of Mussolini were imprisoned, calling for a Federal Europe.[11] Similarly, in 1944 representatives of Resistance movements from nine States set out a draft Declaration for a federal Europe. Following the end of the war European Union enjoyed an unprecedented fashionableness with a raft of organisations being set up.[12] The resolution below contains ideals which were typical of many of these organisations.

European Union of Federalists: Resolutions of the Montreux Conference, August 1947[13]

Having in mind the anxieties and hopes of our time, this Conference of the European Union of Federalists affirms that no national government is any longer capable of assuring to its people liberty, prosperity and peace...

For the first time in history, all the European federalist movements have come together in a single association to make their voice heard - the voice of Europe itself...

European federalism, which alone can provide our peoples with the prospect of salvation, is based on the following foundations:

(1)   The federal idea constitutes a dynamic principle which transforms all human activities. It brings with it not only a new political framework, but also new social, economic and cultural structures. Federalism is a synthesis, and it is made up of two elements indissolubly linked: of organic solidarity and of liberty, or, put differently, the expansion of the human personality in every sphere of daily life...

---

[11]   Weigall, D. & Stirk, P. (eds.) *The Origins and Development of the European Community* (1992, Leicester University Press, Leicester) 31-32. On the link between resistance to the Nazis and the idea of European unity see Stirk, P. *A History of European Integration since 1914* (1996, Pinter, London) 60-69.

[12]   Heater, D. supra n.7, 152.

[13]   Lipges, W. & Loth, W. (eds.) *Documents on the History of European Integration, Volume 4* (1991, De Gruyter, Berlin) 35-36.

(2)   Federalism can be born only from renunciation of all idea of a dictatorial 'New Order' imposed by one of its constituent elements, and of any ideological system ... Each of the nations, each of the elements of which Europe is composed, has its own proper function, its own irreplaceable quality. It follows that, regarded from that angle, a minority has the same human value as a majority. That is why federalism is based on respect for qualities. For example, it is concerned not only with the method of election to a Council of States, but also and above all, with the value of customs, traditions, and the way in which people order their lives ... even if a European Federation can at the beginning unite only some of the States of Europe, the European Union of Federalists will never accept as a *fait accompli* the division of Europe into two hostile blocs.

To start our efforts at unification in the West of Europe means for the West escaping the risk of becoming the victim of power politics, restoring to Europe, at any rate partially, her pride in her legitimate independence, and holding out a hand to the peoples of the East to help them to rejoin the other peoples in a free and peaceful community.

Federalists must declare firmly and without compromise that it is absolute national sovereignty that must be abated, that a part of that sovereignty must be entrusted to a federal authority assisted by all the functional bodies necessary to the accomplishment, on the federal plane, of its economic and cultural tasks, whether in whole or in part. In particular this authority must possess:

(a)   a government responsible to the peoples and groups and not to the federated states;
(b)   a Supreme Court capable of resolving possible disputes between state members of the Federation;
(c)   an armed police under its own control.

Secondly, the Second World War laid bare many of the functional limits of the nation-State. It was clear that many States could not defend their citizens and others, such as the United Kingdom, which could, were close to bankruptcy. Moreover, the increased complexity of the modern age was making it increasingly difficult for States to provide the services expected of them by their citizens.

Milward, A. *The European Rescue of the Nation-State* (1992, Routledge, London) 4-5

From this relatively simple mechanism of national governance, to which allegiance was obtained through a mixture of power, myth and the protection of property, can be seen emerging from the end of the nineteenth century a different conception of the nation-state as a more complex network of mutual political obligations of rulers and ruled. The world wars accelerated this tendency. In both, the nation state was required to take feats of organisation on a scale far greater than anything it had allegiance of its citizens to a degree which it had not previously attempted. To inflict on such huge numbers the experience of relentless war fought with murderous modern technology was not possible without an extension of the state's obligations to them, nor without the changes in the political system which that implied. Through these changes came other demands forcing the state to take a wider interest even in peace in the human condition. Few European nation-states found themselves able in the inter-war period successfully to make the transition to a new form of governance securely founded on this larger pattern of obligations.

Between 1938 and the end of 1940 most of them proved incapable of fulfilling even their oldest and primary duty, the defence of the national territory and the protection of their citizens. Of the twenty-six European nation-states in 1938, by the close of 1940 three had been annexed, ten occupied by hostile powers, one occupied against its wishes by friendly powers, and four partially occupied and divided by hostile powers. Two others had been reduced to a satellite status which would eventually result in their occupation. The only one which had extended its power and triumphantly dominated the continent offered as little hope to mankind as any political organisation which had existed.

The rescue of the nation-state from this collapse, which appeared to make the end of its long domination of European history, is the most salient aspect of Europe's post-war history. The development of the European Community, the process of European integration, was, so runs the argument of this book, a part of that post-war rescue of the European nation-state, because the new political consensus on which this rescue was built required the process of integration, the surrender of limited areas of national sovereignty to the supranation. The history of that surrender is but a small part of the post-war history of the nation-state, though it may eventually seem to have been the most significant. What is described in the detailed studies in this book is the reassertion of the nation as illuminated by the history of the construction of the European Community. Ultimately this will have to take its part in the greater history of the post-war nation-state, a history whose beginnings are only now appearing.

The third consequence of the Second World War was a more direct American involvement in European affairs.[14] The United States contributed to the administration of Germany after the war; then to the economic regeneration of Western Europe through aid granted through the Marshall Plan, and, then became one of the main proponents in the Cold War which developed subsequent to the Marshall Plan. Despite initial misgivings, American policy from 1946 onwards favoured

---

[14]   Beloff, M. *The United States and the Unity of Europe* (1963, Brookings Institution, Washington DC).

European integration. Aid under the Marshall Plan was therefore directed through a common European programme. American involvement also limited the policy options available to different States, thereby preventing any one European State establishing a hegemony over Western Europe. The United States thus thwarted French attempts in the 1940s to limit German industrial production or to prevent Germany from recovering administration of the industrial Ruhr and Saar regions. This, in itself, undoubtedly contributed to an environment within which cooperation was more likely to thrive.

Finally, the shock of the Second World War helped policy-makers rediscover their institutional imagination. As existing traditional structures were weak, the period after the war provided a window of opportunity within which not merely new structures were being proposed by thinkers and non-governmental organisations, but were being actively considered by policy-makers. As early as 1946 Churchill suggested in a speech at Zurich University that there should therefore be a Union of France and Germany which would be a starting point for an eventual wider European union.

The establishment of international and regional organisations proliferated after the war. The United Nation Charter was concluded in San Francisco in 1945. A number of more specialised organisations were set up under its umbrella. In 1946 the Bretton Woods Agreements led to the establishment of the International Monetary Fund (IMF), whose principal role is contributing to the maintenance of price stability, and the International Bank for Reconstruction and Development (World Bank) whose role was to provide financial assistance to Member States. The General Agreements on Tariff and Trade (GATT) was signed in 1947 and this provided the principal framework for the regulation of international trade until its being superseded by the signing of the World Trade Organisation (WTO) in 1993.

Within Europe the Organisation for European Economic Cooperation was established in 1948 to administer aid under the Marshall Plan and prevent trade barriers recurring within Europe. This organisation was succeeded by the Organisation for Economic Cooperation and Development (OECD), a body which exists primarily to facilitate economic cooperation among its members. In 1948 the defence organisation, NATO was set up by the Treaty of Brussels. More ambitiously the Council of Europe was set up in 1949, whose aim was to allow members to discuss all matters of common concern, and to facilitate 'a greater unity between its Members for the purpose of safeguarding the ideals and principles which are their heritage and facilitating their economic and social progress'. The intergovernmental nature of this latter body has obstructed realisation of these aims. Possibly the agreement which had the most far-reaching effects on its members, however, was the customs union set up successfully between the BENELUX States in 1948, which was transformed into an economic union in 1960.[15]

The origins of the European Communities lay in a crisis provoked by the renaissance of Germany. The Federal Republic of Germany was established in 1949. The Ruhr, which was then under the administration of the International High Commission, was due to be handed back to the Federal Republic and the Saar was subsequently to be reunified with the Republic following a plebiscite in the former. French fears of emerging German industrial might were compounded by Germany's increasing share of European steel production. There was already overproduction within Europe and German production was already about to outstrip French production. French isolation on this point meant that it was unable to take any unilateral action which could combat this. The French response was the Schuman Plan,[16] named after the French Finance Minister. Its author was, however, the French civil servant, Jean Monnet. The Plan acted as the blueprint for the European Coal and Steel Community and much of its institutional imprimatur was passed on to the subsequent EEC and EURATOM Treaties.[17]

---

[15] On regional organisations within Europe see Robertson, A. *European Institutions: cooperation, integration, unification* (1973, 3rd Edition, Chapman & Hall, London); Archer, C. *Organising Europe: The Institutions of Integration* (1994, 2nd Ed., Chapman & Hall, New York).

[16] A scholarly account of the plan is contained in Diebold, W. *The Schuman Plan: A Study in International Cooperation* (1959, OUP, Oxford).

[17] Monnet's views are contained in Monnet, J. *Mémoires* (1978, translation, Doubleday, London). A good introduction is also to be found in Holland, M. *European Integration: From Community to Union* (1993, Pinter, London) 5-21. For a biography of this extraordinary man see Duchêne, F. *Jean Monnet - The First Statesman of Interdependence* (1994, Norton, New York).

Robert Schuman, Declaration of 9 May 1950[18]

World peace cannot be safeguarded without the making of creative efforts proportionate to the dangers which threaten it.

The contribution which an organised and living Europe can bring to civilisation is indispensable to the maintenance of peaceful relations. In taking upon herself for more than 20 years the role of champion of a united Europe, France has always had as her essential aim the service of peace. A united Europe was not achieved and we had war.

Europe will not be made all at once or according to a single plan. It will be built through concrete achievements which first create a *de facto* solidarity. The coming together of the nations of Europe requires the elimination of the age-old opposition of France and Germany. Any action which must be taken in the first place must concern these two countries. With this aim in view, the French Government proposes that action be taken immediately on one limited but decisive point. It proposes that Franco-German production of coal and steel as a whole be placed under a common High Authority, within the framework of an organisation open to the participation of the other countries of Europe.

The pooling of coal and steel production should immediately provide for the setting up of common foundations for economic development as a first step in the federation of Europe, and will change the destinies of those regions which have long been devoted to the manufacture of munitions of war, of which they have been the most constant victims.

The solidarity in production thus established will make it plain that any war between France and Germany becomes not merely unthinkable, but materially impossible. The setting up of this powerful productive unit, open to all countries willing to take part and bound ultimately to provide all the member countries with the basic elements of industrial production on the same terms, will lay a true foundation for their economic unification.

There was nothing novel about the suggestion that Franco-German coal and steel production be pooled. This had already been suggested in two earlier reports.[19] There were a number of features which were, however, unusual about the plan. It was the first time the French Government had suggested a commitment with Germany, its wartime foe. Equally importantly, the overture was made to the Germans rather than the British. The reason for this was the most novel

---

[18]   European Parliament, *Selection of Texts Concerning Institutional Matters of the Community for 1950-1982* (1982, OOPEC, Luxembourg) 47.

[19]   Urwin, D. *The Community of Europe: A History of European Integration since 1945* (1995, 2nd Edition, Longman, Harlow) 44.

part of the Plan, its high degree of supranationality. A supranational body, the High Authority, would have a considerable degree of power under the Plan with the result that individual Member States would not be able to veto developments. During negotiations surrounding both the OEEC and the Council of Europe the British had already made clear their preference for intergovernmental bodies, where Member States each had a veto, and their consequent opposition to supranational organisations.

Abelshauser, W. '"Integration à la carte" The Primacy of Politics and the Economic Integration of Western Europe in the 1950s' in Martin, S. (ed.) *The Construction of Europe: Essays in Honour of Emil Noël* **(1994, Kluwer, Dordrecht) 1,3**

the concept of 'integration', specifically in connection with the practice and objectives of the supra-national European Coal and Steel Community, took on functional significance in the process of overcoming the Nation-State principle and strengthening European sovereignty. Just because the advocates and practitioners of a united Europe feared the tenacity of Nation-State thinking, they saw the opportunity, in a behaviour-theory approach, for a gradual, step-by-step approach to a sovereign European community, without major decisions of principle having been required beforehand. 'Integration' thus became, in Talcott Parsons' sense, a

> 'mode of relationship between the units of a system in virtue of which these units work together in such a way as to prevent the system's decay and loss of capacity to maintain its stability, and promote its functioning as a unity.'[20]

Both European politicians in the early days, and supporters of the functionalist theory many years later, bet on the card of the functional, in a sense subversive, federalism, which would, starting with small initial steps, ultimately reach the goal of European sovereignty. The creation of the Coal and Steel Community was accordingly followed by the drafts of further plans for sectoral integration of European agriculture, transport and energy.

This Plan formed the basis of the signing of the Treaty of Paris in 1951 which established the European Coal and Steel Community

---

20   Parsons, T. 'An Analytical Approach to the Theory of Social Stratification' (1940) 45 *American Journal of Sociology* 843.

(ECSC). This Treaty was signed by six States - the BENELUX States, Italy, France and Germany. The United Kingdom had been invited to the negotiations. Its dislike of the supranational elements and the loss of control this would entail over perceived strategic industries resulted in its refusing to take part.

Under the Treaty a highly regulated common market in coal and steel would be established which would be supervised by the High Authority, a body independent from the Member States. This body would have considerable powers to determine the conditions of production and prices within the Member States but would be supervised by a Council, which consisted of Member State representatives.

III. From the Treaty of Paris to the Treaty of Rome

During negotiations for the Treaty of Paris a further external shock hit the European States. This was the opening of the Korean War in 1950. The United States perceived there to be an increased threat from Stalin's Soviet Union and pressed for German rearmament and its entry into NATO, something which was inimical to the French. The French Defence Minister, Pléven, therefore proposed a European Defence Community which would be structured along similar lines to the steel and coal community in the Schuman Plan. There would be a European army under a European Minister of Defence which would be administered by a European Commissariat. This Plan reflected an earlier similar proposal which had been made by the German Chancellor, Adenauer. Once again Britain was invited to join, but it stated that it preferred an expansion of NATO to the establishment of a European Defence Community (EDC). Nevertheless a treaty establishing a European Defence Community was signed between the same six who had signed the ECSC in 1952. The treaty floundered, however, because of France's failure to ratify it. It became clear that the EDC would not obscure American aims. In addition, a less integrationist government under Mendès-France had assumed power and French reverses in South-East Asia had made it more wary about ceding military sovereignty. In 1954 the French National Assembly therefore refused to ratify the treaty.

The failure of the European Defence Community marked a moment at which there was considerable political fluidity. The BENELUX States were increasingly worried by the nationalist policies of the Mendès-France government in France, in particular its attempt to upgrade bilateral relations with Germany at their expense. Whilst there were undoubtedly a number of influential policy-makers in Europe who wished to see European integration proceed, notably the French civil servant, Jean Monnet, and the Belgian Foreign Minister, Henri-Paul Spaak, the method of integration proposed by Monnet, namely functional integration in a limited number of sectors, notably transport and energy, worried the Netherlands, in particular, as it threatened to restrict their efficiencies, particularly in the transport sector.

The reaction of the Netherlands to a proposal by Spaak in 1955 that there should be functional integration in the fields of transport and energy was to reactivate the 1953 Beyen Plan. The 1955 version of this Plan, named after the Dutch Foreign Minister, proposed a common market which would lead to economic union. When it had first been proposed in 1953, it had floundered due to German and Belgian differences about the degree of intervention such a market would require and French reluctance to general economic integration. A meeting of Foreign Ministers was called for Messina, Italy in 1955. The British were invited in addition to the six ECSC Member States but just sent a Board of Trade Official. Despite considerable French scepticism, a Resolution was tabled calling for an Intergovernmental Committee under the Chairmanship of Spaak to be set up to examine the establishment of a common market. As a carrot to the French it was agreed that this should be done in tandem with examining the possibility of integration in the field of atomic energy.[21] British objections to the supranational elements required for a common market entailed that they were unable to participate in the project. They were to wait eighteen years before having the opportunity to do so again.

The Spaak Report, published in 1956, laid the basis for the Treaty Establishing the European Economic Community (EEC Treaty). The Report made a pragmatic distinction between matters affecting the

---

[21]   Legend has it that Spaak had to keep the French delegation up all night to achieve this.

functioning of the common market, which would require a supranational decision-making framework and some supranational supervision of Member States' compliance with their obligations, and more general matters of budgetary, monetary and social policy which would remain within the reserved competence of the Member States. Where these policies had a significant effect on the functioning of the common market, however, Member States should endeavour to coordinate these policies.[22]

An intergovernmental conference was convened in Venice in 1956 whose object was to use the Spaak Report as the basis for negotiations for a new treaty. The result was the signing of the Treaties of Rome in 1957 between the Six - Germany, France, Italy and the BENELUX States. Doubts about difficulties in French ratification led to two treaties being signed, one establishing the European Economic Community, the other the European Atomic Energy Community (EURATOM). The treaties duly entered into force on 1 January 1958.

IV. The EEC Treaty

The central aims of the EEC Treaty, set out in Article 2 EC, were:

'by establishing a common market and progressively approximating the economic policies of Member States, to promote throughout the Community a harmonious development of economic activities, a continuous and balanced expansion, an increase in stability, an accelerated raising of the standard of living and closer relations between the States belonging to it.'[23]

---

[22] Disgracefully, it is extremely difficult to obtain copies of the Spaak Report nowadays. The best description can be found in Kapteyn, P. & Verloren Van Themaat, P. (ed. Gormley, L.) *Introduction to Law of the European Communities* (1990, Kluwer, Deventer) 13-16.

[23] Although it was formally called the EEC Treaty until the Treaty on European Union, the Treaty shall be referred to in the text from now on as the EC Treaty, the name given to it by the Treaty on European Union for purposes of cross-reference and simplicity. Similarly, Article numbers have fluctuated. The numbers given are on the basis of the Treaty in force.

Whilst it was perceived as being no more than instrumental to other objectives, the central concepts within the EC Treaty nevertheless remained the common market. Under the EC Treaty it was to be reached in three phases over a period of twelve years.[24] The description below gives a good description of what this was envisaged to contain.

Kapteyn, P. and Verloren Van Themaat, P. (ed. L. Gormley), *Introduction to Law of the European Communities* (1990, Kluwer, Deventer) 78

The concept of a common market is an essential part of countless obligations imposed by the Treaty. A market can be described as the meeting place of supply and demand; the common market as the meeting place of supply and demand from all the Member States. Because of the fundamental principle of Article 7 of the treaty, the term 'without any discrimination on grounds of nationality by the Member States or by the participants in it' has to be added to this definition. Account also has to be taken of Article 3(f) of the Treaty which requires 'the institution of a system ensuring that competition in the common market is not distorted.' The full definition of the common market thus becomes: the meeting place of supply and demand from all the Member States without any discrimination by the Member States or the participants in it on grounds of nationality or any other distortion of competition. This definition can be somewhat more readily formulated as follows: a common market is a market in which every participant within the Community in question is free to invest, produce, work, buy and sell, to supply or obtain services under conditions of competition which have not been artificially distorted wherever economic conditions are most favourable. This definition emphasises that a common market has a character analogous to that of the domestic market of a single state.

Within the EC Treaty the common market was divided into a number of different elements. The first was the customs union which required the abolition of all customs duties or charges having equivalent effect on the movement of goods between Member States and the establishment of a common external tariff (Articles 9-29 EC). The common market extended beyond the customs union to include the 'four freedoms', so that restrictions on the movements of goods, workers, services and capital were also caught by the EC Treaty (Articles 30-37 EC & 48-73 EC). A procedure was furthermore put in place for harmonising those laws, differences in which were obstructing the four freedoms, and which were thereby preventing the establishment and

---

[24]   Article 7 EC.

functioning of the common market (Article 100 EC). Thirdly, a competition policy was set up to ensure that State barriers to the movement of factors of production would not be replaced by private ones (Articles 85-89 EC). Fourthly, State intervention in the economy which was permitted in the form of State aids and public undertakings was closely regulated (Articles 90-94 EC). Fifthly, Member States' fiscal regimes on goods were regulated so that they could not discriminate against imports (Articles 95-99 EC). Sixthly, a common commercial policy was established to regulate the Community's trade relations with third States (Articles 110-116 EC). Finally, provision was made for more general cooperation in the field of economic policy in order that macroeconomics developments did not disrupt the common market (Articles 102-109 EC).

A number of other policies were established. Arguably the most famous is that of *agriculture*. The inclusion of agriculture was predominantly a response to French and Dutch demands who wished to offset the comparative advantage already being enjoyed by German industry by selling their agricultural surpluses on the German market. At the time agriculture accounted for about 20% of the European labour force and the memory of the severe deflation in the agricultural sector during the 1930s recession and the Second World War had led to the sector being subject to considerable government intervention in all European States. A separate policy was therefore required which Europeanised the system of State intervention in place (Articles 38-47 EC).

In addition, a *transport policy* was included (Articles 74-84 EC). One of the least developed of all Community policies, it required a separate heading like agriculture, because of the heavy intervention by States in their transport sectors. It was included, first, because the Dutch wished to exploit their comparative advantage in this field; secondly, because different transport policies were likely to have an extremely disruptive effect on the common market, and, finally, because it represented an attempt at the sectoral integration which had been so strongly advocated by the likes of Monnet and Spaak.

The EC Treaty also contained a limited *social policy* (Articles 117-128 EC). This owed its inclusion to the view that vastly differing social policies would affect production costs, and hence distort competition, and deter free movement of workers, who without some security, would be disinclined to look in other Member States for work.[25] Finally, an association policy was included to provide for the economic and social development of dependent or formerly dependent territories of the Member States (Articles 131-136 EC).

The most remarkable feature of the EEC Treaty, however, was the institutional arrangement set up to carry out these objectives (Articles 137-198 EC). Whilst not quite as supranational in character as the ECSC, the supranational features given to it over such a wide range of policies was striking. There were four principal institutions. The Commission, a body independent from the Member States, was responsible, *inter alia*, for proposing legislation and checking that the Member States and other institutions complied with the Treaty and any secondary legislation. The Assembly, later to develop into the European Parliament, had initially limited consultative powers, except vis-à-vis the Commission who was accountable to it, but was of considerable symbolic importance in laying the way for the possible development of a future central parliament. Member States still retained considerable control over the process through the Council, which consisted of their representatives, but, crucially, a weighted form of voting known as qualified majority voting allowed for the votes of individual Member States to be overridden in certain areas. Finally, a court, the Court of Justice was established, to check that the Treaty was complied with. Once again, crucially, matters could be brought before it not just by the Member States but also by the supranational Commission and could also be referred to it by national courts.

In light of the failure of the EDC to overcome the bedrock of national sovereignty and the limited success of the ECSC during the 1950s, it may have been principally rhetorical, but the EC Treaty was cast not as a purely 'economic project' but as a step to greater political integration. There is evidence for this not just in the comments of people such as Spaak and Hallstein, the German representative at Messina and

---

[25]   Barnard, C. 'The Economic Objectives of Article 119' 321, 322-324 in Hervey, T. & O'Keeffe, D. (eds.) *Sex Equality Law in the European Union* (1996, John Wiley, Chichester).

the first President of the Commission,[26] at the time, but in the Treaty itself, which, in the Preamble, states that the founders of the Treaty were:

> 'Determined to lay the foundations of an ever closer union among the peoples of Europe ...
>
> Resolved by thus pooling their resources to preserve and strengthen liberty, and calling upon the other peoples of Europe who share their project to join in their efforts.'

The EC Treaty did not fit in neatly with the functionalist model of integration contained within the ECSC, as it did not set up a model of sectoral integration which could then be followed in other sectors but covered the full gamut of economic affairs which touch upon the functioning of a common market. This, combined with the elite-based nature of the process which had resulted in the EEC Treaty - there was little popular clamour for a common market - led to its being initially perceived as a *neo-functionalist* form of integration.[27]

Hix, S. 'The Study of the European Community: The Challenge to Comparative Politics' (1993) 17 *West European Politics* 1, 4-5

In the pluralist tradition, the original formulation of neofunctionalism emphasises the importance of the activities and loyalties of the major societal groups, and in particular the political and economic elites. Neofunctionalist theory argues that a new European 'polity' is emerging because, 'actors in several distinct national settings are persuaded to shift their loyalties, expectations and political activities towards a new centre, whose institutions possess or demand jurisdiction of the pre-existing national states. The motor behind this process is the deterministic 'logic of spillover' whereby a given action, related to a specific goal, creates a situation in which the original goal can be assured only by taking further actions, which in turn create a further condition and a need for more, and so forth. As a result of this spillover process, neofunctionalism predicts the movement

---

[26]   Urwin, D. *The Community of Europe: A History of European Integration since 1945* (1995, 2nd Edition, Longman, Harlow) 76.

[27]   Haas, E. The Uniting of Europe: Political, Social and Economic Forces (1958, Stevens & Sons, London); Lindberg, L. *The Political Dynamics of European Economic Integration* (1963, OUP, Oxford).

from 'negative integration', the removal of barriers to trade (such as the Single Market project), to positive integration, the proactive co-ordination of common policies in order to fulfil economic and welfare objectives (such as the Structural Funds and the Social Charter).

V. The Initial Development of the European Communities

i. De Gaulle and the Luxembourg Accords

Milward has observed that the neo-functionalist school was very squarely rooted in the events of the 1950s.[28] The School has been criticised for failing to account for a number of features, namely the difference between politics and economics; the varying attachments Member States hold for their different sovereign powers and the role external forces, such as economic booms or recessions, play in shaping the differing actors' preferences.[29] Crucially, it could not explain the pace of change, namely when spillover would lead to further action. These weaknesses were to become cruelly apparent in the immediate period following the establishment of the EEC Treaty.[30] For 1958 marked not only the coming into force of the Treaty but also the establishment of Charles de Gaulle as President of France. De Gaulle was well-known for his opposition to the development of any supranational organisation and for his support for an alternative conception, a Europe of the Nation-States, which was based upon inter-governmental cooperation.

---

[28] Milward, A. *The European Rescue of the Nation-State* (1992, Routledge, London) 10-11.

[29] For a strong critique of neofunctionalism see Keohane, R. & Hoffmann, S. 'Conclusions: Community Politics and Institutional Change' in Wallace, W. (ed.) *The Dynamics of European Integration* (1990, RIIA, London).

[30] Haas therefore abandoned neofunctionalism in 1975. Haas, E. *The Obsolescence of Regional Integration Theory* (1975, University of California Press, Berkeley).

President De Gaulle on European Integration - press conference 15 May 1962[31]

Such an [supranational] entity is impossible to achieve in the absence in Europe today of a federator who has the necessary power, reputation and ability. Thus one has to fall back on a sort of hybrid arrangement under which the six states agree to submit to the decisions of a qualified majority. At the same time, although there are already six national Parliaments as well as the European Parliament and, in addition the Consultative Assembly of the Council of Europe... it would be necessary to elect over and above this, yet a further Parliament, described as European, which would lay down the law to the six states.

These are ideas that might appeal to certain minds but I entirely fail to see how they could be put into practice, even with six signatures at the foot of a document. Can we imagine France, Germany, Italy, the Netherlands, Belgium, Luxembourg being prepared on a matter of importance to them in the national or international sphere, to do something that appeared wrong to them, merely because others had ordered them to do so? Would the peoples of France, of Germany, of Italy, of the Netherlands, of Belgium or of Luxembourg ever dream of submitting to laws passed by foreign parliamentarians if such laws ran counter to their deepest convictions? Clearly not. It is impossible nowadays for a foreign majority to impose their will on reluctant nations.

As early as 1961 De Gaulle tried to subvert the supranational qualities of the EEC Treaty through the development of the Fouchet Plan. This proposed a European Political Community whose remit would cover not only economic but also political and social affairs. It would be based on inter-governmental cooperation with each State retaining a veto. This failed to get the support of the other Member States but tensions were raised further in 1963 when De Gaulle vetoed the accession of the United Kingdom who, along with Denmark, Norway and Ireland, had applied for membership in 1961. The grounds which he gave were that the British economy was too different from the European ones and the British Commonwealth links made it difficult for it to join. Undoubtedly, the fear that Britain might be a vehicle for further American influence within Europe played a part. Yet the exercise of the veto on grounds relating to narrow national interests undoubtedly jarred with the ideals set out by the founders and with the interests of some of the other Member States.

---

[31]   Weigall, D. & Stirk, P. *The Origins and Development of the European Community* (1992, Leicester University Press, Leicester) 133-134.

Matters came to a head in 1965. The Commission had made proposals in three areas - increased powers for the Assembly; a system of 'own resources' so that the Communities were financially independent and not dependent on national contributions, and a series of financial regulations which would allow the common agriculture policy to get off the ground. France favoured the last proposal but was strongly opposed to the first two, particularly the supranational elements contained in the concept of own resources. The Commission proposed a 'package deal', however, where all or none would be agreed. When delinkage proved impossible the French walked out of the Council in June 1965, refusing to take part in any more Community business.

De Gaulle came under considerable domestic criticism for walking out. Yet the Commission was also perceived as having adopted a very high-handed approach. The crisis was eventually diffused in January 1966 in Luxembourg, but in a way that would cast a shadow over the development of the Communities for the next twenty years. The Luxembourg Accords, as they came to be known, were an 'agreement to disagree'. Wherever one Member State raised 'very important interests' before a vote in the Council was taken, it was agreed that the matter would not be put to a vote. In essence, it gave every Member State a veto. Whilst this veto was developed at the behest of France, once in place, it was invoked equally freely by all the Member States.[32] Furthermore, it was used for quite minor things. Most notoriously, in 1985 Germany invoked it to prevent a 1.8% decrease in the price of colza.[33]

The Accords had the effect of suppressing many of the supranational qualities of the Communities. As unanimity was effectively required for all legislation, the legislative process was essentially paralysed. Consequently, there were secondary consequences. The Commission, aware that only proposals which had the assent of all the Member States had any prospect of becoming law, became a more passive body which was reluctant to stir up controversy. Furthermore, as it was only by negotiating with all the Member States that legislation

---

[32]   Nicholl, W. 'The Luxembourg Compromise' (1984) 23 *JCMS* 35.
[33]   Vasey, M. 'The 1985 farm price negotiations and the reform of the common agriculture policy' (1985) 22 *CMLRev* 649, 664-666.

could be passed, the Commission focused on its relations with the Council, thereby further sidelining an Assembly which already had very limited powers.[34]

The pace of integration was not merely slowed down. Its direction was also skewed. There was one institution which was not affected by the Accords and that was the Court of Justice.[35] Already in 1963 and 1964 the Court had given its two most significant judgments in *Van Gend en Loos*[36] and *Costa*[37] which held, respectively, that the Community was a sovereign legal order which gave rise to rights which could be invoked before national courts and that in cases of conflict Community law took precedence over national law. Throughout the 1960s and 1970s it continued to give a series of integrationist judgments expanding its 'constitutional' jurisprudence, developing treaty-making powers for the Community, expanding the Treaty provisions on sex equality, the economic freedoms and the competition provisions.[38] These judgments had a number of effects. By opening up new areas of Community competence, restricting possibilities for national governments, enhancing individual Community rights and introducing other actors, such as national courts more fully into the integration process, they provided new channels for the integration process to go down and thereby restructured the form the process took.

---

[34]　The culture of stagnancy and inertia is well captured in the Report of the 'Three Wise Men', EC Bulletin 11-1979, 1.5.2.

[35]　General pieces on the interaction between the Court and the Community legislature include Weiler, J. 'Community, Member States and European Integration: Is the Law Relevant?' (1982) 20 *JCMS* 35; Easson, A. 'Legal Approaches to European Integration: The Role of the Court and Legislator in the Completion of the European Internal Market' (1989) 12 *Journal of European Integration* 101; Lenaerts, K. 'Some Thoughts about the Interaction between Judges and Politicians in the European Community' (1992) 12 *YEL* 1; Wincott, D. 'Political Theory, Law and European Union' in Shaw, J. & More, G. (eds.) *New Legal Dynamics of European Union* (1995, Clarendon Press, Oxford).

[36]　Case 26/62 *Van Gend en Loos v Nederlandse Administratie der Belastingen* [1963] ECR 1, [1963] CMLR 105.

[37]　Case 6/64 *Costa v ENEL* [1964] ECR 585, [1964] CMLR 425.

[38]　On the 'activism' of the Court of Justice see pp 326-330.

A division of responsibilities had also been created within the EC Treaty between the Court and the other Community institutions. The Court was responsible for negative integration, the striking down of national barriers which obstructed the objectives of the EC Treaty. The Community legislative process was responsible for positive integration, the establishment of Community institutions and policies which would replace national ones. The activities of the Court, when juxtaposed next to the inertia of the legislature, risked the danger of an imbalance, where the Community developed an unplanned deregulatory bias under which national policies were prohibited or tightly restricted by the Court without there being any substitute Community legislation available to take their place.[39]

It has also been argued that the institutional imbalance affected not merely the pattern of regulation within the Community, but that the activities of the Court, in so far as they proceeded at a faster pace than the other Institutions, had a braking effect on the legislative process which had to be weighed against the integrative strides they made.

Weiler, J. 'The Community System: the Dual Character of Supranationalism' (1981) 1 *Yearbook of European Law* 267, 291-292

Finally, it may be that the process of approfondissement of normative supranationalism, as described above, had a negative effect on decisional supranationalism both in the Council-Commission relationship and with the Council itself. Normative supranationalism meant that the impact of Community policies and law was perceived as growing not only in scope - to cover more fields - but also in depth - so as to have a more immediate and binding legal effect from which the Member States could not escape. Thus to give one example, the politically delicate issue of supremacy was countered by an insistence of the Member States on their control of the making of this 'supreme' law and their ability to block its making. This view of the role and power of national governments was emphasised strongly by 'pro-marketeers' in the 1975 UK referendum, using it (somewhat misleadingly) as a tool against charges of the 'loss of sovereignty' which Community membership entailed. It is thus suggested that the correlation between

---

[39] The dichotomy between positive and negative integration was established in Tinbergen, J. *International Economic Integration* (1965, 2nd Ed., Elsevier, Amsterdam). The most detailed analysis of these contexts within the field of EC law is Scharpf, F. 'Negative and Positive Integration in the Political Economy of European Welfare States' in Marks, G., Scharpf, F., Schmitter, P., Streeck, W. *Governance in the European Union* (1996, Sage, London).

the approfondissement of normative supranationalism and the diminution of decisional supranationalism is not accidental but at least partly causal.

ii. Institutional Approfondissement

Notwithstanding this inertia, certain significant institutional developments did take place during this period. In 1957 three Communities existed - the European Economic Community, the European Atomic Energy Community and the European Coal and Steel Community - each with a set of institutions. The existence of these parallel sets of institutions threatened to 'balkanise' the Communities. No single set of institutions would be taken seriously. Turf wars might break out over the responsibilities of the different institutions and there would be difficulties of coordinating the activities of the different Communities.

At the signing of the Treaty of Rome a parallel Convention on Relating to Certain Institutions Common to the European Communities was therefore signed which established a single Court and a single Assembly for the three Communities. In 1960 Germany, Netherlands, the EC and EURATOM Commissions and the ECSC High Authority all declared themselves in favour of a single Council and a single Commission for the three Communities, and a Dutch proposal was made to that effect in 1961. As it involved modification of the budgetary provisions, such a proposal could only be put into effect if the Treaties were amended. The French and Luxembourgeois objected, claiming that a Merger of the Institutions was only possible if the Communities were merged, a venture which would have allowed a far more thorough review of the Institutions powers. A compromise was reached in 1963 whereby it was agreed that the Institutions would be merged pending a review of a merging of the three Communities. The latter has never happened, but in 1965 the Merger Treaty was signed which provided for a single Commission and a single Council for the three Communities.[40]

The next significant step was the establishment of the Community Budget, for if many Community policies were to function at

---

[40]   Houben, P-H. 'The Merger of the Executives of the European Communities' (1965) 3 *CMLRev* 37.

all, it was essential that there be resources in place to meet their needs. Initially, the Communities were financed by Member States' contributions, but this gave Member States a financial leverage over the Community Institutions which undermined the latter's autonomy. Under Article 201 EC the Commission was therefore required to examine the conditions under which these contributions could be replaced by the Community's own system of revenue. The Commission's initial proposals, as we have seen, led in part to the crisis which resulted in the Luxembourg Accords. The project had to wait until De Gaulle's death before it could be resurrected. At the Hague in 1969 agreement was reached on the principle of Own Resources which resulted in 1970 in the Own Resources Decision which stipulated the sources of Community revenue[41] and the First Budgetary Treaty which increased the powers of the European Parliament in respect of Community expenditure. In 1975 a Second Budgetary Treaty further increased the Parliament's powers and set up the Court of Auditors, whose duty it was to verify the collection of revenue and the expenditure of Community resources.

The third principal institutional reform during the 1970s concerned the European Parliament. In 1957 the European Parliament consisted of representatives of national parliaments, yet it was envisaged that in due course members would be directly elected. Article 138(3) EC therefore required the European Parliament to submit proposals to the Council for direct elections. This the Parliament duly did in 1961, but for many years the proposals encountered resistance in the Council. The Parliament modified its proposals in 1973 so that a uniform electoral procedure was not required for all Member States. This opened the way for agreement in the Council in 1976 for direct elections.[42] These were duly first held in 1979 and have been held at 5 year periods since.

---

[41]   Decision 70/243/EEC, OJ English Special Edition 1970 (I), 224.
[42]   Decision 76/287/EEC OJ 1976 L 278/1.

iii. European Political Cooperation and European Monetary Cooperation

The direct elections to the European Parliament and the establishment of an independent Community Budget were both required by the EEC Treaty. Beyond that, the Merger Treaty and the Budgetary Treaties increasing the Parliament's powers, whilst important, hardly constituted the significant developments in political integration that the lofty language accompanying the EEC Treaty envisaged. Other important political initiatives began in this era, however, which were to constitute the foundations upon which subsequent developments in the 1980s and 1990s were to be built. In this respect De Gaulle's death in 1968 had a liberating effect leading as it did to a spirit of renewal within the Community which culminated with The Hague Summit in 1969.[43]

Final Communiqué of the Conference of Heads of State of Government on 1 and 2 December 1969 at The Hague[44]

3. ...... Entry upon the final stage of the common market not only means confirming the irreversible nature of the work accomplished by the Communities, but also means paving the way for a united Europe capable of assuming its responsibilities in the world of tomorrow and of making a contribution commensurate with its traditions and its mission.

4. The Heads of State or Government therefore wish to reaffirm their belief in the political objectives which give the Community its meaning and purport, their determination to carry their undertaking through to the end, and their confidence in the final success of their efforts.

8. They reaffirmed their will to press forward with the further developments needed if the

---

[43]   There had been regular summits between the Heads of Government from 1961 onwards. It was agreed in Paris in 1974 that these should take place on a more formal footing. This led to the establishment of the European Council which consists of the Heads of Government and the President of the EC Commission. The Member States take it in turn to hold the Presidency. It is the job of the Presidency to facilitate agreement and mediate between the other Member States. For more details see pp 113-115.

[44]   EC Commission, *Third General Report on the Activities of the Communities* (1970, OOPEC, Luxembourg) 486.

Community is to be strengthened and its development into an economic union promoted. They are of the opinion that the integration process should result in a Community of stability and growth. To this end they agreed that within the Council, on the basis of the memorandum presented by the Commission on 12 February 1969, and in close collaboration with the Commission, a plan in stages should be worked out during 1970 with a view to the creation of an economic and monetary union.
The development of monetary co-operation should be backed up by the harmonization of economic policies.

15. They instructed the Ministers of Foreign Affairs to study the best way of achieving progress in the matter of political unification, within the context of enlargement. The Ministers are to make proposals before the end of July 1970.

The Davignon Report was produced in 1970 by the Member State Foreign Ministers in response to the request that they study the best way to achieve political unification. Their response was that the most appropriate first step was a coordination of foreign policy. Machinery was set up which allowed for regular consultation and constitutes the origins of the second pillar of the Treaty of European Union, that on a common foreign and security policy. It also marked the first attempt by the Member States to develop the integration process in other fields outside the Community machinery on a cooperative intergovernmental basis.

More substantial strides were taken in the monetary field. The Werner Committee in its Report of 1970 set the target of economic and monetary union by 1980.[45] As a first stage, between 1971 and 1973, it proposed that currencies should fluctuate around central parities. In 1972 the 'snake' was set up under which currencies were to fluctuate only by a margin of 2.25% against each other. Both the weakness of its institutional arrangements and unpropitious external circumstances led to the collapse of the snake. The snake contained no mechanism for monetary cooperation or combined financial support when a currency got into trouble nor were there any arrangements to ensure economic cooperation. Various Member States were only partially committed to

---

[45]   EC Bulletin Suppl. 11/70.

it, with the United Kingdom, Ireland, Italy and France all leaving by 1976. In addition to this, the oil crises resulted in the 1970s being a period of considerable turbulence on the world currency markets.

The snake was rendered obsolete by the European Monetary System in 1978 (EMS). The ambition of the latter was principally to curb the destabilising effects of currency movements rather to act as a predecessor for economic and monetary union. Institutionally, it was considerably more solid than the snake. The heart of the EMS was the Exchange Rate Mechanism (ERM). The ERM's operation was dependent on the establishment of a new unit of account, the European Currency Unit (ECU), which was derived from the basket of all the currencies participating in the EMS. National currencies participating in the ERM were set a rate against the ECU and thresholds were set upon the limit against which they could fluctuate against that rate. Two bands were created, a band of 2.25% for the stronger currencies and 6% for the weaker currencies. This flexibility was enhanced by provision being made for realignments where necessary. The system was crucially strengthened by provision for coordinated national central bank intervention to prevent currencies breaching the thresholds. For this purpose all the States placed 20% of their reserves into a European Fund for Monetary Cooperation. Crucially, the European Monetary System enjoyed greater political support than the snake. All EEC States participated in funding it, and all national currencies, except for the pound, participated within the ERM on its establishment in 1979. The system was to work well throughout the 1980s until the early 1990s, when turbulence once again hit the currency markets as a result of German unification.

iv. The Initial Enlargements

a. The United Kingdom, Denmark and Ireland

The United Kingdom had parted with the Six at Messina. It disliked the supranational qualities of the Community, and it feared that the common market entailed both a degree of economic integration into which it did not want to enter and the establishment of a commercial policy vis-à-vis third country goods which would be too protectionist for its own liking and would weaken its links with the Commonwealth. The United Kingdom was all too aware that the establishment of a common market with it on the outside could leave it economically isolated and on the wrong side of a discriminatory trade bloc. From 1956 onwards it therefore pushed for the establishment of a free trade area with other European States which culminated in 1960 with the setting up of the European Free Trade Area (EFTA) between itself Austria, Denmark, Norway, Sweden, Switzerland and Portugal.[46]

1961 brought about a rude awakening. The States within the European Community were experiencing faster economic growth rates than itself and its failure to prevent South Africa's expulsion from the Commonwealth following the Sharpeville massacres brought home to the Foreign Office, at least, Britain's relative decline on the international stage. The United Kingdom therefore made an astonishing *volte-face* and applied alongside Denmark and Ireland for entry to the EEC. The reasons for the latter two States' entry bids are interesting. Politically, European organisations allowed Ireland the opportunity to end its post-war international isolation.[47] Economically, agricultural exports to the United Kingdom played an important part in the Irish economy. Tied in this way to the British economy the Irish needed to follow the British lead. The Danes, by contrast, like the British were sceptical of the Community's supranational qualities. In the wake of the Nordic Council's failure to develop and in the light of the fact that half their exports went to Germany and Britain, there was once again an economic need for their to follow the United Kingdom's lead.[48]

In 1963 the French President, De Gaulle, vetoed the British entry. He did so on the grounds that the United Kingdom was economically out of step with the Six. Its industrial sector was bigger than the Community Member States and he also considered its ties to the

---

[46]   On this see Camps, M. *Britain and the European Community 1955-1963* (1964, OUP, Oxford).

[47]   In the 1950's Ireland was neither a member of the United Nations nor the Commonwealth.

[48]   De Vree, J. & Janssen, M. *The Ordeal of Unity: The Politics of European Integration 1945-1985* (1985, Prime Press, The Hague) 221-213 & 232-234.

Commonwealth to preclude entry. Four years later, in 1967, the three States plus Norway made a second application. The British application was once again vetoed by De Gaulle. This veto left France increasingly isolated and French policy changed in 1969 with the resignation of De Gaulle. The Six agreed in The Hague to open negotiations with the applicants with a view to membership for the latter. The United Kingdom, Denmark and Ireland formally became members on 1 January 1973.[49] Following a referendum, where 53% voted against membership, Norway, however, did not accede to the Community.

b. Greece

Relations between Greece and the Community went back to 1962, when an Association Agreement was signed between the two forming a customs union. Relations were frozen, however, during the period of dictatorship in Greece between 1967-74. Following the advent of democracy Greece applied for membership in 1975. Accession was attractive for both parties. For the Greeks accession was not only economically attractive but symbolised modernisation and a democratic stabilisation. For the Member States Greece was important geopolitically during the Cold War because of its strategic location in the Aegean. Membership was therefore seen as tieing Greece more firmly to the West. The Greek Act of Accession was thus completed in 1979 with Greece becoming a member in 1981.

c. Spain and Portugal

Like Greece, Spain and Portugal emerged from dictatorships and isolationism in the mid 1970s. They made applications to join the Communities only two years after Greece in 1977. Yet accession was

---

[49] A very good account of the United Kingdom's troubled relations with the Community is contained in George, S. *An Awkward Partner: Britain in the European Community* (1994, 2nd Edition, Oxford, OUP).

more problematic. Whilst both saw the Community as a fulcrum through which to achieve economic modernisation and end their relative international isolation, the size of the agricultural sector in Spain resulted in initial French scepticism about entry because of the negative effects this was likely to have on the French agricultural sector. It was therefore only in 1985 that an Act of Accession was signed with Spain and Portugal becoming members in 1986.

VI. The Relance Européen and the Run-Up to the Single European Act

1980 marked the end of a period of failed initiatives during the 1960s and 1970s to regenerate the European Communities. Following the Summit in The Hague in 1969, the Paris Summit in 1972 called for European Union. Like The Hague Summit it had only limited results.[50] In 1975 the Tindemans Report, named after the then Belgian Prime Minister, was drafted to advise on the state of the Community Institutions and on European Union produced no policy response from the Member States.[51] In 1978 the French President, Giscard d'Estaing, proposed that a Committee examine the institutional malaise within the Communities. The Report of the 'Three Wise Men' was duly published, but, once again no action was taken.[52]

By the beginning of the 1980s circumstances had developed so that both the external environment and the internal institutional balance had changed.

Externally, the recession prompted by the oil crisis of 1978 forced national governments to confront the reality of their relative economic decline. Japan had emerged as the preeminent economic force within the world economy. Despite the world recession the United States economy continued to lose less jobs than the European one.

---

[50] It is credited with providing the impetus for the First Community Action Plans in the field of the environment and social policy.

[51] EC Bulletin Supplt. 1/76.

[52] *Report on European Institutions presented by the Committee of the Three to the European Council*, EC Bulletin Supplt. 1-3/78.

Moreover, the raising of interest rates by the United States in 1980 which provoked a double dip recession and its increased defence expenditure, which many saw as a covert form of industrial policy for high tech industries, increased the perception among European governments that the United States was a far from dependable economic ally.

These circumstances prompted the 1981 Genscher-Colombo initiative, named after the German and Italian Foreign Ministers. This saw a 'relance' of the integration process as a way of combatting this decline and set out a draft European 'act' increasing Community competences. These plans met with the opposition of the French Socialist Government who saw them as being too market-led. Nevertheless, a Solemn Declaration on European Union was adopted by the Heads of Government in 1983 which, whilst proposing little concrete reforms, declared that there should be a 'renewed impetus towards the development of Community policies on a broad front', one of which was completion of the internal market, in particular the removal of obstacles to the free movement of goods, services and capital.[53] 1983 also marked the collapse of the Keynesian economic policies being adopted by France. This *volte-face* resulted in the adoption of similar market-orientated policies by all the major economic powers within the EEC and transformed France from being the economic outsider within the Community to being in a position, where as holder of the Presidency in 1984, it could push forward the question of the pace of integration.[54]

During this time a number of other significant developments took place. The first was the mobilisation of major industrialists through organisations such as the European Round Table (ERT) and UNICE into lobbying aggressively across Europe for completion of the common market as a means of promoting European competitiveness.[55] Since the

---

[53]   Solemn Declaration on European Union, EC Bulletin 6-1983, 3.1.6. For critical comment see Weiler, J. 'The Genscher-Colombo Draft European Act: the politics of indecision' (1983) 6 *Journal of European Integration* 129.

[54]   Moravscik, A. 'Negotiating the Single European Act' (1991) 45 *International Organisation* 19, 29-31.

[55]   Sandholtz, W. & Zysman, J. '1992: Recasting the European Bargain' (1989) 42 *World Politics* 95, 116; Cowles, M. 'Setting the Agenda for a New Europe: The ERT and EC 1992' (1995) 33 *JCMS* 527.

1970s transnational pressure groups had begun to locate themselves in Brussels. The number of these groups expanded in the early 1980s suggesting, as two commentators put it, that in addition to organisations such as UNICE and ERT 'there was an organised constituency that was mobilised to support the [single market programme]'.[56] The second was that direct elections had produced a more aggressive European Parliament. Under the chairmanship of Alfiero Spinelli it produced a draft Treaty on European Union which proposed a fully federal Europe with common foreign, macroeconomic and trade policies and a developed system of central institutions.[57] This was presented not to the national governments but to national parliaments. When six of these parliaments expressed favourable opinions with only the Danish Folketing commenting negatively on the proposal, the process threatened to run away from the national governments.

Faced with these pressures, and through astute manoeuvring by the French President, Mitterrand,[58] the Heads of Government agreed at Fontainebleau in 1984 to set up two Committees. One, under the chairmanship of the Irish Senator, John Dooge, would examine the question of institutional reform. The other, the Adoninno Committee, would examine the question of how to develop a 'People's Europe'.[59]

Important as these developments were, however, they were fragmented and uncoordinated. There was a danger that unless harnessed to some overriding objective, these forces would remain peripheral and be held in check by counter integrative pressures. The final piece in the jigsaw came with the appointment of a new Commission in late 1984, headed by the charismatic, former French Finance Minister, Jacques Delors. Delors, in lobbying for the post with

[56] Fligstein, N. & McNichol, J. *The Institutional Terrain of the European Union* (1997, Jean Monnet Harvard Working Paper 97/3, Cambridge, MA) 27. See also Fligstein, N. & Brantley, P. 'The Single Market Program and the interests of business' in Eichengreen, B. & Freiden, J. (eds.) *Politics and Institutions in an Integrated Europe* (1995, Springer, Berlin).

[57] OJ 1984 C 77/33. For comment see Bieber, R., Jacqué, J-P. & Weiler, J. *An Ever Closer Union: a critical analysis of the draft Treaty establishing the European Union* (1985, OOPEC, Luxembourg).

[58] Urwin, D. supra n.19, 224-226.

[59] EC Bulletin Supplt. 7/85.

industry and national governments, had already seized upon the goal of market unity as the principal task of the new Commission to be achieved by the end of 1992. In keeping with the spirit of regeneration, this was no longer talked of as completion of the common market but as completion of the internal market.[60]

Fligstein, N. & Mara-Drita, I. 'How to Make a Market: Reflections on the Attempt to Create a Single Market in the European Union (1996) 102 *American Journal of Sociology* **1, 11-13**

Where did the plan for the [Single Market Programme] SMP come from? It is here that the European Commission played a pivotal role as a collective institutional entrepreneur. The EU had originally been founded to create a common market. The biggest problem of this idea was to define what a single market meant. The SMP initiative began as a modest project proposed by Karl Heinz Narjes, one of the European Commissioners (Directorate General III-Internal Market) in 1981. He viewed a single market as one where there were no barriers to the exchange of goods, services, and labour. His first proposal was relatively modest: he wanted to remove customs booths across Europe, level value-added taxes, and expedite the movement of goods.

This project expanded to include 30 directives that reflected his attempt to broaden the appeal of the proposal and bring other groups along. The European Parliament went on record as favouring the Narjes proposal in the fall of 1982. At the Copenhagen meeting of the European Council in December 1982, Narjes proposed to place the directives on a 'fast track' and consider them as part of a bigger project. This proposal met opposition from the French government.

In spite of this, the initiative began to attract attention from business groups and other organisations within the EU. They resembled an elite social movement with representation of various groups joining the bandwagon for the single market initiative. By 1984, the European Council had agreed in principle to complete the single market. The 'completion of the single market' functioned as a cultural frame in the sense that its content was left unspecified and actors could read anything into it. Only 15 of the 30 original directives had been passed. Narjes began working on a plan that was even more ambitious. He wanted to include 150 directives that would aim to have the single market completed by 1987. This plan was a dress rehearsal for what would ultimately become the SMP.

In 1984, the SMP seemed to be a plan for institutional change that many of the states found attractive precisely because it was an overarching idea that contained few specifics and could be read as broadly consistent with everyone's interest. It had garnered

---

[60]   The use of this term can be traced back to the Solemn Declaration on European Union.

support from the European Commission, European Parliament, and important business groups around Europe. It was sold as one solution to the problem of Europe's lack of competitiveness. It was a deregulatory project that appealed to supporters of Thatcherite and Reaganite economics. Businessmen liked the idea of removing rules hindering trade. States liked the idea that no supranational agency would be created to enforce new rules. It was also an initiative that did not cost any money. From the point of view of the European Commission and European Parliament, it was a way to renew discussions over the future of the EU. In sum, the idea of completing the single market was provocative and its virtue was self-evident.

The SMP was a project on the political agenda of the EU. But, the states had to agree to its provisions. Jacques Delors was the finance minister of France when he was asked to consider being the president of the European Commission in 1984. He took the job only on the condition that a large-scale project be undertaken to reinvigorate the EU. He offered the heads of states three choices: institutional reform, monetary union, or the single market. His preferred project was monetary union. The single market was the only choice that was agreeable.

The SMP was an ill-formed project at this moment. The details were forthcoming in a document prepared by Narjes's successor, a British commissioner named Lord Cockfield. His plan called for 279 directives to be passed by 1992. The white paper that outlined the SMP was a shrewd document. It made arguments that completing the single market was likely to result in great efficiencies across Europe. The directives proposed by the SMP were heterogeneous. Half of them had been floating around the EU for a number of years but were opposed by one or another of the states. The proposed SMP tried to insure that the largest possible coalition could be build. The project was called the 'Completion of the Single Market - Europe 1992'.

This process shows how elements of rational choice and cultural frame models inform the SMP. The organisations and institutions of the EU were set up to resolve the bargaining problems of the EU. The political and economic crisis of the early 1980's gave impetus to the production of new agreements. The SMP started out as a modest initiative and gathered political momentum, becoming a project that could be supported by all of the states. Proposals that states had been resisting for years became attractive when packaged into the SMP. The European Commission started the project, built up support for the project, and, once on the agenda, Jacques Delors and Lord Cockfield skilfully guided the project to completion. Part of the appeal of the project was its central slogans: 'Completion of the Single Market' and 'Europe 1992'.

The success of the 'White Paper' drawn up under the supervision of Lord Cockfield, the British Commissioner, in June 1985, lay partly in casting the measures needed merely as technical steps towards realising the greater political objective of the internal market.[61] It also lay in its listing a finite set of measures. Member States were not therefore committing themselves to an open-ended set of obligations.[62] In addition, at 279, the number of measures needed were not considered excessive. This was due to developments which had occurred within the judicial arena.[63]

Cameron, D. 'The 1992 Initiative: Causes and Consequences' in Sbragia, A. (ed.) *Euro-Politics* (1992, Brookings Institution, Washington DC) 23, 53.

The *Cassis de Dijon* case was brought by a German importer, Rewe Zentral AG, which wished to import the French liqueur into the Federal Republic. Since under German laws the liqueur has too little alcohol to qualify as a liqueur and too much to qualify as a wine, Rewe was not allowed to import it. After the German courts upheld the ruling, Rewe took the case to the European Court of Justice in 1987. It ruled in favor of Rewe, arguing that if the cassis met French standards for a liqueur, then it could be sold as a liqueur in Germany. In so ruling, the Court established the principle of mutual recognition and thereby created a simple standard for resolving trade disputes that would have far-reaching consequences in the years ahead.

The new doctrine uttered in *Cassis de Dijon* greatly facilitated the resolution of trade disputes within the Community. Whereas before the laws of separate states had to be harmonised and made identical in their effects and consequences, the new ruling simply required each state to accept as legitimate the laws of other states as long as certain health and safety concerns were satisfied. As a result, Europe for the first time had available to it a means of bypassing what would otherwise have been a nearly impossible task in the creation of a single internal market — that of harmonising the countless European national laws pertaining to goods, services, capital, and labour. Instead, via mutual recognition, Europe could simply move to the lowest common denominator among the national laws. In fact, the process of creating a single market was greatly

---

[61]   Sandholtz, W. & Zysman, J. '1992: Recasting the European Bargain' (1989) 42 *World Politics* 95, 114-115.

[62]   COM (85) 310 final.

[63]   The case referred to is Case 120/78 *Rewe-Zentral AG v Bundesmonopolverwaltung für Branntwein* [1979] ECR 649, [1979] 3 CMLR 494. There is some doubt as whether the judgment actually says what is alleged here. That is not important. What is important is that it was capable of being interpreted in such a manner by the Commission, OJ 1980 C 256/2. See Alter, K. & Meunier-Aitsahalia, S. 'Judicial Politics in the European Community: European Integration and the Pathbreaking Cassis de Dijon Decision' (1994) 26 *Comparative Political Studies* 535.

accelerated once the Commission could simply codify the lowest common denominators in one domain after another.

For all this, the goal of the internal market was clearly unrealisable whilst unanimity amongst the Member States was required for every single measure. The Dooge Committee had already proposed in March 1985 that the integration process would be enhanced by a return to majority voting. This was firmly opposed by Britain, Denmark and Greece. By linking majority voting to market liberalisation, a goal supported by Britain, the Commission helped soften that government's opposition. Notwithstanding this, when the Italian Government, which held the Presidency, called at the meeting of the Heads of State in Milan in June 1985 for a conference to be held to amend the Treaties, the British, Danes and Greeks all voted against. As, under Article 236 EC, a majority vote was all that was required, the conference was convened. Notwithstanding their opposition all three States who had voted against the conference attended. The result was the signing of the Single European Act in 1986.

VII. The Single European Act

The principal achievements of the Single European Act were fivefold. The first was the development of the internal market.

Article 7a [14] EC. The Community shall adopt measures with the aim of progressively establishing the internal market over a period expiring on 31 December 1992, in accordance with the provisions of this Article and of Articles 8b [19], 8c [20], 28 [26], 57(2) [47(2)], 59 [49], 70(1), 84 [80], 99 [93], 100a [95] and 100b and without prejudice to the other provisions of this Treaty.

The internal market shall comprise an area without internal frontiers in which the free movement of goods, persons, services and capital is ensured in accordance with the provisions of this Treaty.

Tied to the internal market was the second achievement, that of institutional reform. Whereas legislation for the old common market required the consent of all the Member States in the Council,[64] a new legislative procedure, the cooperation procedure, was introduced for the internal market which provided for qualified majority voting in the Council and increased powers for the European Parliament.[65]

Article 100a [95] EC. 1. By way of derogation from Article 100 [94] and save where otherwise provided in this treaty, the following provisions shall apply for the achievement of the objectives set out in Article 7a [14]. The Council shall, acting in accordance with the procedure referred to in Article 189b [251] and after consulting the Economic and Social Committee, adopt the measures for the approximation of the provisions laid down by law, regulation or administrative action in Member States which have as their object the establishment and functioning of the internal market.

2. Paragraph 1 shall not apply to fiscal provisions, to those relating to the free movement of persons nor to those relating to the rights and interests of employed persons.

These two achievements appeared limited for a number of reasons. The internal market, notwithstanding its timetable, looked a less ambitious project than the common market. In particular, it was unclear whether it extended to policies clearly caught by the common market such as competition policy, commercial policy, non-discrimination and economic policy.[66] In addition, the new voting procedure did not apply to core areas such as taxation and freedom of persons. Moreover, in purely logical terms, it was difficult to see how amending the Treaties could affect the Luxembourg Accords as the latter had been concluded outside the Treaty framework. This was especially so, as the United Kingdom, Greece and Denmark insisted upon a Declaration being appended to the Single European Act claiming that nothing within it affected Member States' rights to invoke the Accords.

The third development introduced by the Single European Act also promised to be little more than legal fluff. This was the extension of *express* Community competence to the fields of health and safety at work; economic and social cohesion; research and development and environmental protection. Yet policies in all these areas had already been

---

64   Article 100 [94]EC.

65   This is now contained in Article 189c [252] EC.

66   Pescatore, P. 'Some Critical Remarks on the Single European Act' (1987) 24 *CMLRev* 9, 11.

adopted under the general pre-existing Treaty provisions. It was initially unclear how the 'constitutionalisation' of these policies would immediately benefit them.[67]

The fourth step provided for the laying down of foundations for greater economic and monetary integration which extended beyond the internal market with Article 102a [98] EC stating that greater economic and monetary convergence was necessary for the development of the Community. The terms of the provision were very vague, however, and seemed to do no more than provide a more solid basis for the existing EMS.

Finally, a Title was added to the Treaty on European Cooperation in the Sphere of Foreign Policy. This new Title was, however, little more than a codification of existing practice. It was therefore based almost exclusively upon intergovernmental cooperation with there being no room provided for involvement by the supranational institutions.

VIII. The Response to the Single European Act and the Road to Maastricht

The seemingly modest reforms introduced by the Single European Act resulted in its being described by some as a victory for minimalism.[68] Both the Commission and the Parliament were cool about the Act.[69] The

---

[67] Chalmers, D. 'Environmental Protection and the Single Market: An Unsustainable Development. Does the EC Treaty need a Title on the Environment?' (1995/1) *LIEI* 65.

[68] Bermann, G. 'The Single European Act: A New Constitution for the European Community?' (1989) 27 *Columbia Journal of Transnational Law* 529; Moravscik, A. 'Negotiating the Single European Act' (1991) 45 International Organisation 19.

[69] Ehlermann, C-D. 'The Internal Market Following the Single European Act' (1987) 24 *CMLRev* 361; Weiler, J. 'The Transformation of Europe' (1991) 100 *Yale Law Journal* 2403, 2454; Dehousse, R. & Majone, G. 'The Institutional Dynamics of European Integration: From the Single Act to the Maastricht Treaty' 91, 102-103 in Martin, S. (ed.) *The Construction of Europe: Essays in*

Single European Act confounded expectations, however, and brought about the most radical change in the Community's fortunes in its history. By the end of 1990 all the measures contained in the White Paper had been formally proposed by the Commission.[70] By the end of 1992, on the Commission's estimates, almost 95% of the measures had been enacted and 77% had entered into force in the Member States.[71]

The principal reason for this was that the Single European Act reflected and contributed to a change in political culture which resulted in States being less tolerant of attempts by others to invoke the Luxembourg Accords. This was reflected in the 1987 Council Decision on the 'vote to go to a vote' where it was agreed that if a simple majority of Member States voted to go to a formal vote, then a vote should be taken.[72] This was important as it struck at the heart of the Accords which had always worked upon the basis of other Member States refusing to go to a vote once the Accords had been invoked. This resulted not merely in more legislation being able to be passed because there was no national veto, but it also had a liberating effect on the institutional environment within which that legislation was developed.

Weiler, J. 'The Transformation of Europe' (1991) 100 *Yale Law Journal* 2403, 2460-2461

The sharpest impact, however, of majority voting under the SEA does not turn on these rather fine points. Earlier I explained that, although the language of the Luxembourg Accord suggested its invocation only when asserting a vital national interest, its significance rested in the fact that practically all decision-making was conducted under the shadow of the veto and resulted in general consensus politics.

Likewise, the significance of Article 100a was its impact on all Community decision-making. Probably the most significant text is not the SEA, but the consequently

---

[70] *Honour of Emile Noël* (1994, Kluwer, Dordrecht).
Twenty Fourth Report on the General Activities of the European Communities 1990 (1991, OOPEC, Luxembourg) 53. For an insight into how the Commission operated during this period see Ross, G. *Jacques Delors and European Integration* (1995, Polity Press, London).

[71] *Twenty Sixth General Report on the Activities of the European Communities 1992* (1993, OOPEC, Luxembourg) 35.

[72] Council Rules of Procedure, Article 5, OJ 1987 L 291/27. This is now found in Council Decision of 6 December 1993, OJ 1993, L 340/1, article 7.

changed rules of procedure of the Council of Ministers, which explain the rather simple mechanism for going to a majority vote. Thus, Article 100a's impact is that practically all Community decision-making is conducted under the shadow of the vote (where the Treaty provides for such vote). The Luxembourg Accord, if not eliminated completely, has been rather restricted. For example, it could not be used in the areas in which Article 100a provides the legal basis for measures. In addition, to judge from the assiduousness with which the Member States argue about legal bases, which determine whether a measure is adopted by majority or unanimity, it is rather clear that they do not feel free to invoke the Luxembourg Accord at whim. If the Accord persists at all, it depends on the assertion of a truly vital national interest, accepted as such by the other Member States, and the possibility of any Member State forcing a vote on the issue under the new rules of procedure. In other words, in accordance with the new rules, to invoke the Luxembourg Accord a Member State must persuade at least half the Member States of the 'vitality' of the national interest claimed.

Majority voting thus becomes a central feature of the Community in many of its activities. A parallel with the opposite (Luxembourg Accord veto) practice of the past exists: today, an actual vote by the majority remains the exception. Most decisions are reached by consensus. But reaching consensus under the shadow of the vote is altogether different from reaching it under the shadow of the veto. The possibility of breaking deadlocks by voting drives the negotiators to break the deadlock without actually resorting to the vote. And, as noted above, the power of the Commission as an intermediary among the negotiating members of Council has been considerably strengthened.

The success of the legislative apparatus exposed, however, the technical facade of the White Paper. As legislation was developed, questions which were hidden and which are highly divisive within any society, such as the relationship between State and market and the appropriate method to regulate public goods such as the environment became exposed and prompted divisions. This divisiveness was exacerbated by these debates frequently being cast in Member State versus Community terms.[73]

---

[73]   Dehousse, R. 'Integration v. Regulation? On the Dynamics of Regulation in the European Community' (1992) 30 *JCMS* 383; Goldstein, W. 'The EC: Capitalist or *Dirigiste* Regime?' in Cafruny & Rosenthal (eds.) *The State of the European Community. Vol 2. The Maastricht Debates and Beyond* (1993, Lynne Rieder, Boulder).

Weiler, J. 'The Transformation of Europe' (1991) 100 *Yale Law Journal* 2403, 2476-2477

... the Community political culture which developed in the 1960s and 1970s led both the principal political actors and the political classes in Europe to an habituation of all political forces to thinking of European integration as ideologically neutral in, or ideologically transcendent over, the normal debates on the left-right spectrum. It is easy to understand how this will have served the process of integration, allowing a nonpartisan consensus to emerge around its overall objectives.

1992 changes this in two ways. The first is a direct derivation from the turn to majority voting. Policies can be adopted now within the Council that run counter not simply to the perceived interests of a Member State, but more specifically to the ideology of a government in power. The debates about the European Social Charter and the shrill cries of 'Socialism through the back door,' as well as the emerging debate about Community adherence to the European Convention on Human Rights and abortion rights are harbingers of things to come. In many respects this is a healthy development, since the real change from the past is evidenced by the ability to make difficult social choices and particularly by the increased transparency of the implications of the choice. At the same time, it represents a transformation from earlier patterns with obvious dysfunctional tensions.

The second impact of 1992 on ideological neutrality is subtler. The entire program rests on two pivots: the single market plan encapsulated in the White Paper, and its operation through the new instrumentalities of the Single European Act. Endorsing the former and adopting the latter by the Community and its Member States 'and more generally by the political class in Europe' was a remarkable expression of the process of habituation alluded to above. People were successfully called to rally behind and identify with a bold new step toward a higher degree of integration. A 'single European market' is a concept which still has power to stir. But it is also a 'single European market'. It is not simply a technocratic program to remove the remaining obstacles to the free movement of all factors of production. It is at the same time a highly politicised choice of ethos, ideology, and political culture, the culture of 'the market'. It is also a philosophy, at least one version of which 'the predominant version' seeks to remove barriers to the free movement of factors of production, and to remove distortion to competition as a means to maximise utility. The above is premised on the assumption of formal equality of individuals. It is an ideology the contours of which have been the subject of intense debate within the Member States in terms of their own political choices.

Tensions arose on three fronts. The first was on the degree of regulation needed to complete the internal market. In a speech to the European Parliament in July 1988, the Commission President, Jacques Delors, observed that it could lead to 80% of Member State economic legislation being passed at Community law. The second concerned the social dimension of the Community. From 1986 the Commission tried to link the development of a Community social policy to the realisation of the internal market on the grounds that some harmonisation of social legislation was necessary for the attainment of the latter.[74] In 1988 the Commission promised to develop a draft Charter guaranteeing minimum social rights.

The third front was economic and monetary union. As early as 1987 in the Padoa-Schipoa Report the Commission indicated that due the uncertainty generated by national currency stability the gain anticipated for the single market could not be fully realised without some form of economic and monetary union.[75] Monetary union, in so far as it was perceived to contribute to monetary stability, furthermore fitted in with the anti-inflationary policies adopted by most Member States.[76] Finally, monetary union fitted in with the aspirations of those, notably President Mitterrand of France and President Kohl of Germany, who saw 1992 as being the cantilever to open the door to greater political integration leading to some form of political union. The question of economic and monetary union was therefore placed on the agenda of the Hanover Summit in June 1988. At Hanover the Heads of State asserted that 'the Single European Act confirmed objective of progressive realisation of economic and monetary union'.[77] The Delors Committee, a committee of central bank governors chaired by the Commission President, Jacques Delors, was mandated to examine the concrete steps needed to realise this goal.

All three of these goals were opposed by the British Government, in particular, which saw them variously as being too interventionist and too centralising. This opposition surfaced in a speech given by Mrs Thatcher, the British Prime Minister, at the College of

---

[74] On the attempts to create an 'Espace Social Européenne' see Szyszczak, E. & Nielsen, R. *The Social Dimension of the European Union* (1997, 3rd Edition, Handelshojskolens Forlag, Copenhagen) 29-30.

[75] Padoa-Schipoa, T. with Emerson, M. (et al.) *Efficiency, Stability and Equity: a strategy for the evolution of the economic system of the European Community* (1987, OUP, Oxford).

[76] Sandholtz, W. 'Choosing union: monetary politics and Maastricht' (1993) 47 *International Organisation* 1.

[77] EC Bulletin 6-1988 1.1.1-1.1.5.

Europe in Bruges in September 1988 where she attacked the idea of a new European super-state emerging from Brussels. Yet the British Government was increasingly isolated on both the social dimension and economic and monetary union, as well as its view that the internal market should be an end in itself.

In June 1989 the Delors Report on economic and monetary union was submitted to the Heads of State in Madrid.[78] This Report suggested a gradualist approach to monetary union which should take three stages. The first stage should consist of achievement of the internal market, liberalisation of all capital movements and all States becoming members of the Exchange Rate Mechanism. The second stage required the establishment of an independent European Central Bank, convergence of national economies and a gradual assumption of the national central bank functions by the European Central Bank. The final stage would necessitate the European Central Bank fully taking over national central bank functions and assuming a monopoly over the money supply. Faced with the opposition of all eleven other Member States and the threatened resignation of both her Chancellor of the Exchequer and Foreign Secretary, Mrs Thatcher grudgingly adopted the Report with the other Member States and it was agreed that Member States should go to the first stage on 1 July 1990.

In May 1989 the Commission proposed a Community Charter of Fundamental Social Rights. This was adopted by all of the Member States, apart from Britain, at the Strasbourg European Council in December 1989.[79] The outmanoeuvring of Mrs Thatcher was completed at Strasbourg where it was agreed that an intergovernmental conference should be held to amend the Treaties with a view to economic and monetary union.

Presidents Kohl and Mitterrand, the German and French Presidents, considered that economic and monetary union would not be sustainable without further political unification and launched an initiative to that effect in April 1990. At Dublin in June 1990 it was therefore

---

[78]   Conclusions of Madrid European Council, EC Bulletin 6-1989 1.1.11.
[79]   Conclusions of Strasbourg European Council, EC Bulletin 12-1989, 1.1.1.

agreed that a separate conference should be held on political union.[80] These two parallel intergovernmental conferences opened on 13 December 1990.[81]

IX. The Treaty on European Union

i. The Structure of the Treaty on European Union

The European Union was established by the Treaty on European Union (TEU), which was signed at Maastricht on 10 December 1991. The Treaty follows quite closely the structure of a draft prepared by the Luxembourg Presidency in June 1991. In the initial draft it was stated that the

> 'Treaty marks a new stage in the process leading gradually to a Union with a federal goal'.

Such a statement implied the eventual bringing of macroeconomic, defence, foreign policy under a single central authority and was vigorously opposed by the United Kingdom. The nature of the Union and its objectives were eventually agreed in Articles A [1] and B [2] TEU.

---

[80]   Conclusions of the Dublin European Council, EC Bulletin 6-1990, 1.11. Academic opinion is that political union was added, at least by the Member States, as an afterthought to economic and monetary union and that negotiations were not as well prepared on it as they could have been. See Corbett, R. 'The Intergovernmental Conference on Political Union' (1992) 30 *JCMS* 271; Middlemas, K. *Orchestrating Europe: The Informal Politics of European Union 1973-1995* (1995, Fontana, London) 184-204.

[81]   The most detailed analysis of the negotiations is Laursen, F. & Vanhoonacker, S. *The Intergovernmental Conference on Political Union: Institutional Reforms, New Policies and International Identity of the European Community* (1992, Martijnus Nijhoff, Dordrecht). See also Holland, M. *European Integration: From Community to Union* (1993, Pinter, London) chapter 4.

Article A TEU. By this Treaty, the High Contracting Parties establish among themselves a European Union, hereinafter called 'the Union'.

This Treaty marks a new stage in the process of creating an ever closer union among the peoples in Europe, in which decisions are taken as closely as possible to the citizen.

The Union shall be founded on the European Communities, supplemented by the policies and forms of cooperation established by this Treaty. Its task shall be to organise, in a manner demonstrating consistency and solidarity, relations between the Member States and between their peoples.

Article B TEU. The Union shall set itself the following objectives:

- to promote economic and social progress which is balanced and sustainable, in particular through the creation of an area without internal frontiers, through the strengthening of economic and social cohesion and through the establishment of economic and monetary union, ultimately including a single currency in accordance with the provision of this Treaty;

- to assert its identity on the international scene, in particular through the implementation of a common foreign and security policy including the eventual framing of a common defence policy, which might in time lead to a common defence;

- to strengthen the protection of the rights and interests of the nationals of its Member States through the introduction of a citizenship of the Union:

- to develop close cooperation on justice and home affairs ;

- to maintain in full the 'acquis communautaire' and build on it with a view to considering, through the procedure referred to in Article N(2), to what extent the policies and forms of cooperation introduced by this Treaty may need to be revised with the aim of ensuring the effectiveness of the mechanisms and the institutions of the Community.

The objectives of the Union shall be achieved as provided in this Treaty and in accordance with the conditions and the timetable set out therein while respecting the principle of subsidiarity as defined in Article 3b of the Treaty establishing the European Community.

In the discussions over the institutional structure of the Union both the Commission and the Parliament pressed for 'unicity'. The existing dichotomy between the supranational competences of the Community and European Political Cooperation should be abolished and all the competencies of the Union should be governed by a single institutional structure. It was clear that some Member States, notably the British and the French were opposed to bringing foreign policy within the EC supranational framework. In addition, a tradition of intergovernmental cooperation had developed in the field of Justice and Home Affairs (JHA) on issues such as combating international crime, terrorism and third country national immigration. The British, Irish,

Greeks and Danes were, furthermore, adamant that this was an area where the national veto should be maintained. A single institutional arrangement for all the areas that were to fall within the competence of the Union was simply not feasible.

A 'three pillar' approach was therefore proposed in the Luxembourgeois draft, and it was this that was to become the hallmark of the TEU. The Union is to be composed of three pillars, each with a different institutional balance. The first is that of the European Community; the second, that of Common Security Policy and the third, Justice and Home Affairs.[82]

The integrationist States exacted a price for this tripartite structure in two ways. It was stressed that the EC pillar was the central pillar,[83] with the other two pillars supplementing and building upon it rather than derogating from it. In addition, it was emphasised that the Union was governed by a single institutional framework.

Article C TEU. The Union shall be served by a single institutional framework which shall ensure the consistency and the continuity of the activities carried out in order to attain its objectives while respecting and building upon the 'acquis communautaire'.

The Union shall in particular ensure the consistency of its external activities as a whole in the context of its external relations, security, economic and development policies. The Council and the Commission shall be responsible for ensuring such consistency. They shall ensure the implementation of these policies, each in accordance with its respective powers.

At one level the Treaty, therefore, represented a diplomatic triumph which cleverly accommodated different governments' desires, whilst also bringing all three pillars within a unitary legal framework, so that an understanding of any of the pillars could only be had by reference

---

[82]   The idea was allegedly first suggested by a French negotiator, Pierre de Boissieu, and was constructed around the metaphor of a temple based on three pillars, Middlemas, K., supra n.78, 188.

[83]   Article M [47] TEU. This has since been reaffirmed by the Court of Justice: Joined Case C-64 & C-65/96 *Land Nordrhein-Westfalen v Uecker*; *Jacket v Land Nord-Rhein Westfalen*, Judgment of 5 June 1997.

to the TEU as a whole.[84] Yet the unwieldy nature of the Treaty resulted in its being a technocratic and obscure document with little mobilising force. There was an implicit admission of this within the Treaty itself, as the second price exacted for the structure was that the present Treaty should be but a temporary one. An intergovernmental conference was to be reconvened in 1996 with a view towards furthering the objectives set out in Articles A and B TEU.[85]

Curtin, D. 'The Constitutional Structure of the Union: A Europe of Bits and Pieces' (1993) 30 *Common Market Law Review* 17, 24-26

Insofar as they all shelter under the one 'umbrella' the three main pillars can indeed be said to form an entity as such. But it is a *notional* entity. The popular analogy which has been coined, that of the construction of a 'temple' (comprised by the three pillars), implies a degree of architectural stability and aesthetic finish which is both inaccurate and pretentious. True the 'Union' as such does have the outward shell, in part, of a Constitution - in particular its general principles at the beginning - but this is a *trompe l'oeil*. They are not even justiciable, but exist in a state of suspended animation.

The alteration to the existing structure of the 'Communities' pillar or support reveals more of a *bricoleur's* amateurism than a master brick-layer's strive for perfection and attention to detail. The three existing Communities continue to exist side-by side (Titles II, III and IV) and have not been merged into one although the 'European Economic Community' has been re-christened in a manner apt to cause confusion ('European Community' - the name traditionally used to depict the three Communities). In terms of spring-cleaning the most important of the provisions of the Merger Treaty have been incorporated into the EC Treaty, but there are nevertheless still some provisions of primary law (for example, the Act concerning the election of the European Parliament) which have been incorporated. What is particularly unhappy is the fact that the numbering of some of the fundamental Treaty Articles has changed (for example, Article 7 EEC has suddenly become Article 6 EC and Article 8a EEC became Article 7a EC) augmenting the user-unfriendliness of the whole. Untidiness and failure to sweep away the cobwebs is revealed by the survival of entirely obsolete articles in the EC Treaty as amended. The impression of carelessness is augmented by Article E which fails to refer to the Court of Auditors among the institutions despite the fact that Article 4 EC has newly conferred it with the status of a fully-fledged Community institution.

The Community-method (comprising Titles II, III and IV, respectively containing amendments to the EEC Treaty, ECSC Treaty and EURATOM) stops abruptly. The other two pillars (Titles V and VI, respectively CFSP and CJHA) are

---

[84]   v. Bogdandy, A. & Nettesheim, M. 'Ex Pluribus Unum: Fusion of the European Communities into the European Union' (1996) 2 *ELJ* 267, 279-281.

[85]   Article N.2 TEU. This provision was deleted at Amsterdam.

smaller, more specific in scope, and are, as a general rule, *not adjusted to the Community approach*. They are almost entirely inter-governmental in nature with the result that parliamentary and judicial control is extremely minimal. As a result the legal order of the Union cannot be said to be synonymous with that of the Community, even if the objectives of the Union (Article B) partially overlap with those of the Community. This is one of the reasons why the entire construction can be characterised as 'non-unitary' despite the existence of the overall tarpaulin (Titles I and VI, respectively common provisions and final provisions) and the fact that the Union 'borrows' the EC institutions, money, civil servants etc. With regard to the CJHA 'pillar' it is difficult to avoid the view, given the extent to which the system is liable to generate legal rights and duties (and their importance to individuals in terms of human rights) as well as the impact which they will have on clearly EC matters, that they should have been properly integrated into the EC system. Considerable doubts can rightly be cast as a result on the overall constitutional *coherence* of the system.

ii. Amendments to the EC Treaty

a. Extension of Community Competences

Express EC competencies were extended considerably by the TEU. Relatively uncontroversially, the EC was granted express competencies in the fields of visas for third country nationals,[86] education,[87] culture,[88] public health,[89] consumer protection,[90] the establishment of trans-European networks in transport, energy and telecommunications,[91] industrial policy[92] and development cooperation.[93] There were three further fields which evoked particular controversy, however.

---

[86]   Article 100c EC. This was repealed at Amsterdam.
[87]   Article 126 [*149*] EC .
[88]   Article 128 [*151*] EC.
[89]   Article 129 [*152*] EC.
[90]   Article 129a [*153*] EC.
[91]   Articles 129b-129d [*154-156*] EC.
[92]   Article 130 [*157*] EC.
[93]   Articles 130u-130y [*177-181*] EC. For an overview of the new competencies see Lane, R. 'New Community Competences under the Maastricht Treaty' (1993) 30 *CMLRev* 939.

The first was economic and monetary union.[94] The Treaty followed the three stage structure of the Delors Report. In line with the Madrid European Council, 1 July 1990 was taken as the beginning of the first stage. The second stage was to begin on 1 January 1994. The third stage, and economic and monetary union, is to begin on 1 January 1999.[95] In one crucial respect the Treaty regime was different from that set out in the Delors Report. The latter envisaged the gradual accretion of responsibilities by the European Central Bank during the second stage, whereas the Treaty was founded upon the principle of the indivisibility of monetary sovereignty. The result was that the European Central Bank was not to be set up until the third stage and in its place, during the second stage, a European Monetary Institute was established which had little more than coordinatory and preparatory duties.

The United Kingdom and Denmark were unwilling to give an outright commitment to the abolition of their currencies. Protocols were therefore attached to the Treaty allowing these States to notify the other Member States whether they wished to participate in the third stage.

The second area of controversy was the establishment of Union Citizenship.[96] This posed particular problems for certain governments, notably the Danes and the British, who saw this as a potential replacement, and therefore threat, to national citizenship and national identities.

The final area which proved particularly problematic was that of Social Policy. There was strong support amongst all Member States apart from Britain for an extension of the Community social policy provisions. The British Government opposed on this on the grounds that this was purely a matter of national concern and it did not fit in with that Government's views of a deregulated labour market. The compromise reached was that a Protocol on Social Policy was attached to the EC Treaty. This was signed by all Member States, and authorised all the Member States, apart from the United Kingdom, to establish an

---

[94]   Articles 102a-109m [*98-124*] EC.
[95]   It was initially envisaged that the third stage could begin earlier if certain economic targets, convergence criteria, were met by the Member States. At the Cannes Summit in 1995 it was agreed that the date for the third stage should be 1 January 1999, EU Bulletin 6-1995 I.11.
[96]   Articles 8-8e [*17-22*] EC.

Agreement on Social Policy which would bind only those Member States but would be allowed to use existing EC machinery and resources.

Yet, as in so many areas of the Maastricht Treaty, there was a *quid pro quo* for this extension of express competences. This was the development of the subsidiarity principle which regulated the exercise of EC competences. From now on, in most areas of Community competence it was only to act if the objectives of the proposed action could not be sufficiently achieved by the Member States and by reason of its scale or effects the action could be better achieved by the Community.[97]

b. Institutional Reform

The TEU also modified the institutional arrangements within the Community. The areas within which qualified majority voting took place were increased. Also increased were the European Parliament's powers. Its existing powers were expanded and it was given new powers, notably the power to block legislation in certain areas.

New bodies were also created. The most notable was the Committee of the Regions which, whilst only being given consultative powers, created a voice for the European regions within the Community policy process. Also worthy of note was the establishment of an Ombudsman whose duties were to investigate maladministration by the Community institutions.

i. The Other Two Pillars

The second pillar, Common Foreign and Security Policy, and the third, Justice and Home Affairs, were to be primarily intergovernmental in nature. The Parliament and the Commission are only loosely associated with work in these two pillars and the Court of Justice is almost totally

---

[97]   Article 3b [5] EC.

excluded from reviewing activities which fall within these pillars.[98] Their ambit and objectives are set out below.

Article J. [11] TEU. A common foreign and security policy is hereby established which shall be governed by the following provisions.

Article J.1.1. TEU. The Union and its Member States shall define and implement a common foreign and security policy, governed by the provisions of the Title and covering all areas of foreign and security policy.

2. The objectives of the common foreign and security policy shall be:

— to safeguard the common values, fundamental interests and independence of the Union;

— to strengthen the security of the Union and its Member States in all ways;

— to preserve peace and strengthen international security, in accordance with the principles of the United Nations Charter as well as the principles of the Helsinki Final Act and the objectives of the Paris Charter;

— to promote international co-operation;

— to develop and consolidate democracy and the rule of law, and respect for human rights and fundamental freedoms.

Article K. TEU. Co-operation in the fields of justice and home affairs shall be governed by the following provisions.

Article K.1. TEU. For the purposes of achieving the objectives of the Union, in particular the free movement of persons, and without prejudice to the powers of the European Community, Member States shall regard the following areas as matters of common interest:

1. asylum policy;

2. rules governing the crossing by persons of the external borders of the Member States and the exercise of controls thereon;

3. immigration policy and policy regarding nationals of third countries;

    (a) conditions of entry and movement by nationals of third countries on the territory of Member States;

    (b) conditions of residence by nationals of third countries on the territory of Member States, including family reunion and access to employment;

---

[98] Article L [46] TEU. The one exception is where the Council draws up conventions giving the Court of Justice jurisdiction over matters which fall within Justice and Home Affairs, Article K.3[2](c) [34(2)(d)] TEU.

(c)	combatting unauthorised immigration, residence and work by nationals of third countries on the territory of Member States;
4.	combatting drug addiction in so far as this is not covered by 7 to 9;
5.	combatting fraud on an international scale in so far as this is not covered by 7 to 9;
6.	judicial co-operation in civil matters;
7.	judicial co-operation in criminal matters;
8.	customs co-operation;
9.	police co-operation for the purposes of preventing and combatting terrorism, unlawful drug trafficking and other serious forms of international crime, including if necessary certain aspects of customs co-operation, in connection with the organisation of a Union-wide system for exchanging information within a European Police Office (Europol).

X. The Faltering Ratification of the Treaty on European Union

To come into force the TEU needed to be ratified by all the Member States in accordance with their constitutional arrangements. This appeared to pose little problem. For most States this required little more than parliamentary ratification. Only in Denmark and Ireland were referenda necessary.[99] As we shall see, the process proved to be far from trouble-free with the result that the Treaty did not come into force until 1 November 1993, nearly two years after its signature.

i. The Referenda and the Edinburgh European Council

The first referendum to take place was in Denmark in June 1992. A previous referendum on the Single European Act had received only narrow support. Therefore, it should not have surprised as many as it did when the Danes voted narrowly against ratification by 50.7% to

---

[99]   Strictly speaking a referendum was unnecessary in Denmark as the Treaty could have been ratified with a 5/6 majority in the Danish Parliament. A referendum was considered politically necessary, however, as a means of fostering consensus.

49.3%.[100] Despite the Irish voting conclusively in favour of ratification,[101] this shook the process to the core as the 'all or nothing' nature of the process did not allow the Treaty to enter into effect unless all Member States ratified it. To boost legitimacy for the ratification process within France, President Mitterrand decided to hold a referendum there. What had initially looked a sure thing became a very close contest with only 51% of the vote being in favour of ratification.

If the effect of the referenda were to rattle the politics of Maastricht, events on the world currency markets were to shake its economic foundations. German unification had resulted in Germany pursuing a very tight monetary policy just at the moment when many other Member States were looking for a looser policy.[102] With the Danish referendum putting the process of economic and monetary union in doubt investors increasingly sought to invest in the 'safe' German Mark. The consequence was huge currency speculation during the Autumn 1992 and the Summer of 1993 which shook the EMS to its foundations.[103] The United Kingdom sought to leave the ERM with no immediate prospect of reentry and the ERM was remodelled in such a flexible manner that it allowed for considerable currency fluctuations.[104]

The position was salvaged at the Edinburgh European Council in December 1992. The meeting had to tread a fine line. The other Member States considered the Treaty to be non-negotiable but something had to be done which allowed the Danish Government to say that the Treaty it was offering up for referendum a second time was substantially different from the initial Treaty. The route taken was a

---

[100]   Siune, K. & Svensson, P. 'The Danes and the Maastricht Treaty: The Danish EC Referendum of June 1992' (1993) 12 *Electoral Studies* 99.

[101]   69% of the vote was in favour of ratification.

[102]   Some analyses of these monetary crises therefore pin the blame on the United Kingdom and France seeking to lower interest rates in manners which risked destabilising the markets. See Cobham, D. 'Causes and Effects of the European Monetary Crises of 1992-93' (1996) 34 *JCMS* 585.

[103]   A more detailed description of the crisis can be found in Sandholtz, W. 'Money Troubles: Europe's rough road to monetary union' (1996) 3 *JEPP* 84.

[104]   All the other currencies which remained within the ERM were allowed to fluctuate by plus or minus 15% with the exception of the Dutch Guilder and the German Mark which remained in the narrow 2.25% band.

Decision of unclear legal status 'interpreting' the Treaty.[105] The principal points were:

- The Citizenship provisions of the Treaty did not take the place of national citizenship;
- Denmark gave notification that it was not taking part in the third stage of economic and monetary union;
- Nothing in the Treaty on European Union committed Denmark to membership of the Western European Union;[106]
- The Justice and Home Affairs provisions and the Citizenship provisions could only be enlarged by the Member States in accordance with their constitutional arrangements.[107]

This Decision was seen as giving the Danish Government the necessary breadth to hold a second referendum. This was duly held in May 1993 with 56% voting in favour of ratification.[108]

---

105   Howarth, D. 'The Compromise on Denmark and the Treaty on European Union: A Legal and Political Analysis' (1994) 31 *CMLRev* 465.

106   This was an intergovernmental organisation set up in 1955 which was affiliated to NATO.

107   Conclusions of the Edinburgh European Council, EC Bulletin 12 -1992, Annex 1, Part B.

108   On the referenda see Franklin, M., Marsh, M. & McLaren, L. 'Uncorking the Bottle: Popular Opposition to European Unification in the Wake of Maastricht' (1994) 32 *JCMS* 455; Franklin, M., Van der Eijk C. & Marsh, M. 'Referendum Outcomes and Trust in Government: Public Support for Europe in the Wake of Maastricht' (1995) 18 *WEP* 101; Worre, T. 'First No, Then Yes: The Danish Referendums on the Maastricht Treaty 1992 and 1993' (1995) 33 *JCMS* 235. At the time of the writing, Danish ratification of Maastricht is still not fully settled. Having held that there is a case to answer, the Danish Supreme Court is to give judgment in Autumn 1997 on whether ratification was incompatible with the Danish Constitution on the grounds that it involved a too wideranging transfer of powers to the European Union: Case 272/94 *Carlsen v Prime Minister Rasmussen*. On this see Obradovic, D. 'Repatriation of Powers in the European Community' (1997) 34 *CMLRev* 59.

ii. Difficulties in the British Parliament

In the United Kingdom treaties can be ratified by the executive but if they are to have full internal legislative effect legislation incorporating the treaty in question must be passed by Parliament. Whilst the European Communities Act 1972 incorporated the legal order of the Communities into British law, a 1986 Act stated that any Treaty amendment which increased the powers of the European Parliament would not have the force of law within the United Kingdom unless appropriate legislation had been passed by Parliament. In effect, if Britain were to be able to meet its obligations fully under the Treaty on European Union, parliamentary approval was required.

This posed a problem for the British Government. The Opposition Labour and Liberal Democrat parties opposed ratification on grounds of the United Kingdom's failure to accede the Social Protocol. Many Conservative MPs also opposed ratification but on different grounds. They considered that the Treaty constituted too great a surrender of formal sovereignty particularly in the field of economic and monetary union. Whilst having a formal majority, the Government of John Major had to approach ratification with the caution of a minority Government.

One effect of this was that a large number of amendments were proposed at the Parliamentary Committee stage which considerably slowed down the passage of the Bill. The Opposition parties also sought to make common cause with the Conservative rebels. They sought to do this by trying to ensure that the British Government could not ratify the Treaty without first re-negotiating the Social Protocol. For the Opposition parties this had the advantage that they could argue that they were seeking to have the Protocol applied to the United Kingdom. For the Conservative rebels, on the other hand, the attraction was that they considered it unlikely that the Treaty would be so renegotiated and thus thought it would be likely to fall.

The first step in this strategy was the introduction of a procedural amendment. This only allowed the Act to come into force when the House of Commons had come to a Resolution on a motion tabled by a Minister considering the question of adopting the Social

Protocol. Faced with defeat the Government was forced to accept this amendment.

On 22 July 1993 the motion, as required, was brought to the House of Commons. It was an anodyne motion which merely took note of the current position. It was nevertheless defeated by 324 votes to 316. The only way for the Government to rescue the Bill was to propose a motion of confidence in the Government's policy on the Social Protocol. If this had been defeated, the effect would have been to bring down the Government. Faced with this hardline tactic the rebels towed the line and the Bill was carried by 339 to 299 votes.[109] Following an unsuccessful court action to stop ratification, the Treaty was duly ratified.[110]

iii. Ratification and the German Constitutional Court

The drama of ratification of the Treaty had been played out in the streets and in parliaments. The final act was to be played out in the courts. Challenges to the Treaty had been received before the British, French and Spanish courts.[111] The greatest drama was to occur before the German Constitutional Court on 12 October 1993.

---

[109] Descriptions of this epic Parliamentary battle can be found in Rawlings, R. 'Legal Politics: The United Kingdom and Ratification of the Treaty on European Union' (1994) *PL* 254 & 367; Baker, D., Gamble, A. & Ludlum, S. 'The Parliamentary Siege of Maastricht: Conservative Divisions and British Ratification' (1994) 47 *Parliamentary Affairs* 37.

[110] *R v Secretary of State for Foreign and Commonwealth Affairs ex parte Rees-Mogg* [1994] QB 552.

[111] In France see the decision of the Constitutional Council in *Re Treaty on European Union* (Decision 92-308), Journel Officiel de la République Française 1992, No 5354. In Spain see the decision of the Constitutional Court in *Re Treaty on European Union* [1994] 3 CMLR 101.

Brunner & Others v The European Union [1994] 1 CMLR 57[112]

A challenge was mounted to the Treaty on European Union on the grounds that it violated the German Basic Law. The provision which the German Constitutional Court considered at most length was Article 38 of the Constitution. This provision entitled all Germans to participate in the election of deputies for the German Bundestag. The complainants argued that the Treaty violated this provision, and the democratic principle contained therein, by transferring so many powers to the European Union that the Bundestag was deprived of a substantial part of its decision-making competence. The Constitutional Court considered that the Treaty did not violate the Basic Law but placed clear constraints on the development of the integration process.

39. The European Union is, according to its understanding of itself as a union of the peoples of Europe (Article A.2. of the Union Treaty), a federation of democratic States whose objectives include a dynamic development (see e.g. Article B.1., last indent, and C(1)). If the Union carries out sovereign powers for those purposes, it is first and foremost the national peoples of the member-States who, through their national parliaments, have to provide the democratic legitimation for its so doing.

.....

43. ... What is decisive is that the democratic bases of the European Union are built-up in step with integration, and that as integration proceeds a thriving democracy is also maintained in the member-States. An excess weight of functions and powers within the responsibility of the European federation of States would effectively weaken democracy at national level, so that the parliaments of the member-States could no longer adequately provide the legitimation for the sovereign power exercised by the Union.

44. If the peoples of the individual States provide democratic legitimation through the agency of their national parliaments (as at present) limits are then set by virtue of the democratic principle to the extension of the European Communities functions and

---

[112]   The judgment of the Constitutional Court has provoked considerable controversy. Herdegen, M. 'Maastricht and the German Constitutional Court: Constitutional Restraints for an Ever Closer Union' (1994) 31 *CMLRev* 235; Everling, U. 'The Maastricht Judgment of the German Federal Constitutional Court and Its Significance for the Development of the European Union' (1994) 14 *YBEL* 1; Weiler, J. 'Does Europe Need a Constitution? Demos, Telos and the German Maastricht Decision' (1995) 1 *ELJ* 219; MacCormick, N. 'The Maastricht-Urteil: Sovereignty Now' (1995) 1 *ELJ* 259; Boom, S. 'The European Union after the Maastricht Decision: Will Germany be the "Virginia of Europe?"' (1995) 43 *American Journal of Comparative Law* 177.

powers. Each of the peoples of the individual States is the starting point for a state power relating to that people. The States need sufficiently important spheres of activity of their own in which the people of each can develop and articulate itself in a process of political will-formation which it legitimates and controls, in order thus to give legal expression to what binds the people together (to a greater or lesser degree of homogeneity) spiritually, socially and politically.

45. From all that it follows that functions and powers of substantial importance must remain for the German Bundestag.

46. ...The exercise of sovereign power through a federation of States like the European Union is based on authorisations from States which remain sovereign and which international matters generally act through their governments and control the integration process thereby. It is therefore primarily determined governmentally. If such a community power is to rest on the political will-formation which is supplied by the people of each individual State, and is to that extent democratic, that presupposes that the power is exercised by a body made up of representatives sent by the member-States governments, which in their turn are subject to democratic control. The passing of European legal regulations, too, may (without prejudice to the consequent need for a democratic control of the governments) lie with an institution composed of representatives of the member-States governments, that is to say, on an executive basis, to a greater extent than would be constitutionally acceptable at national level.

.....

49. In view of the fact that the text of an international treaty must be worked out between the parties, the same requirements cannot be set for the certainty and tightness of the rules of a treaty as are imposed in the case of an Act by the requirements of parliamentary jurisdiction. What is decisive is that Germany's membership and the rights and duties that follow there from (and especially the immediately binding legal effect within the national sphere of the Communities actions) have been defined in the Treaty so as to be predictable for the legislature and are enacted by it in the Act of Accession with sufficient certainty. That also means that subsequent important alterations to the integration programme set up in the Union Treaty and to the Union's powers of action are no longer covered by the Act of Accession to the present Treaty. Thus, if European institutions or agencies were to treat or develop the Union Treaty in a way that was no longer covered by the Treaty in the form that is the basis for the Act of Accession, the resultant legislative instruments would not be legally binding with the sphere of German sovereignty. The German state organs would be prevented for constitutional reasons from applying them in Germany. Accordingly the Federal Constitutional Court will review legal instruments within the limits of the sovereign rights conferred on them or transgress them.

XI. Towards a Wider European Union

Challenges to the European Union have come not merely from its internal environment but also from its external environment. The size of the Community doubled between 1973 and 1986. This enlargement occurred at a graduated pace which could be comfortably accommodated by existing Member States, whilst remaining broadly true to its original ideals of being an organisation which was open to any European State.

This was changed by two events. The first was the success of the Single European Act. This made the potential benefits of membership greater. It also increased the cost of non-membership. If the rhetoric of 1992 was realised, the dangers posed by exclusion from the world's largest trading bloc were very great for many other European States. The second event was the collapse of the COMECON and Communism in Eastern Europe. Overnight, it resulted in many additional States, who had previously been antagonistic to the Community, embracing the market-orientated ideals it symbolised.

The process of expansion began with those States who were, economically, most easy to accommodate - the EFTA States. Formal relations went back to 1972 and 1973 where a series of bilateral free trade agreements had been signed between the Community and these States. In 1984 the Luxembourg Declaration stated that economic cooperation should be increased between the Community and these States leading to the creation of a 'European economic space'.[113] This concept was ill-defined and negotiations stagnated until the onset of the Single European Act.

In 1989 Delors proposed that the existing bilateral relations between the Community and individual EFTA States be replaced by a single institutional arrangement. The seven EFTA States (Norway, Sweden, Finland, Iceland, Austria, Liechtenstein and Switzerland)

---

[113]   See Hurni, B. 'EFTA-EC Relations: Aftermath of the Luxembourg Declaration' (1986) 20 *JWTL* 507.

responded positively in the Oslo Declaration.[114] The result was almost three years of negotiations leading to the signing of the Treaty of Oporto in 1991, establishing the European Economic Area.[115]

Under this Treaty EFTA States were required to adopt all Community legislation in the fields of the internal market, research and development policy, social policy, education, consumer protection and environmental protection. Whilst common institutions were set up, they were not built upon any substantive form of reciprocity as their purpose was to ensure the EEA regime complied with the Community one. Whilst allowing EFTA States access to the internal market, it gave them no input in the political process which regulated that market and which, by extension now regulated them. The Agreement was only politically sustainable if perceived as a stepping stone to negotiations.

Austria, Finland and Sweden therefore applied for membership early on during the negotiations with Norway applying soon after. At Lisbon in June 1992 the Member States agreed accession negotiations should immediately follow the signing of the Treaty on European Union. Equally significantly, they looked beyond accession of the EFTA States to accession of other States, noting that any European State whose government was based on the principle of democracy could apply to accede.[116]

At Copenhagen in June 1993 the European Council agreed that membership be offered to the four.[117] Referenda were necessary in all

---

[114] On relations between the EFTA states and the Community prior to the Treaty of Oporto see Luaresen, F. 'The Community's Policy Towards EFTA: Regime Formation in the European Economic Space' (1990) 28 *JCMS* 303.

[115] Although Switzerland signed the Treaty, following a referendum, it decided not to ratify it. The most detailed analysis of the Treaty can be found in Blanchet, T., Piiponen, R. & Westman-Clément, M. *The Agreement on the European Economic Area* (1994, Clarendon Press, Oxford). Other interesting analyses include Weiss, F. 'The Oporto Agreement on the European Economic Area - A Legal Still Life' (1992) 12 *YBEL* 385; Cremona, M. 'The "Dynamic and Homogenous" EEA: Byzantine Structures and Variable Geometry' (1994) 19 *ELRev* 508.

[116] Conclusions of the Lisbon European Council, EC Bulletin 6-1992, I.4.

[117] On the negotiations see Jorna, M. 'The Accession Negotiations with Austria, Finland, Sweden and Norway: A Guided Tour' (1995) 20 *ELRev* 131; Granell, F. 'The European Union's Enlargement Negotiations with Austria, Finland,

four States prior to accession. In Austria and Finland comfortable majorities voted in favour of membership. The majority in favour of membership in Sweden was a narrow one. Norway, once again, voted narrowly against membership. The three new Member States acceded on 2 January 1995.[118]

The Copenhagen meeting established, however, that membership of these former EFTA States was merely part of a process. It was agreed that any European State which had an Association Agreement with the Union should become a member if it so desired provided it was ready to accept the burdens of membership. The size of this commitment can be gauged by the fact that the Community has concluded Association Agreements with twelve other European States.[119] At the Essen European Council in 1994 it was agreed that a 'structured relationship' should be established forthwith between the European Union and the countries of central and eastern Europe preparing the latter for membership.[120]

Following the conclusion of the Intergovernmental Conference, the Commission has stepped the process up a gear with the launch of its Agenda 2000 programme on 16 July 1997. In a 1,300 page document, it assessed how far the ten States currently applying to join the Union met the criteria agreed at Copenhagen. Its conclusions were that Hungary, Poland, Estonia, the Czech Republic and Slovenia came closest to meeting the criteria. Accession negotiations will begin with them and Cyprus in 1998 with a view to possible accession in 2001, although 2003 is held out as being a more likely date.[121] The door is 'left

---

Norway and Sweden' (1995) 33 *JCMS* 117.

[118] On the referenda in Austria, Norway and Finland see the respective articles in (1995) 33 *JCMS*, Issue 3.

[119] These are Bulgaria, Cyprus, the Czech Republic, Estonia, Hungary, Latvia, Lithuania, Malta, Poland, Romania, Slovakia and Turkey. A draft Agreement has been agreed with Slovenia. On these agreements see Peers, S. 'An Ever Closer Waiting Room? The Case for Eastern European Accession to the European Economic Area' (1995) 32 *CMLRev* 187; Evans, A. *The Integration of the European Community and Third States in Europe: A Legal Analysis* (1996, OUP, Oxford).

[120] Conclusions of the Essen European Council, EU Bulletin 12-1994, I.39-I.54.

[121] Malta would have also had the opportunity to begin negotiations but signalled its wish in 1996 not to become a member of the Union.

open' to the other applicants - Bulgaria, Romania, Latvia, Lithuania and Slovakia - yet the conclusions were inevitably divisive in their privileging of one applicant over another.

A Union of potentially 28 States would begin to resemble the pan-European ideal expressed in the Preamble to the Treaty of Rome. Yet, economically and politically it would be very different from the Union today and would produce conflicting pressures. On the one hand it would be less homogenous. A single set of policies might not be suitable for such an entity. On the other hand, if the Union is to retain any set of unity there must at least be core policies or provisions which are applied throughout the Union.

More pressingly, enlargement creates immediate institutional pressures. It has important budgetary consequences as many of the new members are likely to be net recipients. Indeed in Agenda 2000 the Commission puts the cost at ECU 75 billion for the existing 15 members. It is clear, moreover, that if there is not to be a permanent rise in EC expenditure, reform if its main heads of expenditure, the common agricultural policy and the structural funds will be necessary. On present levels of representation, enlargement would result in the membership of all the institutions becoming so large as to make them unwieldy. Finally, it has important implications for the national veto. In 1957 with six Member States unanimity resulted as frequently as not in stalemate and stagnation. In order to function effectively, a Union of 28 States would need to increase its supranational qualities, such as extending qualified majority voting, in certain areas.[122]

These matters were discussed at Amsterdam in 1997.[123] They all proved too divisive, as agreement on any of them entailed a reduction in

---

[122] For contrasting views see Burrows, N. 'The risks of widening without deepening' (1992) 17 *ELRev* 352; Kennedy, D. & Webb, D. 'The Limits of Integration' (1993) 30 *CMLRev* 1095; McMahon, J. '12,16, 20 or 24? The Future Shape of the European Union' (1994) 45 *NILQ* 134; Boos, D. & Forman, J. 'Enlargement: Legal and Procedural Aspects' (1995) 32 *CMLRev* 95.

[123] On discussion of these matters within the context of the IGC see Hughes, K. 'The 1996 Intergovernmental Conference and EU Enlargement' (1996) 72 *International Affairs* 1; Teasdale, A. 'The Politics of Qualified Majority Voting in Europe' (1996) *Political Quarterly* 101, 110-115.

national influence for some or all of the existing Member States. The matter was therefore postponed with a Protocol being signed that a conference shall be convened at least one year before membership of the EU reaches twenty to carry out a comprehensive review of the composition and functioning of the institutions.[124]

XII. The Treaty of Amsterdam

i. The Intergovernmental Conference

The Intergovernmental Conference (IGC) began in Turin on 29 March 1996. At Maastricht topics reserved for consideration at this IGC included:

- revision of the tripartite structure of the TEU;
- extension of the co-decision procedure;[125]
- amendment of the common foreign and security policy and defence provisions;
- extension of express Community competence to energy, civil protection and tourism.
- hierarchy of laws, in particular whether the present classification in Article 189 EC should be replaced by a new typology which distinguishes between primary and implementing laws.

Subsequent areas for discussion which were introduced were reform of the Community Budget and consideration of the number of Commissioners. Serious preparations for the IGC only began at the Corfu European Council in 1994 where a Reflection Group was set up, to be headed by the Spaniard, Westerdorp. This was invited to consider existing topics and other discrete topics such as the question of enlargement and how qualified majority voting should be weighted. It was also given a wider remit. On the basis of reports from the

---

[124]   *Protocol on the institutions with the prospect of enlargement of the European Union.*

[125]   This was the new EC legislative procedure agreed at Maastricht. See pp 172-181.

institutions, the Reflection Group:

'will examine and elaborate ideas relating to the provisions of the Treaty on European Union for which a revision is foreseen and other possible improvements in a spirit of democracy and openness.'[126]

The Report of the Group was submitted to the Madrid European Council in December 1995,[127] and it was accepted as the basis for the IGC.[128] The Report mapped out alternate views and avoided reaching fixed conclusions but stated that the IGC should be based on three broad themes:

- making Europe more relevant to its citizens;
- enabling the Union to work better and preparing it for enlargement;
- giving the Union greater capacity for external action.

At the opening of the Intergovernmental Conference in Turin on 29 March 1996, these themes were outlined to be the guidelines and to provide the mandate for the IGC.[129] The focus had thus changed. The language used in Turin was broader, and the objectives less specific. The reason for this resulted from the legitimacy crisis that the Union was continuing to face, and which the Westerdorp Report had identified as the principal challenge facing the IGC.

Conclusions of the Presidency of the Madrid European Council, EU Bulletin 12-1995, I.98

Men and women of Europe today, more that ever, feel the need for a common project. And yet, for a growing number of Europeans, the rationale for Community integration is not self-evident. This paradox is a first challenge.

---

[126]   Conclusions of the Corfu European Council, EU Bulletin 6-94, I.25.
[127]   Conclusions of the Madrid European Council, EU Bulletin 12-1995, Annex 15. For analysis of its consultation with the different institutions see De Búrca, G. 'The Quest for Legitimacy in the European Union' (1996) 59 *MLR* 349.
[128]   Ibid., I.48.
[129]   Conclusions of the Turin European Council, EU Bulletin 3-1996, I.3-1.8.

When the European Communities were established some 40 years ago, the need for a common design was clear because of the awareness of Europe's failure over the first half of this century.

Now, almost half a century later, the successive enlargements of the Union, the expansion of its tasks, the very complexity of its nature and the magnitude of the problems of our times, make it very difficult to grasp the true significance of, and the continuing need for, European integration.

Let us accept the complexity that is the price that Europe pays to protect our plural identity. But we firmly believe that this creation of Europe's political ingenuity, which cannot take the place of but is now an inseparable counterpart to the Union's Member States, from which its main political legitimacy flows, has been making an invaluable contribution of its own: peace and prosperity based on a definition of common interests and action that is the result not of power politics but of a common body of law agreed by all.

Today Europe has changed, partly because of the Union's success. All those European nations rediscovering their freedom wish to join, or to cooperate more closely with, the European Union. Yet, in Western Europe there is a growing sense of public disaffection despite the Union's contribution to an unprecedented period of peace and prosperity.

We therefore need to explain clearly to our citizens why the Union, which is so attractive to others in Europe, remains necessary for us too.

One reason is that the world outside Europe has also changed. Goods, capital and services nowadays flow globally in an increasingly competitive market. Prices are set worldwide. The prosperity of the Europe of today and tomorrow depends on its ability to succeed in the global marketplace.

The end of the Cold War may have increased the overall security of Europe. But it has also brought greater instability in Europe.

Furthermore, high levels of unemployment, external migratory pressures, increasing ecological imbalances and the growth of international organised crime have stimulated a public demand for greater security that cannot be satisfied by Member States acting alone.

In an increasingly interdependent world, that reality poses new challenges and opens up new opportunities for the Union.

Arguments about legitimacy can confuse and obscure rather than clarify. The legitimacy debate posits some model of governance with which citizens can identify. Many arguments, as the next piece illustrates, on how to legitimate the Union are therefore based upon hidden assumptions about the nature, object and identity of the Union.[130]

---

[130] De Búrca, G. 'The Quest for Legitimacy in the European Union' (1996) 59 *MLR* 349, 352-355.

Obradovic, D. 'Policy Legitimacy and the European Union' (1996) 34 *Journal of Common Market Studies* 191, 208

If the Union is defined as essentially a policy-generating process only, then it could be argued that the issue of how to maintain legitimacy rests with the participating member governments. What counts then is the choices made by those governments about when to take their policy problems to the Union level for resolution and when not to do this. Political loyalty in these circumstances lies at the Member State level, leaving the Union an object of approval or disapproval, not of political affiliation. But if the Union is defined as a partial polity, i.e. as an entity that might develop into a form of direct governance in its own right, the questions concerning the political identity, loyalty and affiliation attached to the Union level of governance, according to H. Wallace, become crucial[131].

She emphasises that the debate on political union that surrounds the Union Treaty is precisely about the shift from policy to polity, and the broaching of metaphysical or basic political values. In other words, it is not merely a matter of adjusting institutional rules and procedures or legal powers to act, important though these are. On the contrary a political union needs a constitution which should be founded on some set of shared values and should express commitment to some form of collective identity. The delineation of some such values and identity would in itself provide some basis for legitimation required for the shift from policy to a more encompassing sociopolitical unit.

The newly emerging integration arrangement introduced by the Maastricht Treaty provides the constitutional basis for the evolving polity at the European level. Apart from economic and monetary union, the Maastricht Treaty expands Community competence proper in fields such as culture, education, health and consumer protection, as well as bringing foreign policy and security and home affairs within the Union structure. Thus the pillars of Maastricht involve areas at the heart of government. The current legitimacy dilemma in the Union concerns precisely the question of the altered polity context in which the decision-making process envisaged by the Union Treaty takes place.

---

[131]   Wallace, H. 'Deepening and Widening: Problems of Legitimacy for the EC' 95, 100 in Garcia, S. (ed.) *European Identity and the Search for Legitimacy* (1993, Pinter, London).

At one level the IGC provided an ideal opportunity for addressing these existential questions. It was, after all, the first conference amending the Treaties where economic integration, be it market integration or monetary integration, was not a central part of the agenda. Yet the very fact that national governments were preoccupied with making the Union better loved and more effective was illustrative of the self-doubt about the project.

The IGC was unsuited to being a radical mechanism for reform. Its membership consisted of national governments, which were the very bodies which had most to lose from an increase in qualified majority voting, an increase in the powers of the supranational institutions or an increase in EU citizens' rights. Furthermore, with every Member State having a veto, the IGC could only operate at the level of the lowest common denominator.[132]

The environment had also changed considerably from the heady days of Maastricht. Rifts between the Member State Governments were becoming increasingly apparent. A number of Member States, notably the Austrian, Greek, German, Irish, Italian and BENELUX Governments wanted to strengthen the supranational qualities of the Union. Some, such as the Portuguese and the Finns, were more equivocal but were amenable to some deepening of the integration process. There were a number of Member States, however, who opposed or expressed reticence about various of the reforms. The Spanish Government was opposed to much increase in majority voting. The French Government was opposed to an increase in the European Parliament's powers and, furthermore, wanted a reaffirmation of national governments' right to veto any measure where significant national interests were at stake. The Danish Government wanted a stronger application of the subsidiarity principle. The most entrenched, however, was the Conservative British Government, which opposed any extension of qualified majority voting or any increase in the powers of the Court of Justice or the European Parliament. Whilst this position was softened

---

[132]   On the vulnerability of the IGC to the external environment see Nugent, N. 'Building Europe - A Need for More Leadership?' (1996) 34 Annual Review of 1995 *JCMS* 1.

Government was opposed to any radical reform of the Treaty.[133]

Secondly, public support for the European Union had diminished.[134] This was, in part, due to the continuing economic recession which was associated in many people's minds with the conditions States were required to meet if monetary union was to proceed.

Finally, relations between the United Kingdom and the other Member States were soured by the BSE crisis. On 20 March 1996 the British Government announced that there was a possible link between bovine spongiform encephalopathy (BSE), a terminal disease which lodged in the nervous systems and brains of cattle, and Creutzfeld-Jakob, a disease which manifested itself in a similar way in humans.[135] Overnight, consumer confidence in the European beef market collapsed. Pushed by the other Member States, the Commission imposed an export ban on all cattle, beef, and beef products from the United Kingdom.[136] This, in turn, had a devastating effect on the British beef industry. The British Government, considering that the link was at best remote and that those parts which posed a risk had been removed from the food chain, lobbied for at least a partial reversal of the ban. When this was not forthcoming, it began a policy of non-cooperation, whereby it would

---

[133] A summary of all the positions taken by the Member States with a view to the 1996 Intergovernmental Conference was prepared by the European Parliament Intergovernmental Conference Task Force. They can be found at http://europa.eu.int/en/agenda/igc-home/ms-doc.

[134] Opinion polls showed that those who considered the European Union a 'good thing' had dropped from 72% in 1990 to 48% in Autumn 1996. EUROBAROMETER, *Public Opinion in the EU, Report No. 46, Autumn 1996* (1997, OOPEC, Luxembourg).

[135] On the crisis, as seen from Britain, see Winter, N. 'Intersecting Departmental Responsibilities, Administrative Confusion and the Role of Science in Government' (1996) 49 *Parliamentary Affairs* 550.

[136] Decision 96/239/EC, OJ 1996, L 78/47.

exercise any veto powers it possessed indiscriminately. A deal was eventually done at Florence in June 1996, but the whole crisis made early negotiations very difficult indeed.[137]

The consequence was that little more than points of difference were identified during the rest of the Italian Presidency.[138] The Florence European Council recommended that the next Presidency, the Irish, present a draft revision of the Treaty at the European Council meeting in Dublin.[139] The Irish draft was divided into five principal sections. The draft was to be amended considerably in the Dutch Presidency which followed with five further versions being presented to the other Member States. It provided, however, the blueprint for the Treaty of Amsterdam which was agreed on 17 June 1997. Finetuning continued throughout the Summer with the Treaty finally being signed on 2 October 1997.

ii. An Outline of the Treaty of Amsterdam 1997

a. The Acquisition of New Competencies

Compared to Maastricht, the number of new competencies added to the TEU was relatively modest. A new Title on Employment was added to the EC Treaty. The most dramatic interventions were, however, in the field of fundamental rights. A first was the introduction of a provision granting the EC institutions the power to take appropriate action to

---

[137] On the deal which was eventually made see Conclusions of the Florence European Council, EU Bulletin 6-1996, I.8.

[138] A progress report was presented at the Florence European Council in June 1996, Conclusions of the Florence European Council, EU Bulletin 6-1996, I.64. The European Parliament had meanwhile declared on 19 June 1996 that it was concerned at 'the visible difficulty in starting on genuine negotiations and considers it vital to move beyond the stage on preliminary discussions'. EP Resolution B4-0833/96, Resolution on the Florence European Council and the Intergovernmental Conference, OJ 1996, C 198/78.

[139] Conference of the Representatives of the Governments of the Member States, *The European Union Today and Tomorrow: Adopting the European Union for the Benefit of Its Peoples and Preparing It for the Future, A General Outline for a Draft Revision of the Treaties*, CONF 2500/96.

combat discrimination based on sex, racial or ethnic origin, religion or belief, disability, age or sexual orientation.[140] The second is more far reaching. It allows a State to be suspended of its rights under the TEU where a finding is made that it has seriously and persistently breached the principles of liberty, democracy, respect for human rights and fundamental freedoms and the rule of law.[141]

b. The Revision of the Tripartite Structure

Amsterdam announced the establishment of an area of Freedom, Security and Justice. This staddles the EC and JHA pillars and places a considerable part of what is currently in the third pillar on JHA within the EC Treaty in a new Title on visas, immigration and other policies related to free movement of persons.[142]

Article 61 EC. In order to establish progressively an area of freedom, security and justice, the Council shall adopt:

(a) within a period of five years after the entry into force of the Treaty of Amsterdam, measures aimed at ensuring the free movement of persons in accordance with Article 14, in conjunction with directly related flanking measures with respect to external borders controls, asylum and immigration, in accordance with the provisions of Article 62(2) and (3), 63(1)(a) and (2)(a), and measures to prevent and combat crime in accordance with the provisions of Article 31(e) of the Treaty on European Union;

(b) other measures in the fields of asylum, immigration and safeguarding the rights of third country nationals, in accordance with the provisions of Article 63;

(c) measures in the field of judicial co-operation in civil matters as provided for in Article 65;

(d) appropriate measures to encourage and strengthen administrative co-operation, as provided for in Article 66;

---

[140]   *Article 13 EC.*
[141]   *Article 7 TEU.*
[142]   *Articles 61-69 EC.*

(e) measures in the field of police and judicial co-operation in criminal matters aimed at a high level of security by preventing and combatting crime within the Union in accordance with the provisions of the Treaty on European Union.

The negotiations took place against the background of a dispute between Belgium and Spain following a finding of a Belgian court that an alleged member of ETA could not be guaranteed a fair trial in Spain and should therefore not be extradited. There was a worry that individuals sought in one Member State might seek to benefit from the freedom given by the Title to seek refuge in another Member State. To combat this a Protocol has been attached to the EC Treaty on Asylum for Nationals of Member States of the European Union. It establishes a presumption that Member States shall be regarded as safe countries of origin for the purposes of asylum and that therefore applications for asylum from nationals of other EU States should be declared inadmissible. The circumstances when this presumption may be rebutted are extremely limited. Furthermore, machinery is put in place to deter Member States from accepting asylum application, as any acceptance must be notified to the Council which will treat it on the basis that the asylum application is manifestly unfounded.[143]

The regime was further complicated by the United Kingdom's refusal to relinquish its border controls. As it formed a common travel area with Ireland, this had implications for the latter. The abandonment of Irish border controls on movement from other Member States, whilst remaining part of the common travel area with the United Kingdom, would have enabled British border controls to be evaded simply through the expedient of entry via Ireland.

Two Protocols to the EC Treaty were therefore signed. The first was the Protocol on the Application of Certain Aspects of Article 14 EC Treaty to the United Kingdom and Northern Ireland. This states that, notwithstanding other EC Treaty provisions, the United Kingdom can retain its rights to verify those entering its territory and to determine whether or not to grant permission for them to enter. As Ireland and the United Kingdom form a common travel area, identical provision was

---

[143] Belgian lodged, however, a Declaration to the Protocol stating that it will continue to examine each individual case on its merits.

made for Ireland. A corollary of this was that other Member States are permitted to retain their border controls vis-à-vis persons entering from the United Kingdom or Ireland.[144] The second Protocol, the Protocol on the Position of the United Kingdom and Ireland, allows the United Kingdom and Ireland not to participate in the adoption of measures taken under this EC Title nor to be bound by them.[145] The consequence of this is not only to protect these Member States from further EC intrusion in this field but also to repatriate powers in the area of visa policy.

The Irish and British participate in that part of the area of Freedom, Security and Justice which is to be realised through the JHA pillar.[146] Following Amsterdam, however, this pillar covers a much narrower range of affairs than previously.

Article 29 TEU. Without prejudice to the powers of the European Community, the Union's objective shall be to provide citizens with a high level of safety within an area of freedom, security and justice by developing common action among the Member States in the fields of police and judicial cooperation in criminal matters and by preventing and combatting racism and xenophobia.

That objective shall be achieved by preventing and combatting crime, organised or otherwise, in particular terrorism, trafficking in persons and offences against children, illicit drug trafficking and illicit arms trafficking, corruption and fraud, through:

- closer cooperation between police forces, customs authorities and other competent authorities in the Member States, both directly and, through the European Police Office (Europol), in accordance with the provisions of Articles 30 and 32;

- closer cooperation between judicial and other competent authorities of the Member States in accordance with the provisions of Articles 31(3) (a)-(d) and 32;

- approximation, where necessary, of rules on criminal matters in the Member States, in accordance with the provisions of Article 31(3)(e).

---

[144] *Protocol on the application of certain aspects of Article 14 of the EC Treaty to the United Kingdom and Ireland.*

[145] *Protocol to the EC Treaty on the position of the United Kingdom and Ireland.*

[146] *Articles 29-42 TEU.*

The provisions establishing the area of freedom, security and justice must be read alongside the Protocol Integrating the *Schengen Acquis* into the framework of the European Union. The Schengen Acquis consists of two agreements, one signed in 1985, the other in 1990, and a number of implementing decisions taken under these agreements. All Member States except Ireland and the United Kingdom are now party to the *acquis*. Iceland and Norway are, in addition, associate members. The purpose of the *acquis* is to provide for the gradual abolition of checks at common frontiers. The Protocol brings the *acquis* within the institutional and legal framework of the Union. It has a *sui generis* position within the Union, however. For it straddles the EC and JHA pillars with the legal base of implementing measures being decided upon an individual basis.[147]

A final complicating feature is the position of Denmark. Denmark is party to the Schengen Acquis. On the other hand, a condition of the 1992 Edinburgh European Council was that Denmark merely participate in *cooperation* in JHA.[148] Like the United Kingdom and Ireland it therefore had reservations about entering the new EC Title on visas, immigration and other policies related to free movement of persons. A Protocol was therefore attached which stated that Denmark would not participate in the adoption of any measures under this Title, nor would it be bound by any measure adopted under this Title. There is one exception to this status of non-involvement. Denmark is bound by the Title and will participate in the adoption of acts taken under it in relation to visa policy.[149] The effect of the Protocol is therefore to preserve the Danish position in this field as it was prior to Amsterdam.

---

[147]   *Protocol integrating the Schengen Acquis into the framework of the European Union, article 2(1).*

[148]   Conclusions of the Edinburgh European Council EC Bulletin 12-1992, I.38.

[149]   *Protocol on the position of Denmark.* The reason for the different policy in relation to visa is that at Maastricht visa policy was placed within the scope of the EC Treaty and not within JHA.

c. Institutional Reforms

In addition to the acquisition of new competencies and the shifting of competencies between the pillars, the TEU's supranational qualities were enhanced in a number of other ways.

First, the powers of the supranational bodies were enhanced. A number of the competencies were shifted to legislative procedures which gave the European Parliament increased powers. The consultative powers of the Committee of the Regions were also extended.[150]

Secondly, the areas where qualified majority voting takes place have been extended. Within the EC Treaty these now include, *inter alia*, employment, countering social exclusion, equality of opportunity and treatment for men and women, public health, transparency, fraud, establishment and research framework programmes. Probably the most significant extension was in the second pillar, CFSP, which, hitherto, had been subject, in practice, to unanimity voting. Qualified majority voting shall now take place for certain implementing measures and in relation to any measure which is taken on the basis of a common strategy.[151]

Thirdly, the Protocol on Social Policy is to be abolished, and instead social policy is to be placed in a Chapter in the EC Treaty on the same footing as all the other policies governed by the EC Treaty. The 'opting-out' by the United Kingdom from the Agreement on Social Policy at Maastricht had caused some irritation amongst other Member States which saw it as trying to obtain an unfair competitive advantage.[152] Concomitantly, there was pressure from within the United Kingdom by those who saw the British failure to participate as evidence that it was moving towards becoming a 'sweat shop' economy. These tensions were resolved by one of the first acts of the Labour Government, on its election in May 1997, which was to indicate its willingness to sign up to the Social Agreement.

As a counterbalance to all the above, which either reduced Member State autonomy or increased the powers of supranational

---

[150]   On this see Chapter 2.
[151]   *Article 23(2) TEU.*
[152]   e.g. Guidelines of the Austrian Government on the subjects likely to be dealt with at the 1996 IGC, June 1995.

institutions, a number of further constraints were added. A Protocol has been set up requiring all consultation documents and Commission proposals to be forwarded in good time so that they can be considered by national Parliaments.[153] Furthermore, a Protocol on Subsidiarity has been signed which not only sets out in more detail the content of the subsidiarity principle, but also requires the Commission to consult more widely in preparing its proposals.[154] Finally, a principle of transparency is entrenched into the EC Treaty with a qualified right of access to EC documents being granted to every citizen of the Union and natural or legal person having its registered office in a Member State.[155]

In terms of institutional reform Amsterdam proved to be, at best, only a partial success. Although it was recognised that institutional reform was necessary to prepare the European Union for enlargement, no agreement was reached on a number of key issues, in particular the weighting of Member State voting within the legislative processes; a formula for determining the number of MEPs from each Member State and the number of future Commissioners. A Protocol, the Protocol on the Institutions with the Prospect of Enlargement of the European Union, was signed. This provides a structure for negotiating institutional reforms which may be necessary to accommodate the first enlargement taking place following Amsterdam. It provides that the Commission shall continue to comprise one national of each Member State - a demand of the smaller Member States - provided that the weighting of voting in the Council is modified in a manner acceptable to all Member States - a demand of some of the larger Member States who saw the smaller Member States as being over represented in the Council. It is recognised, however, that this can only be a short-stop measure and a wider overhaul will be necessary if there is further enlargement. The Protocol therefore requires that another Intergovernmental Conference be convened one year before membership of the Union reaches twenty to review the composition and functioning of the institutions.

---

153   *Protocol on the role of National Parliaments in the European Union.*
154   *Protocol on the application of the principles of subsidiarity and proportionality.*
155   *Article 255 EC.*

d. The Flexibility Provisions

Provision has been made at Amsterdam for allowing some Member States at integrate at a faster rate when others do not wish to. Member States which intend to establish closer cooperation between themselves to make use of the TEU institutions and mechanisms. Various conditions have been imposed, however. In particular, the cooperation must only be used as a last resort, it must concern at least a majority of the Member States and must not affect the competencies, rights and obligations of non-participating Member States.[156] Furthermore, if the cooperation is to take place in areas covered by either the EC Treaty or JHA, authorisation is required with a qualified majority of all Member States being necessary before such cooperation can go ahead.[157]

XIII. Whither the Treaty on European Union?

The Amsterdam Treaty awaits ratification. Experience from Maastricht suggests that it cannot be assumed that it will be unproblematic. The Treaty does seem to have brought the integration process full circle.

The Single European Act developed the Community as a process through the instrument of the internal market. In so doing, it concealed politics behind the facade of economic integration. High politics was dressed as low politics. The TEU took the opposite approach. As Obradovic observed, it went further towards established the European Union as an overt polity with a clear political identity with an extension of express competences in a wide ranging number of areas.[158] Yet the development of this polity was undermined in part by the weakness of its institutional arrangements. More fundamentally, the adverse reaction of the European public to the heady symbols it held up, economic and monetary union and a move towards political union, suggested that, as

---

[156]   *Article 43 TEU.*
[157]   *Article 11 EC* and *Article 40 TEU* respectively.
[158]   See pp 260-266.

currently constructed, a European polity was as much a source of disunity as a source of unity.

Amsterdam seems to take the Union back (if it ever left) towards being a policy-generating process. The Westerdorp Report accepted, for example, that the Union's main political legitimacy stems from the Member States.[159] No doubt federal idealists can pin some of the reasons for this on recidivist, nationalist forces and on the fact that it is national governments rather than national peoples who have negotiated the Treaties. The latter have both harboured power for themselves and rendered the Union obscure to the public. Yet this alone is not sufficient to explain what has happened. There has been little counterweight to these developments. The reason for this may be that, at the end of the day, the idea of Europe still remains obscure to the citizens of Europe. Whilst this is so, it is difficult for it to act as a mobilising force which can give a sufficiently defined identity to any form of polity.[160]

Obradovic, D. 'Policy Legitimacy and the European Union' (1996) 34 *Journal of Common Market Studies* **191, 215**

References are also often made to an impressionistic and superficial notion of a European tradition and heritage, a conglomerate which includes traditions like Roman law, political democracy, parliamentary institutions, Judeo-Christian ethics, cultural heritages such as Renaissance humanism, rationalism and empiricism, and romanticism and classicism, as well as, in its extended version, modern science and the technological breakthroughs of the industrial revolution. According to Euronationalist writings, the unity, the special nature of Europe, is to be found in an entirely unique culture or civilisation, which is rooted in a distant past and therefore has a very long history. However, this concept comes up against two major problems: the indistinctiveness of Europe's boundaries and the imprecise demarcation of Europe as a cultural unity. Consequently, neither an explicatory nor syndrome definition of the notion of European identity has been developed. Given the lack of clear ethno-cultural boundaries and differentiating characteristics, one must expect the idea of European identity to remain relatively vague, the object of lofty reflections rather than the source of spontaneous emotions.

---

[159] Conclusions of the Madrid European Council, EU Bulletin 12-1995 I.48.

[160] See also Weiler, J. 'Fin-de-siècle Europe: On Ideals and Ideology in Post-Maastricht Europe' in Curtin, D & Heukels, T. (eds.) *Institutional Dynamics of European Integration: Essays in Honour of Henry Schermers* (1994, Martijnus Nijhoff, Dordrecht) 23; Laffan, B. 'The Politics of Identity and Political Order in Europe' (1996) 34 *JCMS* 81.

Above all this, the idea of a unified European identity lacks a genuine autochthonous and authentic myth, or in the words of Smith, a pre-modern past - a 'pre-history' which can provide it with emotional sustenance and historical depth[161]. A myth which represents an account of origin, identity and the prepolitical unity of a community - essential components of legitimacy - does not exist at the European level. As a result of these defects, the concept of European identity is prevented from successfully providing a foundation for Union policy legitimacy.

To establish its policy legitimacy, the Union has to have the mythological significance of end values. If the credenda and miranda of legitimate power, the loyalty-evoking symbols, originate in the myth, then the concept of legitimacy in the Union must be based on the mythological discourse operable within the entire European enterprise. The ethos of European integration must be placed in public discourse. People must rally behind and identify with a new, bold step towards a higher degree of integration.

However, the Union simply lacks the mythical ground for reinforcing its policy legitimacy in a way which would stabilise and institutionalise the community. No mythologein is powerfully operative within the Union, no one can win the consent of the entire Union population. At present, the myths embracing ethno-history and collective values and traditions which would merit the European level do not exist. The myth structuring the ethical framework of the Union and thereby establishing its legitimacy has no existence. No mythomoteur serves a moral purpose in structuring the Union. The legitimising myth which would determine the rightness of a cause envisaged by the Maastricht Treaty cannot be invoked on the European scale. Theoretically, therefore, the task of firmly and indisputably establishing Union policy legitimacy is extremely difficult.

Further Reading

Curtin, D. 'The Shaping of a European Constitution and the 1996 IGC' (1995) 50 *Aussenwirtschaft* 237

Dehousse, R. *Europe after Maastricht: An Ever Closer Union?* (1994, Law Books in Europe, Munich)

Duff, A., Pinder, J. & Pryce, R. *Maastricht and Beyond: Building the European Union* (1994, Routledge, London)

Garcia, S. (ed.) *European Identity and the Search for Legitimacy* (1993, Pinter, London)

Hesse, J. & Wright, V. *Federalizing Europe? The Costs, Benefits, and Preconditions of Federal Political Systems* (1996, Clarendon, Oxford)

---

161   Smith, A. 'National Identity and the Idea of European Unity' (1992) 68 *International Affairs* 55, 62.

Janssen, M. & De Vree, J. *The Ordeal of Unity* (1985, Prime Press, Bilthoven)

Martin, S. (ed.) *The Construction of Europe: Essays in Honour of Emile Noël* (1994, Kluwer, Dordrecht)

Middlemas, K. *Orchestrating Europe: The Informal Politics of European Union 1973-1995* (1995, Fontana, London)

Milward, A. *The Reconstruction of Western Europe 1945-51* (1984, Methuen, London)

Pryce, R. *The Dynamics of European Integration* (1985, Croom Helm, London)

Smith, M. (ed.) 'Special Issue on The European Union and a Changing European Order' (1996) 34 *Journal of Common Market Studies*

Urwin, D. *The Community of Europe* (1995, 2nd Edition, Longman, Harlow)

Wistrich, E. *The United States of Europe* (1994, Routledge, London)

Wallace, W. *Regional Integration: The West European Experience* (1994, Brookings Institute, Washington DC)

Winter, J., Curtin, D., Kellermann, A. & De Witte, B. (eds) *Reforming the Treaty on European Union: The Legal Debate* (1996, Kluwer, The Hague)

2. The Institutions of the European Union

I. Introduction

The European Union has been characterised as a system of governance which is more bureaucratic than diplomatic in nature. This arises from the high number of institutions it establishes. These institutions result in conflict-resolution or 'problem solving' not being carried out through a system of ad hoc negotiation but rather through a 'system of institutionalised, constitutional, precedential or otherwise standardised, patterned procedures which all actors commit themselves to use and respect'.[1]

Article D [4] TEU. The European Council shall provide the Union with the necessary impetus for its development and shall define the general political guidelines thereof.

Article E [5] TEU. The European Parliament, the Council, the Commission [*and*] the Court of Justice [*and the Court of Auditors*] shall exercise their powers under the conditions and for the purposes provided for, on the one hand, by the provisions of the Treaties establishing the European Communities and of the subsequent Treaties and Acts modifying and supplementing them and, on the other hand, by the other provisions of the Treaty.

It would be foolish not to recognise that this institutionalisation is at its most apparent and most intense in the EC Treaty. It is within this pillar that those institutions which enjoy the largest degree of *de iure* and

---

[1]   Puchala, D. 'Of Blind Men, Elephants and International Integration' (1972) 10 *JCMS* 267, 279.

de facto independence from the Member States possess the greatest influence.[2]

Article 4 [7] EC. 1. The tasks entrusted to the Community shall be carried out by the following institutions:
- a European Parliament,
- a Council,
- a Commission,
- a Court of Justice,
- a Court of Auditors.

Each institution shall act within the limits of the powers conferred upon it by this Treaty. **2.** The Council and the Commission shall be assisted by an Economic and Social Committee and a Committee of the Regions acting in an advisory capacity.

Article 4a [8] EC. A European System of Central Banks (hereinafter referred to as 'ESCB') and a European Central Bank (hereinafter referred to as 'ECB') shall be established in accordance with the procedures laid down in this Treaty; they shall act within the limits of the powers conferred upon them by this Treaty and by Statute of the ESCB and of the ECB (hereinafter referred to as 'Statute of the ESCB') annexed thereto.

Article 4b [9] EC. A European Investment Bank is hereby established, which shall act within the limits of the powers conferred upon it by this Treaty and the Statute annexed thereto.

Why does this all matter? For lawyers the answer appears self-evident. Member States are formally bound to comply with the procedures governing the operations of these institutions and by the decisions taken by these institutions. For political scientists the answer has traditionally been less obvious. Much international relations scholarship has traditionally perceived international organisations as relatively neutral fora through which collective action could be taken by other actors. These institutions having no real substantive power, they were merely utilised to facilitate realisation of the preferences of other more powerful actors, be they national governments, local elites or

---

[2]   Wessels, W. 'Institutions of the EU system: models of explanation' 20, 21 in Rometsch, D. & Wessels, W. (eds.) *The European Union and the Member States: Towards Institutional Fusion* (1996, Manchester University Press, Manchester).

multinationals. The subservient nature of these organisations was reinforced by the really 'big' decisions being taken outside of the framework of the organisation.[3]

A worrying gap therefore opened up between a tradition of political science which denigrated the importance of transnational institutions and norms in decision-making and a legal tradition which perceived the very existence of these institutions as proof of their centrality. In recent years there have been moves to close this gap. On the one hand, lawyers are increasingly ready to recognise the relativity and contingency of norms and procedures.[4] On the other, a growing number of political scientists have begun to accord a growing influence to procedure and process.[5]

One strand of analysis, the historic institutionalist school, taking a formal view of institutions, noted the extent to which they structured debate. By allocating roles to parties, institutions not only reconfigured power relations but also structured debate. In addition, institutions have a 'lock in' function, namely the decisions taken within them generate expectations amongst all parties which make it difficult for one party to retract if either its preferences change or the decision generates unexpected consequences.[6]

Another strand, new institutionalism, whilst acknowledging the above, focuses on the socialising effects of institutions. The institutional

---

[3]   Examples of this tradition are Keohane, R. & Hoffmann, S. 'Conclusions: Community Politics and Institutional Change' in Wallace, W. (ed.) *The Dynamics of European Integration* (1990, Pintner, London); Moravscik, A. 'Preferences and Power in the European Community: A Liberal Intergovernmentalist Approach' in Bulmer, S. & Scott, A. (eds.) *Economic and Political Integration: Internal Dynamics and Global Context* (1994, Blackwell, Oxford).

[4]   e.g. Snyder, F. 'The Effectiveness of European Community Law: Institutions, Processes, Tools and Techniques' (1993) 56 *MLR* 19. For further on this see, in particular, pp 319-334 & pp 471-475.

[5]   On the differing schools of institutionalism see Hall, P. & Taylor, R. 'Political Science and the New Institutionalisms' (1996) 44 *Political Studies* 936.

[6]   The starting point on 'historic institutionalism' is Steinmo, K., Thelen, K. & Longstreth, F. (eds.) *Structuring Politics - Historic Institutionalism in Comparative Analysis* (1992, CUP, Cambridge). Within the EU context see Pierson, P. 'The Path to European Integration: A Historical Institutionalist Analysis' (1996) 29 *Comparative Political Studies* 123.

context requires actors to engage in a structured manner with others' beliefs, interests and commitment. This process does not actually just structure beliefs, it also has the capacity to transform them. Furthermore, as institutions routinise this dialogue, they have the capacity to entrench not just a formal level but also at a socio-psychological level the new beliefs and commitments.[7]

The socialising effects of institutions has been disputed by the third school of institutionalism - rationalist choice institutionalists.[8] These maintain that the main actors have a fairly fixed and stable set of expectations. Institutions are important as they affect the strategy adopted to realise these expectations. At a macrolevel institutions structure the interaction between the actors and therefore reduce uncertainty about how each will behave. The stable environment this engenders therefore creates more possibilities for agenda-setting and coalition building between actors.

The EU institutions have recently been examined from a new perspective, that of 'fusion' theory.[9] This theory takes, as its starting point, a dichotomy in Member State attitudes. On the one hand, they wished to take efficient measures which would increase the welfare of their citizens. These reasons led to their establishing a number of autonomous institutions. On the other hand, self-interest resulted in their not wishing to see a comprehensive transfer of sovereignty. Unlike the neo-institutionalist critiques outlined above, fusion theory takes an

---

[7] On 'new institutionalism' within the EU context see Bulmer, S. 'The Governance of the European Union: A New Institutionalist Approach' (1993) 13 *Journal of Public Policy* 351; Peterson, J. 'Decision-making in the European Union: towards a framework for analysis' (1995) 2 *JEPP* 69; Kerremans, B. 'Do Institutions Make a Difference? Non-Institutionalism, Neo-Institutionalism, and the Logic of Common Decision-Making in the European Union' (1996) 9 *Governance* 217. For a good comparison of historic institutionalism and new institutionalism see Armstrong, K. 'Regulating the free movement of goods: institutions and institutional change' in Shaw, J. & More, G. (eds.) *New Legal Dynamics of European Union* (1995, Clarendon, Oxford).

[8] The clearest exposé of this within the EU context is Garrett, G. & Tsebelis, G. 'An Institutional Critique of Intergovernmentalism' (1996) 50 *International Organisation* 269.

[9] Wessels, W. 'An Ever Closer Fusion? A Dynamic Macropolitical View on Integration Processes' (1997) 35 *JCMS* 67.

instrumental approach to institutions. It regards institutions as important for a number of reasons. The autonomy of these institutions allows them, once set up, to pursue their own interests. In addition, the centrality of these institutions leads Member States for reasons of self-interest to jockey for influence and participate as fully as possible within these arenas. This leads to 'fusion' whereby national institutions increasingly share responsibilities with other EC actors. The process of sharing and participation also leads to convergence whereby political institutions within the Member States will increasingly undertake 'constitutional, institutional, procedural, organizational and behavioural innovations and adaptations which lead in a similar direction'.[10]

II. The Commission

i. The College of Commissioners: Its Nature and Form

The Commission is a collegiate body consisting of twenty Commissioners. There must be at least one Commissioner from each Member State. The larger Member States - France, Germany, Italy, Spain and the United Kingdom - all have two Commissioners.[11] The TEU changed the procedure for the appointment of the Commissioners giving the European Parliament a greater role to play. Under Article 158 [214] EC the governments of the Member States, after consulting the

---

[10]   Wessels, W. 'Institutions of the EU system: models of explanation' 20, 36 in Rometsch, D. & Wessels, W. (eds.) *The European Union and the Member States: Towards Institutional Fusion* (1996, Manchester University Press, Manchester).

[11]   This number is increasingly being seen as too high, and as threatening the discipline and coherence of the Commission. A view of both part of the Westerdorp Committee and the Commission was that this matter will be exacerbated by enlargement, and that the formula needed rethinking. No agreement was reached on this point at Amsterdam. Commission Opinion to the Intergovernmental Conference, *Reinforcing Political Union and Preparing for Enlargement* (1996) para. 42; Conclusions of the Madrid European Council EU Bulletin 12-1995, I.108.

European Parliament nominate a person to be the President of the Commission. The governments, together with the proposed President, then nominate the other Commissioners. The President and these nominees are then subject to a vote of approval by the European Parliament after which they are appointed by common accord of the Member State governments.

The procedure presented the Parliament with a *fait accompli*. It either approved the Commission or vetoed its appointment en bloc. The procedure has been modified by Amsterdam. It requires the Member State nomination for President to be approved by the Parliament before other potential Commissioners are nominated.[12] This opportunity to veto the appointment of the President will give the Parliament the possibility to enter into a dialogue with the appointee both about the latter's strategic vision for his or her term and about who else should be nominated as Commissioners.

It is the duty of the President, formally incorporated into the EC Treaty at Amsterdam, to provide political guidance.[13] The President starts this process by allocating the portfolios within the Commission. There is a considerable difference in the prestige attached to the different portfolios with considerable bargaining taking place for the most prestigious portfolios.[14] Each Commissioner is serviced by a personal *cabinet*. In addition the Commission is assisted by a permanent secretariat of just over 20,000 officials.[15] This secretariat is organised into Directorates-General, each of which covers a subject matter area,

---

[12]   *Article 214(2) EC.*

[13]   *Article 219 EC.*

[14]   It is not only prospective Commissioners who engage in considerable manoeuvring but also the different Member States who wish their own nationals to have portfolios of importance to that Member State. There is a celebrated instance of Prime Minister Thatcher telephoning Commission President Thorn in 1981 to demand that one of the British Commissioners, Christopher Tugendhat be given a particular portfolio.

[15]   *General Report on the Activities of the European Union 1995* (1996, OOPEC, Luxembourg) 440. An excellent collection of essays on the nature and working of the Commission is Nugent, N. (ed.) *At the Heart of the Union* (1997, Macmillan, Basingstoke).

and further special units providing research, translation and legal services.[16]

Under Article 157 [*213*] EC the Commissioners are to be persons whose 'independence is beyond doubt'. They are required not to seek or take instructions from any government or any other body, and a duty is imposed on Member States to respect this principle. In addition, Commissioners must not find themselves in a position where a 'conflict of interest' arises. They must not therefore engage in any other occupation during their period of office. If any Commissioner breaches any of these operations, the Court of Justice may, on application by either the Council or the Commission, compulsorily retire that Commissioner.

This independence from Member States is made more effective by both the length and security of tenure. Under Article 158 [*214*] EC Commissioners are appointed for a five year renewable term. During its term of office a Commission can expect to see elections in most Member States. Commissioners cannot therefore rely on the same administration who put them up for office in the first place renewing their term of office.[17] Such independence must however be seen in context.

---

[16] The portfolios attributed to Commissioners do not necessarily equate with particular Directorates-General. It is possible that several Directorates-General report to one Commissioner, or even that a particular Commissioner does not have a Directorate General. The purpose of this was to emphasise the collegiality of the Commission. The mismatch between portfolios and the division of labour within the Secretariat is often seen as a source of inefficiency, Ludlow, P. 'The European Commission' 85, 91-93 in Keohane, R. & Hoffmann, S. *The New European Community: Decision Making and Institutional Change* (1991, Westview Press, Boulder). On administrative coordination within the Commission see Spence, D. 'Structure, functions and procedures in the Commission' in Edwards, G. & Spence, D. *The European Commission* (1994, Longman, Harlow).

[17] The Commission is accountable, under Article 144 [*201*] EC, to the European Parliament who can, by a motion of censure, dismiss it.

Christiansen, T. 'Tensions of European Governance: politicised bureaucracy and multiple accountability in the European Commission' (1997) 4 *Journal of European Public Policy* **73, 82-83**

Their [the Commissioners'] role is essentially twofold: on top of their official, sectoral responsibilities they also function as the most senior link between the Commission and the respective national political circuit. Usually, they are members - and appointees - of the major parties in their member state and continue some involvement with national politics after becoming Commissioners. Frequent trips to speak before (and to lecture to) national audiences are common. Again, the metaphor of gate-keeping is perhaps most useful: Commissioners are an easy and efficient way for the Commission to maintain a link with member state governments and domestic political systems. They will know what legislative proposals are politically acceptable in national capitals, while at the same time being in an ideal position to communicate to national elites the requirements of efficient European policy-making.

Yet the unwritten rule that Commissioners also represent member states - and, by association, member states' interests - inside the Commission is only the tip of an iceberg of member state influence inside this supposedly supranational institution. We can look only briefly at a few examples of the way in which the Commission is also an intergovernmental body. On the individual level, for instance, most Commission officials are not just nationals of one of the member states, but also come from an educational, administrative and political system that is profoundly national in orientation. Those entering the Commission with a genuinely European educational formation, like those coming from the College of Europe, the European Institute of Public Administration or the European University Institute, are in a small albeit growing minority. Research on the international organisations indicates the gulf between the theory of a 'neutral' international civil service and the pervasiveness of national identity among the staff of international organisations, even though there this identification tends to be lower than in the wider public. In the end, there is a gulf between 'the myth and the reality' of an international civil service.

There is little empirical work on the identification and socialisation of Commission staff, but where there is confirms the perspective of inherent tension that is advanced here. On the one hand, Commission officials are 'special' for a number of structural reasons associated with the institution:

> [T]he Commission's officials' typical motivational structure is quite different from that of the average national government official...[T]he Commission recruits from people who are highly motivated, risk-oriented, polyglot, cosmopolitan, open-minded and innovative...From the beginnings in the 1960's to the present, it has indeed been officials of a special type who chose to leave the relative security of their national administrations to go to Brussels to do

there a well-paid but extremely challenging job. These people mutually stabilise their motivational structures with a distinct esprit de corps.[18]

On the other hand, there remains the link with national administrative cultures and systems, something which has been the subject of a number of recent studies. Egeberg, for example, finds that 60 per cent of respondents in the Commission state nationality as important for network-building.[19] Considering how important policy networks are in the making of European public policy, this finding - in what is usually considered a supranational institution - is remarkable, even if only 23 per cent of respondents consider nationality as guiding their decisions. Nationality still matters, if only to a limited and perhaps declining extent - this is the credo of such investigations. Even though the Commission is a modern, progressive and innovative organisation, its staff maintain allegiance to national identities and the routines of cultural and linguistic affinity.

The second feature of the Commission is its formal *collegiality*. This principle requires both that the Commission is collectively responsible for all decisions taken and that all Commission decisions should, in principle, be taken collectively.

Case C-137/92P Commission v BASF [1994] ECR I-2555

The Commission adopted a Decision finding BASF, among others, guilty of participating in a PVC cartel. After being adopted by the college of Commissioners, several of the language versions were altered. In addition, only the English, French and German language versions were adopted by the College with the Commissioner for Competition, Peter Sutherland, being delegated to adopt the other language versions.

62. ... the functioning of the Commission is governed by the principle of collegiate responsibility laid down in Article 17 of the Treaty of 8 April 1965 establishing a Single Council and a Single Commission of the European Communities (*Journal Officiel* 1967, 152, p.2, hereinafter referred to as 'the Merger Treaty'), which has now been replaced by Article 163 of the EC Treaty. This provides that: 'The Commission shall act by a majority

---

[18] Eichener, V. *Social Dumping or Innovative Regulation?* (1992, EUI Working Paper SPS 92/28, Florence) 53.

[19] Egeberg, M. 'Organisation and nationality in the European Commission services', (1995) Paper presented for the ECPR Joint Session of Workshops, Bordeaux.

of the number of members provided for in Article 10. A meeting of the Commission shall be valid only if the number of members laid down in its rules of procedure is present'.

63. ... the principle of collegiate responsibility so laid down [is] based on the equal participation of the Commissioners in the adoption of decisions, from which it followed in particular that decisions should be the subject of collective deliberation and that all the members of the college of Commissioners should bear collective responsibility at political level for all decisions adopted.

64. Compliance with that principle, and especially the need for decisions to be deliberated upon by the Commissioners together, must be of concern to the individuals affected by the legal consequences of such decisions, in the sense that they must be sure that those decisions were actually taken by the college of Commissioners and correspond exactly to its intention.

.....

66. Such decisions must state the reasons on which they are based, in accordance with Article 190 of the EEC Treaty. It is settled law that this requires the Commission to set out the reasons which prompted it to adopt a decision, so that the Court can exercise its power of review and Member States and nationals concerned know the basis on which the Treaty has been applied.

67. The operative part of such a decision can be understood, and its full effect ascertained, only in the light of the statement of reasons. Since the operative part of, and the statement of reasons for, a decision constitute an indivisible whole, it is for the college of Commissioners alone to adopt both the operative part and the statement of reasons, in accordance with the principle of collegiate responsibility.

68. As the Court held in its judgment in the *Battery Hens* case [Case 131/86 *United Kingdom v Council* [1988] ECR 905], cited above, that means that only simple corrections of spelling and grammar may be made to the text of an act after its formal adoption by the college of Commissioners, any further alteration being the exclusive province of the college.

The vast amount of Commission activity renders it impracticable for all decisions to be fully considered by all Commissioners. In the interests of administrative expediency the Commission has found two means of tempering the doctrine of collegiality.

The first is the 'written procedure'. Under this procedure a proposal, a *greffe*, is adopted by the Commissioner responsible for the relevant portfolio. After the proposal has been approved by the Legal

Service and associated Directorates-General, it is then circulated to the Cabinets of the other Commissioners. If there is no objection the proposal is adopted as a Commission decision. There are two types of written procedure. The ordinary procedure gives the Cabinets five working days to consider the proposal. The expedited procedure must be authorised by the President. In such circumstances the Cabinets are only given three working days. Whilst the Commission is, formally, collectively responsible for acts adopted under the written procedure, in substance it is one particular Commissioner who is responsible for its development.

The second form of lightening the workload is through internal delegation. Under its rules of procedure the Commission can delegate to particular members well-defined powers of management and administration.[20] It is not self-evident, however, which will be considered to be management powers and which will be considered to be administrative powers. In the *BASF* judgment cited above, for example, the Court considered that a decision requiring undertakings to submit to a Commission investigation into anti-competitive practices was an act of management and so could be delegated. The power to adopt a decision that there had been a violation of EC competition law was not considered to be administrative in nature and was considered to be too wide to be delegated.

ii. The Powers of the Commission

The powers of the Commission are rather tersely set out in Article 155 [*211*] EC.

Article 155 [*211*] EC. In order to ensure the proper functioning and development of the common market, the Commission shall:
- ensure that the provisions of this Treaty and the measures taken by the institutions pursuant thereto are applied;

---

[20]   Rule 27, *Commission Rules of Procedure*, OJ 1975, L 199/43. This was upheld in Case 5/85 *AKZO v Commission* [1986] ECR 2585, [1987] 3 CMLR 716.

- formulate recommendations or deliver opinions on matters dealt with in this Treaty, if it expressly so provides or if the Commission considers it necessary;
- have its own power of decision and participate in the shaping of measures taken by the Council and by the European Parliament in the manner provided for in this treaty;
- exercise the powers conferred on it by the Council for the implementation of the rules laid down by the latter.

This description does not do justice to the range or variety of Commission powers.

a. Legislative and Quasi-Legislative Powers

In two very limited fields the Commission is granted express powers under the EC Treaty to enact legislation. The first is in the field of public undertakings where the Commission can issue Directives to ensure that such undertakings comply with the rules contained in the Treaty, particularly those on non-discrimination and competition.[21] The second is in the field of free movement of workers where the Commission can issue Regulations determining the conditions under which Community nationals may reside in another Member State after having worked there.[22]

Far more wide ranging are the quasi-legislative powers which may be delegated to the Commission. Under Article 145(3)[*202(3)*] EC the Council can confer upon the Commission powers for implementation of the rules which the Council lays down. The powers delegated can be very wide. The Court has found that it is sufficient merely for the general principles to be set out in the Council act, and it is not inconsistent with the notion of implementing powers for the Commission to be granted wide powers of discretion and appraisal.[23] Areas in which the Commission has been frequently delegated wide powers include agriculture, fisheries, external trade relations and competition. These quasi-legislative powers are not unfettered, however. Since the early

---

[21]   Article 90(3) [*86(3)*] EC.
[22]   Article 48(3)(d) [*39(3)(d)*] EC.
[23]   On the width of the powers that may be delegated see pp 487-489.

1960s the Council has conditioned the delegation of these powers by their exercise to be monitored by committees composed of representatives of the national governments.[24] The elaborate system of committees which has since developed is known collectively as *comitology*.[25] There are three principal forms of procedure which are contained in Decision 87/373.[26]

Decision 87/373 EEC laying down the procedure for the exercise of implementing powers conferred on the Commission

Article 2
Procedure I

The Commission shall be assisted by a committee of an advisory nature composed of the representatives of the Member States and chaired by the representative of the Commission.

The representative of the Commission shall submit to the committee a draft of the measures to be taken. The committee shall deliver its opinion on the draft, within a time limit which the chairman may lay down according to the urgency of the matter, if necessary by taking a vote.

The opinion shall be recorded in the minutes; in addition, each Member State shall have the right to ask to have its position recorded in the minutes.

The Commission shall take the utmost account of the opinion delivered by the committee. It shall inform the committee of the manner in which its opinion has been taken into account.

Procedure II

The Commission shall be assisted by a committee composed of the representatives of the Member States and chaired by the representative of the Commission.

The representative of the Commission shall submit to the committee a draft of the measures to be taken. The committee shall deliver its opinion on the draft within a time limit which the chairman may lay down according to the urgency of the matter. The opinion shall be delivered by the majority laid down in article 148(2) of the Treaty in the case of decisions which the Council is required to adopt on a proposal from the Commission. The votes of the representatives of the Member States within the committee shall be weighted in the manner set out in that article. The chairman shall not vote.

---

[24] On how the legal structures arranging relations between these committees and the Commission allow for a variety of values and interests to be introduced into EC policy-making see pp 497-500.

[25] On the development of comitology see Vos, E. 'The Rise of Committees' (1997) 3 *ELJ* 210.

[26] OJ 1987 L 197/33.

The Commission shall adopt measures which shall apply immediately. However, if these measures are not in accordance with the opinion of the committee, they shall be communicated by the Commission to the Council forthwith. In that event:

Variant (a)

The Commission may defer application of the measures which it has decided for a period of not more than one month from the date of such communication;

The Council, acting by a qualified majority, may take a different decision within the time limit referred to in the previous paragraph.

Variant (b)

The Commission shall defer application of the measures which it has decided for a period to be laid down in each act adopted by the Council, but which may in no case exceed three months from the date of communication.

The Council, acting by a qualified majority, may take a different decision within the time limit referred to in the previous paragraph.

Procedure III

The Commission shall be assisted by a committee composed of the representatives of the Member States and chaired by the representative of the Commission.

The representative of the Commission shall submit to the committee a draft of the measures to be taken. The committee shall deliver its opinion on the draft within a time limit which the chairman may lay down according to the urgency of the matter. The opinion shall be delivered by the majority laid down in Article 148(2) of the Treaty in the case of decisions which the Council is required to adopt on a proposal from the Commission. The votes of the representatives of the Member States within the committee shall be weighted in the manner set out in that article. The chairman shall not vote.

The Commission shall adopt the measures envisaged if they are in accordance with the opinion of the committee.

If the measures envisaged are not in accordance with the opinion of the committee, or if no opinion is delivered, the Commission shall, without delay, submit to the Council a proposal relating to the measures to be taken. The Council shall act by a qualified majority.

Variant (a)

If, on the expiry of a period to be laid down in each act to be adopted by the Council under this paragraph but which may in no case exceed three months from the date of referral to the Council, the Council has not acted, the proposed measures shall be adopted by the Commission.

Variant (b)

If, on the expiry of a period to be laid down in each act to be adopted by the Council under this paragraph but which may in no case exceed three months from the date of referral to the Council, the Council has not acted, the proposed measures shall be adopted by the Commission, save where the Council has decided against the said measures by a simple majority.

Nugent has best described the differences between these complex and opaque procedures, stating that under Procedure I the committee can only *advise*, under Procedure II it can *block* and under Procedure III it can *approve*.[27] The key difference between Procedure II and Procedure III is that under Procedure II the committee must actively vote against a measure to prevent it being adopted, whilst under Procedure III the Commission cannot act without the Committee's say so.

Comitology has proliferated since the 1960s. Research has shown that whilst comitology was used in about 20% of all legislation enacted since 1987, the figure is much higher in the case of legislation which authorises either expenditure or which relies upon qualified majority voting with it being used in 66% of all expenditure-authorising legislation in 67% of legislation adopted under Article 100A [95] EC, the internal market legal base.[28] In 1994 in the Budget area alone it was estimated that there were 294 committees in operation.[29] It might be thought that as Commission autonomy is reduced and Member State influence increased in proportion to the powers of the committee, the Commission would push for use of Procedure I (advisory committees) when comitology is required. In fact, it has only proposed use of Procedure I in 29% of all cases.

Comitology has proved more problematic for the Parliament.[30] It has objected to a growth in the committees' powers on two grounds.

---

[27] Nugent, N. *The Government and Politics of the European Union* (1994, 3rd Edition, Macmillan, London) 109. For further analysis of comitology see Bradley, K. 'Comitology and the law: through a glass darkly' (1992) 29 *CMLRev* 693; Blumann, C. 'Le pouvoir exécutif de la Commission à la lumière de l'Acte Unique Européen' (1988) *RTDE* 23; Steunenboldt, B., Koboldt, C. & Schmidtchen, D. 'Policymaking, Comitology and the Balance of Power in the European Union' (1996) 16 *International Review of Law and Economics* 329.

[28] Dogan, R. 'Comitology: Little Procedures with Big Implications' (1997) 20 *WEP* forthcoming.

[29] Docksey, C. & Williams, K. 'The European Commission and the Execution of Community Policy' 125, 133-34 in Edwards, G. & Spence, D. *The European Commission* (1997, 2nd Edition, Longman, Harlow). On the opportunities for influence these committees present see Buitendijk, G. & van Schendelen, M. 'Brussels Advisory Committees: A Channel for Influence?' (1995) 20 *ELRev* 37.

[30] Bradley, K. 'The European Parliament and Comitology: On the Road to Nowhere?' (1997) 3 *ELJ* 230.

The first is that these committees are not accountable to any elected body at either a Community or national level. The other is that it considers the grants to these committees of any power other than an advisory one (i.e. Procedures II and III) allows the Council through manipulation of the comitology to reacquire executive responsibilities which should fall within the Commission's domain.[31] Parliament has managed to exploit some rather sloppy drafting in the TEU. Article 145 [*202*] EC, the enabling provision for delegated powers, merely refers to its being possible where acts are adopted by the Council. Following the TEU acts must be jointly adopted by the Parliament and Council in certain areas of Community competence.[32] The Parliament has claimed that comitology cannot be used in these areas of competence.[33] This clash was partly resolved by the Modus Vivendi of 20 December 1994, an interinstitutional agreement which requires that the Parliament must be consulted over the adoption of any implementing act which falls within a field where acts would normally have to be adopted jointly by the Council and Parliament.[34]

At best the legal status of comitology is highly confused and confusing, and it is likely that it will not go unreformed for much longer. The Westerdorp Report noted a significant majority in favour of simplifying the procedures. There is also a fear that enlargement would put further pressures on comitology in that it might lead to an increase in matters being referred back to the Council. At Amsterdam a Declaration was attached to the Treaty requiring the Commission to submit amendments to the Council by the end of 1998.[35]

---

[31]   Resolution A4-0102/95 on the Functioning of the Treaty on European Union with a view to the 1996 Intergovernmental Conference, para 32(ii).

[32]   See p 174.

[33]   On the difficulties this has produced see Docksey, C. & Williams, K. 'The Commission and the Execution of Community Policy' 125, 149-150 in Edwards, G. & Spence, D. *The European Commission* (1997, 2nd Edition Longman, Harlow).

[34]   OJ 1996, C 102/1.

[35]   *Declaration to the Final Act on the Conferring of Implementing Powers on the Commission.*

b. Initiation of Policy

The Commission is seen as the motor for integration and has responsibility for initiating the policy process. This operates at a number of different levels.[36] The Commission is responsible for *strategic goal setting*, as it is the body which is responsible for deciding what will be the legislative programme for a particular year. In deciding this, it can clearly shape the immediate Community priorities. Secondly, the Commission has the power of *legislative initiative* in all areas, apart from matters falling within the intergovernmental pillar of JHA. Thirdly, the Commission is empowered to *formulate policy more generally* and to act as a stimulus to debate over matters of Union concern. The most celebrated example was the Commission White Paper on Completion of the Internal Market[37] which provided one of the bases for the adoption of the Single European Act and the 1992 project. Finally, the Commission kicks off the budgetary process by placing a *draft budget* before the other Institutions.

The justification for the Commission's being granted the power of proposal was that its autonomy and its expertise would result in its being best able to represent the common European interest.[38] The power to set the agenda results in the Commission being far more politicised than traditional civil services. It has made it a market-place for the development of ideas and accommodation of interests, both Statal and private, with a variety of parties being interested for this reason in its internal workings. This has in turn led to conflicts within the Commission as different DGs seek to adopt their own solutions to similar problems.[39]

---

[36]   For greater detail see Ludlow, P. 'The European Commission' 85, 96-104 in Keohane, R. & Hoffmann, S. (eds.), *The New European Community: Decision Making and Institutional Change* (1991, Westview, Boulder).

[37]   COM (85) doc 310 final.

[38]   Rometsch, D. & Wessels, W. 'The Commission and the Council' 202, 204-205 in Edwards G., & Spence, D. *The European Commission* (1994, Longman, Harlow); Featherstone, K.'Jean Monnet and the "Democratic Deficit" in the European Union' (1994) 32 *JCMS* 149,154-155.

[39]   On the Commission and 'bureaucratic politics' see Peters, G. 'Agenda-Setting

The power of proposal should not be overestimated. It clearly gives the Commission the opportunity to structure the debate. Beyond that, its influence depends upon a number of variables.[40] The reason for this is the agenda-setter's greatest influence exists when it is easier for other relevant actors to adopt the proposal than to amend or reject it. It has, thus, been argued that the Commission's influence will depend, firstly, upon what vote is necessary in the other institutions for a measure to be adopted - the lower the threshold, the higher its influence. Other relevant factors include the extent to which the Commission's preferences coincide with those of the other parties - the greater the coincidence, the higher will be its influence. Finally, a temporal dimension has been identified. If the Commission is impatient, its influence is weakened as it has to accept more readily the views of the other institutions. The reverse is true if the other institutions are impatient for a measure to be adopted.[41]

c. Executive Powers

The Commission has executive powers in a number of areas.[42] The first is in the field of *revenue*. The Commission is responsible for ensuring that the Community's revenue is collected and passed on by national authorities and that the correct rates are applied. It is also responsible for overseeing and coordinating a large part of Community *expenditure*. There are four important funds in this respect, the European Social Fund (ESF), the European Regional Development Fund (ERDF), the European Agricultural Guidance and Guarantee Fund, Guidance Section

---

in the European Community' (1994) 1 *JEPP* 9; Christiansen, T. 'Tensions of European Governance: politicised bureaucracy and multiple accountability in the European Commission' (1997) 4 JEPP 73.

[40] Its variable influence has led various academics to characterise the Commission as an opportunistic 'policy entrepreneur' seeking to expand its agenda-setting competencies wherever possibilities avail themselves. For a survey of this literature see Laffan, B. 'From policy entrepreneur to policy manager: the challenge facing the European Commission' (1997) 4 *JEPP* 422, 423-424.

[41] On this see Pollack, M. 'Delegation, Agency and agenda setting in the European Community' (1997) 51 *International Organisation* 99, 121-124.

[42] These merge to some extent with its quasi-legislative powers.

(EAGFF) and the Financial Instrument for Fisheries (FIFG). In addition, it is responsible for administering Community aid to third countries, most notably under the PHARE programme to Eastern Europe and under the Lomé Convention to African, Caribbean and Pacific (ACP) States. Thirdly the Commission exercises a supervisory role over 'front-line' policy implementation. Whilst national administrations are responsible for Customs and Excise and Agricultural Intervention Boards, the Commission will check to ensure that there is a degree of uniformity. Fourthly, the Commission represents the Community in its external trade relations with third States and in international organisations. It thus represents and acts on behalf of the EC in the GATT negotiations and participates in the work of the UN,[43] the Council of Europe,[44] and the OECD.[45] In addition the Commission handles applications for membership of the EU by carrying out an investigation of the implications of membership and submitting an opinion to the Council.

d. Supervisory Powers

The Commission also acts as the 'conscience of the Community'. In this respect it has a number of supervisory powers. First it, has certain powers of prosecution. Under Article 169 [*226*] EC the EC Commission is appointed guardian of the treaties and may bring actions against the Member States for alleged breaches of EC law. Within the framework of the Commission's limited resources, this power is used frequently. Under Article 173 [*230*] EC a similar power exists to take other EC Institutions before the Court. Secondly, the Commission has certain quasi-judicial powers. It can declare illegal State aids provided by Member States[46] or measures enacted in favour of public undertakings which breach the Treaty.[47] It has also been granted powers to declare

---

43 Article 229 [*302*] EC.
44 Article 230 [*303*] EC.
45 Article 231 [*304*] EC.
46 Article 93 [*88*] EC.
47 Article 90(3) [*86(3)*] EC.

anti-competitive practices by private undertakings illegal and, in certain circumstances, to fine those firms,[48] as well as the power to impose duties on goods coming from third States which are benefitting from 'unfair' trade practices such as dumping or export subsidies.[49]

III. The Council of Ministers

i. The Nature and Composition of the Council: The Representor of National Interests

The Council consists of a representative of each Member State at ministerial level who is authorised to commit the government of that State.[50] The minister in question depends upon the nature of the matter being discussed. Specialised Councils exist in most fields, with the national minister responsible for that area sitting in on the Council.[51] The pattern has been for increasingly Specialised Councils to develop, with 21 such Councils existing as of the end of 1995.[52] Above all these Councils sits the General Affairs Council. This consists of Foreign Ministers and has an overarching competence with the result that it considers matters not claimed as their own by one of the Specialised Councils. This plethora of structures, combined with the floating nature of the participants, has affected the cohesion of the Council and has created difficulties of coordination.[53]

---

[48]   e.g. Regulation 17, OJ Spec Ed. 1962, 204/62, articles 15 and 3 respectively

[49]   e.g. in relation to dumping see Regulation 384/96/EC, OJ 1996, L 56/1, especially articles 7-9.

[50]   Article 146 [*203*] EC.

[51]   The Agriculture Council will consist therefore of Agricultural Ministers; the Environment Council, Ministers for the Environment; Justice and Home Affairs, Ministers of Justice etc.

[52]   On this see Hayes-Renshaw, F. & Wallace, H. *The Council of Ministers* (1997, Macmillan, Basingstoke) 29-33.

[53]   Ibid., 64-65; Edwards, G. 'National sovereignty vs integration? The Council of Ministers' 127, 134-135 in Richardson, J. (ed.) *European Union: Power and Policy Making* (1996, Routledge, London).

The Presidency of the Council rotates around the Member States for six months at a time. It is the role of the President to arrange and to chair Council meetings and to set the agenda for them.[54] The President also liases with the other Institutions. The Presidency has assumed significance in recent years as Member States have used it to develop policy initiatives of interest to them and because the prestige tied to it has resulted in States vying to complete certain initiatives during their term of office in order to benefit from the associated prestige.

There are three systems of voting within the Council - simple majority, unanimity and qualified majority. The system used is important for formal reasons. It obviously contributes to the degree of influence any individual Member State can exert over a proposal. For if a Member State has a veto, its leverage is clearly greater than where simple majority is used. The consequence has been that the system used influences the climate of debate. Scharpf has noted that where there is a requirement of unanimity, a climate of bargaining prevails. Member States, aware of their veto, are inclined to have a heightened sense of self-interest and to look for matching concessions.[55] In circumstances where Member States do not have a veto, they are aware of the possibility of outmanoeuvre. A climate of problem-solving prevails with Member States looking far more towards constructing common solutions and being less protective of their initial positions.[56]

The first, and least frequently used, system of voting is *simple majority* voting. Under this system each Member of the Council has one vote, and eight votes are required for a measure to be adopted. This system is used in only a few areas, principally procedural ones, probably because it fails to protect national interests and because undue weight is

---

[54]   Council Rules of Procedure, OJ 1993, L 304/1.
[55]   Scharpf, F. 'The joint decision trap: lessons from German federalism and European integration' (1988) 66 *Public Administration* 239. This has recently been criticised as providing too generalised an account, thereby failing to take account of the extent to which policy differentiation and policy specialisation may influence voting behaviour and take Member States away from the climate of 'high politics' Peters, B. 'Escaping the Joint Decision Trap: Repetition and Sectoral Politics in the European Union' (1997) 20 *WEP* 22.
[56]   Hayes-Renshaw, F. & Wallace, H. *The Council of Ministers* (1997, Macmillan, Basingstoke) 256-258.

given to the interests of small States at the expense of large ones. These areas are:

- Adoption of the Council's own rules of procedure (Article 151(3) [*207(3)*] EC);
- Extension of time limits for the cooperation and co-decision procedures Articles 189b(7) [*251(7)*] EC and 189c(g) [*252(g)*] EC;
- Request for the Commission to undertake studies or submit proposals (Article 152 [*208*] EC);
- The convening of an intergovernmental conference to amend the Treaty (Article N(1) [*48*] TEU).

The converse of simple majority voting is voting by *unanimity*, whereby every Member State has a veto on any legislation being considered. Unanimity voting is used in those areas of the TEU which are most politically sensitive and where exercise of Community competence is most closely scrutinised. There are a number of institutional matters which can only be resolved by unanimity, such as changes in the number of judges or Advocates-General,[57] or in the number of Commissioners.[58] There are a number of important substantive areas which still require unanimity. The principal ones are:-

- Measures taken under the Citizenship provisions (Articles 8a [*18*], 8b [*19*], & 8e [*22*] EC);
- Coordination of Social Security (Article 51 [*42*] EC);
- Coordination of law governing the professions (Article 57(2) [*47(2)*] EC);
- Authorisation of State aids in exceptional circumstances (Article 93(2) [*88*] EC);
- Harmonisation of indirect taxation (Article 99 [*93*] EC);
- Approximation of laws falling within the common market but outside the internal market (Article 100 [*94*] EC);
- Granting of financial assistance to a Member State in severe economic difficulties (Article 103a(2) [*100(2)*] EC);
- Environmental measures which are primarily of a fiscal nature or concern town and country planning or significantly affect a Member State's choice between energy resources (Article 130s(2) [*175(2)*] EC);
- Action necessary to achieve one of the Community objectives where the powers are not provided elsewhere (Article 235 [*308*] EC);

---

[57] Articles 165 [*221*] & 166 [*222*] EC.
[58] Article 157(1) [*213(1)*] EC.

- Adoption of joint actions or common positions in CFSP (Articles J.2.2., J.3 & J.8 TEU).
Unanimity continues to be the norm in CFSP following Amsterdam for any measure which is not implementing a common strategy, joint action or common position. In the case of implementing measures, votes are to be taken by qualified majority, *Article 23(1) TEU*;
- Adoption of joint positions and action in the field of Justice and Home Affairs (Article K.3(2) TEU). [59] Unanimity continues to be the norm following Amsterdam, except for implementing measures, which are taken by qualified majority, *Article 34 TEU*;
- Transfer of action from the Justice and Home Affairs Pillar to the EC pillar (Article K.9 [*42*] TEU);
- Accession of a new Member State (Article O [*49*] TEU).

The extension of competences and relocation of competences between pillars brought about by Amsterdam will result in the following areas requiring unanimity voting:-

Action to combat discrimination (*Article 13 EC*);
Social policy measures securing social security; protection of workers where their employment contract is terminated; representation and collective defence of the interests of workers; conditions of employment for third country nations legally residing within the European Union, financial contributions for job-creation (*Article 137(3) EC*);
The finding of a serious and persistent breach by a Member State of the principles underlying the Union (*Article 7 TEU*);[60]
Measures adopted under the Title on Visas, Asylum, Immigration and Other Policies Related to Free Movement of Persons for the first five years following ratification of the Treaty of Amsterdam (*Article 67(1) EC*);[61]
The Decision, five years after the coming into effect of the Amsterdam Treaty, whether to make all or some of the other measures adopted under the Title on Visas, Asylum, Immigration and Other Policies Related to Free Movement of Persons subject to the

---

[59] See however Article K.3(2(b)) TEU which allows measures implementing joint actions to be adopted by qualified majority.

[60] The Member State accused of the breach does not take part in the vote, *Article 7(4) TEU*.

[61] There are two exceptions to this - measures establishing lists of third country nationals who must be in possession of visas when crossing an external frontier and procedures establishing a uniform format for visas. These are taken by qualified majority vote, *Article 67(3) EC*.

codecision procedure *(Article 67(2) EC)*;[62]
Measures necessary to implement the Schengen Agreement *(Article 2(1) Protocol
integrating the Schengen Acquis into the framework of the European Union)*.

The most common form of voting, nowadays, is qualified majority voting. This is a weighted form of voting, whereby the Member States are given differing numbers of votes. The number given strives to achieve a balance between the interests of small States and the need to reflect the differing sizes of population within the different Member States. The votes are for Britain, France, Germany, Italy 10 votes each; Spain 8; Belgium, Greece, Portugal, Netherlands 5 votes each; Sweden and Austria 4 votes each; Finland, Ireland and Denmark 3 votes each; Luxembourg 2.

This is a total of 87 votes. The qualified majority is 62 votes if the Council is acting upon a proposal from the Commission. Other cases require at least 62 votes with at least 10 Member States voting in favour. Whilst qualified majority voting has existed since the inception of the EEC Treaty, its usage has only become generalised since the late 1980s. Its initial development was stymied by the 1966 Luxembourg Accords.[63]

The Luxembourg Accords *EEC Bulletin 1966-3, 9.*

I. Where, in the case of decisions which may be taken by majority vote on a proposal of the Commission, very important interests of one or more partners are at stake, the Members of the Council will endeavour within a reasonable time, to reach solutions which can be adopted by all Members of the Council while respecting their mutual interests and those of the Community, in accordance with Article 2 of the Treaty.

Beneath all this language, the result was 'an agreement to disagree'. If one Member State raised the Accords, no vote would be

---

[62]   There is an exception for measures establishing procedures and conditions for issuing a visa and measures establishing rules on a uniform visa. These are to taken automatically by the codecision procedure five years after the coming into effect of Amsterdam, *Article 67(3) EC.*

[63]   Nicoll, W. 'The Luxembourg Compromise' (1984) 23 *JCMS* 35.

taken and the measure dropped. Member States were, *de facto*, granted a veto over all Community legislation, and a universal practice of unanimity. The Accords were not set up, however, under any formal amendment procedures.[64] Juristically, they therefore posed a problem. If a practice continues to prevail despite conflicting with the Treaty, amendment of the Treaty alone will not stop that practice. In addition, some Member States perceived the Accords as a vital safeguard of their national interests.[65] The manner in which this has been resolved has been through an amendment to the Council's rules of procedure. On the proposal of any one Member State, the Council can move to vote on a proposal if a simple majority of the Member States are willing.[66] If a bare majority of Member States refuse to recognise a State's right to invoke the Accords, the Accords are rendered valueless.

The consequence has been that since the SEA the Accords have fallen into disuse. It is probably unwise to view them as extinct, for the Council's Rules of Procedure can be easily modified by a simple majority vote. The possibility of a resurrection of the Luxembourg Accords was raised in the development of the Ioannina Compromise.[67] The dispute arose in 1994 over modifications to the number of votes necessary to secure a qualified majority in the advent of the likely accession of Austria, Finland, Norway and Sweden. The majority considered that 27 votes should be required to block the adoption of legislation.[68] This was

---

[64]   Lasok, D. with Lasok, K. *Law and Institutions of the European Union* (1994, 6th Edition, Butterworths, London) 210.

[65]   The United Kingdom's position therefore at the time of the Single European Act was that the Accords were unaffected. *House of Commons Debates*, 6th series, Vol 96, col 320. This is, formally at least, still the position of the British Government, *A Partnership of Nations: The British Approach to the European Union Intergovernmental Conference 1996* (1996, Cm 3181, HMSO, London) para. 22.

[66]   This was done in Decision 87/508, article 5, OJ 1987 L 291/27. The position is currently regulated by Council Decision of 6 December 1993, article 7(1), OJ 1993, L 304/1. On the history of the Luxembourg Accords following the Single European Act see Teasdale, A. 'The Life and Death of the Luxembourg Compromise' (1993) 31 *JCMS* 567.

[67]   See Editorial Comment (1994) 31 *CMLRev* 453.

[68]   The reason that it was 27 and not 26 was that it was envisaged that Norway would accede to the Union at the time.

based on a mechanical extrapolation of the existing weighting, which set the blocking minority at just under 30% of the total votes cast. This not only reduced the relative weight of existing votes, it also redistributed influence between existing governments.[69] An increase in the thresholds necessary to block a proposal would require Member States having to seek coalitions with additional partners. For some Member States this would be easier than for others. Spain and the United Kingdom therefore considered this extrapolation to be too high.[70]

Council Decision of 29 March 1994 concerning the taking of a Decision by qualified majority by the Council[71]

Article 1. If members of the Council representing a total of 23 to 25 votes indicate their intention to oppose the adoption by the Council of a Decision by qualified majority, the Council will do all in its power to reach, within a reasonable time and without prejudicing obligatory time limits laid down by the Treaties and by secondary law, such as Articles 189B and 189C of the Treaty establishing the European Community, a satisfactory solution that could be adopted by at least 65 votes. During this period, and always respecting the Rules of Procedure of the Council, the President undertakes, with the assistance of the Commission, any initiative necessary to facilitate a wider basis of agreement in the Council. The Members of the Council lend him their assistance.

The significance of the Ioannina Compromise does not lie in the extra 3 votes it suggests will be necessary for a measure to be enacted where the Compromise is invoked. The position is still unsatisfactory from a Spanish viewpoint. For whilst the Compromise can be generally invoked where two large Member States plus any other State other than Luxembourg form a blocking alliance, this is not the case with Spain. It

---

[69] Johnston, R. 'The Conflict over Qualified Majority Voting in the European Union Council of Ministers: An Analysis of the UK Negotiating Stance using Power Indices' (1995) 25 *British Journal of Political Science* 245; Hosli, M. 'Coalitions and Power: Effects of Qualified Majority Voting in the Council of the European Union' (1996) 34 *JCMS* 255.

[70] On the background to the dispute see Westlake, M. *The Council of the European Union* (1995, Cartermill, London) 94-95; Hayes-Renshaw, F. & Wallace, H. *The Council of Ministers* (1996, Macmillan, Basingstoke) 55-56.

[71] OJ 1994 C 105/1. Subsequently modified after Norway's failure to accede to the Union, OJ 1995 C 1/1.

will normally have to be part of an alliance of at least four Member States.[72] The significance lies rather in the reassertion of a culture which suggests there will still be resort to informal instruments where the qualified majority vote is not thought to protect national interests adequately.

The process, however, takes a new turn at Amsterdam. A formulation close to that used in the Luxembourg Accords has been introduced in three areas, where qualified majority voting is otherwise to be the norm. A vote shall not be taken allowing for the establishment of closer cooperation between some Member States in areas governed by the EC Treaty[73] or JHA,[74] or, adopting implementing measures or measures based on a common strategy in the field of CFSP,[75] if a Member State declares that it opposes it for 'important and stated reasons of national policy'. Purists will no doubt be aghast at the incorporation of such a formula into the TEU. Yet this very incorporation may weaken the 'threat' of the Accords. Its introduction in only these limited areas amounts, first to a concession that it cannot be used in other areas of law-making law. Secondly, the process has formalised the Accords in such a way that they probably can not be used in an ad hoc manner even in their narrow field of application. The vote will only not be taken where the reasons are 'important and stated', suggesting that, to be accepted by other Member States, the policy must have been emphatically set out in advance of the meeting by the Member State invoking the formula. The possibility of using it to hijack Council meetings would therefore seem, at a formal level, not to exist.

---

[72] This was recognised at the Treaty of Amsterdam by a Declaration to the Final Act where it was agreed that the Ioannina Compromise would be renegotiated to find a solution for the special case for Spain.

[73] *Article 11(3) EC.*

[74] *Article 40(2) TEU.*

[75] *Article 23(2) TEU.*

ii. The Secretariat and the COREPER

To secure some continuity and coordination the Council is serviced by two bodies, the General Secretariat and the Committee of Permanent Representatives (COREPER). Whilst the former are Community civil servants, the latter consists of members of the national civil services.

Article 151 [*207*] EC. 1. A committee consisting of the Permanent Representatives of the Member States shall be responsible for preparing the work of the Council and for carrying out the tasks assigned to it by the Council.
2. The Council shall be assisted by a General Secretariat, under the direction of a Secretary-General. The Secretary-General shall be appointed by the Council acting unanimously.[76]

The role of the Secretariat is essentially administrative. The role of the COREPER in preparing materials is far more significant. The COREPER developed because it was clear from early on that the Council would be unable to function effectively without proper preparation of Council meetings.[77] It is divided into COREPER I, composed of deputy permanent representatives, which is responsible for issues such as the environment, social affairs, the internal market and transport. COREPER II consists of permanent representatives of ambassadorial rank responsible for the more sensitive issues such as economic and financial affairs and external relations. The COREPER is in turn assisted by about 250 Working Groups of national civil servants.[78] A Commission proposal is first of all passed to these Groups for analysis. These Groups provide Reports which set the agenda for COREPER meetings by indicating points on which there has been agreement within the Working Group (Roman I points) and points which need discussion within the COREPER (Roman II points). COREPER I

---

[76] The Treaty of Amsterdam amends this provision to create the post of Deputy Secretary-General.
[77] Hayes-Renshaw, F., Lequesne, C. & Lopez, P. 'The Permanent Representations of the Member States to the European Communities' (1989) 28 *JCMS* 119.
[78] Westlake, M. The Council of the European Union (1995, Cartermill, London) 312.

and II each meet weekly. In turn COREPER sets the agenda for Council meetings by dividing the agenda into 'A' and 'B' matters. 'A' items are technical matters on which there is agreement and which can be nodded through, whereas 'B' items are considered more contentious requiring discussion in the Council.

There is a strong contrast between the legal characterisation of COREPER and its actual influence. At present the COREPER is recognised purely as having auxiliary capabilities.

Case C-25/94 Commission v Council [1996] ECR I-1469

Both the Community and the Member States were members of the United Nations Food and Agriculture Organisation (FAO). Under a 1991 Arrangement it was agreed that where the thrust of matters fell within EC competence, the Commission would vote in the FAO. If the thrust of the matter fell within national competence, Member States would vote. In 1993 a draft Agreement on the Flagging of Vessels Fishing on the High Seas came up for a vote. The Commission proposed that it should vote. The COREPER, by contrast, proposed that it was a matter which required a Member State vote. The Council 'confirmed the COREPER decision' with the result that the Agreement was adopted in 1993 with the Member States voting upon it. The Commission claimed that the Council had acted illegally. The Council challenged, inter alia, the admissibility of the action, claiming that the decision had been taken by COREPER and not by it.

24. The Court notes that Article 145 of the Treaty provides that the Council shall have power to take decisions.

25. Article 151(1), which forms part of the section relating to the Council, provides that COREPER is responsible for preparing the work of the Council and for carrying out the tasks assigned to it by the Council.

26. It is clear from those provisions that COREPER is not an institution of the Communities upon which the Treaty confers powers of its own but an auxiliary body of the Council, for which it carries out preparation and implementation work.

27. COREPER's function of carrying out the tasks assigned to it by the Council does not give it the power to take decisions which belongs, under the Treaty, to the Council.

28. It follows that COREPER could not adopt, on 21 October 1993, a decision on the right to vote and that the Council's vote on 22 November 1993 cannot therefore be regarded as confirming a previous COREPER decision.

This will be slightly alleviated by the Amsterdam Treaty which amends Article 151 [*207*] EC to allow COREPER to adopt procedural decisions where the Council's rules so provide. Even with this amendment, the law obscures the significance of COREPER.

COREPER is seen both as a useful conduit for informing national capitals of the work of the Community and for enabling national positions to be properly defended.[79] Successive reports on the working of the institutions have thus recognised it as being essential to the effective functioning of the Council, as it both alleviates the general workload of the Council and coordinates the work of the Specialised Councils.[80] The extent to which it does this is reflected by the consensus in the academic literature that the vast majority of matters are not discussed by ministers with decision being in effect taken by the COREPER. The only empirical research on the matter confirms this. In the period considered, of the 500 items placed on the Council agenda, decision-making by the Ministers was only considered to take place on 13% of the items.[81]

The coodinatory role it performs, however, comes at a cost. For there is little doubt that it has created government by 'moonlight'. The meetings of the COREPER are not public, its minutes are not published, and it is not accountable to any parliamentary assembly. As its influence has increased, so one sees accountability and transparency being diminished.

---

[79]   Hayes-Renshaw, F., Lequesne, C. & Lopez, P. supra n.70, 129-131.

[80]   *Report on the European Institutions by the Committee of Three to the European Council (Tindemans Report)*(1979, EC Council, Brussels) 49-54; *Report from the Ad Hoc Committee on Institutional Affairs to the European Council (Dooge Report)* EC Bulletin 3-1985 pt 3.5.1.

[81]   v. Schendelen, M. '"The Council Decides": Does the Council Decide?' (1996) 34 *JCMS* 531. This article also contains a good summary of the literature on the matter.

iii. The Powers of the Council

The powers of the Council are as elliptically defined in Article 145 [*202*] EC as those of the Commission are in Article 155 [*211*] EC.

Article 145 [*202*] EC. To ensure that the objectives set out in the Treaty are attained, the Council shall, in accordance with the provisions of this Treaty:
- ensure co-ordination of the general economic policies of the Member States:
- have power to take decisions:
- confer on the Commission, in acts which the Council adopts, powers for the implementation of the rules which the Council lays down. The Council may impose certain requirements in respect of the exercise of these powers. The Council may also reserve the right, in specific cases, to exercise directly implementing powers itself. The procedures referred to above must be consonant with principles and rules to be laid down in advance by the Council, acting unanimously on a proposal from the Commission and after obtaining the opinion of the European Parliament.

The Council's powers are fivefold. *First*, in areas of policy where responsibility still lies with the Member States, such as general economic policy, foreign and security policy, justice and home affairs, it acts as a forum within which Member States can consult with each other and coordinate their behaviour. *Secondly*, the Council can take the other Institutions before the Court either for actions which contravene EC law[82] or for failing to act when required to by Community law. [83]*Thirdly*, the Council can request the Commission to undertake studies or submit legislative proposals.[84] Nugent notes that the Council has maximised this role, *inter alia*, through the passing of Resolutions which, whilst not having any legal weight, place pressure on the Commission to act, and through the development of machinery, in particular the COREPER Working Groups and the Presidency which act as mechanisms through which ideas can be generated.[85] Whilst, undoubtedly true, the pre-legislative influence of the Council should not be overstated, as whilst

---

[82]   Article 173 [*230*] EC.
[83]   Article 175 [*232*] EC.
[84]   Article 152 [*208*] EC
[85]   Nugent, N. supra n.27, 124-125.

the Council can ask for the submission of proposals it cannot determine their content. *Fourthly*, the Council can delegate legislative powers to the Commission. The *fifth* and most influential role is the power to take the final decision on Commission proposals in most areas of Community policy. This gives the Council a veto over any proposed legislative initiative, which, in turn, bolsters the Council's influence at earlier stages in the decision-making process, as the other institutions are aware that a proposal will only become law if it has the Council's approval, and will tailor their actions accordingly.

IV. The European Council

The European Council consists of the Heads of Government of the Member States and the President of the Commission and is a separate institution from the Council of Ministers.[86] It had been agreed in 1961 in Bonn that the Heads of Government should meet at regular intervals. This practice of 'summitry' was institutionalised at the Paris Summit in 1974 where it was agreed that Heads of Government should meet at least three times a year.[87] The European Council, as a Community Institution, was only formally recognised by the Single European Act 1986, which reduced the times it should meet to twice a year.[88] The strong intergovernmental nature of this institution is reflected in the preparation for the meetings which are organised jointly by national Foreign Ministries and the Council Secretariat.

Article D [4] TEU. The European Council shall provide the Union with the necessary impetus for its development and shall define the general political guidelines thereof.
The European Council shall bring together the Heads of State or of Government

---

[86] On the development and functions of the European Council see Bulmer, S. & Wessels, W. *The European Council* (Macmillan, Basingstoke, 1987); Werts, J. *The European Council* (1992, Asser Instituut, The Hague); Troy Johnston, M. *The European Council, Gatekeeper of the European Community* (1994, Westview Press, Boulder).

[87] *Eighth General Report on the Activities of the Communities* (1974, OOPEC, Luxembourg) 297.

[88] Article 2 SEA.

of the Member States and the President of the Commission. They shall be assisted by the Ministers for Foreign Affairs of the Member States and by a member of the Commission. The European Council shall meet at least twice a year, under the chairmanship of the Head of State or of Government of the Member State which holds the Presidency of the Council.

The European Council shall submit to the European Parliament a report after each of its meetings and a yearly written report on the progress achieved by the Union.

The European Council provides, first, a forum where the Heads of State can discuss matters which fall outside the Treaty. The question of economic and monetary union, for example, was, thus, discussed at length within the European Council in the late 1980s well before the signing of the Treaty on European Union, and it is within the European Council that the Heads of Government are meeting to discuss the current Intergovernmental Conference.

The European Council has developed an increasing role in relation to the internal development of the Union. As Heads of Government have the domestic authority to resolve issues which have reached an impasse within the Council of Ministers, from very early on it was used, informally, to unblock legislative blockages by reaching package deals which would then be implemented by the Council.

The TEU entrenched the 'internal' role for the European Council.[89] It is thus given an overarching role where it is to provide political guidance to the Union.[90] It also has a number of powers in areas where the subject-matter is particularly sensitive. One finds this development within both the EC pillar and the pillar on Common Foreign and Security Policy (CFSP). For example, within the EC pillar, the European Council is entrusted with drawing up broad guidelines on the economic policies of the Member States and the Community.[91] It is within the CFSP pillar, however, that this role is most prevalent, with its

---

[89]   For criticism of this see Eijsbouts, T. 'Constitutional Sedimentation' (1996/1) *LIEI* 52.

[90]   Article D [*4*] TEU.

[91]   Article 103(2) [*99(2)*] EC. The European Central Bank is also required to send its annual report to, amongst others, the European Council, Article 109b(3) [*113(3)*]EC.

being responsible for defining the principles and general guidelines for a common foreign and security policy.[92]

Lodge, J. 'EC Policymaking: institutional considerations' in Lodge, J. (ed.) *The European Community and the Challenge of the Future* **(1989, 1st Edition, Pinter, London) 49-50**

Cynics saw the regularization of summitry in 1974 (on the initiative of French President Giscard d'Estaing) as inimical to European integration, as a crude device by heads of government keen to 'get in on the act' and to grasp a role for themselves in EC affairs before integration eclipsed them as well as the states. Some saw Euro-Councils as reminiscent of the Fouchet Plan to insert a political, intergovernmental directorate over the supranational bodies. Others saw it as potentially integrative in that it was a body that could give direction (hopefully) when the usual institutional dialogue was blocked. Indeed, meeting three times a year (twice per annum since 1987) the European Council soon became a referee in disputes among the Member States, between different sectoral Councils, and the Commission. It was also seen as a court of arbitration when the Council had failed to reach a decision. This role sat uneasily with more grandiose expectations of what it would deliver. Sorting out Council deadlocks detracted from the idea that it was the supreme authority in the EC and from the politically charged business of summitry. Yet, this function almost more than anything served to create the impression that it was an important body in the EC....

From 1974 the European Councils have assumed a 'motor' role in integration. They have launched their own initiatives when a powerful coalition of states (always including France and the FRG) have nudged them along. They have responded to or taken up those launched elsewhere (notably on institutional reform and European Union) and have sanctioned cooperation over a range of areas not necessarily strictly within the EC's competence....In other areas the European Council may simply have sanctioned politically developments occurring in the private sector (for example) whose progress depended on a visible and tangible EC-level commitment....

The European Council's 'motor' role is perhaps less an expression of heads of governments' intention to be seen as the supreme source of authority in the EC than of the reality of contemporary European integration. The EC has become the prime site for promoting cooperation among the Twelve [Fifteen]. It is not a question any more of national goals being 'Europeanized' to improve their chances of attainment. Rather the EC is the reference arena for national goals: the question is whether or not they can be met better, more cheaply or more efficiently and effectively by EC cooperation rather than by individual (often competitive) unilateral national action alone.

---

[92]   Article J.8 TEU. Following Amsterdam this role is now contained in *Article 13(1) TEU.*

V. The European Parliament

i. The Compositional Immaturity of the European Parliament

The European Parliament was initially set up as the European Assembly, and it was not until 1962 that it called itself a Parliament, a description only formally recognised in the Single European Act.[93] Prior to 1979 it consisted merely of representatives of national assemblies or parliaments. Since then, MEPs have been elected by direct universal suffrage at five yearly intervals.[94] Ambivalence about the role of the European Parliament has resulted in its having a number of internal characteristics which would be considered unsatisfactory were it a domestic Parliament operating in a unitary State.

The first concerns the distribution of seats. Parliament is composed of 626 members. These seats are distributed between the Member States on the following basis:- Austria 20, Belgium 25, Denmark 16, Finland 16, France 87, Germany 99, Greece 25, Ireland 15, Italy 87, Luxembourg 6, The Netherlands 31, Portugal 25, Spain 64, Sweden 21 and the United Kingdom 87. Even a rough calculation illustrates that some parts of the Union are better represented than others. For example, Luxembourg with a population of just under 1 million has 1 MEP for roughly every 200,000 inhabitants. Germany, on the other hand, with a population of just over 80 million has 99 MEPs, resulting in there being 1 MEP for approximately every 800,000 inhabitants.[95]

This problem is likely to be exacerbated by enlargement. On current levels of representation enlargement would have resulted in the Parliament having over 1,000 MEPs. Such a number is far too large for

---

[93]   Article 3 SEA.

[94]   The actual Council Decision on direct elections was taken in 1976, Decision 76/787/EEC, OJ 1976, L 278/1.

[95]   A detailed analysis of this imbalance is contained in Herne, K. & Nurmi, H. 'The Distribution of A Priori Voting Power in the EC Council of Ministers and the European Parliament' (1993) 16 *Scandinavian Political Studies* 269.

a deliberative assembly. At Amsterdam the Member States accepted a proposal from the Parliament that an upper limit of 700 be placed upon the size of the Parliament.[96] Yet the small number of representatives of some of the smaller Member States entail that it will be difficult to reduce their representation significantly with the likelihood that it will be the larger Member States which have to make the greater adjustments.

The second is that whilst it is envisaged within the Treaty that uniform election procedures will be drawn up, this has not yet happened.[97] The only current constraint on this freedom enjoyed by Member States is that they allow any citizen of the Union residing in a State of which he or she is not a national to vote or stand as a candidate in the State in which he or she resides.[98] This lack of uniformity has resulted in election to the European Parliament being subject to the vagaries of national procedures, and, consequently to considerable anomalies. For example, in 1984 the European Democratic Group won 50 seats with 6 million votes. The more centrist Liberal Group won only 32 seats with 10 million votes.[99]

The establishment of uniform procedures on which everyone is agreed, however, has proved to be very problematic. A draft proposal was made by the Parliament in 1992 under the threat of Court action brought by the British Liberal Democrat party.[100] The matter has been stalled since then. To facilitate agreement the Amsterdam Treaty suggests that the electoral procedures need not necessarily be uniform

---

[96] *Article 189 EC*. The proposal is contained in Resolution A4-102/95 on the functioning of the Treaty of the European Union with a view to the 1996 Intergovernmental Conference.

[97] Article 138(3) [*190(3)*] EC.

[98] Article 8b(2) [*19(2)*] EC.

[99] Bowler, S. & Farrell, D. 'Legislator Shirking and Voter Monitoring: Impact of European Parliament Electoral Systems upon Legislator-Voter Relationships' (1993) 32 *JCMS* 45; Corbett, R., Jacobs, F. & Shackleton, M. *The European Parliament* (1995, 3rd Edition, Cartermill, London) 19-29.

[100] Resolution A3-0381/92. This was then passed on to the Council as a draft proposal SEC 93(1021). On the background see Case C-41/92 *Liberal Democrats v Parliament* [1993] ECR I-3153.

but could also be 'in accordance with principles common to all Member States'.[101]

The third weakness is that there exists no European political party system. The importance of this was recognised by the TEU.[102]

Article 138a [191] EC. Political parties at European level are important as a factor for integration within the Union. They contribute to forming a European awareness and to expressing the political will of the citizens of the Union.

At the moment, however, MEPs are elected as representatives of national political parties. In establishing lists of candidates for elections these national parties are frequently influenced by narrow domestic issues rather than matters which fall within the remit of the Union, and some commentators suggest that this has an influence on MEP behaviour who, with a view to renomination, have half an eye on what is going on back home.[103] Representatives of national parties sit within less cohesive European 'groupings' once at Strasbourg. There are currently ten groupings within the European Parliament, with 31 MEPs not being attached to any one grouping. The largest grouping is currently the Party of European Socialists, which consists of the principal left of centre parties and which has 221 MEPs. The second largest is the European Peoples Party which consists of MEPs from national Christian democratic parties and which has 173 MEPs affiliated to it.[104]

---

[101]   *Article 190(3) EC.*

[102]   Attina, F. 'The voting behaviour of the European Parliament members and the problem of Europarties' (1990) 5 *European Journal of Political Research* 557; Attina, F. 'Parties, Party System and Democracy in the European Union' (1992) 27 *International Spectator* 67; Gaffney, J. (ed.) *Political Parties and the European Community* (1994, Routledge, London).

[103]   Abélès, M. 'Political Anthropology of a Transnational Institution: The European Parliament' (1993) 11 *French Politics and Society* 1, 11-17; Brzinski, J. 'Political Group Cohesion in the European Parliament, 1989-1994' 135, 143-144 in Rhodes, C. & Mazey, S. (eds.) *The State of the European Union volume 3: Building a European Polity* (1995, Longman, Harlow)

[104]   Lodge, J. (ed.) *The 1994 Elections to the European Parliament* (1995, Pinter, London).

ii. The Powers of the European Parliament

a. Supervisory Powers

If the Commission represents the 'conscience of the Community' vis-à-vis the Member States, it might be expected that the Parliament should, to a large extent, assume that role vis-à-vis the Community institutions. For, as Raworth observes, in a parliamentary system, it is the legislature which is directly elected and, for that reason, is the supreme organ of the State. The executive, on the other hand, which is appointed, can only derive its legitimacy from its accountability to the legislature.[105] There is, however, a proviso. Whilst this argument is tenable within a unitary or federal state, the Union has not yet evolved to that status. The presence of the Council, as representative of national interests, is a reminder that the Community exists somewhere between international regime and incipient federal State. Whilst in the latter one might expect the other institutions to be accountable to the Parliament, within the former it would not. The consequence is that whilst, therefore, there would seem little objection to the other supranational institutions, in particular the Commission, being accountable to the Parliament, it would be surprising if this were the case with an institution as strongly intergovernmental as the Council.

The system of controls that Parliament can impose can be divided into three; controls to ensure that other institutions do not break EC law; controls to restrict practices which, whilst not being breaches of EC law, constitute acts of maladministration, and controls to regulate the exercise of policy-making more generally.

In the original EC Treaty there was no explicit mention of the Parliament having the power to bring other EC Institutions to Court. The closest was Article 175 [232] EC, the provision which allows Institutions to be taken to Court for failing to act where legally required

---

[105] Raworth, P. 'A Timid Step Forwards: Maastricht and the Democratisation of the European Community' (1994) 19 *ELRev* 16,16-17.

to do so, which was sufficiently open textured for *locus standi* to be easily extended to the Parliament.[106] The position was more difficult in respect of Article 173 [*230*] EC, the provision allowing acts of the Community institutions to be annulled.[107] When the matter first came up before the Court, it considered that the textual arguments were so strong that Parliament was denied standing.[108] This was modified by the judgment below which provides the basis for the amendment introduced by the Treaty on European Union.

Article 173 [*230*] EC. 3. The Court shall have jurisdiction ... in actions brought by the European Parliament and by the ECB for the purpose of protecting their prerogatives.

The rationale for this limited locus standi is that of institutional balance, namely that Parliament should have some mechanism available to it to ensure that the other institutions do not transgress on its powers.[109]

Case C-70/88 European Parliament v Council (Chernobyl) [1990] ECR 2041, [1992] 1 CMLR 91

A Regulation governing the maximum levels of radioactivity permitted in feeding stuffs following the Chernobyl disaster was adopted under Article 31 EURATOM. This provision allowed Council to adopt a measure on a proposal from the Commission without the need to consult Parliament. The Parliament protested, claiming that Article 100A [*95*] EC, the legal base for harmonisation of legislation necessary to secure the establishment and functioning of the internal market, was the appropriate legal base.

---

106   Article 175 [*232*] EC states that Member States and 'other institutions of the Community' may bring an action for failure to act, Case 13/83 *European Parliament v Council* [1985] ECR 1513, [1986] 1 CMLR 138.

107   Prior to the TEU Article 173 [*230*] EC read: 'It [the Court of Justice] shall for this purpose have jurisdiction in actions brought by a Member State, the Council or the Commission on grounds of.....'

108   Case 302/87 *European Parliament v Council* (Comitology) [1988] ECR 5615.

109   Weiler, J. 'Pride and Prejudice - Parliament v Council' (1989) 14 *ELRev* 334, 336-338; Bradley, K. 'Sense and Sensibility: Parliament v Council *continued*' (1991) 16 *ELRev* 245.

13. First of all, in the first paragraph of Article 173 or Article
Parliament is not included among the institutions which, like †
bring an action for annulment against any measure of another

14. Furthermore, since the Parliament is not a legal person i
before the Court under the second paragraph of the Articles
173(4) EC], the scheme of which would, in any event, be inap
annulment brought by the Parliament.

15. In the judgment in Case 302/87, after having stated the reasons why the Parliament
did not have capacity to bring an action under Article 173 of the EEC Treaty, the Court
pointed out that various legal remedies were available to ensure that the Parliament's
prerogatives were defended. As was observed in that judgment, not only does the
Parliament have the right to bring an action for failure to act, but the Treaties provide
means for submitting for review by the Court acts of the Council or the Commission
adopted in disregard of the Parliament's prerogatives.

16. However, the circumstances and arguments adduced in the present case show that the
various legal remedies provided for both in the Euratom Treaty and in the EEC Treaty,
however effective and diverse they may be, may prove to be ineffective or uncertain.

17. First, an action for failure to act cannot be used to challenge the legal basis of a
measure which has already been adopted.

18. Secondly, the submission of a reference for a preliminary ruling on the validity of
such an act or the bringing of an action by Member States or individuals for the
annulment of the act are mere contingencies, and the Parliament cannot be sure that they
will materialise.

19. Finally, while the Commission is required to ensure that the Parliament's prerogatives
are respected, that duty cannot go so far as to oblige it to adopt the Parliament's position
and bring an action for annulment which the Commission itself considers unfounded.

20. It follows from the foregoing that the existence of those various legal remedies is not
sufficient to guarantee, with certainty and in all circumstances, that a measure adopted
by the Council or the Commission in disregard of the parliament's prerogatives will be
reviewed.

21. Those prerogatives are one of the elements of the institutional balance created by the
Treaties. The Treaties set up a system for distributing powers among the different
Community institutions, assigning to each institution its own role in the institutional
structure of the Community and the accomplishment of the tasks entrusted to the
Community.

e of the institutional balance means that each of the institutions must powers with due regard for the powers of the other institutions. It also at it should be possible to penalise any breach of that rule which may occur.

he Court, which under the Treaties has the task of ensuring that in the interpretation d application of the Treaties the law is observed, must therefore be able to maintain the institutional balance and, consequently, review the observance of the Parliament's prerogatives when called upon to do so by the Parliament, by means of a legal remedy which is suited to the purpose which the parliament seeks to achieve.

24. In carrying out that task the Court cannot, of course, include the Parliament among the institutions which may bring an action under Article 173 of the EEC Treaty or Article 146 of the Euratom Treaty without being required to demonstrate an interest in bringing an action.

25. However, it is the Court's duty to ensure that the provisions of the Treaties concerning the institutional balance are fully applied and to see to it that the Parliament's prerogatives, like those of the other institutions, cannot be breached without it having available a legal remedy, among those laid down in the Treaties, which may be exercised in a certain and effective manner.

26. The absence in the Treaties of any provision giving the Parliament the right to bring an action for annulment may constitute a procedural gap, but it cannot prevail over the fundamental interest in the maintenance and observance of the institutional balance laid down in the Treaties establishing the European Communities.

27. Consequently, an action for annulment brought by the Parliament against an act of the Council or the Commission is admissible provided that the action seeks only to safeguard its prerogatives and that it is founded only on submissions alleging their infringement. Provided that condition is met, the Parliament's action for annulment is subject to the rules laid down in the Treaties for actions for annulment brought by the other institutions.

28. In accordance with the Treaties, the Parliament's prerogatives include participation in the drafting of legislative measures, in particular participation in the cooperation procedure laid down in the EEC Treaty.

29. In the present case, the Parliament claims that the contested regulation is based on Article 31 of the Euratom Treaty, which provides only that the Parliament is to be consulted, whereas it ought to have been based on Article 100A of the EEC Treaty, which requires implementation of the procedure for cooperation with the Parliament.

30. The Parliament infers from that that the Council's choice of legal basis for the contested regulation led to a breach of its prerogatives by denying it the possibility, which the cooperation procedure offers, of participating in the drafting of the measure more closely and actively than it could in the consultation procedure.

31. Since the Parliament claims that its prerogatives were breached as a result of the choice of legal basis for the contested measure, it follows from all the foregoing that the present action is admissible. The Council's objection of inadmissibility must therefore be dismissed and the proceedings must be continued with regard to the substance of the case.

The second area in which Parliament has flexed its muscles before the Court concerns the question of whether it has been adequately consulted by the other institutions, notwithstanding that the appropriate legal base has been chosen.

Case C-21/94 Parliament v Council [1995] ECR I-1827

In 1993 a Directive had been adopted on the application of taxes on certain vehicles used for carriage of goods by road and tolls and charges for the use of certain infrastructures. The Directive had been adopted on the bases of Articles 75 [*71*] and 99 [*93*] EC, both of which require that the Parliament be consulted. The Parliament was consulted but the Directive was amended subsequently without its being reconsulted.

17. It must first of all be borne in mind that due consultation of the Parliament in the cases provided for by the Treaty constitutes an essential formal requirement breach of which renders the measure concerned void (see, for example, the judgment in Case 417/93 *Parliament v Council* [1995] ECR I-1185, paragraph 9). The effective participation of the Parliament in the legislative process of the Community, in accordance with the procedures laid down by the Treaty, represents an essential factor in the institutional balance intended by the treaty. Such power reflects the fundamental democratic principle that the people should take part in the exercise of power through the intermediary of a representative assembly (see, for example, the judgment in Case C-65/93 *Parliament v Council* [1995] ECR I-643, paragraph 21).

18. The duty to consult the European Parliament in the course of the legislative procedure, in the cases provided for by the Treaty, implies the requirement that the Parliament should be reconsulted whenever the text finally adopted, viewed as a whole, departs substantially from the text on which the Parliament has already been consulted, except where the amendments essentially correspond to the wish of the Parliament itself (see, for example, the judgment in Case C-388/92 *Parliament v Council* [1994] ECR I-2067, paragraph 10, and in Case C-280/93 *Germany v Council* [1994] ECR I-4973, paragraph 38).

19. The Court must therefore consider whether or not the amendments referred to by the Parliament affect the actual substance of the text, viewed as a whole.

.....

22. As the Advocate General pointed out in paragraph 49 of his Opinion, it is apparent from a comparison between the Commission's initial proposal and the directive not only that the Council is no longer obliged to adopt a harmonized system by 31 December 1998 at the latest, but also that the Commission is no longer required to submit, in the report to be presented to the Council, proposals for establishing cost-charging arrangements based on the principle of territoriality. Those amendments go to the very essence of the system introduced and must be classified as substantial.

23. It is, moreover, not disputed that those amendments do not correspond to any wish expressed by Parliament.

24. Nevertheless, the Council believes that even if the text finally adopted, viewed as a whole, did depart substantially from the text on which the Parliament had been consulted, it was not required to reconsult that institution provided that, as in this case, the Council was sufficiently well informed as to the opinion of the Parliament on the essential points at issue.

25. That argument must be rejected.

26. Proper consultation of the Parliament in the cases provided for by the Treaty constitutes one of the means enabling it to play an effective role in the legislative process of the Community (see, in particular, the judgment in Case C-316/91 *Parliament v Council* [1994] ECR I-625, paragraph 17); to accept the Council's argument would result in seriously undermining that essential participation in the maintenance of the institutional balance intended by the treaty and would amount to disregarding the influence that due consultation of the Parliament can have on adoption of the measure in question.

.....

28. Consequently, the fact that the Parliament was not consulted for a second time during the legislative procedure laid down in Articles 75 and 99 of the EEC Treaty constitutes an infringement of essential formal requirements as a result of which the measure at issue must be annulled.

The third area where Parliamentary prerogatives are at stake is where implementing powers are delegated to the Commission which are to be exercised either exclusively or, as more usually happens, under the comitology procedure. Such procedures preempt the normal legislative procedures in the Treaty and, if abused, could result in a downgrading of the Parliamentary interest. That being said, the Court has yet to give judgment on any action brought before it by the Parliament which claims that an instrument grants too wide implementing powers.

It has been suggested that it may be misguided to place too much emphasis on institutional autonomy as a reason for Parliament having standing.

Weiler, J. 'Pride and Prejudice - Parliament v Council' (1989) 14 *European Law Review* 334, 338-339 & 342-343

In principle, privileged status is conceded to bodies which in some way represent a general interest ....

...The European Parliament has its own constituency which is different from that of Council and Member States: European citizens as a whole, whose interests, it must be remembered, may differ from those of their governments. If the system of privileged locus standi is conceived, at least in part, as an attempt to fuse different layers of the general interest, Parliament would add an important complexion to this fusion. To the extent that Parliament's decisional role has increased, there could also be the interest in not inducing it to fight every measure with all its political powers simply because it believes the measure is illegal.

... It is true that the right of Parliament to sue another institution would appear to be outside the normal province of legislatures. I have already pointed out in reply it has been suggested this is so because in most systems the legislature is very powerful and has plenary political power to approve legislation, something not existing in the Community. But one can go further. First of all there is a 'federal logic' in allowing Parliament to bring an action when its own prerogatives are at stake. And instead of looking to the other side of the Atlantic one may look to that repository of federal experience within the Community - the Federal Republic. Under German Constitutional law, the Bundesrat may sue the President of the Republic for adoption of acts, the legal basis of which excluded Bundesrat participation. Analogous reasoning could apply to the Community system as well. In addition, whereas it may be argued that traditionally legislatures do not have as their function the bringing of legal suits, this cannot be said to be reflected in the EEC Treaty. If this were so, why, one may ask, has the Council, *in addition to the Member States*, standing to sue under Article 173 EC?

The second form of supervisory power possessed by the Parliament is that of considering acts of maladministration carried out by any EC institution or body. Since 1953, citizens of the European Union or natural or legal persons resident in the Union have been entitled to petition the Parliament.[110] In 1987 the Parliament set up a Committee of Petitions consisting of MEPs to consider the petitions.[111] Each year the Parliament receives about 1,000 petitions which take two forms. They either express views on a particular issue, such as human rights or animal protection, or seek redress for a particular grievance, which may have been committed by an EC institution, national authority or private body.[112] In the latter two cases the Parliament will usually seek the assistance of the Commission, which has wider enforcement powers than it.

At Maastricht Denmark considered that acts of maladministration should be considered by a body independent from the Parliament and pushed for the appointment of the Community Ombudsman.[113]

Article 138e [195] EC.1. The European Parliament shall appoint an Ombudsman empowered to receive any complaints from any citizen of the Union or any natural or legal person residing or having its registered office in a Member State concerning instances of maladministration in the activities of the Community institutions or bodies, with the exception of the Court of Justice and the Court of First Instance acting in their judicial role.

In accordance with his duties, the Ombudsman shall conduct inquiries for which he finds grounds, either on his own initiative or on the basis of complaints submitted to him direct or through a member of the European Parliament, except where the alleged facts are or have been the subject of legal proceedings. Where the Ombudsman establishes an instance of maladministration, he shall refer the matter to the institution concerned, which shall then have a period of three months in which to inform him of its views. The Ombudsman shall then forward a report to the European Parliament and the institution concerned. The person lodging the complaint shall be informed of the outcome of such inquiries.

The Ombudsman shall submit an annual report to the European Parliament on the outcome of his inquiries.

---

[110] This is now formally recognised in Article 138d [194] EC.

[111] This Committee has now been given a formal basis in Article 138c [193] EC.

[112] Corbett, R., Jacobs, F. & Shackleton, M. *The European Parliament* (1995, 3rd Edition, Cartermill, London) 290-292.

[113] The current Ombudsman is a Finn, Jacob Söderman, who was sworn in on 27 September 1995. On the Ombudsman see Marias, E.(ed.) *The European Ombudsman* (1994, EIPA, Maastricht); Magliveras, K. 'Best Intentions but empty words: The European Ombudsman' (1995) 20 *ELRev* 401,

2. The Ombudsman shall be appointed after each election of the European Parliament for the duration of its term of office. The Ombudsman shall be eligible for reappointment.

The Ombudsman may be dismissed by the Court of Justice at the request of the European Parliament if he no longer fulfils the conditions of his duties or if he is guilty of serious misconduct.

3. The Ombudsman shall be completely independent in the performance of his duties. In the performance of those duties he shall neither seek nor take instructions from any body. The Ombudsman may not, during his term of office, engage in any other occupation, whether gainful or not.

4. The European Parliament shall, after seeking an opinion from the Commission and with the approval of the Council acting by a qualified majority lay down the regulations and general conditions governing the performance of the Ombudsman's duties.

The conditions regarding the performance of the Ombudsman's duties have now been set out in Decision 94/262 EC.[114] In the main this Decision fleshes out Article 138e [*195*] EC. The complaint must allow the Ombudsman to identify the person making the complaint, must be made within two years of the facts on which it is based coming to the attention of the complainant, and must be preceded by appropriate administrative approaches to the institution concerned. In addition, no complaint may be made concerning the working relations between the Institutions and their employees unless all internal procedures have been exhausted. Crucially, however, it extends the Ombudsman's powers, so that EC institutions are obliged to supply it with the information it requests which is necessary to carry out its investigations.[115] This duty is extended to Member States in so far as national laws on secrecy or otherwise do not prevent the information being disclosed.[116]

The Ombudsman is obliged to seek solutions with the institutions concerned.[117] Whilst this duty of cooperation might facilitate settlements, it raised doubts as to how inquisitorial the Ombudsman would be. The early evidence is mixed. In 1996 the Ombudsman began 210 inquiries, and made decisions in 114 cases. In 32 of those it addressed a critical

---

[114]   OJ 1994 L 113/15.
[115]   Ibid., article 3(2).
[116]   Ibid., article 3(3).
[117]   Ibid., article 3(5).

remark to the institution in question.[118] This seems a high proportion until it is realised that 27 of those 32 cases related to one instance, the Commission's handling of a complaint about the failure of the British Government to carry out an environmental assessment before authorising work to be carried out on the Newbury bypass.[119]

The third level at which Parliament has supervisory powers is that certain institutions are accountable to it. The level of accountability varies considerably according to the institution concerned:

The Court of Justice and the Court of First Instance: The institutions least accountable to the Parliament are the two Courts. Neither institution nor, in the absence of misconduct, any of the individual judges are in any way accountable to the Parliament.

The European Council: The European Council is required by Article D [4] TEU to submit a report to Parliament after each of its meetings and an annual written report on the progress of the Union.

The Council of Ministers: Formally, apart from the Courts, the Council of Ministers is the least accountable of all the Community institutions to the Parliament. The need for inter-institutional dialogue has resulted in the development of a limited accountability. First, it is customary for the President of the Council to present before the Parliament the proposed work of the Council for the forthcoming six months. The only difficulty with this is that the President is not a representative of the Council and can only express that government's view and not views on behalf of the Council itself.[120] Secondly, a convention has grown whereby the Council will answer questions put to it by members of the Parliament. A formal corollary of this is that the Council has a right to be heard by the Parliament.[121]

---

[118]   The European Ombudsman, *European Ombudsman Annual Report* (1997, OOPEC, Luxembourg) 18-19.

[119]   Ibid., 58-67.

[120]   Westlake, M. *A Modern Guide to the European Parliament* (1994, Pinter, London) 41.

[121]   Article 140(3) [*197(3)*] EC.

The European Central Bank: The European Central Bank will be required to submit an Annual Report to all the institutions including the Parliament.[122] In addition the President of the ECB or members of the Executive Council may, at the request of the European Parliament, or on their own initiative be heard by the competent Committees of the Parliament.[123]

The Commission: The Commission is the institution over which the Parliament has most control. It is required to submit an Annual Report which is debated and voted on by the Parliament[124] and is required to reply to questions put by Parliament or its members.[125] The most draconian power the Parliament has over the Commission is the motion of censure.[126] If a motion of censure is passed by a two-thirds majority of the votes cast representing a majority (i.e. more than 313) of the members of the European Parliament, the Commission is obliged to resign as a body. This power to dismiss, essentially, the Commission has proved to be of limited effect. It is an 'all or nothing' power. It does not allow Parliament to criticise or dismiss individual Commissioners, and this, combined with the Parliament not traditionally having any input in the appointment of the new Commission, resulted in its being occasionally threatened but never exercised.[127]

The TEU may have tilted the balance in this respect. Parliament now has the right, first, to be consulted by the Member States over the nominations for Commissioner and, secondly, to veto the appointment of the Commission as a body.[128] As discussed earlier, this power was reinforced at Amsterdam by Parliament being given the additional power to veto the nominated President of the Commission.[129] Whereas

---

122   Article 109b(3)(1) [*113(3)(1)*] EC.
123   Article 109b(3)(2) [*113(3)(2)*] EC. Jacobs, F. 'The European Parliament and Economic and Monetary Union' (1991) 28 *CMLRev* 361.
124   Article 143 [*200*] EC.
125   Article 140(3) [*197(3)*] EC.
126   Article 144 [*201*] EC.
127   Westlake, M. *The Commission and the Parliament* (1994, Butterworths, London) 28; Corbett, R., Jacobs, F. & Shackleton, M. supra n.112, 246-247.
128   Article 158(2) [*214(2)*] EC.
129   See p 87.

Parliament previously had no influence over who would be the replacements for a Commission subject to a motion of censure, it now has considerable influence.

In addition the extension of the Commission term to five years has synchronised its mandate with that of the Parliament. The result is that all prospective Commissioners are subject to questioning by Parliamentary Committees before assent is given to their appointment. The combination of all this is that the Commission is likely to be increasingly responsive to the views of Parliament in the future.

b. The Budgetary Powers of the Parliament

The 'Own Resources' Decision of 1970 made the Community financially independent from the Member States and gave it its own system of revenue.[130] Within the elaborate system regulating the Community Budget, Parliament enjoys extensive powers in relation to expenditure.[131]

It has, firstly, the power, acting by a majority of its Members and two thirds of the votes cast, to reject the draft Budget if there are 'important reasons' and ask for a new draft to be submitted to it by the Commission.[132] Secondly, a distinction is made between non-compulsory expenditure (NCE) and compulsory expenditure (CE). The latter is considered to be all expenditure that the Community is obliged to enter into in order to enable it to meet its obligations, both internally and externally, under the Treaty and secondary legislation.[133] In relation to CE the Parliament can propose modifications to the draft Budget which has been agreed by the Council on the basis of the Commission's proposal, but the final say remains with the Council. In regard to NCE

---

[130] Decision 70/243/EEC, OJ 1970, L 94/1.

[131] For a good description of the formal and informal processes at work see Laffan, B. *The Finances of the European Union* (1997, Macmillan, Basingstoke) 70-88.

[132] Article 203(8) [*272(8)*] EC.

[133] Joint Declaration by the Community Institutions on 30 June 1982 on the Community Budgetary Procedure, OJ 1982, C 194/1. For analysis see Dankert, P. 'The Joint Declaration by the Community Institutions on 30 June 1982 on the Community Budgetary Procedure' (1983) 20 *CMLRev* 707.

the Parliament can not only propose amendments to the draft Budget but, within limits, also has the last say.[134]

The system is, however, fraught with difficulties at two levels. The first is that an unhealthy distinction is made between the legislative and budgetary powers of the Community. The Council will, for example, adopt legislation under one of the legislative procedures which excludes the Parliament but which has considerable implications for the Budget.[135] Conversely, much legislation cannot function effectively without adequate provision being made for it within the Budget. The differing division of powers made between the Institutions within the budgetary and legislative fields thus inevitably provokes tensions. Secondly, the distinction between NCE and CE is an unhappy one. Not only is there little rationale for the distinction, but it leads to jockeying between the institutions as to the head under which a particular item of expenditure should fall.

The Parliament's final say in relation to NCE has also to be put into perspective. The amount by which the Parliament can increase NCE is limited. The Commission must prior to 1 May of the year preceding the Budget establish a maximum rate of increase for Community expenditure.[136] Parliament cannot exceed that maximum rate unless through agreement with the Council.[137] Secondly, Parliament's powers to raise revenue do not match its powers in the field of expenditure. It is the Council, acting unanimously on a proposal from the Commission, after having only consulted the Parliament, which determines the Community's revenue system of own resources for financing the Budget.[138] This imposes an additional constraint on expenditure in the

---

[134] Article 203(5) [*272(5)*] EC.
[135] See Chapter 3.
[136] This maximum rate is based on the trend in GNP within the Community, budgetary increases within the Member States and increase in the cost of living.
[137] There is one slight exception to this. Where the Council establishes a draft Budget which has further increased expenditure as a whole by over one and a half times the maximum rate, Parliament is entitled to propose amendments to NCE which allow for a further increase of up to one half the maximum rate. The whole procedure is contained in Article 203(9) [*272(9)*] EC.
[138] Article 201 [*269*] EC. The current system of own resources is contained in Decision 94/728/EC, OJ 1994, L 293/9.
     Article 2. 1. Revenue from the following shall constitute own

light of the requirement that revenue and expenditure be balanced.[139] The third constraint is the small size of the Community Budget. The limit placed on the size of the EC Budget rises to a maximum of 1.27% of Community GNP in 1999,[140] which is a minuscule fraction of the amount available to most central authorities.[141]

---

resources entered in the budget of the Communities:

(a) levies, premiums, additional or compensatory amounts, additional amounts or factors and other duties established or to be established by the institutions of the Communities in respect of trade with non-member countries within the framework of the common agricultural policy, and also contributions and other duties provided for within the framework of the common organization of the markets in sugar;

(b) common customs tariff duties and other duties established or to be established by the institutions of the Communities in respect of trade with non-member countries and customs duties on products coming under the Treaty establishing the European Coal and Steel Community;

(c) the application of a uniform rate valid for all Member States to the VAT assessment base which is determined in a uniform manner for member states according to Community rules. However, the assessment base to be taken into account for the purposes of this decision shall, from 1995, not exceed 50 % of GNP in the case of Member States whose per capita GNP, in 1991 was less than 90 % of the Community average; for the other Member States the assessment base to be taken into account shall not exceed:

- 54 % of their GNP in 1995,
- 53 % of their GNP in 1996,
- 52 % of their GNP in 1997,
- 51 % of their GNP in 1998,
- 50 % of their GNP in 1999;

the cap of 50 % of their GNP to be introduced for all Member States in 1999 shall remain applicable until such time as this decision is amended;

(d) the application of a rate - to be determined pursuant to the budgetary procedure in the light of the total of all other revenue - to the sum of all the Member States' GNP.....

[139] Article 199 [268] EC.
[140] Conclusions of the Edinburgh European Council, EC Bulletin 12-1992, I.46.
[141] Harden, I. 'The Constitution of the European Union' (1994) *PL* 609.

c. The Legislative Powers of the European Parliament

The basis for Parliament's legislative powers is contained in Article 138b [*192*] EC.

Article 138b [*192*] EC. In so far as provided in this Treaty, the European Parliament shall participate in the process leading up to the adoption of Community acts by exercising its powers under the procedures laid down in Articles 189b [*251*] and 189c [*252*] and by giving its assent or delivering advisory opinions.

The European Parliament may, acting by a majority of its members, request the Commission to submit an appropriate proposal on matters on which it considers that a Community act is required for the purpose of implementing the EC Treaty.

The formal legislative powers of the Parliament vary according to the legislative procedure adopted. A bald statement of its formal powers will not always fully capture the significance of the Parliament's input. During the legislative stage, Parliament will frequently seek to influence the agenda by using its powers to propose modifications and amendments.[142]

Parliament will also be consulted at a pre-legislative stage prior to adoption of a proposal by the Commission in any area where its opinion is formally required. The Parliament has sought to maximise its influence at this stage by astute use of its Committee System.[143] Committees of MEPs have existed since the Parliament's inception. Their principal role is to prepare Reports on legislative proposals. In recent years they have proliferated and become increasingly specialised with 19 Standing Committees currently existing. This specialisation allows Parliament to garner its resources effectively and target its comments more incisively.[144] This is particularly important at the pre-legislative stage where parties' positions are still in a state of flux. Committees

---

[142]   There is further discussion of all this in Chapter 3.

[143]   For greater detail see Corbett, R., Jacobs, F. & Shackleton, M. *The European Parliament* (1995, 3rd Edition, Catermill, London) 105-137.

[144]   Bowler, S. & Farell, D. 'The Organizing of the European Parliament: Committees, Specialization and Co-ordination' (1995) 25 *British Journal of Political Science* 219.

sought to maximise their influence by often preparing reports on their own initiative.[145] It is in this last area that Parliament has sought to maximise its influence.

Judge, D. and Earnshaw, D. 'Weak European Parliament Influence? A Study of the Environment Committee of the European Parliament' (1994) 29 *Government and Opposition* **262, 264-266**

In using these procedures the Environment Committee again sought to involve itself at the *pre-legislative* stage through a conscious strategy of agenda setting. There are several dimensions to this strategy. One was to use 'Rule 63' reports to encourage action on the part of the Commission. On many occasions the Commission might already have been considering such action, and so the intention of the Committee was either to accelerate this process, and so advance the issue up the Commission's overcrowded agenda, or to focus the Commission's attention upon an issue and so determine the priorities and relative policy-making of the Commission. Aware, for example, that the Commission was formulating proposals on waste management, the Environment Committee initiated its own investigation in the subject with the intention of 'guiding' the Commission's own internal deliberations. The influence of the Committee's report is partially observable in the Commission's eventual proposals on the incineration of hazardous waste and on land-fill of waste. Rather than simply waiting, therefore, to react to formal Commission proposals as part of the consultation process, the Environment Committee engaged in a pro-active strategy of articulating its own policy concerns to the Commission. Exactly how much direct influence this strategy had upon the final Commission proposal is difficult, if not impossible, to assess; but the Committee itself would probably claim no more than that it sought to articulate the concerns of the EP at the formative stage of legislation alongside other interested parties considered by the Commission.

On occasion, however, EP initiatives have been openly acknowledged by the Commission's Directorate General for Environment, Nuclear Safety and Civil Protection (DG XI) as being of importance in prompting action or changing its own priorities. Perhaps the clearest, and most publicly acknowledged, example was the genesis of the Commission's *Green Paper on the Urban Environment*. In the preface to the Green Paper the then Commissioner, Ripa di Meana, openly recorded that the paper was a 'practical response to the resolution tabled in December 1988 by a Member of the European Parliament, Ken Collins, urging that the problems facing the urban environment be studied in greater detail'. Rarely is the influence of MEPs proclaimed in such a public manner. As a consequence, the informal dimension of agenda-setting and initiation are often overlooked in standard texts on, and 'guides' to the EC decision-making process.

---

[145]   European Parliament, *Rules of Procedure* (1996, 11th Edition, OOPEC, Luxembourg) Rule 148.

The degree of influence that the European Parliament can bring to bear is not a constant but will vary. Based on a number of case studies, pioneering work by Judge, Earnshaw and Cowan suggested that there were a number of variables which will affect the level of that influence.[146]

- The type of policy. Low-visibility policies, normally formulated on a sectoral basis, characterised by a high-degree of cooperation between the actors concerned, set up quite a closed and interconnected world with little room for Parliamentary intrusion and influence in the development of such policies. There was greater room for Parliamentary influence in the case of regulatory policies, environmental protection being an example, which were seen as affecting a less specialised, less closed group of actors.
- The extent to which the field concerned is dominated by intergovernmentalism. In some areas, notably those where unanimity is required in the Council, exercise of Community competence is less readily accepted than in other areas. In such areas Parliamentary influence is diminished both by national resistance to Community intrusion and by there being no possibilities for it to exploit divisions between the Member States.
- Inter-institutional relations. These exist at a formal level, depending upon the particular legislative procedure used. They also exist at an informal level. The authors thus noted the manner in which Parliament had been able to increase its pre-legislative influence by ensuring that a Rapporteur for a Committee was appointed once the Commission's Annual Programme was announced rather than later when the formal proposal for a legislative measure was announced. This allowed it to influence the content of the Commission's legislative proposal.
- Institutional resources, namely the quantity and quality of personnel involved with any measure. It was noted therefore that the existence of an expert in biochemistry on the Environmental Committee of the Parliament had undoubtedly increased its influence in the field of biotechnology.

---

[146]   Judge, D., Earnshaw, D. & Cowan, N. 'Ripples or Waves: the European Parliament in the European Community policy process' (1994) 1 JEPP 27.

VI. The Court of Justice and the Court of First Instance

i. The Court of Justice

a. The Remit of the Court

The duty of the Court of Justice is to ensure that in the interpretation and the application of the Treaty 'the law is observed'.[147] This duty is tempered, first, by the jurisdictional rules which dictate the circumstances in which particular actors may bring actions before it.[148] The second is that the Court's powers vary across the three pillars of the TEU. Whilst it has full jurisdiction to consider any matter which falls within the first pillar, that of the EC Treaty, it is excluded from ruling on the second pillar, CFSP. Prior to Amsterdam the Court was similarly excluded from ruling on the vast majority of the provisions contained in the third pillar, JHA,[149] the one exception being conventions drawn up by the Council within the context of JHA which may confer jurisdiction upon the Court to interpret their provisions and to rule on any disputes regarding their application.[150]

The Court's powers in the field of JHA are extended by Amsterdam. It will still have no power to rule on the Treaty provisions. It is given, however, the power to adjudicate upon secondary acts adopted under JHA. Its exact powers depend upon the secondary act in question.[151] It has the power not only to interpret but also to review and declare illegal framework decisions and decisions taken in this area.[152] Its powers are more limited in relation to the other secondary legislation,

---

[147] Article 164 [*220*] EC. A good summary of the Court's mode of operation and the problems it faces are contained in British Institute of International and Comparative Law, *The Role and Future of the European Court of Justice* (1997, BIICL, London).

[148] See Chapters 6, 8 and 10.

[149] Article L TEU.

[150] Article K.3.2(c) TEU.

[151] On these different forms of legislation see Chapter 3 in Volume 2.

[152] *Article 35(1) & 35(7) TEU.*

namely common positions and conventions, which it can only interpret, and may not review.[153] A further constraint in this area is that the Court has no power to review the validity or proportionality of operations carried out by the police or enforcement agencies of a Member State or the exercise of the responsibilities incumbent upon Member States with regard to the maintenance of law and order and the safeguarding of internal security.[154]

The Court's jurisdiction is extended in one other area by Amsterdam, and that is in relation to *Article 7 TEU*, the provision which allows action to be taken against a Member State in cases where it seriously and persistently breaches the principles underlying the Union. Action taken by the institutions under it may be reviewed by the Court in so far as 'the Court has jurisdiction under the treaties establishing the European Communities and under this Treaty'.[155] As action taken under *Article 7 TEU* will clearly cut across all three pillars, the consequence of this is that the Court will only be able to review action in those areas where it has jurisdiction, notably in the EC and JHA pillars.

b. The Composition of the Court

The Court is made up of fifteen judges, one from each Member State. They are appointed by common accord of the Member States for a renewable period of 6 years,[156] and are required to be persons whose independence is beyond doubt and are either suitable for the highest judicial office in their respective countries or 'jurisconsults of recognised competence'.[157] The Court then elects a President from among its members and, in addition, appoints a Registrar to deal with the administration of the Court. Whilst the number of women judges or

---

[153]   *Article 35(1) & 35(7) TEU.*
[154]   *Article 35(5) TEU.*
[155]   *Article 46 (c) TEU.*
[156]   This is done on a three yearly cycle so that every three years half the Court is replaced.
[157]   Article 167 [*223*] EC.

judges coming from ethnic minorities is disappointing,[158] judges have come from a wide variety of professional backgrounds, notably from national judiciaries, private practice, academia and national ministries.[159] This notwithstanding, there has been some criticism of the method of appointment. The system excludes the Community institutions, notably the Parliament, from the process and a fear has also been expressed that the renewability of the term of office might compromise the independence of the judges. In practice, this never seems to have been a problem. Independence is undoubtedly helped by the length of the term of office, which results in there being a good chance that the administration which appointed the judge will no longer be in office when the judge is up for reappointment, and the principle of collegiality which makes it impossible for judgments to be associated with individual judges. Despite this the Committee of the European Parliament endorsed a Report in 1993 that judges should be elected by the Parliament for a non-renewable term of nine years.[160]

c. The Operation of the Court

To assist with workload, cases need not be decided in plenary session, that is to say by the full Court but can be decided in chambers, consisting of either three or five judges, if the Court so wishes. The only circumstance in which a case cannot be heard in chambers is when a Member State or a Community Institution that is party to the

---

[158]   Within the Court of Justice there has been no judge appointed who has come from an ethnic minority, and whilst there has been one woman Advocate-General, Advocate-General Rozès, there has never been a woman judge.

[159]   For a description of the backgrounds of some of the past and present judges see Neville Brown, L. & Kennedy, T. *The Court of Justice of the European Communities* (1994, 4th Edition, Sweet & Maxwell, London) 55-59.

[160]   The so-called 'Rothley Report'. European Parliament Session Document A3-0228/93. The Court of Justice has indicated that it would not object to such a revision. *Report of the European Court of Justice for the 1996 Intergovernmental Conference*, Proceedings of the Court 15/95, 11. No such revision was made.

proceedings requests that the case be heard in plenary session.[161] Whether giving a judgment in plenary session or in chambers, the Court works under the principle of collegiality. A single judgment will be given representing the view of the Court with there being no possibility for either dissenting or concurring opinions. The consequence is that the judgments are often terse in nature, and in many ways, are analogous in their wording to some form of international treaty, as they try to accommodate the varying views of the judges giving them.

This style of judgment has some benefits. First, it protects the anonymity of the judges, and so protects their independence. Secondly, the Court is perceived by those associated with it as deriving much of its intellectual dynamism from the debate generated by a single judgment. It allows for a considerable exchange of views and differing national legal traditions to filter through into the judgment.[162] Thirdly, at one level, a single judgment enhances the authority of the Court. Member States are unable to point to sympathetic dissenting opinions or their national judge siding with them as a means of undermining the authority of a particular judgment.

On the down side, however, there is a danger, as the size of the Court grows, that the Court might, in its own words, 'cross the invisible boundary between a collegiate court and a deliberative assembly'.[163] Fifteen judges is already a large number and there is a danger that any increase would result in a diminishing of the dialectic which is meant to characterise the current preparation of judgments. On the other hand, if membership of the Court does not grow with the accession of new Member States, the result will be that some national legal traditions will not be represented on the Court, and there is a danger of a feeling of exclusion developing in that Member State. The second problem is that as the judgment is built on compromise, this affects the quality of its

---

161   Article 165 [*221*] EC.

162   Koopman, T. 'The Future of the Court of Justice of the European Communities' (1991) 11 *YBEL* 15, 24; Kapteyn, P. 'The Court of Justice of the European Communities after the Year 2000' 135, 139 in Curtin, D. & Heukels, T. (eds.) *Institutional Dynamics of European Integration: Liber Amicorum Schermers, Volume 1* (1994, Martijnus Nijhoff, Dordrecht).

163   *Report of the European Court of Justice for the 1996 Intergovernmental Conference*, Proceedings of the Court 15/95, 10.

reasoning. This has resulted in criticism that often the Court either seems not to counter a point or consider a question and that, often, its judgments are insufficiently reasoned.[164]

d. The Advocate General

The Court is assisted by eight Advocates General.[165] The same procedure and conditions of appointment apply to them as to judges of the Court of Justice. The function of the Advocate General is to make, in open court, impartial and independent submissions on any case brought before the Court.[166] In other words, they act not as a legal representative of one of the parties but as a legal representative of the public interest. These Opinions are published in advance of the judgment in order to allow the Court sufficient time to consider them. These Opinions are not binding on the Court, although they are increasingly being explicitly used as a source of law by the Court of Justice. Even when the conclusions reached are similar, it is difficult to know whether the reasoning is necessarily so, given that the Opinion is often very discursive in nature. From a lawyer's perspective the Opinions are interesting as they often provide a more detailed analysis of the context and the argument than is found in the judgment of the Court itself.

ii. The Court of First Instance

The structure of the Community judicial system resulted, from early on, in the Court having a heavy workload and the development of a backlog. As new Member States acceded to the Community, awareness of

---

[164] Bishop, W. 'Price Discrimination under Article 86: Political Economy in the European Court' (1981) 44 *MLR* 282, 294-295.

[165] For greater analysis of the work of the Advocates General see Dashwood, A., 'The Advocate General in the Court of Justice of the European Communities' (1982) 2 *Legal Studies* 202; Borgschmidt, K. 'The Advocate General at the European Court of Justice: A Comparative Study' (1988) 13 *ELRev* 106.

[166] Article 166 [*222*] EC.

Community law grew and Community law penetrated into new areas of social life, the problem grew more acute. In 1987 the Court sent a request to the Council for the establishment of a Court of First Instance to help ameliorate these difficulties, a request the Council acceded to in Decision 88/591/EEC.[167] The position of the Court of the First Instance has now been formally recognised in the EC Treaty.

Article 168A [*225*] EC. 1. A Court of First Instance shall be attached to the Court of Justice with jurisdiction to hear and determine at first instance, subject to a right of appeal to the Court of Justice on points of law only and in accordance with the conditions laid down by the Statute, certain classes of action or proceeding defined in accordance with the conditions laid down in paragraph 2. The Court of First Instance shall not be competent to hear and determine questions referred for a preliminary ruling under Article 177 [*234*].

2. At the request of the Court of Justice and after consulting the European Parliament and the Commission, the Council acting unanimously, shall determine the classes of action or proceeding referred to in paragraph 1 and the composition of the Court of First Instance and shall adopt the necessary adjustments and additional provisions to the Statute of the Court of Justice. Unless the Council decides otherwise, the provisions of this Treaty relating to the Court of Justice, in particular the provisions of the Protocol on the Statute of the Court of Justice, shall apply to the Court of Justice.

3. The members of the Court of First Instance shall be chosen from persons whose independence is beyond doubt and who possess the ability required for appointment to judicial office; they shall be appointed by common accord of the governments of the Member States for a term of six years. The membership shall be partially renewed every three years. Retiring members shall be eligible for re-appointment.

---

[167]   OJ 1988 L 241/1. The literature on the CFI is considerable. Due, O. 'The Court of First Instance' (1988) 8 *YBEL* 1; Kennedy, T. 'The Essential Minimum: the Establishment of the Court of First Instance' (1989) 14 *ELRev* 7 and 'The Essential Minimum: A Postscript' (1990) 15 *ELRev* 54; Da Cruz Vilaça, J. 'The Court of First Instance of the European Communities: a Significant Step Towards the Consolidation of the European Community as a Community Governed by the Rule of Law' (1990) 10 *YBEL* 1; Millett, T. *The Court of First Instance of the European Communities* (1990, Butterworths, London); Vesterdorp, B. 'The Court of First Instance of the European Communities after Two Full Years in Operation' (1992) 29 *CMLRev* 897; Brown, N. 'The First Five Years of the Court of First Instance and Appeals to the Court of Justice: Assessment and Statistics' (1995) 32 *CMLRev* 743.

4. The Court of First Instance shall establish its rules of procedure in agreement with the Court of Justice. Those rules shall require the unanimous approval of the Council.

The Court of First Instance (CFI) has fifteen judges. It can operate in chambers in much the same way as the Court of Justice, and although no Advocates General are assigned to it, one of the judges can, if desired, act as Advocate General in any particular case. In relation to the EC Treaty the CFI's jurisdiction is still quite limited. The Council has only assigned it jurisdiction in respect of:

- actions by natural or legal persons either seeking annulment of acts of the Community Institutions under Article 173 [*230*] EC, challenging under Article 175 [*232*] EC the failure of the Institutions to act or seeking damages against the Community Institutions under Article 178 [*235*];
- staff disputes between the Community Institutions and its employees (Article 179 [*236*] EC)
- matters referred to the Court of Justice under an arbitration clause in a contract (Article 181 [*238*] EC).[168]

It is prevented from hearing references from national courts by the EC Treaty. Furthermore, jurisdiction has not been extended to allow it to hear any case brought by an EC institution against another or to hear any case brought against a Member State either by the Commission or another Member State.

There is a right to appeal from the CFI to the Court of Justice within two months of notification of the decision. This right exists not just for parties to the dispute but also for Member States and EC Institutions.[169]

---

[168]   Decision 88/591/EEC, OJ 1988 L 241/1, as amended by Decision 93/350/EC, OJ 1993 L 144/21, and Decision 94/149/EC, OJ 1994 L 66/29.

[169]   Protocol on the Statute of the Court of Justice as amended by Council Decision of 24 October 1988 establishing a Court of First Instance, as amended by Decision 88/591/EEC, OJ 1988 L 241/1, as amended by Decision 93/350/EC, OJ 1993 L 144/21, and Decision 94/149/EC, OJ 1994 L 66/29, article 49.

Article 51, Protocol on the Statute of the Court of Justice. An appeal to the Court of Justice shall be limited to points of law. It shall lie on the grounds of lack of competence of the Court of First Instance, a breach of procedure before which it would adversely affect the interests of the appellant as well as the infringement of Community law by the Court of First Instance.

If the Court of Justice finds the appeal to be well-founded, it will quash the decision of the CFI. It then has the discretion to give the final judgment, or to refer the matter back to the CFI. If it adopts the latter course of action, the CFI is bound by the Court of Justice's decision on the point of law.[170]

This last point raises the question of the relationship between the Court of Justice and the CFI. It might be thought that the hierarchical relationship which exists between the two would result in the latter being formally bound by the decisions of the former. This is not the view of the CFI. It takes the view that it is not bound by the judgments of the Court except in two narrow sets of circumstances. The first is the one referred to above where its decision has been quashed by the Court of Justice and the matter is referred back to it. The second is where the principle of *res judicata* applies, namely that a dispute involving the same parties, the same subject-matter and the same cause of action had already been decided by the Court of Justice.[171]

Nevertheless the circumstances in which the CFI will not follow judgments of the Court of Justice will be rare. If the CFI were to ignore judgments of the Court of Justice on a habitual basis, it would generate considerable instability. This would stem not merely from the increased unpredictability in the CFI's judgment, but also from the systemic conflict it would put in place between the two Courts, whereby the CFI would take one decision reversing established ECJ case law only for the ECJ, on appeal, to reaffirm the existing law.

---

[170] Ibid., article 54.
[171] Case T-162/94 *NMB France & Others v Commission* [1996] ECR II-427.

VII. The European Central Bank[172]

In principle, a decision has to be taken before 1 July 1998 as to which Member States will participate in the third stage of Economic and Monetary Union.[173] Following this decision the President, Vice-President and Executive Board of the European Central Bank (ECB) will be appointed by common accord of those Heads of Government participating in the third stage after they have consulted the European Parliament and the European Monetary Institute (EMI).[174] With the appointment of its Executive Board the ECB is established. It initially takes over the tasks of the EMI, which is then liquidated,[175] and only fully exercises the powers conferred upon it from the beginning of the third stage.

The ECB has its own independent legal personality,[176] and has two decision-making bodies. The first is the Executive Board, which consists of the President and Vice-President of the European Central Bank and four other members.[177] The other is the Governing Council. This consists of members of the Executive Board plus the governors of those national central banks whose Member States are participating in the third stage of monetary union. The President of the Council and a member of the Commission may participate in its meetings but do not

---

172   Only an outline of the ECB's composition and functions is given here. More detailed analysis of both the European Central Bank and the European System of Central Banks is to be found in the Chapter on Free Movement of Capital and Economic and Monetary Union in Volume II.

173   Article 109j(4) [121(4)] EC.

174   Article 109l(1) [123(1)] EC; Protocol on the Statute of the European System of Central Banks and of the European Central Bank (hereinafter known as the Statute), article 50. The European Monetary Institute is the predecessor of the ECB and has been in operation since 1 January 1994. Its principle functions are to prepare for the third stage of economic and monetary union and to assist in the coordination of monetary policy, Article 109(f) [117] EC. For more detail see the Chapter on Free Movement of Capital and Economic and Monetary Union in Volume II.

175   Article 109l(2) [123(2)] EC.

176   Article 106(2) [107(2)] EC.

177   Statute, article 11. Members of the Executive Board are appointed for an 8 year non-renewable term.

have the right to vote.[178] In general, each body votes by a simple majority.[179]

The ECB operates within the context of the European System of Central Banks (ESCB). The ESCB is composed of the ECB and the national central banks.[180] Its membership is therefore identical to the Governing Council of the ECB. Unlike the ECB, the ESCB has no legal personality and has been described as 'a set of rules and an institutional framework, rather than an institution in itself'.[181] It provides no more than a structure through which the ECB and national central banks can conduct the monetary policy of the European Union. Its functions are described below.

Article 105 [*105*] EC 1. The primary objective of the ESCB shall be to maintain price stability. Without prejudice to the objective of price stability, the ESCB shall support the general economic policies of the Community with a view to contributing to the achievement of the objectives of the Community as laid down in Article 2 [*2*]. The ESCB shall act in accordance with the principle of an open market economy with free competition, favouring an efficient allocation of resources, and in compliance with the principles set out in Article 3a [*4*].

2. The basic tasks to be carried out through the ESCB shall be:
- to define and implement the monetary policy of the Community;
- to conduct foreign exchange operations consistent with the provisions of Article 109 [*111*];
- to hold and manage the official foreign reserves of the Member States;
- to promote the smooth operation of payment systems.

---

[178]   Article 109b [*113*] EC.

[179]   Statute, articles 10.2 and 11.5. The biggest exception to this concerns decisions relating to the income of national central banks, the capital of the ECB and subscription to that capital, the transfer of foreign reserves and the allocation of ECB profits where decisions are taken by a weighted form of voting which excludes members of the Executive Board, Statute, article 10(3).

[180]   Article 106(1) [*107(1)*] EC.

[181]   Snyder, F. 'EMU - Metaphor for European Union? Institutions, Rules and Types of Regulation' 63, 80 in Dehousse, R. *Europe After Maastricht: An Ever Closer Union?* (1994, Law Books in Europe, Munich).

3. The third indent of paragraph 2 shall be without prejudice to the holding and management by the governments of Member States of foreign exchange working balances.

4. The ECB shall be consulted:
- on any proposed Community act in its field of competence;
- by national authorities regarding any draft legislative provision in its fields of competence, but within the limits and under the conditions set out by the Council in accordance with the procedure laid down in Article 106(6) [*107(6)*].
The ECB may submit opinions to the appropriate Community institutions or bodies or to national authorities on matters in its field of competence.

5. The ESCB shall contribute to the smooth conduct of policies pursued by the competent authorities relating to the prudential supervision of credit institutions and the stability of the financial system.

6. The Council, acting unanimously on a proposal from the Commission and after consulting the ECB and after receiving the assent of the European Parliament, confer upon the ECB specific tasks concerning policies relating to the prudential supervision of credit institutions and other financial institutions with the exception of insurance undertakings.

The central power of the ECB is the exclusive right to authorise the issue of bank notes within the Community.[182] This allows it to control the money supply and gives it the power to set short-term interest rates.

The ECB is also responsible for governing the ECSB.[183] It has two sets of powers to enable it to do this. The first are a set of quasi-legislative powers which enable it to adopt regulations, decisions and recommendations necessary to carry out those tasks entrusted to the ESCB.[184] It also has certain enforcement powers. It will be able to bring national central banks before the Court of Justice who do not comply with their obligations under the EC Treaty and the Statute of the ESCB.[185] In addition, within limits to be set by the Council, it also has

---

182   Article 105a [*106*] EC.
183   Article 106(3) [*107(3)*] EC.
184   Article 108a(1) [*110(1)*] EC.
185   Article 180(d) [*237(d)*] EC.

the power to impose fines and penalty payments on undertakings which do not comply with these regulations or decisions.[186]

The internal division of powers within the ECB is based upon the crude principle that the Governing Council is responsible for developing policy, whilst the Executive Board is responsible for implementing it. The Governing Council of the ECB is responsible for adopting the guidelines and taking the decisions necessary for the performance of the tasks entrusted to the ESCB. These include formulating EC monetary policy by taking decisions relating to intermediary monetary objectives, key interest rates and supply of reserves. The Executive Board is responsible for implementing these guidelines and giving the necessary instructions to national central banks. It may also have certain powers delegated to it by the Governing Council.[187]

VIII. Other Bodies

i. The Court of Auditors

The fifth institution mentioned in Article 4 [4] EC is the Court of Auditors. First established in 1977, the Court of Auditors only received formal recognition with the coming into force of the TEU. The Court consists of 15 members, who are appointed by the Council acting unanimously after having consulted the Parliament for a term of 6 years. The duty of the Court of Auditors is to audit the Community.[188] For this purpose it is required to examine all the revenue and expenditure of the EC. The audit is to be based on the records of the Community and, if necessary, performed on the spot in the other Community institutions or the Member States. For these purposes the Court of Auditors is required to establish links with national audit bodies or, where appropriate, with national departments.

---

[186]   Article 108a(3) [*110(3)*] EC.

[187]   The respective powers of the bodies are contained in the Statute, article 12.

[188]   Article 188a [*246*] EC.

Formally the Court of Auditors is little more than a supervisory body. It can submit observations or deliver opinions on specific matters at the request of the other Community institutions, and it can also assist the Parliament and the Council in exercising their powers of control over the implementation of the Community Budget. Its greatest voice comes, however, from the requirement that it publish an Annual Report on the finances of the Community at the end of each financial year.[189] These Reports have been quite trenchant in their criticism on the management of the Community finances, both at a national and at a Community level, and have been influential in the development of Community instruments to tackle fraud.[190]

ii. The Economic and Social Committee

This is an advisory body. Article 193 [*257*] EC states that it is to comprise representatives of producers, farmers, carriers, workers, dealers, craftsmen, professional occupations and the general public. There are 222 members appointed by the Council for a four year renewable term. The members must be independent and act in the general interest of the EC. In considerable parts of the Treaty consultation of the Committee is mandatory, whilst in others consultation by the Council and Commission is voluntary. Weatherill and Beaumont consider that the Committee is an unnecessary waste of time and expense, as there are plenty of other avenues for interest groups to make clear their views.[191] Others see it as instrumental to improving the

---

[189] Article 188c(4) [*248(4)*] EC.

[190] On the Court of Auditors see O'Keeffe, D. 'The Court of Auditors' in Curtin, D. & Heukels, T. *Institutional Dynamics of European Integration: Liber Amicorum Professor Schermers, Volume 1* (1994, Martijnus Nijhoff, Dordrecht); Harden, I., White, F. & Donnelly, K. 'The Court of Auditors and Financial Control and Accountability in the European Community' (1995) 1 European Public Law 599.

[191] Weatherill, S. & Beaumont, P. *EC Law: The Essential Guide to the Legal Workings of the European Community* (1995, 2nd Edition, Penguin, Harmondsworth) 151.

drafting process in EC law.[192] The Treaty of Amsterdam seems to have taken the latter view with consultative powers being extended to public health policy and to the new areas of employment and social policy.

iii. The Committee of the Regions

This was established by the TEU to give regional authorities greater input in the decision-making process.[193] The Committee has 222 members who are appointed by the Council acting unanimously on proposals from the Member States for a four-year renewable term. The role of this Committee is similar to the Economic and Social Committee in that it has merely an advisory status. Furthermore, whilst the Council or Commission can consult whenever they wish, the circumstances in which they are obliged to consult it are quite limited.[194] There is only an obligation to consult it in those parts of the Treaty which explicitly refer to education, culture, public health and economic and social cohesion. In a host of other areas in which measures can have a significant impact on the regions, there is no need to consult it.[195]

The position has been improved by the Treaty of Amsterdam which adds to those areas where the Committee of the Regions should be consulted. There is thus provision for consultation in the fields of employment, social matters, public health, the social fund, vocational training and the environment. There still remain a number of areas, such as the internal market, competition, industrial policy and consumer

---

[192]   Gordon-Smith, D. 'The Drafting Process in the European Community' (1989) 10 *Statute Law Review* 56.

[193]   Article 198a [*263*] EC.

[194]   Article 198c [*267*] EC. The Treaty of Amsterdam adds Parliament to this list, *Article 267(4) EC.*

[195]   On the Committee of the Regions and the input of regions more generally into the decision-making process see Schaefer, G. 'Regions in the Policy Process of the EC: Reflections on the Innovations of the Maastricht Treaty' (1993) 3 *European Institute of Public Administration* 8; Scott, A., Peterson, J. & Miller, D. 'Subsidiarity: A "Europe of the Regions" v. the British Constitution' (1994) 32 *JCMS* 47; Taylor, K. 'European Union: The Challenge for Local and Regional Government' (1995) 66 *Political Quarterly* 74.

protection, which have an important regional dimension in which no consultation is required. Furthermore, preliminary evidence suggests that the opinions of the Committee carry only limited weight with the other institutions.[196]

iv. The Growth of Regulatory Agencies

One paradigm used to explain the development of the European Union is that of the 'regulatory state'. The author most closely associated with this view, Majone, identifies three functions of government in the socio-economic sphere. The first is a redistribution one, which involves the transfer of resources from one group of society to another. The second is a stablisation one, which is concerned with maintaining certain levels of growth, employment and price stability. The final one is a regulatory one. This is concerned with correcting the various forms of market failure which prevent goods being allocated in the most efficient manner possible.[197] Majone sees the EC as traditionally only pursuing this latter function. From this he accounts, first, for the EC's considerable regulatory powers but limited finances. It also accounts for contrast in the considerable development of certain EC policies - such as protection of the environment; health and safety; competition; financial services - with the failure of the EC to develop other policies in a substantial manner, notably social policy.[198]

The Commission has, indeed, many of the functions of a regulatory agency.[199] Yet, from early on, Member States have been wary

---

[196]   McCarthy, R. 'The Committee of the Regions: an advisory body's tortuous path to influence' (1997) 4 *JEPP* 439.

[197]   These distinctions are most explicitly drawn in Majone, G. 'The rise of statutory regulation in Europe' in Majone, G. (ed.) *Regulating Europe* (1996, Routledge, London).

[198]   Majone, G. 'The European Community between Social Policy and Social Regulation' (1993) 31 *JCMS* 153; Majone, G. 'The Rise of the Regulatory State in Europe' (1994) 17 *WEP* 77.

[199]   On this see Majone, G. 'The European Commission as regulator' & Laudati, L. 'The European Commission as regulator: the uncertain pursuit of the competitive market' in Majone, G. (ed.) *Regulating Europe* (1996, Routledge,

about using it as a repository for further regulatory competencies, preferring, instead, to set up a series of independent agencies and offices.[200] To date there are ten such bodies.[201]

Shapiro, M. 'The problems of independent agencies in the United States and the European Union' (1997) 4 *Journal of European Public Policy* 262, 281-282

The standard, overt rationale for the creation of EU agencies is that they ought to be partially or wholly independent of the Commission because they are 'managerial', perform 'technical' tasks or are engaged in 'information' gathering and analysis only. In the US it may make sense to say that managerial, technical, informational functions should be separated from the regular cabinet departments or ministries because those departments are part of the Executive Branch which is political. Both in the sense that it is headed by a democratically elected President and in the sense that the President is his political party's leader. This is the get-technology-out-of-politics theme. But the separation of powers in the EU is entirely different. The Commission-Council separation is itself a supposed separation of technocracy (the Commission) from intergovernmental politics (the Council). Therefore, to assert a managerial-technical-informational rationale for separating the agencies from the Commission is, in a certain sense, absurd. It is the assertion that the technical ought to be separated from the technical.

Is all this managerial-technical-informational talk simply a smoke screen for the more fundamental argument that, because Europeans don't like the technocrats in Brussels and fear concentrating even more governance there, if we want more EU

---

[200]   London).
Everson, M. 'Independent Agencies: Hierarchy Beaters?' (1995) 1 *ELJ* 180; Kreher, A. (ed.) *The New European Agencies* (RSC 96/49, EUI, Florence); Kreher, A. 'Agencies in the European Community - a step towards administrative integration in Europe' (1997) 4 *JEPP* 225.

[201]   These are the European Centre for the Development of Vocational Training, Regulation 337/75, OJ 1975, L 39/1; European Foundation for the Improvement of Living and Working Conditions, Regulation 1365/75, OJ 1975, L 139/1; European Environment Agency, Regulation 1210/90, OJ 1990, L 120/1; European Training Foundation, Regulation 1360/90, OJ 1990, L131/1; European Monitoring Centre for Drugs and Drug Addiction, Regulation 302/93, OJ 1993, L 36/1; European Agency for the Evaluation of Medicinal Products, OJ 1993, L 214/1; Office for Harmonisation in the Internal Market (Trade Marks and Designs), Regulation 40/94, OJ 1994, L 11/1; European Agency for Health and Safety at Work, Regulation 2062/94, OJ 1994, L 216/1; Community Plant Variety Office, Regulation 2100/94, OJ 1994, L 227/1; Regulation 1035/97/EC, OJ 1997, L151/1.

technocrats, we need to split them up and scatter them about Europe? I think the answer to this question is largely yes but not entirely.

A second motive is, I believe, a kind of 'neo-functionalism'. If currently direct routes to further political integration of the Union are blocked, following Haas's old arguments about the World Health Organisation and the UN, further growth can be achieved indirectly through the proliferation of small, limited jurisdictions, allegedly 'technical agencies' that will appear politically innocuous. That is why it is not enough to say that the agencies are not in Brussels. It must also be said that they are merely technical or informational.

A third motive is about technocracy. The member state composed management boards were no doubt a political necessity. But by stressing the technical and informational functions of these agencies, by making each highly specialised to a particular technology and by incorporating large components of scientific personnel, there is undoubtedly the hope that the technocrats will take over these agencies from the politicians. And the technocrats for each of these agencies, it is hoped will create Europe-wide epistemic communities whose technical truths transcend intergovernmental politics. As Americans say 'there is no Republican or Democratic way to pave a street', Europeans may be able to say there is no French or Greek way. Thus, while the proffered technocratic rationale do not really explain why the agencies should be independent of the Commission, they do explain why the agencies should each take a small slice of allegedly technical-informational activity. That kind of organisation is most likely, over time, to assure the internal dominance within each agency of its transnational technocrats over its national politicians.

With the exception of those agencies which have a narrow remit, there has been an aversion against giving any of these bodies formal coercive or normative powers. Thus, whilst the Office for Harmonisation, Plant Variety Office have the power to register the European trade mark and European plant variety rights, and the Agency for Evaluation of Medicinal Products the power to authorise the marketing of those medicines derived from biotechnology, all the other agencies have little more than coordinatory roles linked to the provision of information. Yet the ability to supply information is a powerful one when coupled with the reputation that is bestowed upon that information as a result of an agency's expertise.[202] As Shapiro has noted, information that German brown coal is resulting in deforestation in Sweden will

---

[202]   The starting point on 'information by regulation' is Magat, W. & Viscusi, W. *Informational Approaches to Regulation* (1992, MIT, Cambridge).

almost certainly have policy implications.[203] Other commentators have talked, therefore, of these agencies regulating by information in that the information they supply will serve to forge expectations and preferences.[204] Others consider that they will, additionally, bring about policy convergence through the networks they establish and the contacts these provide between administrations.[205]

Further Reading

Andersen, S. & Eliassen, K. *The European Union: How Democratic is It?* (1996, Sage, London) chapters 8-11.

Hayes-Renshaw, F. & Wallace, H. 'Executive Power in the European Union: the functions and limits of the Council of Ministers' (1995) 2 *Journal of European Public Policy* 559

    The Council of Ministers (1996, Macmillan, Basingstoke)

Keohane, R. & Hoffmann, S. *The New European Community: Decision Making and Institutional Change* (1991, Westview Press, Boulder)

Nugent, N. *The Government and Politics of the European Union* (1994, 3rd Edition, Macmillan, London)

    'The leadership capacity of the European Commission' (1995) 2 *Journal of European Public Policy* 603

Peters, G. 'Agenda-setting in the European Community' (1994) 1 *Journal of European Public Policy* 9

Sbragia, A. (ed.) *Euro-Politics* (1992, Brookings Institute, Washington DC)

Scharpf, F. 'The Joint Decision Trap: lessons from German federalism and European integration' (1988) 66 *Public Administration* 239

Westlake, M. *A Modern Guide to the European Parliament* (1994, Pinter, London)

---

[203] Shapiro, M. 'The problems of independent agencies in the United States and the European Union' (1997) 4 JEPP 262, 285.

[204] Majone, G. 'The new European agencies: regulation by information' (1997) 4 *JEPP* 262, 271-274.

[205] Dehousse, R. 'Regulation by networks in the European Community: the role of European agencies' (1997) 4 *JEPP* 246, 258.

----- *The Commission and the Parliament: Partners and Rivals in the European Policy-Making Process* (1994, Butterworths, London)
----- *The Council of the European Union* (1995, Cartermill, London)

3. Law-Making by the European Community

I. Introduction

The primary legislative instrument, the Basic Law of the European Union, is the TEU. It is only, however, a framework treaty. Whilst it sets out a number of obligations, these alone are insufficient to realise its objectives. It therefore also contains a variety of law-making procedures and processes. One cannot point to one simple legislative instrument, however, generated by the Union legislature which is applicable to the range of activities covered by the TEU. Instead, there are a bewildering array of instruments peculiar to each pillar. The EC pillar alone contains six types of formal legislative act. Both CFSP and JHA contain a number of further instruments, all with differing legal effects.[1] The position is exacerbated by Amsterdam, which extends to four the number of instruments available in CFSP and JHA respectively. In addition to this, practice has resulted in a large number of informal instruments being developed to supplement these formal instruments.

II. EC Legislation

i. Binding Instruments

Whilst the EC institutions have a discretion as to which legislative

---

[1]   In order to avoid undue repetition, we have decided to deal with the instruments and law-making processes in CFSP and JHA in the Chapters in Volume II which deal with those two pillars.

instrument to use in many areas of EC competence, in others, they are limited to the choice of one particular instrument. Article 189 [*249*] EC describes all but one of the formal legislative instruments.

Article 189 [*249*] EC. In order to carry out their tasks and in accordance with the provisions of this Treaty, the European Parliament acting jointly with the Council, the Council and the Commission shall make regulations and issue directives, take decisions, make recommendations or deliver opinions.

A regulation shall have general application. It shall be binding in its entirety and directly applicable in all Member States.

A directive shall be binding as to the result to be achieved, upon each Member State to which it is addressed, but shall leave to the national authorities the choice of form and methods.

A decision shall be binding in its entirety upon those to whom it is addressed.

Recommendations and opinions shall have no binding force.

Regulations. The piece of secondary legislation which most closely resembles a domestic statute is the Regulation. The first hallmark of regulations is their general application. In principle, they do not apply to individualised circumstances but to:

'objectively determined situation and produce(s) legal effects with regard to categories of persons described in a generalised and abstract manner.'[2]

The second hallmark of regulations is their direct applicability. They enter into force twenty days following their publication in the Official Journal or the date which is specified in the regulation.[3] From that date onwards they are automatically incorporated into the domestic legal order of each Member State, and require no further transposition. Indeed, it is normally illegal for a Member State to seek to incorporate a regulation into its legal order through implementing legislation. The reasons for this are threefold. The first is that the national implementing measure, if it comes into force on a different date from the regulation, can obscure the date when the regulation comes into force. The second

---

[2]   Joined Cases 789 & 790/79 *Calpak et al. v Commission* [1980] ECR 1949, [1981] 1 CMLR 26.

[3]   Article 191 [*254*] EC.

is that national implementing measures may contain changes which affect the uniform application of the regulation.[4] The third reason which has been given is that regulations are direct sources of rights and obligations. National implementing measures obscure the Community nature of these rights and obligations to citizens who are subject to them.[5]

These features make regulations the most centralising of all EC instruments, and they are used wherever there is a need for uniformity. Regulations are thus required to be used in a very limited number of areas[6] and are the most frequent instrument used in external trade law, transport, competition, agriculture, fisheries and the transition to economic and monetary union.

It is important to note that these features are descriptive and are not conditions for the legality of regulations. One thus finds regulations, which have been characterised as 'disguised decisions' in that they apply to an individualised set of circumstances, but which have not been found to be illegal simply by reason of that feature.[7] Similarly, there are examples of regulations requiring implementing measures to be adopted by national authorities. A failure to do so in such circumstances will be a breach of EC law. In *Commission v United Kingdom* therefore the United Kingdom was required by a regulation to take the necessary measures to ensure tachographs were installed in commercial vehicles. Its failure to do so was declared to be illegal by the Court.[8]

Directives. The directive is different from the regulation in that whilst it is binding as to the result to be achieved, it leaves the choice as to form and methods used to the discretion of the Member States. Whilst a directive is similar to a regulation in that it will come into force twenty days after publication or on the date stipulated in the directive,[9] typically it will give a deadline - usually eighteen or twenty four months after

---

4   Case 39/72 *Commission v Italy* [1973] ECR 101, [1973] CMLR 439.

5   Case 34/73 *Variola v Amministrazione delle Finanze* [1973] ECR 981.

6   Article 48(3)(d) [*39(3)(d)*] EC (rights of residence workers following employment in another Member State); Article 94 [*89*] EC (Council Regulations on State aids); Article 209(a) [*280*] EC (budgetary arrangements).

7   e.g. Joined Cases 41-4/70 *International Fruit Company v Commission* [1971] ECR 411.

8   Case 128/78 *Commission v United Kingdom* [1978] ECR 2429.

9   Article 191 [*252*] EC.

publication - by which Member States must transpose its obligations into national law. A distinction is therefore made between ends and means with Member States having discretion as to the latter but not as to the former. This discretion given to Member States is merely a convention. There are thus cases where the obligations imposed by the Directive are so detailed that the Court has stated that they vitiate the discretion granted to Member States and must be transposed into national law verbatim.[10]

Whilst transposition rates by all Member States are quite high, the sheer number of Directives results in failure to transpose being one of the most frequently cited breaches of EC law.[11] To confront this the Commission has adopted a policy in the 1990s of automatically bringing a Member State before the Court of Justice if it fails to transpose a Directive by the time-limit.[12]

The areas in which only directives may be used are quite limited.[13] In practice, the autonomy granted to Member States by a

---

[10]   Case 38/77 *ENKA v Inspecteur der Invoerrechten* [1977] ECR 2203.

[11]   At the end of 1995 the Commission estimated that the number of Directives applicable ranged from 1,252 in the case of Finland to 1,267 in the cases of Germany and Spain. The State with the best record for notifying the Commission of measures taken to implement directives was Denmark with a notification rate of 97.9%. The worst was Finland with a notification rate of 70.5%. This was due to the autonomy enjoyed by the Faro Islands which required additional implementing measures to be taken for them. The next worst was Austria with a notification rate of 84.2%. In the case of Austria this meant that there were 199 directives for which no implementing measure had been notified. EC Commission, *Thirteenth Annual Report on monitoring the application of Community law*, OJ 1996, C 303/1, 12.

[12]   EC Commission, *Eighth Annual Report to the European Parliament on the Monitoring of the Application of Community Law*, OJ 1991, C 138/1.

[13]   Article 54(2) [*44(2)*] EC (General Programme abolishing restrictions on freedom of establishment); Article 56(2) [*46(2)*] EC (special treatment for foreign nationals establishing themselves); Article 57(2) [*47(2)*] EC (mutual recognition of qualifications); Article 63(1) [*52(1)*] EC (restrictions on freedom to provide services); Article 100 [*94*] EC (approximation of laws directly affecting the common market); Article 101 [*96*] EC (elimination of distortions of competition on the common market); Article 113(3) [*133(3)*] EC (framework for Commission negotiations with third countries for international agreements on commercial policy); Article 118a(2) EC [deleted by Amsterdam](minimum requirements for health and safety).

directive have resulted, however, in its being preferred over regulations in many other areas. One thus finds that directives are the most common instrument used in the fields of harmonisation of laws, environment, consumer protection, company law, intellectual property and social policy.

Decisions. The third instrument mentioned in Article 189 [*249*] EC is the decision. Decisions differ from regulations in that they are not intended to have general application but are addressed to particular parties. They are binding upon those to whom they are addressed. For this reason there is a requirement that the addressee must be notified of any decision which is addressed to it.[14] There is only a requirement of publication, however, if the decision is adopted under the co-decision procedure.[15]

The power to take decisions is, in essence, the exercise of an executive power. Decision-making powers can be, thus, found in most areas of EC competence. In some areas these are conferred expressly by the EC Treaty. Examples include the power of the Commission to take decisions declaring state aids to be incompatible with the common market[16] and the power of the Council to fine a Member State participating in the third stage of economic and monetary union which is running an excessive budget deficit.[17] In many other areas, notably competition policy and regional policy, institutions, the Commission, in particular, are delegated decision-making powers.

International Agreements. Although not mentioned in Article 189 [*249*]EC, international agreements with third States should also be considered as a form of secondary legislation. Article 228 [*300*] EC provides for the conclusion of such agreements by the Community and Member States, and these agreements bind both the EC institutions and the Member States.[18] The Court has also established that the EC succeeds to agreements made by the Member States where competence in that area is then transferred to it. These agreements bind it in the same manner as agreements actually concluded by it.

---

[14]   Article 191(1) [*254(1)*] EC.
[15]   Ibid. On the co-decision procedure see pp 172-181.
[16]   Article 93(2) [*88(2)*] EC.
[17]   Article 104c(11) [*104(11)*]EC.
[18]   Article 228(7) [*300(7)*] EC.

ii. Hierarchy of Norms

In the run-up to Maastricht both the Parliament and the Commission expressed dissatisfaction with Article 189 [249] EC on the grounds that it did not distinguish between legislation and quasi-legislation. In both their views a distinction should be drawn between framework laws and implementing laws.[19] The matter was not resolved at Maastricht, but it was agreed that 'hierarchy of norms' should be placed on the agenda for the next IGC.[20]

Framed in these terms, the debate is a slightly odd one. When the Commission is delegated implementing powers, it is true that the acts it adopts are regulations, decisions etc. Despite the use of similar terminology, a hierarchy of sorts already exists as the Court has always stated that these implementing acts are subordinate to the act from which they derive.[21]

The rationale for the distinction is an institutional one, and was suggested in order to limit the volume of legislation considered by the Parliament and the Council. Responsibility for enacting the subordinate implementing legislation would be primarily transferred to the Commission.[22] The issue never really got off the ground at Amsterdam. There were difficulties of classification in determining which acts would be considered to be legislative ones and which implementing ones. Furthermore, the British Government was opposed to any such

---

[19]   OJ 1991, C 129/136, 139 and EC Bulletin 2/1991, 127-134. On this debate see Bieber, R. & Salomé, I. 'Hierarchy of Norms in European Law' (1996) 33 *CMLRev* 907; Tizzano, A. 'The Instruments of Community Law and the Hierarchy of Norms' in Winter, J., Curtin, D., Kellermann, A. & de Witte, B. (eds.) *Reforming the Treaty on European Union* (1996, Asser Instituut, Kluwer, The Hague).

[20]   Declaration 16 TEU.

[21]   e.g. Case 38/70 *Tradax v Einfuhr- und Vorratstelle* [1971] ECR 145; Case 145/79 *Roquette v France* [1980] ECR 2917.

[22]   Resolution A4-0102/95 on the functioning of the Treaty on European Union with a view to the 1996 Intergovernmental Conference, para. 32(ii).

development, fearful that it might lead to an increase in Commission powers.[23]

iii. Soft Law

The final paragraph of Article 189 [*249*] mentions recommendations and opinions. Although these are informal instruments, they have no binding force. They are therefore best taken together with a variety of other instruments mentioned in the EC Treaty or developed through practice. These include resolutions and declarations of the institutions or Member States; action programmes indicating a future course of conduct; decisions of the representatives of the Member States meeting in Council;[24] guidelines issued by institutions as to how they will exercise their powers[25] and inter-institutional arrangements.[26] These measures do not create 'hard' obligations which can be invoked before a court.[27] Instead, they all form under the generic 'soft law'.

Soft law has been described as 'rules of conduct which, in principle, have no legally binding force but which nevertheless may have practical effects'.[28] It often locates the peripheries of the integration process. Wellens and Borchardt, for example, note that the closer a

---

23   *A Partnership of Nations: The British Approach to the European Union Intergovernmental Conference 1996* (HMSO, Cm. 3181, London) para. 23.

24   Wellens, K & Borchardt, G. 'Soft Law in the European Community' (1989) 14 *ELRev* 267, 301.

25   Della Cananea, G. 'Administration by Guidelines: The Policy Guidelines of the Commission in the Field of State Aids' in Harden I. (ed.) *State Aid: Community Law and Policy* (1993, Bundesanzeiger).

26   Monar, J. 'Inter-Institutional Agreements: The Phenomenon and Its New Dynamics after Maastricht' (1994) 31 *CMLRev* 693, 698-699.

27   Although on their role as a source of legal reasoning see Case C-322/88 *Grimaldi v Fonds des Maladies Professionelles* [1989] ECR 4407, [1991] 2 CMLR 265; Klabbers, J. 'Informal Instruments before the European Court of Justice' (1994) 31 *CMLRev* 997.

28   Snyder, F. 'The Effectiveness of European Community Law: Institutions, Processes, Tools and Techniques' (1993) 56 *MLR* 19, 32; Snyder, F. *Soft Law and Institutional Practice in the European Community* (EUI Working Paper Law No. 93/5, 1993, Florence) 2.

measure is perceived to be to the central objectives of the Community, the more concrete its normative expression is likely to be. If uniformity is required a Regulation will be used. If convergence is merely required, the most likely instrument is a Directive. The existence of soft law will often reflect consensus that the matter is one of Community concern, yet it also suggests that there are strong extrapetal forces pushing towards diversity being maintained in the area in question.

Frequently, soft law has been the starting point of the 'Communitarisation' of a particular policy area, acting as the precursor to the development of hard law. In the field of environment protection, for example, the process first began in a systematic way with the development of soft law, in the form of an Action Programme.[29] These programmes were then realised through the development of relevant legislation. It may also orientate the conduct of the EC institutions by providing a framework for the organisation of relations between themselves. The most obvious examples are the institutional arrangements in the field of the budget, and the institutional arrangements on democracy, transparency and subsidiarity and the proceedings of the conciliation committee.[30] It may also take the form of commitments on the part of institutions to respect certain values.[31] Finally, it may take the form of an institution indicating how it is going to conduct its affairs. This in turn generates expectations on the part of individuals as to their position under Community law.[32]

Soft law can also orientate the behaviour of the Member States. Member States may legislate on the basis of soft law. Even if they do not legislate, soft law may still constrain their behaviour. For example, a series of criteria are set out in a Protocol to the Treaty on European Union which the Member States should meet, should they wish to

---

[29] On the First Action Programme see OJ 1973 C 112/1. The adoption of Action Programmes is now explicitly recognised in Article 130s(3) [*175(3)*] EC.

[30] On this see Monar J. supra n.26, 709-715.

[31] The most obvious example of this is the Joint Declaration by the European Parliament, the Council and the Commission on Human Rights, OJ 1977, C 103/1, which commits the institutions to respect these rights.

[32] The *de minimis* notice in competition law is a good example of this, where the Commission indicates that it will only pursue cartels above a certain size, OJ 1986 C 231/2, as amended by OJ 1994 C 368/20.

participate in the third and final stage of economic and monetary union. In formal terms, these criteria do not add up to much. They can both be altered and ignored by the Council.[33] Yet as they are regarded as the yardstick for assessing whether a national economy is up to economic and monetary union, they have had a considerable impact upon national behaviour.

Snyder has estimated that the amount of soft law is likely to develop for a number of reasons.[34] The first is that the drive towards subsidiarity is relocating the margins of Community law with increasing resort being made to soft law at the expense of 'hard law'.[35] Soft law has also been generated through the Community, and particularly the Commission, assuming greater administrative functions in fields such as the internal market, competition, state aids, external relations and regional policy.[36] Soft law enables the Commission to set out its views upon a particular policy area in broad terms and in a proactive manner without its having to negotiate with the other institutions.[37]

Some commentators see the importance of soft law as transcending this, and of providing the basis for a new form of multi-level governance. Within such a system the relationship between the EC Institutions and other societal actors is non-hierarchical, with the EC Institutions seeking to guide and persuade these actors to take action rather than to force them to take action. A mutual dependence thus develops between these actors which leads them to seek common solutions to shared problems.[38]

---

[33] See Article 109j(2) [121(2)] EC and Protocol on the Convergence Criteria referred in Article 109j [121] of the EC Treaty, article 6.

[34] Snyder, F. 'Soft Law and Institutional Practice' supra n.28, 2-8.

[35] Conclusions of the Edinburgh European Council, EC Bulletin 12-1992, I.19.

[36] This follows administrative developments elsewhere see Baldwin, R. & Houghton, J. 'Circular Arguments: The Status and Legitimacy of Administrative Rules' (1986) *PL* 239.

[37] Snyder, F. 'Soft Law and Institutional Practice' supra n.28, 27.

[38] On multi-level governance see Jachtenfuchs, M. 'Theoretical Perspectives on European Governance' (1995) 1 *ELJ* 115; Kohler-Koch, B. 'Catching up with Change: The Transformation of European Governance' (1996) 3 *JEPP* 359; Christiansen, T. 'Reconstructing European Space: From Territorial Politics to Multilevel Governance' in Jørgensen, K. (ed.) *Reflective Approaches to European Governance* (1997, Macmillan, Basingstoke).

Multilevel governance has been subject to increased criticism recently. It has been convincingly argued that it obscures the extent to which hierarchies and formal decision-making processes shape EC government and the extent to which the constraints imposed by the EC shape national redistributional policies.[39] Soft law has also been criticised from a normative perspective for constraints for avoiding all the substantive constraints with which hard law must comply. It thus occupies an opaque demi-monde, where there are doubts about its legality, reviewability and availability to parties affected.[40]

III. EC Legislative Procedures

i. Introduction

Excluding the procedures for delegated legislation, there are twenty two different legislative processes within the TEU.[41] Most of these, however, are variations of the four principal legislative procedures described in more detail below. Others - such as where the Commission can enact legislation acting alone,[42] or where the Council can enact legislation on the basis of a Commission proposal without having to consult the

---

[39]   Hix, S. 'The Study of the European Union II: The "New Governance" Agenda and Its Rival' (1998) 5 *JEPP* forthcoming.

[40]   Harlow, C. 'Codification of EC Administrative Procedures? Fitting the Foot to the Shoe or the Shoe to the Foot' (1996) 2 *ELJ* 3, 20.

[41]   Commission Report for the Reflection Group for the Intergovernmental Conference 1996 (1995, OOPEC, Luxembourg) Annex 8.

[42]   These are the conditions under which Community nationals may remain in another Member State after having been employed there, Article 48(3)(d) [*39(3)(d)*] EC, and directives and decisions ensuring that public undertakings comply with the provisions of the EC Treaty, Article 90(3) [*86(3)*] EC.

Parliament[43] - occur in narrow fields, and will not be dwelt upon further.[44]

ii. The Consultation Procedure

The Consultation Procedure was the predominant legislative procedure until the SEA, and is still widely used, particularly in those areas where Member States are more cautious about the development of Community legislation.[45] The procedure is the simplest of all the legislative procedures. It follows three stages:

(a) The Commission submits a proposal to the Council
(b) The Council consults the Parliament
(c) The Council adopts the measure, either by qualified majority or by unanimity, depending upon the field in question.

---

[43] This is the case for recommendations taken under Article 126(4) [*149(4)*] EC (education), Article 128(5) [*151(5)*] EC (culture) and Article 129(4) [*152(4)*] EC (health); Decisions taken under Article 4(2) of the Agreement on Social Policy [*139(2) EC*] (implementation of Community-wide agreements between management and labour); autonomous measures and international agreements taken under the banner of commercial policy (Articles 113(4) [*133(4)*] & 228(3) [*300(3)*] EC), sanctions (Article 228a [*301*] EC) and measures taken appropriate to the economic situation in the case of severe difficulties in the supply of certain products (Article 103a [*100*] EC).

[44] The procedures used in the pillars on Justice and Home Affairs and Common Foreign and Security Policy and those used in relation to economic and monetary union will be discussed in the relevant chapters in Volume II.

[45] e.g. Articles 8a, b & e [*18, 19 & 22*] EC (citizenship); Article 43(2) [*37(2)*] EC (agriculture); Article 94 EC [*89*] (state aids); Article 99 [*93*] EC (indirect taxation); Article 100 [*94*] EC (common market); Article 100c EC (visa policy) [repealed at Amsterdam]; Article 130(3) [*157(3)*] EC (industrial policy); Article 130o(1) [*172(1)*] EC (certain aspects of research and development); Article 130s(2) [*175(2)*] EC (environmental taxes, planning and measures significantly affecting Member States' choice of energy policy) and Article 235 [*308*] EC.

In *Roquette Frères* the Court characterised the consultation of the Parliament as reflecting at Community level:

> '... the fundamental democratic principle that the peoples should take part in the exercise of power through the intermediary of a representative assembly.'[46]

From this the Court has derived a right for the Parliament to be reconsulted wherever the text adopted by the Council differs substantially from the text on which the Parliament has been consulted.[47]

Case C-65/90 Parliament v Council [1992] ECR I-4593[48]

Regulation 4059/89, based on Article 75 [71] EC, was adopted under the consultation procedure and provided a system whereby hauliers could apply for an authorisation to run road haulage services in another Member State for a limited period of time. The Parliament challenged this, noting that the proposal upon which it had been consulted had given non-resident hauliers an unlimited right to operate road haulage services within another Member State.

16.The case-law of the Court indicates that the duty to consult the European Parliament in the course of the legislative procedure, in the cases provided for by the Treaty, includes the requirement that the Parliament be reconsulted on each occasion when the text finally adopted, viewed as a whole, departs substantially from the text on which the Parliament has already been consulted, except in cases where the amendments essentially correspond to the wishes of the Parliament itself (see the judgments in Case 41/69 *Chemiefarma v Commission* [1970] ECR 661 and Case 817/79 *Buyl v Commission* [1982] ECR 245).

17. Article 1 of the regulation originally proposed by the Commission, on which the Parliament gave its opinion, provided that any road haulier for hire or reward established in a Member State and authorized to carry on business as an international road haulier should be allowed to carry out national road haulage operations for hire or reward in a Member State other than the one in which he is established. According to Article 3 of the

---

46   Case 138/79 *Roquette Frères v Council* [1980] ECR 3333.
47   See also recently Case C-392/95 *Parliament v Council*, Judgment of 10 June 1997.
48   Amended legislation was introduced following this judgment but this was also annulled for failure to consult the Parliament adequately, Case C-388/92 *Parliament v Council* [1994] ECR I-2067.

original proposal, national transport operations were to be subject to the rules in force in the Member State where the transport operations were carried out, provided that such rules were applied by that State to non-resident and national carriers alike.

18. On the other hand, the regulation adopted by the Council provides only that carriers established in a Member State and authorized to carry on business as international road hauliers should be entitled to operate on a temporary basis national road haulage services in another Member State (Article 1). Cabotage may be carried out only within a Community quota of 15 000 cabotage authorizations valid for two months (Article 2). In addition, the regulation applies only until 31 December 1992 and the Council is to adopt before 1 July 1992 a regulation laying down the definitive cabotage system (Article 9).

19. A comparison between the Commission's original proposal and the contested regulation shows that temporary authorization within the framework of a Community quota has been substituted for the principle of freedom of cabotage in Member States for carriers established in another Member State. Those amendments affect the very essence of the instrument adopted and must therefore be regarded as substantive. They do not correspond to any wish of the Parliament. On the contrary, in its opinion of 12 September 1986 the Parliament favoured greater liberalization, proposing that a paragraph should be added to Article 1, ensuring that Member States in which authorization to carry out national transport operations is subject to quantitative restrictions should increase the number of authorizations appropriately in order to allow carriers from other Member States to participate in domestic transport operations when additional authorizations are issued.

Even allowing for this reconsultation Parliament remains extremely marginalised under this procedure. Whilst the Council cannot adopt a measure without first having consulted the Parliament, it is not required to wait until Parliament has been consulted before it considers a proposal, and the Court has even stated that the Council is making good use of time if it does consider the matter prior pending consultation of the Parliament.[49] Political agreement is thus often reached within the Council without Parliament's opinion having been heard.[50] Consultation is thus a procedural requirement with the Council not being required to take account of its views or to give reasons for rejecting them.

---

[49]   Case C-417/93 *Parliament v Council* [1995] ECR I-1185.

[50]   On this see Westlake, M. *The Commission and the Parliament* (1994, Butterworths, London) 34.

The lack of leverage that the Parliament has over the Council also harms its relations with the Commission. As Parliament's views count for so little, there are no incentives for the Commission to coordinate or even consult with it. It has also been suggested that the procedure reduces the autonomy of the Commission. In areas where the measure can only be passed through the Council by a unanimity vote, the Commission is only likely to submit proposals which it knows are acceptable to all the Member States. This can reduce its role to finding the lowest common denominator.[51]

Despite its relative lack of complexity, the procedure is also one of the most opaque. No time-limits are imposed upon any of the institutions, allowing the possibility of stalling, if need be. Furthermore, there is no Treaty requirement upon the part of the Council to give reasons for why it has accepted, modified or rejected the Parliament's views with the result that the procedure results in very little dialogue between those two institutions.

iii. The Cooperation Procedure

Dissatisfaction with the consultation procedure led the Member States to set up an additional procedure at the time of the Single European Act, the cooperation procedure, now set out in Article 189c [252] EC.[52]

---

[51] On this see the *Report by the Ad Hoc Group examining the question of increasing the Parliament's powers* (the 'Vedel' Report) EC Bulletin Supplt. 4/72; Committee of Three, *Report on the European Institutions* (1980, OOPEC, Luxembourg) 74-75.

[52] Areas governed by the cooperation procedure include Article 6(2) EC (non-discrimination on grounds of nationality); Article 75(1) EC (transport); Articles 104a, 104b, & 105a [*102, 103 & 106*] EC (certain aspects of economic and monetary union); Article 118a2 EC (health and safety at work); Article 125 EC (European Social Fund); Article 127(4) EC (vocational training); Articles 130j, 130k, 130l, and 130o(2) EC (certain aspects of research and development); Article 130s(1) EC (environment); Article 130w EC (development) and article 2(2) of the *Social Protocol*. With the exception of the economic and monetary union procedures, these provisions will use co-decision following ratification of Amsterdam.

Article 189c [252] EC. The Commission submits a proposal to both the Council and the Parliament. The Council, having obtained Parliament's opinion and acting by qualified majority, adopts a 'common position' on the proposal, which is then communicated back to the Parliament for a second reading. The procedure then depends upon the reaction of the Parliament.

(a) If the Parliament does not act within the time limit of three months or approves the common position, the Council then adopts the act in accordance with its common position.

(b) If Parliament rejects the common position by an absolute majority (i.e. 314 votes), the Council may still adopt the measure, but it can only do so if it acts by *unanimity*.

(c) If the Parliament, acting by absolute majority, proposes amendments to the common position, these amendments are then communicated back to the Commission. If the Commission accepts them, they can be adopted by the Council, acting by qualified majority. If the Commission rejects them, they can only be adopted by the Council acting by unanimity.[53]

The most prominent feature distinguishing the cooperation procedure from the consultation procedure is that of greater Parliamentary engagement. First, the Parliament has two readings, one prior to the Council's adoption of its common position, the other subsequent to it. Secondly, Parliament can alter the way the Council votes. If the Parliament approves the common position, the Council can adopt the act by *qualified majority*, if Parliament rejects the common position, it can only be adopted by the Council if it acts unanimously. Put another way, Parliament plus one Member State can always block a measure. In addition, the Parliament, in principle, acting with the Commission can always block a measure, as the Commission can always withdraw a proposal any time before its adoption. This second

---

[53]   On the cooperation procedure see Bieber, R., Pantalis, J. & Schoo, J. 'Implications of the Single Act for the European Parliament' (1986) 23 *CMLRev* 767; Edward, D. 'The Impact of the Single Act on the Institutions' (1987) 24 *CMLRev* 19; Bieber, R. 'Legislative Procedure for the Establishment of the Single Market' (1988) 26 *CMLRev* 711; Fitzmaurice, J. 'An Analysis of the European Community's cooperation procedure' (1988) 26 *JCMS* 389; Corbett, R. 'Testing the New Procedures: The European Parliament's First Experiences with its New "Single Act" Powers' (1989) 27 *JCMS* 359; Lodge J., 'The European Parliament - from "assembly" to co-legislature: changing the institutional dynamics' 58, 68-77 in Lodge, J. (ed.) *The European Community and the Challenge of the Future* (1989, 1st Edition, Pinter, London).

possibility is less likely for the simple reason that the Commission must have initially approved the draft measure in order to propose it. A subsequent withdrawal of the measure involves a *volte-face* which needs some justifying.

The initial criticisms of the procedure were, first, that the Council could still ultimately overrule the Parliament, and, secondly, that the Parliament had been given a power - namely the power to hinder the adoption of Community legislation - which it did not really want, as it was far more in its interest to facilitate the adoption of Community legislation, and which was difficult to exercise, as it required an absolute majority in Parliament.[54] This latter criticism is supported by legislative practice. As of 31 July 1997, 400 measures had been adopted under the Cooperation Procedure.[55] In only six instances had Parliament exercised its power to reject the common position.[56] The power to reject the common position may have been of limited formal value, but it could be used to gain the Parliament not only considerable informal influence but also to enable it to set the agenda.

Tsebelis, G. 'The Power of the European Parliament as a Conditional Agenda Setter' (1994) 88 *American Political Science Review* 128, 131

Agenda-setting players have power when it is impossible, difficult, or costly for decision makers to modify their proposals. Modification of proposals may be precluded by the prevailing institutions. For example, when the president of the United States nominates a candidate for the Supreme Court, the Senate cannot modify the proposal. In the first theoretical paper analysing the importance of agenda control, the agenda setter could make a series of proposals that would be voted under 'closed rule' that is, without amendments. This agenda setter had quasi-dictatorial powers, being able to drive a society through a series of successive votes to select the agenda setter's ideal point. However, an agenda setter loses this power under open rule, because the proposals can subsequently be modified by amendments of the deciding body. Agenda setters also have power if the deciding body is impatient, that is, if it pays a price as long as there is no

---

[54]   See Resolutions of the European Parliament, OJ 1987 C 7/83 and OJ 1988 C 187/229.

[55]   European Parliament Progress Report on the Delegations to the Conciliation Committee. Annex II, 6. PE 223.209.

[56]   Reply of the President of the European Parliament to Question 39/97 by Richard Corbett. PE 259.385/BUR.

agreement. Impatience creates an asymmetry in favour of the proposal of the agenda setter and against its modifications.

The co-operation procedure presents a different mechanism for agenda-setting power. Regardless of impatience, it is more difficult for the Council to modify a Parliamentary proposal (provided it is accepted by the Commission) than to accept it. Indeed, qualified majority is needed for acceptance but unanimity for modification. This procedure may enable the EP to offer a proposal that makes a qualified majority of the Council better off than any unanimous decision. If such a proposal exists, if the EP is able to make it, and if the Commission adopts it, then the EP has agenda-setting powers. If, however, these conditions are not met, the EP loses its agenda-setting power. This is why I characterise the EP's agenda power under the co-operation procedure as conditional.

This view has been critiqued as overstating the Parliament's influence. In particular, it has been argued that the Parliament only has the position to set the agenda where the positions of the other players are very fluid.[57] Nevertheless, the statistics illustrate that the Parliament's influence increased significantly. At the end of July 1997, 54% of the Parliament's amendments proposed at first reading were accepted by the Commission, and 41% by the Council. On the second reading, with attitudes hardening, the figures were 43% and 21% respectively.[58]

The final feature of the procedure is that it is tighter than the consultation procedure. Both the Commission and the Council are obliged to inform the Parliament of the reasons which led the Council to adopt its common position, and also of the Commission's position.[59] In addition, there is a system of time limits from the time the Council has adopted the common position. The Parliament is thus under an obligation to conclude its second reading within three months if its voice

---

[57]   Moser, P. 'The European Parliament as a Conditional Agenda Setter: What are the Conditions? A Critique of Tsbelis' (1996) 90 *American Political Science Review* 834; Hubschmid, C. & Moser, P. 'The Co-Operation Procedure in the EU: Why was the European Parliament Influential in the Decision on Car Emission Standards?' (1997) 35 *JCMS* 225.

[58]   Supra n.55, 6. The impact is not merely quantitative. Many qualitatively significant amendments proposed by the Parliament have been accepted, Earnshaw, D. & Judge, D. 'From co-operation to co-decision: The European Parliament's path to legislative power' 96, 101-106 in Richardson, J (ed.) *European Union: Power and Policy Making* (1996, Routledge, London).

[59]   Article 189c(b) [*252(b)*] EC.

is not to be ignored.[60] The Commission must come to a view on any Parliamentary amendments within one month.[61] Finally, the Council is required to act within three months of receiving the draft following the Parliament's second reading.[62] Some disquiet was expressed at the time that no time limit was imposed on the Council to reach a common position.[63] The better view is that as proposals vary considerably in their complexity and the extent to which they intrude upon national sensitivities, it is too constraining to hedge the Council into some form of fixed deadline. As the adoption of a common position is the first point at which these issues get formally addressed by the Member States, it was unduly restrictive to impose a time limit.[64]

iv. The Co-Decision Procedure

The TEU added a further legislative procedure, the co-decision procedure, contained in Article 189b EC.[65] The route taken is identical to the Cooperation Procedure up until the second reading.[66]

---

60   Article 189c(b) [252(b)] EC.

61   Article 189c(d) [252(d)] EC.

62   Article 189c(f) [252(f)] EC. Both the Council's and Parliament's deadlines can be extended by one month by common accord, Article 189c(g) [252(g)] EC.

63   Bieber, R., Pantalis, J. & Schoo, J. 'Implications of the Single Act for the European Parliament' (1986) 23 CMLRev 767, 780.

64   Edward, D. 'The Impact of the Single Act on the Institutions' (1987) 24 CMLRev 19, 24.

65   The areas covered by this procedure include Article 49 [40] EC (free movement of workers); Article 54(2) [44(2)] EC (freedom of establishment); Articles 57(1), 57(2) & 66 [47(1), 47(2) & 55] EC (provisions for the self-employed); Articles 100a [95] & 100b [repealed] EC (internal market); Article 128(5) [151(5)] EC (culture); Article 129(4) [152(4)]EC (public health); Article 129a(2) [153(2)] EC (consumer protection); Article 129d [156] EC (trans-European networks); Article 130i [166]EC (framework programme for research and development); Article 130s(3) [175(3)] EC (environment action programmes).

66   Article 189b(2) EC. There are two provisions which use the co-decision procedure, yet the Council may only take decisions acting by unanimity - Article 128 [151] EC (culture) and Article 130i [166] EC (framework programmes for

If Parliament adopts the Council's common position, or does nothing within three months, then the measure is adopted by the Council in an identical manner to that under the Cooperation Procedure.[67]

If Parliament proposes amendments to the common position, these amendments can be accepted by the Council in the same way as under the cooperation procedure, namely by qualified majority if the Commission agrees with the amendments, and by unanimity if the Commission does not. If the Council does not accept the amendments it must convene the Conciliation Committee.[68]

If Parliament, by an absolute majority, rejects the Council's common position, the Council has a choice. It can either convene the Conciliation Committee or allow the measure to fall.[69]

The Conciliation Committee has 30 members, 15 representatives from the Council, one from each of the Member States, and 15 representatives from the Parliament. Its task is to approve a joint text. For a text to be adopted, a qualified majority vote is required from the Council members and a simple majority from the Parliament members. The Commission sits in on the proceedings, and, whilst it cannot vote, its duty is to attempt to reconcile the positions of the Council and the Parliament.[70]

If the Committee approves a joint text within six weeks, that text will be adopted as law if it is approved both by the Parliament, acting by absolute majority (i.e. 314 votes), and the Council, acting by qualified majority. If either fails to approve the measure, the measure falls.[71]

If the Conciliation Committee fails to approve a joint text, the measure, in principle, falls. The one exception is where the Council takes the confrontational step of reaffirming its common position, possibly taking Parliament's amendments into account (this can be done by qualified majority).[72] In which case the act will be adopted in accordance with the common position unless the Parliament, acting by absolute majority, rejects the text within a further six weeks.[73]

---

research and development).

[67] Article 189b(2)(a) & (b) EC.

[68] Article 189(b)(3) EC.

[69] Article 189b(2)(c) EC.

[70] Article 189b(4) EC.

[71] Article 189b(5) EC.

[72] The Council did this in relation to the draft Directive on open network provision of voice telephony. The Parliament duly rejected the text, Corbett R., Jacobs F. & Shackleton M., *The European Parliament* (1995, 3rd Edition, Cartermill, London) 207.

[73] Article 189b(6) EC.

The procedure operates within a series of strict time limits. These limits only start from the time the Council has adopted its common position. The Council is under a duty to communicate the reasons for the common position to the Parliament, and the Commission must also fully inform the Parliament of its position.[74] The Parliament is then under a duty to complete its second reading within three months if account is to be taken of its views.[75] Once the Parliament has given its second reading, the Council has three months to convene a Conciliation Committee in the case of Parliamentary amendments it does not accept,[76] and an unlimited period where the Parliament has rejected the common position. From that moment on the institutions and the Conciliation Committee are under a series of six week deadlines to act.[77] The deadlines of three months and six weeks can be extended to four months and eight weeks respectively by the common accord of the Council and the Parliament.[78]

In substantive terms the co-decision procedure increases the formal powers of the Parliament in three ways. In instances where a Conciliation Committee is convened the Parliament now has a third reading to consider a measure after the Committee has met. In those instances where a joint text is approved by the Conciliation Committee that text is jointly adopted by the Parliament and the Council, not simply adopted by the Council. Finally, and most importantly, Parliament can *veto* any measure.It has been questioned, however, whether this veto amounts to the genuine co-decision the title of the procedure implies.

Curtin, D. 'The Constitutional Structure of the European Union: A Europe of Bits and Pieces' (1993) 30 *Common Market Law Review* 17, 37-38

The crux of the new co-decision procedure is that unless Council and Parliament agree on the final text of the legislation, neither is given the last word and the legislation simply falls. Parliament can exercise its power of *amendment* at two points: on first reading... and in the context of the conciliation procedure, where it can influence the text on equal terms with the Council and with the Commission mediating. In the event that such

---

[74]   Article 189b(2) EC.
[75]   Article 189b(2)(b) EC.
[76]   Article 189b(3) EC.
[77]   Article 189b(5) & (6) EC.
[78]   Article 189b(7) EC.

agreement is not forthcoming the co-decision procedure allows the Council to adopt by qualified majority a text in the event of conciliation not reaching an agreement; this Council text then stands unless rejected by a majority of the members of the European Parliament. This could arguably mean that there would be little incentive for the Council to negotiate a compromise in the conciliation procedure unless it was clear that there would be the required majority in Parliament. Parliament would also have to be willing to take the blame for the legislative procedure ending without result, a negative role it would normally be reluctant to assume. Thus the procedure is formally one of co-decision but with the effective balance of power indisputably weighed towards the Council. In the final analysis, the Council is not even bound, when deciding by qualified majority, to incorporate into its post-conciliation text those amendments made by the European Parliament earlier in the process which were accepted by the Commission.

The position in terms of informal influence is more complicated. Parliamentary influence is increased not simply through the creation of a veto but through the regularisation and formalisation of contacts between the Council and the Parliament through the Conciliation Committee.[79] It was certainly the Parliament's hope that over time the Committee would develop an autonomy of its own which would increase that body's influence.[80] It is possible, however, that, paradoxically, the Conciliation Committee might reduce the Parliament's influence at earlier stages in the procedure. The reason for this is that under the Cooperation procedure a lower vote is required for the Council to accept Parliament's amendments than to modify them. The possibility therefore existed for Parliament to exert influence by making amendments that were acceptable to a qualified majority within the

[79]   Earnshaw, D. & Judge, D. 'From co-operation to co-decision: The European Parliament's path to legislative power' 96, 124-125 in Richardson, J. (ed.) *European Union: Power and Policy Making* (1996, Routledge, London).

[80]   European Parliament, *Report on the First Application of the Co-Decision Procedure* (1994, Conciliation Secretariat, Brussels) 15.The Committee appears to have arisen out of proposal from the Parliament for a body similar to the Mediations Committee in Germany which has the duty of providing compromise solutions to the two federal legislative assemblies, the Bundestag and the Bundesrat. See Foster, N. 'The new Conciliation Committee under Article 189b' (1994) 19 *ELRev* 185. On the working of the Conciliation Committee see the Parliament Resolution, 'The Arrangements for the proceedings of the Conciliation Committee under Article 189b EC', OJ 1993 C 329/132; Corbett, R., Jacobs, F. & Shackleton, M. supra n.72, 205-207.

Council. The existence of the Conciliation Committee reduces this possibility, as it allows members of the Council, albeit acting within the framework of the Committee, to make amendments by qualified majority. As the voting threshold for Council modifications is reduced from unanimity to qualified majority, so it becomes easier for the Council to act proactively and recapture the agenda from Parliament.[81]

Experience suggests that the Conciliation Committee has been reasonably effective. As of 31 July 1997 96 measures had been adopted under Article 189b EC, 35 of those had been on the basis of a joint text agreed within the Conciliation Committee. Only once had a text of the Committee, that on the draft directive for Open Network Provision of Telephony Services, been rejected and only once, on a draft directive for patenting of biotechnological inventions, had it failed to come to an agreement.[82]

The TEU required that the scope of the procedure should be considered at the IGC with a view to its possibly being widened.[83] The relationship between the cooperation and co-decision procedures was problematic. Member States' blocking rights were identical in both procedures, as both relied upon a qualified majority vote. It was difficult, therefore, to argue that one should be used over the other in areas of greater national sensitivity. Indeed, there was no evidence this is the case, for, as the Commission notes, the distribution of areas under co-decision is 'fragmentary and arbitrary'.[84] Parliament therefore pushed for an abolition of the cooperation procedure.[85] The Commission was less forthright.

---

[81] Tsbelis, G. 'Maastricht and the Democratic Deficit' (1997) 52 *Aussenwirtschaft* 26, 43-45.

[82] Supra n.55, 3-4.

[83] Article 189b(8) EC. 212 proposals have in fact been made by the Commission under Co-Decision representing 25% of EC legislative activity. Supra n.55, 3.

[84] Commission report on the Scope of the codecision procedure, EU Bulletin 7/8-1996, 192.

[85] Resolution A4-0102/95, para. 29(i).

2. On purely democratic grounds, codecision should be extended to all the Community's legislative activity. But how should this be defined?

Giving a legal definition of a legislative instrument would in practice entail moving towards a hierarchy of norms.

On the other hand, the Commission considers that the criteria commonly used to define what constitutes a legislative instrument could be used as a guideline; it would have no legal effect and would not be formalised in the Treaty, but would make it possible to determine which of the various areas in the Treaty should come under codecision and which should not.

In short, to meet these criteria legislative instruments would have to meet the following description:

*   be directly based on the Treaty;
*   be binding;
*   determine essential elements of Community action in a given area; and
*   be general in scope.

The Commission thus considered that a simple substitution of the codecision procedure for the cooperation procedure would not be fully satisfactory. There were, first, some areas, such as citizenship and agriculture, where the consultation procedure was used. These should be replaced by codecision. It, secondly, noted that the cooperation procedure was used for some tasks of an essentially administrative nature. Codecision was not needed here.

At Amsterdam the Member States followed the broad outlines of the Commission proposal. The one proviso to this was that they were unwilling to extend codecision to as many fields where the consultation procedure currently applies as the Commission would have wished. Nevertheless, the remit of the codecision procedure has been considerably extended.[86] Conversely, the remit of the cooperation

---

[86]   The additional areas where codecision will apply following Amsterdam are *Article 12 EC* (discrimination on grounds of nationality); *Article 18(2) EC* (citizens' rights to move and reside freely within the territory of the Member States); *Article 42 EC* (social security for immigrant workers); *Article 46(2) EC* (special treatment for foreign nationals); *Article 47 EC* (coordination of provisions on the self-employed and the professions); *Article 71 EC* (common

procedure is reduced to a few administrative tasks in the field of economic and monetary union.[87]

The second matter considered at Amsterdam was reform of the codecision procedure itself. There had been growing criticism of its complexity.[88] Agreement was reached to simplify the procedure.

Article 251 EC. 1. Where reference is made in this Treaty to this Article for the adoption of an act, the following procedure shall apply.

2. The Commission shall submit a proposal to the European Parliament and the Council.

The Council, acting by a qualified majority after obtaining the opinion of the European Parliament,
- if it approves all the amendments contained in the European Parliament's opinion, may adopt the proposed act thus amended;

---

rules on transport); *Article 80(2) EC* (sea and air transport); *Article 116 EC* (customs cooperation); *Article 129 EC* (incentive measures on employment); *Article 137(3) EC* (social policy with the exception of all areas which require unanimity); *Article 138(3) EC* (equal pay); *Article 148 EC* (implementing decisions relating to the European Social Fund); *Article 150(4) EC* (vocational training); *Article 152(4) EC* (public health); *Article 156 EC* (Trans-European Networks); *Article 162 EC* (implementing decisions of the European Regional Development Fund); *Article 172 EC* (multiannual frameworks for research and development): *Article 175(1) EC* (environment); *Article 179 EC* (development cooperation); *Article 255 EC* (transparency); *Article 280 EC* (countering fraud); *Article 285 EC* (customs cooperation); *Article 286 EC* (establishment of advisory authority on data protection).

[87] *Article 99(5) EC* (rules for multilateral surveillance of economic policy); *Article 102(2) EC* (prohibition of measures not based on prudential grounds which establish privileged access by EC institutions, Member States or public bodies to financial institutions); *Article 103(2) EC* (overdraft facilities with ECB or national central banks and liability of EC institutions and Member States for commitments of other Member States or public bodies); *Article 106(2) EC* (denominations and technical specifications of the euro).

[88] This was taken on board at an early stage, with there being a consensus in the Reflection Group that codecision required simplifying, *Report of the Reflection Group*, SN 520/95, para. 86.

- if the European Parliament does not propose any amendments, may adopt the proposed act;
- shall otherwise adopt a common position and communicate it to the European Parliament. The Council shall inform the European Parliament fully of the reasons which led it to adopt its common position. The Commission shall inform the European Parliament fully of its position.

If, within three months of such communication, the European Parliament:
(a) approves the common position or has not taken a decision, the act in question shall be deemed to have been adopted in accordance with that common position;
(b) rejects, by an absolute majority of its component members, the common position, the proposed act shall be deemed not to have been adopted;
(c) proposes amendments to the common position by an absolute majority of its component members, the amended text shall be forwarded to the Council and to the Commission, which shall deliver an opinion on those amendments.

3. If, within three months of the matter being referred to it, the Council, acting by a qualified majority, approves all the amendments of the European Parliament, the act in question shall be deemed to have been adopted in the form of the common position thus amended; however, the Council shall act unanimously on the amendments on which the Commission has delivered a negative opinion. If the Council does not approve all the amendments, the President of the Council, in agreement with the President of the European Parliament, shall within six weeks convene a meeting of the Conciliation Committee.

4. The Conciliation Committee, which shall be composed of the members of the Council or their representatives and an equal number of representatives of the European Parliament, shall have the task of reaching agreement on a joint text, by a qualified majority of the members of the Council or their representatives and by a majority of the representatives of the European Parliament. The Commission shall take part in the Conciliation Committee's proceedings and shall take all the necessary initiatives with a view to reconciling the positions of the European Parliament and the Council. In fulfilling this task, the Conciliation Committee shall address the common position on the basis of the amendments proposed by the European Parliament.

5. If, within six weeks of its being convened, the Conciliation Committee approves a joint text, the European Parliament, acting by an absolute majority of the votes cast, and the Council, acting by a qualified majority, shall each have a period of six weeks from that approval in which to adopt the act in question in accordance with the joint text. If either of the two institutions fails to approve the proposed act within that period, it shall be deemed not to have been adopted.

6. Where the Conciliation Committee does not approve a joint text, the proposed act shall be deemed not to have been adopted.

7. The periods of three months and six weeks referred to in this Article shall be extended by a maximum of one month and two weeks respectively at the initiative of the European Parliament or the Council.

Article 251 EC brings about some simplification. In particular, it allows a text to be adopted at first reading if the Parliament and Council are in agreement. In addition, the time limits are tightened up, so that if the Council does not approve the Parliament's amendments, it must convene a Conciliation Committee within six weeks, extendable to eight weeks if necessary.[89] A Declaration is also attached to the Treaty stating that in no case should the period between the Parliament's second reading and the outcome of the Conciliation Committee exceed nine months.

More subtly, the amendments tilt the legislative balance more in Parliament's favour. At a formal level this is done by preventing the Council from continuing where Parliament has rejected a measure. It will therefore no longer have the discretion to convene the Conciliation Committee following a rejection by the Parliament of its common position at second reading. It will also no longer have the possibility of seeking to re-establish its common position in situations where the Conciliation Committee has failed to agree a joint text. A greater formal equality is therefore established between the institutions.

Parliament's influence has also been increased through the limiting of the Conciliation Committee's discretion. Whereas previously the Committee had complete discretion to come up with a joint text, its mandate is now limited. It must now address the 'common position on the basis of the amendments proposed by the Parliament'.[90] This amendment was introduced by the Member States to stop MEP's on the Committee trying to hijack the process through the raising of completely fresh points for the first time at Committee stage. Paradoxically, it may serve to entrench Parliament's agenda setting capabilities. It does this, first, by limiting the autonomy of the Commitee. Secondly, the status of Parliamentary amendments is strengthened, as, even where not accepted

---

[89]   There is currently no time limit here.
[90]   *Article 251(4) EC.*

by the Council, they will be used as the formal starting point for setting the agenda of the Conciliation Committee.

v. The Assent Procedure

The legislative procedure under which the Parliament enjoys greatest powers is the assent procedure. First developed under the Single European Act, its ambit was extended considerably by the TEU[91] and altered slightly at Amsterdam.[92] The procedure is extremely simple.

(a) A proposal is made by the Commission,[93] ECB,[94] Parliament[95] or applicant Member State.[96]
(b) The Council then adopts a common position on the proposal, normally by unanimity.[97]
(c) The Parliament must then give its approval.
(d) It is only if the Parliament gives its approval ('assent') that the Council can then adopt the measures.

---

[91]   The procedure applies to Article 8a(2) EC (movement and residence rights for Union citizens); Article 105(6) [105(6)] EC (the conferral of prudential supervision over credit institutions on the ECB); Article 106(5) [107(5)] EC (amendments to the Protocol of the ESCB); Article 130d [161] EC (the establishment and rules governing the Cohesion Fund; Article 138(3) [190(3)] EC (uniform procedures for Parliament elections); Article 228(3) [300(3)] EC (association agreements and international agreements having budgetary or certain legislative implications); Article O [49] TEU (accession of new Member States).

[92]   One new Treaty provision uses the assent procedure *Article 7 TEU*(the finding of a serious and persistent breach by a Member State of the principles underlying the Union). Meanwhile, codecision replaces assent as the procedure used in *Article 18(2) EC* (movement and residence rights for Union citizens).

[93]   Articles 8a(2) EC; 105(6) [105(6)] EC; 106(5) [107(5)] EC;130d [161] EC & 228(3) [300(3)] EC.

[94]   Article 106(5) [107(5)] EC

[95]   Article 138(3) [190(3)] EC

[96]   Article O [49] TEU.

[97]   The exception to this is Article 106(5) [107(5)] EC where the proposal comes from the ECB, in which case the voting requirement is qualified majority.

The advantages for the Parliament of the assent procedure over the co-decision procedure are two-fold. The first is a change in presumptions. Under the co-decision procedure a measure can be adopted unless an absolute majority of members actively vote *against* the measure. In some cases Parliament might be sufficiently divided that this will be difficult to achieve. Under the assent procedure a measure will only be adopted if a majority of members actively vote *for* that measure, an absolute majority in the case of accession and adoption of a uniform electoral system, a simple majority otherwise. The second is that no time-limits are imposed upon Parliament, within which it must act. Even where it might eventually approve a measure, it therefore has a power of delay which it can use to maximise its influence within the decision-making process.[98]

IV. The 'Democratic Deficit' and the Legislative Process

The question of democratic legitimacy, in Euro-speak the 'democratic deficit', has dominated debate over the Community legislative processes. Within the Union the debate is complicated by the Union not being a mature federation but a supranational organisation which must reconcile national and central interests. The debate has therefore been framed in a number of ways. At one level it is an institutional debate, whereby there should be an executive fully accountable to an elected legislature.[99]

---

[98]   On the assent procedure see Corbett, R., Jacobs, F. & Shackleton, M. supra n.72, 211-217.

[99]   The literature on this area is immense. Some of the more significant recent contributions are Curtin, D. 'The Constitutional Structure of the European Union: A Europe of Bits and Pieces' (1993) 30 *CMLRev* 17 Featherstone, K. 'Jean Monnet and the "Democratic Deficit" in the European Union' (1994) 32 JCMS 149; Boyce, B. 'The Democratic Deficit of the European Community' (1993) 46 *Parliamentary Affairs* 458; Raworth, P. 'A Timid Step Forwards: Maastricht and the Democratisation of the European Community' (1994) 19 *ELRev* 16; Piris, J-C. 'After Maastricht, are the Community Institutions more Efficacious, More Democratic, More Transparent?' (1994) 19 *ELRev* 449; Lodge, J. 'Transparency and Democratic Legitimacy' (1994) 32 *JCMS* 343; Curtin, D. & Meijers, H. 'The Principle of Open Government in Schengen and

At this level debate inevitably focuses on the relatively weak powers of the European Parliament and the extent to which they vary according to the legal base.

Piris, J-C. 'After Maastricht, are the Community Institutions more Efficacious, More Democratic, More Transparent?' (1994) 19 *European Law Review* 449, 462-463

... many people refer to what is called in the Brussels jargon the 'democratic deficit'. This expression became all the rage in the European Parliament and was taken over by a number of commentators. It takes the following circumstance as its point of departure: the transfer of powers from the Member States to the European Community has not been accompanied by a corresponding transfer of powers from the national powers to the European Parliament. Therefore the Council, composed of representatives of national executives, adopts acts which were formerly subject to a national parliamentary procedure. So much for the celebrated 'democratic deficit'.

In actual fact, the number of texts adopted by the Council which fell within the powers of the national parliaments before the creation of the European Communities is not that great. For the most part, regulations and directives of the Communities are technical texts, which formerly fell within national executive powers.

So far as concerns the texts which in the past fell within the powers of national legislatures, the following points may be made:
(1) that every vote in the Council can (some say 'should') be preceded by national procedures for consulting national parliaments;
(2) that the members of the Council are politicians, members of their national government and, for many of them, members of their national parliament;
(3) that, in the Member States of the Communities, the national governments which were appointed democratically, are responsive to their public opinion and accountable to their national parliaments and that any important vote in the Council may bring about immediate reactions, and may even be politically 'punished' at national level.

the European Union: Democratic Retrogression' (1995) 32 *CMLRev* 391; Tillikainen, T. 'The Problem of Democracy in the European Union' in Rosas A. & Antola E. (eds.) *A Citizens' Europe* (1995, Sage, London); Armingeon, K. 'The Democratic Deficit of the European Union' (1995) 50 *Aussenwirtschaft* 67; Grimm, D. 'Does Europe Need a Constitution?' (1995) 1 *ELJ* 282; Habermas, J. 'Comment on Paper by Dieter Grimm: "Does Europe Need a Constitution?"' (1995) 1 *ELJ* 303; Andersen, S. & Eliassen, K. *The European Union: How Democratic Is It?* (1996, Sage, London).

In light of the manner in which the Council conducts its business, a rider must be added to these points. Debate does not take place within the Council in the public manner that it takes place within national parliaments or, for that matter, the European Parliament. As a general rule, the public neither have access to the meeting nor are the debates broadcast. Until recently, furthermore, public access to the minutes of these meetings was denied. There is therefore considerably less public awareness of what takes place within the Council and the Council is thus less accountable than is the case with national legislatures within the European Union.

The question of the democratic deficit should not be seen purely in terms of institutional accountability. The democratic deficit has been examined so far purely from a unitary *European perspective*.[100] For some this can only be done if there exists an underlying European *Demos*, a collective sense of identity and loyalty. The essence of demos is described below by a critic of the term.[101]

Weiler, J. 'Does Europe need a Constitution? Reflections on Demos, Telos and the German Maastricht Decision' (1995) 1 *European Law Journal* 219, 225-226

The people of a polity, the *Volk*, its demos, is a concept which has a subjective socio-psychological-component which is rooted in objective, organic conditions. ...

The subjective manifestations of peoplehood, of the demos, are to be found in a sense of social cohesion, shared destiny and collective self-identity which, in turn, result in (and deserve) loyalty. These subjective manifestations have thus both a descriptive and normative element.

The subjective manifestations are a result of, but also conditioned on some, though not necessarily all, of the objective elements: common language, common history, common cultural habits and sensibilities and - this is dealt with more discretely since the twelve years of National Socialism - common ethnic origin, common religion. All these factors alone do not capture the essence of Volk - one will always find allusions to some spiritual, even mystic, element as well. Whereas different writers may throw a different mix of elements into the pot, an insistence on a relatively high degree of homogeneity, measured by these ethno-cultural criteria, is typically an important, indeed critical element of the discourse. Here rests the most delicate aspect of the theory since the

---

[100]   For an excellent analysis of this problem see the essays in Hayward J. (ed.) *The Crisis of Representation* in (1995) 18(3) *Western European Politics.*
[101]   See Grimm, D. 'Does Europe Need a Constitution?' (1995) 1 *ELJ* 303.

insistence on homogeneity is what conditions in its statal operationalisation the rules for inclusion and exclusion. When, say, Jews were excluded from full membership in many European Nation-States as equal citizens it was often on the theory that being a Christian was essential to the homogeneity of the people. The 'organic' nature of the *Volk* is a delicate matter. I call 'organic' those parts of the discourse which make, to a greater or lesser degree, one or more of the following claims: The *Volk* pre-dates historically, and precedes politically the modern State. Germany could emerge as a modern Nation-State because there was already a German *Volk*. The 'nation' is simply a modern appellation, in the context of modernist political theory and international law, of the pre-existing *Volk* and the State is its political expression.

For such people, whilst a strong sense of national identity exists within much of Europe, the sense of European identity is more questionable. To them therefore the idea of a European democracy is a contradiction in terms. Whilst this is part of a much more wide ranging debate, touching as it does on the legitimacy of the Union, it also has considerable implications for the institutional structure of the Union.[102] In institutional terms, qualified majority voting poses a threat to national democracy, in so far as it results in a transfer of powers from the regions and the Member States to the EC institutions and a corresponding loss of power for regional and national parliamentary assemblies. For those who perceive questions in terms of national *demos*, it is no answer to argue the loss of their national assembly's legislative powers is compensated for by an increase in the European Parliament's influence.

Weiler, J. 'After Maastricht: Community Legitimacy in Post-1992 Europe' in Adams W. (ed.) *Singular Europe: Economy and Polity of the European Community after 1992* (1992, University of Michigan Press, Ann Arbor) 11, 23-24.

... in terms of democratic theory, the final objective of a unifying polity is to recoup the loss of democracy initiated by the process of integration. This 'loss' is recouped when the

---

[102]   On this debate see Weiler, J. 'After Maastricht: Community Legitimacy in Post-1992 Europe' in Adams W. (ed.) *Singular Europe: Economy and Polity of the European Community after 1992* (1992, University of Michigan Press, Ann Arbor); Neunreither, K. 'The Syndrome of Democratic Deficit in the European Community' in Parry G. (ed.) *Politics in an Interdependent World* (1994, Elgar, Aldershot).

social fabric and discourse is such that the electorate accepts the new boundary as defining the polity and then totally accepts the legitimacy of being subjected to majority rule in a much larger system comprising the integrated polities. ...

Even today, after adoption of the SEA, it can be argued plausibly that the electorate in most member states accepts only grudgingly the notion that crucial areas of public life should be governed by a decision process in which their national voice becomes a minority that may be overridden by a majority of representatives from other European countries. In theoretical terms, there is still no legitimacy to the notion that the boundaries within which a minority will accept (as democratically legitimate) a majority decision must now be national rather than European.

At its starkest, one could claim that, in terms of social legitimacy, there is no difference between a decision made in the Council of Ministers and a decision made in the European Parliament. To the electorate, both present themselves as legislative chambers with representatives of the member states. In both cases, until this dimension of legitimacy is resolved by time and other factors, the electorate of a minority member state may find it hard to swallow and could consider it socially illegitimate that they have to abide by a majority decision of a redefined polity.

On this premise, the single most legitimating element (from a social point of view) was the Luxembourg Accord and the veto power. To be sure, one paid a huge cost in terms of efficient decision making and progress. But it was the device that enabled the Community to legitimate its program and its legislation, for it provided both an ex ante 'insurance policy' to the national electorates that nothing could get through without their voice having a controlling say and it presented ex-post legitimation as well. Everything that the Community did, however unpopular it might have been, was passed with the assent of national ministers. To the extent that the output of the Community decision process was legitimate, it was so at least partially because of the knowledge that it is controllable in this way.

If the question of democracy within the legislative processes of the European Union becomes inextricably linked to the question of *demos*, there is a danger of a dialogue of the deaf developing with those who believe in a European *demos* shouting past those who do not, and vice versa. The most sustained challenge to this linkage between *demos* and democracy has come from Habermas. In Habermas' view it is both futile and dangerous, even within national systems, to search in contemporary pluralistic societies for some collective pre-existing identity which can be used to legitimate institutional processes. For him the value of institutional processes in the public sphere is inherent in that they provide a context where strangers can be brought together and communicate with each other.

Habermas, J. 'Remarks on Dieter Grimm's "Does Europe Need a Constitution?"' (1995) 1 *European Law Journal* 303, 306-307

The core is formed a by political public sphere which enables citizens to take positions at the same time on the same topics of the same relevance. This public sphere must be deformed neither through external nor internal coercion. It must be embedded in the context of a freedom-valuing political culture and be supported by a liberal associational structure of a civil society. Socially relevant experience from still-intact private spheres must flow into such a civil society so that they may be processed there for public treatment. The political parties - not state-dependent - must remain rooted in this complex so as to mediate between the spheres of informal public communication, on the one hand, and the institutionalised deliberation and decision processes, on the other. Accordingly, from a normative perspective, there can be no European Federal state worthy of the name of a democratic Europe unless a European-wide integrated public sphere develops in the ambit of a common political culture: a civil society with interest associations; non-governmental organisations; citizens' movements, etc; and naturally a party system appropriate to a European arena. In short, this entails public communication that transcends the boundaries of the until now limited national public spheres.

Certainly, the ambitious functional requirements of democratic will-formation can scarcely be fulfilled in the nation-state framework; this is all the more true for Europe. What concerns me, however, is the perspective from which these functional prerequisites are normatively justified; for this, as it were, prejudices the empirical evaluation of the present difficulties. These must, for the time being, seem insuperable if a pre-political collective identity is regarded as necessary, that is an independent cultural substrate which is articulated only in the fulfilment of the said functional requirements. But a communications-theoretical understanding of democracy, one that Grimm also seems to favour, can no longer rest upon such a concretistic understanding of 'the people'. This notion falsely pretends homogeneity, where in fact something still quite heterogeneous is met.

The ethical-political self-understanding of citizens in a democratic community must not be taken as an historical-cultural a priori that makes democratic will-formation possible, but rather as the flowing contents of a circulatory process that is generated through the legal institutionalisation of citizens' communication. This is precisely how national identities were formed in modern Europe. Therefore it is to be expected that the political institutions to be created by a European constitution would have an inducing effect. Europe has been integrating economically, socially and administratively for some time and in addition can base itself on a common cultural background and the shared historical experience of having happily overcome nationalism. Given the political will, there is no a priori reason why it cannot subsequently create the politically necessary communicative context as soon as it is constitutionally prepared to do so. Even the requirement of a common language - English as a second first language - ought not be an insurmountable obstacle with the existing level of formal schooling. European identity can in any case mean nothing other than unity in national diversity.

Habermas provides an alternative basis for evaluating the democratic foundations of the European Union. Yet the institutional context within which these processes have developed has shown them to be bedevilled by questions of identity and demos. Particularly sensitive policy areas almost always require unanimity within the Council, whilst, at the other end of the scale Parliament enjoys its greatest powers where the national interest is seen as being less strident. The result is a bewildering range of legislative procedures which is perceived to be one of the causes of the democratic deficit within the Union.[103]

The centrality of national identity was underscored by the TEU recognising the need for a greater involvement by national parliaments in the EC legislative process.[104] A Declaration is attached to the TEU stating that it is important for contacts and exchange of information between national Parliaments and the European Parliament to be stepped up, and that national parliaments should receive Commission proposals for legislation in good time for information or examination.[105]

In addition, since 1989 representatives of the European Parliament have six monthly meetings with those organs of the national parliaments who are responsible for EU matters. The meetings are held in the Member State which is holding the Presidency. Since 1991 they

---

[103] See Report of the Commission on the operation of the Treaty on European Union, SEC (95) 731 final, 10 May 1995.

[104] See Westlake, M. 'The European Parliament, national parliaments and the 1996 IGC' (1995) 66 *Political Quarterly* 59. On national parliaments and the legislative process see Norton, F. (ed.) National Parliaments and the European Union (1996, Frank Cass, London); Smith, E. (ed.) *National Parliaments as Cornerstones of European Integration* (1996, Kluwer, The Hague); Bergman, T. 'National parliaments and EU Affairs Committees: notes on empirical variation and competing explanations' (1997) 4 *JEPP* 373.

[105] Declaration 13 TEU. On the system within the United Kingdom for examination of proposed legislation by the British Parliament and its experiences see Campbell, A. 'The Single European Act and the Implications' (1986) 35 *ICLQ* 932; Kennon, A. 'The Single Market - A Legislative Perspective' (1992) 13 *Company Lawyer* 25; Birkinshaw, P. & Ashiagbor, D. 'National Participation in Community Affairs: Democracy, the UK Parliament and the EU' (1995) 33 *CMLRev* 499.

have been placed on a formalised basis and operate under the acronym of COSAC (Conference of European Affairs Committees).

Both national parliamentary participation in the EC legislative procedure and the role of COSAC were addressed at Amsterdam in a Protocol.[106] In relation to information for national parliaments, the Protocol requires the Commission to forward promptly all consultation documents to them. In addition, Commission proposals for legislation shall be made in sufficiently good time to enable each national government to ensure that its parliament receives the proposal as appropriate. To facilitate this the Council is required, subject to exceptions on grounds of urgency, to allow a six week period to elapse before it places on its agenda either a Commission proposal on EC legislation or on action in JHA.

The role of COSAC is also beefed up. It may make any contribution it deems appropriate for the attention of the EU institutions. In particular, it may examine legislative proposals in the area of freedom, security and justice which have a direct bearing on the rights and freedoms of individuals. It may address the Council, Commission and Parliament on the legislative activities of the Union, particularly on questions of subsidiarity, fundamental rights and on the area of freedom, security and justice.

Better coordination between the European Parliament and national parliaments, whilst undoubtedly desirable, should not be seen as a panacea.

Neunreither, K. 'The Democratic Deficit of the European Union: Towards Closer Cooperation between the European Parliament and the National Parliaments' (1994) 29 *Government and Opposition* 299, 312-313

Legitimacy also depends on the consent of the citizen, not necessarily on individual decisions taken, but on the system itself. There must exist some kind of identification between the citizen and the political system. Some authors have tried to distinguish between 'formal legitimacy' and 'social legitimacy'. Social legitimacy would then mean that the citizens feel part of the political entity in which decisions are taken. Without retaining the above distinction which is certainly controversial, it is obvious that the

---

[106]   *Protocol to the TEU on the role of National Parliaments in the European Union.*

citizens in Europe identify themselves much more closely with their member states and, to some extent, their regions than with the European Union.

If we return to the democratic deficit and the possible contribution of both the European and the national parliaments to reducing it, we could say that a solution might be found for the institutional deficit, especially the parliamentary one. This solution should certainly not consist in increasing unilaterally the powers of the European Parliament at the expense of the national parliaments. During the last three or four years it has been increasingly acknowledged that the two parliamentary sides are complementary, that both the EP would benefit from an increased role of the national parliaments and that the national parliaments could greatly benefit from a number of facilities and offers of cooperation from the EP. The condition for such an evolution is that both the EP and the national parliaments stay within their respective areas of competences and that above all, the national parliaments do not give way to the temptations to get involved directly in the EU institutional system. This would lead to confusion and be counter-productive.

But the more difficult questions about the democratic deficit lie beyond institutional competences. It is the acceptance of the system as such which is under scrutiny: can the ambitious goal for deepening the European Union, both in the field of the economy, including a common currency, in social matters but also in external relations and security be reached without a transformation of major elements of the European political culture? Do we not dramatically need European political parties, European trade unions, a far-reaching European organisational structure, a web of government in the broadest sense including social and cultural life, with emphasis on the media, if we want to move forward substantially on the road which Maastricht has put on the map? In that context the European Parliament and the national parliaments are challenged far beyond the catalogue of their competences or functions.

V. Transparency and the Legislative Process

The volume of legislation passed following the Single European Act drew increasing attention to the byzantine and, to the outside, obscure policy-making processes within the Community. A reaction to this was a clamour in the 1990s for increased participation and transparency.

Shapiro, M. 'Codification of Administrative Law: The US and the Union' (1996) 2 *European Law Journal* 26, 43.

Regulation versus deregulation is even more central to the politics of the Union than to the politics of each of its Member States. The movement of regulatory authority from Member States capitals to Brussels accelerates the fear of technocracy and the desire for transparency and participation both among the people and national economic elites. The key lies in the elites. Accustomed to a style of regulation in which business elites and government technocrats formed an intimate 'in group' which negotiated mutually satisfactory regulatory compromises, the regulated firms now faced a more distanced, less intimate regulation from Brussels in which national business leaders are less 'in'. If you are 'in', you do not concern yourself with participation and transparency, that is to the interests of the 'outs'. But if you are beginning to fall 'out', participation and transparency suddenly seem more attractive. Just as the regulated elites now support a large lobbying industry in Brussels (if you are 'in' you do your own lobbying - if you are 'out' you have to pay someone else to do it), they are likely to support an administrative law that opens ups regulatory decision-making to outside influences.

The general principle of open government was seriously addressed for the first time in the run up to the TEU when the Dutch Government proposed that the Council be given a competence to adopt regulations on access to information.[107] This was not accepted by the other Member States but a Declaration was attached to the TEU.

Declaration No. 17 TEU. The Conference considers that transparency of the decision-making process strengthens the democratic nature of the institutions and the public's confidence in the administration. The Conference accordingly recommends that the Commission submit to the Council no later than 1993 a report on measures designed to improve public access to the information available to the institutions.

i. The Legislative Process and the Lobby

The question of transparency has parted into two debates. The first has been on the use of information to convince interested parties of the need for Community action. Lodge has suggested that subsidiarity, by placing an onus on the Commission to justify the need for Community legislation, created a premium on its being 'able to ensure support in the

---

[107]   Curtin, D. & Meijers H., 'The Principle of Open Government in Schengen and the European Union: Democratic Retrogression' (1995) 32 *CMLRev* 391, 419-421.

marketplace for its proposed action'.[108] Persuasion of the need for a measure would require that these people first of all be informed of the proposed content of the measure.

Lodge, J. 'Transparency and Democratic Legitimacy' (1994) 32 *Journal of Common Market Studies* 343, 350-351

...the presentation of transparency in this way was a means of suggesting that attempts were being made to enhance participatory opportunities and the EU institutions' capacities for making informed choices. Beyond this, several additional steps have been taken to improve the following: access to data bases; the existing relay network (of information on the EC); and the drafting of a code of conduct by interest groups who are supposed to regulate themselves...

Early warning of Commission thinking has always been one of the criteria of successfully influencing subsequent decisions, whether on the content of legislation or on the acquisition of funds and contracts. Accordingly, the following measures have been agreed. Lists of COM documents on general topics are now published in the *Official Journal* each week. Papers of general interest that formerly would not have been published are included in the COM series. Work programmes and legislative programmes are published in the Official Journal to publicize action planned by the Commission. Those forthcoming proposals suitable for wide-ranging preliminary consultation are highlighted. A list of topics on which Green or White Papers will be prepared, and plans to consolidate legislation, are published in the legislative programme. An interinstitutional yearbook describing the internal organization of the institutions in more detail is being prepared. These measures and those on accelerating access to and the transmission of information (such as the strengthening of the CELEX system) are likely to benefit particularly those groups who are already aware of the EU and its broad objectives rather than the public at large.

The provision of information as a means of enlisting support and establishing a marketplace of ideas at the pre-legislative stage was formalised at Amsterdam.

---

[108]   Lodge, J. 'Transparency and Democratic Legitimacy' (1994) 32 *JCMS* 343, 345-346.

9. Without prejudice to its right of initiative, the Commission should:
- except in cases of particular urgency or confidentiality, consult widely before proposing legislation and, wherever appropriate, publish consultation documents.

The process contains dangers, however. As Lodge states above, it benefits primarily insiders who already have an understanding of the system. It is thus indissociable from the question of the lobby and the extent to which public processes should respond to private influences.[109]

Mazey, S. and Richardson, J. 'The Commission and the lobby' in Edwards, G. & Spence, D. *The European Commission* (1997, 2nd Edition, Longman, Harlow) 178, 191-193

According to the Secretariat General of the European Commission, there are now approximately 3,000 special-interest groups in Brussels, with up to 10,000 employees working in the lobbying sector.[[110]] These figures include more than 500 European and international federations, whose constituent members belonging to national associations number more than 5,000. In addition, there are 50 offices in Brussels representing regional and local authorities, more than 200 firms with direct representation, about 100 consultancies in Brussels itself and 100 law firms specialising in Community law. It is little wonder then that for the past four years both the Commission and the Parliament have been considering the possibility of regulating lobbying. The primary catalyst for this lobbying explosion was, of course, the Single European Act 1986, which committed EC Member States to complete the internal market by the end of 1992 and reformed the EC decision-making process in such a way as to reduce the power of individual national governments to block EU policies. The further extension of the Community's legislative competence and changes to the EC decision-making process introduced by the Maastricht Treaty have given fresh impetus to this trend. The gradual extension of Qualified Majority Voting (QMV) has, of course, been of special importance. Though much of the public and academic debate about the consequences of QMV has focused on the threat to Member States, little attention has been paid to its possible effects on lobbying. Under

---

[109]   Peterson, J. 'Playing the Transparency Game: Consultation and Policy-Making in the European Commission' (1995) 73 *Public Administration* 473.

[110]   EC Commission, *An Open and Structured Dialogue between the Commission and Special Interest Groups* SEC (92) 2272 final, 4.

QMV no national government can be relied upon to 'deliver' preferred policy outcomes and groups must take note of that in further developing their lobbying strategies. If nothing else, QMV is bound to make these strategies more transnational in their focus. The pluralistic nature of the EC decision-making process, combined with the reliance of Commission officials upon outside expertise (be it from conventional interest groups or from epistemic communities) will facilitate the continued development of sectoral (and increasingly cross-sectoral) policy networks centred upon the European Commission.

These developments outlined above represent an unplanned and pragmatic response to the growing importance of European policy-making. In terms of the policy process, the development of effective EC level policy networks would be functionally beneficial. However, the considerable influence wielded by organised interests within the European Commission and the close - often informal - links which exist between some groups and Commission officials have served to increase public unease about the 'democratic deficit'. In 1991 the European Parliament began to debate the need for a register of lobbyists. Partly in response to these pressures the Secretariat General of the European Commission in 1992 reviewed Commission procedures regarding group consultation. Allegations concerning the political influence of corporate groups and other special interests are, of course, not unique to the European Community. Liberal democratic theorists and political scientists have for many years studied and debated the impact of organised interests on public policy-makers. However, unlike national executives, the European Commission is not an elected government, democratically accountable to the electorate. Nor is the EU policy-making process as transparent as many national-level procedures. Indeed, the debate over links between special interests and EC Commission officials forms part of a much wider, current debate within the Community on the need to increase the openness and transparency of the EU decision-making process.

There are at present no explicit Commission regulations (such as accreditation, registration, code of conduct) with respect to interest groups. Paradoxically, this is due to the Commission's longstanding commitment to maintaining an open dialogue with as many special interests as possible. As a general policy, therefore, it has consistently refused to grant formal privileges such as the issuing of entry passes and favoured information to selected groups. However, the growth of EC lobbying, aggressive lobbying styles and 'misdemeanours', such as lobbyists selling draft documents and misrepresenting themselves to the public by the use of Commission symbols, has persuaded the Commission Secretariat General of the need 'to clarify and better structure the Commission's relations with special interest groups' [111].

Both the Parliament and the Commission now take the view that something must be done to prevent abuses by lobbyists. In this respect Parliament wants to take a harder line than the Commission. The Galle

---

[111]   Ibid., 6.

Report in 1991 suggested that a Register of lobbyists be set up which should be controlled by a Bureau of the European Parliament and which could strike lobbyists from the Register.[112] The Commission has suggested a lighter touch, namely a Directory of lobbyists should be established. This Directory would however be self-selecting, and would be the first step towards lobbyists creating their own professional association with its own Code of Conduct.[113] This latter approach has met with only limited success, however. Part of the problem is the sheer diversity of number of groups, very few of whom are organised on a European rather than a national scale.[114]

There is, however, a second more intractable problem with the lobby. Whilst the dialogue with organised interests that it provides is informative for all Community institutions, that very dialogue allows differing interest groups varying degrees of influence. To the extent that these degrees of influence might not represent society's interests as a whole, and to the extent that the lack of transparency within the system prevents one from gauging the amount of influence wielded by different interest groups, there is a lacuna in the system.[115]

---

[112] PE 200.405 fin. 1992. For further discussion see McLaughlin, A. & Greenwood, J. 'The Management of Interest Representation in the European Union' (1995) 33 *JCMS* 143.

[113] EC Commission, *An Open and Structured Dialogue between the Commission and Special Interest Groups* SEC (92) 2272 final.

[114] McLaughlin, A. & Greenwood, J. supra n.112, 149; McLaughlin, A., Jordan, G. & Maloney, W. 'Corporate Lobbying in the European Community' (1993) 31 *JCMS* 191.

[115] On this see Streeck, W. & Schmitter, P. 'From national corporatism to transnational pluralism: Organised Interests in the Single Market' (1991) 19 *Politics and Society* 133; Harlow, C. 'A Community of Interests? Making the Most of European Law' (1992) 55 *MLR* 331; Mazey, S. & Richardson, J. (eds.), *Lobbying in the European Community* (1993, OUP, Oxford); Greenwood, J. & Ronit K. 'Interest Groups in the European Community: Newly Emerging Dynamics and Forums' (1994) 17 *WEP* 31; Peters, G. 'Agenda-Setting in the European Community' (1994) 1 *JEPP* 9; Pedler, R. & van Schendelen, P. (eds.), *Lobbying the European Union: Companies, Trade Associations and Interest Groups* (1994, Dartmouth, Aldershot).

ii. Transparency and the Right to Information

The second prong to the transparency debate has been its potential for reducing the democratic deficit within the European Union. In particular the dissemination of information about the policy-making process were seen as central to any assertion of public control over that process. Two initial suggestions were made to open up by the proceedings of the Council to the public. The first was the provision of information on the Council's meetings through the publication of its minutes. The second was the granting of direct access to the public of the Council's proceedings. Whilst limited headway has been made on this second point, wide access has been given to the public on documents held by the Commission and the Council.[116]

Code of Conduct concerning Public Access to Council and Commission Documents, OJ 1993 L 340/41

General Principle
　　　　The public will have the widest possible access to documents held by the Commission and the Council. 'Document' means any written text, whatever its medium, which contains existing data and is held by the Council or the Commission.
Exceptions
　　　　The institutions will refuse access to any document whose disclosure could undermine:
- the protection of the public interest (public security, international relations, monetary stability, court proceedings, inspections and investigations),
- the protection of the individual and of privacy,
- the protection of commercial and industrial secrecy,
- the protection of the Community's financial interests,
- the protection of confidentiality as requested by the natural or legal persons that supplied the information or as required by the legislation of the Member State that supplied the information.
　　　　They may also refuse access in order to protect the institution's interest in the confidentiality of its proceedings.

---

[116]　　Piris, J-C. 'After Maastricht, are the Community Institutions More Efficacious, More Democratic, More Transparent?' (1994) 19 *ELRev* 449 esp. 470 *et seq.*

The Code was adopted by two implementing Decisions of the Council and Commission which transposed the Code into their internal rules of organisation.[117] The use of internal rules of organisation as the principal instrument governing public access to Council and Commission documents was regarded as deeply unsatisfactory by both the Dutch and Danish Governments. For it cast access to these documents not in terms of some general overarching principle of open government providing an organic link between the individual and the government but rather as one simply of good administration.[118]

This characterisation was furthermore not simply an academic point. It went to the culture of governance and thus the circumstances in which documents would be disclosed. If access was characterised as stemming from a principle of open government, one would expect a more liberal regime to operate. The converse was true with its being characterised simply as part of the institutions' internal organisation. For the Council systematically refused access to all documents in the first six months following its decision.

Case C-58/94 Netherlands v Council [1996] ECR I-2169, [1996] 2 CMLR 996

The Netherlands brought an action both against the Code of Conduct concerning Public Access to Council Documents and against Council Decision 93/731 on public access to Council documents. It claimed the Code of Conduct did not have legal effects, but that, if it were to, it would be illegal as it contained no reference to its legal basis. The Dutch government considered the Council Decision to be illegal on the grounds that it was adopted as part of the Council's internal rules

---

[117]   Decision 93/731/EC, OJ 1993 L 340/43, in the case of the Council; Decision 94/90/EC, OJ 1994 L 46/58, in the case of the Commission.

[118]   Curtin, D. & Meijers, H. 'The Principle of Open Government in Schengen and the European Union: Democratic Retrogression' (1995) 32 *CMLRev* 391, 427 *et seq*; Armstrong, K. 'Citizenship of the Union? Lessons from Carvel and The Guardian' (1996) 59 *MLR* 582; Curtin, D. 'Betwixt and Between: Democracy and Transparency in the Governance of the European Union' in Winter, J., Curtin, D., Kellermann, A. & de Witte, B. (eds.) *Reforming the Treaty on European Union: The Legal Debate* (1996, Kluwer, The Hague); Shaw, J. 'European Union Citizenship: The IGC and Beyond' (1997) 3 *European Public Law* (forthcoming).

of procedure. The Dutch considered that this could not be the case as it was expressly envisaged to have legal effects vis-à-vis citizens.

25. It appears, however, in particular from the preamble and the penultimate paragraph of the Code of Conduct, entitled 'Implementation', that the Code reflects the agreement reached between the Commission and the Council on the principles governing access to the documents of the two institutions, while inviting the institutions to implement those principles by means of specific regulations.

26. In those circumstances, the Code of Conduct merely foreshadows subsequent decisions intended, unlike the Code, to have legal effects. In so far as it traces out the general lines on the basis of which the two institutions are to adopt measures relating to the confidentiality and disclosure of papers held by them, the Code responds to the concern of the Council and the Commission to prevent major divergences in their subsequent actions in this field.

27. The application must be dismissed as inadmissible in so far as it is directed against the Code of Conduct, since the Code is an act which is the expression of purely voluntary coordination and is therefore not intended in itself to have legal effects.

.....

34. As the Advocate General emphasized in sections 14 and 15 of his Opinion, the domestic legislation of most Member States now enshrines in a general manner the public's right of access to documents held by public authorities as a constitutional or legislative principle.

35. In addition, at Community level, the importance of that right has been reaffirmed on various occasions, in particular in the declaration on the right of access to information annexed (as Declaration 17) to the Final Act of the Treaty on European Union, which links that right with the democratic nature of the institutions. Moreover, as appears from paragraphs 3 and 6 of this judgment, the European Council has called on the Council and the Commission on several occasions to implement that right.

36. It was in order to conform to this trend, which discloses a progressive affirmation of individuals' right of access to documents held by public authorities, that the Council deemed it necessary to amend the rules governing its internal organization, which had hitherto been based on the principle of confidentiality.

37. So long as the Community legislature has not adopted general rules on the right of public access to documents held by the Community institutions, the institutions must take measures as to the processing of such requests by virtue of their power of internal organization, which authorizes them to take appropriate measures in order to ensure their internal operation in conformity with the interests of good administration.

38. The fact that Decision 93/731 has legal effects vis-à-vis third parties cannot call in question its categorization as a measure of internal organization. There is nothing to prevent rules on the internal organization of the work of an institution having such effects (see, in particular, Case C-69/89 *Nakajima v Council* [1991] ECR I-2069, paragraphs 49 and 50, and Case C-137/92 P *Commission v BASF and Others* [1994] ECR I-2555, paragraphs 75 and 76).

The status of public access to documents was discussed at Amsterdam. The Treaty was amended so as to make transparency, in principle at least, one of its hallmarks.

Article 1(2) TEU. The Treaty marks a new stage in the process of creating an ever closer union among the peoples of Europe, in which decisions are taken as openly as possible and as closely as possible to the citizen.

The principle has been accordingly entrenched within the EC Treaty.

Article 255(1) EC.1. Any citizen of the Union and any natural or legal person residing or having its registered office in a Member State shall have a right of access to European Parliament, Council and Commission documents, subject to the principles and the conditions to be defined in accordance with paragraphs 2 and 3.

2. General principles and limits on grounds of public or private interest governing this right of access to documents shall be determined by the Council, acting in accordance with the procedure referred to in Article 251 EC within two years of entry into force of the EC Treaty.

3. Each institution referred to above shall elaborate in its own rules of procedure specific provisions regarding access to its documents.

Article 207(3) EC. The Council shall adopt its Rules of Procedure. For the purpose of applying Article 255(3), the Council shall elaborate in these Rules the conditions under which the public shall have access to Council documents. For the purpose of this paragraph, the Council shall define the cases in which it is to regarded as acting in its legislative capacity, with a view to allowing greater access to documents in those cases, while at the same time preserving the effectiveness of its decision-making process. In any event, when the Council acts in its legislative capacity, the results of votes and explanations of vote as well as statements in the minutes shall be made public.

Despite all this, the status of the right to access to documentation is no less clear. Whilst Amsterdam moves some way to establishing a general principle of open government, whose general conditions shall be determined in a unitary manner under the codecision procedure, specific conditions of access are still regarded as a matter of internal organisation for each institution.

Indeed, in one sense, Amsterdam has restricted the principle of open government. The current situation is that the 'public' have the right to seek access to documentation. This is limited by *Article 255(1) EC* to citizens of the Union or those residing or having a registered office in the Union. A whole class of natural and legal persons are thus excluded from access to documents. Examples will include third country immigrants not formally resident in the Union; third country exporters; beneficiaries of EC development aid; traders subject to EC extraterritorial jurisdiction. All of these persons can be as adversely affected by action by the EC institutions as anyone who is a national of the Union or who is resident or established there. Cast in this way, the right of access to documentation becomes a source of division rather than a simple exercise in participatory government.

The problems of characterisation have been offset to some extent by the CFI's taking a restrictive approach to the circumstances in which access to documents may be legitimately refused.

The first example of this was *Carvel*.[119] The European Affairs editor of the British Guardian Newspaper was refused Justice and Agriculture Council documents on grounds of confidentiality. Documents may be refused on grounds of confidentiality, but the Court ruled that, in exercising its discretion the Council must be engaging in a balancing exercise, weighing the interest of citizens in obtaining access to these documents against its own interest in maintaining confidentiality. From the Council's own documentation and from declarations by the Danish and Dutch governments the Court found that no such balancing exercise had been carried out. It therefore found

---

[119]   Case T-194/94 *Carvel & Guardian Newspapers v Council* [1995] ECR II-2765, [1995] 3 CMLR 359.

access had been wrongfully refused.[120] The matter was explored in further detail in *WWF*.

Case T-105/95 World Wildlife Fund for Nature (WWF) v Commission, Judgment of 5 March 1997, [1997] 2 CMLR 55

In 1991 the Irish authorities decided to build a visitor's centre at Mullaghmore in the Burren Natural Park with the help of EC Structural Funds. The Commission opened an investigation into the project at the request of the WWF to see if it constituted a wrongful use of the Structural Funds. It considered that there was no need for it to take action. Following two unsuccessful court actions, the WWF asked for access for documents relating to the Commission's examination of the project. The Commission refused access on two grounds, that of the public and that of confidentiality.

57. The Court considers that the Code of Conduct contains two categories of exception to the general principle of citizens' access to Commission documents and these correspond to the provisions of Article 4 of Decision 93/731.

58. According to the working of the first category, drafted in mandatory terms, 'the institutions will refuse access to any document where disclosure could undermine...[in particular] the protection of the public interest (public security, international relations, monetary stability, court proceedings and investigations)...' (see paragraph [9] above). It follows that the Commission is obliged to refuse access to documents falling under any one of the exceptions contained in this category once the relevant circumstances are shown to exist (see, in relation to the corresponding provisions of Decision 93/731. Case T-194/94 *Carvel and Guardian Newspapers v EU Council* [1995] ECR II-2765).

59. By way of contrast, the wording of the second category, drafted in discretionary terms, provides that the Commission 'may also refuse access in order to protect the institution's interest in the confidentiality of its proceedings' (see paragraph [9] above). It follows, accordingly, that the Commission enjoys a margin of discretion which enables it, if need be, to refuse a request for access to documents which touch upon its deliberations. The Commission must nevertheless exercise this discretion by striking a genuine balance between, on the one hand, the interest of the citizen in obtaining access to those documents and, on the other, its own interest in protecting the confidentiality of its deliberations (see, in relation to the corresponding provisions of Decision 93/731, the

---

[120]   The Council, under a Supplementary Code, has now undertaken to examine systematically whether to make public documents submitted to it, and decisions and conclusions adopted where these relate to the adoption of legislation, EU Bulletin 10-1995, 1.9.1.

judgment in Case T-194/94 *Carvel and Guardian Newspapers v EU Council* [1995] ECR II-2765).

60. The Court considers that the distinction between these two categories of exception in the Code of Conduct is explained by the nature of the interest which the categories seek respectively to protect. The first category, comprising the 'mandatory exceptions', effectively protects the interest of third parties or of the general public in cases where disclosure of particular documents by the institution concerned would risk causing harm to persons who could legitimately refuse access to the documents if held in their own possession. On the other hand, in the second category, relating to the internal deliberations of the institution, it is the interest of the institution alone which is at stake.

61. The Commission, however, entitled to invoke jointly an exception within the first category and one within the second in order to refuse access to documents which it holds, since no provision of Decision 94/90 precludes it from doing so. In effect, the possibility cannot be ruled out that the disclosure of particular documents by the Commission could cause damage both to interests protected by the exceptions of the first category and to the Commission's interest in maintaining the confidentiality of its deliberations.

62. Having regard to these factors, it is necessary to consider, secondly, whether the documents relating to an investigation into a possible breach of Community law, leading potentially to the opening of a procedure under Article 169 of the Treaty, satisfy the conditions which must be met for the Commission to be able to rely upon the public interest exception, which is one of the exceptions within the first category provided for in the Code of Conduct.

63. In this regard, the Court considers that the confidentiality which the Member States are entitled to expect of the Commission in such circumstances warrants, under the heading of protection of the public interest, a refusal of access to documents relating to investigations which may lead to an infringement procedure, even where a period of time has elapsed since the closure of the investigation.

64. It is important, nevertheless, to point out that the Commission cannot confine itself to invoking the possible opening of an infringement procedure as justification, under the heading of protecting the public interest, for refusing access to the entirety of the documents identified in a request made by a citizen. The Court considers, in effect, that the Commission is required to indicate, at the very least by reference to categories of documents, the reasons for which it considers that the documents detailed in the request which it received are related to the possible opening of an infringement procedure. It should indicate to which subject matter the documents relate and particularly whether they involve inspections or investigations relating to a possible procedure for infringement of Community law.

65. The duty identified in the preceding paragraph does not, however, mean that the Commission is obliged in all cases to furnish, in respect of each document, 'imperative reasons' in order to justify the application of the public interest exception and thereby risk jeopardising the essential function of the exception in question, which follows from the very nature of the public interest to be protected and the mandatory character of the exception. It would be impossible, in practical terms, to give reasons justifying the need for confidentiality in respect of each individual document without disclosing the content of the document and, thereby, depriving the exception of its very purpose.

66. Thirdly, it is necessary to consider whether the Contested Decision meets the requirement to state reasons which flows from Article 190 of the Treaty.

The Court then found that the Commission Decision did not state in sufficient detail the reasons why access should be refused. It therefore annulled the Decision.

The *Carvel* and *WWF* decisions highlight a further problem, however. As the Code and implementing Decisions only apply to what takes place in the Council and the Commission, there is a danger that real negotiations will just be shifted to discussions between capitals or within the COREPER, and the process will remain no more transparent than before. This danger of government by moonlight has been exacerbated by Amsterdam which includes a Declaration that states:

> *The Conference agrees that the principles and conditions referred to in Article 255(1) will allow a Member State to request the Commission or the Council not to communicate to third parties a document originating from that State without its prior agreement.*

The intention of the Declaration is quite clear - to partition an arena of national government immune from any public access to documentation. It awaits to be seen, whether as a corollary, much of the negotiation and consultation which form parts of EC policy-making is shifted towards this demi-monde.

Further Reading

Andersen, S. & Burns, T. 'The European Union and the Erosion of Parliamentary Democracy: A Study of Post-parliamentary Governance' in Andersen, S. & Eliassen, K. *The European Union: How Democratic Is it?* (1996, Sage, London)

Boyron, S. 'Maastricht and the Codecision Procedure: A Success Story' (1996) 45 *International and Comparative Law Quarterly* 293

Dashwood, A. 'Community Legislative Procedures in the Era of the Treaty on European Union' (1994) 19 *European Law Review* 343

Gosalbo Bono, R. 'Co-decision: an Appraisal of the Experience of the European Parliament as Co-legislator' (1994) 14 *Yearbook of European Law* 21

Grimm, D. 'Does Europe Need a Constitution?' (1995) 1 *European Law Journal* 282

Marks, G. & McAdam, D. 'Social Movements and the Changing Structure of Political Opportunity in the European Union' in Marks, G., Scharpf, F., Schmitter, P. & Streeck, W. *Governance in the European Union* (1996, Sage Press, London)

Raworth, P. 'A Timid Step Forwards: Maastricht and the Democratisation of the European Community' (1994) 19 *European Law Review* 16

Streeck, W. & Schmitter, P. 'From national corporatism to transnational pluralism: Organised Interests in the Single Market' (1991) 19 *Politics & Society* 133

Tsebelis, G. & Garrett, G. 'Agenda Setting Power, Power Indices, and Decision Making in the European Union' (1996) 16 *International Review of Law & Economics* 345

Westlake, M. 'The European Parliament, national parliaments and the 1996 IGC' (1995) 66 *Political Quarterly* 59

4. The Competences of the Union

I. The Division of Powers between the Union and the Member States

Any system which provides for different levels of decision-making has the inherent problem of dividing responsibility between those differing levels of government. In all federal constitutions there is thus some mechanism for allocating and regulating responsibilities between federal and local authorities.[1] Until the mid-1980s the mechanism used was the Luxembourg Accords, which allowed a Member State to veto any proposal it disliked. The problem therefore never arose of a Member State being forced to observe a piece of legislation whose adoption it opposed. The fall into disuse of the Accords and the corresponding volume of legislation generated by the Single European Act provoked a legitimacy crisis, as it resulted in one mechanism for regulating competences between the EC and Member States being abolished without a substitute being put up in its place.[2]

Reestablishment of the Accords was not really an attractive option for it would simply lead to a stymying of the Community interest and a resurrection of the paralysis of the 1960s and 1970s. What was needed was a mechanism which sought not to place one interest, be it Community or national, over the other but sought an accommodation of both. This mechanism was the subsidiarity principle. Mention of the principle can be traced back to the Commission's submissions to the

---

[1] Dehousse, R. 'Community Competences: Are There Limits to Growth' 103, 118-119 in Dehousse, R. *Europe after Maastricht: An Ever Closer Union?* (1994, Law Books in Europe, Munich)

[2] Weiler, J. 'The Transformation of Europe' (1991) 100 *Yale Law Journal* 2403, 2462-2463.

Tindemans Report in 1975,[3] and it was also part of the federal solution proposed by the European Parliament in its draft Treaty on European Union.[4] It became formally a part of EC law when the SEA introduced it into the limited field of the environment.[5] It was only at Maastricht, however, that it was transformed into an overarching principle of EC law. Its importance is underscored by its place near the beginning of the EC Treaty.

Article 3b [5] EC. The Community shall act within the limits of the powers conferred upon it by this Treaty and of the objectives assigned to it therein.

In areas which do not fall within its exclusive competence, the Community shall take action, in accordance with the principle of subsidiarity, only if and in so far as the objectives of the proposed action can not be sufficiently achieved by the Member States and can therefore, by reason of the scale or effects of the proposed action, be better achieved by the Community.

Any action by the Community shall not go beyond what is necessary to achieve the objectives of this Treaty.

The division of competences is more tersely regulated in the other two pillars of the Union.

Article A [1] TEU. ... This Treaty marks a new stage in the process of creating an ever closer union among the peoples of Europe, in which decisions are taken [*as openly as possible and*] as closely as possible to the citizens.

Article F [6] TEU (1) [3]. The Union shall respect the national identities of its Member States...

---

[3] On the historical origins of the principle within the Community see Cass, D. 'The Word that Saves Maastricht? The Principle of Subsidiarity and the Division of Powers within the European Community' (1992) 29 *CMLRev* 1107, 1110-1128; Teasdale, A. 'Subsidiarity in Post-Maastricht Europe' (1993) 64 *Political Quarterly* 187, 187-189.

[4] OJ 1984, C 77/33, Article 12. On the links between federalism and subsidiarity see Emiliou, N. 'Subsidiarity: An Effective Barrier Against the "the Enterprises of Ambition"?' (1992) 17 *ELRev* 383.

[5] Article 130r(4) EEC.

There are no articles explaining how this will affect the powers of the Institutions in these two pillars. The reason for this has no doubt to do with the lack of supranational qualities of these two pillars. There is little scope for qualified majority voting or for enforcement of decisions by the supranational institutions of the Community, be it the Court or the Commission. The instrument used to protect national autonomy is still the national veto. This remains the case following Amsterdam. Whilst the scope for qualified majority voting has been enlarged in both CFSP, in areas where qualified majority has been installed it has been established that a State may invoke the Luxembourg Accords, so that if a member for the Council declares that it intends, for important and stated reasons of national policy to oppose the adoption of a decision to be taken by qualified majority, then a vote shall not be taken.[6] The national veto results rather in the national interest being asserted over the EC one in an ad hoc manner. For that reason, it is difficult to make broad statements about the underlying principles dividing Member State and Union powers in the second and third pillars, and the rest of this Chapter shall concentrate on the EC pillar.

II. Community Competences

i. Express Powers and Implied Powers

The first paragraph of Article 3b [5] EC places the crudest but, arguably, the most important limit on the exercise of EC powers, namely that the EC can only exercise those powers conferred upon it by the Treaty. As the Community can only act through its institutions, this provision must be placed alongside Article 4(1) [7(1)] EC, which requires that each institution must act within the limits of the powers conferred upon it by the Treaty. The doctrine has inevitably meant that the question of the

---

6   *Article 23(2) TEU* in the case of CFSP. There is only very limited provision made for qualified majority voting in the field of JHA by Amsterdam, namely measures taken to implement Decisions already adopted may be taken by qualified majority, *Article 34(2)(c) TEU.*

powers of the institutions has become conflated with that of textual analysis of the EC Treaty. Language is open-ended in nature, however. Moreover, when the Treaty was established, it was not possible for its founders to foresee all the circumstances when the EC should, or should not, have competence. The Court has therefore adopted a pragmatic approach to the doctrine of conferred powers, holding that the Community has competence not only where expressly granted by a provision, but also that it has the implied competences to carry out the tasks expressly allocated to it.

Joined Cases 281, 283-5, 287/85 Germany, France, Netherlands, Denmark and United Kingdom v Commission [1987] ECR 3203, [1988] 1 CMLR 11

Article 118(2) [*140(2)*] EC empowers the Commission to arrange consultations with the Member States with a view to promoting cooperation in the social field. In 1985 the Commission adopted a Decision *requiring* Member States, first, to inform it of any draft measures that they proposed to take vis-à-vis third country nationals. One of the purposes of this information was to enable the Commission to determine whether the proposed measure complied with EC policies in related fields. A number of Member States claimed the decision was *ultra vires*. They claimed, in particular, that the Article could be used neither as a basis for taking binding decisions nor as an instrument through which to vet national immigration policies.

27. ... it must be considered whether the second paragraph of Article 118, which provides that the Commission is to act, *inter alia*, by arranging consultations, gives it the power to adopt a binding decision with a view to the arrangement of such consultations.

28. In that connection it must be emphasized that where an Article of the EEC Treaty - in this case Article 118 - confers a specific task on the Commission it must be accepted, if that provision is not to be rendered wholly ineffective, that it confers on the Commission necessarily and *per se* the powers which are indispensable in order to carry out that task. Accordingly, the second paragraph of Article 118 must be interpreted as conferring on the Commission all the powers which are necessary in order to arrange the consultations. In order to perform that task of arranging consultations the Commission must necessarily be able to require the Member States to notify essential information, in the first place in order to identify the problems and in the second place in order to pinpoint the possible guidelines for any future joint action on the part of the Member States; likewise it must be able to require them to take part in consultations.

29. Indeed, the collaboration between Member States required by Article 118 is only possible within the framework of organized consultations. In the absence of any action to initiate it that collaboration might remain a dead letter, even though provision is made for it in the Treaty. Since the Commission was specifically given the task of promoting such collaboration and arranging it, it is entitled to initiate consultation procedures within the social field referred to in Article 118.

30. It must be borne in mind that that power of the Commission must be confined to arranging a procedure for the notification of information and consultation and that in the present stage of development of Community law the subject-matter of the notification and consultation falls within the competence of the Member States. It must also be pointed out that the power which the Commission seeks to exercise under Article 118 is simply a procedural one to set up the notification and consultation machinery which is to result in the adoption of a common position on the part of the Member States.

31. Consequently, since Article 118 provides a specific basis for the Commission's decision there is no need to consider whether the outcome sought by the decision in question might have been achieved through other general provisions of the Treaty or other procedures necessitating action on the part of other institutions.

32. Now that it has been established that the Commission is empowered under Article 118 to adopt a binding decision vis-à-vis the Member States establishing a communication and consultation procedure, it must be considered whether the contested decision does not go beyond the limits of such a procedure, as the applicant Member States claim.

33. The Member States maintain that the decision does not merely arrange a consultation procedure, but, by assigning an aim to that consultation, seeks to determine its outcome and hence exceeds the Commission's powers, which are of a procedural nature. The second indent of article 3 of the contested decision provides, in fact, that the purpose of the consultation procedure is to ensure that the agreements and measures communicated are in conformity with Community policies in the fields covered by the decision, including policy on development aid.

34. Since the Commission has a power of a purely procedural nature to initiate a consultation procedure it cannot determine the result to be achieved in that consultation and cannot prevent the Member States from implementing drafts, agreements and measures which it might consider not to be in conformity with Community policies and actions.

35. As a result, in so far as the second indent of article 3 lays down a precise obligation on the Member States and is intended to debar them from adopting national measures or concluding agreements that the Commission considers not to be in conformity with Community policies and actions, it must be regarded, as the applicant Member States rightly argue, as exceeding the scope of the Commission's powers under Article 118.

The doctrine of implied powers can be seen as merely an example of the Court's celebrated teleological style of reasoning, where the Court interprets provisions in the light of the provisions' underlying objectives.[7] The problem with this form of analysis is that these guiding objectives are often contested, and are in many cases merely 'discovered' through *ex post facto* analysis in the judgment of the Court. An alternative explanation is that the Court became frustrated by the institutional effectiveness of the Community being dependent upon the vagaries of the exact limits to interpretation of particular provisions. This was particularly the case where this significantly impeded the work of the Community in areas where it clearly had *some* competence. It has therefore been willing to round up the Treaty wherever this was 'necessary' to secure the autonomy of a clearly established power.

ii. The Subverting of Conferred Powers and Article 235[*308*] EC

The philosophy underlying conferred powers is that of limited government. Government is only possible in that narrow area authorised by the constituent instrument. This philosophy has been undermined in two ways. The first is that the doctrine will not be applied where the Community institutions are mandated to perform executive tasks by the Member States.

Case C-316/91 Parliament v Council [1994] ECR I-625

The Parliament challenged the legal basis of a development fund set by the Council to finance development cooperation under the Fourth Lomé Convention. The fund of 12 billion ECU had been established on the basis of an internal agreement between the Member States under which the Commission would prepare a draft which the Council would adopt, and to which the Member States would directly contribute rather than from the Community Budget. The Parliament claimed that the correct legal procedure was Article 209 [*279*] EC, the

---

[7]   On this form of analysis see Schermers, H. & Waelbroeck, D. *Judicial Protection in the European Communities* (1992, 5th Edition, Kluwer, Deventer) 18-26.

main budgetary provision. In the alternative, it alleged that if the fund had been set up outside the framework of the Treaty, the Commission had no power to propose a draft.

Advocate General Jacobs

83. Nor does it follow from Article 4(1) of the Treaty, on which the Parliament placed much reliance in its written submissions, that a Community institution may never act on the mandate of the Member States. Article 4(1) provides that each Community institution shall act within the limits of the powers conferred upon it by the treaty. Its main objective is to define the constitutional position of the Community institutions vis-à-vis that of the Member States. It makes clear that the Community institutions do not have inherent powers but only those which, expressly or by implication, are conferred upon them by the Treaty. Powers which are not thus conferred upon them lie with the Member States. It follows from Article 4(1) that a Community institution may not encroach upon the competence of the Member States nor may it act in such a way as to evade the requirements of the Treaty. It is not the purpose of that provision, however, to rule out the possibility of a Community institution undertaking functions on the mandate of the Member states.

84. It is therefore possible for a Community institution to undertake on behalf of the Member States certain functions outside the framework of the Treaty provided that such functions, and the way in which it performs them, are compatible with its Treaty obligations. Whether that is the case is subject to the control of the Court.

85. As a general rule, a distinction can perhaps be drawn between executive functions and legislative functions. It will be easier to accept that a Community institution may undertake an executive function on the mandate of the Member States, such as to coordinate action decided by the Member States or to represent their collective interests vis-à-vis third countries, than to accept that a Community institution, especially the Council, may undertake a legislative function on the mandate of the Member States. That is because the Council is the main legislative organ of the Community and, as a general rule, it may not operate in a legislative capacity on the mandate of the member states in parallel with its legislative function under the Treaty. Such action might have the result that the procedures provided for in the Treaty were evaded, and might also cause confusion with regard to the nature of the acts adopted by the Council.

The more wide-ranging exception is that of Article 235 [*308*] EC, which is a 'catch-all' provision giving the Community institutions far-ranging powers where those powers are not provided for elsewhere in the Treaty.

Article 235 [*308*] EC. If action by the Community should prove necessary to attain, in the course of the operation of the common market, one of the objectives of the Community and this Treaty has not provided the necessary powers, the Council shall, acting unanimously on a proposal from the Commission and after consulting the European Parliament take the appropriate measures.

The objectives of the Community are wide ranging indeed, including such broad goals as raising the standard of living. The Article has been used expansively. In the 1970s, for example, it was used to allow the Community to grant development aid to Africa, a matter which did not seem closely related to any of the Community's then-existing competences.[8] Until 1996 no judicial limits seemed to have been placed on the ambit of Article 235 [*308*] EC. The control which existed was that action based on the Article required the consent of all Member States. There had to be consensus therefore about the appropriateness of Community competence before action could be taken. Such a provision made a mockery of the principle of limited government. The practice had another effect. As national representatives of the Council were ministers, and thus members of national executives, Article 235 [*308*] EC resulted in the expansion of national executive power at the expense of national parliaments. In 1996 the Court moved to prevent abuse of Article 235 [*308*] EC.[9]

Opinion 2/94, Accession to the European Convention for the Protection of Human Rights and Freedoms [1996] ECR I-1759, [1996] 2 CMLR 265

The Council asked the Court whether the Community was competent to accede the European Convention on Human Rights and Freedoms.

---

[8]   Weiler, J. 'The Transformation of Europe' (1991) 100 *Yale Law Journal* 2403, 2445.

[9]   The language of *Opinion 2/94* bears more than a passing resemblance to that used by the German Constitutional Court in *Brunner v Treaty of European Union* [1994] 1 *CMLR* 57, see pp 19-20. It provides a good example of how Community law developments sometimes occur through a dialectic established between national courts and the Court of Justice.

27. No Treaty provision confers on the Community institutions any general power to enact rules on human rights or to conclude international conventions in this field.

28. In the absence of express or implied powers for this purpose, it is necessary to consider whether Article 235 of the Treaty may constitute a legal basis for accession.

29. Article 235 is designed to fill the gap where no specific provisions of the Treaty confer on the Community institutions express or implied powers to act, if such powers appear none the less to be necessary to enable the Community to carry out its functions with a view to attaining one of the objectives laid down by the Treaty.

30. That provision, being an integral part of an institutional system based on the principle of conferred powers, cannot serve as a basis for widening the scope of Community powers beyond the general framework created by the provisions of the Treaty as a whole, and in particular, by those that define the tasks and the activities of the Community. On any view, Article 235 cannot be used as a basis for the adoption of provisions whose effect would, in substance, be to amend the Treaty without following the procedure which it provides for that purpose.

.....

34. Respect for human rights is ... a condition of the lawfulness of Community acts. Accession to the Convention would, however, entail a substantial change in the present Community system for the protection of human rights in that it would entail the entry of the Community into a distinct international institutional system as well as integration of all the provisions of the Convention into the Community legal order.

35. Such a modification of the system for the protection of human rights in the Community, with equally fundamental institutional implications for the Community and for the Member States, would be of constitutional significance and would therefore be such as to go beyond the scope of Article 235. It could be brought about only by way of Treaty amendment.

iii. The Legal Base Game

The far-reaching nature of Community competences has meant that rarely is Community competence challenged. Each Community act must be based, however, on a specific legal base. Much more common is a challenge to the legal base upon which the individual measure is based. A typology of legal bases can be made in this respect. There are first of all legal bases, such as agriculture, which govern particular vertically integrated sectors. Secondly, there are Articles 100A [*95*] EC and 100 [*94*] EC, which regulate the establishment and functioning of the internal market and common market respectively. Thirdly, there are legal bases which regulate horizontal activities, such as environment, consumer and health policy, which cut across different sectors and touch upon the exercise of nearly all economic activity. Fourthly, there are bases establishing flanking policies, such as culture, education, industry and development cooperation, which are more self-contained than horizontal policies but do not relate to particular sectors. Finally, there is the residuary base of Article 235 [*308*] EC.

These legal bases have two functions. The first is an *enabling* one. It is the existence of the legal base which allows the Community legislature to legislate. The second is a *protective* one. The limits provided by the legal base offer Community institutions, individuals and Member States the guarantee that the Community is acting within the limits of its powers.[10] The base will determine the legislative procedure to be used, which will, in turn, determine the balance of power between the institutions and the influence enjoyed by individual Member States. These two functions pull in opposing tensions, however - one towards expanding Community action, the other towards limiting it. This, put together with the large number of legal bases which exist, has inevitably given rise to disputes about delimitation over particular legal bases.

The initial response of the Court was to establish a formal hierarchy between legal bases. At the bottom of the pecking order was Article 235 [*308*]EC, as all legal bases enjoyed precedence over it in cases of overlap.[11] At the apex of the hierarchy was the agricultural base, Article 43 [*37*] EC. In the *Hormones* judgment[12] the United Kingdom brought an action against a Directive outlawing the use of certain hormones in livestock farming. The Directive had been based on Article

---

[10]   The distinction is taken from Barents, R. 'The Internal Market Unlimited: Some Observations on the Legal Basis of Community Legislation' (1993) 30 *CMLRev* 85, 92.

[11]   Case C-295/90 *Parliament v Council* [1992] ECR I-4193, [1992] 3 CMLR 281.

[12]   Case 68/86 *United Kingdom v Council* [1988] ECR 855, [1988] 2 CMLR 543. See Barents, R. 'Hormones and the Growth of Community Agricultural Law' (1989/2) *LIEI* 1.

43 [*37*] EC, which only required qualified majority voting in the Council. The United Kingdom argued that it should have been based on Article 100 [*94*] EC, which required unanimity. The Court ruled that Article 43 [*37*] EC was the appropriate legal base on the grounds that Article 38(2) [*32(2)*)] EC stated that the common market rules applied 'save as otherwise provided in Articles 39 to 46', and thus established a hierarchy between Article 43 EC and 100 EC.[13]

The internal market provision, Article 100A [*95*] EC, enjoyed a similar precedence over horizontal policies to that enjoyed by Article 43 [*37*] EC over it.

Case 300/89 Commission v Council ('Titanium Dioxide') [1991] ECR I-2867, [1993] 3 CMLR 359.

The Commission brought an action for annulment under Article 173 [*230*] EC of Council Directive 89/428/EEC on procedures for harmonising the programmes for the reduction and eventual elimination of pollution caused by waste from the titanium dioxide industry. The Directive had been unanimously adopted by the Council on the basis of Article 130S [*175(1)*] EC. The original Commission proposal, however, had suggested Article 100 [*94*] EC as the legal base for the measure, altering it to Article 100A [*95*] EC with the entry into force of the SEA.

10. It must first be observed that in the context of the organisation of the powers of the Community the choice of the legal basis for a measure may not depend simply on an institution's conviction as to the objective pursued but must be based on objective factors which are amenable to judicial review (see the judgment in Case 45/86 *Commission v Council* [1987] ECR 1493, paragraph 11). Those factors include in particular the aim and content of the measure.

11. As regards the aim pursued, Article 1 of Directive 89/428 indicates that it is intended, on the one hand, to harmonise the programmes for the reduction and ultimate elimination of pollution caused by waste from existing establishments in the titanium dioxide industry and, on the other, to improve the conditions of competition in that industry. It thus

---

[13] Paradoxically the Court has not adopted a similar approach to that other sectoral policy, transport. See Joined Cases 209-213/84 *Ministère Public v Asjes* [1986] ECR 1425, [1986] 3 CMLR 173.

pursues the twofold aim to environmental protection and improvement of the conditions of competition.

12. As regards its content, Directive 89/428 prohibits, or, according to strict standards, requires reduction of the discharge of waste from existing establishments in the titanium dioxide industry and lays down time limits for the implementation of the various provisions. By thus imposing obligations concerning the treatment of waste from the titanium dioxide production process, the directive conduces, at the same time, to the reduction of pollution and to the establishment of greater uniformity of production conditions and therefore of conditions of competition, since the national rules on the treatment of waste which the directive seeks to harmonise have an impact on production costs in the titanium dioxide industry.

13. It follows that, according to its aim and content, as they appear from its actual wording, the directive is concerned, indissociably, with both the protection of the environment and the elimination of disparities in conditions of competition.

14. Article 130s of the Treaty provides that the Council is to decide what action is to be taken by the Community concerning the environment. Article 100a(1), for its part, is concerned with the adoption by the Council of measures for the approximation of the provisions laid down by law, regulation or administrative action in Member States which have as their object the establishment and functioning of the internal market. According to the second paragraph of Article 8a of the EEC Treaty, that market is to comprise 'an area without internal frontiers in which the free movement of goods, persons, services and capital is ensured'. By virtue of Articles 2 and 3 of the Treaty, a precondition for such a market is the existence of conditions of competition which are not distorted.

15. In order to give effect to the fundamental freedoms mentioned in Article 8a [now Article 7a], harmonising measures are necessary to deal with disparities between the laws of the Member States in areas where such disparities are liable to create or maintain distorted conditions of competition. For that reason, Article 100a empowers the Community to adopt measures for the approximation of the provisions laid down by law, regulation or administrative action in member states and lays down the procedure to be followed for that purpose.

16. It follows that, in view of its aim and content, the Directive at issue displays the features both of action relating to the environment with which Article 130s of the Treaty is concerned and of a harmonising measure which has as its object the establishment and functioning of the internal market, within the meaning of Article 100a of the Treaty.

17. As the Court held in Case 165/87 *Commission v Council* [1988] ECR 5545, paragraph 11, where an institution's power is based on two provisions of the Treaty, it is bound to adopt the relevant measures on the basis of the two relevant provisions. However, that ruling is not applicable to the present case.

18. One of the enabling provisions at issue, Article 100a, requires recourse to the co-operation procedure provided for in Article 149(2) of the Treaty, whereas the other, Article 130s, requires the Council to act unanimously after merely consulting the European parliament. As a result, use of both provisions as a joint legal basis would divest the co-operation procedure of its very substance.

19. Under the co-operation procedure, the Council acts by a qualified majority where it intends accepting the amendments to its common position proposed by the parliament and included by the Commission in its re-examined proposal, whereas it must secure unanimity if it intends taking a decision after its common position has been rejected by the parliament or if it intends modifying the Commission's re-examined proposal. That essential element of the co-operation procedure would be undermined if, as a result of simultaneous reference to Articles 100a and 130s, the Council were required, in any event, to act unanimously.

20. The very purpose of the co-operation procedure, which is to increase the involvement of the European Parliament in the legislative process of the Community, would thus be jeopardised. As the Court stated in its judgments in Case 138/79 *Roquette Frères v Council* [1980] ECR 3333 and Case 139/79 *Maizena v Council* [1980] ECR 3393, paragraph 34, that participation reflects a fundamental democratic principle that the peoples should take part in the exercise of power through the intermediary of a representative assembly.

21. It follows that in the present case recourse to the dual legal basis of Articles 100a and 130s is excluded and that it is necessary to determine which of those two provisions is the appropriate legal basis.

22. It must be observed in the first place that, pursuant to the second sentence of Article 130r(2) of the Treaty 'environmental protection requirements shall be a component of the Community's other policies'. That principle implies that a Community measure cannot be covered by Article 130s merely because it also pursues objectives of environmental protection.

23. Secondly, as the Court held in its judgments in Cases 91/79 and 92/79 *Commission v Italy* [1980] ECR 1099 and 1115 provisions which are made necessary by considerations relating to the environment and health may be a burden upon the undertakings to which they apply and, if there is no harmonisation of national provisions on the matter, competition may be appreciably distorted. It follows that action intended to approximate national rules concerning production competitions in a given industrial sector with the aim of eliminating distortions of competition in that sector is conducive to the attainment of the internal market and thus falls within the scope of Article 100a, a provision which is particularly appropriate to the attainment of the internal market.

24. Finally, it must be observed that Article 100a(3) requires the Commission, in its proposals for measures for the approximation of the laws of the member states which have as their object the establishment and functioning of the internal market, to take as a base a high level of protection in matters of environmental protection. That provision thus expressly indicates that the objectives of environmental protection referred to in Article 130r may be effectively pursued by means of harmonising measures adopted on the basis of Article 100a.

25. In view of all the foregoing considerations, the contested measure should have been based on Article 100a of the EEC Treaty and must therefore be annulled.

This hierarchical approach proved problematic. There now exists a wide variety of legal bases. The establishment of a hierarchy between all of them would result in too complicated and convoluted a system. Moreover, the approach came in for considerable criticism following the *Titanium Dioxide* judgment. The wide ranging nature of Article 100A [*95*] EC resulted in its providing a general competence which obscured other legal bases. Bases such as Article 130S(1) [*175(1)*] EC, the environmental base, were marginalised, as almost all the legislation which would have been enacted under these bases affected conditions of competition and thus had to be based on Article 100A [*95*] EC. It was therefore argued that *Titanium Dioxide* distorted the scheme of the Treaty and the institutional balance which was maintained by this scheme.[14] Three years later the Court went a considerable way towards dismantling this hierarchy.

Case C-155/91 Commission v Council [1993] ECR I-939

The Council adopted Directive 91/156/EEC, the Framework Directive on Waste, on the basis of Article 130s(1) [*175(1)*] EC. The Commission brought an action for annulment of the Directive, claiming it should have been based on Article 100A [*95*] EC.

7. As the Court has consistently held, in the Community's institutional framework, the choice of the legal basis of an act must be determined by objective factors which can be judicially reviewed. These factors include, *inter alia*, the aim and content of the act (see Case C-295/90 *Parliament v Council* [1992] ECR I-4193).

---

[14]   Crosby, S. 'The Single Market and the Rule of Law' (1991) 16 *ELRev* 451.

The Court then examined the Directive.

10. The above considerations show that, from its aim and content, the object of the Directive is to ensure the management of waste, be it of industrial or domestic origin, with a view to complying with the requirements of environmental protection.

11. However, the Commission further observed that the Directives implements the principle of free movement of waste destined for reuse and submits waste to be disposed of to conditions complying with the rules of the internal market.

12. It is true that waste, whether recyclable or not, must be considered as goods the movement of which under Article 30 EEC should not be hindered (Case C-2/90 *Commission v Belgium* [1992] ECR I-4431, para. 28).

13. However, the Court stated that mandatory requirements relating to the protection of the environment may be regarded as justifying exceptions to the rules on free movement of goods. Against this background, the Court acknowledged the principle whereby environmental damage should be rectified at source - as laid down in Article 130r(2) EEC for action by the Community in the field of the environment - implies that it is for each region, commune or other local authority to take the appropriate measures to ensure reception, processing treatment and disposal of its own waste. Consequently waste should be disposed of as close as possible to the place where it was produced in order to keep transport to a minimum (Case C-2/90, *Commission v Belgium*, *op cit.*, para. 34).

14. The object of the Directive is precisely to implement these guidelines. Article 5 in particular embodies the principle of proximity of the place where the waste is to be disposed of in relation to the place where it is produced in order to ensure, insofar as possible, that each Member States is responsible for the disposal of its own waste. Furthermore, Article 7 of the Directive permits Member States to prohibit the movement of waste, whether it is to be reused or disposed of which does not comply with their management plans.

15. Under these conditions, the Directive cannot be regarded as aiming to implement the free movement of waste, as admitted by the Commission at the hearing.

.....

18. It has to be admitted that some provision in the Directive, and in particular the definitions [on waste] in Article 1, have an impact on the functioning of the internal market.

19. However, and despite the Commission's allegations to the contrary, the sole fact that the establishment or the functioning of the internal market is concerned is not sufficient for Article 100a EEC to apply. Indeed, as the Court has consistently held, the legal basis of Article 100a is not justified where harmonisation of the conditions of the market within the Community are only ancillary to those adopted (see Case C-70/88 *Parliament v Council* [1991] ECR I-4529).

20. This is the case in the present situation. Harmonisation, as provided for by Article 1 of the Directive, seeks principally with a view to protecting the environment, to ensure efficient management of waste in the Community, whatever its origin, and its effects on the conditions of competition and on the flow of trade are only ancillary. For this reason, the Directive must be distinguished from Directive 89/428/EEC which was the subject of the aforementioned 'titanium dioxide case' and whose aim is to approximate national laws on the conditions of production in a given industrial sector for the purpose of eliminating distortions of competition in this particular sector.

21. It follows from these considerations that the Directive at issue was correctly based on Article 130s EEC. ...

The room for overlap, and thus for the formal hierarchy to come into play, is considerably reduced if in every case one must examine the instrument's predominant aim and content. In determining the appropriate base for a particular instrument, the Court will have to examine whether it adopts the principles of a particular policy. Is the purpose of an instrument market liberalisation, for example, in which case Article 100A [*95*] EC, or does it follow principles of environmental protection, such as the 'polluter pays' or the 'proximity principle'? Such an assessment will invite an initial characterisation of the different policies of the Community. The consequence is the development of a number of autonomous, segregated Community policies, each characterised by an autonomous set of principles.[15]

Yet, at the parameters, considerable uncertainty remains. It will often not be clear what the predominant purpose of a Community instrument will be, particularly as such instruments are the result of considerable negotiations with different sides perceiving themselves to be gaining different benefits from any instrument. While differing legal bases exist, the consequence is that this uncertainty will result in continued litigation. Weatherill has observed that this is a problem which is likely to remain whatever test is adopted by the Court. The underlying

---

[15]   Chalmers, D. 'The Single Market: From Prima Donna to Journeyman' 55, 69-71 in Shaw, J. & More, G. (eds.) *New Legal Dynamics of the European Union* (1995, Clarendon, Oxford).

problem is the byzantine structure of the Treaty with its proliferation of legal bases and legislative procedures.[16] Ultimately, only an overhaul of the Treaty is likely to bring a close to the 'legal base game'.[17]

III. Subsidiarity

i. The Remit of the Subsidiarity Principle

The principle of subsidiarity contained in paragraph 2 of Article 3b [5] EC regulates areas of mixed or concurrent competence, namely those areas within which both the Community and the Member States can legislate. Obviously, it cannot apply in fields where the Community has no competence. Perhaps less obviously, it cannot apply in areas where the Member States have no competence, namely in areas where the Community has exclusive competence. The Court has only ever explicitly ruled that the Community has exclusive competence in three fields: the common customs tariff,[18] common commercial policy[19] and fisheries.[20] In those fields Member States are unable to act without prior authorisation from the Community.[21] In its Communication to the

---

[16]   Weatherill, S. 'Regulating the Internal Market: Result Orientation in the House of Lords' (1992) 17 *ELRev* 299, 312-313. On the deleterious effect the legal base game has had in one area, the environment, see Chalmers, D. 'Environmental Protection and the Single Market: An Unsustainable Development. Does the EC Treaty Need a Title on the Environment?' (1995/1) *LIEI* 65.

[17]   On legal base see also Emiliou, N. 'Opening Pandora's box: The Legal Basis of Community Measures before the Court of Justice' (1994) 19 *ELRev* 488.

[18]   Case C-125/94 *Aprile Srl, en liquidation v Amministrazione delle Finanze dello Stato* [1995] ECR I-2919.

[19]   *Opinion 1/75, Understanding on a Local Costs Standard* [1975] ECR 1361, [1976] 1 CMLR 85.

[20]   Case 804/79 *Commission v United Kingdom* [1981] ECR 1072, [1982] CMLR 543. See Temple Lang, J. 'The ERTA Judgement and the Court's Case Law on Competence and Conflict' (1986) 6 *YBEL* 183.

[21]   Ibid. See also Case 41/76 *Donckerwolcke v Procureur de la République* [1976] ECR 1921, [1977] 2 CMLR 1.

Edinburgh European Council the Commission suggested that the concept was wider.

Commission Communication to the Council and the European Parliament SEC (92) 1990 final, 27 October 1992:

So that the Community can attain its objectives, certain obligations to act have been imposed upon it. These include, in particular, the creation of an area without internal frontiers, the strengthening of economic and social cohesion, and the establishment of economic and monetary union.

(a) At the present stage in the Community's development it is impossible, legally speaking, to determine whether all these objections to act entail exclusive powers for the Community and in particular whether they deprive the Member States of the right to act.

Historically the concept of exclusive competence originally grew out of the obligation to establish the 'common market', which was spelled out in very firmly binding terms, including the fixing of a deadline under the Single Act.

In this sense it is possible to speak of a genuine obligation to act leading, in the course of time and through the rulings of the Court of Justice, to the formation of a block of exclusive powers centred around the four fundamental freedoms and certain common policies essential to, or a corollary of, the establishment of an internal market.

What is involved here is:
- the removal of barriers to the free movement of goods, persons, services and capital
- the common commercial policy
- the general rules on competition
- the common organisation of the agricultural markets
- the conservation of fisheries resources
- the essential elements of transport policy

(b) The demarcation lines of this block of exclusive powers will have to change as European integration progresses. They can not remain frozen. For one thing the Maastricht Treaty provides for future single monetary and exchange rate policies which should ultimately lead to exclusive Community competence in the final stage of EMU.

Furthermore, it is clearly not easy to draw a line between implementing the four freedoms and what some people refer to as the smooth operation of the single market. The dynamics of the four freedoms generate an impetus towards flanking policies which in turn call for the introduction of genuine policies (environment and cohesion, for example) albeit ones that do not at present involve Community competence - that is the possibility of depriving Member States of the power to act.

3. The exercise of exclusive powers

One consequence of the existence of a block of exclusive powers, joined by the common thread of an internal market, is that the Community does not have to demonstrate the need for action on each occasion where free movement is involved.

... It must be assumed that the exclusive powers flowing from an obligation to act are strictly construed because they represent an exception to Community powers as a whole. The exclusiveness of powers is not determined by the matter covered but by the imperatives of free movement. This is why not all measures associated with the smooth operation of the internal market fall under exclusive Community competence. For example while harmonisation of the VAT base does fall within the area of exclusive powers, it is doubtful whether uniform VAT rates are essential to free movement.

This interpretation was largely accepted by the European Council.

Conclusions of the Edinburgh European Council, Annex I to Part A: EC Bulletin 12-1992, 14

1.15. Paragraphs 2 and 3 of Article 3b apply only to the extent that the Treaty gives the institution concerned the choice whether to act and/or a choice as to the nature and extent of the action.

ii. The Content of the Subsidiarity Principle

The essence of the subsidiarity principle is twofold; first, the objectives of the proposed action cannot be sufficiently achieved by the Member States; secondly, the proposed action, by reason of its scale or effects, can be better achieved by the Community. The burden of proof is upon the Community to justify any Community action. Beyond that, however, the meaning of the principle is famously opaque. The uncertainty surrounding the principle prompted the Edinburgh European Council to attempt to 'flesh out' the principle, as part of the package that would allow a second referendum to be held in Denmark on ratification of the

TEU. At Amsterdam, many of the Edinburgh conclusions have been made formally part of the EC Treaty via a Protocol.[22]

Conclusions of the Edinburgh European Council, Annex I to Part A: EC Bulletin 12-1992, 14.[23]

1.18. For Community action to be justified the Council must be satisfied that both aspects of the subsidiarity criterion are met: the objectives of the proposed action can not be sufficiently achieved by Member States' action and they can therefore be better achieved by action on the part of the Community.

The following guidelines should be used in examining whether the abovementioned condition is fulfilled:
- the issue under consideration has transnational aspects which can not be satisfactorily regulated by action by the Member States; and/or
- actions by Member States alone or lack of Community action would conflict with the requirements of the Treaty (such as the need to correct distortion of competition or avoid disguised restrictions on trade or strengthen economic and social cohesion) or would otherwise significantly damage Member States' interests; and/or
- the Council must be satisfied that action at Community level would produce clear benefits by reason of its scale or its effects compared with action at the level of the Member States.

The reasons for concluding that a Community objective can not be sufficiently achieved by the Member States but can be better achieved by the Community must be substantiated by qualitative or, wherever possible, quantitative indicators.

The extent to which these guidelines aid interpretation is unclear. The implementation of these guidelines will depend upon the context against which a measure is judged, the criteria used and the ethos of the institution making the decision.

---

[22] *Protocol to EC Treaty on the application of the principles of subsidiarity and proportionality.*

[23] These can now be found in *Protocol to EC Treaty on the application of the principles of subsidiarity and proportionality, paras. 4 & 5.*

Protocol to EC Treaty on the application of the principles of subsidiarity and proportionality

3.... Subsidiarity is a dynamic concept and should be applied in the light of the objectives set out in the Treaty. It allows Community action within the limits of its powers to be expanded where circumstances so require, and conversely, to be restricted or discontinued where it is no longer justified.

The breadth of the principle has resulted in a variety of underlying functions being ascribed to it. As the next piece makes clear, the conflicts and contradictions brought about by this have resulted in the principle being intractable at best.[24]

Steiner. J. 'Subsidiarity under the Maastricht Treaty' in O'Keeffe, D. and Twomey, P. (eds.) *Legal Issues of the Maastricht Treaty* (1994, Wiley Chancery Law, London) 49, 49-51

Despite the central importance of subsidiarity (established under the Maastricht Treaty 1991, and affirmed at the Edinburgh Summit in December 1992) as a guiding principle of Community law, the meaning and scope of this principle and its practical application are riddled with uncertainty. Discussion of the principle in the Community context, even before its incorporation into the Maastricht Treaty, reveals that it is capable of no less than 30 different meanings. Designed to determine the appropriate level of action across the whole spectrum of public activity, international (in the widest sense), Community, national, regional and local, it has been invoked in the Community context to assist in determining the appropriate allocation of powers as between the Community and its Member States, and to control the exercise of Community powers. In this context it has been described variously, as a principle of necessity, of proportionality, of effectiveness, an elementary principle of good government, or simply a principle of good sense. It has been interpreted as meaning that the Community should only act:

1. where the objective cannot be achieved by regulation at national level;
2. where the objective can be better, or more effectively achieved, by action at Community level (the 'efficiency by better results' criterion; or

---

[24]   Wilke, M. & Wallace, H. *Subsidiarity: approaches to power sharing in the European Community* (1990, RIIA, London); Van Kersbergen, K. & Verbeek, B. 'The Politics of Subsidiarity in the European Union' (1994) 32 JCMS 215; Peterson, J. 'Subsidiarity: A Definition to Suit any Vision' (1994) 47 *Parliamentary Affairs* 116.

3. where the matter in question can be more effectively regulated at the Community (the 'administrative efficiency' criterion).

Furthermore the principle of effectiveness contained in (2) and (3) can be interpreted with reference to specific criteria, that Community action is more effective because of the scale, or cross border, or spillover effect of the matter subject to regulation; or simply in terms of administrative efficiency in order to achieve improved 'coherence'. The concept of cross border or spillover effect may itself be construed strictly, as meaning that the problem in question because of its dimensions, cannot be dealt with effectively at national level, or broadly, as meaning that regulation at national level is undesirable because of the repercussions, or potential repercussions, on the single market.

If the principle of effectiveness is to be judged according to the weaker criteria of administrative efficiency or potential impact on the single market, its logic will inevitably operate in favour of increased centralization. Even though many activities could be regulated (in the sense of problems dealt with) effectively at national level, or broadly, as meaning that regulation at national (or even at the regional or local) level, such regulation can interfere with the functioning of the single market, by:

(1) erecting barriers to the free movement of goods, persons, services and capital; or
(2) undermining competition within the Community by giving a competitive advantage to states with less rigorous standards.

However, the effectiveness principle must be set against another, different meaning of subsidiarity, its original, philosophical meaning, as a principle concerned with promoting social responsibility, a guarantee for individual liberty. In the words of Pope Pius XI:

'It is an injustice, a grave evil and disturbance of right order for a larger and higher association to arrogate to itself functions which can be performed efficiently by smaller and lower societies.'

In pursuit of this principle it is said that decisions affecting individuals should be made as closely as possible to the individual concerned.

This aspect of subsidiarity, at least as between the Community and Member States, was recognised, albeit not expressly, in the original EEC Treaty, which allowed for derogation, even from the basic Treaty freedoms, in order to preserve national autonomy in fundamental matters of public morality, public policy, public security and public health. Under Article 235 the Community institutions were only empowered to act where this was 'necessary' in order to achieve Community objectives: the Directive itself has been cited as an example of this principle, although here it is only executive and administrative power, the 'choice of form and methods' of implementation, which rests with Member States: States have little discretion in matters of policy. The principle can also be found in the Court of Justice's...jurisprudence, for example the *Cassis de Dijon* 'rule of reason', which allows States to derogate from the strict rules of Article 30 in order to protect certain 'mandatory requirements', and in the proportionality principle, adopted by the Court as a means of protecting individuals from excessive interference by public authorities. Moreover, while opinions may differ as to the degree to which a 'level' Community 'playing field' is desirable, there is widespread agreement that certain matters should be left to Member States, even if they do affect competition in the single market. A totally level field, requiring harmonisation of *ALL* matters relevant to the functioning of the single market has never been advocated nor does it exist in any mature federation. With few exceptions, and regardless of the authors' integrationist leanings, references to subsidiarity point to the dangers of excessive centralization and the need to protect diversity. Indeed it was the German *Länder*, which sought to invoke the principle as a means of preserving the competence of the regions against further encroachments of Community law, threatened as a result of the Single European Act 1986, which rekindled the debate on subsidiarity and led to the incorporation of the principle at Maastricht.

Thus, it is clear that the principle of subsidiarity can be used, legitimately, both ways to justify as well as to resist centralization. Moreover, given its chameleon quality, its capacity to 'mean all things to all men', and the inherent conflict between criteria based on effectiveness and concern to foster social responsibility, it is not surprising that it has been used, by pro- and anti-federalists alike, sometimes in respect of the same issues, to argue for, or against, Community, as opposed to national regulation.

iii. The Justiciability of the Principle

At first sight there would appear to be little doubt about the justiciability of Article 3b [*5*] EC. It is an Article of the EC Treaty, and, as such, one would think that it can be ruled upon like any other EC Treaty Article.[25] The Edinburgh European Council certainly took that view in 1992. For although it considered that the principle did not have direct effect (no doubt to prevent perennial litigation), it considered that the Court of Justice was responsible both for interpreting the principle and for

---

[25]   On the justiciability of Article 3b EC see Emiliou, N. 'Subsidiarity: An Effective Barrier against the Enterprises of Ambition' (1992) 17 *ELRev* 383; Toth, A. 'The Principle of Subsidiarity in the Maastricht Treaty' (1992) 29 *CMLRev* 1079; Toth, A. 'Is Subsidiarity Justiciable?' (1994) 19 *ELRev* 268; Gonzàlez, J-P. 'The Principle of Subsidiarity (A guide for lawyers with a particular community orientation)' (1995) 20 *ELRev* 355; Partan, D. 'The Justiciability of Subsidiarity' in Rhodes, C. & Mazey, S. (eds.) *The State of the European Union: volume 3 - Building a European Polity* (1995, Longman, Harlow).

reviewing compliance with it by the other Community institutions.[26] There are also suggestions that this is the view of the Court.

In *Bosman*[27] a UEFA rule restricting football players moving from one club to another after their contract of employment had expired was challenged on the grounds that it breached Article 48 [*39*] EC, the provision requiring free movement of workers. The German Government intervened to argue that the principle of subsidiarity required that the provision should not bind private organisations such as UEFA. The Court rejected this and stated that fundamental rights, such as Article 48 [*39*] EC, were not to be interpreted in the light of the subsidiarity principle. At the very least it would therefore appear that the Court can take cognisance of the subsidiarity principle. The matter was discussed at greater length in the *Working Time* judgment.

Case C-84/94 United Kingdom v Council [1996] ECR I-5755, [1996] 3 CMLR 671

The Council had adopted Directive 93/104/EC on certain aspects of the organisation of working time. This Directive prescribed, *inter alia*, maximum weekly working times as well as minium periods of daily rest, weekly rest and annual leave for a number of working activities. The United Kingdom challenged the Directive on the ground that it should not have been based on Article 118A EC which provided for the setting of minimum health and safety standards for workers. For, the United Kingdom argued, the measure did not, in reality, concern health and safety. In addition, the United Kingdom argued that the measure was disproportionate.

---

[26]   *Conclusions of the Edinburgh European Council, Annex I to Part A*: 'The principle of subsidiarity can not be regarded as having direct effect; however interpretation of this principle, as well as review of compliance with it by the Community institutions are subject to control by the Court of Justice. ...' EC Bulletin 12-1992, I.15.

[27]   Case C-415/93 *Union Royale Belge des Sociétés de Football Association ASBL v Bosman* [1995] ECR I-4921, [1996] 1 CMLR 645. The matter has also been considered by the Court of First Instance. It did not rule on the matter, however, as the alleged illegal act took place before the entry into force of the TEU. See Case T-29/92 *Vereniging van Samenwerkende Prijsregelende Organisaties in de Bouwnijverheid v Commission* [1995] ECR II-289.

46. The applicant further maintains that the Community legislature neither fully considered nor adequately demonstrated whether there were transnational aspects which could not be satisfactorily regulated by national measures, whether such measures would conflict with the requirements of the EC Treaty or significantly damage the interests of Member States or, finally, whether action at Community level would provide clear benefits compared with action at national level. In its submission, Article 118a should be interpreted in the light of the principle of subsidiarity, which does not allow adoption of a directive in such wide and prescriptive terms as the contested directive, given that the extent and the nature of legislative regulation of working time vary very widely between Member States. The applicant explains in this context, however, that it does not rely upon infringement of the principle of subsidiarity as a separate plea.

47. In that respect, it should be noted that it is the responsibility of the Council, under Article 118a, to adopt minimum requirements so as to contribute, through harmonisation, to achieving the objective of raising the level of health and safety protection of workers, which in terms of Article 118a(1), is primarily the responsibility of the Member States. Once the Council has found that it is necessary to improve the existing level of protection as regards the health and safety of workers and to harmonise the conditions in this area while maintaining the improvements made, achievement of that objective through the imposition of minimum requirements necessarily presupposes Community-wide action, which otherwise, as in this case, leaves the enactment of the detailed implementing provisions required largely to the Member States. The argument that the Council could not properly adopt measures as general and mandatory as those forming the subject-matter of the directive will be examined below in the context of the plea alleging infringement of the principle of proportionality.

.....

54. Fourth, a measure will be proportionate only if it is consistent with the principle of subsidiarity. The applicant argues that it is for the Community institutions to demonstrate that the aims of the directive could be better achieved at Community level than by action on the part of the Member States. There has been no such demonstration in this case.

55. The argument of non-compliance with the principle of subsidiarity can be rejected at the outset. It is said that the Community legislature has not established that the aims of the directive would be better served at Community level than at national level. But that argument, as so formulated, really concerns the need for Community action, which has already been examined in paragraph 47 of this judgment.

56. Furthermore, ... , the applicant bases its argument on a conception of 'minimum requirements' which differs from that in Article 118a. That provision does not limit Community action to the lowest common denominator, or even to the lowest level of protection established by the Member States, but means that Member States are free to provide a level of protection more stringent than that resulting from Community law, high as it may be.

229

There is something curiously unsatisfactory about the reasoning in this judgment. On the one hand, the Court seems ready to entertain arguments about subsidiarity. On the other, it provides no indication that if the Council considers there to be a need for EC legislation it will second-guess the Council and strike down the legislation. This encourages doubts as to whether the principle can be used as an effective basis for judicial review. The House of Lords Select Committee on the European Communities stated, for example:-

> 'The Committee does not believe that subsidiarity can be used as a precise measure against which to judge legislation. The test of subsidiarity can never be wholly objective or consistent over time - different people regard collective action as more effective than individual action in different circumstances ... to leave legislation open to annulment or revision by the European Court on such subjective grounds would lead to immense confusion and uncertainty in Community law.'[28]

The practice of federal systems supports this view. Traditionally, both the US Supreme Court and the German Constitutional Court have been extremely reluctant to mediate in disputes between federal and local authorities over the exercise of concurrent powers precisely because it is so difficult to locate a boundary.[29] If federal courts are reluctant to intervene, it is placing a heavy burden indeed upon a supranational institution such as the Court of Justice to make rulings on issues that are inevitably contentious, as they touch upon national identity and autonomy where there is so little to guide it.

Dehousse has also noted that for the Court to strike down measures on grounds of their having failed to comply with the subsidiarity principle would be a considerable break from its previous practice. Having examined the Court's case law in a number of areas he considered that where the Treaty left a margin of discretion to the other

[28]   House of Lords Select Committee on European Communities, *Political Union* (Session 1990-91, 17th Report, HMSO, London).

[29]   Constantinesco, V. 'Who's Afraid of Subsidiarity?' (1991) 11 *YBEL* 33, 38-41; Scharpf, F. 'Community and autonomy: multi-level policy making in the European Union' (1994) 1 *JEPP* 219, 223-225.

institutions as to the extent of their powers, the Court was reluctant to intervene to substitute its own view as to the extent of their powers.[30]

The first solution, suggested by Emiliou, is a compromise one.[31] The Court should restrict itself to a marginal review of subsidiarity and should only intervene where there has been a patent error or a misuse of power. In most cases this will merely require the Court examining whether the other institutions have addressed the question of subsidiarity in exercising their powers.[32]

EC Interinstitutional declaration on democracy, transparency and subsidiarity, EC Bulletin 10-1993, 118

In exercising its right of initiative, the Commission shall take into account the principle of subsidiarity and show that it has been observed. The European Parliament and Council shall do likewise in exercising the powers conferred upon them.

The explanatory memorandum for any Commission proposal shall include a justification of the proposal under the principle of subsidiarity.

Any amendment which may be made to the Commission's text whether by the European Parliament or the Council, must if it entails more extensive or intensive intervention by the Community be accompanied by a justification under the principle of subsidiarity and Article 3b EC.

The three institutions shall, under their internal procedures, regularly check that action envisaged complies with the provisions concerning subsidiarity as regards both the choice of legal instruments and the content of a proposal. Such checks must form an integral part of the substantive examination.

Scharpf has gone further and suggested that substantive review is possible. He noted that the practice of federal systems suggests that it is difficult for courts to review action where the constitution is constructed according to a unipolar logic under which the constitution merely seeks to limit the scope of central government. Such a

---

[30] Dehousse, R. 'Community Competences: Are there Limits to Growth?' 103, 115-116 in Dehousse, R. (ed) *Maastricht: An Ever Closer Union?* (1994, Law Books in Europe, Munich).

[31] Supra n.25, 405 *et seq.*

[32] Following Amsterdam any proposal for legislation must state why it satisfies the subsidiarity principle, *Protocol to the EC Treaty on the application of the principles of subsidiarity and proportionality, para. 4.*

constitution often leads courts to prefer the explicitly stated central competences against the more murkily defined competences of local government. Very soon competence-creep begins as more competences accrue to central government. This can be avoided if a bipolar logic is adopted by the constitution, so that the responsibilities of both central and local government are set out.

Scharpf, F. 'Community and autonomy: multi-level policy-making in the European Union' (1994) 1 *Journal of European Public Policy* **219, 225**

The recognition of a bipolar constitutional order prevents the one-sided orientation of judicial review towards the enumerated powers of the central government, which is otherwise characteristic of federal states. It requires the court to balance competing jurisdictional claims with a view not only to their substantive justification, but also to the manner in which powers are exercised. The criterion is mutual compatibility, and the characteristic outcome is not the displacement of one jurisdiction by the other, but the obligation of both to choose mutually acceptable means when performing the proper functions of government at each level.

Applying this logic to the European Union, one would have to demand judicial recognition or, better still, the explicit specification of reserved powers of national (and subnational) governments in the constitutive treaties. The Maastricht Treaty already makes a start in this direction by postulating in Article F(1): 'The Union shall respect the identities of its Member States, whose systems of government are founded on the principles of democracy.' This would need to be further developed. Ultimately, of course, the content of the identity-related reserved powers of member states must be defined by political processes rather than scholarship. There is reason to think, however, that in the relationship between the Union and its members, just as in federal-state relations within the nation state, the core of reserved rights would lie in the protection of the cultural and institutional identity of the members.

It may also be that justiciability is just a side issue in the discussion about the impact of the subsidiarity principle. Arguably more far-reaching is the effect that it has had upon the political culture of the European Union. It has already been seen that the subsidiarity issue must be addressed in the statement of reasons which precedes any issue. Since the Edinburgh European Council, the Commission has, in addition, been required to submit an Annual Report on the application of the subsidiarity principle.[33] The impact of this, according to Commission figures, is that whilst it made 61 significant proposals in 1990, only 19 were made in 1996.[34] It is possible that the difference results from the near completion of the single market programme resulting in less legislation. Similarly, it is possible that this lull in proposals is merely a transient one. These statistics create a presumption, however, that subsidiarity is making an impact right at the heart of the government of the EC.[35]

iv. The Proportionality Principle

The proportionality principle contained in Article 3b(3) [*5(3)*] EC differs from the principle outlined in the second paragraph in two ways. First, it applies to Community action in all fields of competence. Secondly, it does not regulate whether or not they should be Community action but rather the content of any measure, in particular whether the measure places unnecessary burdens on either Member States or individuals. In this latter respect it has a strong libertarian feel to it which is not necessarily present in the subsidiarity principle contained in Article 3b(2)[*5(2)*] EC, as it suggests that individual liberty and autonomy are natural states which should be curbed by the Community institutions only exceptionally, and then only to the minimum extent necessary.

Commission Communication to the Council and the European Parliament SEC (92) 1990 final, 27 October 1992

The purpose of the subsidiarity principle is to give general application to the rule that the means should be proportionate to the ends.

---

33   This is formalised in the *Protocol on the application of the principles of subsidiarity and proportionality, paragraph 9(4)*.

34   EC Commission, *Commission Work Programme for 1996* COM (95) 512, 15.

35   On the implementation of the subsidiarity principle see Maher, I. 'Legislative Review by the EC Commission: Revision without Radicalism' in Shaw, J. & More, G. (eds.) *New Legal Dynamics of the European Union* (1995, Clarendon, Oxford).

In practical terms, subsidiarity means that, when exercising its powers, the Community must, where various equally effective options are available, choose the form of action or measure which leaves the Member States, individuals or businesses concerned the greatest degree of freedom.

Beyond this general rule, though is the implication that if a binding rule proves necessary, the actual degree of regulation should be kept to a minimum.

The main choice where subsidiarity is concerned is between binding and non-binding measures. The decision whether or not to legislate should be based on an assessment of:

- the importance of uniformity in the field in question and, in particular, the need for non-discrimination and certainty as to the law; and

- where appropriate, the degree of technical complexity of the area in question.

2. The Intensity of Legislative Action

... If legislative action is necessary, the subsidiarity principle dictates that Community legislation and national measures each be given its own respective role: Community legislation forms the framework into which national action must be fitted.

For this purpose the Treaty of Rome devised an original instrument which typifies subsidiarity: the Directive sets the result to be achieved but leaves it to the member States to choose the most appropriate means of doing so.

... If the subsidiarity exercise is to produce any overall tangible results, then it must unquestionably be by systematically reverting to the original concept of the directive as a framework of general rules, or even simply of objectives, for the attainment of which the Member States have sole responsibility.

Similarly, preference must be given to the technique of minimum standards and mutual recognition.

Regulations should remain the exception, to be resorted to only where there is an overriding need for uniform rules, in particular to guarantee the rights and obligations of individuals and firms.

Conclusions of the Edinburgh European Council, Annex I to Part A: EC Bulletin 12-1992, 15

Third Paragraph:

1.19. This paragraph applies to all Community action, whether or not within exclusive competence.

Any burdens, whether financial or administrative, falling upon the Community, national governments, local authorities, economic operators and citizens should be minimised and should be proportionate to the objective pursued.

Community measures should leave as much scope for national decisions as possible, consistent with securing the aim of the measure and observing the requirements of the Treaty. While respecting Community law, care should be taken to respect well established national arrangements and the organisation and working of Member States' legal systems. Where appropriate and subject to the need for proper enforcement, Community measures should provide Member States with alternative ways to achieve the objectives of the measures.[36]

Where it is necessary to set standards at Community level, consideration should be given to setting minimum standards, with freedom for Member States to set higher national standards not only in the areas where the Treaty so requires but also in other areas where this would not conflict with the objectives of the proposed measure or with the Treaty.

The form of action should be as simple as possible, consistent with satisfactory achievement of the objective of the measure and the need for effective enforcement. The Community should legislate only to the extent necessary. Other things being equal, directives should be preferred to regulations and framework directives to detailed measures.[37] Non-binding measures such as recommendations should be preferred where appropriate. Consideration should also be given where appropriate to the use of voluntary codes of conduct.

... Where difficulties are localised and only certain member States are affected, any necessary Community action should not be extended to other Member States unless this is necessary to achieve an objective of the Treaty.

Whilst the institutions are urged to adopt a greater lightness of touch, care should be taken not to exaggerate. In *Germany v Parliament* the German Government challenged a Directive which required all credit institutions to enter guarantee schemes which provided cover for depositors.[38] The German Government argued that the compulsory nature of the scheme resulted in its failing to take account of established national practices. In particular, by preventing Member States from adopting alternate solutions to achieve the objectives of depositor protection, it was forcing Germany to scrap the voluntary scheme it had in place. The Court was dismissive of such arguments. It noted that harmonisation measures could not result in all 'well established national practices' being tolerated. It was therefore permissible for the EC legislature to outlaw some.

The judgment suggests that a bipolar logic grips not just the subsidiarity principle but also the proportionality principle. Whilst the

---

[36]   This paragraph is also contained in *Protocol to the EC Treaty on the application of the subsidiarity and proportionality principles, para 7.*

[37]   This subparagraph is contained in *Protocol to the EC Treaty on the application of the subsidiarity and proportionality principles, para 6.*

[38]   Case C-233/94 *Germany v Parliament*, Judgment of 13 May 1997.

proportionality principle would militate against legislation which unnecessarily sought to replace diversity with uniformity, it clearly allows for the EC legislature to have a sufficient margin of discretion to bring about the convergence it considers necessary to attain its objectives. Whilst there is nothing innately unattractive about this method, the complex balancing approach it requires makes it particularly unamenable to judicial control.

IV. Pre-emption and the Protection of Community Competence

i. Pre-emption - A Chameleon Concept

The establishment of Community competence is only one half of the coin. Instruments must also exist to protect Community competence. If not, Community activity would be fully contingent on Member State consent and the system would enjoy little meaningful autonomy. The doctrine of supremacy of Community law performs that function by holding that where there is a conflict between Community and national law EC law must prevail.[39] Such a doctrine is dependent, however, on a mechanism which will determine when there is an actual or potential conflict. This role is fulfilled by the doctrine of pre-emption.[40] The operation of the doctrine depends considerably upon the surrounding legal context.

Waelbroeck, M. 'The Emergent Doctrine of Community Pre-emption - Consent and Re-delegation' in Sandalow, T. & Stein, E. (eds.) *Courts and Free Markets: Perspectives from the United States and Europe. Volume II* (1982, Clarendon, Oxford) 548, 551

From an analysis of the case law, it appears that the Court is influenced by two conflicting approaches to the pre-emption problem.

---

[39]   Case 6/64 *Costa v ENEL* [1964] ECR 585, [1964] CMLR 425.
[40]   Cross, E. 'Pre-emption of Member State Law in the European Economic Community: A Framework for Analysis' (1992) 29 *CMLRev* 447.

Under the first approach, which we will call 'the conceptualist-federalist' approach, the essential problem is to define the scope of the Community competence. Once this is done, the consequence - i.e. the absence of power for the Member States to deal with the subject-matter included within the Community's competence - automatically follows. In other words, the Community competence is construed as being necessarily exclusive.

In opposition to this approach, the 'pragmatic' approach accepts that the Community's competence is not necessarily exclusive. The Member States retain a concurrent power to regulate matters falling within the reach of the Community's power, as long as in so doing they do not create a conflict with the rules adopted by the Community. The problem is not one of tracing the boundary between the powers of the Community and those of the Member States but of identifying whether or not the exercise by Member States of their powers is contrary to rules adopted by the Community.

ii. Exclusive Powers

As mentioned earlier, the Community has exclusive competence in the fields of common commercial policy, common customs tariff and fisheries.[41] The traditional legal effects of exclusivity are described below.

Opinion 1/75 Re Understanding on a Local Costs Standard [1975] ECR 1355, [1976] 1 CMLR 85

An Opinion[42] of the Court was sought as to whether the Community was exclusively competent under Article 113 [*133*] EC, the common commercial policy provision, to conclude an OECD Understanding on a Local Costs Standard. Under the Understanding participating governments agreed not to provide credit for more than 100% of the value of the goods or services exported to other participating States. The reason for this was that the provision of such a disproportionate amount of credit amounted to an export subsidy.

---

[41]   See pp 221.

[42]   A procedure exists under Article 228(6) [*300(6)*] EC where the Council, Commission or any of the Member States can ask for an Opinion of the Court upon whether the Community is acting lawfully in concluding a draft treaty. The reason for this procedure is that international agreements, being binding upon the international plane, cannot be annulled as easily as internal acts.

Such a policy [Article 113 EC] is conceived in that article in the context of the operation of the Common Market, for the defence of the common interests of the Community, within which the particular interests of the Member States must endeavour to adapt to each other.

Quite clearly, however, this conception is incompatible with the freedom to which the Member States could lay claim by invoking a concurrent power, so as to ensure that their own interests were separately satisfied in external relations, at the risk of compromising the effective defence of the common interests of the Community.

In fact any unilateral action on the part of the Member States would lead to disparities in the conditions for the grant of export credits, calculated to distort competition between undertakings of the various Member States in external markets. Such distortion can be eliminated only by means of a strict uniformity of credit conditions granted to undertakings in the Community, whatever their nationality.

It cannot therefore be accepted that, in a field such as that governed by the understanding in question, which is covered by export policy and more generally by the common commercial policy, the Member States should exercise a power concurrent to that of the Community, in the Community sphere and in the international sphere. the provisions of Articles 113 and 114 concerning the conditions under which, according to the Treaty, agreements on commercial policy must be concluded show clearly that the exercise of concurrent powers by the Member States and the Community in this matter is impossible.

To accept that the contrary were true would amount to recognizing that, in relations with third countries, Member States may adopt positions which differ from those which the Community intends to adopt, and would thereby distort the institutional framework, call into question the mutual trust within the Community and prevent the latter from fulfilling its task in the defence of the common interest.

The establishment of exclusive competence can lead to the emergence of *regulatory gaps*. A regulatory gap exists where Member States are barred from regulating in a particular area, but there exists no substitute Community legislation in place. Exclusivity debars Member States from acting in the area, yet they can, simultaneously, prevent the Community from acting by blocking measures in the Council. The danger exists in such circumstances that the subject-matter which provided the rationale for the regulation in the first place will go unprotected.

To prevent this, in all the fields where the Community has exclusive powers national measures are permitted, provided prior authorisation has been given for these measures.[43] Yet this exposes the myth of exclusivity, for it results in national measures and Community existing side-by-side in areas which are supposed to be the sole domain of the Community legislator. The difference between these fields and others is that of the power of authorisation granted to Community institutions which shifts the balance of power in their favour.

iii. Field Occupation

The most common form of pre-emption is that of 'field occupation'. Where Community legislation occupies a field, Member States are prohibited from enacting legislation within that field.

Case 60/86 Commission v United Kingdom ('Dim Dip') [1988] ECR 3921

The Commission brought an action against a British prohibition on cars being used on the roads which were not equipped with dim-dip lighting devices. Annex I to Directive 76/756/EEC, on the installation of lighting and light-signalling devices on motor vehicles, imposed a number of requirements before Member States could authorise cars be used on the roads. The installation of dim-dips was not one of them. Article 2(1) of the Directive stipulated, however, that Member States could *not* refuse to authorise those cars which met the Directive's requirements.

10. It is clear from the documents before the Court that the reason for which dim-dip devices were not included in the provisions, even as optional devices, is that the technical committee of national experts did not consider them acceptable given the state of technical progress at the time. In addition, it was not considered appropriate to adapt Directive 76/756/EEC, after its entry into force, so as to take account of technical progress in accordance with the procedure laid down in article 13 of Directive

---

43   In the case of the commercial policy see Case 41/76 *Donckerwolcke v Procureur de la République* [1976] ECR, [1977] 2 CMLR 535; fisheries, Case 801/79 *Commission v United Kingdom* [1981] ECR 1045, and the common customs tariff, Case 70/77 *Simmenthal v Italian Finance Administration* [1978] ECR 1453.

70/156/EEC and article 5 of Directive 76/756/EEC, by bringing dim-dip devices within the scope of the latter Directive.

11. Such an interpretation of the exhaustive nature of the list of lighting and light-signalling devices set out in Annex I to the Directive is consistent with the purpose of Directive 70/156/EEC which is to reduce, and even eliminate, hindrances to trade within the Community resulting from the fact that mandatory technical requirements differ from one Member State to another (see the first and second recitals in the preamble to Directive 70/156/EEC). In the context of Directive 76/756/EEC that objective is reflected in the obligation imposed on the Member States to adopt the same requirements 'either in addition to or in place of their existing rules' (second recital).

12. It follows that the Member States cannot unilaterally require manufacturers who have complied with the harmonized technical requirements set out in Directive 76/756/EEC to comply with a requirement which is not imposed by that Directive, since motor vehicles complying with the technical requirements laid down therein must be able to move freely within the common market.

Within the context of the single market this form of pre-emption is particularly important. Otherwise, the maintenance of differing national regimes, while not directly conflicting with the Community instrument, would lead to commercial uncertainty, as operators would be unsure as to what was required of them. In addition, distortions of competition and restrictions to trade caused by these differing regimes would remain, with the consequence that the harmonisation process would be robbed of much of its effect. Pre-emption in this form, however, runs the risk that it creates a regime which is both difficult to achieve and stifling in its effect.

Weatherill, S. 'Beyond Preemption? Shared Competence and Constitutional Change in the European Community' in O'Keeffe, D. and Twomey, P. (eds) *Legal Issues of the Maastricht Treaty* (1994, Wiley Chancery, London) 13, 18-19.

There are enormous advantages for commercial certainty in fixing a Community rule, susceptible to neither unilateral national alteration nor the judicial weighing exercise inherent in the *Cassis* approach to Article 30. Yet preemption in its traditional form has flaws, arising from the broad perception that it may be neither feasible nor desirable to suppose that a rigid rule of preemption can serve an increasingly heterogenous Community. Preemption is difficult to achieve, given the unfeasibility of replacing 12 regimes with one. This leads to a legislative logjam, an obstacle firmly fixed, until 1987, by the practice of unanimous voting in Council which forced the Community to move at the pace of the slowest member. Even if a single Community rule is agreed, its stifling effect on national initiatives may prove undesirable. A uniform Community rule may ossify practice, discouraging innovation.

...

Yet failure to achieve the rapid adaptation of obsolete norms in response to technical innovation will cause inefficiency within the Community market, which will also affect the competitiveness of Community operators in world markets. Preemption risks creating a level but barren playing field.

The fears posed by field-occupation led some Member States, notably Germany and Denmark, to worry at the time of the Single European Act that the introduction of Article 100A [*95*] EC and qualified majority voting might lead to the undermining of existing high national standards. The response was to introduce Article 100A(4) EC.

Article 100A(4) EC. If, after the adoption of a harmonisation measure by the Council acting by a qualified majority, a Member State deems it necessary to apply national provisions on grounds of major needs referred to in Article 36, or relating to protection of the environment or the working environment, it shall notify the Commission of these provisions.

The Commission shall confirm the provisions involved after having verified that they are not a means of arbitrary discrimination or a disguised restriction on trade between Member States.

By way of derogation from the procedure laid down in Articles 169 and 170, the Commission or any Member State may bring the matter directly before the Court of Justice if it considers that another Member State is making improper use of the powers provided for in this Article.

Fears were expressed at the time that frequent resort to Article 100A [4] EC would prevent realisation of the single market have not been realised.[44] Article 100A(4) EC has only been invoked twice by Germany and Denmark, who consider the concentrations of a wood

---

[44] Pescatore, P. 'Some Critical Remarks on the Single European Act' (1987) 24 *CMLRev* 9. For analysis of the difficulties of Article 100A(4) EC see Flynn, J. 'How will Article 100A(4) Work? A Comparison with Article 93' (1987) 24 *CMLRev* 689.

chemical, pentachlorophenol, authorised to be marketed by a 1991 Directive to be too lenient.[45] The reason that Article 100A(4) EC has been invoked so rarely is that diversity can be accommodated within Community legislation, with different standards being applied to different parts of the Community.

Article 7c [15] EC. When drawing up its proposals with a view to achieving the objectives set out in Article 7a [14], the Commission shall take into account the extent of the effort that certain economies showing differences in developments will have to sustain during the period of establishment of the internal market and it may propose appropriate provisions.

If these provisions take the form of derogations, they must be of a temporary nature and must cause the least possible disturbance to the functioning of the common market.

The existence of Article 7c [15] EC undermines one of the central pillars supporting field-occupation which was that it prevented distortion of competition and barriers to trade. For through differing standards being applied within a Community instrument these are simply reintroduced at the Community level. Moreover, it is very difficult to see how any differences introduced can be subjected to judicial control given that the rationale for their introduction can be as diffuse as differences in economic development.[46]

Experience has also suggested that at the time Article 100A(4) EC was established by the SEA, too much attention was focused on establishing a single market and insufficient on the difficulties of

---

45   The Commission authorisation of the German derogation was challenged successfully on the grounds that Germany had put the measure in force prior to Commission authorisation and that the Commission failed to supply adequate reasons as to why it authorised the German measure, Case C-41/93 *France v Commission* [1994] ECR I-1829, [1995] 3 CMLR 179. The Commission renewed the authorisation, Decision 94/783/EC, OJ 1994, L 316/43. This is under fresh challenge, Case C-127/97 *Burstein v Freistaat Bayern*, OJ 1997, C181/2. The Danish derogation was only formally authorised in 1996, Decision 96/211/EC, OJ 1996, L 68/32.

46   Chalmers, D. 'Environmental Protection and the Single Market: An Unsustainable Development. Does the EC Treaty Need a Title on the Environment?' (1995/1) *LIEI* 65, 91-93.

regulating that market. In particular, the harmonisation process was a cumbersome one which reacted only slowly to scientific developments.[47] Yet the doctrine of pre-emption prevented Member States acting on their own initiative. This problem was addressed in two ways at Amsterdam. The first was to allow Member States to seek a derogation from existing legislation where new scientific evidence justified it. The other was to provide that harmonisation measures could include safeguard clauses allowing Member States to derogate from the legislation in question in limited circumstances.[48]

Article 95 EC 4. *If, after the adoption by the Council or by the Commission of a harmonisation measure, a Member State deems it necessary to maintain national provisions on grounds of major needs referred to in Article 30, or relating to the protection of the environment or the working environment, it shall notify the Commission of these provisions as well as the grounds for maintaining them.*

5. Moreover, without prejudice to the previous subparagraph, if, after the adoption by the Council or by the Commission of a harmonisation measure, a Member State deems it necessary to introduce national provisions based on new scientific evidence relating to the protection of the environment or the working environment on grounds of a problem specific to that Member State arising after the adoption of the harmonisation measure, it shall notify the Commission of the envisaged provisions as well as the grounds for introducing them.

6. The Commission shall, within six months of the notifications as referred to in paragraphs 4 and 5, approve or reject the national provisions involved after having verified that they are not a means of arbitrary discrimination or a disguised restriction on trade between Member States and whether or not they shall not constitute an obstacle to the functioning of the internal market.

In the absence of a decision by the Commission within this period the national provisions referred to in paragraphs 4 and 5 shall be deemed to have been approved.

---

[47] Dehousse, R., Joerges, C., Majone, G., Snyder, F., Everson, M. *Europe after 1992 - New Regulatory Strategies - EUI Working Paper 92/31* (1992, EUI, Florence) 4-6.

[48] The ground must be a non-economic one and must be for the reasons referred to in *Article 30 EC*. These are public morality, public policy or public security; protection of health of life of humans, animals and plants; protection of national treasures possessing artistic, historic or archaeological value, and the protection of industrial and commercial property.

When justified by the complexity of the matter and in the absence of danger for human health, the Commission may notify the Member State concerned that the period referred to in this paragraph may be extended for a further period of up to six months.

7. When, pursuant to paragraph 6, a Member State is authorised to maintain or introduce national provisions derogating from a harmonisation measure, the Commission shall immediately examine whether to propose an adaptation to that measure.

8. When a Member State raises a specific problem on public health in a field which has been the subject of prior harmonisation measures, it shall bring it to the attention of the Commission which shall immediately examine whether to propose appropriate measures to the Council.

9. By way of derogation from the procedure laid down in Articles 226 and 227, the Commission and any Member State may bring the matter directly before the Court of Justice if it considers that another Member State is making improper use of the powers provided for in this Article.

10. The harmonisation measures referred to above shall, in appropriate cases, include a safeguard clause authorising the Member States to take, for one or more of the non-economic reasons referred to in Article 36, provisional measures subject to a Community control procedure.

iv. Minimum Harmonisation

The doctrine of field occupation is tailored very much to the needs of the single market. In other fields, EC competences do not require such a monolithic regime. It would be perverse, for example, if EC environmental policy, for example, prevented Member States from maintaining higher environmental standards. In such circumstances, the development of Community policies would automatically result in the 'levelling down' of some national policies. It would also prevent the national experimentation with legislation which is the key to the evolution of effective risk management regimes. As Community competences expanded with the SEA and the TEU, so minimum harmonisation provisions were added in the fields of the environment, consumer protection and health and safety at work.[49] These provisions made clear that Community competences exercised under these Titles created merely a 'bed of rights' which did not prevent Member States enacting more restrictive provisions.

Article 130t [*176*] EC. The protective measures adopted pursuant to Article 130s [*175*] shall not prevent any Member State from maintaining or introducing more stringent measures compatible with this Treaty.

The automatic casting of legislation taken under certain legal bases as minimum harmonisation led to difficulties. The rationale leading to minimum harmonisation being established in these instances could equally well be applied to other legal bases. This was particularly so as EC policies often cut across several legal bases. Community environmental policy, for example, was as affected by measures taken under Article 100A [*95*] EC as those taken under Article 130s [*175*] EC. This problem was considered at the Edinburgh European Council.

Conclusions of the Edinburgh European Council, Annex I to Part A: EC Bulletin 12-1992, 15

1.19 Where it is necessary to set standards at Community level, consideration should be given to setting minimum standards, with freedom for Member States to set higher standards, not only in the areas where the Treaty so requires ... but also in other areas where this would not conflict with the objectives of the proposed measure or with the Treaty.

The Edinburgh European Council knocked the doctrine of field occupation off its pedestal. Whilst it still applies in certain areas of Community law, it can no longer be said to be central, as many measures will now explicitly state that they are minimum harmonisation measures. This expansion of concurrent competence, whereby both Member States

---

[49]   In addition to Article 130t [*176*] EC, see Article 118a(3) [*137(5)*] EC on health and safety at work; Article 129a(3) [*153(3)*] EC on consumer protection and, following Amsterdam, *Article 152(4)(a) EC* on public health.

and Community institutions act within a particular field, has happened not just as a result of Treaty amendments and changes in the political culture but also through contributions by the Court of Justice.

The Court has done this, first, by narrowing the field covered by the Community instrument where the doctrine of field occupation applies. In those instances where the national legislation is perceived to be pursuing a public good effectively the Court will often interpret the EC legislation in a manner so that it does not unduly restrict the national policy in question.

Case C-11/92 R v Secretary of State for Health, ex parte Gallaher Ltd. [1993] ECR I-3545, [1994] 3 CMLR 179

Articles 3 and 4 of Directive 89/622/EEC required that health warnings on packets of cigarettes cover at least 4% of the surface area. Article 8(1) stated that Member States could not restrict the sale of cigarettes which complied with the Directive on grounds of labelling. The United Kingdom followed the Directive in respect of imported packets of cigarettes. In relation to domestic products it maintained its pre-existing regime which required that the health warning cover at least 6% of the surface area. Gallaher and a number of other British manufacturers brought an action, claiming this was precluded by the Directive.

10. It should be borne in mind that the Directive, which was adopted pursuant to Article 100a of the EEC Treaty, is designed to eliminate barriers to trade which might arise as a result of differences in national provisions on the labelling of tobacco products and thereby impede the establishment and operation of the internal market. With that end in view, the Directive contains common rules concerning the health warnings to appear on the unit packet of tobacco products and the indications of the tar and nicotine yields to appear on cigarette packets.

11. These common rules are not always identical in nature.

12. Some of them give Member States no discretion to impose requirements stricter than those provided for in the Directive, or even to impose more detailed or at any rate different requirements, with regard to the labelling of tobacco products.

.....

14. Other provisions of the Directive allow the Member States a degree of discretion to adapt the labelling of tobacco products to the requirements of public health protection.

One such provision is article 4(2), which allows the Member States to select the specific warnings which must appear on cigarette packets by choosing them from those listed in the Annex to the Directive. Another is article 4(3), which allows Member States to stipulate that the general warning `tobacco seriously damages health', as well as the specific warnings, must be combined with the indication of the authority that is their author.

.....

16. Member States which have made use of the powers conferred by the provisions containing minimum requirements cannot, according to article 8 of the Directive, prohibit or restrict the sale within their territory of products imported from other Member States which comply with the Directive.

17. In order to reply to the question referred by the national court, it is therefore necessary to determine whether articles 3(3) and 4(4) of the Directive still allow the Member States a degree of latitude to require, with regard to domestic production, that the indications and warnings in question cover in each case more than 4% of the relevant surface area.

.....

20. Articles 3(3) and 4(4) of the Directive contain provisions directed to the Member States, to whom the Directive is addressed, and not to the manufacturers of tobacco products, who have no interest in using a greater surface area for the indications and warnings in question. The expression 'at least' contained in both articles must be interpreted as meaning that, if they consider it necessary, Member States are at liberty to decide that the indications and warnings are to cover a greater surface area in view of the level of public awareness of the health risks associated with tobacco consumption.

.....

22. Admittedly, as the applicants in the main proceedings have pointed out, this interpretation of the provisions may imply less favourable treatment for national products in comparison with imported products and leaves in existence some inequalities in conditions of competition. However, those consequences are attributable to the degree of harmonization sought by the provisions in question, which lay down minimum requirements.

23. The answer to the question referred by the national court must therefore be that articles 3(3) and 4(4) of Council Directive 89/622/EEC are to be interpreted as allowing the Member States to require, so far as domestic production is concerned, that the indications concerning tar and nicotine yields provided for in article 3 of that Directive and the general and specific warnings provided for in article 4 of the Directive be printed on cigarette packets so as to cover at least 6% of each of the relevant surface areas.

There are also extreme circumstances in which, even though the Community legislation occupies the field and does not take the form of minimum harmonisation legislation, the Court will refuse to disapply national legislation.

Case C-57/89 Commission v Germany [1991] ECR I-883

Member States were required by Article 4(1) of Directive 79/409/EEC to designate the most suitable habitats in their territory for certain species of wild bird. Under Article 4(4), once designated, these habitats were to be preserved and appropriate steps taken to prevent their deteriorating. The Directive was based on Article 235 [*308*] EC and envisaged no circumstances in which measures could be taken to reduce the size of the special protection areas. Germany wished to build a dyke which cut across, and therefore impaired, one of its designated areas in the Leybucht region near the North Sea. It argued this was necessary as, otherwise, the coast would be washed.

19. With regard to the powers of the Member States to review in that way a decision to classify an area as a special protection area, it must be stated that a reduction in the geographical extent of a protected area is not expressly envisaged by the terms of the Directive.

20. Although the Member States do have a certain discretion with regard to the choice of the territories which are most suitable for classification as special protection areas pursuant to Article 4(1) of the Directive, they do not have the same discretion under Article 4(4) of the Directive in modifying or reducing the extent of the areas, since they have themselves acknowledged in their declarations that those areas contain the most suitable environments for the species listed in Annex I to the Directive. If that were not so, the Member States could unilaterally escape from the obligations imposed on them by Article 4(4) of the Directive with regard to special protection areas.

21. That interpretation of Article 4(4) of the Directive is borne out, moreover, by the ninth recital in the preamble, which underlines the special importance which the Directive attaches to special conservation measures concerning the habitats of the birds listed in Annex I in order to ensure their survival and reproduction in their area of distribution. It follows that the power of the Member States to reduce the extent of a special protection area can be justified only on exceptional grounds.

22. Those grounds must correspond to a general interest which is superior to the general interest represented by the ecological objective of the Directive. In that context the interests referred to in Article 2 of the Directive, namely economic and recreational requirements, do not enter into consideration. As the Court pointed out in its judgments in Case 247/85 (*Commission v Belgium* [1987] ECR 3029) and Case 262/85 (*Commission v Italy* [1987] ECR 3073), that provision does not constitute an autonomous derogation from the general system of protection established by the Directive.

23. With regard to the reason put forward in this case, it must be stated that the danger of flooding and the protection of the coast constitute sufficiently serious reasons to justify the dyke works and the strengthening of coastal structures as long as those measures are confined to a strict minimum and involve only the smallest possible reduction of the special protection area.

v. Article 5 [*10*] EC and the Management of Concurrent Competences

In the case of both exclusive competence and field occupation the limits on national activity are relatively well-defined. In the case of exclusive competence Member States cannot act anywhere within the area of competence without Community authorisation. In the case of field occupation Member States cannot act in the field circumscribed by the Community legislation. No such demarcation exists in the case of concurrent competences. This blurring of competences can lead to dysfunction and uncertainty. A good example are international agreements where often the Community and Member States will have shared competence. The give-and-take nature of negotiating these agreements means that neither will be able to negotiate effectively unless they cooperate with the other, or unless one is nominated to negotiate on behalf of the other. Relations in such areas are structured by the duty of cooperation contained in Article 5 [*10*]EC.

Article 5 [*10*] EC. Member States shall take all appropriate measures, whether general or particular, to ensure fulfilment of the obligations arising out of this Treaty or resulting from action taken by the institutions of the Community. They shall facilitate the achievement of the Community's tasks.

They shall abstain from any measure which could jeopardise the attainment of the objectives of this Treaty.

While the provision is only addressed to Member States the Court extended its remit in *Zwartveld* to bind EC institutions.[50] The provision has thereby been transformed into an overarching principle which, in the words of one commentator has the role of 'drawing all relevant institutions into the job of effectively sustaining Community policy'.[51]

Case 2/88-Imm Criminal proceedings v Zwartveld and Others [1990] ECR I-3365, [1990] 3 CMLR 457.

The examining magistrate in Groningen, the Netherlands, was examining charges that Zwartveld and others had been illegally selling fish. To assist with his investigations he asked for inspection reports carried out by Commission officials and to question the officials themselves. The Commission refused to cooperate claiming that the Dutch magistrate had no power to force it to hand over the documents and that producing these documents, which were internal ones, might jeopardise its relations with the Member States. The magistrate referred the matter to the Court.

15. In order to assess whether the objection of inadmissibility lodged by the Commission is well founded, it should be recalled that the Court has already held in its judgment in Case 6/64 *Costa v ENEL* [1964] ECR 585, that, by contrast with ordinary international treaties, the EEC Treaty has created its own legal system which, on the entry into force of the treaty, became an integral part of the legal systems of the Member States.

16. In its judgment in Case 294/83 *Les Verts v European Parliament* [1986] ECR 1357, the Court established the principle that the European Economic Community is a Community based on the rule of law, inasmuch as neither its Member States nor its Institutions can avoid a review of whether the measures adopted by them are in conformity with the basic constitutional charter, the Treaty (paragraph 23). The EEC

---

[50]   Arnull, A. 'Does the Court Have Inherent Jurisdiction?' (1990) 27 *CMLRev* 683.

[51]   Weatherill, S. 'Beyond Preemption? Shared Competence and Constitutional Change in the European Community' 13, 31 in O'Keeffe, D. & Twomey, P. (eds.) *Legal Issues of the Maastricht Treaty* (1994, Chancery, Chichester). For a description of the forms these obligations can take see Temple Lang, J. 'Community Constitutional Law: Article 5 EEC Treaty' (1990) 27 *CMLRev* 645.

Treaty established the Court of Justice as the judicial body responsible for ensuring that both the Member States and the Community Institutions comply with the law.

17. In that Community subject to the rule of law, relations between the Member States and the Community Institutions are governed, according to Article 5 of the EEC Treaty, by a principle of sincere cooperation. That principle not only requires the Member States to take all the measures necessary to guarantee the application and effectiveness of Community law, if necessary by instituting criminal proceedings (see the judgment in Case 68/88 *Commission v Greece* [1989] ECR 2965, at p. 2984, paragraph 23) but also imposes on Member States and the Community Institutions mutual duties of sincere cooperation (see the judgment in Case 230/81 *Luxembourg v European Parliament* [1983] ECR 255, paragraph 37).

18. This duty of sincere cooperation imposed on Community Institutions is of particular importance vis-à-vis the judicial authorities of the Member States, who are responsible for ensuring that Community law is applied and respected in the national legal system.

.....

22. In this case, the request has been made by a national court which is hearing proceedings on the infringement of Community rules, and it seeks the production of information concerning the existence of the facts constituting those infringements. It is incumbent upon every Community Institution to give its active assistance to such national legal proceedings, by producing documents to the national court and authorizing its officials to give evidence in the national proceedings; that applies particularly to the Commission, to which Article 155 of the EEC Treaty entrusts the task of ensuring that the provisions of the Treaty and the measures taken by the Institutions pursuant thereto are applied.

23. The Court, which is responsible under Article 164 of the EEC Treaty for ensuring that in the interpretation and application of the Treaty the law is observed, must have the power to review, at the request of a national judicial authority and by means of a legal procedure appropriate to the objective pursued by that authority, whether the duty of sincere cooperation, incumbent on the Commission in this case, has been complied with.

.....

25. Under those circumstances, the Commission must produce to the Rechter-Commissaris the documents which it has requested, unless it presents to the Court imperative reasons relating to the need to avoid any interference with the functioning and independence of the Communities justifying its refusal to do so.

Weatherill, S. 'Beyond Preemption? Shared Competence and Constitutional Change in the European Community' in O'Keeffe, D. & Twomey, P. (eds.) *Legal Issues of the Maastricht Treaty* (1994, Chancery, Chichester) 13, 31-32

The Court's shaping of Article 5 into a general constitutional principle, far beyond its explicit wording, is emblematic of the Court's self-evolution into a general constitutional court possessed of inherent jurisdiction to ensure the observance of the rule of law in the Community, beyond the Treaty structure of enumerated powers. This may be seen as a response to the fragmentation of Community law in that the Court itself is strengthening its own capacity to supervise the overall structure of the Community, just as, in a specific case of fragmentation, the Court has energetically controlled failure to implement Directives. Justification for the Court's activism lies in the overall aims of the Treaty - the constitutional rule of law.

Accordingly, Article 5 is likely to be vigorously employed by the Court as a basis for an obligation to manage the varying patterns of integration so that the Community structure does not fragment. Where competence is shared, as under the minimum harmonisation formula, this can readily take the concrete form, of, for example, obligations to co-operate and notify. Critically, it is much more difficult to extend this idea into the fields of the 'opt-outs', which represent a denial of Community competence.

V. The Evasion of Pre-emption

It can be seen that as the competences of the Community grew, so its effects on national legal regimes became more heterogeneous. There is a single strand which unites exclusive competence, field-occupation and Article 5 [*10*] EC. By subjecting Member States-Community relations to the jurisdiction of the Court of Justice, all create an institutional structure with the Court of Justice at its apex. It is the Court who has the last say and thus ultimately structures relations between Member States and the Community. Increasingly since the TEU, new patterns of integration are being created which have little or no pre-emptive effect and which marginalise or exclude the Court.

A considerable move away from pre-emption has occurred through the expansion of soft law.[52] This expansion is explicitly provided

---

[52]   On soft law see Chapter 3.

for by the TEU in a number of areas notably in the fields of education,[53] culture,[54] public health[55] and consumer protection[56] The development of subsidiarity has also led to an expansion of soft law in other areas.[57] Soft law cannot be invoked directly before courts, and therefore would seem to have no pre-emptive effect. Some provision is still made for the adjustment of national legal orders and other Community law to soft law. The Court ruled in *Grimaldi*[58] that Recommendations have an interpretative function, as Community instruments and national legislation should, where possible, be interpreted in accordance with them.

A full move away from pre-emption has been made, however, in the other two pillars of the Union, CFSP and JHA. Prior to Amsterdam almost everything which fell within these pillars was non-justiciable and would therefore appear to have little pre-emptive effect.[59] The Court will have competence, following ratification at Amsterdam, to rule on framework decisions, conventions, and their implementing measures, which are adopted under JHA.[60] The pre-emptive qualities of such measures are yet to be determined, however.

Few would consider that a uniform, inflexible legal structure is appropriate for the range of activities now carried out by the Union. Heterodoxy creates its own problems, however. The various policies of the European Union are not self-contained in a way which allows them to be packaged into neatly compartmentalised politico-legal orders.

There are first of all policies which formally straddle two pillars. The most obvious example of this is sanctions. These are adopted by the Council on a qualified majority vote within the framework of the EC Treaty. Yet before these sanctions can be adopted, provision must be

---

[53]   Article 127(4) [*150(4)*] EC.
[54]   Article 128(5) [*151(5)*] EC.
[55]   Article 129(4) [*152(4)*] EC.
[56]   Article 129a(1)(b) [*153(2)(b)*] EC.
[57]   Conclusions of the Edinburgh European Council, EC Bulletin 12-1992, I.19.
[58]   Case 322/88 *Grimaldi v Fonds des Maladies Professionelles* [1989] ECR 4407, [1991] 2 CMLR 265; Case C-188/91 *Deutsche Shell v Hauptzollamt Hamburg-Harburg* [1993] ECR I-363.
[59]   Article L TEU.
[60]   *Article 35(1) TEU.*

made for them through measures adopted by unanimity within the framework of CFSP. The Commission has noted that the unanimity requirement in CFSP has undermined the possibility of sanctions being taken by qualified majority vote within the EC pillar, for dissenting States veto the measures at the CFSP stage.[61]

Policies also spill across pillars in an informal manner. An example of this is immigration of third country nationals which transcends both the EC and JHA. Whilst immigration policy of third country nations primarily falls within JHA,[62] various aspects of it such as visa policy and family members of EC migrants fall within the competence of the EC. In addition, the EC has competence by virtue of Article 238 [*310*] EC to conclude Association Agreements with third countries which can deal, *inter alia*, with matters of immigration. The result was a hotchpotch of a policy. The right to family reunion within a particular Member State depended upon whether one was an EC migrant or not, for that brought one within the EC Treaty. More generally, the rights of third country nationals would vary according to whether their State had signed an Association Agreement with the EC and the terms of that agreement.[63]

There are finally delimitation problems between the different pillars. The most celebrated example concerned visa-free travel for school pupils from third countries who were resident in a Member State. The Commission considered that this was a matter of visa policy and therefore fell within EC competence by virtue of Article 100c EC, which provides for the establishment of a common visa policy. The Council, meanwhile, considered that as this concerned conditions of entry and movement for third country nationals within the Union, it fell within JHA. It duly adopted the measure under that pillar.[64]

---

[61]   EC Commission, *Report for the Reflection Group* (1995, OOPEC, Luxembourg) paras. 131 & 132.

[62]   Article K.1.3 TEU. This will be changed by the entry into force of Amsterdam which will bring it into the EC Treaty, *Article 61(a) EC*.

[63]   For more on this see the Chapter on External Relations in Volume II.

[64]   Decision 94/795 JHA on joint action concerning travel facilities for school pupils form third countries resident in a Member State, OJ 1996, L 327/1. For discussion see Hix, S. & Niessen, J. *Reconsidering European Migration Policies: The 1996 Intergovernmental Conference and the Reform of the*

VI. Differentiated Integration and the Treaty on European Union

i. Towards Increased Differentiation at Maastricht

Maastricht marked an increase in differentiated integration. This has traditionally been described as 'institutional arrangements which permit the differential participation of Member States in certain policy areas'.[65] It thus allows both for a multi-speed Europe, whereby Member States integrate at different paces to one another, and for a multidimensional Europe where Member States integrate in differing areas to one another.

The differentiation pursued at Maastricht was principally an 'à la carte' one with opt-outs being established on an ad hoc basis by Member States developing various forms of exemptions from policies to which they took exception.[66]

The first kind of opt-out can equally be described as an opt-in. It is provided for in Protocols No.11 and 12, on EMU and the United Kingdom and Denmark respectively.

Protocol 11, TEU. 1. The United Kingdom shall notify the Council whether it intends to move to the third stage before the Council makes its assessment...

Unless the United Kingdom notifies the Council that it intends to move to the third stage, it shall be under no obligation to do so.

---

[65] *Maastricht Treaty* (1996, Migration Policy Group, Brussels) 23-24.
Harmsen, R. 'A European Union of Variable Geometry: Problems and Perspectives' (1994) 45 *NILQ* 109, 118. Harmsen calls this 'jurisdictional variability'. He considers that variable geometry also consists of 'structural variability', which involves the applying of differing institutional arrangements to different sectors. Variable geometry is used in its traditional sense here. Whilst the importance of the phenomenon has increased, it is not a new one. Ehlermann, C. 'How Flexible Is Community Law? An Unusual Approach to the Concept of "Two Speeds"' (1984) 82 *Michigan Law Review* 1274.

[66] Europe à la carte is a system of integration under which Member States can pick and choose between different policies. On this see Stubb, A. 'A categorisation of differentiated integration' (1996) 26 *JCMS* 283.

If no date is set for the beginning of the third stage ... the United Kingdom may notify its intention to move to the third stage before 1 January 1998.

10. If the United Kingdom does not move to the third stage, it may change its notification at any time after the beginning of that stage...[67]

Such an opt-out provides a formal mechanism for eventual convergence. It also does not exempt a Member State in that field of policy from other Treaty obligations. British monetary policy, for example, is still subject to the obligations on coordination and on free movement of capital which are contained elsewhere in the Treaty.

Greater detachment is provided by the opt-out secured by the United Kingdom in the field of social policy. This opt-out took the form of a Protocol which established an Agreement signed by the other eleven (now fourteen) Member States setting up a social policy between themselves. The United Kingdom is excluded from the Agreement, and its participation would require a Treaty amendment to which all the other Member States would have to consent. Yet such a route does not take British social policy outside the reach of EC law. Provisions exist elsewhere in the EC Treaty which allow elements of that policy to be introduced in a manner which binds the United Kingdom.[68]

Complete opt-outs from EU policy are only possible where the national area of policy is defined in order that it can be ringfenced against intrusion by the Union. The first example of this is the Protocol which states that nothing in the Treaty shall affect Danish legislation on the acquisition of second homes. The second is Protocol 17 on the Irish abortion laws.[69]

---

[67] Protocol 12 on Denmark and EMU does not contain this last option. Denmark notified at the Edinburgh European Council that it was not going to the third stage.

[68] A good example of this is the 'Working Hours Directive' which was introduced on the basis of Article 118A EC, the health and safety provision. Directive 93/104/EC, concerning the organisation of working time, OJ 1993 L 307/18. See Case C-84/94 *United Kingdom v Council* [1996] ECR I-5755, [1996] 3 CMLR 671.

[69] The background to this Protocol was the judgment of Case C-159/90 *SPUC v Grogan* [1991] ECR I-4685, [1991] 3 CMLR 849. For the follow-up see *Attorney-General v X* [1992] 2 CMLR 277.

Protocol 17. Nothing in the Treaty on European Union or in the Treaties establishing the European Communities, or in the Treaties or Acts modifying or supplementing those Treaties, shall affect the application in Ireland of Article 40.3.3. of the Constitution of Ireland.

The third is in the field of defence. As part of the Edinburgh Agreement enabling Denmark to have a second referendum on the TEU it was stipulated that Denmark would not participate in the elaboration and implementation of those decisions and actions of the Union which have defence implications.[70]

The final feature of à la carte geometry which began to take shape at Maastricht was in the field of economic and monetary policy. It concerned the decision which States are to participate in the third stage of economic and monetary union.

Article 109j(4) *[121(4)]* **EC.** If by the end of 1997 the date for the beginning of the third stage has not been set, the third stage shall start on 1 January 1999. Before 1 July 1998, the Council meeting in the composition of Heads of State or of Government ... shall, acting by a qualified majority and on the basis of the recommendations of the Council ..., conform which Member States fulfill the necessary conditions for adoption of a single currency.

This last form of differentiation is best described as a 'lock-out', for it allows a Member State to be excluded from a policy in which it wishes to participate. The decision is a structured one in that it is taken according to criteria which suggest that State's economy is insufficiently convergent for it to form a monetary union safely with other Member States. Yet it sets a disquieting precedent. For whilst all the other examples of differentiation were attempts to reconcile difference, albeit in an ad hoc manner, differentiation is being used here as a form of imposed exclusion, which creates new forms of association to which not all States of the Union can be members.

---

[70]   Conclusions of the Edinburgh European Council, Annex 1 to Part B: EC Bulletin 12-1992, I.37.

ii. The Continuation of Europe à la Carte at Amsterdam

The phenomenon of Member States securing opt-outs in respect of particular policies continued apace at Amsterdam:

Germany: The weakest opt-out is the German Declaration on public credit institutions obtained by the German Government. This noted that the arrangements for making available a comprehensive and efficient financial infrastructure in its regions is a matter for the organisation of that Member State. The Declaration does not seek a complete opt-out from the EC competition rules, however, as it states that such facilities should not adversely affect conditions of competition to an extent beyond that required to perform their tasks and which is contrary to the interests of the Community. The Declaration sends therefore, at best, an ambiguous signal.

Belgium: Slightly stronger is the Declaration Belgium obtained in relation to the Protocol on Asylum for nationals of EU Member States. The Protocol establishes a presumption that all Member States are safe countries of origin for asylum purposes. The corollary of this is a presumption is established that an application for asylum by a national of another Member State shall be declared inadmissible. The Belgian Declaration states that it will carry out an individual examination of any asylum request made by a national of another Member State in accordance with its obligations under international refugee law. At the very least it suggests therefore every case will be considered on its merits. It seems therefore to exempt Belgium from the Protocol. The difficulty with this argument, however, is the use by Belgium of a Declaration. Declarations can be of interpretive value at best and cannot justify a *contra legem* interpretation of the Protocol which seems to suggest that requests should normally be refused.

United Kingdom and Ireland: More far-reaching are the opt-outs from the new EC Title on Free Movement of Persons, asylum and immigration granted to Ireland and the United Kingdom. The Protocol on the Position of the United Kingdom and Ireland allows for non-participation by those States in the adoption of measures taken under the new Title in the EC Treaty on Visas, Asylum Immigration and Other Policies Related to Free Movement of Persons.[71] It also stipulates that any such measure shall not bind them.[72] Both Member States have been granted two forms of 'opt-in', however. The first allows them to participate in the adoption of any measure by notifying the President of the Council in writing within three months of a proposal.[73] The second applies once a measure has been adopted. Either may notify either the Council or the Commission that it intends to be bound by the measure.[74] Ireland, a reluctant partner to the Protocol, has already indicated in a Declaration that it intends to participate in the adoption of measures pursuant to this Title to the maximum extent compatible with the Common Travel Area.[75]

The Protocol does not deal with the possibility that the Court of Justice might interpret existing provisions, in particular Article 7a EC, to outlaw border controls. A further Protocol, the Protocol on the Application of Certain Aspects of Article 14 EC to the United Kingdom and to Ireland, therefore asserts the United Kingdom's right to exercise frontier controls on any person seeking to enter the United Kingdom.[76] As a corollary it entitles other Member States to impose controls on persons entering from the United Kingdom or Ireland.[77]

Denmark: There is a Protocol on the Position of Denmark.[78] This grants opt-outs both in relation to the Visas, Asylum Immigration and Other Policies Related to Free Movement of Persons and in relation to defence. At any time Denmark may, in accordance with its constitutional requirements, opt in by informing other Member States that it no longer

---

[71] *Protocol to the TEU on the position of the United Kingdom and Ireland, article 1.*
[72] Ibid., *article 2.*
[73] Ibid., *article 3.*
[74] Ibid., *article 4.*
[75] *Declaration to the Final Act by Ireland.*
[76] *Protocol to the EC Treaty on the application of certain aspects of Article 14 EC to the United Kingdom and to Ireland, article 1.*
[77] Ibid., *article 3.*
[78] *Protocol to the TEU on the position of Denmark.*

wishes to avail itself of all or part of the Protocol.[79] In relation to defence, the Edinburgh European Council Decision is reaffirmed. Denmark shall not participate in the adoption or implementation of EU acts with defence implications.[80]

The position in respect of free movement of persons, asylum and immigration is complicated by existing Danish commitments under Schengen and the existing EC Treaty. The consequence is that whilst Denmark shall not participate in the adoption of or be bound by any measures taken under the Title in the EC Treaty,[81] an exception is made in relation to measures determining which nationals must possess a visa and the format of that visa. Denmark is to participate fully in relation to the adoption of these measures and is bound by them.[82]

Special provision is also made in relation to the *Schengen Acquis*.[83] Whilst it is bound by the existing *acquis*, if the Council decides to build upon that *acquis*, Denmark must decide within 6 months whether or not it will implement that decision. If it decides to implement the decision, an obligation will be created binding only in international law. If it decides not to implement the decision, the other Schengen States can consider what appropriate measures should be taken.

iii. Towards a More Generalised Variable Geometry at Amsterdam

a. The Structuring of a Differentiated Europe

In September 1994 two German Parliamentarians, Schäuble and Lammers, published a paper which suggested that the IGC should consider mechanisms which would allow some Member States to integrate at a faster rate when others did not wish to. Flexible or variable integration is different from Europe à la carte as it recognises deeper

---

[79]   Ibid., *article 7.*
[80]   Ibid., *article 6.*
[81]   Ibid., *articles 1 & 2.*
[82]   Ibid., *article 4.*
[83]   Ibid., *article 5.*

underlying differences over the level of integration sought by providing for a more structured separation between a core group of countries seeking greater integration and others more reticent about it. This notion of 'flexible integration' was taken up by the French, German and British Governments and was placed on the IGC agenda at Turin.[84]

The matter proved to be one of the most hotly contested and problematic. There was a danger that any mechanism could breed a 'hard core Europe' which would not only undermine the spirit of cohesiveness and community at heart of integration project but would lead to the exclusion of other Member States and would impair the latter's existing rights and competences under other TEU provisions. The result agreed at Amsterdam was a system hedged with conditions and provisos.

Article 43 TEU. 1. Member States which intend to establish closer co-operation between them may make use of the institutions, procedures and mechanisms laid down by this Treaty and the Treaty establishing the European Communities provided that the co-operation:

(a) is aimed at furthering the objectives of the Union and at protecting and serving its interests;

(b) respects the principles of the Treaties and the single institutional framework of the Union;

(c) is only used as a last resort, where the objectives of the Treaties could not be attained by applying the relevant procedures laid down therein;

(d) concerns at least a majority of Member States;

(e) does not affect the 'acquis communautaire' and the measures adopted under the other provisions of the Treaties;

(f) does not affect the competences, rights, obligations and interests of those Member States which do not participate therein;

---

[84]   On the debate see Stubb, A. 'The 1996 Intergovernmental Conference and the management of flexible integration' (1997) 4 *JEPP* 37, esp. 48-50.

(g) is open to all Member States and allows them to become parties to the cooperation at any time, provided that they comply with the basic decision and with the decisions taken within that framework;

(h) complies with the specific additional criteria laid down in Article 11 of the Treaty establishing the European Community and Article 40 of this Treaty, depending on the area concerned and is authorised by the Council in accordance with the procedures laid down therein.

2. Member States shall apply, as far as they are concerned, the acts and decisions adopted for the implementation of the cooperation in which they participate. Member States not participating in such cooperation shall not impede the implementation thereof by the participating Member States.

Article 44. (1) For the purposes of the adoption of the acts and decisions necessary for the implementation of the cooperation referred to in Article 43, the relevant institutional provisions of this Treaty and of the Treaty establishing the European Community shall apply. However, while all members of the Council shall be able to take part in the deliberations, only those representing participating Member States shall take part in the adoption of decisions. The qualified majority shall be defined as the same proporiotn of the weighted votes of the members of the Council concerned as laid down in Article 205(2) of the Treaty establishing the European Community. Unanimity shall be constituted only by those Council members concerned.

Article 45. The Council and the Commission shall regularly inform the European Parliament of the development of closer cooperation established on the basis of this Title.

These conditions protect against exclusion in a number of ways. The formal rights and competences of non-participating Member States are protected both by the explicit proviso that closer cooperation should not affect them or the *acquis communautaire*. There were also a fear of marginalisation, whereby existing Union processes would become increasingly supplanted by new procedures. This has been accommodated by the requirements that the institutional framework of the Union be respected and that the procedure be used only as measure of last resort. The final worry was one of closure, namely that a hard core elite of Member States would form secretive arrangements which were not open to all. These concerns have been addressed through the requirements that increased cooperation concern at least a majority of Member States and that it be open to all at any time.

Article 43 TEU. is not justiciable, however. The main protection offered is authorisation and further conditions are required before increased cooperation between a select number of States can take place in the EC and JHA pillars.[85] The centrality of this vote of authorisation was underscored by considerable debate as to whether it should be by qualified majority or unanimity. Member States wishing to proceed at a faster pace perceived a unanimity vote as not only allowing more sceptical States the power to continue to obstruct the pace of integration but also granting them the power of veto over arrangements, which, in territorial terms, did not concern them. Less integrationist States, aware of how they could be easily outmanoeuvred in a qualified majority vote, considered that only unanimity could give then sufficient guarantees against exclusion and marginalisation. The compromise agreed was that the vote would normally be taken by qualified majority, but that Member States would retain the right to invoke the Luxembourg Accords.

Article 11 EC. 1. Member States which intend to establish closer co-operation between themselves may be authorised, subject to Articles 43 and 44 of the TEU, to make use of the institutions, procedures and mechanisms laid down by this Treaty, provided that the co-operation proposed:

(a) does not concern areas which fall within the exclusive competence of the Community;

(b) does not affect Community policies, actions or programmes;

(c) does not concern the citizenship of the Union or discriminate between nationals of Member States;

---

[85] The relevant provision in JHA is *Article 40 TEU.* The voting requirements are identical to *Article 11 EC.* There is no requirement of a proposal for closer cooperation from the Commission in regard to the former. In addition, the substantive conditions are looser. Cooperation need only respect the powers of the EC and the objectives of JHA, and have the aim of enabling the Union to develop more rapidly into an area of freedom, security and justice for it to proceed.

(d) remains within the limits of the powers conferred upon the Community by this Treaty;

(e) and does not constitute a discrimination or a restriction of trade between Member States and does not distort the conditions of competition between the latter.

2. The authorisation referred to in paragraph 1 shall be granted by the Council, acting by a qualified majority on a proposal from the Commission and after consulting the European Parliament.

If a member of the Council declares that, for important and stated reasons of national policy, it intends to oppose the granting of an authorisation by qualified majority, a vote shall not be taken. The Council may, acting by a qualified majority, request that the matter be referred to the European Council for decision by unanimity.

Member States which intend to establish closer co-operation as referred to in paragraph 1 may address a request to the Commission, which may submit a proposal to the Council to that effect. In the event of the Commission not submitting a proposal, it shall inform the Member States concerned of the reasons for not doing so.

Once established, increased cooperation operates in much the same way as other areas of the Treaty. Only those Member States participating will vote in the Council, however, with a proportionate rebalancing of the vote where qualified majority is required. Furthermore, any expenditure, except administrative expenditure, will be borne by the participating Member States unless the Council, acting unanimously, decides otherwise.[86]

One example of increased cooperation was taken at Amsterdam. It was the Protocol Integrating the *Schengen Acquis* into the European Union framework. The aim of this *acquis*, to which all States other than the United Kingdom and Ireland are party, seems to be identical to the Area on Freedom, Security and Justice, namely to establish a common immigration policy and an area without internal border of controls. Yet it has set up a far more evolved system of judicial, police and immigration authority cooperation than currently exists within the TEU framework. The Protocol provides that if, within a reasonable period, either the United Kingdom or Ireland have not notified the President of

---

[86]   *Article 44(2) TEU.* See also *Article 40(4) TEU* and *Article 11 (4) EC.*

the Council in writing that they wish to participate, an authorisation for closer cooperation will be deemed to have been given.[87]

Paradoxically the Protocol does not meet the conditions set out in *Article 11 EC*. By providing for the abolition of borders between a number, but not all, of the Member States, it contains a number of features which were problematic. In particular, it was arguable that it discriminated between nationals of Member States and that it affected a Community policy, that of securing an areas of freedom, security and policy. To avoid legal difficulties, it was therefore stated that Article 11 EC was without prejudice to the Protocol integrating the *Schengen Acquis*.[88]

b. Flexibility and Non-Participating States

Both *Articles 11 EC* and *40 TEU* provide specific processes for allowing non-participating States to accede to areas of increased cooperation in the EC and JHA pillars.

Article 11 EC. 3. Any Member State which wishes to become a party to co-operation set up in accordance with this Article shall notify its intention to the Council and to the Commission, which shall give an opinion to the Council within three months of receipt of that notification. Within four months of the date of that notification, the Commission shall decide on it and on possible specific arrangements as it may deem necessary.[89]

The provision is dangerously vague, and the perils of Member States who do not participate in closer cooperation form the State being

---

[87]   *Protocol integrating the Schengen Acquis into the framework of the European Union, article 5(1).*

[88]   *Article 11(5) EC.*

[89]   There is one difference between *Article 40(3) TEU* and *Article 11(3) EC*. In the case of *Article 40(3) TEU* a favourable decision is deemed to be taken within four months of notification unless the Council, acting by qualified majority, decides to hold the application in abeyance. There is no equivalent provision in *Article 11(3) EC*.

permanently locked-out are illustrated by *the Protocol Integrating the Schengen Acquis into the Framework of the European Union*. This states that the United Kingdom and Ireland may at time request to take part in some or all of the *acquis*. It will require a unanimous vote from those participating, however, for them to be allowed to do so.[90] The possibility, therefore, exists, that one State could bar participation indefinitely.

c. The Political Economy of Flexibility

The Amsterdam Treaty does not reflect a complete break from the à la carte differentiation of Maastricht. Whilst providing a future framework for increased cooperation between select numbers of Member States, it its noticeable that this framework governs none of the exceptions sought by individual Member States at Amsterdam. Furthermore, whilst Amsterdam does seek to provide mechanisms which accommodate in a transparent manner the desires for autonomy present in some Member States against those for increased integration in others, it is not clear to what extent it can stop informal processes developing outside the formal Treaty framework evolving in the same manner that the Schengen Agreement developed outside the EC Treaty framework.

The dangers with the development of 'Europe à la carte' are twofold. The first is that the integration process is built upon a system of compromise, with one Member State surrendering policy in an area that is of benefit to others in return for reciprocal concessions. If Member States increasingly opt-out of areas they dislike, there is a danger of the process unravelling, as, increasingly, they offer no reason for others to integrate with them. The second difficulty with 'Europe à la carte' is that it does not address more fundamental differences between Member States about the depth of integrative structure sought.

Indeed, the most significant impact of the flexibility provisions is likely to be in the dynamic they provide and their effect on voting patterns within the Council in those areas in which all Member States

---

[90]   Supra n.87, article 4.

currently participate. One of the features of the debate on economic and monetary union had been that some national governments were more willing to accommodate the integrationist arguments because they were worried about the costs of exclusion. They were thus willing to countenance the 'second-best' option of participation in an arrangement with which they were not happy, considering it preferable to the worse option of exclusion. The impact of the flexibility provisions in those areas where the costs of exclusion are perceived to be high will therefore be to engender a spirit of increased cooperation, even in areas subject to unanimity voting. The opposite pattern occurs, however, in those areas, of which social regulation is the most obvious, where the national government perceives there to be no costs, or even to be benefits, to exclusion. There are not only few incentives for it to accommodate the interests of other government, but, in addition, there are few incentives for the latter to water down their proposals to accommodate the interests of the former. In such areas, incentives provided by flexibility would suggest increased fragmentation.

Harmsen, R. 'A European Union of Variable Geometry: Problems and Perspectives' (1994) 45 _Northern Ireland Law Quarterly_ 109, 129-131

If 'variable geometry' corresponds to deep-seated political trends, it nonetheless also poses significant problems with respect to both the maintenance of system legitimacy and the practical functioning of institutions. As regards the legitimacy of the politico-legal system, extensive recourse to variable institutional structures risks undermining the minimal sense of 'community' necessary for the creation or maintenance of a cohesive political unit. At a more practical level, problems are presented by the coexistence of parallel legal orders as well as by the need to redesign common political institutions in a way which corresponds to jurisdictional variations. Straddling the line between abstract considerations of legitimacy and more practical problems of institutional design, the overall level of systemic complexity further gives cause for concern.

Potential problems of legitimacy most obviously attach to national opt-outs, given that they may easily be perceived as unfairly benefiting a particular Member State. The case of the British Social Protocol opt-out is paradigmatic. As pointedly demonstrated by the so-called 'Hoover Affair' of 1992. British non-participation in the new areas of common social policy rapidly sparks allegations in other Member States of a fundamental inequity. In effect, a situation has been created in which either the UK is allowed to enjoy the perceived relative advantage of lower social costs or the other Member States must accept a lower level of social protection so as not to be a competitive disadvantage. In either case a high corrosive dynamic is produced. The logic of the integration process to date has been very much one of complex political trade-offs resulting in 'package deals' which, though far from seamless webs, ensure a minimum of cohesion. A simple 'agreement to disagree' breaks with even this minimalist search for cohesiveness and, consequently, risks a more general unravelling of the overarching political compromises which define the Community. Indeed, in this light, it is difficult to envisage the UK's social policy opt-out being a workable long-term arrangement. The opening of a substantial breach may perhaps be avoided in the short term only because of a quite limited enthusiasm on the part of the 11 participatory States to move much beyond the level of a declaration of principles.

Graduated integration on the EMU model avoids some of the pitfalls associated with opt-outs of the Social Protocol type. In so far as the graduated EMU model appears to differentiate States on the basis of 'objective' criteria rather than subjective political will it is unlikely to provoke similar sentiments of fundamental unfairness. However, as already became clear when the idea was first mooted by Brandt and Tindemans in the 1970s, graduated integration does threaten to marginalise those States regulated to the 'second tier'. For example, in the specific case of EMU, the fears of the Union's poorer Member States that their transitional 'derogations' may become a form of permanent 'second-class' status have been strongly and repeatedly voiced. In this way, questions of system legitimacy may also be raised. Involuntary exclusion, no less than the perceived inequities of voluntary non-participation, may tear at the fabric of political community.

At the level of institutional practice, the logic of 'variable geometry' poses the problem of co-ordinating parallel legal orders. Jurisdictional variability, by definition, involves the creation of parallel legislative or regulatory regimes. Nevertheless, the differentiation thus admitted must in some way be controlled if it is not to vitiate or distort the core principles upon which the Union is based. This problem was quite explicitly addressed, and in good part resolved, by the negotiators of the EEA Agreement, albeit at the cost of severely limiting the input of the EFTA States into the decision-making process. In worrying contrast, however no mechanism has been envisaged to deal with the potential emergence of competing social policy regimes under the terms of Social Protocol.

'Variable geometry' also presents clear and as yet only partially resolved problems for the structure of the Union's political institutions. Some forms of institutional asymmetry have already been adopted which correspond to the jurisdictional asymmetry accepted as part of the Maastricht process. Thus, for example, the UK has no voting rights on matters decided under the Social Protocol Agreement, with the arithmetic of the qualified majority being adjusted accordingly. Similarly, as noted earlier, Denmark has renounced its right to exercise the Union Presidency when defence matters are under consideration. Nevertheless, other questions raised by such opt-outs remain unresolved. For example, no clear decision has been taken (at the time of writing) concerning the extent to which British MEPs may properly participate in parliamentary deliberations concerning social-policy matters covered by the opt-out. It might also be asked if the Danish renunciation of the Union Presidency with respect to defence matters is at all a viable model for dealing with future opt-outs. If this single case is in itself relatively unproblematic, it is difficult to imagine the operation of an indefinite number of such variations within the rotating structure of the Union Presidency.

It is at this point that considerations of legitimacy and practicality overlap. In part, as suggested by the preceding discussion of institutional mechanics, the limits of variability are set by the practical capacity of a legal or political system to cope with the complexity. However, beyond the internal manageability of the system, attention must also be paid to its external intelligibility. Similarly put, institutional variability, though it may correspond to a very real political necessity, also renders the politico-legal system as a whole exceptionally opaque. For the European Union, already sharply criticised for a relatively low degree of intelligibility, there is a very real danger that further moves down the path of 'variable geometry' will render still more difficult its legitimation in the eyes of often sceptical national publics.

Further Reading

Bieber, R. 'On the Mutual Completion of Overlapping National Legal Systems: The Case of the European Communities and National Legal Systems' (1988) 13 *European Law Review* 147

Dashwood, A. 'The Limits of European Community Powers' (1996) 21 *European Law Review* 113

Dehousse, R. 'Comparing National and EC Law: The Problem of the Level of Analysis' (1994) 42 *American Journal of Comparative Law* 761

Hauser, H. & Müller, A. 'Legitimacy: The Missing Link for Explaining EU-Institution Building' (1995) 50 *Aussenwirtschaft* 17

Ladeur, K-H. 'European Community Institutional Reforms: Extra-National Management as an Alternative Model to Federalism' (1990/1) *Legal Issues of European Integration* 1

Marks, G., Scharpf, F., Schmitter, P. & Streeck, W. *Governance in the European Union* (1996, Sage, London)

Reich, N. 'Competition between legal orders: A New Paradigm of EEC Law' (1992) 29 *Common Market Law Review* 861

Shaw, J. 'European Legal Studies in Crisis? Towards a New Dynamic' (1996) 16 *Oxford Journal of Legal Studies* 231

Stubb. A. 'The 1996 Intergovernmental Conference and the management of flexible integration' (1997) 4 *Journal of European Public Policy* 37

Temple Lang, J. 'The Division of Powers between the Community and Member States' (1988) 39 *Northern Ireland Law Quarterly* 209

----- 'What Powers Should the European Community Have?' (1995) 1 *European Public Law* 97

Usher, J. 'Variable Geometry or Concentric Circles: Patterns for the European Union' (1997) 46 *International and Comparative Law Quarterly* 243

Weatherill, S. *Law and Integration in the European Union* (1996, Clarendon, Oxford) Chapter 5

5. Constitutionalism and the European Communities

I. Introduction

A feature of the late twentieth century has been the growth in public international organisations. The powers, nature and membership of these organisations is diverse, but they all share one common feature - the manner of their creation. All are set up by international treaty. The Communities were no different - set up by the ECSC, EEC and EURATOM Treaties, which were amended, when considered necessary, once again by treaties, notably the Single European Act and the Treaty on European Union.

This common origin has allowed public international lawyers to develop a body of rules for international organisations, the traditional starting point for which is the doctrine of conferred powers.[1] This doctrine asserts that international organisations only have those legal rights and duties which are specified or implicit in their constituent documents and are developed in practice.[2] It thus suggests, first, material limits, set out in the founding treaty, as to what the organisation can do. Secondly, it posits hierarchical relations between the States establishing the organisation and the organisation itself. As the source of the organisation's power is their grant by the Member States, it would appear that the organisation must occupy a subordinate position to those States, as it derives its powers from the pre-existing legal settlement.[3]

---

[1] Schermers, H. & Blokker, N. *International Institutional Law* (1995, 3rd Edition, Kluwer, Dordrecht) 141-142.

[2] e.g. *Reparations for Injuries Suffered in the Service of the United Nations* ICJ Reports (1949) 174, 180.

[3] Schilling, T. 'The Autonomy of the Community Legal Order: An Analysis of Possible Foundations' (1996) 37 *Harvard International Law Journal* 389, 391.

Weiler, J. & Haltern, U. 'The Autonomy of the Community Legal Order - Through the Looking Glass' (1996) 37 *Harvard International Law Journal* 411, 417-419

The European legal order was begotten from public international law in the normal way that these things happen: there was a communion among some Member States - the High Contracting Parties - which negotiated, signed, and subsequently ratified the constituent Treaties that brought into being, first the nascent European Coal and Steel Community and then, its twin siblings, the European Economic Community and Euratom. We know their progeny today as the three-pillared European Union. This manner of conception would, in the normal course of international life, determine the genetic - as well as legal - code of the new infant: an international organisation with a separate legal personality but with no measure of independence or power to eradicate its subordination to its States' parents and its subjection to the classical laws governing the States' treaty relations. The States, like the Olympian gods, would forever remain ultimate Masters of their creation. The Germans have a nice phrase for this: the Member States are called the 'Herren der Verträge'.

This mastery of the States over their offspring does not prevent, as with other Almighties, acts of self-limitation: in the begetting of an international organisation through an international treaty, the High Contracting Parties may decide to bestow on their offspring the power to make decisions that will bind them. They may even privilege a few States in the process. But, at any point, as long as the Member States act in unison, they may change the status or the capacities of the organisation. The basic principles of the law of treaties would apply to privilege the makers of the treaty at all critical junctures in the life of a treaty - treaty-making, amendment, interpretation and termination. As masters of the treaty, states are also masters of the organisation. Thus, for example, not infrequently will states amend a treaty- including one setting up an international organisation - in violation of its specific amendment procedures. As long as the amendment is in accord with the collective will of all parties, it would be considered valid. Likewise, should there be a disagreement over the interpretation of a clause within a treaty, an agreement of all parties will normally be the final word as either an authentic interpretation or a de facto amendment.

There is a different manner in which disparate states may bring into being a new legal order, by 'constitutional' fusion. Birth may take different forms, from constitutional convention to treaty. Arguably each new creature inherits a genetic and legal code altogether different from that of their parents. The constitutive act may explicitly or implicitly extinguish the separate existence of the constituent units to the new creation. Thus, it is sometimes thought that whereas the subjects of a treaty (or a treaty-based international organisation) are the states composing it, the subjects of, say, a federal constitutional order are not only its constituent states, but also its common citizenry. This difference is thought to create a different level of legitimacy for the constitutional order, one where its legitimacy does not come only from the consent of the citizens of those constituent units.

There was little to suggest either in the format of the EC Treaties or in the processes leading to their formation that they did not correspond to the initial model set out by Weiler and Haltern. The drafting of the Treaty was carried out by diplomats and foreign offices rather than legislatures or statutory draughtsmen. The processes of ratification were left up to the independent constitutional processes of each Member State. In the Treaties themselves, there is no express provision stating that they are to have an organic or 'constitutional' character. Indeed, when one examines the Treaties they looked very different from those national constitutions which have developed in the Western liberal tradition. There was no attempt to set out, in a universal manner, a catalogue of civil and political rights; to provide for a delimitation of judicial, legislative and executive functions in the manner that most Member-State constitutions purport to do; or to set out express constitutive principles delineating the exercise of national and Community competences.[4]

Indeed, in the early years, it was assumed that the Communities corresponded to traditional models. In the 1950s the Member States twice sought to amend the European Coal and Steel Community informally, abandoning the formal legal structures set up for amendment in Article 36 ECSC.[5] In 1962 a House of Lords Committee asked to report to the Lord Chancellor on the legal implications of British membership of the European Communities stated:

> **12.** The transfer of legislative power ... does not of course mean, from the point of view of the constitutional law of the United Kingdom, a surrender of any part of the ultimate sovereignty of Parliament. An Act of Parliament applying the Treaties can be repealed by a subsequent Act, and if this happens, the Treaties will cease to be law in this country and the power of the European Council to make regulations having effect as law in this country will come to an end. If we did this without the agreement of other member countries, we would be in

---

[4]   On this see Schilling, T. supra n.3, 393-394.

[5]   Weiler, J. & Modrall, J. 'Institutional Reform: Consensus or Majority' (1985) 10 *ELRev* 316; De Witte, B. 'Rules of Change in International Law: How Special Is the European Community?' (1994) 25 *Netherland Yearbook of International Law* 299.

breach of our international obligations and would be liable to proceedings under public international law.[6]

These assumptions were overturned on 5 February 1963.

Case 26/62 Van Gend en Loos v Nederlandse Administratie der Belastingen [1963] ECR 1, [1963] CMLR 105

Van Gend en Loos had imported a chemical, ureaformaldehyde, from Germany into the Netherlands. The Dutch customs and excise had changed the tariff classification of the chemical thus increasing the amount of import duty payable. Van Gend en Loos argued that this was in breach of Article 12 [25] EC, which prohibited, inter alia, increases in the customs duties which, at that time, applied to trade between Member States. The Netherlands is however a monist State, which allows certain treaties to be invoked before domestic courts independently of national implementing legislation. The Dutch tax court, the Tariefcommissie, before whom this matter came, asked the Court of Justice whether 'Article 12 of the EEC Treaty has direct application within the territory of a Member State, in other words, whether nationals of such a State can on the basis of the Article in question lay claim to individual rights which the courts must protect.'

As the Belgian and Dutch governments observed in their submissions, the question was ambiguous. It could be read as asking, whether as a matter of Dutch domestic law, this was the type of treaty provision which could be invoked before Dutch courts. The Court of Justice could not rule on such a question as it only has jurisdiction over questions of Community law. The Court dismissed this objection, claiming that it was clear from the wording of the question that the Dutch court was asking whether as a matter of EEC law the provision could be invoked in domestic courts. This posed a further problem as there is no rule of international law which *requires* Member States to allow treaty provisions to be invoked before domestic courts. The Court would therefore have to distinguish the EEC Treaty from all other international treaties if it was to answer the question in the affirmative.

To ascertain whether the provisions of an international treaty extend so far in their effects it is necessary to consider the spirit, the general scheme and the wording of those provisions.

---

[6]   Public Record Office LCO 29/108.

The objective of the EEC Treaty, which is to establish a Common Market, the functioning of which is of direct concern to interested parties in the Community, implies that this Treaty is more than an agreement which merely creates mutual obligations between the contracting states. This view is confirmed by the preamble to the Treaty which refers not only to governments but to peoples. It is also confirmed more specifically by the establishment of institutions endowed with sovereign rights, the exercise of which affects Member States and also their citizens. Furthermore, it must be noted that the nationals of the states brought together in the Community are called upon to cooperate in the functioning of this Community through the intermediary of the European Parliament and the Economic and Social Committee .

In addition the task assigned to the Court of Justice under Article 177, the object of which is to secure uniform interpretation of the Treaty by national courts and tribunals, confirms that the states have acknowledged that Community law has an authority which can be invoked by their nationals before those courts and tribunals.

The conclusion to be drawn from this is that the Community constitutes a new legal order of international law for the benefit of which the states have limited their sovereign rights, albeit within limited fields, and the subjects of which comprise not only Member States but also their nationals. Independently of the legislation of Member States, Community law therefore not only imposes obligations on individuals but is also intended to confer upon them rights which become part of their legal heritage. These rights arise not only where they are expressly granted by the Treaty, but also by reason of obligations which the Treaty imposes in a clearly defined way upon individuals as well as upon the Member States and upon the institutions of the Community.

The mind-numbing technicality and arcanity of the subject-matter of the dispute can mask the importance of this judgment. The key to its understanding lies in the phrase 'new legal order of international law for the benefit of which the states have limited their sovereign rights'. Stated more simply, the Court has claimed a sovereign authority for the EEC Treaty. Such a claim breaks from the doctrine of conferred powers, for it no longer sees the basis of Community powers as derived from the Member States but as autonomous and original.[7] For sovereignty is traditionally perceived as having both a dichotomous and a constitutive character:

'in the context of the internal structure of a political society, the concept of sovereignty has involved the belief that there is an absolute power within the community. Applied to problems which arise in the relations between political

---

[7]   The second paragraph cited from the judgment would seem to suggest that the Court considered this to lie in the Community's qualities as a common market.

communities, its function has been to express the antithesis of this argument - the principle that internationally, over and above the collection of communities, no supreme authority exists ...'[8]

During the eighteenth and nineteenth centuries a link was developed between the concept of sovereignty and that of the nation-State.[9] In international relations there was therefore the growth of the State system. Internally, sovereignty was formally vested in national constitutional settlements. Constitutions were therefore considered to have a constitutive nature in that they gave 'origin to a political entity and ... sanction its nature and primary ends'.[10] The assertion of sovereignty in *Van Gend en Loos* is thus essentially a claim that the Treaty has a constitutional character.[11] This point was acknowledged most explicitly in *Opinion 1/91* where it stated:

> ... the EEC Treaty, albeit concluded in the form of an international agreement, none the less constitutes the constitutional charter of a Community based on the rule of law.[12]

---

[8]   Hinsley, F. 'Sovereignty' (1986, Cambridge University Press, Cambridge) 158. The literature on this concept is enormous. Useful starting points are Bartelson, J. *A Geneaology of Sovereignty* (1995, Cambridge University Press, Cambridge); Fowler, M. & Bunck, J. *Law, Power and the Sovereign State. The Evolution and the Application of the Construct of Sovereignty* (1995, Peen State University, Pennsylvania); London Fell.

[9]   Ibid., 60-99. On this see Giddens, A. 'The Nation-State and Violence' (1985, Polity, Cambridge); James, A. *Sovereign Statehood* (1986, Allen & Unwin); Biersteker, T. & Weber, C. (eds.) *State Sovereignty as a Social Construct* (1996, Cambridge University Press, Cambridge)

[10]   Castiglione, D. 'The Political Theory of the Constitution' 5, 8 in Bellamy, R. & Castiglione, D. (eds.) *Constitutionalism in Transformation: European and Theoretical Perspectives* (1996, Blackwell, Oxford).

[11]   For a useful analysis of the utility of 'sovereignty' as a tool of discussion within the context of the European Union see Neuman, M. *Democracy, Sovereignty and the European Union* (1996, St. Martin's Press, New York) 4-15.

[12]   Opinion 1/91, *Re European Economic Area*, [1991] ECR I-6079, [1992] 1 CMLR 245.

Thus began the process of 'constitutionalisation' which was to have both tremendous symbolic value and also enormous formal and socio-political implications for the Communities. For it not only challenges traditional assumptions about sovereignty being the property of the nation-State,[13] but makes the aggressive claim that, at least within the area of its jurisdiction, ultimate political authority lies with the Communities.[14]

II. The Formal Implications of Constitutionalism

i . The Supremacy of EC Law

The narrow point at issue in *Van Gend en Loos* was whether Treaty provisions could be invoked before national courts. The categorisation of the EC Treaty as constituting a new sovereign legal order suggested, however, that final legal authority vested in the EC Treaty and not national constitutions or national legislation.

---

[13]   Stone has observed that it therefore breaks down the distinction between, on the one hand, international regimes governing relations between States and domestic constitutional arrangements governing relations within States, Stone, A. 'What is a Supranational Constitution? An Essay in International Relations Theory' (1996) 56 *Review of Politics* 441, 473-474.

[14]   The literature on constitutionalism is enormous. Starting points include Stein, E. 'Lawyers, Judges and the Makings of a Transnational Constitution' (1981) 75 *AJIL* 1; Hartley, T. 'Federalism, Courts and Legal Systems: the emerging constitution of the EC' (1986) 34 *AJCL* 229; Mancini, G. 'The Making of a Constitution for Europe' (1989) 26 *CMLRev* 595; Lenaerts, K. 'Constitutionalism and the Many Faces of Federalism' (1990) 38 *AJCL* 25; Walker, N. 'European Constitutionalism and European Integration' (1996) *PL* 266; Bellamy, R., Bufacchi, V. & Castiglione, D. (eds.) *Democracy and Constitutional Culture in the European Union* (1995, Lothian Foundation, London); Weiler, J. 'The Reformation of European Constitutionalism' (1997) 35 *JCMS* 97.

Case 6/64 Costa v ENEL [1964] ECR 585, [1964] CMLR 425

In 1962 an Italian Law was passed nationalising the electricity production and distribution industries. Costa, a shareholder of Edison Volta, a company affected by the nationalisation, refused to pay his electricity bill, claiming the nationalisation breached EC law. The matter was referred to the Court of Justice by the national court. The Italian Government claimed the Court had no jurisdiction to rule on the matter, as the Italian domestic legislation was the relevant applicable law, and the Court had no competence to rule upon national law.

The Italian Government submits that the request of the Giudice Conciliatore is 'absolutely inadmissible', inasmuch as a national court which is obliged to apply a national law cannot avail itself of Article 177.

By contrast with ordinary international treaties, the EEC Treaty has created its own legal system which, on the entry into force of the Treaty, became an integral part of the legal systems of the Member States and which their courts are bound to apply.

By creating a Community of unlimited duration, having its own institutions, its own personality, its own legal capacity and capacity of representation on the international plane and, more particularly, real powers stemming from a limitation of sovereignty or a transfer of powers from the States to the Community, the Member States have limited their sovereign rights, albeit within limited fields, and have thus created a body of law which binds both their nationals and themselves.

The integration into the laws of each Member State of provisions which derive from the Community, and more generally the terms and the spirit of the Treaty, make it impossible for the States, as a corollary, to accord precedence to a unilateral and subsequent measure over a legal system accepted by them on a basis of reciprocity. Such a measure cannot therefore be inconsistent with that legal system. The executive force of Community law cannot vary from one State to another in deference to subsequent domestic laws, without jeopardizing the attainment of the objectives of the Treaty set out in Article 5 (2) and giving rise to the discrimination prohibited by Article 7.

The obligations undertaken under the Treaty establishing the Community would not be unconditional, but merely contingent, if they could be called in question by subsequent legislative acts of the signatories. Wherever the Treaty grants the States the right to act unilaterally, it does this by clear and precise provisions (for example Articles 15, 93 (3), 223, 224 and 225). Applications, by Member States for authority to derogate from the Treaty are subject to a special authorization procedure (for example Articles 8 (4), 17 (4), 25, 26, 73, the third subparagraph of Article 93 (2), and 226) which would lose their purpose if the Member States could renounce their obligations by means of an ordinary law.

The precedence of Community law is confirmed by Article 189, whereby a regulation 'shall be binding' and 'directly applicable in all Member States'. This provision, which is subject to no reservation, would be quite meaningless if a state could unilaterally nullify its effects by means of a legislative measure which could prevail over Community law.

It follows from all these observations that the law stemming from the Treaty, an independent source of law, could not, because of its special and original nature, be overridden by domestic legal provisions, however framed, without being deprived of its character as Community law and without the legal basis of the Community itself being called into question.

The transfer by the States from their domestic legal system to the Community legal system of the rights and obligations arising under the Treaty carries with it a permanent limitation of their sovereign rights, against which a subsequent unilateral act incompatible with the concept of the Community cannot prevail. Consequently Article 177 is to be applied regardless of any domestic law, whenever questions relating to the interpretation of the Treaty arise.

A hierarchy of norms was thus established between Community law and national law. The process took two further developments. The first was that if Community law is to take precedence over national law in cases of conflict, then, logically, it has to develop rules to determine when a conflict exists. This was done through the development of the doctrine of pre-emption.[15]

The second development was a jurisdictional one. *Costa* only directly addressed the narrow question of what a national court should do when it finds a conflict between national law and Community law. In many national legal systems, a division of duties is made between national courts which allows only administrative or constitutional courts to strike down administrative or legislative acts respectively. These are procedural rules which do not set out to disapply EC law but merely to allocate to particular national courts the duty of controlling the executive or the legislature. Their effect, however, is that certain courts would not be able to apply EC law if this meant disapplying a national executive or legislative act. This problem could only be resolved if EC law expanded the jurisdiction of such courts by conferring such powers upon them. The effect of this would be that the doctrine of supremacy would no longer be being used merely to regulate conflicts, but would instead be replacing national law with EC law.[16] This, in turn, required the Court

---

[15]   This was discussed earlier, see pp 236-249.

[16]   Weiler, J. 'The Community System: the Dual Character of Supranationalism' (1981) 1 *YBEL* 267, 275.

to address questions of procedure and jurisdiction that it would otherwise have been able to leave wholly within the domain of the domestic legal system.[17]

Case 106/77 Amministrazione delle Finanze dello Stato v Simmenthal [1978] ECR 629, [1978] 3 CMLR 263

The Court of Justice had earlier ruled in a reference sent to it by a Pretore (magistrate) in Susa, Italy that a system of veterinary fees on imports of beef set up by a 1970 Italian law breached Article 12 [25] EC.[18] The Italian magistrate asked whether he was required to disapply the national legislation, a power up until that time only enjoyed by the Italian Constitutional Court.

13. The main purpose of the first question is to ascertain what consequences flow from the direct applicability of a provision of Community law in the event of incompatibility with a subsequent legislative provision of a Member State.

14. Direct applicability in such circumstances means that rules of Community law must be fully and uniformly applied in all the Member States from the date of their entry into force and for so long as they continue in force.

15. These provisions are therefore a direct source of rights and duties for all those affected thereby, whether Member States or Individuals, who are parties to legal relationships under Community law.

16. This consequence also concerns any national court whose task it is as an organ of a Member State to protect, in a case within its jurisdiction, the rights conferred upon individuals by Community law.

17. Furthermore, in accordance with the principle of the precedence of Community law, the relationship between provisions of the Treaty and directly applicable measures of the institutions on the one hand and the national law of the Member States on the other is such that those provisions and measures not only by their entry into force render automatically inapplicable any conflicting provision of current national law but - in so far as they are an integral part of, and take precedence in, the legal order applicable in the territory of each of the Member States - also preclude the valid adoption of new national

---

[17]   In turn the question of what was a court for the purpose of Community had therefore to be addressed, On this see pp 443-447.

[18]   Case 35/76 *Simmenthal v Italian Minister for Finance* [1976] ECR 1871, [1977] 2 CMLR 1.

legislative measures to the extent to which they would be incompatible with Community provisions.

18. Indeed any recognition that national legislative measures which encroach upon the field within which the Community exercises its legislative power or which are otherwise incompatible with the provisions of Community law had any legal effect would amount to a corresponding denial of the effectiveness of obligations undertaken unconditionally and irrevocably by Member States pursuant to the Treaty and would thus imperil the very foundations of the Community.

19. The same conclusion emerges from the structure of Article 177 of the Treaty which provides that any court or tribunal of a Member State is entitled to make a reference to the court whenever it considers that a preliminary ruling on a question of interpretation or validity relating to Community law is necessary to enable it to give judgment.

20. The effectiveness of that provision would be impaired if the national court were prevented from forthwith applying Community law in accordance with the decision or the case-law of the Court.

21. It follows from the foregoing that every national court must, in a case within its jurisdiction, apply Community law in its entirety and protect rights which the latter confers on individuals and must accordingly set aside any provision of national law which may conflict with it, whether prior or subsequent to the Community rule.

22. Accordingly any provision of a national legal system and any legislative, administrative or judicial practice which might impair the effectiveness of Community law by withholding from the national court having jurisdiction to apply such law the power to do everything necessary at the moment of its application to set aside national legislative provisions which might prevent Community rules from having full force and effect are incompatible with those requirements which are the very essence of Community law.

23. This would be the case in the event of a conflict between a provision of Community law and a subsequent national law if the solution of the conflict were to be reserved for an authority with a discretion of its own, other than the court called upon to apply Community law, even if such an impediment to the full effectiveness of Community law were only temporary.

ii. The Development of the Court as an Incipient Constitutional Court

The constitutionalisation of the EC Treaty has immediate institutional implications for the Court of Justice. The authority of a written constitution is dependent upon granting to some central body, normally a constitutional court or council, certain exclusive, formal powers. For, without such a central authority, there is a danger of the polity descending into institutional chaos, as there would be no mechanism to accommodate different organisations' competing and conflicting interpretations of the constitution. The powers granted to a central authority would include:

- the formal power to have the final say over the legal authority of the constitution;
- the power to give rulings on the constitution, which are accepted as final, in so far as they cannot be challenged without a formal amendment to the constitution, and which are to be accepted as authoritative not just between parties to the dispute but by third parties;
- a monopoly over the review of the compatibility of legislative acts with the constitution.

The logic of constitutionalising the EC Treaty was that the Court of Justice would have to claim these powers for itself.[19] Implicit in its claim for the sovereign qualities of the EC legal order is the claim that the Court has what is known in German as the *Kompetenz-Kompetenz*, the final authority to rule on the legal status of the EC Treaty. For if it

---

[19]   On this see Barrington, D. 'Emergence of a Constitutional Court' in O'Reilly, J. (ed.) *Human Rights and Constitutional Law: essays in honour of Brian Walsh* (1992, Dublin, Round Hall Press); Due, O. 'A Constitutional Court for the European Communities' & Jacobs, F. 'Is the Court of Justice of the European Communities a Constitutional Court?' in Curtin, D. & O'Keeffe, D. *Constitutional Adjudication in European Community and National Law* (1992, Butterworths, Dublin);   Rinze, J. 'The Role of the ECJ as a Federal Constitutional Court' (1993) *PL* 426.

did not have that authority, then what was it doing making the claim in the first place? Once again, the Court was more explicit in *Opinion 1/91*.

Opinion 1/91 Re Draft Treaty on a European Economic Area [1991] ECR I-6079, [1992] 1 CMLR 245

In 1991 in Oporto a Treaty was signed between the European Community and the EFTA States setting up a 'European Economic Area' (EEA). The thrust of the agreement was the extension of the EC's *acquis communautaire* on trade and competition law to the EFTA States. The Agreement also set up institutional machinery to ensure sufficient homogeneity of law throughout the EEA. This included the establishment of an EEA Court to settle disputes between the Contracting Parties. The Contracting Parties were defined in the Agreement as the Community, the Member States and the EFTA States. An Opinion was sought under Article 228(1)[*300(1)*] EC as to whether the Agreement was compatible with EC law.[20]

34. This means that, when a dispute relating to the interpretation or application of one or more provisions of the agreement is brought before it, the EEA Court may be called upon to interpret the expression 'Contracting Party', ... in order to determine whether, for the purposes of the provision at issue, the expression 'Contracting Party' means, the Community, the Community and the Member States, or simply the Member States. Consequently, the EEA Court will have to rule on the respective competences of the Community and the Member States as regards the matters governed by the provisions of the agreement.

35. It follows that the jurisdiction conferred on the EEA Court ... is likely adversely to affect the allocation of responsibilities defined in the Treaties and, hence, the autonomy of the Community legal order, respect for which must be assured by the Court of Justice pursuant to Article 164 of the EEC Treaty. This exclusive jurisdiction of the Court of Justice is confirmed by Article 219 of the EEC Treaty, under which Member States undertake not to submit a dispute concerning the interpretation or application of that treaty to any method of settlement other than those provided in the Treaty.

---

[20]   The Agreement was revised and declared compatible with EC law in *Opinion 1/92, Re Draft Treaty on a European Economic Area (No.2)* [1992] ECR I-2821, [1992] 2 CMLR 217.

The second hallmark of a constitutional court, the capacity to make rulings on the constitution which are accepted as authoritative and binding by other courts, has proved more difficult for the Court to establish. Its dependence on national courts to enforce Community law has rendered it unwilling to adopt too hierarchical an attitude vis-à-vis national courts.[21]

The most direct point of contact between national courts and the Court of Justice is through Article 177 [*234*] EC.[22] This provision confers no appellate function upon the Court of Justice but entitles, or in certain cases obliges, national courts to refer questions of EC law to the Court which have been raised in cases before them and are necessary to resolution of the dispute. The Court commented on the status of the answers it gave in *Wünsche*:

> A judgment in which the Court gives a preliminary ruling on the interpretation or validity of an act of a Community Institution conclusively determines a question or questions of Community law and is binding on the national court for the purposes of the decision to be given by it in the main proceedings.[23]

The Article 177 [*234*] EC reference machinery tempers the binding qualities of Court's judgments. In *Da Costa*,[24] a case which involved facts materially identical to those in *Van Gend en Loos*, the Court stated the power given to national courts to refer questions of EC law to the Court of Justice includes the power to refer matters back on which the Court had already given a ruling.[25]

More problematic has been the question of the effects of Court judgments on other courts. An easy answer would be to assert that, as

---

21   For further on this see pp 319.

22   See Chapter 8.

23   Case 69/85 *Firma Wünsche Handelsgesellschaft v Federal Republic of Germany* [1986] ECR 947.

24   Joined Cases 28-30/62 *Da Costa v Nederlandse Belastingadministratie* [1963] ECR 31, [1963] CMLR 224. For further analysis see Toth, A. 'The Authority of Judgments of the European Court of Justice: Binding Force and Legal Effects' (1984) 4 *YBEL* 1.

25   For an example of this see Case 104/79 *Foglia v Novello* [1980] ECR 745, [1981] 1 CMLR 45; Case 244/80 *Foglia v Novello (No.2)* [1981] ECR 3045, [1982] 1 CMLR 585.

the doctrine of stare decisis and precedent do not formally exist in EC law, judgments of the Court of Justice have only a declaratory effect on the state of EC law. Yet, if this were so, Court judgments would have no predictive value whatsoever. This is not the case. The Court follows and cites its previous case law as habitually as courts in jurisdictions which have a formal system of precedent.[26]

The *erga omnes* effects of Court judgments - that is to say the extent to which they bind national courts other than the referring court - are less clear. Whilst some Advocates General have asserted that all Court rulings have general *erga omnes* effects,[27] others have asserted that they do not.[28] The Court, meanwhile, has not ruled, generally, upon this matter. It has ruled, however, on the more limited question of the *erga omnes* effects of judgments which declare an act of a Community Institution, such as a Regulation, Directive or Decision, to be invalid.

Case 66/80 International Chemical Corporation v Amministrazione delle Finanze dello Stato [1981] ECR 1191, [1983] 2 CMLR 593

In a series of judgments the Court had previously declared illegal a Regulation setting the price at which milk powder was to be purchased.[29] The plaintiff, who had not been a party in any of these judgments, sought to recover certain securities which had been demanded on the basis of this Regulation. The tribunal in Rome referred the question whether the findings of invalidity in the previous

---

[26] It has thus stated that its case law definitively settles legal situations, Case C-308/93 *Bestuur van de Sociale Verzekeringsbank* [1996] ECR I-2097, [1996] 2 CMLR 729. On the broader question of precedent see Koopmans, 'Stare Decisis in European Law in O'Keeffe, D. & Schermers, H. (eds.) *Essays in European Law and Integration* (1982, Kluwer, Deventer); Arnull, A. 'Owning up to Fallibility: Precedent and the Court of Justice' (1993) 30 *CMLRev* 247.

[27] e.g. Advocate General Darmon in Case 338/85 *Pardini v Ministerio del Commercio con L'Estero* [1988] ECR 2041; Advocate General Van Gerven in Case 145/88 *Torfaen BC v B & Q* [1989] ECR 765, [1990] 1 CMLR 337.

[28] e.g. Advocate General Lenz in Case 103/88 *Fratelli Constanzo v Milano* [1989] ECR 1839, [1990] 3 CMLR 239.

[29] These were a series of judgments known as the 'Skimmed-Milk Powder' cases. they were Case 114/76 *Bela-Mühle* [1977] ECR 1211, [1979] 2 CMLR 83; Case 116/76 *Granaria* [1977] ECR 1247, [1979] 2 CMLR 83; Joined Cases 119 & 120/76 *Öhmühle Hamburg* [1977] ECR 1269, [1979] 2 CMLR 83.

judgments only bound the national courts, who determined those cases, or whether the rulings applied *erga omnes* and bound all EC courts.

11. The main purpose of the powers accorded to the Court by Article 177 is to ensure that Community law is applied uniformly by national courts. Uniform application of Community law is imperative not only when a national court is faced with a rule of Community law the meaning and scope of which need to be defined; it is just as imperative when the Court is confronted by a dispute as to the validity of an act of the institutions.

12. When the Court is moved under Article 177 to declare an act of one of the institutions to be void there are particularly imperative requirements concerning legal certainty in addition to those concerning the uniform application of Community law. It follows from the very nature of such a declaration that a national court may not apply the act declared to be void without once more creating serious uncertainty as to the Community law applicable.

13. It follows therefrom that although a judgment of the Court given under Article 177 of the Treaty declaring an act of an Institution, in particular a Council or Commission regulation, to be void is directly addressed only to the national court which brought the matter before the Court, it is sufficient reason for any other national court to regard that act as void for the purposes of a judgment which it has to give.

14. That assertion does not however mean that national courts are deprived of the power given to them by Article 177 of the Treaty and it rests with those courts to decide whether there is a need to raise once again a question which has already been settled by the Court where the Court has previously declared an act of a Community institution to be void. There may be such a need in particular if questions arise as to the grounds, the scope and possibly the consequences of the invalidity established earlier.

15. If that is not the case national courts are entirely justified in determining the effect on the cases brought before them of a judgment declaring an act void given by the Court in an action between other parties.

The special status the Court has attached to declarations of invalidity was followed a few years later by a ruling that only it could declare acts of the EC Institutions to be illegal or invalid.[30] In other

---

[30]   As a corollary to its assertion of a monopoly of review over EC acts, the Court has now stated that only it can review EC institutions for failure to act, Case C-68/95 *Port v Bundesanstalt für Landwirtschaft und Ernährung*, [1996] ECRI-6065.

words, it asserted that in relation to acts of the EC Institutions, only it had the powers of review which would normally be exercised by administrative or constitutional courts within domestic jurisdictions.[31]

Case 314/85 Firma Fotofrost v Hauptzollamt Lübeck-Ost [1987] ECR 4199, [1988] 3 CMLR 57

In 1983 the Commission issued a Decision addressed to the German authorities stating that Fotofrost, a trader in photographic goods, would be required to pay import duties on binoculars imported from the eastern part of Germany. Fotofrost challenged the matter before a Hamburg court claiming that the Commission Decision conflicted with the 1957 Protocol on German Internal Trade and was therefore illegal. The Hamburg court referred the question, *inter alia*, as whether it could declare the Commission Decision to be invalid.

12. Article 177 confers on the Court jurisdiction to give preliminary rulings on the interpretation of the Treaty and of acts of the Community institutions and on the validity of such acts. The second paragraph of that Article provides that national courts may refer such questions to the Court and the third paragraph of that Article puts them under an obligation to do so where there is no judicial remedy under national law against their decisions.

13. In enabling national courts, against those decisions where there is a judicial remedy under national law, to refer to the Court for a preliminary ruling questions on interpretation or validity, Article 177 did not settle the question whether those courts themselves may declare that acts of Community institutions are invalid.

14. Those courts may consider the validity of a Community act and, if they consider that the grounds put forward before them by the parties in support of invalidity are unfounded, they may reject them, concluding that the measure is completely valid. By taking that action they are not calling into question the existence of the Community measure.

15. On the other hand, those courts do not have the power to declare acts of the Community institutions invalid. As the Court emphasized in the judgment of 13 May 1981 in Case 66/80 International *Chemical Corporation v Amministrazione delle Finanze* (1981) ECR 1191, the main purpose of the powers accorded to the Court by Article 177 is to ensure that Community law is applied uniformly by national courts. That requirement of uniformity is particularly imperative when the validity of a Community

---

[31]   Bebr, G. 'The Reinforcement of the Constitutional Review of Community Acts under Article 177 EEC Treaty' (1988) 25 *CMLRev* 667.

act is in question. Divergences between courts in the Member States as to the validity of Community acts would be liable to place in jeopardy the very unity of the Community legal order and detract from the fundamental requirement of legal certainty.

16. The same conclusion is dictated by consideration of the necessary coherence of the system of judicial protection established by the Treaty. In that regard it must be observed that requests for preliminary rulings, like actions for annulment, constitute means for reviewing the legality of acts of the community institutions. As the Court pointed out in its judgment of 23 April 1986 in Case 294/83 Parti Ecologiste 'Les Verts' v European Parliament (1986) ECR 1339), 'in Articles 173 and 184, on the one hand, and in Article 177, on the other, the Treaty established a complete system of legal remedies and procedures designed to permit the Court of Justice to review the legality of measures adopted by the institutions'.

17. Since Article 173 gives the Court exclusive jurisdiction to declare void an act of a Community institution, the coherence of the system requires that where the validity of a Community act is challenged before a national court the power to declare the act invalid must also be reserved to the Court of Justice.

18. It must also be emphasized that the Court of Justice is in the best position to decide on the validity of Community acts. Under Article 20 of the Protocol on the Statute of the Court of Justice of the EEC, Community Institutions whose acts are challenged are entitled to participate in the proceedings in order to defend the validity of the acts in question. Furthermore, under the second paragraph of Article 21 of that Protocol the Court may require the Member States and institutions which are not participating in the proceedings to supply all information which it considers necessary for the purposes of the case before it.

19. It should be added that the rule that national courts may not themselves declare Community acts invalid may have to be qualified in certain circumstances in the case of proceedings relating to an application for interim measures; however, that case is not referred to in the national court's question.

iii. The Development of a Liberal Agenda

The establishment of a sovereign legal order did not take place within a vacuum but within a context. The context was that of a common market. A common market is, at least in part, a liberal idea. For its foundations include a number of individual economic freedoms, such as the freedoms to trade and move across borders. The constitutionalisation of the common market therefore had strong ideological overtones. It suggests the entrenchment of a liberal agenda to be enforced by private individuals through the courts.[32]

Chalmers, D. 'Judicial Preferences and the Community Legal Order' (1997) 60 *Modern Law Review* 164, 170

Whilst it is not stipulated anywhere in the EC Treaty that the Court should be guided by a liberal ethos, the objectives of the EC Treaty and the Court's position within its institutional framework militated in favour of such an adoption. The common market being underpinned by a market ideology presupposes a discourse based upon individual rights. Whilst liberal rights, when viewed normatively, guarantee individual freedoms, the protection of individual autonomy they allow, in functional terms, constitutes the institutionalisation of the market economy. Liberalism also serves to entrench the judicial identity of the Court. For liberal ideology perceives the jurisdictional basis of courts to be the protection of individual rights. The centrality of individual rights therefore places courts at the core of any liberal system of governance. When the Europeanisation of its discourse is placed next to its judicial identity, it is not difficult to deduce why, therefore, the Court developed a liberal identity which first manifested itself in *Van Gend en Loos* and which has been strongly present ever since.

---

32   On this see Petersmann, E-U. 'Constitutionalism, Constitutional Law and European Integration' (1991) *Aussenwirtschaft* 233; Mestmäcker, E. 'On the Legitimacy of European Law' (1994) 58 *Rabels Zeitschrift* 615; Streit, M. & Musler, W. 'The Economic Constitution of the European Community: From "Rome" to "Maastricht"' (1995) 1 *ELJ* 5; Petersmann, E-U. 'Proposals for a New Constitution for the European Union: Building Blocks for a Constitutional Theory and Constitutional Law of the EU'(1995) 32 *CMLRev* 1123; Ball, C. 'The Making of a Transnational Capitalist Society: The Court of Justice, Social Policy, and Individual Rights under the European Community's Legal Order' (1996) 37 *Harvard International Law Journal* 307.

iv. Fundamental Rights

a. The Incorporation of Fundamental Rights into the Community Legal Order

The granting of individual rights to private parties invocable in domestic courts has made the European Union less remote from the population than most international organisations. Individuals are given a part in the government of the European Union and protected by the Union regime in a manner which does not occur in those traditional international organisations modelled along inter-State bargains.[33]

There is a difficulty, however. In normative terms the Court has constitutionalised the EC Treaty by suggesting it enjoys a higher legal status to that enjoyed by national constitutions. Yet the EC Treaty does not resemble those Western Constitutions, developed in the republican tradition. These establish a series of reciprocal claims between the State and citizen which are formalised into a series of legally entrenched civil and political rights protected from legislative and executive infringement.[34] The EC Treaty, however, contains a number of economic rights but only very limited civil, political and social rights. As Weiler has observed, in these circumstances, the constitutionalisation of the EC Treaty has only a limited emancipating effect. To argue that the EC Treaty, or even secondary legislation, must be applied in national courts is an empty statement if the Treaty and secondary legislation gives individuals very little. It is, in essence, the granting of a 'constitution without constitutionalism'.[35]

---

[33]   Mancini, F. & Keeling, D. 'Democracy and the European Court of Justice' (1994) 57 *MLR* 175, 182 *et seq.*; Szyszczak, E. 'How to Make Europe more Relevant to Its Citizens: Effective Judicial Process' (1996) 21 *ELRev* 556.

[34]   See Bellamy, R. 'The Political Form of the Constitution: the Separation of Powers, Rights and Representative Democracy' in Bellamy, R. & Castiglione, D. (eds.) *Constitutionalism in Transformation: European and Theoretical Perspectives* (1996, Blackwell, Oxford).

[35]   Weiler, J. 'European Neo-constitutionalism: in Search of Foundations for the European Constitutional Order' 105, 106 in Bellamy, R. & Castiglione, D.

This problem was initially not acknowledged by the Court, for it was initially extremely reticent about developing fundamental rights which were not explicitly mentioned in the EC Treaty. In a series of early judgments it refused to countenance arguments based on the alleged breach by the Community Institutions of some right which was protected in national constitutions.[36]

Towards the end of the 1960s the Court softened its approach slightly, by admitting a secondary, interpretive role for such rights. In *Van Eick* the Court stated that EC Institution staff disciplinary procedures had to be exercised:

> 'bound in the exercise of [their] powers to observe the fundamental principles of the law of procedure'.[37]

It was more explicit still in *Stauder*.[38] In that instance the Commission adopted a Decision designed to reduce Community butter stocks by allowing butter to be sold at a reduced price to people who were on certain social welfare schemes. To claim the butter the beneficiaries had to produce a coupon which, in the German and Dutch version, had to indicate their name but which, in the French and Italian versions, merely needed to refer to them. Stauder, a German national, challenged the requirement that his name be on the coupon, claiming that it violated his right to respect for privacy. When the question was referred to the Court as to which language version should prevail, the Court indicated that, looking at the objective of the decision, the more liberal French and Italian version should be adopted. It then stated:

> 'Interpreted in this way the provision at issue contains nothing capable of prejudicing the fundamental human rights enshrined in the general principles of Community law and protected by the Court.'

(eds.) *Constitutionalism in Transformation: European and Theoretical Perspectives* (1996, Blackwell, Oxford).

[36] Case 1/58 *Stork v High Authority* [1959] ECR 17; Joined Cases 36,37,38 & 40/59 *Geitling v High Authority* [1960] ECR 423; Case 40/64 *Sgarlata v Commission* [1965] ECR 215, [1966] CMLR 314.

[37] Case 35/67 *Van Eick v Commission* [1968] ECR 329.

[38] Case 29/69 *Stauder v City of Ulm* [1969] ECR 419, [1970] CMLR 112.

Human rights still occupied no more than a soft role in Community law. References in both *Van Eick* and *Stauder* can be seen as no more than rhetorical flourishes which were in no sense central to the decisions taken by the Court in each instance. Whilst stressing the consonance between EC law and established notions of fundamental rights regimes, the Court did not grant these fundamental rights an organic status which would allow them to be used both as a basis for steering the actions of public authorities and as a ground for judicial review.

The absence of individual guarantees in EC law threatened, however, the very supremacy of EC law so boldly asserted by the Court of Justice. For if EC law did not offer similar safeguards of fundamental liberties to those found in national constitutions, it would lead to situations arising where national courts would be given a choice between either refusing to apply Community law or forsaking fundamental liberties enshrined in their national constitutions.[39] It was therefore no surprise that in the first judgment where the Court had to deal with the relationship between EC law and provisions of a national constitution, it also had to reconsider the place of fundamental rights within the EC legal order.

Case 11/70 Internationale Handelsgesellschaft v Einfuhr- und Vorratstelle für Getreide und Futtermittel [1970] ECR 1125, [1972] CMLR 255

Under an EC Regulation Internationale Handelsgesellschaft had been awarded a licence to export maize on condition that it set down a deposit which would be forfeited if it failed to export the maize within the time stipulated in the licence. Upon forfeiture Internationale Handelsgesellschaft challenged the Regulation before the administrative court in Frankfurt. The court considered that the Regulation violated the provisions in the German Constitution which protected the freedom to trade and required all public action to be proportionate.

3. Recourse to the legal rules or concepts of national law in order to judge the validity of measures adopted by the institutions of the Community would have an adverse effect on the uniformity and efficacy of Community law. The validity of such measures can only be

---

[39]   Scheuner, U. 'Fundamental Rights in European Community Law and in National Constitutional Law' (1975) 12 *CMLRev 171*, 173-174.

judged in the light of Community law. In fact, the law stemming from the Treaty, an independent source of law, cannot because of its very nature be overridden by rules of national law, however framed, without being deprived of its character as Community law and without the legal basis of the Community itself being called in question. Therefore the validity of a Community measure or its effect within a Member State cannot be affected by allegations that it runs counter to either fundamental rights as formulated by the constitution of that State or the principles of a national constitutional structure.

4. However, an examination should be made as to whether or not any analogous guarantee inherent in Community law has been disregarded. In fact, respect for fundamental rights forms an integral part of the general principles of law protected by the Court of Justice. The protection of such rights, whilst inspired by the constitutional traditions common to the Member States, must be ensured within the framework of the structure and objectives of the Community. It must therefore be ascertained, in the light of the doubts expressed by the Verwaltungsgericht, whether the system of deposits has infringed rights of a fundamental nature, respect for which must be ensured in the Community legal system.

The development of guarantees in EC law to protect fundamental rights as a *quid pro quo* for acceptance of the precedence of EC law over even national constitutions would be transparent even were it not for the juxtaposition of the two in the judgment. Why else would the Court refer to national constitutions - many of which are impoverished and outdated sources of fundamental rights? Indeed, there is consensus amongst both the proponents and opponents of the Court that the threat to the supremacy of Community law provided the context and, certainly to a partial extent, the rationale for the incorporation of fundamental rights in the EC legal order.[40] Yet merely to perceive the development of fundamental rights as part of some introverted discourse between the

---

[40]   e.g. Mancini, G. 'A Constitution for Europe' (1989) 26 *CMLRev* 595, 611; Coppell, J. & O'Neill, A. 'The European Court of Justice: Taking Rights Seriously?' (1992) 29 *CMLRev* 669, 672. It should be noted, however, that members of the Court had been considering the question of fundamental rights separately from the question of supremacy for some time. See Pescatore, P. 'Les droits de l'homme et l'intégration européenne' (1968) 4 *CDE* 629; Pescatore, P. 'Fundamental Rights and Freedoms in the System of the European Communities' (1970) 18 *AJCL* 343.

national courts and the Court of Justice is to obscure their integrative and disintegrative potential.[41]

Clapham, A. 'A Human Rights Policy for the European Community' (1990) 10 *Yearbook of European Law* 309, 311

Talking about human rights may sometimes bestow identity on Community citizens. This has a subjective dimension with citizens finding they have rights in common; as well as containing an objective perspective with the discovery of a common concern about the rights of others (inside or outside the Community). Where these rights move beyond 'God-given' or 'self-evident' rights they result in an intense 'contract' or relationship with the right giver. Should the Community realize its role in distributing rights to Community citizens it could expect some increased loyalty. However such a symbiotic relationship could only occur should the Community respond to the demands of its citizens rather than reinforcing rights which are primarily geared to its own objectives.

Clearly, rights have an important role to play in the process of European Integration, but, it must be said that they may well operate as a double-edged sword. Not only are they a cohesive force but they may well be divisive. Should the Community move to tackle questions such as divorce, contraception, abortion, blasphemy, surrogacy, etc., rights might no longer be handy tools for integration but vehicles of division and disintegration. Furthermore, not only will moral diversity have to be tolerated in the move towards unity, but it is clear that effective rights to challenge Community decisions or provisions could well slow up or completely ensnare new initiatives or progress at the Community level.

b. The Application of Fundamental Rights Within the Community Legal Order

Simple resort to the rhetoric of fundamental rights will not, however, have any of the effects claimed above for fundamental rights. The proof

---

[41] On this debate see also Kunhardt, L. 'European Courts and Human Rights' in Greenberg, D. (ed.) *Constitutionalism and Transitions in the Contemporary World* (1993, OUP, New York); Bellamy, R. 'The Constitution of Europe: Rights or Democracy' in Bellamy, R. Bufacchi, V. Castiglione, D. (eds.) *Democracy and Constitutional Culture in the Union of Europe* (1995, Lothian Foundation Press, London).

of the pudding is in the application. In *Internationale Handelsgesellschaft*, for example, the Court of Justice, having stated that acts of the Community Institutions must respect fundamental rights, went on to claim that no fundamental right had been breached. The matter was taken, further, before the German Constitutional Court, which stated that it would disapply EC law if it violated fundamental rights protected in the German Constitution, although it did not find this to be the case in that instance.[42] The matter was further complicated by a similar assertion being made by the Italian Constitutional Court.[43] Indeed, this line of authority has continued in both jurisdictions to this day.[44] The clear assertion that EC law can be reviewed by national courts for its compatibility with rights contained in the latter's constitutions implied that the Court of Justice could only be assured of the continued supremacy of EC law if it applied fundamental rights in a manner that was at least as protective of individual liberties as the jurisprudence of those courts.

Speculation thus arose as to whether the Court would adopt a 'maximalist approach' to fundamental rights, namely whether it should protect any fundamental right mentioned in the constitution of any

---

[42] *Internationale Handelsgesellschaft mbH v Einfuhr und Vorratstelle für Getreide und Futtermittel* [1974] 2 CMLR 540.

[43] *Frontini v Ministero delle Finanze* [1974] 2 CMLR 372. On these judgments see Edeson, W. & Wooldridge, F. 'European Community Law and Fundamental Human Rights: Some Recent Decisions of the European Court and National Courts' (1976/1) *LIEI* 1; De Witte, B. 'Community Law and National Constitutional Values' (1991/2) *LIEI* 1.

[44] In Italy see *Fragd v Amministrazione delle Finanze*, Decision 232 of 21 April 1989, (1989) 72 RDI. For comment see Gaja, G. 'New Developments in a Continuing Story: The Relationship between EEC Law and Italian Law' (1990) 27 *CMLRev* 83. For recent developments in Germany see Reich, N. 'Judge-Made "Europe à la carte": Some Remarks on Recent Conflicts between European and German Constitutional Law provoked by the Bananas Litigation' (1996) 7 *EJIL* 103; Everling, U. 'Will Europe Slip on Bananas? The Bananas Judgment of the Court of Justice and National Courts' (1996) 33 *CMLRev* 401; Zuleeg, M. 'The European Constitution under Constitutional Constraints: The German Scenario' (1997) 22 *ELRev* 19, 33-34.

Member State.[45]   If the supremacy of EC law were to be protected throughout the Union, such an approach would be necessary, as was suggested by Advocate General Warner:

'No Member State can, in my opinion, be held to have included in its partial transfer of sovereignty to the Community power for the Community to legislate in infringement of rights protected by its own Constitution. To hold otherwise would involve attributing to a Member State the capacity, when ratifying the Treaty, to flout its own Constitution.'[46]

Yet to draw-up a broad ever-expanding list of fundamental rights undermines these rights' fundamentality. Furthermore, it supposes a political consensus which may be lacking in a society as diverse as that within the European Union. There is no mechanism therefore for societies with conflicting constitutional provisions. For to address questions of fundamental rights in terms of institutional politics obscures and trivialises the underlying roots which give fundamental rights their rhetorical and emotional resonance.

Weiler, J. 'Fundamental Rights and Fundamental Boundaries: On Standards and Values in the Protection of Human Rights' 51, 52-53 in Neuwahl, N. & Rosas, A. *The European Union and Human Rights* **(1995, Martijnus Nijhoff, The Hague)**

I think the appeal of rights has to do with two roots. The first of these two roots regards fundamental rights (and liberties) as an expression of a vision of humanity which vests the deepest values in the individual which, hence, may not be compromised by anyone. Probably one of the oldest and most influential sources of this vision is to be found in the Pentateuch: *And God created man in His own image, in the image of God created He him.* (Gen. I:27). With this trademark, what legislator has the authority to transgress the

---

[45]   On this see Mendelson, M. 'The European Court of Justice and Human Rights' (1981) 1 *YBEL* 125, 153-156; Clapham, A. 'A Human Rights Policy for the European Community' (1990) 10 *YBEL* 309, 331-332; Weiler, J. 'Fundamental Rights and Fundamental Boundaries: On Standards and Values in the Protection of Human Rights' 51, 56-66 in Neuwahl, N. & Rosas, A. *The European Union and Human Rights* (1995, Martijnus Nijhoff, The Hague).

[46]   Case 7/76 *IRCA* [1976] ECR 1213, 1237.

essential humanity of the species? Naturally, there are secular, humanist parallels to this vision a plenty.

The other root for the great appeal of right, and part of the justification, even if counter-majoritarian, looks to them as an instrument for the promotion of the *per se* value of putting constraints on power. Modern democracy emerges, after all, also as a rejection of absolutism - and absolutism is not the prerogative of kings and emperors. Similar sentiments inform the great appeal of fundamental boundaries in non-unitary systems such as federal states and the European Union. I use the term Fundamental Boundaries as a metaphor for the principle of enumerated powers or limited competences which are designed to guarantee that in certain areas communities (rather than individuals) should be free to make their own social choices without interference from above. If you wish, if fundamental rights are about the autonomy and self-determination of the individual, fundamental boundaries are about the autonomy and self-determination of communities. The appeal of fundamental boundaries rests as well on two parallel roots. First as an expression of a vision of humanity which vests the deepest values in communities (potentially existing within larger polities) which, thus, must be protected. This Community vision of humanity derives from an acknowledgement of the social nature of humankind, as a counterbalance to the atomistic view of the individual which is reflected in the concept of individual rights and liberties. It too finds a powerful Biblical expression in the Pentateuch: *And the Lord God said: It is not good that man should be alone* (Gen. II:18). Fundamental boundaries around communities-of-value become the guarantee against existential aloneness - the protection of the *Gemeinschaft* against the *Gesellschaft*. Its second root is a reflection at the level of social organisation of that same *per se* value of non-aggregation of power. Fundamental boundaries constitute and thus ensure different realms of power.

Even if the motivations for the development of fundamental rights were a cynical attempt to secure the precedence of EC law, such an attempt would only be successful if it pulled on these very same structures which gave fundamental rights such a powerful social presence within the respective national systems. This required, at the very least, that the Court place its cards on the table and explain what vision of humanity and which central values provided the inspiration for its development of fundamental rights. For if these rights were to confer legitimacy on the EC, at their heart there must be set out an autonomous Community vision of human values or principles, which had organic qualities of their own and were not parasitic on the content of various national instruments.

Case 44/79 Hauer v Land Rheinland-Pfalz [1979] ECR 3727, [1980] 3 CMLR 42

Miss Hauer was refused authorisation to plant vines on her land by the authorities in Rhineland Pfalz, Germany. One of the bases for this decision was a 1976 EC Regulation which imposed a three year prohibition on the planting of new vines. She challenged the decision before a German administrative court which considered that the Regulation might violate her rights to property and to pursue a trade, as protected under the German constitution.

14. As the Court declared in its judgment of 17 December 1970, *Internationale Handelsgesellschaft* (1970) ECR 1125, the question of a possible infringement of fundamental rights by a measure of the Community institutions can only be judged in the light of Community law itself. The introduction of special criteria for assessment stemming from the legislation or constitutional law of a particular Member State would, by damaging the substantive unity and efficacy of Community law, lead inevitably to the destruction of the unity of the Common Market and the jeopardizing of the cohesion of the Community.

15. The Court also emphasized in the judgment cited, and later in the judgment of 14 May 1974, *Nold* (1974) ECR 491, that fundamental rights form an integral part of the general principles of the law, the observance of which it ensures; that in safeguarding those rights, the Court is bound to draw inspiration from constitutional traditions common to the Member States, so that measures which are incompatible with the fundamental rights recognized by the Constitutions of those States are unacceptable in the Community; and that, similarly, international treaties for the protection of human rights on which the Member States have collaborated or of which they are signatories, can supply guidelines which should be followed within the framework of Community law. That conception was later recognized by the joint declaration of the European Parliament, the Council and the Commission of 5 April 1977, which, after recalling the case-law of the Court, refers on the one hand to the rights guaranteed by the constitutions of the Member States and on the other hand to the European Convention for the Protection of Human Rights and Fundamental Freedoms of 4 November 1950.

The effect of this development is well illustrated by *Orkem*. The establishment of certain organic Community principles, in this instance the rights of defence, as the underlying basis for the Court's reasoning resulted in a right being developed, protection against self-incrimination in competition proceedings, which was not present in either national constitutional traditions or international human rights treaties.[47]

Joined Cases 374/87 & 27/88 Orkem SA & Solvay v Commission [1989] ECR 3283, [1991] 4 CMLR 502

The applicants sought to annul a Decision taken by the Commission after an inquiry into the existence of anti-competitive practices in the thermoplastics industry. Under Article 11 of Regulation 17 the Commission is entitled to request, or even require, undertakings it is investigating to supply information. In this instance the undertakings complained that the Commission used this power to force the undertakings to incriminate themselves.

18. The applicant claims, essentially, that the Commission used the contested decision to compel it to incriminate itself by confessing to an infringement of the competition rules and to inform against other undertakings. By doing so, the Commission has, in its view, infringed the general principle that no one may be compelled to give evidence against himself, which forms part of Community law in so far as it is principly upheld by the laws of the Member states, by the European Convention for the Protection of Human Rights and Fundamental Freedoms of 4 November 1950 ... and by the International Covenant on Civil and Political Rights of 19 December 1966 ... It has thus, in the applicant's view, infringed the rights of the defence.

.....

28. In the absence of any right to remain silent expressly embodied in Regulation No 17, it is appropriate to consider whether and to what extent the general principles of Community Law, of which fundamental rights form an integral part and in the light of which all Community legislation must be interpreted, require, as the applicant claims, recognition of the right not to supply information capable of being used in order to establish against the person supplying it, the existence of an infringement of the competition rules.

---

47   Lenaerts, K. 'Fundamental Rights to be Included in a Community Catalogue' (1991) 16 *ELRev* 367, 381-382; Clapham, A. 'A Human Rights Policy for the European Community' (1990) 10 *YBEL* 309, 336-337. The position has now been revised under the European Convention on Human Rights and Freedoms by *Funke v France*, Series A, No. 256A. For comment see Van Overbeek, W. 'The Right to Remain Silent in Competition Investigations' (1994) 15 *ECLR* 127.

29. In general, the laws of the Member States grant the right not to give evidence against oneself only to a natural person charged with an offence in criminal proceedings. A comparative analysis of national law does not therefore indicate the existence of such a principle, common to the laws of the Member States, which may be relied upon by legal persons in relation to infringements in the economic sphere, in particular infringements of competition law.

30. As far as Article 6 of the European Convention is concerned, although it may be relied upon by an undertaking subject to an investigation relating to competition law, it must be observed that neither the wording of that Article nor the decisions of the European Court of Human Rights indicate that it upholds the right not to give evidence against oneself.

31. Article 14 of the International Covenant, which upholds, in addition to the presumption of innocence, the right (in paragraph 3(g)) not to give evidence against oneself or to confess to guilt, relates only to persons accused of a criminal offence in court proceedings and thus has no bearing on investigations in the field of competition law.

32. It is necessary, however, to consider whether certain limitations on the Commission's powers of investigation are implied by the need to safeguard the rights of the defence which the Court has held to be a fundamental principle of the Community legal order (Judgment of 9 November 1983 in Case 322/82 *Michelin v Commission* (1983) ECR 3461, paragraph 7).

33. In that connection, the Court observed recently, in its judgment of 21 September 1989 in Joined Cases 46/87 and 227/88 *Hoechst v Commission* (1989) ECR 2859, paragraph 15, that whilst it is true that the rights of defence must be observed in the administrative procedures which may lead to the imposition of penalties, it is necessary to prevent those rights from being irremediably impaired during preliminary inquiry procedures which may be decisive in providing evidence of the unlawful nature of the conduct engaged in by undertakings and for which they may be liable. Consequently, although certain rights of the defence relate only to contentious proceedings which follow the delivery of the statement of objections, other rights must be respected even during the preliminary inquiry.

34. Accordingly, whilst the Commission is entitled, in order to preserve the useful effect of Article 11(2) and (5) of Regulation No 17, to compel an undertaking to provide all necessary information concerning such facts as may be known to it and to disclose to it, if necessary, such documents relating thereto as are in its possession, even if the latter may be used to establish, against it or another undertaking, the existence of anti-competitive conduct, it may not, by means of a decision calling for information, undermine the rights of defence of the undertaking concerned.

35. Thus, the Commission may not compel an undertaking to provide it with answers which might involve an admission on its part of the existence of an infringement which is incumbent upon the Commission to prove.

There has, as a result, been a heated debate surrounding the ethical values which have provided the backdrop to the development of these fundamental rights. The principal criticism has been that the doctrine has been used to protect not just civil liberties but also economic rights, such as the right to trade and the right to own property.[48] From this common starting point critics have parted company. Phelan has argued that by market concerns being placed on an equal plane to civil liberties, the latter are diminished. They no longer enjoy a privileged status over all other interests and there will inevitably be circumstances where market freedoms will be balanced against civil liberties - a process which is unsuited to the protection of civil liberties.[49]

Coppell and O'Neill have gone further and argued that the Court never took fundamental rights (sic) seriously. They were only used instrumentally by the Court to temper resistance to market integration, and that, in practice, wherever a conflict has arisen between the pressures of market integration and civil liberties, the former has triumphed.[50]

As Weiler and Lockhart have observed, when a panoramic view of the Court's case law is taken, there is little evidence to support the last contention.[51] The argument that market values should not be placed on the same pedestal as civil values is less easy to dismiss.

There are a number of longstanding objections. The first, derived

---

[48] Which interests are protected will be dealt with in Chapter 10.

[49] See Phelan, D.'Right to Life of the Unborn v. Promotion of Trade in Services: The European Court of Justice and the Normative Shaping of the European Union' (1992) 55 *MLR* 670. The example of this which is cited is Case C-159/90 *Society for the Protection of the Unborn Child v Grogan* [1991] ECR I-4685, [1991] 3 CMLR 849.

[50] Coppell, J. & O'Neill, A. 'The European Court of Justice: Taking Rights Seriously' (1992) 29 *CMLRev* 669.

[51] Weiler, J. & Lockhart, N. '"Taking Rights Seriously" Seriously: The European Court and Fundamental Rights Jurisprudence - Part I' (1995) 32 *CMLRev* 51; Weiler, J. & Lockhart, N. '"Taking Rights Seriously" Seriously: The European Court and Fundamental Rights Jurisprudence - Part II' (1995) 32 *CMLRev* 579.

from the neo-Marxist critique of capitalism, stems from the dual nature of the market economy. In such an economy trade can only occur as a result of the specialisation brought about by the division of labour. A concomitant of the freedom to trade is the subordination of labour to employment relations which are hierarchical in nature, commodify human beings and can lend themselves to exploitation and abuse.[52] In the post-Marxist tradition it is also argued that the market enterprise is inherently unstable. The market can only exist autonomously without supporting mechanisms if there is a strict correlation between the accumulation of private capital and an increase in 'social wealth'. This could only occur if the holder of any private capital relinquished a corresponding share of any increase in that capital. Evidence that this does not happen takes the form of the competition process, which leads to the weakening and bankruptcy of other holders of capital, and unemployment.[53] Other social and political institutions have therefore to be developed to accommodate this failure. Both these objections focus on the market's potentially exploitative qualities. Weber has also criticised its suppressive qualities:

> 'The market community as such is the most impersonal relationship of practical life into which humans can enter with one another. This is not due to the potentiality of struggle among the interested parties which is inherent in the market relationship ... The reason for the impersonality of the market is its matter-of-factness, its orientation to the commodity and only to that. Where the market is allowed to follow its own autonomous tendencies, its participants do not look towards the persons of each other but only towards the commodity; there are no obligations of brotherliness or reverence, and none of those spontaneous human relations that are sustained by personal unions.'[54]

---

[52]   An outstanding example of this critique is Polanyi, K. *The Great Transformation* (1957, Beacon Hill, Boston).

[53]   Habermas, J. *Legitimation Crisis* (1973, Beacon Press, Boston) 24-31.

[54]   Weber, M. *Economy and Society: Volume 2* (1968, translated by Roth, G. & Wittich, C., Bedminster, New York) 636.

A further twist has been added by Ward who has argued that debate about the ethics of the market is misplaced within this context and misunderstand the nature of legal reasoning.

Ward, I. 'Making Sense of Integration: A Philosophy of Law for the European Community' (1993) 17 *Journal of European Integration* 101, 128-129 & 132-133

Unlike pure ethics, the subjective and practical nature of legal problems established, in one sense, a peculiar dimension. Thus legal hermeneutics, like theological hermeneutics, in order to avoid radical interpretive contingency, demanded a particular, synthetic *a priori*, conceptual determination. In other words, a particular 'method'. Yet, at the same time, the legal problem retains its essentially hermeneutic nature. At root, Gadamer stressed that legal hermeneutic interpretation, like any other form of hermeneutics, was historical. This 'historical consciousness' both presented the unavoidable contingency of the legal text - which can be any material from which a judge derives meaning - but at the same time trains it, such that 'the recognition of the meaning of a legal text and its application in a particular legal instance are not separate actions, but one process.'[55] The task of hermeneutics, like that of the judge, is to emphasise a unit of reasoning, or integrity of reasoning. A judge cannot, and should not, try to avoid the 'prejudices' which he or she inherits from the text or the immediate legal situation. Interpretation and reasoning is always an interface of text, text author and text reader. The 'constraint' which lies on the hermeneutically aware judge is the demand of integrity or 'fidelity to the text,' in other words, the desirability of interpreting and reasoning in complete faith with the 'purpose' of text, as 'understood' in the immediate historical circumstance.

.....

To suggest that the right to life, or any other ethical position, could be a 'legal norm,' is to completely misunderstand the nature of what a rights-based philosophy of law is. Moral and legal norms are rationally quite distinct. Similarly, when the same person suggests that the decision in the *Grogan* case showed that the European Court 'adopted an approach with enormous moral implications by a recharacterisation of the rights issue, based on economic principle which denies the validity of the Irish constitutional position in the EC,' it might be better argued that the European Court gave a ruling which the judicial order of the Community demanded. If there are unpalatable moral implications, then it is for politicians to rectify the problem, and to redesign the political order. It is not an excuse for lawyers to strip down the legal order, and rebuild it in someone's particular ethical image. This is the unavoidable truth which drove Kant to produce his third *Critique* and to set the philosophical tone for the following two centuries. Any

---

55   Gadamer, H-G. *Truth and Method* (1975, London) 276.

substantive ethics is built in someone's image. To suggest that the Community's ethics are not really 'fundamental' is to seize the obvious. Of course, they are not 'fundamental.' There are no fundamental ethics to be challenged. At best, there are ethics contingently established, or 'constructed,' by a community. In the Europe of the 1990's, this is the European Community, and its fundamental rights are precisely fundamental to it. If a series of such substantive or ethical rights contingently 'fundamental' to certain communities is to be established, then it will require the building of a more integrated, most obviously federal, Community political structure, with a sovereign power which can enforce the ethical norms. Until there is such a structure, then the current juridical order will continue to operate such norm controls, perhaps best described as 'confederal' or 'quasi-federal,' as it possesses, and we as morally driven 'citizens' of the Community will live in accordance with them. So if, at present the Court possesses the 'principle' of proportionality, to maintain the coherence of its own order, it must exercise this principle. Of course, the exercise of such a principle might have ethical repercussions. But if that is the 'principle' which the Court possesses, and can exercise in its bid to present judicial reasoning of 'integrity' and judgements of immanent fairness, then that is the principle which must be used.

Despite its sophistication Ward's analysis does beg a number of questions. Whilst he may be right to assert that courts are not privileged actors, they are political actors, nonetheless, even if operating within a hermeneutic straitjacket. They cannot be absolved from all responsibility for their actions by a simple defence of 'integrity' to the text. For it may well be the case that the Court has to choose between a number of traditions of 'integrity to the text'. Ward's analysis does not tell us which tradition led the Court to develop its doctrine of fundamental rights in the first place.

c. Fundamental Rights and the Member States

All the instances described above concerned challenges directed at acts of the Community institutions. If the development of the doctrine was confined to merely this arena, then, from a practical sense, there was little to concern Member State governments directly. For the doctrine of fundamental right would act as an additional constraint on the functioning of the Community institutions whilst not compromising national governments. The position was radically altered, however, if the doctrine was extended to cover Member State action. The autonomy of national governments and legislatures would be reduced. Equally significantly, the EC would be given a stronger civilian and political identity, as action occurring within the national sphere would not be struck down simply because it violated economic norms but also for infringing civil liberties.

Unsurprisingly, the Court was initially reticent about holding Member State action to be bound by fundamental rights. Whilst there were a number of instances in which fundamental rights were alluded to as an interpretive tool by the Court,[56] the matter was only addressed directly for the first time in *Cinéthèque*.

Joined Cases 60 & 61/84 Cinéthèque v Fédération Nationale des Cinémas Français [1985] ECR 2605, [1986] 1 CMLR 365

A French law provided that no film shown in cinemas could be sold or hired in video form for twelve months after it had been released. Cinéthèque, a video vendor, alleged that the French law was contrary to Article 30 [*28*] EC, the free movement of goods provision, and also constituted a unjustifiable restriction on freedom of expression.

24. ... Article 30 [of the EEC Treaty] must be interpreted as meaning that it does not apply to national legislation which regulates the distribution of cinematographic works by imposing an interval between one mode of distributing such works and another by prohibiting their simultaneous exploitation in cinemas and in video-cassette form for a limited period, provided that the prohibition applies to domestically produced and imported cassettes alike and any barriers to intra-Community trade to which its implementation give rise do not exceed what is necessary for ensuring that the exploitation in cinemas of cinematographic works of all origins retains priority over other means of distribution.

---

[56]   Case 36/75 *Rutili v Minister for the Interior* [1975] ECR 1219, [1976] 1 CMLR 140; Case 118/75 *Watson and Belmann* [1976] ECR 1185; Case 222/84 *Johnston v Chief Constable of the RUC* [1986] ECR 1651, [1986] 3 CMLR 53. For discussion see Drzemczewski, A.'The Domestic Application of the Human Rights Convention as European Community Law' (1981) 30 *ICLQ* 118.

25. The plaintiffs and the interveners in the main action also raised the question whether Article 89 of the French law on audio-visual communication was in breach of the principle of freedom of expression recognised by Article 10 of the European Convention for the Protection of Human Rights and Fundamental Freedoms and was therefore incompatible with Community law.

26. Although it is true that it is the duty of this Court to ensure observance of fundamental rights in the field of Community law, it has no power to examine the compatibility with the European Convention of national legislation which concerns, as in this case, an area which falls within the jurisdiction of the national legislator.

The Court adopted similar reasoning in *Demirel*.[57] In this instance, a Turkish national had come to visit her family in Germany on a tourist visa rather than a family reunification visa. On the expiry of her visa, she challenged the deportation on the grounds that it breached both the 1967 EEC-Turkey Association Agreement and Article 8 of the European Convention on Human Rights and Freedoms, which protected the right to respect for family life. The Court found that the Agreement did not lay down conditions under which Member States were required to permit family reunification of Turkish workers. In those circumstances, the Court considered that it did not have jurisdiction to assess the compatibility of Member State action with the European Convention on Human Rights.

With the Community Institutions having limited political and economic resources, most administration regulated by Community law is carried out by national authorities. Clearly, the coherence and unity of the Community legal order would be compromised if the EC Institutions were subject to a regime where they were bound by fundamental rights, and the national authorities were subject to another, where they were not, or if different national authorities were subject to different regimes.[58] This anomaly was particularly apparent in those

---

[57]   Case 12/86 *Demirel v Stadt Schwabisch Gmund* [1987] ECR 3719, [1989] 1 CMLR 421.

[58]   Lenaerts, K. 'Fundamental Rights to be Included in a Community Catalogue' (1991) 16 *ELRev* 367, 368; Temple Lang, J. 'The Sphere in Which Member States Are Obliged to Comply With the General Principles of Law and Community Fundamental Rights Principles' (1991/2) *LIEI* 23, 28-29.

circumstances where national authorities were implementing EC obligations.[59]

Case 5/88 Wachauf v Germany [1989] ECR 2609, [1991] 1 CMLR 328

Wachauf, a tenant, had transformed some land to milk production. On the expiry of the tenancy a tenant farmer in Germany requested compensation for the discontinuance of milk production Such compensation was available under Council Regulation 857/84 but there was a proviso that where the application was made by a tenant farmer, the lessor must give written consent. In Wachauf's case the lessor had withdrawn consent and the German authorities refused Wachauf's request. The German court considered that such a refusal to grant compensation would be incompatible with the right to own property protected by the German Constitution.

17. The Court has consistently held ... that fundamental rights form an integral part of the general principles of law, the observance of which is ensured by the Court. In safeguarding those rights, the Court has to look to the constitutional traditions common to the Member States, so that measures which are incompatible with the fundamental rights recognised by the constitutions of those States may not find acceptance in the Community. International treaties concerning the protection of human rights on which the Member States have collaborated or to which they have acceded can also supply guidelines to which regard should be had in the context of Community law.

18. The fundamental rights recognized by the Court are not absolute, however, but must be considered in relation to their social function. Consequently, restrictions may be imposed on the exercise of those rights, in particular in the context of a common organization of a market, provided that those restrictions in fact correspond to objectives of general interest pursued by the Community and do not constitute, with regard to the aim pursued, a disproportionate and intolerable interference, impairing the very substance of those rights.

19. Having regard to those criteria, it must be observed that Community rules which, upon the expiry of the lease, had the effect of depriving the lessee, without compensation,

---

[59]   There is earlier, although less explicit authority, for the proposition that Member States when implementing EC obligations are bound by fundamental rights, Joined Cases 201-202/85 *Klensch v Sécrétaire d'Etat* [1986] ECR 3477. See Weiler, J. 'The European Court at a Crossroads: Community Human Rights and Member State Action' in *Liber Amicorum Pierre Pescatore: Du droit International au droit de l'Integration* (1987, Nomos, Baden Baden).

of the fruits of his labour and of his investments in the tenanted holding would be incompatible with the requirements of the protection of fundamental rights in the Community legal order. Since those requirements are also binding on the Member States when they implement Community rules, the Member States must, as far as possible, apply those rules in accordance with those requirements.

20. In the present case, it is clear from Article 7(4) of Regulation No 857/84, as amended, that in the case of rural leases due to expire where the lessee is not entitled to an extension of the lease, the Member States may decide to allow the departing lessee to keep all or part of the reference quantity if he intends to continue milk production. It is also clear from Article 4(1)(a) of Regulation No 857/84 that in order to complete the restructuring of milk production Member States may grant compensation to producers who undertake to discontinue milk production definitively. It is true that, if that provision is read in conjunction with Article 4(2) of the same Regulation, pursuant to which the reference quantities thereby freed are to be added, as necessary, to the national reserve, it may be inferred that, in so far as the reference quantity corresponding to the holding returns to the lessor, it cannot be taken into account when compensation is granted.

21. However, that conclusion does not preclude the possibility for a departing lessee to obtain compensation calculated on the basis of all or part of the relevant reference quantity when that is justified by the extent of the lessee's contribution to the building-up of milk production on the holding. In that event, the quantity taken into consideration for the purposes of calculating the compensation must be treated as a freed quantity and, consequently, may not be put at the disposal of the lessor who repossesses the holding.

Once it had been accepted that, in principle, there were some circumstances in which Member State action falling within the arena of Community law was governed by fundamental rights, it became hard, however, for the Court to deny the proposition that Member States were bound by fundamental rights whenever they acted within the field of application of EC law.[60]

---

[60] By contrast, where they act outside the field of application of EC law, Member States continue not to be bound by the EC doctrine of fundamental rights. See Case C-299/95 *Kremzow v Austria*, Judgment of 29 May 1997.

Case 260/89 Elliniki Radiophonia Tileorassi (ERT) v Dimitiki (DEP) [1991] ECR I-2925, [1994] 4 CMLR 540

ERT, a Greek radio and television company, enjoyed exclusive broadcasting rights under Greek statute. It sought an injunction against an information company (DEP) and Mr Kouvelas, the Mayor of Thessaloniki, who had set up a rival television station. The respondents argued that ERT's exclusive rights infringed the free movement and competition provisions of EC and Article 10 of the European Convention on Human Rights and Fundamental Freedoms relating to freedom of expression.

41. With regard to Article 10 of the European Convention on Human Rights, ... the Court has consistently held, fundamental rights form an integral part of the general principles of law, the observance of which it ensures. For that purpose the Court draws inspiration from the constitutional traditions common to the Member States and from the guidelines supplied by international treaties for the protection of human rights on which the Member States have collaborated or of which they are signatories (see in particular Case C-4/73 *Nold v Commission* [1974] ECR 491, paragraph 13). The European Convention on Human Rights has special significance in that respect (see in particular Case C-222/84 *Johnston v Chief Constable of the RUC* [1986] ECR 1651, paragraph 18). It follows that, as the Court held in its judgment in Case 5/88 *Wachauf v Federal Republic of Germany [1989] ECR 2609*, paragraph 19, the Community cannot accept measures which are incompatible with observance of human rights thus recognised and guaranteed.

42. As the Court has held (see the Judgment in Joined Cases 60 & 61/84 *Cinéthèque v Fédération National de Cinemas Françaises [1985] ECR 205*, paragraph 25 and Case 12/86 *Demirel v Stadt Schwabisch Gmund* [1987] ECR 3719, paragraph 28), it has no power to examine the compatibility with the European Convention on Human Rights of national rules which do not fall within the scope of Community law. On the other hand, where such rules do fall within the scope of Community law, and reference is made to the Court for a preliminary ruling, it must provide all the criteria of interpretation needed by the national court to determine whether those rules are compatible with the fundamental rights the observance of which the Court ensures and which derive in particular from the European Convention on Human Rights.

43. In particular, where a Member State relies on the combined provisions of Articles 56 and 66 in order to justify rules which are likely to obstruct the exercise of the freedom to provide services, such justification, provided for by Community law, must be interpreted in the light of the general principles of law and in particular of fundamental rights. Thus the national rules in question can fall under the exceptions provided for by the combined provisions of Articles 56 and 66 only if they are compatible with the fundamental rights the observance of which is ensured by the Court.

309

44. It follows that in such a case it is for the national court, and if necessary, the Court of Justice to appraise the application of those provisions having regard to all the rules of Community law, including freedom of expression, as embodied in Article 10 of the European Convention on Human Rights, as a general principle of law the observance of which is ensured by the Court.

The protection of fundamental rights within the domestic sphere has a number of institutional consequences. It would suggest a vigorous policing of the application of those rights. In so far as this might entail matters being referred to the Court of Justice, it would require that institution to intrude upon a number of civil and political choices which had traditionally been the reserve of Member States. Subsequent practice suggests a reticence upon the part of the Court to do this.

One area where it has been called upon to make rulings is that of broadcasting. In *TV 10* the Court was called upon to consider the legality of the Dutch broadcasting regime, which sought to promote cultural pluralism by only allowing broadcasting associations, associations established to represent a particular social, cultural, religious or philosophical persuasion, to broadcast.[61] TV 10, a commercial cable network, managed from the Netherlands and owned by the Dutch nationals, but which sought to broadcast from Luxembourg, challenged a refusal to allow it to broadcast. The Court considered the matter to be an essentially domestic matter, therefore falling outside the remit of EC law, and the affair could have been left there. It had also been asked to consider whether the Dutch regime violated Article 10 of the European Convention on Human Rights, protecting freedom of expression. The Court was brief. It considered that a system, such as the present one, which promoted cultural pluralism, did not infringe that principle.[62] Yet this judgment contrasts with a ruling of the European Court on Human Rights which stated that whilst cultural pluralism was of great value, technological development entailed that this could be achieved in a manner less restrictive of

---

[61] Case C-23/93 *TV 10 SA v Commissariaat voor de Media* [1994] ECR I-4795, [1995] 3 CMLR 284.

[62] There is a proviso, however, that the measure not discriminate against foreign nationals, Case C-353/89 *Commission v Netherlands* [1991] ECR I-4069.

freedom of expression than by preventing certain people broadcasting, namely by imposing conditions in the licence.[63]

The other arena in which issues of fundamental rights in the domestic sphere have come before the Court is that of agriculture. In *Bostock* similar issues were raised to those in *Wachauf*. The only difference was that it did not concern a matter where Community legislation might be interpreted as preventing national authorities from granting compensation, but concerned a situation where national authorities had a discretion as to whether to grant compensation or not.[64]

Case C-2/92 R v Ministry of Agriculture, Fisheries and Food, ex parte Bostock [1994] ECR I-955, [1994] 3 CMLR 547

Bostock had been a tenant on a farm since 1962. The farm already had existing facilities but Bostock improved them and increased milk production. Bostock received a reference quantity, a quota for the milk production. In 1985 he sold his tenancy to his landlord. The British legislation implementing the EC Regulation required that the reference quantity be transferred to the landlord and that Bostock be allocated no compensation.

13. In *Wachauf*, ... [T]he national court in that case asked in particular whether that regulation could be interpreted in a manner compatible with the constitutional guarantees that precluded a lessee from being deprived, without compensation, of the fruits of his labour on expiry of the lease.

14. The Court held that the Community regulation in question left the competent national authorities a sufficiently wide margin of appreciation to enable them to apply that regulation without depriving the lessee, on the expiry of the tenancy, of the fruits of his labour and his investments in the let holding without any compensation ....., that is, without disregarding the requirements of the protection of fundamental rights in the Community legal order ...

15. The judgment in *Wachauf* does not therefore address the question, raised by the national court in this case, of the rights to compensation which a tenant may in

63   *Informationsverein Lentia v Austria* A/276 (1993).

64   In the view of Advocate General Gulmann in *Bostock*, the discretion this gave to the British authorities meant that the matter fell outside the doctrine of fundamental rights.

appropriate circumstances derive from Community law when he surrenders his lease.

16. However, the Court pointed out ... in its judgment in *Wachauf* ... that the requirements flowing from the protection of fundamental rights in the Community legal order are also binding on Member States when they implement Community rules and that the Member States must therefore, as far as possible, apply those rules in accordance with those requirements. In that connection the Court held in its judgment in Case C-260/89 *ERT v DEP* [1991] ECR I-2925, at paragraph 42, that where such national rules fall within the scope of Community law and reference is made to the Court for a preliminary ruling, it must provide all the criteria of interpretation needed by the national court to determine whether those rules are compatible with the fundamental rights whose observance the Court ensures.

17. It is therefore necessary to examine the fundamental rights relied on by Mr Bostock in order to enable the national court to decide whether the rules in question are compatible with those rights.

The right to property:

18. Mr Bostock argues that the right to property is a fundamental right which requires a Member State to introduce a scheme for payment by a landlord of compensation to an outgoing tenant, or indeed confers directly on the tenant a right to compensation from the landlord.

19. That argument cannot be accepted. The right to property safeguarded by the Community legal order does not include the right to dispose, for profit, of an advantage, such as the reference quantities allocated in the context of the common organization of a market, which does not derive from the assets or occupational activity of the person concerned (judgment in Case C-44/89 *Von Deetzen v Hauptzollamt Oldenburg* (*Von Deetzen II*) [1991] ECR I-5119, paragraph 27).

20. It follows that the protection of the right to property guaranteed by the Community legal order does not require a Member State to introduce a scheme for payment of compensation by a landlord to an outgoing tenant and does not confer a right to such compensation directly on the tenant.

It is difficult to reconcile this judgment with *Wachauf*, as in the latter the Court considered that somebody should not be deprived of the fruits of their labour without good reason, yet that is precisely what happened in *Bostock*.[65] The essential difference is not a legal one, but one of institutional context. In *Wachauf* the Court stopped an EC Regulation attacking national constitutional traditions. No such tradition was at stake in *Bostock*, rather it was being proposed by the applicant that fundamental rights should intrude in an area of national authority discretion. The lodestar of both judgments seems therefore to be that of national autonomy.[66] In such circumstances, one would not expect a rigorous expansion of the doctrine by the Court within the domestic sphere. And indeed this is what has happened. In *ex parte Country Landowners Association*, a Regulation had been passed allocating quotas for sheep and goat producers. The quota was granted to the producer rather than the landowner, and could be transferred by the producer. It was acknowledged that such a regime would lower the capital value of the land, but the British regime implementing the Regulation provided no compensation for the land owners. The Court, taking *Bostock* as its starting point, asserted that as these quotas were similar to reference quantities, the right to property did not extend to protect them.[67] This was notwithstanding that implementation of this regime substantially diminished the landowners' assets. Less controversially, in *Duff*, a case which originated in Ireland, the Court held that a regime which imposed a levy on those whose production exceeded their allocated milk quota did not infringe the fundamental right to property.[68]

All this suggests a reluctance on the part of the Court to provide rigorous criteria for the review by national courts of domestic action for its compatibility with EC fundamental rights. This has spillover effects for the review of actions of the EC institutions. For it is inconceivable

---

[65] For further criticism see Weiler, J. & Lockhart, N. '"Taking Rights Seriously" Seriously: The European Court and Its Fundamental Rights Jurisprudence - Part II' (1995) 32 *CMLRev* 579, 605-617.

[66] The criticism that the Court fails to explain sufficiently the reasons for different intensities of review is not a new one. See De Búrca, G. 'Fundamental Human Rights and the Reach of EC Law' (1993) 13 *OJLS* 283, 304-305 .

[67] Case C-38/94 *R v Minister of Agriculture, Fisheries and Food, ex parte Country Landowners Association* [1995] ECR I-3875.

[68] Case C-63/93 *Duff et al. v Minister for Food & Attorney General* [1996] ECR I-569.

that one regime of fundamental rights can apply to national authorities acting within the scope of EC law and another to the EC institutions themselves. In *O'Dwyer* the CFI thus had to consider a decision by the Council to reduce the size of producers' milk quotas without the provision of any compensation.[69] Relying upon *Bostock* it held that no issue of an infringement of the right to property was raised in this instance, as a quota was not an interest protected by the right to property.

There is a second, deeper reason why the actions of national authorities should be bound by fundamental rights. This reasoning transcends the case law outlined above and goes to the heart of the Union's identity. Weiler has argued that the heart of the European project cannot be to replace the nation-State with some identical European construct. The qualities of the nation-State are that it can give individuals a sense of community, identification and cultural differentiation. The task of the European project, he sees, as being to regulate the less attractive character of the nation-State - the potential it offers for xenophobia, exclusionary practices and introspection. The qualities of the European demos would therefore be:

'a commitment to the shared values of the Union as expressed in its constituent documents, a commitment, inter alia, to the duties and rights of a civil society covering discrete areas of public life, a commitment to membership in a polity which privileges exactly the opposites of nationalism - those human features which transcend the differences of organic ethno-culturalism.'[70]

---

[69] Joined Cases T-466/93, T-469/93, T-473/93, T-474/93, T-477/93 *O'Dwyer et al. v Council* [1995] ECR II-2071.

[70] Weiler, J. 'The Reformation of European Constitutionalism' (1997) 35 *JCMS* 97, 119. See also Weiler, J. 'Does Europe need a Constitution? Reflections on Demos, Telos and the German Maastricht Decision' (1995) 1 *ELJ* 219; Weiler, J. 'Legitimacy and Democracy of Union Governance' 249, 269-271 in Edwards, G. & Pijpers, A. (eds.) *The Politics of European Treaty Reform: The 1996 Intergovernmental Conference and Beyond* (1997, Cassell, London).

Respect for fundamental rights would clearly form part of such a civilian identity.[71] Yet one of the appeals of fundamental rights are that they are the property of the individual - they can be asserted against all other interests. Although not explicitly asserted by Weiler, implicit in his vision is a scenario where fundamental rights are protected against infringement by all authorities, whether EC or national.

The bestowal of human rights, *per se*, is insufficient, as Preuss has noted, to ensure protection of human dignity.[72] Any discourse which seeks to protect this dignity must also provide institutions and processes through which individuals may be represented and protected. It is this institutional dimension which has proved more contentious. In *Opinion 2/94*, where the possibility of future EC accession to the European Convention on Human Rights and Freedoms was considered, the Court rejected the idea of any existing institutional competence to enact rules on human rights or to conclude international conventions.[73] Indeed, it noted that accession would entail such a substantial change for the Community system that it could not be achieved without amendment of the EC Treaty.

If the grand vision of fundamental rights as central to a new European civilian identity was not adopted in *Opinion 2/94*, matters are less clear following the Treaty of Amsterdam.[74] This includes, first, an

---

[71]   The closest the Court has come to accepting this idea was Opinion of Advocate General Jacobs in *Case C-168/91 Konstantinidis v Stadt Altemsteig [1993] ECR I-1191*, who considered that the status of European citizen could be invoked to oppose any violation of fundamental rights. This suggestion was not taken up by the Court and was even disavowed by Advocate General Gulmann in Case C-2/92 *R v Minister of Agriculture, Fisheries and Food, ex parte Bostock* [1994] ECR I-955.

[72]   Preuß, U. 'Problems of a Concept of European Citizenship (1995) 1 *ELJ* 267, 274.

[73]   Opinion 2/94 *Re Accession by the Community to the European Convention for the Protection of Human Rights and Fundamental Freedoms* [1996] ECR I-1759, [1996] 2 CMLR 265. For discussion within the human rights context see Arnull, A., Schermers, H. & Dashwood, A. *The Human Rights Opinion of the ECJ and Its Constitutional Implications* (1996, CELS Occasional Paper No. 1, Cambridge).

[74]   The Westerdorp Report for the IGC appears to have borrowed Weiler's language. It states 'The Union is not and does not want to be a super-State. Yet is far more than a market. It is a unique design based on common values' SN

---

extension of the non-discrimination principle to cover not merely discrimination on nationality, as is currently the case,[75] but many other forms of discrimination.

Article 13 EC. Without prejudice to the other provisions of this Treaty and within the limits of the powers conferred by it upon the Community, the Council, acting unanimously on a proposal from the Commission and after consulting the European Parliament may take appropriate action to combat discrimination based on sex, racial or ethnic origin, religion or belief, disability, age or sexual orientation.

Although couched in the language of non-discrimination, implicit in *Article 13 EC* is the entrenchment of a number of civil values within the EC legal order, such as respect for sexual, biological or ethnic identity, freedom of belief, inclusion of the old and the disabled. It suffers from two constraints, however. The first is the institutional weakness of the consultation procedure used.[76] The second is that the provision is not entirely free-standing. It can only be applied to those areas in which the EC has already been conferred powers by other EC Treaty provisions. A provision which operates within the superstructure of other EC Treaty provisions cannot be recognised as making a fundamental shift in the identity of the EC Treaty. More far-reaching is *Article 6 TEU.*

Article 6 TEU. 1. The Union is founded on the principles of liberty, democracy, respect for human rights and fundamental freedoms, and the rule of law, principles which are common to the Member States.

2. The Union shall respect fundamental rights, as guaranteed by the European Convention for the Protection of Human Rights and Fundamental Freedoms signed in Rome on 4ᵗʰ November 1950 and as they result from the constitutional traditions common to the Member States, as general principles of Community law.

3. The Union shall respect the national identities of its Member States.

520/95, December 1995.
[75] Article 6 [*12*] EC.
[76] See pp 165-168.

4. The Union shall provide itself with the means necessary to attain its objectives and carry through its policies.

Amsterdam also provides mechanisms to enforce these principles. Respect for them is now a formal precondition to membership of the European Union.

Article 49 TEU. Any European State which respects the principles set out in Article 6(1) may apply to become a member of the Union ...

Article 49 TEU formalised existing practice.[77] More radically a Memorandum was submitted by the Foreign Ministers of the BENELUX Governments on 7 March 1996 which called for sanctions to be imposed on Member States who violated fundamental rights. These proposals have been incorporated in *Article 7 TEU*.[78]

Article 7. TEU. 1. The Council, meeting in the composition of the Heads of State or Government and acting by unanimity on a proposal by one third of the Member States or by the Commission and after obtaining the assent of the European Parliament, may determine the existence of a serious and persistent breach by a Member State of principles mentioned in Article 6(1), after inviting the government of the Member State concerned to submit its observations.

2. Where such a determination has been made, the Council, acting by a qualified majority, may decide to suspend certain of the rights deriving from the application of this Treaty to the State in question, including the voting rights of the representative of the Government of that Member State in the Council. In doing so, the Council shall take into account the possible consequences of such a suspension on the rights and obligations of natural and legal persons.

The obligations of the Member State concerned under this Treaty shall in any case continue to be binding on that State.

---

[77] Conclusions of the Lisbon European Council EC Bulletin 6-1992, I.4.

[78] A similar procedure is created in relation to the EC part of the TEU by *Article 309 EC.*

3. The Council, acting by a qualified majority, may decide subsequently to vary or revoke measures taken under paragraph 2 in response to changes in the situation which led to their being imposed.

4. For the purposes of this Article, the Council shall act without taking into account the vote of the representative of the Member State concerned. Abstentions by members present in person or represented shall not prevent the adoption of decisions referred to in paragraph 1. A qualified majority shall be defined as the same proportion of the weighted votes of the members of the Council concerned as laid down in Article 205(2) of the Treaty establishing the European Community. The provisions of this paragraph shall also apply in the event of voting rights being suspended pursuant to paragraph 2.

5. For the purposes of this Article, the European Parliament shall act by a two thirds majority of the votes cast, representing a majority of its members.

In normative terms, the Union has set itself up as guarantor of a series of civil values. It can no longer therefore be denied that it has a civil identity. The institutional dimension of *Article 7 TEU* renders it a very impoverished one. Whilst the procedure can be initiated by the Commission and requires the assent of the Parliament, it also requires a unanimous finding by the Heads of Government (minus the State accused) of a persistent and serious breach of the principles in *Article 6(1) TEU*. If one of the appeals of fundamental rights is the constraints they place on governmental power, there is a paradox that the process used to enforce them actually increases that power in the round. This, in turn, weakens the other root of the appeal of fundamental rights, namely that rights not only act as a negative constraint on governments but empower individuals. They do this not simply by preserving individual autonomy but by providing a connection and a bond between the individual and the polity. They act therefore as 'a medium of communication, association and solidarity'.[79] This role is diminished within the European Union for as possession of the EU's civil identity is largely placed in the hands of national governments, the link between the citizen and the EU polity is disrupted and made more remote with the

---

[79]   Cohen, J. & Arato, A. *Civil Society and Political Theory* (1992, MIT Press, New Baskerville) 297.

consequence that not only will the citizen's rights be less effectively protected but that the identification of EU citizens with this new civilian identity will, at best, be a weak one.

III. European Union Constitutionalism in Context

There is a suspension of disbelief in the previous discussion. It presupposes that the Court of Justice operates within a vacuum with its judgments being uncontestingly accepted both by the European Union and Member State political processes, on the one hand, and within the wider social context, on the other. Yet to have even a formal validity, the doctrine espoused by the Court of Justice must be accepted by national courts.[80] A claim to sovereignty extends beyond national judicial duties, however, as it is also a claim to political authority. Any analysis must locate the position of constitutional legal discourse within the integration process more generally. This entails examining both the integrative effect of constitutionalism and the possible socio-cultural bases which might give authority to EC constitutionalism. Failure to address the latter can weaken the ties of allegiance which that order can call upon.

Allott, P. 'The European Community is Not the True European Community' (1991) 100 *Yale Law Journal* 2485, 2498

The problem of forming and institutionalising an adequate conception of the relationship between the public power system of a society and the society as a cultural totality is as old as organised human society. In modern democracies, we have learned that it is not only the tyrant of the absolute monarch who can take over the whole of society in the name of the state. When the idea of popular democracy seemed, misleadingly, at last to identify the people with the state, it became easy to take another false step: to identify the state with society. A similar process has been at work in the European Community. Since the EC has seemed to be some sort of excrescence from the national societies, formed by the coalescing of political activity originating within the national societies, a self-standing

---

[80]   Eleftheriardis, P. 'Aspects of European Constitutionalism' (1996) 21 *ELRev* 32.

political system outside all national societies, existing in a sort of social vacuum.

The absence of a transcendent social framework for the Community powersystem has generated a cascade of consequences in the constitutional development of the EC over the last forty years. It has meant that the EC system, a particular political and legal system, reminiscent of national state systems, has come to be equated with the idea of 'Europe' for many people. It has meant that the EC has seemed to have no reason for existing other than the continued willing of the state systems of the states that formed it. Above all, it has meant that EC communal interest has come to be perceived as an aggregated interest, aggregated from separate national interests. In other words, it has meant that the EC has tended to revert to a pre-modern democratic model, of individualism aggregated rather than communalism distributed. This in turn means that there is a sense of retrograde motion in the development of democracy in Western Europe, as politicians and civil servants take over the negotiation of new laws as if they were negotiating treaties. The process of EC legislation has thereby managed to detach itself from the national political accountability, feeble as it now is in all the Member States, which is applicable to national legislation.

Allott has therefore argued that Europe's constitutional crisis can only be resolved at the level of consciousness. He argues that the first step must be the reintegration of European unification into the historical consciousness of the peoples of Europe. This will require both the bringing about of a collective consciousness and a transcendental debate about the idea of Europe and its relationship with the other ideas which capture Europeans' loyalties.[81]

Whilst Allott concentrates on the revival of the European idea as an escape from the crisis, others argue that the discourse of constitutionalism has a sufficient internal appeal, such, that when asserted by any public body, its potentialities should not be underestimated.

Walker, N. 'European Constitutionalism and European Integration' (1996)
***Public Law* 266, 272-275**

Difficulties and dangers associated with the tendency to overestimate the importance of constitutionalism as a legitimating measure are examined in due course, but it is equally imperative not to underestimate its potential. Although legitimation of a system of

---

[81]   Allott, P. 'The Crisis of European Constitutionalism: Reflections on the Revolution in Europe' (1997) 34 *CMLRev* 439.

government is a more modest task than the legitimation of the socio-political order which underpins that system of government, it is still vital in its own right. In line with the general analytical framework, the contribution of constitutionalism may be either affirmative or negative. In many national constitutional cultures, for example, there is arguably a historical symbiosis between the framework of constitutional government and a broad ethic of constitutionalism, embracing such ideas as fundamental right, the separation of powers, the federal division of powers, or, even more generally, limited government and the rule of law, or Rechtsstaat, principle itself.

Ideas and the institutions with which they are culturally entwined need not, however, be mutually supportive. A cursory glance at American or British constitutional theory, for example, reveals how often the language of constitutionalism is invoked in criticism of the prevailing system. In many cases, moreover, the two registers of constitutionalism are combined, the normative critique underpinned by cultural argument. In this mode, it is typically claimed that the extant constitutional law is untrue to constitutional traditions; and that, in order to answer a popular perception of constitutional failure and/or to restore a normatively superior standard of government, the ailing constitution should be reformed in line with these traditions.

This type of argument is not restricted to the national context. The debate about the so-called 'democratic deficit' of the European Union may be at least partly understood in these terms. The view that such a deficit exists - a view which, despite successive reforms increasing the powers of the European Parliament, continues to focus on that body - presupposes some democratic ideal to which the institutions of the European Union should aspire. In turn, this ideal is often grounded in an argument about the best traditions of the Member States of the Union and the expectations which attended its formation and later development; in other words, it is based upon an argument about the nature of European constitutionalism, not only as a set of abstract beliefs about good government, but as a set of immanent expectations within European constitutional culture.

A second reason not to underestimate the significance of constitutionalism is that, although the legitimacy of the constitutional system of government may be analytically separate from the legitimacy of the underlying socio-political order, the two are linked empirically. There are both minimalist and maximalist points in support of this proposition. Minimally, a defensible system of constitutional government is a necessary, if insufficient, condition for the legitimation of the underlying socio-political order. An additional minimalist point is one of form rather than substance. It concerns the indispensability of a language and culture of constitutionalism which are distinctive to the polity in question. The legacy of the historical bond between State and constitution ensures that the acceptance of a body such as the European Union as a reckonable socio-political entity depends upon the existence of a constitutional belief system and related network of institutions which are identifiable with that socio-political entity. As a mark of political maturity the existence of such a constitutional domain will not guarantee the legitimacy of the European Union as an autonomous socio-political order, but its absence will certainly signify the failure, or at least the incompleteness of that project.

The maximalist argument suggests that sometimes the constitution and its associated belief system have a much more central role in the legitimation of the underlying socio-political order. As regards post-war Germany, it has been persuasively argued that the absence of nationalism as an acceptable candidate to mobilise support for the new State and the dark legacy of a totalitarian political system helped to foster a new 'constitutional patriotism' - involving the treatment of the constitution itself as an object of allegiance and as a rallying-point for the cultivation of a new set of values to sustain the reconstructed State. Arguably, the United States Constitution provides another example of the maximalist thesis. Although some content that its venerable status has made it resistant to rational public critique and transparent reform - to the ultimate detriment of the underlying socio-political order - others insist that its symbolic centrality to American public life has permitted it; and its surrounding culture of debate, a central place in the development and legitimation of the multi-ethnic United States as an integrated society.

A final point underlining the significance of constitutionalism concerns other indirect links with the legitimacy and security of the underlying socio-political order. Constitutional beliefs create or reinforce the conditions which make possible other developments which themselves are vital to the legitimation of the socio-political order. To return to the German case, the social state (Sozialstaat) principle, enshrined in Article 20 of the Basic Law, centres a cluster of constitutional doctrines which arguably have helped to underpin the distinctive post-war German version of social democracy. This is closely tied to a commitment to the 'Rhine model' of social market capitalism, and incorporates a strong emphasis upon high minimum living standards and the fostering of political and economic harmony and co-operation between social classes and territorial groups; in turn, the fruits of German social democracy have been crucial in cementing the legitimacy of its post-war order. Another example is from the early history of the Community itself. Economic prosperity is one of the ideals which motivated and sustained the Community through its first generation. A factor contributing to this was the entrenchment of the Four Freedoms of movement of persons, goods, services and capital within the Treaty of Rome, as principles informing the actions of the major constitutional actors within the new entity.

Yet, used as a mirror to the European Union, constitutionalism also serves to highlight its deficiencies, such as the 'democratic deficit' and the dichotomy it draws between granting extensive economic rights whilst leaving civil, political and social rights to be determined predominantly at a national level.[82] Walker's thesis suggests that constitutionalism has potentially integrative features which has been contested by others. Shaw has argued that law reflects rather than reconciles deep-seated political trends and tensions. The integrative,

---

[82]   On this see Joerges, C. 'Taking the Law Seriously: On Political Science and the Role of Law in the Process of European Integration' (1996) 2 *ELJ* 105.

centripetal dynamic of the Community legal order is matched by an equally strong disintegrative, centrifugal dynamic, which, whilst perhaps less evident, is nevertheless there. It is, thus, misleading, in her view, to portray one dynamic as having a privileged position over the other.[83]

Walker acknowledges that within the context of the European Union constitutionalism's integrative potential has limits. The shared traditions of constitutionalism within the European Union are few. Walker considers, thus, that whilst it is possible to trace shared traditions surrounding the structural features of constitutionalism - those norms which concerns the decision-making processes of the State and the relationship between the different bodies - the same is not true, however, of the substantive features of constitutionalism - namely those norms, such as Bills of Rights, which define the goals or values which should direct government. It is difficult for the European Union to develop such a set of structural features, however, because of the problem of constitutional denial. This is the phenomenon whereby those who are opposed to the development of the European Union as a separate polity will not wish to see it develop constitutional features because of the strong interlinkages between the development of a socio-political entity and its constitutional form.[84]

These tensions are leading legal theorists to think of ways of reconfiguring constitutionalism. It is increasingly being argued that the sovereign qualities of EC law cannot simply entail a subordination of national legal orders to the EC legal order. The Member States still remain masters of the Treaties, in so far as it is they who can alter the existing settlement. It is also argued that such a view fails to account for the internal dynamics of the present settlement by failing to respect the political autonomy of Member States and to account for the central role Member States have, acting within the Council and as administrators of EC law, with the EC system of governance.[85]

---

[83] Shaw, J. 'European Union Legal Studies in Crisis? Towards a New Dynamic' (1996) 16 *OJLS* 231, 240-252.

[84] Walker, N. 'European Constitutionalism and European Integration' (1996) *Public Law* 266, 275-279.

[85] Maccormick, N. 'The Maastricht-Urteil: Sovereignty Now' (1995) 1 *ELJ* 259, 263-264; Maccormick, N. 'Liberalism, Nationalism and the Post-Sovereign State' 141, 147-149 in Bellamy, R. & Castiglione, D. (eds.) *Constitutionalism*

Maccormick, who has led the debate here, argues, however, that this does not lead to a rejection of the sovereign qualities of the EC legal order. He argues that it is perfectly possible to detach sovereignty from Statehood. He points, as examples, to the systems of internal regulation of Brazilian *favelas*, shanty-towns, which have developed quite autonomously from the State. The EC is similarly, in his view, a legal system which has its own autonomous normative qualities.[86] The relationship between these distinct legal systems, EC and national, need not be hierarchical, but a pluralistic conception would be that they be interacting.

Maccormick, N. 'The Maastricht Urteil: Sovereignty Now' (1995) 1 *European Law Journal* 259, 264-265

On the whole, therefore, the most appropriate analysis of the relations of legal systems is pluralistic rather than monistic, and interactive rather than hierarchical. The legal systems of Member States and their common legal system of EC law are distinct but interacting systems of law, and hierarchical relationships of validity within criteria of validity proper to distinct systems do not add up to any sort of all-purpose superiority of one system over another. It follows also that the interpretative power of the highest decision-making authorities of the different systems must be, as to each system, ultimate. It is for the European Court of Justice to interpret in the last resort and in a finally authoritative way the norms of Community law. But equally, it must be for the highest constitutional tribunal of each Member State to interpret its constitutional and other norms, and hence to interpret the interaction of the validity of EC law with higher level norms of validity in the given state system. Interpretative competence-competence is a feature of the highest tribunal of any normative system.

On this analysis, taking a pluralistic view of the systems of law operative in Europe, the systems are distinct and partially independent of each other, but partially overlapping and interacting. It must then follow that the constitutional court of a Member State is committed to denying that its competence to interpret the constitution by which it was established can be restricted by decisions of a tribunal external to the system, even one whose interpretative advice on points of EC law the constitutional court is obligated to accept under Article 177 EC. Conversely, the European Court of Justice is by the same

---

in *Transformation: European and Theoretical Perspectives* (1996, Blackwell, Oxford); Joerges, C. 'Taking the Law Seriously: On Political Science and the Role of Law in the Process of European Integration' (1996) 2 *ELJ* 105, 116-117.

[86] Maccormick, N. 'Beyond the Sovereign State' (1993) 56 *MLR* 1, 14 *et seq.*

logic committed to denying that its competence to interpret its own constitutive treaties can be restricted by decisions of Member State tribunals.

What this indicates is that acceptance of a pluralistic conception of legal systems entails acknowledging that not all legal problems can be solved legally. The problem in principle is not that of an absence of legal answers to given problems, but of a superfluity of legal answers. For it is possible that the European Court interprets Community law so as to assert some right or obligation as binding in favour of a person within the jurisdiction of the German Court, while that Court in turn denies the validity of such a right or obligation in terms of the German Constitution. In principle, the same conflict is possible as between any Member State system and EC law. The problem is not logically embarrassing, because strictly the answers are from the point of view of different systems. But it is practically embarrassing to the extent that the same human beings or corporations are said to have and not have a certain right. How shall they act? To which system are they to give their fidelity in action?

Resolving such problems, or, more wisely still, avoiding their occurrence in the first place, is a matter for circumspection and for political as much as legal judgement. The European Court of Justice ought not to reach its interpretative judgements without regard to their potential impact on national constitutions. National Courts ought not to interpret laws or constitutions without regard to the resolution of their compatriots to take full part in European Union and European Community. If despite this conflicts come into being through judicial decision-making and interpretation, there will necessarily have to be some political action to produce a solution. None of this seems at all surprising.

A pluralist account which requires account to be taken of the Community interest entails that a detailed account be given of what that Community interest represents. A space has to be found for it which it can fill. Joerges has gone further in articulating what this space may include. He argues the Community interest requires Member States to take account of their neighbours. Supremacy of EC law for him has an organisational role. It requires that the interests and concerns of 'foreigners' be taken account of by national legislatures, executives and judges.[87] This would suggest that EC membership entail as a minimum that EC law be given precedence in any area where 'foreign interests' are considered to be at stake. Whether establishing a functional link between EC competence and the precedence of EC law represents the best way of reconciling the national and the Community interest is unsure. The concept of foreign interests or concerns is so wide that it almost serves

---

[87]   Joerges, C. 'Taking the Law Seriously: On Political Science and the Role of Law in the Process of European Integration' (1996) 2 *ELJ* 105, 117.

to eliminate the pluralism set out by Maccormick's model. For example, would the emotional concerns of EU citizens in other Member States about bullfighting in Spain or foxhunting in the United Kingdom justify both EC legislation on the matter, and that legislation being granted precedence over national law. The answer might be that the foreign interest is too remote in such an instance. The scenario could be changed, however, were it to be found that non-Spanish bulls were being used for the bullfighting. This account suggests that if supremacy of EC law is to be genuinely pluralist in nature, the Community interest it represents must be a bipolar one, which carries an assessment of the relative weight of both the communal and the autonomous interests at stake.[88]

IV. The 'Activism' of the Court of Justice

Constitutions are normally established by civil ferment, coups d'Etat or plebiscite. Rare is the constitutional settlement created by a court, given the culture of judicial restraint within which most courts operate and the confines of the interpretive task allocated to them. Whilst the charge of 'judicial activism' is one that has been levied at the activities of the Court across the board, it is perhaps most appropriate to consider it here, where its impact has been most salient.

i. The Court of Justice has overstepped the functions of a court

In introducing a 1996 Bill before the British House of Commons which would have enabled British Ministers to make Orders disapplying judgments of the Court, the MP bringing the Bill stated:

---

[88]   On this see Scharpf, F. 'Community and Autonomy: Multilevel Policy-Making in the European Union' (1994) 1 *JEPP* 219.

'the European court is a political court, and it sees its role as the architect of European integration.'[89]

There are, in effect, two charges being made. The first is that the Court of Justice has abandoned the traditional limits of the judicial functions, and is adopting functions typically carried out by other bodies, such as legislatures.[90] The other is that there is an essentially one-sidedness to the Court's judgments, which fails to give sufficient weight to concerns such as national autonomy.

The most recent detailed exposition of the first position has been given by Hartley.[91] He distinguishes three types of ruling. The first are rulings within the interpretation of the text. The second are rulings outside the text. These are rulings which are not supported by the text, and which have no basis in the text, but are not contrary to the text. The third type of ruling is one which contradicts the text. In Hartley's view, the Court has given a number of judgments which clearly fall within this category. As examples he cites, *inter alia*, *Van Gend en Loos*, *Fotofrost*,[92] *Les Verts* [93] and *Chernobyl*.[94] His categorisation of these judgments has been hotly contested with others arguing that such judgments are textually consistent.[95]

Hartley and his critics adopt a common starting point. They all share the positivist assumptions that legal texts contain a central meaning

---

[89] Ian Duncan-Smith MP, HC Deb vol 276 col 198.

[90] This charge can be found in Neill, P. *The European Court of Justice: A Case Study in Judicial Activism* (1995, European Policy Forum, Frankfurter Institut) 47. For a critique see Cornish, W. 'Judicial Legislation' 359, 365-368 in Rawlings, R. (ed.) *Law, Society and Economy* (1997, Clarendon Press, Oxford).

[91] Hartley, T. 'The European Court, Judicial Objectivity and the Constitution of the European Union' (1996) 112 *LQR* 95.

[92] Case 314/85 *Firma Foto-Frost v HZa Lübeck Ost* [1987] ECR 4199, [1988] 3 CMLR 57.

[93] Case 294/83 *Parti Ecologiste 'Les Verts' v Parliament* [1986] ECR 1339, [1987] 2 CMLR 343.

[94] Case C-70/88 *Parliament v Council* [1990] ECR I-2041, [1992] 1 CMLR 91.

[95] Arnull, A. 'The European Court and Judicial Objectivity: A Reply to Professor Hartley' (1996) 112 *LQR* 111; Tridimas, T. 'The Court of Justice and Judicial Activism' (1996) 21 *ELRev* 199.

and are essentially autonomous and closed. The marginalisation of extra textual considerations runs the risk, first, however, of claiming a more fixed, strait jacketed meaning for language than it actually possesses. Hartley's critics are thus able to counter his arguments precisely by claiming that he takes too narrow textual interpretations. They, conversely, encounter the other danger of positivism - the 'hard case'. They argue that it is the open-texture of the language of the EC Treaty which has allowed and legitimated the Court to reach the judgments it has. It is unconvincing, in the extreme, to argue that courts simply have a free hand wherever linguistic rigour allows it. It obscures the moral, social and historical context within which judges operate. Moreover, it denigrates one of the functions of the law, which is to generate a stable set of expectations as to its operation, as it implies radical indeterminacy in many, if not the majority of, cases.[96]

The other criticism of the Court is that it has not had sufficient regard to its surrounding social context. The principal critic, in this regard, is Hjalte Rasmussen. At the time, an outspoken lone voice, Rasmussen's work was pathbreaking in that it opened the Court of Justice to the critical tradition to which so many courts in the domestic context are subject.[97] Rasmussen begins by laying out the trichotomy between rulings within the text, and rulings on which the text is silent, which was later to be adopted by Hartley. Like Hartley, Rasmussen considers that the text should be followed wherever possible. Also like Hartley, he claims examples where, in his view, the Court has blatantly disregarded the text.

Rasmussen's account becomes more interesting, however, in respect of that large number of situations where he considers the text to be silent. The critique at this point ceases to be formalistic - possibly, because, as was stated earlier, formalism cannot provide any answers in these circumstances. Rasmussen suggests that here the Court should take account of 'institutionalised responses' to its case law. These include

---

[96]   For more discussion on this, and an excellent summary of the literature see Habermas, J. *Between Facts and Norms* (1996, Polity Press, Oxford) 195-237.

[97]   Rasmussen, H. *On Law and Policy in the European Court of Justice* (1986, Martijnus Nijhoff, Dordrecht). See also Weiler, J. 'The Court of Justice on Trial' (1987) 21 *CMLRev* 555; Capelletti, M. 'Is the European Court of Justice "Running Wild"' (1987) 12 *ELRev* 3.

the other EC institutions, national courts, national governments, and independent expert opinion. For these are considered to channel societal reaction to the Court's doctrine. Rasmussen considers that the Court's integrationist zeal has, damningly, caused it to fail to do this.[98]

There is an elementary truth at the heart of Rasmussen's thesis which is that courts' legitimacy does not rest simply on procedural grounds. That is to say that no matter how much a court follows the rules of due process and is seen to reach decisions in an impartial manner, it will not enjoy support if it consistently reaches decisions which are unacceptable to society at large.[99] From that it does not follow that his solution should be adopted. For a start, the heterogeneity of institutionalised responses means that the circumstances will be rare where they all speak with a sufficiently clear, single voice. Even if they were, it is not clear that the Court should follow such responses. Were it to do so, it would merely become the mouthpiece for majoritarianism, in so far as it accurately reflected public opinion, or, more likely intergovernmentalism, in so far as national governments would become the interlocutors between the Court and the European citizenry. Neither is an enchanting prospect. Liberal rationales given for judicial review are precisely to avoid these phenomena. For, otherwise, there is a danger that minorities will be persecuted and higher values obscured.[100]

Rasmussen's model also threatens to destroy the premises of legal validity. Habermas has argued that these are twofold. The first is that of legal certainty. The utility of law stems in part from the existence of established law which generates a series of stable expectations. The other facet is that of legitimacy. The procedural rationality which applies both to the making and application of law generates an expectation that norms deserve to be obeyed.[101] Rasmussen's model threatens both these dimensions. The whims of popularism destroy the illusion of any prior certainty. Furthermore, in so far as public opinion attaches to outcomes rather than procedures, it renders the procedural validity upon which law

---

[98] Ibid., 377-383.
[99] Tyler, *Why People Follow the Law: Procedural Justice, Legitimacy and Compliance* (1990, Yale University Press, Belhaven).
[100] Ely, J. *Democracy and Distrust* (1980, Harvard University Press, Cambridge, Mass).
[101] Habermas, J. n.96, 198.

is based otiose and irrelevant. This, in the long term, undermines faith in the institution itself, for the institution seems to confer no added value to the other surrounding political processes.

ii. The Court of Justice as a Transnational Institution

The Court of Justice is not simply a court. It is a transnational court. It is not clear, therefore, whether analogies with domestic courts operating within an exclusively domestic context are entirely appropriate.[102] For, some see the European Union as no more than a highly institutionalised form of international relations. Within such an approach, different interests and perspectives come to the fore.

Where does the EC legal order fit within such a scheme? The starting point is the realist critique offered by Garrett.[103] Such an approach perceives national governments to be the principal actors in international relations. Garrett perceives the EC, as an international organisation, to be no more than an aggregation of the preferences of the Member State governments. The EC legal order plays a vital role in enabling it to meet these preferences in two ways. The first is that it solves the 'prisoner's dilemma' facing national governments, whereby there are no incentives to comply with their obligations unless they can be sure that there are guarantees that other Member States will comply with their obligations. Secondly, it solves the 'incomplete contract'

---

[102] On this problem more generally see Dehousse, R. 'Comparing National and EC Law: The Problem of the Level of Analysis' (1994) 42 *AJCL* 761.

[103] There has been a fierce debate on this with the Statist view offered by Garrett challenged by the elite-based approach advocated by Mattli and Slaughter. As the latter focuses on relations between the Court of Justice, national courts and national professions, it is analysed in more detail in Chapter 6. Garrett, G. 'International Cooperation and institutional choice: the European Community's internal market' (1992) 46 *International Organisation* 533; Burley, A-M. & Mattli, W. 'Europe Before the Court: A Political Theory of Legal Integration' (1993) 47 International Organisation 41; Garrett, G. 'The politics of legal integration in the European Union' (1995) 49 *International Organisation* 171; Mattli, W. & Slaughter, A-M. 'Law and Politics in the European Union: a reply to Garrett' (1995) 49 *International Organisation* 183.

problem. As it would entail considerable administrative costs for Member States to detail out exhaustively (if that were possible!) the 'rules of the game', it is more efficient to sketch out a broad schema and to delegate to the Court the task of 'filling in' the rest.

Garrett's analysis is more sophisticated than merely suggesting that the Court blindly follows the suggestions of national governments in its case law. He acknowledges that the Court will reject Member State arguments in particular cases. For he notes that whilst the wider benefits of a decision - e.g. greater trade liberalisation - may outweigh the immediate costs -e.g. the opening up to competition of a hitherto protected domestic industry - it may still be in the interest of the national government to argue vigorously in favour of the latter, for this allows it to hide behind the skirts of the Court in case of adverse domestic reaction. Garrett's analysis does suggest, however, that, in the long run, the Court is the captive of the national governments. If it were to give judgments that run counter to their preferences, not only would it encounter difficulties in implementation, but it would also undermine the foundations upon which its jurisdiction is based.

For all its intelligence, Garrett's argument does have some weaknesses. The first is that the notion of national government preference is left so vague as to be almost without predictive value. It is difficult to evaluate the weight attached to completion of the internal market by national governments when placed alongside the development of supranationalism with the increasing loss of political autonomy that the latter concept implies for them. The second difficulty with Garrett's view is that it takes rather a monolithic view of society. Increasingly, in other areas, such as the push towards the Single European Act, research has emphasised the importance of non-governmental actors.[104] There is little reason to assume that legal integration is different. To see EC law as merely a cumulation of governmental preferences is to obscure the role of national courts, legal professions, academics, ideologies. This appears counterintuitive. As a specialised discourse, these are the very people upon whom development of any legal system is dependent. The final criticism that can be made of Garrett's theory is that it understates the autonomy of law. Joerges has observed that the normative basis of

---

[104]   See pp 33-34.

law gives it an internal structure and principled autonomy which mean it cannot simply be resolved to a configuration of political interests.[105] Without these features it would lack both utility and legitimacy and, ultimately, could not even serve the functions to which it is ascribed by Garrett.

iii. The Centrality of the Court

The preceding analysis considers the possible justifications for the Court's actions. There is however, another question which can be asked. This is not whether what the Court has done was principled within its own terms of reference as a transnational court, but whether it was wise. Such analysis focuses upon the implications of the Court's enjoying such a central position within the integration process. To be sure, such a position was not carved out for itself exclusively by the Court. The stagnation within the Council prior to the Single European Act gave a salience to the Court's rulings they might otherwise not have had, and emphasised the centrality of law to the integration process. Similarly, the willingness of national courts to refer matters to the Court of Justice gave it a constituency and process for the enforcement of its judgments without which many of the developments could not have taken place.[106] Such an analysis would take a slightly broader perspective of the Court, which would consider it as part of a surrounding political backdrop, and as a fixture, albeit a central one, within a general process. It is no defence to argue that the centrality of the Court is necessary to ensure that the EC is a Community based upon the rule of law. For it is difficult to perceive the judicial process of dispute resolution as a socially detached one. The adjudicative process, not being a mechanistic one, will inevitably engage in law-making, in so far as it will both expand the law and have predictive effects. For the reasons explained above, this socially, highly-charged feature is particularly prominent in the case of

---

[105]   Supra n.87, 120.
[106]   Alter, K. 'The European Courts' Political Power' (1996) 18 *WEP* 458.

the Court of Justice. The rule of law in such circumstances does equate with the rule of the Court.[107]

Within this context there are two considerations which might militate against the Court's being a central institution of governance. The first is that it is an obscure, remote institution to most of the citizens of Europe. In a survey taken in 1992 only 4.5% of EU citizens claimed to be 'very aware' of the Court.[108] Furthermore, of those who showed some awareness, support for the institution was not high. Three forms of support were measured. The first was *diffuse support*, namely was the Court 'a good thing'. The second was the *index of acceptance* of the Court, namely would people comply with a judgment with which they disagreed and how likely it was that they would try to have the Court's decision reversed. The third were *procedural perceptions* of the Court, namely whether respondents considered decisions of the Court are made in fair way. It was found that the Court enjoyed no support on any of these three items amongst 45% of those surveyed who were aware of its existence.

It is not clear that this can be cured by a process of judicial reform. The process of dispute resolution which determines the court's jurisdiction also limits its policy-making capacities. The process of dispute resolution not only provides asymmetries of representation and information but it also structures the horizons of the court's decision. Focused on the process of adjudication, broader issues inevitably are considered to be more peripheral.[109] The danger of unintended

---

[107] Wincott, D. 'The role of law or the rule of the Court of Justice? An "institutional" account of judicial politics in the European Community' (1995) 2 *JEPP* 583.

[108] Gibson, J. & Caldeira, G. 'The Legitimacy of Transnational Legal Institutions: Compliance, Support and the European Court of Justice' (1995) 39 *American Political Science Review* 459.

[109] An infamous example of this was the *Barber* judgment. In this judgment, on the basis of Article 119 [*141*] EC, the provision requiring equal pay for work of equal value for men and women, the Court required Member States to equalise occupational pension schemes for men and women. Realising the financial implications of this, the Court stated the judgment could not be relied upon 'to claim entitlement to a pension with effect from a date prior to this judgment'. The difficulty was that this could be interpreted so that (i) it only applied to new pension schemes set up after the judgment; (ii) only workers who joined a

consequences, thus, becomes more obvious. Yet, paradoxically, with courts, these consequences are harder to rectify, as there is little which is systematic about what is decided.[110] For courts being reactive bodies, the matter can only become rectified when, in the absence of EC Treaty amendment, a third party decides to litigate a matter. Even when this first step is taken, if the matter is coming through the national courts under the Article 177 [*234*] EC reference mechanism, the backlog of cases before the Court entails that the process can still take years.[111]

Further Reading

De Búrca, G. 'Fundamental Human Rights and the Reach of EC Law' (1993) 13 *Oxford Journal of Legal Studies* 283
Coppel, J. & O'Neill, A. 'The European Court of Justice: Taking Rights Seriously?' (1992) 29 *Common Market Law Review* 669
Joerges, C. 'Taking Law Seriously: On Political Science and the Role of Law in the Process of European Integration' (1996) 2 *European Law Journal* 105
Lenaerts, K. 'Fundamental Rights to be Included in a Community Catalogue' (1991) 16 *European Law Review* 367
Maccormick, N. 'Liberalism, Nationalism and the Post-Sovereign State' in Bellamy, R. & Castiglione, D. (eds.) *Constitutionalism in Transformation: European and Theoretical Perspectives* (1996, Blackwell, Oxford)

---

pension scheme after the judgment could benefit from it; (iii) it applied only to benefits in respect of employment carried out after that date; or (iv) the judgment applies to all pensions payment made after the judgment. Case C-262/88 *Barber v Guardian Royal Exchange* [1990] ECR I-1889, [1990] 2 CMLR 513. For comment see Honeyball, S. & Shaw, J. 'Sex, law and the retiring man' (1991) 16 *ELRev* 47. The third interpretation was adopted by the Court in Case C-109/91 *Ten Oever v Stichting Bedrijspensioenfonds voor het Galzenwassers-en Schoonaakbedrijf* [1993] ECR I-4879 and by the Member States in a Protocol attached to the TEU, Protocol No.2 on Article 119.

[110] This is especially true of EC Treaty provisions. Secondary legislation can of course be amended by the other EC institutions.

[111] See pp 476.

Schilling, T. 'The Autonomy of the Community Legal Order: An Analysis of Possible Foundations' (1996) 37 *Harvard International Law Journal* 389

Shaw, J. 'European Union Legal Studies in Crisis? Towards a New Dynamic' (1996) 16 *Oxford Journal of Legal Studies* 231

Stone, A. 'What is a Supranational Constitution? An Essay in International Relations Theory' (1996) 56 *Review of Politics* 441

Szyszczak, E. 'Making Europe More Relevant to Its Citizens' (1996) 21 *European Law Review* 351

Weiler, J. 'The Reformation of European Constitutionalism' (1997) 35 *Journal of Common Market Studies* 97

----- & Lockhart, L. '"Taking Rights Seriously" Seriously: The European Court and Fundamental Rights Jurisprudence' (1995) 32 *Common Market Law Review* 51 & 579

de Witte, B. 'Community Law and National Constitutional Values' (1991/2) *Legal Issues of European Integration* 1

6. Member States and The Court of Justice

I. Introduction

The EC politico-legal process has been considered to have four distinct phases.[1] The first consists of the *adoption* of EC legislation through one of the EC legislative processes. The second involves the *incorporation* of EC law into the national legal systems - the transposition of a Directive being the most obvious example of this. The third is the application of EC law by those subject to its obligations. The fourth is that of *enforcement*.

Member States play an important role in the adoption of legislation, both directly through the Council of Ministers, and indirectly through the COREPER and the influence they will exert individually upon the Commission and Parliament. The near-monopoly States enjoy over what Giddens calls 'the means of violence within a society'[2] results in their influence growing through the cycle. It is normally only they who have the powers to incorporate EC law into the national legal orders. At the stage of applying EC law, Member States' monopoly over the

---

[1] Krislov, Weiler, J. & Ehlermann, C-D. 'The Political Organs and the Decision-Making Process in the United States and the European Community' 61, 62 in Capelletti, M., Seccombe, M. & Weiler, J. (eds.) *Integration through Law, Volume 1: Methods, Tools and Institutions, Book 2: Political Organs, Integration Techniques and Judicial Process* (1986, de Gruyter, Berlin). Whilst adopted here, this paradigm is not unproblematic. It has been criticised as being too top down and thus obscuring the extent to which the specific constitutional qualities of the different parties at the various points in the chain can affect the process. Snyder, F. 'The Effectiveness of European Community Law: Institutions, Processes, Tools and Techniques' (1993) 56 *MLR* 19, 25.

[2] Giddens, A. *Social Theory and Modern Sociology (1987, Stanford University Press, Stanford) 172.*

regulation of societal activities and their importance as participants in the market place - through activities such as public procurement, State aids and public undertakings - result in their overshadowing any private actor at this stage of process. Finally, Member States have the exclusive power to enforce EC law within their jurisdiction. For this reason Member States enjoy a paradoxical position within the EC legal order. On the one hand, their actions contribute to the development and flourishing of EC law. On the other, it is Member States who pose the greatest systemic challenge to the effective functioning of the EC legal system. Control of Member State behaviour at the post-legislative stage is therefore one of the central problems of EC governance.

Two procedures were initially expressly provided in the EC Treaty to accommodate this. The first, and most frequently used, provides for the Commission to bring Member States before the Court for failing to comply with EC law.[3]

Article 169 [*226*] EC. If the Commission considers that a Member State has failed to fulfil an obligation under this Treaty, it shall deliver a reasoned opinion on the matter after giving the State concerned the opportunity to submit its observations.

If the State concerned does not comply with the opinion within the period laid down by the Commission, the latter may bring the matter before the Court of Justice.

The opportunity to bring a Member State before the Court of Justice is also given to other Member States. The number of instances where it has been taken are rare, as it is less costly and provokes less

---

[3] There are a number of specific provisions which regulate when the Commission or another Member State may bring a Member State to Court for breach of a particular Article. These are Article 93(2) [*88(2)*] EC (failure to comply with a Commission decision that a State aid is illegal) Article 100A(4) [*95(9)*] EC (measures derogating from an EC harmonisation measure); Article 225 [*298*] EC (invocation by a Member State of Article 223 [*296*] or 224 [*297*] EC, which allows derogations from EC law on grounds of essential security, war, serious internal disturbance or serious international tension constituting a threat of war).

confrontation for Member States to induce the Commission to bring an action against other Member States than to do it themselves.[4]

Article 170 [227] EC. A Member State which considers that another Member State has failed to fulfil an obligation under this Treaty may bring the matter before the Court of Justice.

Before a Member State brings an action against another Member State for an alleged infringement of an obligation under this Treaty, it shall bring the matter before the Commission.

The Commission shall deliver a reasoned opinion after each of the States concerned has been given the opportunity to submit its own case and its observation on the other party's case both orally and in writing.

If the Commission has not delivered an opinion within three months of the date on which the matter was brought before it, the absence of such an opinion shall not prevent the matter from being brought before the Court of Justice.

Amsterdam expanded the Court's jurisdiction in JHA.[5] A corollary of this was the extension of its central enforcement powers.

Article 35(7) TEU. The Court of Justice shall have jurisdiction to rule on any dispute between Member States regarding the interpretation or the application of acts adopted under Article 34(2) whenever such dispute cannot be settled by the Council within six months of its being referred to the Council by one of its members. The Court shall also have jurisdiction to rule on any dispute between Member States and the Commission regarding the interpretation or the application of conventions established under Article 34(2)(d).[6]

This provision seems less developed than Articles 169 [226] and 170 [227] EC. In particular, it does not set out any procedure to be followed unlike those two Articles. This is something which is likely to be set out in future secondary legislation.

---

[4]   Only once has an Article 170 [227] EC action been taken fully through. Case 141/78 *France v United Kingdom* [1979] ECR 2923.

[5]   See pp 136-137.

[6]   The acts referred to in *Article 34(2) TEU* are the legislative acts which may be adopted under JHA.

II. Common Features to Articles 169 [*226*] EC and 170 [*227*] EC

i. Causes of Action

Breach of any binding norm of EC law by a State will justify a finding of non-compliance.[7] Thus, Member States can be subject to an enforcement action not just for failure to comply with the EC Treaty but also for breach of regulations, directives and decisions, as well as failure to comply with fundamental rights in so far as the national action falls within the field of application of EC law. Failure by a Member State to respect an international agreement concluded by the EC institutions can also be the basis for an Article 169 [*226*] EC action. The Court therefore accepted a Commission action against Germany which alleged that the latter had failed to comply with the International Dairy Agreement, an agreement to which the EC was party.[8] It held that the Commission's duty to ensure Member State compliance with the EC Treaty included a duty to ensure compliance with international agreement concluded by the EC, as these bound not merely the institutions but also the Member States. Frequently such agreements will set up institutional machinery to achieve their effective machinery. Although the Court has not ruled directly upon the matter, it seems that an enforcement action can be used to ensure Member State compliance with decisions taken by institutions set up under these agreements. In *Greece v Commission* the Court therefore found that decisions taken within the institutional framework of the EEC-Turkey Association constituted an integral part of the Community legal order as they were directly concerned with the agreement.[9]

More problematic is the position of a large number of

---

[7] For a typology of the types of act which will constitute an infringement see Dashwood, A. & White, R. 'Enforcement Actions under Articles 169 and 170 EEC' (1989) 14 *ELRev* 388, 391-396.

[8] Case C-61/94 *Commission v Germany* [1996] ECR I-3959.

[9] Case 30/88 *Greece v Commission* [1989] ECR 3911.

Conventions which have been developed within the aegis of the Community, but are not EC law proper. These fall into three categories. The first is where the EC Treaty mandates Member States to enter into agreements with each other to secure a particular objective. An example of this is the Brussels Convention on Jurisdiction and Enforcement of Judgments and Civil Matters which was entered into within the framework of Article 220 [293] EC which requires Member States to enter negotiations to simplify formalities governing the reciprocal recognition and enforcement of judgments. The Convention in this instance can be traced back to a binding EC norm. It may be that an action could therefore be brought for breach of the Convention on the basis of Article 5 [10] EC, which requires Member States to facilitate the Community's tasks.[10] The second scenario concerns Conventions such as the Community Patent Convention. These are concluded within the aegis of the EC framework but their roots cannot be traced back to any provision or principle of EC law. It seems very difficult to argue that enforcement actions can be brought in relation to these. The final scenario concerns conventions agreed within the framework of JHA. The Court's jurisdiction depends prior to ratification of Amsterdam simply upon the terms of the Convention.[11] It will have automatic jurisdiction under *Article 35(7) TEU* to rule on these conventions should Amsterdam be ratified.

ii. Measures for which States are Liable

a. The Concept of the State

Only Member States can be the subject of actions brought under Articles 169 [226] and 170 [227] EC. The question arises therefore as to what

---

[10]   Commission practice has not been to instigate Article 169 [226] EC proceedings but to issue recommendations in this area, OJ 1985, L 44/2.

[11]   Article K.3.2(c)TEU. No convention signed under this provision has granted either Member States or the Commission competence to bring another Member State before the Court for breach of its terms.

is considered to be State action for the purposes of these Articles. Although formally actions are brought against the State, in practice it is the central government which is proceeded against. The Court has held that it is responsible for the acts or omissions of all State agencies 'even in the case of a constitutionally independent institution'.[12] The central government is thus responsible not only for all acts of central government but also for all acts of local government.[13]

The definition creates problems of compliance. It is otiose to hold central government responsible for the acts of bodies which are constitutionally independent from it. This very constitutional independence often prevents central government from taking any effective measures to curtail the breach. In many jurisdictions, notably federal ones, therefore, national authorities have no power to sanction the actions of local or regional authorities.[14] In all Member States, the area in which this is most apparent is in relation to acts of the judiciary. There is a feeling that an enforcement action brought against a Member State in these circumstances is asking it to compromise the independence of the judiciary and to provoke a constitutional crisis. There is thus some uncertainty on this point. Advocate General Warner stated in *Bouchereau* that Article 169 [*226*] EC could not be used in cases of simple judicial error but would only be available in circumstances where a national court deliberately disregarded or ignored EC law.[15] The Commission is also ambivalent on the matter. Whilst it initiated proceedings against Germany in 1974 in relation to the *Internationale Handelsgesellschaft* decision of the German Constitutional Court,[16] those proceedings were subsequently dropped, and it has not instigated Article 169 [*226*] EC actions in respect of judicial actions since.[17]

---

12   Case 77/69 *Commission v Belgium* [1970] ECR 237.
13   e.g. Case 199/85 *Commission v Italy* [1987] ECR 1039; Case C-2/90 *Commission v Belgium* [1992] ECR I-4431, [1993] 1 CMLR 365.
14   Hessels, B. & Mortelmans, K. 'Decentralized Government and Community Law: Conflicting Institutional Developments?' (1993) 30 *CMLRev* 905.
15   Case 30/77 *Bouchereau* [1979] ECR 1999, 2220.
16   On this decision see p 295.
17   On this and the debate on this matter see Schermers, H. & Waelbroeck, D. *Judicial Protection in the European Communities* (1992, 5th Edition, Kluwer, Deventer) 305-307.

Such a monolithic view of State responsibility poses other problems. It seems clear that where a Member State is exercising control over a body, then it will be liable for the actions of that body no matter what the latter's functions. In *Commission v Ireland* the Irish Government was found liable for the actions of a private body, the Irish Goods Council, which was running a 'Buy Irish' campaign.[18] The reasons for this were that the latter was considered to have relatively little autonomy as the Irish Government provided the overwhelming majority of its funding, appointed the members of its Management Committee and defined the broad outlines of its campaign.

In an age when activities carried out by publicly owned bodies in some Member States are carried out by a variety of quasi-autonomous, autonomous and private bodies in other Member States, it is increasingly difficult to determine which functions are the responsibility of the State in the absence of such control.

Case C-24/91 Commission v Spain [1992] ECR I-1989

In 1989, the University of Complutense, a public university in Madrid awarded a contract for the extension and renovation of the Faculty of Political Science and Sociology and the School of Social Work without following the procedures laid out under EC public procurement law. Although not discussed by the Court, Advocate-General Lenz first considered whether an Article 169 [*226*] EC action was admissible for such a breach.

Advocate General Lenz

9. In an action for failure to fulfil Treaty obligations, it is essential to establish whether the defendant State may be held responsible for the offending conduct. The problem arises in particular when the State uses the machinery of private law in carrying out its functions. In such cases the possibility of State influence must be established positively.

10. The situation is different where the conduct of a primary State authority is concerned. The Member State is thus responsible, vis-à-vis the Community, for independent bodies even where there is no provision for direct Government intervention in specific areas of conduct.

---

[18]   Case 249/81 *Commission v Ireland* [1982] ECR 4005, [1983] 2 CMLR 104.

11. A State university, even if independent from an organizational point of view, is as a rule a State institution. The type of 'legal person governed by public law' chosen by the Member State when setting up the university is therefore not so very important. The State may therefore be held responsible, in the context of an action for failure to comply with Treaty obligations, for legal acts of the university.

b. Actions of Private Parties for Which Member States are Responsible

Member States cannot be responsible for all illegal acts which occur upon their territory at all times. To impose such a duty would not only transform them into guarantors of EC law but would impose an overwhelming burden upon their resources. A process of attributing responsibility has also to take place to determine which acts fall within the responsibility of the State. This has been done through the medium of Article 5 [*10*] EC, which requires Member States to take measures to ensure the application of EC law. Member States are therefore not only under a negative duty not to break substantive provisions of EC law themselves, but are also under a positive duty to enforce private compliance with EC law upon their territory.

Case 68/88 Commission v Greece [1989] ECR 2965, [1991] 1 CMLR 31

In 1986 a Greek company, ITCO, exported two consignments of maize to Belgium which it fraudulent passed off as Greek when, in fact, they came from the former Yugoslavia. By doing this it was able to avoid the agricultural levies payable to the EC own resources which were charged on imports of maize from third countries which entered the Community. There was evidence of complicity by Greek civil servants in this fraud. In addition, no attempt was made by the Greek authorities to prosecute ITCO for its behaviour.

23. It should be observed that where Community legislation does not specifically provide any penalty for an infringement or refers for that purpose to national laws, regulations and administrative provisions, Article 5 of the Treaty requires the Member States to take all measures necessary to guarantee the application and effectiveness of Community law.

24. For that purpose, whilst the choice of penalties remains within their discretion, they must ensure in particular that infringements of Community law are penalized under conditions, both procedural and substantive, which are analogous to those applicable to infringements of national law of a similar nature and importance and which, in any event, make the penalty effective, proportionate and dissuasive.

25. Moreover, the national authorities must proceed, with respect to infringements of Community law, with the same diligence as that which they bring to bear in implementing corresponding national laws.

26. In the present case, it does not appear from the file on the case that the Greek authorities have instituted criminal or disciplinary proceedings against the persons who took part in the commission and concealment of the fraud denounced by the Commission or that there was any impediment to the institution of such proceedings.

c. Defences to Enforcement Actions

Member States have attempted to raise a number of defences in enforcement actions against them, to which the Court has, generally, been unsympathetic. It will not therefore accept defences based on the economic costs or administrative difficulties in compliance[19] or those invoking provisions of domestic law.[20] Member States have also tried to argue that the provision of EC law on which infringement proceedings were brought is illegal. This argument will not be accepted unless the Court considers the EC provision to contain such serious and manifest defects as not merely to be illegal but to justify a declaration of non-existence.[21] The reason for this is that the functions of Articles 169 [*226*] and 170 [*227*] EC are considered to be to allow a declaration that a Member State has not complied with their obligations and not to be a route to judicially review acts of the EC institutions.[22] The only defence which the Court has been ready to accept in principle, albeit it has never

---

19   Case C-42/89 *Commission v Belgium* [1990] ECR I-2821, [1992] 1 CMLR 22.

20   Case 1/86 *Commission v Belgium* [1987] ECR 2797.

21   On this see Case C-137/92P *Commission v BASF* [1994] ECR I-2555.

22   Case 226/87 *Commission v Greece* [1988] ECR 3611, [1989] 3 CMLR 569; Case C-74/91 *Commission v Germany* [1992] ECR I-5437.

accepted in practice, is that of *force majeure*. Whilst the content of this concept varies according to the context in which it is used, it refers to the occurrence of an event outside the Member State's control which makes it extraordinarily difficult for the State to comply with EC law.[23] *Force majeure* is to be understood as:

> 'not limited to absolute impossibility but must be understood in the sense of abnormal and unforeseeable circumstances, the consequence of which, in spite of the evidence of all due care,... could not have been avoided except at the cost of excessive sacrifice.'[24]

The circumstances in which there will be a successful defence are therefore very rare indeed. In *Commission v Italy* the Italian Government was required to provide statistical returns on the carriage of goods by road.[25] The Court accepted that the bombing in January 1979 of the data-processing plant which compiled the returns could constitute *force majeure*. It did not accept it as a defence for the Italian Government's providing only partial returns for 1979 and none for 1980. For the Court considered the defence could only justify non-compliance for that period which an administration, acting with due diligence, would require to replace the equipment.

---

[23]   Thompson, J. 'Force Majeure: The Contextual Approach of the Court of Justice' (1987) 24 *CMLRev* 259; Magliveras, K. 'Force Majeure in Community Law' (1990) 15 *ELRev* 460.

[24]   Case C-124/92 *An Bord Bainne Cooperative v Intervention Board* [1993] ECR I-5061.

[25]   Case 101/84 *Commission v Italy* [1985] ECR 2629.

III. The Article 169 [*226*] EC Procedure

Article 169 [*226*] EC contains an administrative process which must be entered into before the Commission can bring a Member State before the Court of Justice. The purpose of this process is to afford the Member State concerned both the opportunity to remedy the infringement alleged and the opportunity to answer any allegations before the Commission takes the confrontational step of taking it to Court.

The first stage in the administrative process is an informal one, whereby the Commission will set out its allegations and seek a response from the Member State in question. This informal process is not formally required by Article 169 [*226*] EC. It is secretive in nature with little scope for public comment or influence on the proceedings.[26] Yet it is at this stage that most issues are resolved through a process of negotiation and consultation. In 1995, a not atypical year, the Commission considered 5,068 cases. Of these it only commenced proceedings in 1,016, about 20% of the cases.[27] Whilst the reason for not proceeding in many instances will be that the Commission will consider no illegal act to have been committed, many proceedings will not be started as a result of informal dispute resolution between the Commission and the Member State concerned.

The process formally begins with the Commission's issuing a letter of formal notice. The reason for this is that Article 169(1) [*226(1)*] EC states that the Commission must issue a reasoned opinion having given the State concerned the opportunity to submit observations. Member States have to know first upon what they are to submit observations.

---

[26]   Szyszczak, E. 'L'Espace Sociale Europeenne: Reality, Dreams, or Nightmares?' (1990) 33 *German Yearbook of International Law* 284, 299.

[27]   EC Commission, *Thirteenth Annual Report on monitoring the application of Community law*, OJ 1996, C 303/1, 10

Case 211/81 Commission v Denmark [1982] ECR 4547

The Commission brought an action against the Danish Government for failing to transpose Directive on electrical energy meters. The Danish Government claimed that the letter of formal notice was insufficient as it merely noted Denmark's failure to act.

7. It should be recalled that by virtue of Article 169 of the Treaty the Commission may bring before the Court an action for failure of a State to fulfil its obligations only after giving the Member State concerned the opportunity of submitting its observations.

8. it follows from the purpose assigned to the pre-contentious stage of the proceedings for failure of a state to fulfil its obligations that a letter giving formal notice is intended to delimit the subject-matter of the dispute and to indicate to the Member State which is invited to submit its observations the factors enabling it to prepare its defence.

9. As the Court held in its judgment of 17 February 1970 in Case 31/69 *Commission v Italy* [1970] ECR 25, the opportunity for the Member State concerned to submit its observations constitutes an essential guarantee required by the Treaty and, even if the Member State does not consider it necessary to avail itself thereof, observance of that guarantee is an essential formal requirement of the procedure under Article 169.

10. It appears from the documents before the Court that by a letter dated 23 May 1979 giving formal notice the Commission merely asserted that in its view the Danish Government had not put into force the measures necessary to transpose Directive 76/891 into national law but refrained from specifying the obligations which, in its view, were imposed on that State by virtue of the directive and which had been disregarded.

11. In the present case, however, that fact did not have the effect of depriving the Danish government of the opportunity of submitting its observations to good effect. On 7 June 1978 the Commission had addressed to the Danish Government a letter setting out the precise reasons which led it to conclude that the Kingdom of Denmark had failed to fulfil one of the obligations imposed on it by Directive 76/891. It was by reference to the position adopted by the Commission in that letter of 7 June 1978 that the Danish Government submitted its observations on 22 August 1979.

The Member States will then submit their observations on the letter of formal notice. If agreement is still not reached, the Commission will then reach the final phase of the administrative stage, the issuing of a reasoned opinion. As the subject-matter of the dispute is delimited by the formal letter of notice, the reasoned opinion can not modify the subject-matter of the dispute by introducing new claims. It should therefore not amend conclusions contained in the letter of notice.[28] That said, the Court will allow some account to be taken of changes in circumstances. In *Commission v Belgium* the Commission challenged the system of broadcasting regulation set up by the Flemish Communities. In its letter of formal notice it challenged the 1987 law.[29] The 1987 law was then replaced by a 1994 law. It was this latter regime that was challenged in the reasoned opinion. The Court rejected a Belgian claim that this amendment compromised the latter's rights of defence, noting that the national provisions mentioned need not be identical if the change in legislation resulted in the system as a whole not being altered.

The reasoned opinion is not merely a repetition of the letter of formal notice. Whilst the latter need do no more than give a summary of the complaints,[30] the reasoned opinion must give a coherent and detailed statement of reasons, which should include a detailed statement of the legal and factual context to the dispute.[31] The reasoned opinion must also take account of any resolutions submitted by the Member State.[32] Finally, and importantly, the reasoned opinion must also give a reasonable period for compliance by the Member State to comply with it. The minimum length of the period the Commission must lay down will depend upon a number of factors. These include the urgency of the matter and when the matter was first brought to the attention of the Member State by the Commission.[33]

Case 293/85 Commission v Belgium [1988] ECR 305, [1989] 2 CMLR 527

Under a 1985 law Belgian universities were authorised to charge a supplementary fee (a 'minerval') on nationals from other Member States who

---

[28] Case 124/81 *Commission v United Kingdom* [1983] ECR 203, [1983] 2 CMLR 1; Case 278/85 *Commission v Denmark* [1987] ECR 4065.

[29] Case C-11/95 *Commission v Belgium* [1996] ECR I-4115.

[30] Case 74/82 *Commission v Ireland* [1984] ECR 317.

[31] Case C-247/89 *Commission v Portugal* [1991] ECR I-3659.

[32] Case C-266/94 *Commission v Spain* [1995] ECR I-1975.

[33] This is not when the letter of formal notice was sent but when informal contacts were first made. Case C-56/90 *Commission v United Kingdom* [1993] ECR I-4109; Case C-473/93 *Commission v Luxembourg* [1996] ECR I-3207.

enrolled with them. The Commission considered such action to be illegal following the *Gravier* judgment, given on 13 February 1985.[34] It had an informal meeting with Belgian officials on 25 June 1985 where it expressed that view but also stated that it was still considering the effects of the judgment. On 17 July 1985 it issued a letter of formal notice stating that, in view of the onset of the new academic year, the Belgian Government should submit its observations within 8 days. The Belgian authorities asked for more time. On 23 August 1985 the Commission issued a reasoned opinion with the Belgian Government being given 15 days to comply. The Belgians claimed that the action was inadmissible given the limited periods offered for compliance.

13. It should be pointed out first that the purpose of the pre-litigation procedure is to give the Member State concerned an opportunity, on the one hand, to comply with its obligations under Community law and, on the other, to avail itself of its right to defend itself against the complaints made by the Commission.

14. In view of that dual purpose the Commission must allow Member States a reasonable period to reply to the letter of formal notice and to comply with a reasoned opinion, or, where appropriate, to prepare their defence. In order to determine whether the period allowed is reasonable, account must be taken of all the circumstances of the case. Thus, very short periods may be justified in particular circumstances, especially where there is an urgent need to remedy a breach or where the Member State concerned is fully aware of the Commission's views long before the procedure starts.

15. It is therefore necessary to examine whether the shortness of the periods set by the Commission was justified in view of the particular circumstances of this case. ...

16....., the imminent start of the 1985 academic year may indeed be regarded as a special circumstance justifying a short time-limit. However, the Commission could have taken action long before the start of the academic year because the major part of the Belgian provisions were already part of its legislation before the law of 21 June 1985. They were therefore known to the Commission at the latest when the judgment of 13 February 1985 was delivered, which was six months before the start of the 1985 academic year. Furthermore, it should be noted that at the time the Commission had not made any criticism of the minerval and had even given the impression, prior to the entry into force of the law in question, that it accepted that the minerval was compatible with Community law. In those circumstances the Commission cannot rely on urgency which it itself created by failing to take action earlier.

17. As for the Commission's alternative argument that the time-limits laid down were not absolute and that consequently replies given after their expiry would have been accepted,

---

[34]   Case 293/83 *Gravier v City of Liège* [1985] ECR 593, [1985] 3 CMLR 1.

it should be remarked that that factor is not relevant. A Member State to which a measure subject to a time-limit is addressed cannot know in advance whether, and to what extent, the Commission will if necessary grant it an extension of that time-limit. In this case, moreover, the Commission did not reply to the Kingdom of Belgium's request for an extension of time.

18. As regards the question whether the Kingdom of Belgium was aware sufficiently in advance of the Commission's views, it is common ground that although the commission had expressed its views to the competent officials of the Belgian ministries of national education on 25 June 1985, at a meeting of the education committee of 27 and 28 June 1985 it stated that it was still considering the effects of the judgments of the Court in the field of university education. It follows that the Kingdom of Belgium was not fully informed of the definitive views of the Commission before these proceedings were brought against it.

It is only if compliance does not occur, that the matter may be brought before the Court. Indeed, once the period set out in the reasoned opinion has elapsed there is nothing a Member State can do to prevent the matter being heard by the Court. For the Court has repeatedly stated that it will consider the position at the end of the period laid down in the reasoned opinion, and will not take account of subsequent changes.[35] Compliance by the Member State with the reasoned opinion after the deadline set out in the latter but before judgment will not therefore prevent the Court's declaring that it has acted illegally. There are two reasons for this. The first is that given the unwieldy nature of the procedure, it would otherwise be unable to capture breaches of a relatively short duration.[36] The other is that there would otherwise be opportunities for Member States to manipulate the procedures by simply bringing their conduct to an end shortly before judgement was given.[37]

---

[35] Case C-200/88 *Commission v Greece* [1990] ECR I-4299; Case C-105/91 *Commission v Greece* [1992] ECR I-5871; Case C-133/94 *Commission v Belgium* [1996] ECR I-2323.

[36] Advocate General Lenz in Case 240/86 *Commission v Greece* [1988] ECR 1835, 1844.

[37] Advocate General Lagrange in Case 7/61 *Commission v Italy* [1961] ECR 317, 334.

IV. Article 170 [*227*] EC

The procedure in Article 170 [*227*] EC is activated by a Member State bringing the matter to the attention of the Commission. From that point the procedure closely resembles Article 169 [*226*] EC. The Commission will issue a letter of formal notice followed by a reasoned opinion. The only difference is that the Commission must give both Member States, the complainant and the defendant, the opportunity to submit observations and observations on the other party's case before issuing a reasoned opinion. It is only if the Commission does not issue a reasoned opinion within three months that the complainant Member State may bring an action. Even under this provision, therefore, its role in enforcing EC law is still cast very much as a supplementary one.

V. Interim Measures

Within any judicial procedure there is a need for interim measures to prevent any judgment from being pre-empted by 'events on the ground'.

Article 186 [*243*] EC. The Court of Justice may in any cases before it prescribe any necessary interim measures.

The Commission can only seek interim measures once it has brought a matter before the Court. The most extensive recent discussion of interim relief was given in the *FYROM* judgment.[38]

---

[38] This action was brought under Article 225 [*298*] EC which is a provision allowing the Commission to take enforcement action if it considers a Member State is misusing Article 224 [*297*] EC. The issues are identical, however, to interim measures sought under Articles 169 [*226*] or 170 [*227*] EC.

Case C-120/94R Commission v Greece [1994] ECR I-3037

In 1994 the Greek Government imposed sanctions on the Former Yugoslav Republic of Macedonia (FYROM) claiming that the latter had ambitions on Greek territory. The Commission considered that these sanctions violated EC legislation on common rules for imports from third countries. The Greek Government sought to justify the sanctions under Article 224 [*297*]EC which allows Member States to derogate from EC law in the 'event of serious international tension constituting a threat of war'. The Commission considered this an improper use of the provision, and brought an action against Greece. It then sought interim measures.

42. Article 186 of the Treaty empowers the Court to prescribe any necessary interim measures in cases before it. It makes no exceptions or distinctions according to the nature of the case.

.....

44. Pursuant to Article 83(2) of the Rules of Procedure an order prescribing interim measures may only be made in the presence of circumstances giving rise to urgency and on the basis of pleas of fact and law establishing a prima facie case for the interim measures applied for.

45. According to Article 86(4) of the Rules of Procedure and the third paragraph of Article 36 of the EEC Statute of the Court of Justice such an order may in no way prejudice the decision of the Court on the substance of the case.

.....

67. The measures adopted unilaterally by the Hellenic Republic with regard to the FYROM are undoubtedly contrary to the fundamental Community rules regarding the free movement of goods and the common commercial policy.

68. However, the Hellenic Republic relies on Article 224 of the Treaty, a provision which, at first sight, permits a Member State in certain exceptional circumstances to derogate even from fundamental Community rules.

69. In order to ascertain whether, as the Commission submits, the essential requirements for the application of Article 224 are not met in this case and whether, as the Commission also claims, the Greek Government has made improper use of the powers referred to in that Article, it would be necessary to consider complex legal questions, including the determination of the scope of the judicial review to be exercised in the context of the procedure laid down in the second paragraph of Article 225 of the Treaty.

70. Those questions require thorough consideration of argument from both sides. At the stage of the application for interim measures, it is sufficient to note that the arguments put forward by the Commission appear, at first sight, to be sufficiently pertinent and serious to establish a prima facie case justifying the interim measures.

71. It is therefore necessary to consider whether the condition of urgency is satisfied.

.....

89. As regards the requirement of urgency, it should be noted that the Court has consistently held (see in particular the order in Case C-280/93R *Germany v Council* [1993] ECR I-3667, paragraph 22) that the urgency of the interim measures, referred to in Article 83(2) of the Rules of Procedure, must be considered in the light of the need to adopt provisional measures in order to avoid serious and irreparable harm resulting from application of the measure which is the subject-matter of the main action.

90. The various types of harm alleged by the Commission must be considered in turn.

91. As regards in the first place the harm to the common commercial policy, to freedom of transit for goods within the Community and to the internal market, it should be observed that the arguments put forward by the Commission are based on the link between the harm alleged and the breach of Community law by the Hellenic Republic. According to the Commission, the seriousness of the harm results from the manifest nature of the breach.

92. However, applying the considerations set out in paragraphs 67 to 70, above, although the Commission's arguments may be sufficient to establish a prima facie case it is not possible to confirm that the Hellenic Republic has committed a manifest breach of Community law, as the Commission maintains, since without detailed consideration of the matter it is not possible to establish that the Greek Government relied improperly on Article 224 of the Treaty or made an improper use of the powers provided for by that Article.

93. The existence of harm in that respect has therefore not been established.

94. As regards in the second place the breach of the general political guidelines laid down by the European Council and the harm resulting from the exacerbation of tension in the Balkans and of the risk of war, which is alleged to have been caused by the maintenance of the measures adopted by the Hellenic Republic against the FYROM, it must be noted that even if the Court were competent to make the political judgments which would be indispensable in order to assess the existence of harm and, above all, of a link between that harm and the conduct of the Greek Government, it could not, in any event, form an opinion at this stage of the procedure for interim measures. The assessments it might make would inevitably encroach upon the powers of the Court in the context of Articles 224 and 225 of the Treaty and, therefore, prejudice the decision on the substance of the case.

95. As regards in the third place the irreparable harm suffered by Community traders, the Commission has merely made general assertions without any attempt to support them with adequate facts. That harm has therefore not been established.

96. As regards in the last place the harm suffered by the FYROM, the information supplied by the Commission appears to be sufficient to establish its existence.

97. Nevertheless, it is necessary to consider whether the Commission is entitled in these proceedings on an application for the adoption of interim measures to rely 'regardless of any harm to Community interests' on harm suffered by a non-Member country as a result of measures which the Hellenic Republic considers justified under Article 224 of the Treaty.

98. In view of the fact that the proceedings on the application for interim measures are accessory to the main action, the urgency of the interim measures must be considered in the light of the interests which Articles 224 and 225 of the Treaty seek to protect, those provisions being applicable to the case before the Court.

99. Article 224 requires the Member States to consult each other with a view to taking together the steps needed to prevent the functioning of the common market being affected by measures which a Member State may be called upon to take in certain exceptional circumstances. Article 225, by contrast, provides in the first paragraph for the Commission to intervene only where measures taken under Articles 223 and 224 have the effect of distorting the conditions of competition in the common market.

100. Without prejudice to a more detailed interpretation of those provisions in the course of the main proceedings, it would seem that the task entrusted to the Commission by Article 225, with regard to Article 224, is intended to safeguard the interests of the Community.

101. Accordingly, the Court considers that it cannot take into account in these proceedings for interim measures the harm suffered by the FYROM.

102. In those circumstances the application for interim measures must be dismissed.

VI. Penalties under Article 171 [*228*] EC

Member States have always been under an obligation to take the necessary measures to comply with a judgment of the Court of Justice.[39] Until the TEU, whilst failure to do so might possibly result in their being pursued in national courts,[40] there were no Community level sanctions.

Article 171(1) [*228(1)*] EC. If the Court of Justice finds that a Member State has failed to fulfil an obligation under this Treaty, the State shall be required to take the necessary measures to comply with the judgment of the Court of Justice.

2. If the Commission considers that the Member State concerned has not taken such measures it shall, after giving that Member State the opportunity to submit its observations, issue a reasoned opinion specifying the points on which the Member State concerned has not complied with the judgment of the Court of Justice.

If the Member State concerned fails to take the necessary measures to comply with the Court's judgment within the time-limit laid down by the Commission, the latter may bring the case before the Court of Justice. In so doing it shall specify the amount of the lump sum or penalty payment to be paid by the Member State concerned which it considers appropriate in the circumstances.

If the Court of Justice finds that the Member State concerned has not complied with its judgment it may impose a lump sum or penalty payment on it.

This procedure shall be without prejudice to Article 170 [*227*].

The procedure which now exists is a convoluted one. The Commission must, in essence, repeat the process of a formal letter of notice, submission of observations and the issuing of a reasoned opinion.

The sanctions incurred at the end of a successful Article 171 [*228*] EC action may also have little deterrent or preventive effect. The existing procedure, in only allowing a one-off lump sum or penalty payment to be imposed upon a defaulting State, is, meanwhile fairly inflexible in the sanctions it allows to be imposed upon a Member

---

[39]   Article 171 EEC.
[40]   See pp 398-422.

State.[41] In relation to persistently recurring offences, a system of periodic fines may have a greater deterrent effect. Conversely, if the purpose of Article 171 [228] EC is not merely to penalise the State involved but also to stop the egregious behaviour, then there may be circumstances where it would have been appropriate for a series of injunctive remedies to have been provided which would allow the Commission to seek relief in the national courts of the State in question.[42]

No sanctions have yet been imposed by the Court under Article 171 [228] EC. The reason for this is that it was not until early 1997 that the Commission sought to instigate the procedure for the first time.[43] In preparation the Commission issued a Memorandum in 1996 setting out the criteria which will determine the size of the fine it seeks.

Memorandum on applying Article 171 of the EC Treaty[44]

3. Under Article 171, if a member State has failed to take the necessary measures to comply with a judgment of the Court of Justice within the time limit laid down in the reasoned opinion addressed to it by the Commission, the latter may bring the case before the Court of Justice. In so doing, the Commission specifies '*the amount of the lump sum or penalty payment to be paid by the Member State concerned which it considers appropriate in the circumstances*'.

Within this procedure, the Commission has *a discretion in deciding* whether to refer the case to the Court but, if it does decide to do so, it is required to *give its view as to the penalty and the amount thereof* when lodging its application.

This does not, however, in the Commission's view, mean that it must ask for a penalty to be imposed in every case. Where circumstances warrant (e.g. where the infringement is minor or there is no risk of the offence being repeated), the Commission may refrain from asking for a penalty to be imposed; it must nevertheless state its reasons.

---

[41]   Article 172 [229] EC provides for the Parliament and the Council to adopt jointly regulations giving the Court unlimited jurisdiction with the regard to the penalties it may impose. No such regulations have yet been adopted.

[42]   Curtin, D. 'The Constitutional Structure of the Union: A Europe of Bits and Pieces' (1993) 30 *CMLRev* 17, 33.

[43]   The first actions were brought against Germany, Case C-121/97 *Commission v Germany*, Case C-122/97 *Commission v Germany*, OJ 1997 C 166/7.

[44]   OJ 1996 C 242/7.

4. Article 171 offers a choice between two types of pecuniary sanction, a lump sum or a penalty payment. The basic object of the whole infringement procedure is to secure compliance as rapidly as possible, and the Commission considers that a penalty payment is the most appropriate instrument for achieving it.

This does not, however, mean that it will never ask for a lump sum to be imposed.

5. Decisions as to the amount of the penalty must be taken with an eye to its actual purpose, which is to ensure that Community law is effectively enforced. The Commission considers that the amount must be calculated on the basis of three fundamental criteria:
- the seriousness of the infringement
- its duration
- the need to ensure that the penalty itself is a deterrent to further infringements.

6. As regards seriousness, an infringement in the form of failure to comply with a judgment is always quite clearly serious. However, for the specific purpose of fixing the amount of the penalty, the Commission will also take account of two parameters closely linked to the underlying infringement which gave rise to the original judgment, vis the importance of the Community rules which have been infringed and the effects of the infringement on general and particular interests.

6.1. In assessing the importance of the community provisions which have been infringed, the Commission will have regard to their nature and scope rather than to their standing in the hierarchy of norms. Thus, for example, an infringement of the principle of non-discrimination must always be regarded as very serious, regardless of whether it has come about through a breach of the principle laid down by the EC Treaty itself or of the principle as set out in a regulation or directive. Generally speaking, for example, attacks on fundamental rights and on the four fundamental freedoms enshrined in the Treaty should be regarded as serious and a penalty appropriate to that degree of seriousness should be imposed in such cases.

6.2. The effects of the infringement on general or particular interests will have to be gauged on a case-by-case basis. Examples of such effects would be a loss of own resources resulting from an infringement or the particularly damaging effects of pollution arising from an action in breach of Community law. Where the effects of an infringement on the general interest are concerned, its impact on the functioning of the Community must be taken into account. Clearly, an unwarranted prohibition on the marketing in one Member State of goods manufactured in another has an immediate and obvious effect on the functioning of the common market, but other, less drastic measures, or even in some cases a failure by a Member State to act, may have just as much effect on the functioning of the Community.

6.3. More specifically, when taking the interests of individuals into account for the purpose of calculating the amount of a penalty, the Commission does not set out to obtain redress for the damage and loss sufferer as a result of an infringement, since such redress may be obtained by commencing proceedings before the national courts. The Commission's purpose is rather to take into consideration the effects of an infringement from the point of view of the individual and the economic operators concerned; thus, for example, consequences are not the same where the breach concerns, either an individual case of misapplication (non-recognition of a diploma), or the failure to implement a directive on the mutual recognition of diplomas, which would prejudice the interests of an entire profession.

7. The Commission will also take into account the duration of an infringement in deciding the amount of a penalty. In proceedings whose object is to establish that a judgment of the Court of Justice has not been complied with, the duration will, as a rule, be considerable.

8. From the point of view of the effectiveness of the penalty, it is important to set amounts such that the penalty has a deterrent effect. To impose purely symbolic penalties would negate the whole purpose of this addition to the infringement procedure and run counter to the ultimate objective of the procedure, which is to ensure that Community law is fully enforced.

A decision as to whether to ask for a penalty to be imposed will depend on the circumstances of the case, as stated at point 3. But, once it has been found that a penalty should be imposed, for it to have a deterrent effect it must be set at a higher figure if there is any risk of a repetition (or where there has been a repetition) of the failure to comply, in order to cancel out any economic advantage which the Member State responsible for the infringement might derive in the case in point.

VII. The Effectiveness of Centralised Enforcement

a. The Prosecutorial Discretion of the Commission

The marginality of Article 170 [227] EC results in the effectiveness of centralised enforcement processes resting almost entirely in the hands of the Commission. This is not simply because only the Commission can bring an Article 169 [226] EC action, but also because it has a discretion whether to bring proceedings or not.

Case 247/87 Star Fruit Co. v Commission [1989] ECR 291, [1990] 1 CMLR 733

A Belgian banana trader alleged that it was prejudiced by the organisation of the French banana market which it believed was contrary to EC law. It tried to use Article 175 [*232*]EC arguing that the EC Commission's failure to initiate Article 169 [*226*] EC proceedings constituted a failure to act which could be proceeded against.

11. However, it is clear from the scheme of Article 169 of the Treaty that the Commission is not bound to commence the proceedings provided for in that provision but in this regard has a discretion which excludes the right for individuals to require that institution to adopt a specific position.

12. It is only if it considers that the Member state in question has failed to fulfil one of its obligations that the Commission delivers a reasoned opinion. Furthermore, in the event that the state does not comply with the opinion within the period allowed, the institution has in any event the right, but not the duty, to apply to the Court of Justice for a declaration that the alleged breach of obligations has occurred.

13. It must also be observed that in requesting the Commission to commence proceedings pursuant to Article 169 the applicant is in fact seeking the adoption of acts which are not of direct and individual concern to it within the meaning of the second paragraph of Article 173 and which it could not therefore challenge by means of an action for annulment in any event.

14. Consequently, the applicant cannot be entitled to raise the objection that the Commission failed to commence proceedings against the French republic pursuant to Article 169 of the Treaty.

This discretion has been criticised in the academic literature as diminishing the effectiveness of EC law.[45] Repeated attempts to oblige the Commission to take action have all been turned down.[46] The Court

---

[45] Mastroianni, R. 'The Enforcement Procedure under Article 169 of the EC Treaty and the Powers of the European Commission: *Quis Custodiet Custodes*?' (1995) 1 *European Public Law* 535. By contrast see Evans, A. 'The Enforcement Procedure of Article 169 EEC: Commission Discretion' (1979) 4 *ELRev* 442.

[46] The discretion enjoyed by the Commission has been repeatedly reaffirmed, e.g. Case T-575/93 *Koelman v Commission* [1996] ECR II-1; Case T-277/94

will not look at the Commission's motive for bringing an action,[47] nor are there any time limits within which an action should be brought.[48] In the light of this, complainants have recently sought to involve the Ombudsman, arguing that whilst the Commission may not be compelled to bring an action, failure to do so constitutes an act of maladministration. In an inquiry into the Commission's refusal to bring Article 169 [226] EC proceedings against the British Government for failure to carry out an environmental impact assessment before authorising the Newbury bypass, the Ombudsman moved some way towards giving complainants procedural rights. It found that there had been an act of maladministration in the Commission's releasing a press statement stating that it was not going to start proceedings before it had informed the complainants of its decision:

'An administrative process of this kind normally concludes with a reasoned decision communicated to those who have participated in the process. The Ombudsman considers that, as a matter of good administrative behaviour, the Commission should have informed the registered complainants of its decision before, or at least at the same time as announcing the decision publicly through a press release.'[49]

In a subsequent Decision the Ombudsman stated that it was not enough for the Commission to notify a complainant of a refusal to take action, it must give reasons for that refusal.[50] Following its Decision on the Newbury Bypass the Ombudsman set out a few more comments. It considered that before making its final decision the Commission might

---

	AITEC v Commission [1996] ECR II-351.
47	Case 416/85 *Commission v United Kingdom* [1988] ECR 3127.
48	Case 7/68 *Commission v Italy* [1968] ECR 423, [1969] CMLR 1; Case 7/71 *Commission v France* [1971] ECR 1003, [1972] CMLR 453 . It has been suggested, however, that an action may be declared inadmissible if an excessive delay prevents a Member State from being able to defend itself. There are no cases of this having happened yet. Case C-96/89 *Commission v Netherlands* [1991] ECR I-2461.
49	Decision 206/27.10.95/HS/UK, para. 3.2. European Ombudsman, *European Ombudsman Annual Report for 1996* (1997, OOPEC, Luxembourg) 64.
50	Decision 132/21.9.95/AH/EN. Ibid., 67.

come to a provisional conclusion that there had been no breach of EC law with an invitation to submit observations within a defined period. The Ombudsman saw this as having the advantages of both allowing the Commission to receive criticisms in time for it to evaluate and respond, and of allowing citizens to participate more effectively in the administrative process.[51]

Evidence suggests that external considerations will influence which cases are pursued by the Commission. Enforcing EC law is but one of the Commission's policies. Its other powers, notably its agenda-setting powers, have influenced its enforcement policy. The prioritisation of particular policies by the Commission has also resulted in the prioritisation of enforcement of those policies by the Commission. Thus, whilst there is considerably more legislation in the field of the agriculture than in that of the internal market, there is no evidence to suggest Member State compliance in one is worse than in the other. Research suggested that between 1978 and 1993 the internal market accounted for over 35% of all letters of formal notice and over 40% of all reasoned opinions, whilst agriculture accounted for just under 25% of all letters of formal notice and 18% of all reasoned opinions.[52]

b. Article 169 [*226*] EC as a Negotiation Process

The process remains fluid even after the Commission has started an investigation. In particular, two factors militate against the Commission taking a draconian line against Member States. The first is the remoteness of the sanctions provided under Article 171 [*228*] EC. The tortuousness of the procedures involved result in the weight of any threat by the Commission being extremely limited. Secondly, it is rarely in the Commission's interest to adopt a confrontational approach vis-à-vis a particular Member State. It will require that State's cooperation in a host of other policy areas. In every instance there is, thus, a conflict of

---

[51]   Ibid., 66.

[52]   Mendrinou, M. 'Non-compliance and the European Commission's role in integration' (1996) 3 *JEPP* 1, 9-10.

interest within the Commission which results in its having to weigh the benefits of compliance against the costs of obstruction by a Member State in other areas.[53]

Even after the formal instigation of Article 169 [*226*] EC proceedings the procedure continues to be one of negotiation and compromise.[54] In 1995 1,016 letters of formal notice were issued. This figure was not dissimilar from the previous two years. 974 were issued in 1994 and 1,209 in 1993. On average over the last three years, only just over 30% of those letters result in a reasoned opinion. Thus, 192 reasoned opinions were issued in 1995, 546 in 1994, and 352 in 1993. The number of cases referred to the Court is even smaller. 72 new cases were referred in 1995, 89 in 1994 and 44 in 1993. The figures suggest that in only about 7% of the cases where the Commission issues a letter of formal notice will the matter actually arrive at the Court.[55] This is a very small percentage, as it should be remembered that the Commission will only issue a letter of formal notice if it considers that there has been a breach and the Member State has not responded satisfactorily to its inquiries.

Further Reading

Craig, P. 'Once upon a Time in the West: Direct Effect and the Federalization of EEC Law' (1992) 12 *Oxford Journal of Legal Studies* 453
EC Commission, Annual Reports on the Monitoring and Application of EC Law
Evans, A. 'The Enforcement Procedure of Article 169 EEC: Commission Discretion' (1979) 4 *European Law Review* 442
Mastroianni, R. 'The Enforcement Procedure under Article 169 of the

---

[53]   Craig, P. 'Once upon a Time in the West: Direct Effect and the Federalization of EEC Law' (1992) 12 *OJLS* 453, 455-456.
[54]   Snyder, F. 'The Effectiveness of European Community Law' (1993) 56 *MLR* 19, 30.
[55]   EC Commission, *Thirteenth Annual Report on monitoring the application of Community law*, OJ 1996, C 303/1.

EC Treaty and the Powers of the European Commission: *Quis Custodiet Custodes?*' (1995) 1 *European Public Law* 535

Mendrinou, M. 'Non-compliance and the European Commission's role in integration' (1996) 3 *Journal of European Public Policy* 1

Snyder, F. 'The Effectiveness of European Community Law: Institutions, Processes, Tools and Techniques' (1993) 56 *Modern Law Review* 19

White, R. and Dashwood, A. 'Enforcement Actions Under Articles 169 and 170 EEC' (1989) 14 *European Law Review* 388

7. Enforcement of EC Law Through National Courts

I. Introduction

The weaknesses of Article 169 [226] EC and 170 [*227*] EC stem not just from Member State dilatoriness and overstretched Commission resources. They also arise from a too monolithic view of Member States which adopted the international law fiction that central governments can and therefore should be responsible for the acts of all public bodies. Furthermore, whilst the last Chapter began by emphasising the importance of Member States within the whole process, the phase within which they enjoy least influence is that of the application of EC law. In a market economy, many EC legal obligations, most notably in the fields of competition, consumer, social and environmental law, can only be applied by private parties, and in such areas governments are reduced to, at best, a policing role.

There is some recognition of the diversity of State institutions and the importance of private actors in ensuring the effectiveness of EC law in the development of centralised enforcement mechanisms since the Treaty of Rome. Article 180(d) [*237(d)*] EC was added at Maastricht, allowing the ECB, under conditions analogous to Article 169 [226] EC, to bring national central banks before the Court of Justice for failure to meet their obligations in EC law.

Both the Commission and the ECB have also been given limited enforcement powers against private undertakings in a limited number of fields. In the field of competition the Commission has the power to fine undertakings and require infringements to be brought to an end.[1] In the field of external trade, it can impose duties on third country undertakings which are engaging in unfair trade practices.[2] The ECB, on its inception, will have the powers to fine undertakings which do not comply with any regulations or decisions it may adopt on the minimum reserves of banks, the prudential supervision of banks as well clearing and payment systems.[3]

Such centralised systems of enforcement do not get round the problem of the limited resources of central institutions. In addition, they create dangers of a 'denial of justice', as individuals will always be dependent upon the assent of these enforcement agencies to action against illegal conduct affecting the former's interests. With limited resources, there is always a danger that even the best-intentioned institution will have to prioritise with the result that individuals will perceive justice not to be done.

From an early stage, EC law has been able to ameliorate many of these problems by creating mechanisms through which EC law can be enforced in a decentralised manner through national courts. The relative success of decentralised enforcement has meant that in many areas of EC law national courts are seen as the primary agents of enforcement.[4]

---

[1] e.g. Regulation 17, OJ Spec Ed. 1962, 204/62, Articles 15 and 3 respectively.

[2] e.g. in relation to dumping see Regulation 384/96/EC, OJ 1996, L 56/1, especially Articles 7-9.

[3] Article 108a [*110*] EC.

[4] Curtin, D. 'The Decentralised Enforcement of Community Law Rights: Judicial Snakes and Ladders' in Curtin, D. & O'Keeffe, *Constitutional Adjudication in European Community and National Law* (1992, Butterworths, Dublin).

i. The Development of Direct Effect

The need for a decentralised system of enforcement pursued by private individuals through national courts propelled the process of constitutionalisation. In *Van Gend en Loos*, it will be remembered, the Court held that the EC Treaty had sovereign legal qualities in response to a question from a Dutch court as to whether it gave rise to rights which should be protected by national courts.[5] The Court then held that, as a result of these qualities:

> '... the subjects of [the Community] comprise not only Member States but also their nationals. Independently of the legislation of Member States, Community law therefore not only imposes legislation on individuals but is also intended to confer upon them rights which become part of their heritage. These rights arise not only where they are expressly granted by the Treaty, but also by reason of obligations which the Treaty imposes in a clearly defined way upon individuals as well as upon the Member States and upon the institutions of the Community.'

The doctrine of direct effect through which these rights were to be realised was a very narrow one. The provision in question, Article 12 [*25*] EC prohibiting the imposition of customs duties or charges having equivalent effect on imports, was only found to give rise to individuals because it satisfied a number of narrow criteria: that it was a clear, unconditional, negative prohibition which was not dependent upon any further implementing measures at the EC or national level.

The criteria appear restrictive and implied a narrow vision of which provisions could be invoked before national courts. In practice, they have been interpreted liberally. The requirement that provisions contain a negative prohibition was dropped in *Reyners*.[6] Positively

---

[5] Case 26/62 *Van Gend en Loos v Nederlandse Administratie der Belastingen* [1963] ECR 1, [1963] CMLR 105.

[6] Case 2/74 *Reyners v Belgium* [1974] ECR 631, [1974] 2 CMLR 305.

phrased provisions in the EC Treaty are more open-ended, stipulating a particular objective from which a set of corollary duties flow.

Case 43/75 Defrenne v SABENA [1976] ECR 455, [1976] 2 CMLR 98

Under Belgian law female air stewards were required to retire at forty, unlike their male counterparts. Gabrielle DeFrenne had been forced to retire from the Belgian national carrier, SABENA on this ground in 1968. She brought an action claiming that the lower pension payments this entailed breached the principle in Article 119 [*141*] EC that 'each Member State shall ensure and maintain the principle that men and women should receive equal pay for work of equal value'. On its face there appeared to be a number of obstacles to the provision being directly effective. The principle seemed to be neither sufficiently clear or unconditional, as complete implementation of the principle would require elaboration of further criteria for recognising discrimination and implementing measures to abolish.

16. Under the terms of the first paragraph of Article 119, the Member States are bound to ensure and maintain 'the application of the principle that men and women should receive equal pay for equal work'.

17. The second and third paragraphs of the same Article add a certain number of details concerning the concepts of pay and work referred to in the first paragraph.

18. For the purposes of the implementation of these provisions a distinction must be drawn within the whole area of application of Article 119 between, first, direct and overt discrimination which may be identified solely with the aid of the criteria based on equal work and equal pay referred to by the Article in question and, secondly, indirect and disguised discrimination which can only be identified by reference to more explicit implementing provisions of a Community or national character.

19. It is impossible not to recognize that the complete implementation of the aim pursued by Article 119, by means of the elimination of all discrimination, direct or indirect, between men and women workers, not only as regards individual undertakings but also entire branches of industry and even of the economic system as a whole, may in certain cases involve the elaboration of criteria whose implementation necessitates the taking of appropriate measures at Community and national level.

.....

21. Among the forms of direct discrimination which may be identified solely by reference to the criteria laid down by Article 119 must be included in particular those which have their origin in legislative provisions or in collective labour agreements and which may be detected on the basis of a purely legal analysis of the situation.

22. This applies even more in cases where men and women receive unequal pay for equal work carried out in the same establishment or service, whether public or private.

23. As is shown by the very findings of the judgment making the reference, in such a situation the court is in a position to establish all the facts which enable it to decide whether a woman worker is receiving lower pay than a male worker performing the same tasks.

24. In such situation, at least, Article 119 is directly applicable and may thus give rise to individual rights which the courts must protect.

In the 1970s, following judgments such as *DeFrenne*, the strict criteria set out in *Van Gend en Loos* were relaxed in favour of a more flexible test, namely whether the provision was sufficiently precise and unconditional to be invoked in national courts.[7] In the eyes of one judge, the invocability of EC Treaty provisions was therefore reduced to a simple question of justiciability.[8]

Direct effect, however, does no more than give individuals the right to invoke provisions of EC law before a national court. Increasingly, EC legislation has stipulated that Member States should provide remedies and secure effective judicial protection for the substantive provisions set out in the legislation. A good example of this

---

[7] e.g. Case 148/78 *Ratti* [1979] ECR 1629, [1980] 1 CMLR 96; Case 8/81 *Becker v Finanzamt Münster-Innenstadt* [1982] ECR 53, [1982] 1 CMLR 499. On this development see Dashwood, A. 'The Principle of Direct Effect in European Community Law (1978) 16 *JCMS* 229; Craig, P. 'Once upon a time in the West: Direct Effect and the Federalization of EEC Law' (1992) 12 *OJLS* 453, 460-470; Schermers, H. & Waelbroeck, *Judicial Protection in the European Communities* (1992, 5th Edition, Kluwer, Deventer) 141-148. For a slightly different perspective see Prechal, S. *Directives in European Community Law: A Study of Directives and Their Enforcement in National Courts* (1995, Clarendon, Oxford) 132-144.

[8] Pescatore, P. 'The Doctrine of Direct Effect: An Infant Disease of Community Law' (1983) 8 *ELRev* 155, 176-7.

is Article 6 of Directive 76/207/EEC, the Equal Treatment Directive which stipulates:

> 'Member States shall introduce into their national legal systems such measures as are necessary to enable all persons who consider themselves wronged by failure to apply the principle of equal treatment to pursue their claims by judicial process, possibly after recourse to other competent authorities.'[9]

A simple test of justiciability does not facilitate the enforcement of such provisions as all would appear to be dependent upon implementing measures taken by the national authorities. The Court has indicated that it may still be possible to invoke these.

Case C-271/91 Marshall v Southampton and South West Hampshire Area Health Authority (No. 2) [1993] ECR I-4367, [1993] 3 CMLR 293

Ms Marshall, a dietician, was required to retire at an earlier age than her male counterparts in breach of Directive 76/207/EEC. Under the Sex Discrimination Act 1975 the remedy available for unlawful discrimination was compensation, with the maximum amount to be awarded being £6250, whilst her damage assessed was considered to be £18,405. Ms Marshall claimed that the cap on damages was in breach of Article 6 of the Directive.

22. Article 6 of the Directive puts Member States under a duty to take the necessary measures to enable all persons who consider themselves wronged by discrimination to pursue their claims by judicial process. Such obligation implies that the measures in question should be sufficiently effective to achieve the objective of the directive and

---

[9]   OJ 1976 L 39/40. Other examples include Directive 89/48/EEC on a general system for the recognition of higher education diplomas awarded on completion of professional education and training of at least three years' duration, OJ 1989, L 19/16, Article 8(2); Directive 89/665/EEC, remedies in the field of public procurement, OJ 1989 L 395/34; Directive 92/49 (Third Non-Life Insurance Directive) on the coordination of laws, regulations and administrative provisions relating to direct insurance other than life assurance OJ, 1992, L 228/1, Article 56; Directive 92/59/ EC on General Product Safety, OJ 1992, L 228/24, Article 14(2).

should be capable of being effectively relied upon by the persons concerned before national courts.

23. As the Court held in Case 14/83 *Von Colson and Kamann v Land Nordrhein-Westfalen* [1984] ECR 1891, paragraph 18, Article 6 does not prescribe a specific measure to be taken in the event of a breach of the prohibition of discrimination but leaves Member States free to choose between the different solutions suitable for achieving the objective of the Directive, depending on the different situations which may arise.

24. However, the objective is to arrive at real equality of opportunity and cannot therefore be attained in the absence of measures appropriate to restore such equality when it has not been observed. As the Court stated in paragraph 23 of the judgment in *Von Colson and Kamann* cited above those measures must be such as to guarantee real and effective judicial protection and have a real deterrent effect on the employer.

25. Such requirements necessarily entail that the particular circumstances of each breach of the principle of equal treatment should be taken into account. In the event of discriminatory dismissal contrary to Article 5(1) of the Directive, a situation of equality could not be restored without either reinstating the victim of discrimination or, in the alternative, granting financial compensation for the loss and damage sustained.

26. When financial compensation is the measure adopted in order to achieve the objective indicated above, it must be adequate, in that it must enable the loss and damage actually sustained as a result of the discriminatory dismissal to be made good in full in accordance with the applicable national rules.

.....

34. It follows from the considerations set out above as to the meaning and scope of Article 6 of the Directive, that that provision is an essential factor for attaining the fundamental objective of equal treatment for men and women, in particular as regards working conditions, including the conditions governing dismissal, referred to in Article 5(1) of the Directive, and that where, in the event of discriminatory dismissal, financial compensation is the measure adopted in order to restore that equality, such compensation must be full and may not be limited *a priori* in terms of amount.

35. Accordingly, the combined provisions of Article 6 and Article 5 of the Directive give rise, on the part of a person who has been injured as a result of discriminatory dismissal, to rights which that person must be able to rely upon before the national courts as against the State and authorities which are an emanation of the State.

36. The fact that Member States may choose among different solutions in order to achieve the objective pursued by the directive depending on the situations which may arise, cannot result in an individual's being prevented from relying on Article 6 in a situation such as that in the main proceedings where the national authorities have no discretion in applying the chosen solution.

37. It should be pointed out in that connection that, as appears in particular from the judgment in Joined Cases C-6/90 and C-9/90 *Francovich and Others v Italian Republic* [1991] ECR I-5357, at paragraph 17, the right of a State to choose among several possible means of achieving the objectives of a directive does not exclude the possibility for individuals of enforcing before national courts rights whose content can be determined sufficiently precisely on the basis of the provisions of the directive alone.

In Banks Advocate General van Gerven therefore stated:

> '... in so far as a provision of Community law is *sufficiently operational* in itself to be applied by a court, it has direct effect. The clarity, precision, unconditional nature, completeness or perfection of the rule and its lack of dependence on discretionary implementing measures are in that respect merely aspects of one and the same characteristic feature which that rule must exhibit, namely it must be capable of being applied by a court to a specific case.'[10]

Operationality is a peculiarly fuzzy concept because it implies that the matter which must be addressed is no longer simply the specificity of the language but whether the matter is amenable to judicial resolution. Furthermore, increasingly, extra-judicial remarks were being made by judges of the Court that there were limits on what matters could be decided by courts.[11]

Case C-236/92 Comitato di Coordinamento per la Difesa della Cava v Regione Lombardia [1994] ECR I-483

A non-governmental organisation sought to oppose the siting of a waste dump by the regional authorities in Lombardy. It sought to invoke Article 4 of Directive

---

[10]   Case C-128/92 *Banks v British Coal* [1994] ECR I-1209, 1237.

[11]   Koopmans, T. 'The Role of Law in the Next Stage of European Integration' (1986) 35 *ICLQ* 925; Mancini, F. & Keeling, D. 'Language, Culture and Politics in the Life of the European Court of Justice' (1995) 1 *Columbia Journal of European Law* 397, 405.

75/442/EEC, the Framework Directive on waste, which stated, 'Member States shall take the necessary measures to ensure that waste is disposed of without endangering human health and without harming the environment ...' On its wording the provision seemed as precise as Article 119 [*141*] EC in *DeFrenne*. A consequence of its being directly effective would be that the national court would have to become engaged in deciding the difficult question of the best site for the dump.

8. The Court has consistently held (see in particular the judgments in Case 8/81 *Becker v Finanzamt Münster-Innenstadt* [1982] ECR 53 and Case 103/88 *Fratelli Costanzo v Commune di Milano* [1989] ECR 1839) that wherever the provisions of a directive appear, as far as their subject-matter is concerned, to be unconditional and sufficiently precise, those provisions may be relied upon by an individual against the State where the State fails to implement the directive in national law by the end of the period prescribed or where it fails to implement the directive correctly.

.....

11. The provision in question does not display the above characteristics.

12. Considered in its context, Article 4 of the directive, which essentially repeats the terms of the third recital in the preamble, indicates a programme to be followed and sets out the objectives which the Member States must observe in their performance of the more specific obligations imposed on them by Articles 5 to 11 of the directive concerning planning, supervision and monitoring of waste-disposal operations.

13. It must also be noted that the Court has already held, in relation to the Member States' obligations under Article 10 of the directive, that the provision does not lay down any particular requirement restricting the freedom of the Member States regarding the way in which they organize the supervision of the activities referred to therein but that that freedom must be exercised having due regard to the objectives mentioned in the third recital in the preamble to the directive and Article 4 thereof (see the judgment in Joined Cases 372 to 374/85 *Ministère Public v Traen* [1987] ECR 2141).

14. Thus, the provision at issue must be regarded as defining the framework for the action to be taken by the Member States regarding the treatment of waste and not as requiring, in itself, the adoption of specific measures or a particular method of waste disposal. It is therefore neither unconditional nor sufficiently precise and thus is not capable of conferring rights on which individuals may rely as against the State.

The siting of a waste dump is indeed one of those questions which is particularly unsuited to substantive resolution by a court. The decision will require a considerable degree of scientific expertise relating both to the composition of the waste and the geology of the area. There may well also be parties affected who will not be able to appear before the court for reasons of standing or cost. Yet the types of dispute susceptible to judicial resolution is not likely to be clear-cut, but will rather resemble a sliding scale, which will result in increasing references to the Court about whether a particular provision is directly effective or not.

ii. Vertical Direct Effect and Horizontal Direct Effect

The only provisions which were negatively phrased in the EC Treaty were those which restrained State intervention in the economy. A consequence of the holding in *Van Gend en Loos* that only negatively phrased provisions could be directly effective was that the neo-liberal qualities in the Treaty were reinforced. Direct effect was thus most frequently invoked by traders challenging Member State regulation of their transactions. The extension of direct effect to positively phrased provisions altered this. Positively phrased provisions committed Member States to take measures intervening in the economy. They were qualitatively different from negatively phrased provisions. In the case of the latter the right arises as a consequence of the duty imposed upon the State. The duty therefore precedes the right. Van Gend en Loos' right not to pay customs duties therefore arose as a consequence of the obligation on the Dutch Government not to levy them. This is not the case with positively phrased provisions. In the case of Article 119 [*141*] EC, therefore, the right to equal pay for work of equal value for men and women commits the Member State to take certain action. The State's duties follow the right. This is significant because it gives the right an indefeasible quality. As it is no longer a corollary of a duty addressed to one particular party, it can be asserted not just against that party but against all parties.[12]

---

[12]   On the application of this distinction within EC law see Coppel, J. 'Rights, Duties and the End of Marshall' (1994) 57 *MLR* 859, 864-866. Whilst the

The action was brought against SABENA, who, both parties acknowledged for these purposes was a private person. It was argued that Article 119 [*141*] EC could only be invoked against States.

30. It is also impossible to put forward arguments based on the fact that Article 119 only refers expressly to 'Member States'.

31. Indeed, as the Court has already found in other contexts, the fact that certain provisions of the Treaty are formally addressed to the Member States does not prevent rights from being conferred at the same time on any individual who has an interest in the performance of the duties thus laid down.

32. The very wording of Article 119 shows that it imposes on States a duty to bring about a specific result to be mandatorily achieved within a fixed period.

33. The effectiveness of this provision cannot be affected by the fact that the duty imposed by the Treaty has not been discharged by certain Member States and that the joint institutions have not reacted sufficiently energetically against this failure to act.

34. To accept the contrary view would be to risk raising the violation of the right to the status of a principle of interpretation, a position the adoption of which would not be consistent with the task assigned to the Court by Article 164 of the Treaty.

35. Finally, in its reference to 'Member States', Article 119 is alluding to those States in the exercise of all those of their functions which may usefully contribute to the implementation of the principle of equal pay.

36. Thus, contrary to the statements made in the course of the proceedings this provision is far from merely referring the matter to the powers of the national legislative authorities.

37. Therefore, the reference to 'Member States' in Article 119 cannot be interpreted as excluding the intervention of the courts in direct application of the Treaty.

---

issue of horizontal direct effect was first dealt with at length in *DeFrenne*, the Court had recognised in an earlier judgment that EC Treaty provisions could impose obligations on private parties, Case 36/74 *Walrave & Koch v Association Union Cycliste Internationale* [1974] ECR 1405, [1975] 1 CMLR 320.

38. Furthermore it is not possible to sustain any objection that the application by national courts of the principle of equal pay would amount to modifying independent agreements concluded privately or in the sphere of industrial relations such as individual contracts and collective labour agreements.

39. In fact, since Article 119 is mandatory in nature, the prohibition on discrimination between men and women applies not only to the action of public authorities, but also extends to all agreements which are intended to regulate paid labour collectively, as well as to contracts between individuals.

.....

69. The Governments of Ireland and the United Kingdom have drawn the Court's attention to the possible economic consequences of attributing direct effect to the provisions of Article 119, on the ground that such a decision might, in many branches of economic life, result in the introduction of claims dating back to the time at which such effect same into existence.

70. In view of the large number of people concerned such claims, which undertakings could not have foreseen, might seriously affect the financial situation of such undertakings and even drive some of them to bankruptcy.

71. Although the practical consequences of any judicial decision must be carefully taken into account, it would be impossible to go so far as to diminish the objectivity of the law and compromise its future application on the ground of the possible repercussions which might result, as regards the past, from such a judicial decision.

72. However, in the light of the conduct of several of the Member States and the views adopted by the Commission and repeatedly brought to the notice of the circles concerned, it is appropriate to take exceptionally into account the fact that, over a prolonged period, the parties concerned have been led to continue with practices which were contrary to Article 119, although not yet prohibited under their national law.

73. The fact that, in spite of the warnings given, the Commission did not initiate proceedings under Article 169 against the Member States concerned on grounds of failure to fulfil an obligation was likely to consolidate the incorrect impression as to the effects of Article 119.

74. In these circumstances, it is appropriate to determine that, as the general level at which pay would have been fixed cannot be known, important considerations of legal certainty affecting all the interests involved, both public and private, make it impossible in principle to reopen the question as regards the past.

75. Therefore, the direct effect of Article 119 cannot be relied on in order to support claims concerning pay periods prior to the date of this judgment, except as regards those workers who have already brought legal proceedings or made an equivalent claim.

A distinction has been drawn between vertical direct effect and horizontal direct effect. Taking a rather hierarchical view of the relationship between individual and State, vertically directly effective provisions are ones which can be invoked by individuals against an emanation of the State. Horizontally directly effective provisions, by contrast, are those which can be invoked against other private parties.

The socio-economic consequences of the finding of horizontal direct effect in *DeFrenne* were considerable. On the one hand protection for women in the workplace was significantly enhanced. On the other, the financial implications were also considerable as the immediate burden of compliance fell upon all parties against whom the right can be asserted. The Irish Government argued that the costs of compliance would exceed Irish receipts from the European Regional Development Fund for the period 1975-77 and the British Government argued that it would add 3.5% to labour costs - a considerable admission on the part of those two governments on the degree of exploitation of women in their respective jurisdictions.

With such large adjustment costs the only manner through which the Court could feel confident about compliance was through limiting the temporal effects of the ruling. Individuals would not be able to bring actions for that discrimination which had occurred since the Treaty had come into force - the normal rule. Instead, except in regard to proceedings which had already been commenced, Article 119 [*141*] EC was only to have direct effect in relation to discrimination which occurred after the judgment. The circumstances when rulings limiting the temporal effects of judgments in this way are rare.[13] Their symbolism is considerable, however. For, as Rasmussen has observed, it destroys the

---

[13] See Alexander, W. 'The Temporal Effects of Preliminary Rulings' (1988) 8 *YBEL* 11. Other examples include Case 24/86 *Blaizot v University of Liege* [1988] ECR 379, [1989] 1 CMLR 57; Case C-262/88 *Barber v GRE* [1990] ECR 1889, [1990] 2 CMLR 513; Case C-308/93 *Cabanis Issarte v Bestuur* [1996] ECR I-2097.

illusion that the Court is engaging in some neutral exercise of merely giving life to the text, as it is impossible 'to maintain this myth while ruling that Article 119 was deprived of direct effects until the day of pronouncement of the Court's decision; only to produce such effects from that day onwards'.[14]

iii. Direct Effect and Regulations

The bulk of EC law is not contained in the EC Treaty but in secondary legislation. The effective enforcement of EC law thus required that these be also able to be invoked in national courts.

Regulations were the least controversial of the instruments mentioned in Article 189 [*249*] EC. They are quasi-legislative and normative in nature, normally leaving little discretion as to their implementation to Member States.[15] Furthermore, the characterisation of regulations in Article 189(2) [*249(2)*] EC as being 'directly applicable' was closely associated, in some commentator's eyes at least, with the notion of direct effect.[16]

In *Leonesio* regulations were held to be capable of direct effect.[17] In that instance Ms Leonesio had slaughtered five dairy cows. Under the terms of two regulations she was entitled to slaughter premiums for these cows which were to be payable within two months. For budgetary reasons she was not paid by the Italian authorities. The Court held she could invoke the regulations against the Italian authorities on the grounds that the general nature of regulations and their direct applicability resulted in their being capable of direct effect.

---

14 Rasmussen, H. On *Law and Policy in the European Court of Justice* (1986, Martijnus Nijhoff, Dordrecht) 441.

15 See pp 156-157.

16 On the various views on the relationship between the terms see Steiner, J. 'Direct Applicability in EEC Law: A Chameleon Concept' (1982) 98 *LQR* 229.

17 Case 93/71 *Leonesio v Italian Ministry of Agriculture* [1972] ECR 293, [1973] CMLR 343.

iv. Direct Effect, Decisions and Directives

The position of Directives was more complicated. A number of objections were posited against directives being capable of direct effect.[18] It was stated, first, that the discretion given by Article 189 [*249*] EC to Member States to implement Directives resulted in individuals only being able to derive rights from the executory acts of national authorities. Secondly, it was argued that to give direct effect to Directives would blur the distinction between them and regulations which was so clearly spelt out in Article 189 [*249*] EC. Thirdly, it was argued that the use of only Directives in some sectors of the EC Treaty envisaged that the EC would not have direct legislative powers in these areas, a schema which would be destroyed by giving direct effect to Directives. Lastly, it was argued that, as there was no formal requirement that Directives be published, legal certainty would be prejudiced by according them direct effect.[19]

The path for granting direct effect to Directives was, however, eased by the Court's judgment in *Grad* that Decisions are capable of direct effect.[20]. In *Grad* a Decision putting in place the common system of value added taxation was invoked before a German court. The Court of Justice ruled that it would be incompatible with the binding effect of this Decision for it not to be capable of direct effect. As all the objections listed above in relation to Directives apply equally to Decisions, and Directives are also binding, it would have been contradictory for the Court subsequently to refuse Directives direct effect.

---

[18]   These objections are summarised in Lauwaars, R. *Lawfulness and legal force of Community decisions* (1973, Sijthoff, Leiden) 33.

[19]   This is no longer the case. Since the entry into force of the TEU there is a formal requirement that all regulations and directives be published, Article 191(2) [*254(2)*]EC.

[20]   Case 9/70 *Grad v Finanzamt Traustein* [1970] ECR 838, [1971] CMLR 1.

Case 41/74 Van Duyn v Home Office [1974] ECR 1337, [1975] 1 CMLR 1

Van Duyn was refused leave to enter the United Kingdom in order to take up an offer of a secretarial post at the Church of Scientology, as the United Kingdom government had imposed a ban on foreign scientologists entering the United Kingdom. Ms van Duyn challenged the ban on the grounds, *inter alia*, that it breached Directive 64/221/EEC, which required that any ban must be based upon the personal conduct of the individual. The Court considered that her association with the Church of Scientology met the requirements of the Directive. It considered, first, whether the Directive was capable of direct effect.

12.... It would be incompatible with the binding effect attributed to a directive by Article 189 to exclude, in principle, the possibility that the obligation which it imposes may be invoked by those concerned. In particular, where the Community authorities have, by directive, imposed on Member States the obligation to pursue a particular course of conduct, the useful effect of such an act would be weakened if individuals were prevented from relying on it before their national courts and if the latter were prevented from taking it into consideration as an element of Community law. Article 177, which empowers national courts to refer to the Court questions concerning the validity and interpretation of all acts of the Community institutions, without distinction, implies furthermore that these acts may be invoked by individuals in the national courts. It is necessary to examine, in every case, whether the nature, general scheme and wording of the provisions in question are capable of having direct effects on the relations between Member States and individuals.

The reasoning used is weak and starts from an *a contrario* position of whether there is any good reason why Directives should not have direct effect.[21] Indeed, Mancini, a former judge at the Court, has admitted that 'this judgment goes beyond the letter of Article 189'.[22] More significantly, the ruling provoked a strong counter reaction from both French and German courts.[23]

---

[21]   Hartley, T. *The Foundations of European Community Law* (1994, 3rd Edition, Clarendon, Oxford) 211-213.

[22]   Mancini, G. & Keeling, D. 'Language, Culture and Politics in the Life of the European Court of Justice' (1995) 1 *Columbia Journal of European Law* 397, 401.

[23]   The German Federal Fiscal Court similarly refused to allow a directive to be invoked before it in *Re Value Added Tax Directives* [1982] 1 CMLR 527.

Minister of the Interior v Cohn-Bendit, Judgment of 22 December 1978
[1980] 1 CMLR 543

Daniele Cohn-Bendit was a German national who had been a leader of the
student disturbances in 1968 had been offered a job as a broadcaster back in
France. The Minister of the Interior sought to deport him. Cohn-Bendit invoked
Directive 64/221 stating that it required that any decision be both formally
reasoned and that the grounds for the decision be made known to the immigrant.
As this had not happened here, the decision was therefore illegal. The matter
went up to the Conseil d'Etat, the highest administrative court in France.

... it appears clearly from the provisions of Article 189 of the Treaty that if directives bind
Member States 'with regard to the result to be achieved' and if, in order to achieve the
results which they define, the national authorities of Member States are under an
obligation to adapt their legislative and regulatory provisions to the directives which are
addressed to them, these authorities remain the only competent authorities to determine
the form to give to the implementation of these directives and to determine themselves,
under the control of the national judicial authorities their own method for producing their
effect in internal national law;
... directives cannot be invoked by persons within the jurisdiction of those Member States
in order to support a legal action undertaken against any administrative action with regard
to an individual;
... it follows from the foregoing that M. Cohn-Bendit cannot hope to succeed in his
argument ... to annul the decision of the Minister of the Interior. ...

The Court of Justice refined its reasoning in subsequent cases,
adding a further ground as to why directives were to be capable of
direct effect, the 'estoppel argument'. This argument ran that directives
imposed a duty upon Member States to adopt the appropriate
implementing measures by a certain date. Member States could not rely
upon their failure to carry out these obligations. They were thus
estopped or prevented from denying the direct effect of directives.

This argument was relied upon, first, to establish the contingent
direct effect of directives. In *Ratti* a trader was prosecuted for not
labelling his solvents in accordance with Italian law.[24] He sought to rely
upon two directives. Whilst the transitional period for one of these had

---

[24]   Case 148/78 *Pubblico Ministero v Ratti* [1979] ECR 1629, [1980] 1 CMLR
96.

expired, it had not for the other. The Court therefore held that he could only rely upon the first directive. The Member State was estopped by its failure to take the necessary implementing measures from denying this directive's direct effect. The other directive was not directly effective, however, as the Member State was still within its period of grace. Directives will only be directly effective, therefore, from the end of transposition, and, even then, will only be capable of direct effect if the Member State has failed to implement them or has not implemented them correctly.[25] Individual rights flow from the national provisions in the case of correctly implemented directives.[26]

The estoppel argument had other implications. Predicated on fault on the part of the Member State, it could be easily used to justify individual actions against Member States.[27] Directives were addressed to Member States and imposed obligations of transposition on them. Directives were not addressed to individuals, however, and they could not be at fault for a Directive which had not been transposed. A consequence of the 'estoppel' argument would be to suggest that Directives were incapable of horizontal direct effect.[28]

---

[25] For an example of inadequate implementation see Case 51/76 *Verbond van Nederlandse Ondernehmingen v Inspecteur der Inverrechten en Accijnzen* [1977] ECR 113, [1977]1 CMLR 413.

[26] Case 102/79 *Commission v Belgium* [1980] ECR 1473.

[27] Case 8/81 *Becker v Finanzamt Münster-Innenstadt* [1982] ECR 53, [1982] 1 CMLR 696.

[28] There was a considerable literature on this see Dashwood, A. 'The Principle of Direct Effect in European Community Law' (1978) 16 *JCMS* 229, 242-244; Easson, A. 'Can Directives Impose Obligations on Individuals' (1979) 4 *ELRev* 67; Timmermans, C. 'Directives: Their Effects within the National Legal Systems' (1979) 16 *CMLRev* 533, 541-545; Wyatt, D. 'The Direct Effect of Community Social Law: Not Forgetting Directives' (1983) 8 *ELRev* 241, 245-247; Green, N. 'Directives, Equity and the Protection of Individual Rights' (1984) 9 *ELRev* 295.

Case 152/84 Marshall v Southampton and South West Hampshire Area Health Authority [1986] ECR 723, [1986] 1 CMLR 688

Under the Sex Discrimination Act 1975 Ms Marshall had no redress for being forced to retire at an earlier age that her male counterparts. The British Government argued that she could not invoke Directive 76/207/EEC, as it could not be relied upon against undertakings.

48. With regard to the argument that a directive may not be relied upon against an individual, it must be emphasised that according to Article 189 of the EEC Treaty, the binding nature of a directive, which constitutes the basis for the possibility of relying on the directive before a national court, exists only in relation to 'each Member state to which it is addressed'. It follows that a directive may not of itself impose obligations on an individual and that a provision of a directive may not be relied upon as such against such a person.

49. In that respect it must be pointed out that where a person involved in legal proceedings is able to rely on a directive as against the State he may do so regardless of the capacity in which the latter is acting, whether employer or public authority. In either case it is necessary to prevent the State from taking advantage of its own failure to comply with Community law.

.....

51. The argument submitted by the United Kingdom that the possibility of relying on provisions of the directive against the respondent *qua* organ of the State would give rise to an arbitrary and unfair distinction between the rights of State employees and those of private employees does not justify any other conclusion. Such a distinction may easily be avoided if the Member state concerned has correctly implemented the directive in national law.

If Marshall was an attempt to assuage some of the criticism which had been levelled at the Court since *Van Duyn*, it also created problems of its own. The most immediate of these was that if Directives were only able to be invoked against organs of the State, then this latter concept would have to be defined. As Curtin astutely observed, such a task is a fruitless choice. Not only do a multitude of different legal structures exist but the legal status of many bodies which perform economic duties on the one hand or public duties on the other is as much a product of historical happenstance as the consequence of any thought-out strategy.[29]

Case C-188/89 Foster and others v British Gas plc [1990] ECR I-3313, [1990] 2 CMLR 833

Ms Foster was forced to retire at 60, whereas men could continue working until 65. She and four other women invoked the Equal Treatment Directive against her former employer, British Gas. The latter was at the time a nationalised industry. Its board members were appointed by the Secretary of State, who could only also give them directions and instruments. In addition, they were required to submit periodic reports to the Secretary of State. The corporation also had to run a balanced budget over two years, and the power to propose legislation.

16. As the Court has consistently held (see the judgment in Case 8/81 *Becker v Hauptzollamt Münster-Innenstadt* [1982] ECR 53, paragraphs 23 to 25), where the Community authorities have, by means of a directive, placed Member States under a duty to adopt a certain course of action, the effectiveness of such a measure would be diminished if persons were prevented from relying upon it in proceedings before a court and national courts were prevented from taking it into consideration as an element of Community law. Consequently, a Member State which has not adopted the implementing measures required by the directive within the prescribed period may not plead, as against individuals, its own failure to perform the obligations which the directive entails. Thus, wherever the provisions of a directive appear, as far as their subject-matter is concerned, to be unconditional and sufficiently precise, those provisions may, in the absence of implementing measures adopted within the prescribed period, be relied upon as against any national provision which is incompatible with the directive or in so far as the provisions define rights which individuals are able to assert against the State.

17. The Court further held in its judgment in Case 152/84 *Marshall, paragraph 49*, that where a person is able to rely on a directive as against the State he may do so regardless of the capacity in which the latter is acting, whether as employer or as public authority. In either case it is necessary to prevent the State from taking advantage of its own failure to comply with Community law.

18. On the basis of those considerations, the Court has held in a series of cases that unconditional and sufficiently precise provisions of a directive could be relied on against organizations or bodies which were subject to the authority or control of the State or had

---

[29]   Curtin, D. 'The Province of Government: Delimiting the Direct Effect of Directives in the Common Law Context' (1990) 15 *ELRev* 195,198-199.

special powers beyond those which result from the normal rules applicable to relations between individuals.

19. The Court has accordingly held that provisions of a directive could be relied on against tax authorities (the judgments in Case 8/81 *Becker, cited above*, and in Case C-221/88 *ECSC v Acciaierie e Ferriere Busseni (in liquidation)* [1990] ECR I-495), local or regional authorities (judgment in Case 103/88 *Fratelli Costanzo v Comune di Milano* [1989] ECR 1839), constitutionally independent authorities responsible for the maintenance of public order and safety (judgment in Case 222/84 *Johnston v Chief Constable of the Royal Ulster Constabulary* [1986] ECR 1651), and public authorities providing public health services (judgment in Case 152/84 *Marshall, cited above*).

20. It follows ... that a body, whatever its legal form, which has been made responsible, pursuant to a measure adopted by the State, for providing a public service under the control of the State and has for that purpose special powers beyond those which result from the normal rules applicable in relations between individuals, is included in any event among the bodies against which the provisions of a directive capable of having direct effect may be relied upon.

Adopting a definition of the State which ran beyond the classical duties of maintaining law and order highlighted the unsatisfactory nature of the reasoning. The basis of the distinction was flawed as it was impossible to argue that health authorities or nationalised industries were any more responsible for transposing directives than private parties. It also created an arbitrary two tier legal system where parties had greater protection against public bodies than private ones, notwithstanding that their functional relationship with the two was the same. Increasingly, the distinction came to be criticised by both Advocates-General[30] and academics.[31]

---

[30]   See Advocate General Van Gerven in Case C-271/91 *Marshall v Soton AHA* [1993] ECR I-4367, [1993] 3 CMLR 293; Advocate General Jacobs in Case C-316/93 *Vaneetveld v Le Foyer* [1994] ECR I-763; Advocate General Lenz in Case C-91/92 *Faccini Dori v Recreb* [1994] ECR I-3325, [1995] 1 CMLR 665.

[31]   Curtin, D. 'Directives: The Effectiveness of Judicial Protection of Individual Rights' (1990) 27 *CMLRev* 709; Prechal, S. 'Remedies after *Marshall*' (1990) 27 *CMLRev* 451; Coppel, J. 'Rights, Duties and the End of Marshall' (1994) 57 *MLR* 859.

Case C-316/93 Vaneetveld v Le Foyer [1994] ECR I-763

Ms Vaneetveld was injured in a car accident and wished to know in action against the insurance company whether she was protected by Directive 84/5/EEC on insurance against civil liability in respect of the use of motor vehicles. Whilst the question of horizontal direct effect was not addressed by the Court, it was considered by Advocate General Jacobs.

Advocate General Jacobs

20. In deciding the issue, the Court relied [in *Marshall*] - and relied exclusively - on the wording of Article 189 of the Treaty. As is well known, and for good reasons, such reliance on the wording of the Treaty has not generally been decisive in the Court's interpretation of it. Moreover the argument based on the wording, although it carries some weight, is not wholly convincing. Article 189 says that a directive 'shall be binding, as to the result to be achieved, upon each Member State to which it is addressed ...'. Quite apart from the fact that Article 189 does not expressly exclude the possibility of derived obligations arising for persons other than Member States, it may be noted that, on the basis of such an argument from the text, it would have been wholly impossible to maintain that Article 119 of the Treaty, for example, imposed obligations on private employers as the Court had held as long ago as 1976. Moreover, if a directive can impose obligations only on Member States, it is by no means easy to justify imposing obligations on a body such as the Southampton and South-West Hampshire Area Health Authority (Teaching). The well-known attempt at a rationale for assigning direct effect to a directive as against a Member State, namely that a Member State ought not to be allowed to rely upon its own failure to implement a directive, is singularly inapposite in relation to such a body, which has no responsibility for that failure.

21. In any event, once the Court had accepted that directives did have such a reach, it became difficult to justify distinctions between, for example, employers in the public sector and employers in the private sector. Moreover, once direct effect, although limited, had been recognized, some of the general arguments of principle against assigning horizontal direct effect to directives - for example, the argument that, under Article 189 of the Treaty, directives leave to the national authorities the choice of form and methods - could no longer be sustained.

22. It becomes difficult, also, in my view, to sustain a distinction in this respect between directives - which are, after all, the main, and often the only, form of Community legislation provided for under many areas of the Treaty - and other binding provisions of Community law, namely treaties, regulations and decisions, all of which, it is accepted, may impose obligations on individuals.

23. Similarly, if horizontal direct effect were to be denied to directives as having an insufficient democratic basis - the role of the European Parliament in the enactment of directives having been very limited at the outset and having increased only gradually - then again it is difficult to see why that argument should apply only to directives and not to other Community provisions, such as regulations, in which the role of the Parliament has been identical. Moreover it cannot be objected against horizontal direct effect that the measures have not been implemented by a democratically elected national parliament, since the directives in question *ex hypothesi* leave no discretion to the national legislature.

24. Nor in my view can an argument be based on the absence of a requirement in the Treaty that directives should be published. That lacuna, remedied by the Treaty on European Union, can be explained by the limited role envisaged for directives in the original Treaty, and is of little significance given the invariable practice of publishing in the Official Journal all legislative directives of the type addressed to all Member States. No doubt, if a particular directive had not been published, the absence of publication might have prevented it, like any other measure, from producing legal effects.

25. The above considerations do not in my view obviate the important differences which still remain between directives and regulations. In *Marshall I* the Court rightly, in my view, refrained from relying on the argument (mentioned in the Opinion of Advocate General Slynn) that to make directives directly enforceable against individuals would obliterate the distinction between directives and regulations. To recognize that even the provisions of a directive may be directly enforceable, in the exceptional case where they have not been correctly transposed, in no way affects the obligation of Member States to take all measures necessary to implement them; while regulations, being directly applicable, do not normally require implementation. Moreover, a directive, as we have seen, will produce legal effects only after the period which it lays down for its implementation has expired. Regulations and directives will remain different instruments, appropriate in different situations and achieving their aims by different means, even if it is recognized that in certain circumstances a directive which has not been correctly implemented may impose obligations on certain private entities.

.....

29. There are sound reasons of principle for assigning direct effect to directives without any distinction based on the status of the defendant. It would be consistent with the need to ensure the effectiveness of Community law and its uniform application in all the Member States. It would be consistent, in particular, with the recent emphasis in the Court's case-law on the overriding duty of national courts to provide effective remedies for the protection of Community rights. It is perhaps because a new approach to directives is required by the Court's recent case-law that the views of commentators have tended, recently, to advocate assigning horizontal direct effect to directives. As for the argument based on the need for uniform application of Community law, the case is self-evident; but it is necessary to ensure that Community legislation is uniformly applied not only as between Member States but within Member States. Distortions will obviously result, both between and within Member States, if directives are enforceable, for example, against employers or suppliers of goods or services in the public sector but not in the private sector. It is no answer to suggest that such distortions will be removed if the directive is properly implemented; the situation which has to be envisaged is one in which the directive has not been properly implemented.

.....

31.It cannot, I think, be objected that imposing obligations on individuals will prejudice legal certainty. On the contrary, perhaps the most significant feature of the existing case-law on this point is that it has generated uncertainty. It has led, first, to a very broad interpretation of the notion of Member State so that directives can be enforced even against commercial enterprises in which there is a particular element of State participation or control, notwithstanding that those enterprises have no responsibility for the default of the Member States, and notwithstanding that they might be in direct competition with private sector undertakings against which the same directives are not enforceable.

.....

33. There are, of course, circumstances in which it will be clear that a directive which has not been implemented by a Member State will not impose obligations on individuals. Thus a directive cannot of itself give rise to any criminal liability. Nor perhaps should a directive be construed as imposing obligations on individuals where that would confer rights on the defaulting State.

34. In general, however, it seems to me that directives whose very object is that rights should be conferred on individuals, and that obligations should be imposed on individuals, should be enforceable at the suit of the plaintiff unless the legitimate expectations of the defendant would thereby be defeated.

The Court did turn its attention to the matter later in the year.

Case C-91/92 Dori v Recreb Srl [1994] ECR I-3325, [1995] 1 CMLR 665

Ms Dori concluded a contract with Interdiffusion Srl for an English language correspondence course at Milan railway station. She then had second thoughts and cancelled her contract, relying upon the provisions of Directive 85/577/EEC, concerning the protection of the consumer in respect of contracts negotiated away from business premises. Italy had not taken any steps to implement the Directive.

The Court was asked whether the Directive could be invoked against another individual. Six Member States and the Commission intervened to argue against horizontal direct effect with only the Greek Government intervening in favour.

20. As the Court has consistently held since its judgment in Case 152/84 *Marshall v Southampton and South-West Hampshire Health Authority* [1986] ECR 723, paragraph 48, a directive cannot of itself impose obligations on an individual and cannot therefore be relied upon as such against an individual.

21. The national court observes that if the effects of unconditional and sufficiently precise but untransposed directives were to be limited to relations between State entities and individuals, this would mean that a legislative measure would operate as such only as between certain legal subjects, whereas, under Italian law as under the laws of all modern States founded on the rule of law, the State is subject to the law like any other person. If the directive could be relied on only as against the State, that would be tantamount to a penalty for failure to adopt legislative measures of transposition as if the relationship were a purely private one.

22. ... the case-law on the possibility of relying on directives against State entities is based on the fact that under Article 189 a directive is binding only in relation to 'each Member State to which it is addressed'. The case-law seeks to prevent 'the State from taking advantage of its own failure to comply with Community law'.

24. The effect of extending that case-law to the sphere of relations between individuals would be to recognise a power in the Community to enact obligations for individuals with immediate effect, whereas it has competence to do so only where it is empowered to adopt regulations.

25. It follows that, in the absence of measures transposing the directive within the prescribed time-limit, consumers cannot derive from the directive itself a right of cancellation as against traders with whom they have concluded a contract or enforce such a right in a national court.

Constitutional reasons, namely a lack of competence, are therefore asserted for Directives' not having horizontal direct effect. Indeed, since *Faccini Dori* the Court has asserted in a number of judgments that directives are incapable of horizontal direct effect.[32] The position has been muddied by the Court's holding that, whilst an

---

[32]   Case C-472/93 *Luigi Spano v Fiat Giotech* [1995] ECR I-4321; Case C-192/94 *El Corte Ingles v Rivero* [1996] ECR I-1281. Case C-168/95 *Arcaro* [1996] ECR I-4705.

individual may not found an action against another individual on the basis of a Directive, a Directive may be invoked as a 'shield' in a dispute between private parties to prevent a provision of national law being invoked by one against the other.

Case C-194/94 CIA Security International SA v Signalson SA and Securitel SPRL [1996] ECR I-2201, [1996] 2 CMLR 781

CIA marketed a burglar alarm, Andromede, on the Belgian market. This alarm had won a prize but had not received prior approval by the Belgian authorities, as required under Belgian regulation. CIA brought an action against Signalson, a competitor, who had made a number of derogatory statements about the alarm practice, one of which was that the alarm had not been authorised for the Belgian market. CIA argued that the Belgian system of prior authorisation could not be invoked against it as the former had not been notified to the Commission as required by Directive 83/189/EEC.

Advocate General Elmer

68. Consideration must, however, be given to the question whether the direct effect of the notification procedure in the Directive can be relied upon in a case such as that in the main proceedings, where the action is between two individuals. Under the Court's case-law a directive cannot, as stated, of itself impose obligations on an individual. A provision in a directive cannot therefore be relied upon as such against an individual, in the same way as the Community may not issue rules in the form of a directive which impose obligations on an individual. On the other hand, when applying national law, national courts must interpret national legal provisions, as far as possible, in the light of the wording and purpose of the directive so as to achieve the result it has in view. That obligation applies both to provisions in a law which has been specifically introduced in order to implement the directive and to provisions in other legislation, and it applies regardless whether the legislation preceded the directive or vice versa.

69. In the main proceedings Signalson and Securitel have claimed that C.I.A. should cease marketing the Andromede system since it has not received type approval under the provisions contained in the Law and 1991 Decree. They have further claimed that C.I.A. should be ordered to pay a periodic penalty payment as a result. Those claims are based on national regulations which have not been notified in accordance with the Directive, namely the Law and the 1991 Decree. On the basis of the Belgian Law on Commercial Practices it is claimed that those regulations should be enforced in relation to a trader by way of an order that he cease marketing and pay a periodic penalty. Such enforcement must, in my view, be contrary to the direct effect of the notification procedure set out in

Articles 8(1) and 9 of the Directive. That would, under the Court's case-law hitherto, be clear without more if it was the State which, as prosecutor, consumer ombudsman or similar had brought proceedings against C.I.A. The fact that the question in this case has been raised in the context of a private action, however, in my view can make no difference whatsoever. It is the State which lays down rules on penalties, prohibitions on marketing, etc. and it is the courts which must impose such sanctions regardless of who, under the national rules on procedure, might have brought the case.

70. In the main proceedings C.I.A. claimed that Signalson and Securitel should be fined for having acted in breach of good commercial practice by stating that the Andromede system was not approved in accordance with regulations contained in the Law and the 1991 Decree. That claim is based on the fact that C.I.A. was not obliged to seek type approval since the Belgian regulations had not been notified in accordance with the Directive. The question might be raised whether it can be said that if C.I.A.'s claim is upheld that would amount to allowing the Directive to impose obligations on individuals (in this case Signalson and Securitel).

71. The notification procedure in the Directive imposes a number of obligations on the Member States. The Directive does not, however, on its wording, aim to impose duties on individuals and therefore no question arises as to whether the Directive should have direct effect as far as individuals' obligations are concerned. The Directive is thus essentially different from Directive 85/577/EEC which was at issue in Case C-91/92 Faccini Dori.

72. C.I.A.'s claim is itself based on national law. The purpose of the reference to the Court would appear, in the light of C.I.A.'s claims, to obtain the necessary basis for the national court's interpretation of the Belgian Law on Commercial Practices. I would refer to what was stated above concerning the national court's duty, as far as possible, to interpret national law in the light of Community law. Such interpretation of national law in the light of Community law can naturally indirectly be of significance for the claims relating to Signalson and Securitel, but that is no different from the situation in other cases, whether the Court has indicated the rule of interpretation to be applied (see, for example, Case C-106/89 Marleasing [1990] ECR I-4135).

73. If it were held that C.I.A. was not able to point to the incompatibility of the Belgian regulations with Community law in its claims against Signalson and Securitel that would, in my view, create an unsatisfactory and incomprehensible situation where Community law would on the one hand be seeking to prevent a Member State from prosecuting an individual who had not complied with a non-notified technical provision, but on the other hand would debar the same individual from relying on the same circumstance in a case against a competitor who had stated that the individual in question had conducted himself unlawfully by not complying with the (unlawful) national regulation.

The Court

48. For such a consequence [the technical regulations to be inapplicable] to arise from a breach of the obligations laid down by Directive 83/189, an express provision to this effect is not required. As pointed out above, it is undisputed that the aim of the directive is to protect freedom of movement for goods by means of preventive control and that the obligation to notify is essential for achieving such Community control. The effectiveness of Community control will be that much greater if the directive is interpreted as meaning that breach of the obligation to notify constitutes a substantial procedural defect such as to render the technical regulations in question inapplicable to individuals.

.....

50. In the present case ... the aim of the directive is not simply to inform the Commission. ..., the directive has, precisely, a more general aim of eliminating or restricting obstacles to trade, to inform other States of technical regulations envisaged by a State, to give the Commission and the other Member States time to react and to propose amendments for lessening restrictions to the free movement of goods arising from the envisaged measure and to afford the Commission time to propose a harmonizing directive. Moreover, the wording of Articles 8 and 9 of Directive 83/189 is clear in that those articles provide for a procedure for Community control of draft national regulations and the date of their entry into force is made subject to the Commission's agreement or lack of opposition.

.....

54. In view of the foregoing considerations, it must be concluded that Directive 83/189 is to be interpreted as meaning that breach of the obligation to notify renders the technical regulations concerned inapplicable, so that they are unenforceable against individuals.

The distinction drawn by *CIA* results in considerable uncertainty. It would appear that in *Dori*, for example, if Ms Dori had paid for the course, she could not invoke the directive to return the goods and recover the money. If, however, she had merely contracted for the course but not yet paid any money, she would be in a better position. For she could defeat any claim brought in contract by Recreb on the grounds that the national law was incompatible with the directive and therefore inapplicable. The arbitrary nature of this distinction also suggests that it is false to assume that the use of the Directive as a shield will not penalise individuals. In the latter example given above, Recreb was affected as severely by the Directive as if the latter had horizontal direct effect. The Court therefore finds itself in a compromised and unconvincing position. If the basis of the direct effect of the directives is the failure of the State to transpose the directive in question, then *CIA* seems to be very harsh. If there is a duty on national courts to disapply national laws which conflict with Directives, however, then the question arises as to what is the basis for such a duty. If the basis is to further the effectiveness of EC law, then that would suggest in turn recognition that directives be capable of horizontal direct effect.

III. Indirect Effect

The Court has repeatedly stated that it views direct effect as providing no more than a minimum guarantee and that direct effect, *per se*, does not secure complete implementation of an individual's rights.[33] With the cul-de-sac it found itself in over the horizontal direct effect of directives, it increasingly looked to other instruments to expand the juridical effects of EC law. The first of these was the doctrine of indirect effect, which requires national courts to interpret and apply national legislation in conformity with EC law.

Case 14/83 Von Colson and Kamann v Land Nordrhein-Westfalen [1984] ECR 1891, [1986] 2 CMLR 430

Two female applicants had been refused posts as social workers on grounds of their sex. By way of a remedy they asked to be appointed to the relevant posts or six months salary. Under German law they could only claim 'reliance loss' - in this case the reimbursement of travelling expenses. A reference was made to the Court to ask if Article 6 of the Equal Treatment Directive, 76/207/EEC required that the discrimination be remedied by the appointment of the claimant to the post.

---

[33]   e.g. Case 72/85 *Commission v Netherlands* [1986] ECR 1219; Case 168/85 *Commission v Italy* [1986] ECR 2945; Case C-159/89 *Commission v Greece* [1991] ECR I-691.

26. However, the Member States' obligation arising from a directive to achieve the result envisaged by the directive and their duty under Article 5 of the Treaty to take all appropriate measures, whether general or particular, to ensure the fulfilment of that obligation, is binding on all the authorities of Member States including, for matters within their jurisdiction, the courts. It follows that, in applying the national law and in particular the provisions of national law specifically introduced in order to implement Directive 76/207, national courts are required to interpret their national law in the light of the wording and purpose of the Directive in order to achieve the result referred to in the third paragraph of Article 189.

.....

28. ... It is for the national court to interpret and apply the legislation adopted for the implementation of the directive in conformity with the requirements of Community law, in so far as it is given a discretion to do so under national law.

As the basis for indirect effect is not the State's failure to act but the duty of cooperation set out in Article 5 [*10*] EC, the Court has ruled that it takes effect not from the date of implementation of the Directive but from its date of publication. In *Kolpinghuis* a cafe owner selling bottles of ordinary water labelled as 'mineral water' was charged with infringing Dutch laws on water purity.[34] The national court asked whether a Directive on the marketing of mineral water could be taken into account in determining the contents of the offence. At the time the directive had not yet been implemented in The Netherlands. Notwithstanding this, the Court ruled that it made no difference to the duty of interpretation whether the period for implementation had expired or not.

As indirect effect is formulated as no more than a rule of interpretation, the individual's rights still stem formally from the national law. As the Court is not dealing, formally, with which instruments generate rights, it has taken a liberal view of the instruments capable of indirect effect.

---

[34]   Case 80/86 *Kolpinghuis Nijmegen BV* [1987] ECR 3969, [1989] 2 CMLR 18.

Case C-322/88 Grimaldi v Fonds des Maladies Professionelles [1989] ECR 4407, [1991] 2 CMLR 265

Grimaldi worked as a miner in Belgium. In 1983 he asked for official recognition that he suffered from an occupational disease which had been listed in a 1962 Commission Recommendation. This Recommendation had not transposed, and the Belgian court asked what legal effects it possessed.

16. In these circumstances there is no reason to doubt that the measures in question are true recommendations, that is to say measures which, even as regards the persons to whom they are addressed, are not intended to produce binding effects. Consequently, they cannot create rights upon which individuals may rely before a national court.

17. In this regard, the fact that more than 25 years have elapsed since the first of the recommendations in question was adopted, without its having been implemented by all the Member States, cannot alter its legal effect.

18. However, in order to give a comprehensive reply to the question asked by the national court, it must be stressed that the measures in question cannot therefore be regarded as having no legal effect. The national courts are bound to take recommendations into consideration in order to decide disputes submitted to them, in particular where they cast light on the interpretation of national measures adopted in order to implement them or where they are designed to supplement binding Community provisions.

The doctrine still appeared to be a relatively nondescript one because of the narrow set of circumstances in which it applied. It only applied in circumstances where the legislation was ambiguous, and, even then, it only applied in the case of national legislation which was considered to be implementing a provision of EC law.[35] This assumption was blown apart in *Marleasing*.

---

[35] Advocate General Slynn in Case 152/84 *Marshall v Soton AHA* [1986] ECR 723; Advocate General Mischo in Case 80/86 *Kolpinghuis Nijmegen* [1987] ECR 3969, 3979. See contra Advocate General Van Gerven in Case C-188/90 *Foster v British Gas* [1990] ECR I-3313, 3341.

Case C-106/89 Marleasing SA v La Commercial Internacionale de Alimentacion SA [1990] ECR I-4135, [1992] 1 CMLR 305

The plaintiff company brought an action against La Commercial in order to have its company's articles of association declared void as having been created for the sole purpose of defrauding and evading creditors. The Spanish Civil Code stated that contracts made with 'lack of cause' were void. Directive 68/151 contained an exhaustive list of reasons under which companies could be declared void. Avoidance of creditors was not on that list.

8. ... as the Court pointed out in its judgment in ... Case 14/83 *Von Colson and Kamann v Land Nordrhein-Westfalen* [1984] ECR 1891, paragraph 26, the Member States' obligation arising from a directive to achieve the result envisaged by the directive and their duty under Article 5 of the Treaty to take all appropriate measures, whether general or particular, to ensure the fulfilment of that obligation, is binding on all the authorities of Member States including, for matters within their jurisdiction, the courts. It follows that, in applying national law, whether the provisions in question were adopted before or after the directive, the national court called upon to interpret it is required to do so, as far as possible, in the light of the wording and the purpose of the directive in order to achieve the result pursued by the latter and thereby comply with the third paragraph of Article 189 of the Treaty.

Indirect effect has been expanded, first by its being given a more wide-ranging content of requiring *all* national legislation to be interpreted in the light of all EC law, irrespective of whether it is implementing legislation or not and irrespective of whether it was enacted prior or subsequent to the provision of EC law in question. In addition, the interpretive duty has been strengthened. As Docksey and Fitzpatrick observe:

'... it is no longer sufficient for a national court to turn to Community law only if the national provision is "ambiguous". Its first priority must be to establish the meaning of the Community obligation and only then to conclude whether it is possible to achieve the necessary reconciliation with the national law.'[36]

---

[36]   Docksey, C. & Fitzpatrick, B. 'The Duty of National Courts to Interpret Provisions of National Law in Accordance with Community Law' (1991) 20 *ILJ* 113, 119.

The strength of this duty was ambiguous. At its widest it would come close to requiring national judges to read national law as giving effect to EC law, almost irrespective of the wording of the provision of national law. Such an interpretation would have been tantamount to granting directives horizontal direct effect in all circumstances except where there was no national legislation to interpret. For in every other case the national judge would have been given jurisdiction to hear the matter by the relevant provision of national law, but would then consider the matter on the basis of EC law. Such a strong interpretive obligation was considered, however, to pose considerable problems for legal certainty.

De Búrca, G. 'Giving Effect to European Community Directives' (1992) 55 *Modern Law Review* 215, 230-231

This confusion as to the legal rights and responsibilities of individuals will obviously be extreme in cases of clear difference between the terms of the national measure and that of the Directive. For example, domestic law which purports to implement a Directive might create certain exceptions to it, on which one party may rely. The court would have to penalise that party for relying on the validity of a clear provision of national law, if another party called upon it to interpret that law in the light of the Directive which contained no such exception. Since *Marleasing* does seem to require the interpretation of domestic law as against individuals, the EC evidently considers that this does not breach the EC's protection of the legitimation expectations principle. One possibility is that the ECJ does not consider expectations in such a situation to be legitimate. The implication of the ECJ's ruling seems to be that individuals must now be as much aware of the provisions of EC Directive as they are of Regulations or of Treaty Articles. The corollary of this is that a private party, basing itself on the ECJ's earlier case law, might legitimately rely on the national courts to read the provisions of the Directive into domestic legislation in the area. The ECJ's ruling seems to imply that the other party who is disadvantaged by its indirect enforcement should not be surprised. This view is not formally in accordance with the doctrine of direct effect (by virtue of which only Regulation and Treaty Articles are enforceable against individuals), though it is arguably more realistic in so far as the existence of expectations are concerned. If private individuals and companies are actually familiar with EC law, it is as likely that they will be familiar with the provisions of Directives as with provisions of Regulations and Treaty Articles. This is particularly likely if the ECJ has been interpreting a specific Directive for some time.

For this reason Advocate General Van Gerven argued in a number of cases that indirect effect should not require *contra legem* interpretations of national law. That is to say that the strength of the interpretive obligation should be so strong as to require the national provision to be given a meaning which contradicted its 'ordinary' meaning.[37] The Court accepted this advice in *Wagner-Miret*.

Case C-334/92 Wagner-Miret v Fondo de Garantia Salarial [1993] ECR I-6911

Directive 80/987/EEC required Member States to establish a guarantee fund which would secure employees' back pay in cases where an undertaking went insolvent. Under an Annex Member States could exempt particular categories from this protection. The only category Spain placed in this Annex were maids. The Spanish legislation in question stipulated, however, that company directors were not eligible for such payments.

20. ... it should be borne in mind that when it interprets and applies national law, every national court must presume that the State had the intention of fulfilling entirely the obligations arising from the directive concerned. As the Court held in its judgment in Case 106/89 *Marleasing SA v La Commercial Internacional de Alimentacion SA* [1990] ECR I-4135, paragraph 8, in applying national law, whether the provisions in question were adopted before or after the directive, the national court called upon to interpret it is required to do so, so far as possible, in the light of the wording and the purpose of the directive in order to achieve the result pursued by the latter and thereby comply with the third paragraph of Article 189 of the Treaty.

21. The principle of interpretation in conformity with directives must be followed in particular where a national court considers, as in the present case, that the pre-existing provisions of its national law satisfy the requirements of the directive concerned.

22. It would appear from the order for reference that the national provisions cannot be interpreted in a way which conforms with the directive on the insolvency of employers and therefore do not permit higher management staff to obtain the benefit of the guarantees for which it provides. If that is the case, it follows from [Joined Cases 6/90 and C-9/90 *Francovich v Italian Republic* [1991] ECR I-5352], that the Member State

---

37   Case C-262/88 *Barber v GRE* [1990] ECR I-1889, [1990] 2 CMLR 513; Joined Cases 63 & 64/92 *Jackson v Chief Adjudication Officer* [1992] ECR I-4737; Case C-271/91 *Marshall (No.2)* [1993] ECR I-4367, [1993] 3 CMLR 293.

concerned is obliged to make good the loss and damage sustained as a result of the failure to implement the directive in their respect.

IV. State Responsibility

i. The Establishment of State Responsibility

As early as 1960 the Court stated in *Humblet* that there was a duty upon Member States to make reparation for the consequences of unlawful acts.[38] It returned to the theme in 1975 where it stated in its suggestions on European Union that persons affected by a failure of a Member State to comply with EC law should be able to seek reparation before a national court.[39] Yet assumptions had always been made that such a remedy could not exist whilst remedies remained primarily a matter of discretion for the national courts

With the refusal of the Court to allow Directives to be capable of horizontal direct effect in *Marshall*, arguments were increasingly raised that, as further obligations could not be placed on private parties, effective judicial protection of EC law was only possible if individuals were given a right to sue the State before a national court for any damage suffered as a result of that State's failure to comply with EC law.[40] Indeed, as Steiner later observed, in the context of Directives, such a principle enjoyed more legitimacy than either direct or indirect effect, for the principle of State liability allowed an action against those

---

[38]   Case 6/60 *Humblet v Belgium* [1960] ECR 559.

[39]   EC Bulletin Supplt. 9/75, 18.

[40]   Barav, A. 'Damages in Domestic Courts for Breach of Community Law by National Public Authorities' in Schermers, H., Heukels, T. & Mead, P. (eds.) *Non-Contractual Liability of the European Communities* (1988, Martijnus Nijhoff, Dordrecht); Curtin, D. 'Directives: the Effectiveness of Judicial Protection of Individual Rights' (1990) 27 *CMLRev* 709; Prechal, S. 'Remedies after Marshall' (1990) 27 *CMLRev* 451.

who were really at fault for the non-transposition, the central authorities.[41]

Joined Cases C-6/90 & 9/90 Francovich and Bonifaci v Italy [1991] ECR I-5357

An Article 169 [226] EC action had already been successfully brought against Italy for its failure to implement Directive 80/987 EEC, protecting employees in the case of insolvency, by setting up a guarantee fund to protect their back pay in the case of insolvency.[42] Francovich was owed LIT 6,000,000 by his employer whilst Bonifaci and 33 other colleagues were owed LIT 256,000,000 by their employer. The Italian courts asked whether the Italian state was liable to pay them the sums owed.

(a) The existence of State liability as a matter of principle

31. It should be borne in mind at the outset that the EEC Treaty has created its own legal system, which is integrated into the legal systems of the Member States and which their courts are bound to apply. The subjects of that legal system are not only the Member States but also their nationals. Just as it imposes burdens on individuals, Community law is also intended to give rise to rights which become part of their legal patrimony. Those rights arise not only where they are expressly granted by the Treaty but also by virtue of obligations which the Treaty imposes in a clearly defined manner both on individuals and on the Member States and the Community institutions (see the judgments in Case 26/62 *Van Gend en Loos* [1963] ECR 1 and Case 6/64 *Costa v ENEL* [1964] ECR 585).

32. Furthermore, it has been consistently held that the national courts whose task it is to apply the provisions of Community law in areas within their jurisdiction must ensure that those rules take full effect and must protect the rights which they confer on individuals (see in particular the judgments in Case 106/77 *Amministrazione delle Finanze dello Stato v Simmenthal* [1978] ECR 629, paragraph 16, and Case C-213/89 *Factortame* [1990] ECR I-2433, paragraph 19).

33. The full effectiveness of Community rules would be impaired and the protection of the rights which they grant would be weakened if individuals were unable to obtain redress when their rights are infringed by a breach of Community law for which a Member State can be held responsible.

---

[41]   Steiner, J. 'From direct effects to Francovich: shifting means of enforcement of Community law' (1993) 18 *ELRev* 3, 9-10.

[42]   Case 22/87 *Commission v Italy* [1989] ECR 143.

34. The possibility of obtaining redress from the Member State is particularly indispensable where, as in this case, the full effectiveness of Community rules is subject to prior action on the part of the State and where, consequently, in the absence of such action, individuals cannot enforce before the national courts the rights conferred upon them by Community law.

35. It follows that the principle whereby a State must be liable for loss and damage caused to individuals as a result of breaches of Community law for which the State can be held responsible is inherent in the system of the Treaty.

36. A further basis for the obligation of Member States to make good such loss and damage is to be found in Article 5 of the Treaty, under which the Member States are required to take all appropriate measures, whether general or particular, to ensure fulfilment of their obligations under Community law. Among these is the obligation to nullify the unlawful consequences of a breach of Community law (see, in relation to the analogous provision of Article 86 of the ECSC Treaty, the judgment in Case 6/60 *Humblet v Belgium* [1960] ECR 559).

37. It follows from all the foregoing that it is a principle of Community law that the Member States are obliged to make good loss and damage caused to individuals by breaches of Community law for which they can be held responsible.

(b) The conditions for State liability

38. Although State liability is thus required by Community law, the conditions under which that liability gives rise to a right to reparation depend on the nature of the breach of Community law giving rise to the loss and damage.

39. Where, as in this case, a Member State fails to fulfil its obligation under the third paragraph of Article 189 of the Treaty to take all the measures necessary to achieve the result prescribed by a directive, the full effectiveness of that rule of Community law requires that there should be a right to reparation provided that three conditions are fulfilled.

40. The first of those conditions is that the result prescribed by the directive should entail the grant of rights to individuals. The second condition is that it should be possible to identify the content of those rights on the basis of the provisions of the directive. Finally, the third condition is the existence of a causal link between the breach of the State's obligation and the loss and damage suffered by the injured parties.

41. Those conditions are sufficient to give rise to a right on the part of individuals to obtain reparation, a right founded directly on Community law.

42. Subject to that reservation, it is on the basis of the rules of national law on liability that the State must make reparation for the consequences of the loss and damage caused.

In the absence of Community legislation, it is for the internal legal order of each Member State to designate the competent courts and lay down the detailed procedural rules for legal proceedings intended fully to safeguard the rights which individuals derive from Community law (see the judgments in Case 60/75 *Russo v AIMA* [1976] ECR 45, Case 33/76 *Rewe v Landwirstschaftskammer Saarland* [1976] ECR 1989 and Case 158/80 *Rewe v Hauptzollamt Kiel* [1981] ECR 1805).

43. Further, the substantive and procedural conditions for reparation of loss and damage laid down by the national law of the Member States must not be less favourable than those relating to similar domestic claims and must not be so framed as to make it virtually impossible or excessively difficult to obtain reparation (see, in relation to the analogous issue of the repayment of taxes levied in breach of Community law, inter alia the judgment in Case 199/82 *Amministrazione delle Finanze dello Stato v San Giorgio* [1983] ECR 3595).

A constitutional significance was detected by some academics in *Francovich* whose logic parallelled that of the early cases on horizontal direct effect of EC Treaty provisions. Prior to *Francovich* individual rights created by directives arose as a consequence of duties imposed upon Member States either as a result of their wrongful failure to implement the directive or as a result of the duties imposed upon national courts. In *Francovich*, however, the starting point for state responsibility is that it arises as a consequence of the individual rights set out in the directive.[43]

This suggested a new style of reasoning whereby direct effect, indirect effect and state responsibility could not be seen as discrete ends in themselves but merely as manifestations of a more general principle which required individual rights to be judicially protected - a requirement of effective judicial process.[44] On such a reading, the Court would be

---

[43] Coppel, J. 'Rights, Duties and the End of Marshall' (1994) 57 *MLR* 859.
[44] On 'effective protection' see Ross, M. 'Beyond Francovich' (1993) 56 *MLR* 55; Tesauro, G. 'The Effectiveness of Judicial Protection and Co-operation between the Court of Justice and National Courts' (1993) 13 *YBEL* 1; Tash, A. 'Remedies for European Community Law Claims in Member State Courts: towards a European Standard' (1993) 31 *Columbia Journal of Transnational Law* 377; Caranta, R. 'Judicial Protection against Member States: a New Jus Commune Takes Shape' (1995) 32 *CMLRev* 703; Van Gerven, W. 'Bridging the Unbridgeable: Community and National Tort Laws after *Francovich* and *Brasserie*' (1996) 45 *ICLQ* 507.

increasingly innovative in finding ways to protect individual rights. Thus in *Francovich* the lack of direct effect of the provisions in question did not prevent the 'rights' they contained being protected through an action in damages against the State.

Such a reading of the judgment is not without its problems. It begs the question that if there is a new doctrine of effective judicial process, then why was this not articulated by the Court rather than its creating this convoluted system of three separate overlapping doctrines. This argument also seemed to run counter to developments in *Dori* and *Wagner-Miret* which limited the extent to which direct and indirect effect could be used to protect individual rights. Most crucially, the theory of effective judicial process never stipulated which precise legal actions it should give rise to, for in all systems there are limits on the type of legal provision and the type of action which may be brought in court.

At a practical level, *Francovich* was incontestably significant. It was seen as securing greater individual protection in a number of ways.[45] It would prevent breaches of EC law, as it provided incentives for Member States to comply with EC law and to implement directives properly. The possibility of being awarded damages would also provide incentives for individuals to bring more actions to court. Finally, it would narrow the lacuna in judicial protection which arose out of the limits of direct and indirect effect.[46]

Yet tort actions against the State are a problematic method of securing protection of individual rights. They involve, *inter alia*, decisions about the allocation of State resources which are arguably inconsistent with the judicial function.

---

[45] Although not it appears for the luckless Sr. Francovich whose employer was found to fall outside the scope of the directive, Case C-479/93 *Francovich v Italian State* [1995] ECR I-3843.

[46] Curtin, D. 'State Liability under Community Law: a New Remedy for Private Parties' (1992) 21 *ILJ* 74, 80-81; Plaza Martin, C. 'Furthering the Effectiveness of EC Directives and the Judicial Protection of Individual Rights Thereunder' (1994) 43 *ICLQ* 26, 45.

In a passage from *Francovich* not noted for its lucidity, it was said that:

'the full effectiveness of Community rules would be impaired and the protection of the rights which they grant would be weakened if individuals were unable to obtain compensation when their rights are infringed by a breach of Community law for which a Member State can be held responsible.'

Redolent of the language of rights, the Opinion of AG Tesauro in *Brasserie* searches for a rights based solution within the structural framework of EC law. Tesauro characterises rights-based liability as 'civilised'. He sees it as the inevitable result of the emergence of 'the state governed by the rule of law' and as representing 'a shift of emphasis, at least in the more advanced legal systems, from the conduct of the perpetrator of the damage to the rights of the injured party'.

The American academic, Rosenberg, has suggested a 'rights-based' theory of tortious liability centred around the principle that those who benefit from an undertaking should bear a commensurate share of its burdens so that there is 'no unjustified sacrifice of some for others'.[47] This formulation mirrors the French principle of *égalité devant les charges publics*. It differs little from the theory of state liability constructed by Professors Cohen and Smith[48] on the basis of 'social entitlement', equality, and collective or mutual insurance. It echoes, but does not go as far as, Professor Patrick Atiyah's general theory of accident compensation based on social insurance.[49] The beauty of these theories is that they are all propounded by academics.

Far-reaching and hard to distinguish from the general welfare function of the modern State, they lock courts into 'tragic choices' (Calabresi's famous phrase) over the allocation of resources - a function strictly reserved in western constitutional theory for executive and legislature. The issues are not made easier by the presentation of polycentric problems as claims by 'individuals' in what Chayes terms the 'bi-polar lawsuit'.[50] The jurist Lon Fuller insisted that awarding compensation in a polycentric or 'on-going venture' moves a court infallibly from an adjudicative to an administrative

---

47 Rosenberg, 'The Causal Connection in Mass Exposure Cases: a Public Law Vision of the Tort System' (1984) 97 *Harvard Law Review* 851 at note 107.
48 Cohen and Smith, 'Entitlement and the Body Politic: Rethinking Negligence in Public Law' (1986) 24 *Canadian Bar Review* 1; Cohen, 'Responding to Government Failure' (1995) 6 *National Journal of Constitutional Law* 23.
49 Cane and Atiyah, *Accidents, Compensation and the Law* (Weidenfeld & Nicolson, 6th Ed., 1993).
50 Chayes,'The Role of the Judge in Public Law Litigation' (1976) 89 *Harvard Law Review* 1281.

function.[51] For slightly different reasons, Epstein warns against compensation, both for economic loss and for invasions of constitutional rights, on the ground that they involve too great a conflict of interest:

'To give legal protection against these forms of harms is to undertake an enormous expansion of the legal system. People's sympathies in individual cases might incline many to start down this road even if they are not quite sure how far they are willing to go. But the temptation should be resisted: for these types of harms, the only correct legal response is the simple one of no compensation.'[52]

ii. The Conditions of Liability

Equally problematic was the extent of the *Francovich* remedy. Whilst the language of the judgment suggested a very open-ended remedy which could be invoked by any individual who could point to a loss suffered as a result of State's failure to comply with a provision of EC law which conferred rights upon that individual. The circumstances of the judgment were very narrow. Indeed, it was hard to think of a more culpable pattern of behaviour than that of the Italian Government. Thus, whilst some commentators suggested that *Francovich* created a situation where Member States were strictly liable for breach of any provisions which created individual rights,[53] others claimed it was only authority for the proposition that Member States incurred liability where they failed to transpose a directive.[54]

Whatever the intention of the Court, analyses suggested that there were other considerations which needed to be addressed. In no Member State is there an open-ended system of strict governmental liability. The reason for this is that public bodies have to operate within

---

51   Cited in Allison, 'The Procedural Reason for Judicial Restraint' (1994) *PL* 452, 459. See also Fuller, 'The Forms and Limits of Adjudication' (1978) 92 *Harvard Law Review* 353.

52   Epstein, *Simple Rules for a Complex World* (Harvard University Press, 1995) 109.

53   Caranta, R. 'Governmental Liability after Francovich' (1992) 52 *CLJ* 272, 285.

54   Lewis, C. & Moore, S. 'Duties, Directives and Damages in European Community Law' (1993) *PL* 151, 161-163.

a complex legislative framework where it is easy to make mistaken evaluations of the legal situation. If every potential mistake exposed them to litigation not only would they be more wary of acting but even where they did act, government could be crippled by continual litigation from disgruntled individuals. These policy considerations had also influenced the regime on non-contractual liability of EC institutions under Article 215(2) [*288(2)*] EC.[55] The iniquity of Member States being subject to a more wide-ranging liability than EC institutions would be most obvious where national authorities were implementing a Community act. For the situation might arise that whilst an act of an EC institution was not sufficiently egregious to incur liability under Article 215(2) [*288(2)*] EC, its implementation by national authorities might fall foul of the *Francovich* judgment.

More thoughtful analyses therefore suggested that either a fault based system of liability should be adopted whereby Member States only incurred liability if they breached provisions of EC law which were sufficiently clear and precise[56] or a model should be adopted which parallelled that of Article 215(2) [*288(2)*] EC.[57] These considerations influenced the Court when it returned to the question of State liability.

Joined Cases C-46/93 Brasserie du Pêcheur SA v Federal Republic of Germany and C-48/93 R v Secretary of State for Transport ex parte Factortame Ltd [1996] ECR I-1029, [1996] 1 CMLR 889

Brasserie du Pêcheur, a French firm, had been forced to discontinue exports of beer to Germany in 1981. This was due to a German 'Purity Law' which did not allow beers lawfully marketed according to different rules in other Member States to enjoy the designation 'Bier' and did not allow the marketing of beer which contained additives. This law was declared illegal in 1987 on the grounds that it contravened Article 30 [*28*] EC, the provision outlawing quantitative restrictions or measures having equivalent effect on the free movement of

---

[55]   See pp 586-593.

[56]   Steiner, J. 'From direct effects to Francovich: Shifting Means of Enforcement of Community Law' (1993) 18 *ELRev* 3, 17-18.

[57]   Craig, P. 'Francovich, Remedies and the Scope of Damages Liability' (1993) 109 *LQR* 595, 610.

goods.[58] Brasserie du Pêcheur sought compensation of DM 1,800,000 for the loss of sales between 1981 and 1987.

In 1988 Factortame and a number of other Spanish fishermen challenged a British statute which imposed a system of registration imposing, *inter alia*, residence, nationality and domicile requirements on the owners of fishing vessels. In 1989 parallel proceedings were brought by the Commission against the nationality requirements imposed by the system of registration.[59] It also applied and was granted interim relief by the Court requiring the United Kingdom to suspend the nationality requirement.[60] The system of registration was declared illegal by the Court in March 1991.[61] The applicants claimed for damages against the British Government, and their case was joined with that of Brasserie du Pêcheur.

27. Since the Treaty contains no provision expressly and specifically governing the consequences of breaches of Community law by member States, it is for the Court, in pursuance of the task conferred on it by Article 164 of the Treaty of ensuring that in the interpretation and application of the Treaty the law is observed, to rule on such a question in accordance with generally accepted methods of interpretation, in particular by reference to the fundamental principles of the Community legal system and, where necessary, general principles common to the legal systems of the Member States.

28. Indeed, it is to the general principles common to the laws of the Member States that the second paragraph of Article 215 of the Treaty refers as the basis of the non-contractual liability of the Community for damage caused by its institutions or by its servants in the performance of their duties.

29. The principle of the non-contractual liability of the Community expressly laid down in Article 215 of the Treaty is simply an expression of the general principle familiar to the legal systems of the Member States that an unlawful act or omission gives rise to an obligation to make good the damage caused. That provision also reflects the obligation on public authorities to make good damage caused in the performance of their duties.

30. In any event, in many national legal systems the essentials of the legal rules governing State liability have been developed by the courts.

---

[58]   Case 178/84 *Commission v Germany* [1987] ECR 1227, [1988] 1 CMLR 780.

[59]   Case C-246/89 *Commission v United Kingdom* [1991] ECR I-4585, [1991] 3 CMLR 706.

[60]   Case 246/89R *Commission v United Kingdom* [1989] ECR 3125.

[61]   Case C-221/89 *R v Secretary of State for Transport ex parte Factortame* [1991] ECR I-3905, [1991] 3 CMLR 589.

31. In view of the foregoing considerations, the Court held in *Francovich and Others,* at paragraph 35, that the principle of State liability for loss and damage caused to individuals as a result of breaches of Community law for which it can be held responsible is inherent in the system of the Treaty.

32. It follows that that principle holds good for any case in which a Member State breaches Community law, whatever be the organ of the State whose act or omission was responsible for the breach.

33. In addition, in view of the fundamental requirement of the Community legal order that Community law be uniformly applied (see, in particular, Joined Cases C-143/88 and C-92/89 *Zuckerfabrik Süderdithmarschen and Zuckerfabrik Soest* [1991] ECR I-415, paragraph 26), the obligation to make good damage caused to individuals by breaches of Community law cannot depend on domestic rules as to the division of powers between constitutional authorities.

34. As the Advocate General points out in paragraph 38 of his Opinion, in international law a State whose liability for breach of an international commitment is in issue will be viewed as a single entity, irrespective of whether the breach which gave rise to the damage is attributable to the legislature, the judiciary or the executive. This must apply *a fortiori* in the Community legal order since all State authorities, including the legislature, are bound in performing their tasks to comply with the rules laid down by Community law directly governing the situation of individuals.

35. The fact that, according to national rules, the breach complained of is attributable to the legislature cannot affect the requirements inherent in the protection of the rights of individuals who rely on Community law and, in this instance, the right to obtain redress in the national courts for damage caused by that breach.

.....

Conditions under which the State may incur liability for acts and omissions of the legislature contrary to Community law

.....

38. Although Community law imposes State liability, the conditions under which that liability gives rise to a right to reparation depend on the nature of the breach of Community law giving rise to the loss and damage (*Francovich and Others,* paragraph 38).

39. In order to determine those conditions, account should first be taken of the principles inherent in the Community legal order which form the basis for State liability, namely first, the full effectiveness of Community rules and the effective protection of the rights which they confer and, second, the obligation to cooperate imposed on Member States by Article 5 of the Treaty (*Francovich and Others,* paragraphs 31 to 36).

40. In addition, as the Commission and the several governments which submitted observations have emphasized, it is pertinent to refer to the Court's case-law on non-contractual liability on the part of the Community.

41. First, the second paragraph of Article 215 of the Treaty refers as regards the non-contractual liability of the Community, to the general principles common to the laws of the Member States, from which, in the absence of written rules, the Court also draws inspiration in other areas of Community law.

42. Second, the conditions under which the State may incur liability for damage caused to individuals by a breach of Community law cannot, in the absence of particular justification, differ from those governing the liability of the Community in like circumstances. The protection of the rights which individuals derive from Community law cannot vary depending on whether a national authority or a Community authority is responsible for the damage.

43. The system of rules which the Court has worked out with regard to Article 215 of the Treaty, particularly in relation to liability for legislative measures, takes into account, inter alia, the complexity of the situations to be regulated, difficulties in the application or interpretation of the texts and, more particularly, the margin of discretion available to the author of the act in question.

44. Thus, in developing its case-law on the non-contractual liability of the Community, in particular as regards legislative measures involving choices of economic policy, the Court has had regard to the wide discretion available to the institutions in implementing Community policies.

45. The strict approach taken towards the liability of the Community in the exercise of its legislative activities is due to two considerations. First, even where the legality of measures is subject to judicial review, exercise of the legislative function must not be hindered by the prospect of actions for damages whenever the general interest of the Community requires legislative measures to be adopted which may adversely affect individual interests. Second, in a legislative context characterised by the exercise of a wide discretion, which is essential for implementing a Community policy, the Community cannot incur liability unless the institution concerned has manifestly and gravely disregarded the limits on the exercise of its powers (Joined Cases 83/76, 94/76, 4/77 and 40/77 *HNL and Others v Council and Commission* [1978] ECR 1209, paragraphs 5 and 6).

46. That said, the national legislature - like the Community institutions - does not systematically have a wide discretion when it acts in a field governed by Community law. Community law may impose upon it obligations to achieve a particular result or obligations to act or refrain from acting which reduce its margin of discretion, sometimes to a considerable degree. This is so, for instance, where, as in the circumstances to which the judgment in *Francovich and Others* relates, Article 189 of the Treaty places the member State under an obligation to take, within a given period, all the measures needed in order to achieve the result required by a directive. In such a case, the fact that it is for the national legislature to take the necessary measures has no bearing on the member State's liability for failing to transpose the directive.

47. In contrast, where a Member State acts in a field where it has a wide discretion, comparable to that of the Community institutions in implementing Community policies, the conditions under which it may incur liability must, in principle, be the same as those under which the Community institutions incur liability in a comparable situation.

48.In the case which gave rise to the reference in Case C-46/93, the German legislature had legislated in the field of foodstuffs, specifically beer. In the absence of Community harmonization, the national legislature had a wide discretion in that sphere in laying down rules on the quality of beer put on the market.

49. As regards the facts of Case C-48/93, the United Kingdom legislature also had a wide discretion. The legislation at issue was concerned, first, with the registration of vessels, a field which, in view of the state of development of Community law, falls within the jurisdiction of the Member States and, secondly, with regulating fishing, a sector in which implementation of the common fisheries policy leaves a margin of discretion to the Member States.

50.Consequently, in each case the German and United Kingdom legislatures were faced with situations involving choices comparable to those made by the Community institutions when they adopt legislative measures pursuant to a Community policy.

51. In such circumstances, Community law confers a right to reparation where three conditions are met: the rule of law infringed must be intended to confer rights on individuals; the breach must be sufficiently serious; and there must be a direct causal link between the breach of the obligation resting on the State and the damage sustained by the injured parties.

52. Firstly, those conditions satisfy the requirements of the full effectiveness of the rules of Community law and of the effective protection of the rights which those rules confer.

53.Secondly, those conditions correspond in substance to those defined by the Court in relation to Article 215 in its case-law on liability of the Community for damage caused to individuals by unlawful legislative measures adopted by its institutions.

54. The first condition is manifestly satisfied in the case of Article 30 of the Treaty, the relevant provision in Case C-46/93, and in the case of Article 52, the relevant provision in Case C-48/93. Whilst Article 30 imposes a prohibition on Member States, it

nevertheless gives rise to rights for individuals which the national courts must protect (Case 74/76 *Iannelli & Volpi v Meroni* [1977] ECR 557, paragraph 13). Likewise, the essence of Article 52 is to confer rights on individuals (Case 2/74 *Reyners* [1974] ECR 631, paragraph 25).

55. As to the second condition, as regards both Community liability under Article 215 and Member State liability for breaches of Community law, the decisive test for finding that a breach of Community law is sufficiently serious is whether the Member State or the Community institution concerned manifestly and gravely disregarded the limits of its discretion.

56. The factors which the competent court may take into consideration include the clarity and precision of the rule breached, the measure of discretion left by that rule to the national or Community authorities, whether the infringement and the damage caused was intentional or involuntary, whether any error of law was excusable or inexcusable, the fact that the position taken by a community institution may have contributed towards the omission, and the adoption or retention of national measures or practices contrary to Community law.

57. On any view, a breach of Community law will clearly be sufficiently serious if it has persisted despite a judgment finding the infringement in question to be established, or a preliminary ruling or settled case-law of the Court on the matter from which it is clear that the conduct in question constituted an infringement.

58. While, in the present cases, the Court cannot substitute its assessment for that of the national courts, which have sole jurisdiction to find the facts in the main proceedings and decide how to characterize the breaches of Community law at issue, it will be helpful to indicate a number of circumstances which the national courts might take into account.

59. In Case C-46/93 a distinction should be drawn between the question of the German legislature's having maintained in force provisions of the Biersteuergesetz concerning the purity of beer prohibiting the marketing under the designation 'Bier' of beers imported from other Member States which were lawfully produced in conformity with different rules, and the question of the retention of the provisions of that same law prohibiting the import of beers containing additives. As regards the provisions of the German legislation relating to the designation of the product marketed, it would be difficult to regard the breach of Article 30 by that legislation as an excusable error, since the incompatibility of such rules with Article 30 was manifest in the light of earlier decisions of the Court, in particular Case 120/78 *Rewe-Zentral* [1979] ECR 649 ('Cassis de Dijon') and Case 193/80 *Commission v Italy* [1981] ECR 3019 ('vinegar'). In contrast, having regard to the relevant case-law, the criteria available to the national legislature to determine whether the prohibition of the use of additives was contrary to Community law were significantly less conclusive until the Court's judgment of 12 March 1987 in *Commission v Germany*, cited above, in which the Court held that prohibition to be incompatible with Article 30.

60. A number of observations may likewise be made about the national legislation at issue in Case C-48/93.

61. The decision of the United Kingdom legislature to introduce in the Merchant Shipping Act 1988 provisions relating to the conditions for the registration of fishing vessels has to be assessed differently in the case of the provisions making registration subject to a nationality condition, which constitute direct discrimination manifestly contrary to Community law, and in the case of the provisions laying down residence and domicile conditions for vessel owners and operators.

62. The latter conditions are *prima facie* incompatible with Article 52 of the Treaty in particular, but the United Kingdom sought to justify them in terms of the objectives of the common fisheries policy. In the judgment in *Factortame II*, cited above, the Court rejected that justification.

63. In order to determine whether the breach of Article 52 thus committed by the United Kingdom was sufficiently serious, the national court might take into account, *inter alia*, the legal disputes relating to particular features of the common fisheries policy, the attitude of the Commission, which made its position known to the United Kingdom in good time, and the assessments as to the state of certainty of Community law made by the national courts in the interim proceedings brought by individuals affected by the Merchant Shipping Act.

64. Lastly, consideration should be given to the assertion made by Rawlings (Trawling) Ltd, the 37th claimant in Case C-48/93, that the United Kingdom failed to adopt immediately the measures needed to comply with the Order of the President of the Court of 10 October 1989 in *Commission v United Kingdom*, cited above, and that this needlessly increased the loss it sustained. If this allegation - which was certainly contested by the United Kingdom at the hearing - should prove correct, it should be regarded by the national court as constituting in itself a manifest and, therefore, sufficiently serious breach of Community law.

65. As for the third condition, it is for the national courts to determine whether there is a direct causal link between the breach of the obligation borne by the State and the damage sustained by the injured parties.

66. The aforementioned three conditions are necessary and sufficient to found a right in individuals to obtain redress, although this does not mean that the State cannot incur liability under less strict conditions on the basis of national law.

67. As appears from paragraphs 41, 42 and 43 of *Francovich and Others*, cited above, subject to the right to reparation which flows directly from Community law where the conditions referred to in the preceding paragraph are satisfied, the State must make reparation for the consequences of the loss and damage caused in accordance with the domestic rules on liability, provided that the conditions for reparation of loss and damage laid down by national law must not be less favourable than those relating to similar domestic claims and must not be such as in practice to make it impossible or excessively difficult to obtain reparation (see also Case 199/82 *Amministrazione delle Finanze dello Stato v San Giorgio* [1983] ECR 3595).

68. In that regard, restrictions that exist in domestic legal systems as to the non-contractual liability of the State in the exercise of its legislative function may be such as to make it impossible in practice or excessively difficult for individuals to exercise their right to reparation, as guaranteed by Community law, of loss or damage resulting from the breach of Community law.

69. In Case C-46/93 the national court asks in particular whether national law may subject any right to compensation to the same restrictions as apply where a law is in breach of higher-ranking national provisions, for instance, where an ordinary Federal law infringes the Grundgesetz of the Federal Republic of Germany.

70. While the imposition of such restrictions may be consistent with the requirement that the conditions laid down should not be less favourable than those relating to similar domestic claims, it is still to be considered whether such restrictions are not such as in practice to make it impossible or excessively difficult to obtain reparation.

71. The condition imposed by German law where a law is in breach of higher-ranking national provisions, which makes reparation dependent upon the legislature's act or omission being referral to an individual situation, would in practice make it impossible or extremely difficult to obtain effective reparation for loss or damage resulting from a breach of Community law, since the tasks falling to the national legislature relate, in principle, to the public at large and not to identifiable persons or classes of person.

72. Since such a condition stands in the way of the obligation on national courts to ensure the full effectiveness of Community law by guaranteeing effective protection for the rights of individuals, it must be set aside where an infringement of Community law is attributable to the national legislature.

73. Likewise, any condition that may be imposed by English law on State liability requiring proof of misfeasance in public office, such an abuse of power being inconceivable in the case of the legislature, is also such as in practice to make it impossible or extremely difficult to obtain effective reparation for loss or damage resulting from a breach of Community law where the breach is attributable to the national legislature.

.....

The actual extent of the reparation

82. Reparation for loss or damage caused to individuals as a result of breaches of Community law must be commensurate with the loss or damage sustained so as to ensure the effective protection for their rights.

83. In the absence of relevant Community provisions, it is for the domestic legal system of each Member State to set the criteria for determining the extent of reparation. However, those criteria must not be less favourable than those applying to similar claims based on domestic law and must not be such as in practice to make it impossible or excessively difficult to obtain reparation.

84. In particular, in order to determine the loss or damage for which reparation may be granted, the national court may inquire whether the injured person showed reasonable diligence in order to avoid the loss or damage or limit its extent and, whether, in particular he availed himself in time of all the legal remedies available to him.

85. Indeed, it is a general principle common to the legal systems of the Member states that the injured party must show reasonable diligence in limiting the extent of the loss or damage, or risk having to bear the damage himself (Joined Cases C-104/89 and C-37/90 *Mulder and Others v Council and Commission* [1992] ECR I-3061, paragraph 33).

.....

87. Total exclusion of loss of profit as a head of damage for which reparation may be awarded in the case of a breach of Community law cannot be accepted. Especially in the context of economic or commercial litigation, such a total exclusion of loss of profit would be such as to make reparation of damage practically impossible.

88. As for the various heads of damage referred to in the Divisional Court's second question, Community law imposes no specific criteria. It is for the national court to rule on those heads of damage in accordance with the domestic law which it applies, subject to the requirements set out in paragraph 83 above.

89. As regards in particular the award of exemplary damages, such damages are based under domestic law, as the Divisional Court explains, on the finding that the public authorities concerned acted oppressively, arbitrarily or unconstitutionally. In so far as such conduct may constitute or aggravate a breach of Community law, an award of exemplary damages pursuant to a claim or an action founded on Community law cannot be ruled out if such damages could be awarded pursuant to a similar claim or action founded on domestic law.

95. ... to make the reparation of loss or damage conditional upon the requirement that there must have been a prior finding by the Court of an infringement of Community law attributable to a Member State would be contrary to the principle of the effectiveness of Community law, since it would preclude any right to reparation so long as the presumed infringement had not been the subject of an action brought by the Commission under Article 169 of the Treaty and of a finding of an infringement by the Court. Rights arising for individuals out of Community provisions having direct effect in the domestic legal systems of the Member states cannot depend on the Commission's assessment of the expediency of taking action against a Member State pursuant to Article 169 of the Treaty or on the delivery by the Court of any judgment finding an infringement (see, to this effect, Joined Cases 314/81, 315/81, 316/81 and 83/82 *Waterkeyn and Others* [1982] ECR 4337, paragraph 16).

A dichotomy initially appeared to have been drawn in *Brasserie du Pêcheur* between those circumstances in which national authorities are left no discretion as to achieve a particular result and those where they have a wide discretion to make legislative choice with different tests applying to the two categories.[62] More recently, in *Dillenkofer* the Court has suggested that a unitary test will be applied where liability will be incurred if three conditions are met.[63] These are:

- the provisions infringed must be intended to confer rights on individuals;
- the breach must be sufficiently serious;
- there must be a direct causal link between the breach by the Member State and the damage sustained by the injured parties.[64]

---

[62] This dichotomy was subsequently reasserted in Case C-392/93 *R v HM Treasury, ex parte British Telecommunications* [1996] ECR I-1631, [1996] 2 CMLR 887; Case C-5/94 *R v Ministry of Agriculture, Fisheries and Food, ex parte Hedley Lomas* [1996] ECR I-2553, [1996] 2 CMLR 391.

[63] Joined Cases C-178-9 & C-188-190/94 *Dillenkofer v Germany* [1996] ECR I-4845, [1996] 3 CMLR 469. See also Case C-66/95 *R v Secretary of State ex parte Sutton*, Judgment of 22 April 1997.

[64] There is already a burgeoning literature on *Brasserie du Pêcheur*. In addition to the articles cited elsewhere see Emiliou, N. 'State Liability under Community Law: Shedding More Light on the Francovich Principle?' (1996) 21 *ELRev* 399; Gravells, N. 'State Liability in Damages for Breach of European Community Law' (1996) *PL* 567; Convery, J. 'State Liability in

That said, the Court has suggested that in areas where Member States enjoy no discretion, simple illegality may be treated as being sufficiently serious, *per se*, to incur liability. One example the Court has given of such a circumstance is where a Member State fails to take any action to transpose a Directive. *Francovich* was an example of this. A similar case was *Dillenkofer*. Germany had failed to transpose Directive 90/314/EC on package holidays by the implementation date of 21 December 1992. The directive gives consumers a right to repatriation and a refund of the money passed over in the case of insolvency of the organiser. The Court therefore held that the German Government had to compensate a group of holiday makers who had either been unable to leave Germany or had been stranded in their country of destination following the insolvency of two tour operators in 1993.

The other scenario in which the Court seems to be willing to impose strict liability is in cases where the national authorities are not required to make a *legislative* choice. This has already been criticised on the grounds that not only is it often difficult to classify acts as legislative or administrative, but administrative acts are often taken against as complex a background as legislative acts.[65] It remains to be seen how viable is this, particularly as, in the only case on this point, the breach of the Member State was so flagrant that liability would have been incurred under almost any test.

In *Lomas* the British Ministry of Agriculture, Fisheries and Food was pursuing a policy of refusing to issue licences for exports of live animals for slaughter to Spain on the grounds that the conditions of Spanish slaughterhouses did not meet those set out in Directive 74/577/EEC. The only evidence relied upon by the British Government were press reports. In such circumstances, the measures in question were clearly an illegal restriction on trade. Whilst the Court noted that the refusal to issue an export licence was an administrative act so that mere infringement of Community law might be sufficient, its finding of

---

[65]   the United Kingdom after Brasserie du Pêcheur' (1997) 34 CMLRev 603; Oliver (1996) 34 CMLRev 635.

Craig, P, 'Once more unto the breach: The Community, the State and Damages Liability' (1997) 113 *LQR* 67, 81.

liability was based in part on the British Government's inability to produce any evidence to support its allegations.

In areas where Member States enjoy a legislative discretion, liability will only be incurred where it is shown that they have manifestly and gravely disregarded the limits of this discretion. In reality, the test is a circular one, for it is difficult to argue that Member States enjoy a discretion to act in such an arbitrary way where the acts in question are so clearly illegal. Three scenarios have so far been described where liability will be incurred.

The first, and the one likely to be least frequent, is where a Member State breaches an interim order by the Court. In *Factortame* it will be remembered that the Court had issued already an interim order in the action brought by the Commission against the United Kingdom government requiring the latter to suspend the national requirements imposed for registration of fishing vessels. There was some evidence to suggest that the United Kingdom had not complied with this order. The Court noted that if that were the case, the United Kingdom would be liable for any loss suffered.

The second scenario is where there is settled case-law which makes it clear that the conduct by the national authorities is illegal. In *Brasserie du Pêcheur* the Court intimated therefore that the refusal to allow the designation 'Bier' to foreign beer manufactured according to different processes in other Member States was a serious breach, as there was established case law pronouncing such behaviour to be illegal. Conversely, the Court did not consider the case law on national regulation of additives in food to be sufficiently settled to justify a finding of liability. A similar approach was taken in *Factortame* where the Court ruled that as it was settled that discrimination against other nationals was outlawed, and as the registration requirements were discriminatory, the breach was probably sufficiently serious to justify liability.

The final scenario on which the Court has ruled is where, although there is no settled law on the matter, the provision is so clear and precise that the meaning is not in doubt. This is the most problematic, as it assumes a core meaning to provisions which is not contested.

Case C-392/93 R v HM Treasury ex parte British Telecommunications plc
[1996] ECR I-1631, [1996] 2 CMLR 887

Directive 90/531/EEC established, *inter alia,* procurement procedures which must be followed by those enjoying special rights in the field of telecommunications. Article 8(1) of the directive stated that it would not apply 'where other entities are free to offer the same services in the same geographical area and under substantially the same conditions'. The United Kingdom considered that it was for it to decide when this was the case. British Telecommunications claimed the question was one of fact and did not require determination by the national authorities. The Court accepted British Telecommunications' argument. British Telecommunications then sought damages for the loss caused by its being wrongfully required to follow the procedures in the Directive.

41. Whilst it is in principle for the national courts to verify whether or not the conditions governing State liability for a breach of Community law are fulfilled, in the present case the Court has all the necessary information to assess whether the facts amount to a sufficiently serious breach of Community law.

42. According to the case-law of the Court, a breach is sufficiently serious where, in the exercise of its legislative powers, an institution or a Member State has manifestly and gravely disregarded the limits on the exercise of its powers (judgments in *HNL and Others v Council and Commission,* cited above, paragraph 6, and in *Brasserie du Pêcheur and Factortame,* paragraph 55). Factors which the competent court may take into consideration include the clarity and precision of the rule breached (judgment in *Brasserie du Pêcheur and Factortame,* paragraph 56).

43. In the present case, Article 8(1) [of the Directive] is imprecisely worded and was reasonably capable of bearing, as well as the construction applied to it by the court in this judgment, the interpretation given to it by the United Kingdom in good faith and on the basis of arguments which are not entirely devoid of substance. That interpretation, which was also shared by other Member States, was not manifestly contrary to the wording of the directive or to the objective pursued by it.

44. Moreover, no guidance was available to the United Kingdom from case-law of the Court as to the interpretation of the provision at issue, nor did the Commission raise the matter when the 1992 Regulations were adopted.

45. In those circumstances, the fact that a Member State, when transposing the directive into national law, thought it necessary itself to determine which services were to be excluded from its scope in implementation of Article 8, albeit in breach of that provision, cannot be regarded as a sufficiently serious breach of Community law of the kind intended by the Court in its judgment in *Brasserie du Pecheur and Factortame*.

Quite a formalistic approach has therefore been adopted with liability being confined to a limited number of strict circumscribed circumstances. There are undoubted advantages to such an approach. The predictability generated will undoubtedly allow national administrations a space to govern without fear of litigation. A formal approach can never generate complete certainty, however, because of the multiplicity of factual and legal situations which such rules must attempt to cover. In every instance, it is possible to think of circumstances where the legal situation is unclear, and the difficulty with a formalist approach is that it is precisely there where the rules 'run out' that few indicators are given as to how the matter should be decided. In relation to measures which generate strict liability, the example of administrative acts has already been given? Another example might be where a Member State takes no action to transpose a directive, considering its existing law to meet the directive's requirements. If this subsequently turns out not to be the case, will it be liable as, formally at least, it has not transposed the directive?

The examples given as to when a Member State has manifestly and gravely disregarded the limits of its discretion also pose as many questions as answers. Will a Member State be liable where it breached settled case law which has been widely criticised or where it is not clear that the case law in question covers the State's behaviour? What will be the position, if an interim order is breached where the terms of that order are ambiguous? Finally, exactly how clear does a provision have to be before it generates liability?[66]

Uncertainty has already manifested itself in relation to which loss may be recovered. In *Sutton* a mother who cared for an ill daughter had been refused Invalidity Care Allowance on the grounds that she, the

---

[66] It has been argued for example that the provision in *British Telecommunications* was unambiguous, Oliver, P. (1996) 34 *CMLRev* 635, 664.

mother, had reached pensionable age and was entitled to a pension.[67] Because of the difference in ages within the United Kingdom - with women reaching pensionable age at 60 whilst men did not reach it until 65 - this breached Directive 79/7. Mrs Sutton was duly awarded £5,588 in benefits by the British courts. As this was treated as benefits and not compensation, no interest was awarded for it being in arrears. She brought an action claiming for the interest. The Court remained ambiguous on the matter. It repeated that Member States were under a duty to compensate for loss caused, but then stated that they enjoyed a discretion as to the calculation of damages provided that this was not less than for similar claims made under domestic law and did not render it practically impossible or excessively difficult to obtain compensation. In other words, it offered no guidance to the national court as to whether the interest could be claimed or not.

The doctrine of State responsibility is not a static doctrine, but must be seen as part of a process. In this respect there is uncertainty about the dynamic of its development and where it will lead to. The first question which has been raised is whether it will lead to a form of private liability where an action can be brought against individuals for loss caused by their illegal actions.

Case C-128/94 Banks v British Coal Corporation [1994] ECR I-1207

Banks, a competitor of British Coal alleged that the latter had been engaging in anti-competitive practices in securing supply contracts from the British Electricity Supply Industry. The British court asked whether the relevant provisions of the ECSC could be invoked before national courts. The Court found that they were not directly effective. The more general question of private liability was discussed by Advocate General Van Gerven.

Advocate General Van Gerven

43. The general basis established by the Court in the *Francovich* judgment for State liability also applies where an individual infringes a provision of Community law to which he is subject, thereby causing loss and damage to another individual. The situation

---

[67]   Case C-66/95 *R v Secretary of State ex parte Sutton*, Judgment of 22 April 1997.

then falls within the terms stated by the Court in paragraph 31 of the *Francovich* judgment (and even earlier in *Van Gend en Loos*), namely breach of a right which an individual derives from an obligation imposed by Community law on another individual. Once again, the full effect of Community law would be impaired if the former individual or undertaking did not have the possibility of obtaining reparation from the party who can be held responsible for the breach of Community law - all the more so, evidently, if a directly effective provision of Community law is infringed: in that regard the Court has already pointed out in *Simmenthal* that such provisions are:

'a direct source of ... duties for all those affected thereby, whether Member States or individuals, who are parties to legal relationships under Community law.'[68]

It has been generally acknowledged for some considerable time ... that such provisions of Community law as have direct effect in relation to individuals include Articles 85 and 86 of the EEC Treaty: as shown earlier in this Opinion the same is true of Articles 4, 65(1) and 66(7) of the ECSC Treaty. When an undertaking subject to those rules infringes them, it can be held responsible for that infringement, according to the reasoning in the *Francovich* judgment, and it must be held liable for the loss and damage resulting from that breach of Community law.

44. In a field such as competition law, moreover, there are powerful additional arguments which militate in favour of undertakings having the possibility under Community law of obtaining reparation for loss and damage which they sustain as a result of a failure by other undertakings to fulfil their obligations under Community law. I shall confine myself to two of those arguments.

To begin with, recognition of such a right to obtain reparation constitutes the logical conclusion of the horizontal direct effect of the rules concerned: the rulings in *Simmenthal* and *Factortame* (paragraph 39 above) offer no solution where a national court has to adjudicate not on a rule of national legislation or administrative law which it can refrain from applying, but on a situation governed by private law in which one or more undertakings infringe a rule of competition, as a result of which a third party suffers loss and damage. The only effective method whereby the national court can in those circumstances fully safeguard the directly effective provisions of Community law which have been infringed is by restoring the rights of the injured party by the award of damages. Even a declaration that the legal relationship between the parties is void - for which there is an express basis in Community law - is not capable of making good the loss and damage (already) suffered by a third party.

In addition, such a rule on reparation plays a significant role in making the Community rules of competition more operational, particularly since the Commission, as guardian of those rules, itself acknowledges that it is dependent on the cooperation of

---

[68]   Case 106/77 *Amministrazione delle Finanze v Simmenthal* [1978] ECR 629, [1978] 3 CMLR 263.

the national courts in enforcing them. Individual actions for damages have for some time proved useful for the enforcement of federal anti-trust rules in the United States as well.

Even if such an argument were accepted, the extent of the doctrine is unclear. It would be assumed that directives could not generate private liability as they are not capable of horizontal direct effect. Yet if the system of liability established by *Francovich* will be available in all areas where direct effect is available, questions are posed about the future of direct effect. For, from a litigant's perspective, it seems quite a weak form of action compared to a liability-based regime.

The final question to be addressed is the impact of *Francovich* on domestic regimes. Whilst the extent of the duty of the reparation is a matter for national jurisdictions, this discretion is limited by a proviso that the reparation be commensurate to the loss,[69] and that the national regime on remedies not make it impossible or excessively difficult for the applicant to obtain reparation. These provisos have resulted in the EC regime on State responsibility imposing liability on national authorities in circumstances where they would incur no liability for breach of an equivalent domestic law. For example, *Factortame* suggested a general right to claim economic loss which is not available in English law. Similarly, in *Brasserie du Pêcheur*, the Court stated that acts of the legislature could attract liability - something that is not otherwise the case in German law. The need to secure a 'base level of protection' has led to suggestions that liability regimes across the European Union will converge both as a result of direct intrusion from the Court of Justice and as a result of the incorporation of new doctrines into national legal systems.[70] Others advocate a convergence of rules not to do justice to

---

[69]   Retroactive application to the applicant by the Member State of national measures implementing EC law will normally be sufficient, unless the applicant can show that the illegal act resulted in its suffering complementary loss sustained on account of its being unable to benefit from a financial advantage granted by EC law. Joined Cases C-94 & 95/95 *Bonifaci v INPS*, Judgment of 10 July 1997; Case C-373/95 *Maso et al. v INPS*, Judgment of 10 July 1997.

[70]   For an early view see Schwarze, J. 'Tendencies Towards a Common Administrative Law in Europe' (1991) 16 *ELRev* 3; Waelbroeck, D. 'Treaty Violations and Liability of Member States and the European Community' in

those asserting EC rights, but as the only way of securing the interests of those, such as public administrations, who may wish to contest EC rights.[71] Such arguments run the danger, however, of being too seduced by the internal logic of EC law and failing to pay sufficient attention to the environment within which it may operate. It may well be that the specificity and extrapetal tendencies of different social and legal cultures will obstruct such a development, leaving the existing dichotomy between EC rights and national procedures largely intact.[72]

V. Remedies and Procedure in National Courts

Francovich created not just a new cause of action. It also prescribed a particular remedy, namely governmental liability, that should be used in national courts. In that sense, it was one of a number of cases which marked a departure from the traditional position that whilst there may be duties upon national courts to allow provisions of EC law to be invoked before them, as a result of either the direct effect or indirect effect doctrines, the remedies and procedures to be applied were a matter for the national legal order.[73]

---

[71] Curtin, D. & Heukels, T. (eds.) *Institutional Dynamics of European Integration* (1994, Martijnus Nijhoff, Dordrecht); Caranta, R. 'Judicial Protection against Member States: a New Jus Commune takes Shape' (1995) 32 *CMLRev* 703 Van Gerven, W. 'Bridging the Unbridgeable: Community and National Tort Laws after Francovich and Brasserie' (1996) 45 *ICLQ* 507. Himsworth, C. 'Things Fall Apart: The Harmonisation of Community Judicial Procedural Protection Revisited' (1997) 22 *ELRev* 291.

[72] Legrand, P. 'European Legal Systems are Not Converging' (1996) 45 ICLQ 52. Along similar lines see Legrand, P. 'Against a European Civil Code' (1997) 60 *MLR* 44.

[73] For comment see Bridge, J. 'Procedural Aspects of the Enforcement of EC Law Through the Legal Systems of the Member States' (1984) 9 *ELRev* 28; Barav, A. & Green, N. 'Damages in the national Courts for Breach of Community Law' (1986) 6 *YBEL* 55; Oliver, P. 'Enforcing Community Rights in English Courts' (1987) 50 *MLR* 881; Steiner, J. 'How to make the Action Fit the Case: Domestic Remedies for Breach of EC Law' (1987) 12 *ELRev* 102.

Case 45/76 Comet v Produktschap [1976] ECR 2043

Comet had paid sums to Produktschap in 1968 and 1969 on the export of plants and bulbs which were contrary to Article 16 EC [*repealed at Amsterdam*], a provision requiring the abolition of customs duties or charges having equivalent effect on exports by 1962. Produktschap argued that reimbursement of the sums was time barred under Dutch law. Comet, meanwhile, argued that the national rule should be disapplied as it constituted an obstacle to the primacy of EC law.

12.... in application of the principle of cooperation laid down in Article 5 of the Treaty, the national courts are entrusted with ensuring the legal protection conferred on individuals by the direct effect of the provisions of Community law.

13. Consequently, in the absence of any relevant Community rules, it is for the national legal order of each Member State to designate the competent courts and to lay down the procedural rules for proceedings designed to ensure the protection of the rights which individuals acquire through the direct effect of Community law, provided that such rules are not less favourable than those governing the same right of action on an internal matter.

14. Articles 100 to 102 and 235 of the Treaty enable the appropriate steps to be taken as necessary, to eliminate differences between the provisions laid down in such matters by law, regulation or administrative action in Member States if these differences are found to be such as to cause distortion or to affect the functioning of the common market.

15. In default of such harmonization measures, the rights conferred by Community law must be exercised before the national courts in accordance with the rules of procedure laid down by national law.

16. The position would be different only if those rules and time-limits made it impossible in practice to exercise rights which the national courts have a duty to protect.

Whilst the precise remedy to be applied is a matter for the national judicial discretion, the provision of guidelines as to how this is to be applied has been described as marking the second generation of EC law.[74] Whilst in the first phase the Court was concerned with describing

---

[74] This was first used in De Wilmars, M. 'L'éfficacité des différentes techniques nationales de protection juridique contre les violations du droit communautaire par les autorités nationales' in *FIDE, Remedies for Breach of Community Law* (1980, London, Sweet & Maxwell). It was taken up more

some of the hallmarks of EC constitutionalism, in this second phase it examines in more detail the assimilation of the EC and national legal orders. This process of assimilation suggested the development of two forms of consistency. On the one hand, there was an internal consistency which required EC law not to be undervalued in relation to the enforcement of national law. On the other, the setting of a minimum standard, namely that national rules not make it impossible to exercise EC rights suggests an external consistency in the form of a minimum level of enforcement.[75] The difficulty with this approach, however, was that the vagueness of the guidelines and the discretion left to the national judge detracted from the goal of uniformity of EC law. In the late 1980's and early 1990's, albeit sporadically, the Court began to develop a third generation of EC law, whose hallmarks was a more specific system of remedies and procedures.

The first example of this occurring was in the area of restitution of illegally levied tax. In *Deville* a French tax on motor vehicles had been declared unlawful. A time limit had been imposed on claims for refunds.[76] Deville, having been refused a refund on these grounds, claimed that the bar was illegal. The Court ruled that a corollary of the direct effect of EC law was that any sum unlawfully levied should be capable of recovery. It therefore considered that any measure which specifically reduced the possibilities for bringing proceedings for recovery of illegally levied taxes was illegal. The effectiveness of this right to restitution is tempered, however, by the discretion Member States enjoy not to refund money where this will lead to unjust enrichment,[77] such as where a trader has passed the costs of the tax onto the customer and then seeks double enrichment through reclaiming the tax in question.

---

more recently in Curtin, D. & Mortelmans, K. 'Application and Enforcement of Community Law by the Member States: Actors in Search of a Third Generation Script' in Curtin, D. & Heukels, T. (eds.) *Institutional Dynamics of European Integration* (1994, Martijnus Nijhoff, Dordrecht).

[75] Szyszczak, E. 'Making Europe More Relevant to Its Citizens: Effective Judicial Process' (1996) 21 *ELRev* 351, 352.

[76] Case 240/87 *Deville v Administration des Impôts* [1988] ECR 3513.

[77] Case C-212/94 *FMC* [1996] ECR I-389.

In *Société Comateb*, a case involving 27 traders claiming for dock dues illegally levied in Guadeloupe, the Court indicated that this exception was a narrow one.[78] In the first place, the Court stated that a Member State could resist repayment only where it had been shown by the Member State that the entirety of the charge had been borne by someone other than the trader. If only part of the burden had been passed on, them the remainder should be refunded. Furthermore, even where the whole of tax had been passed on, the Court ruled that the Member State may still not be able to plead the unjust enrichment exception. This would be the case where the effect of the tax was such as to lead to a restriction in the volume of the imports and a corresponding loss for the trader.

The next field where specific remedies were developed was in the field of interim relief in the context of Article 177 [*234*] EC references. In a series of judgments the Court has ruled that national courts should suspend national measures where this is necessary to protect the rights of the parties.[79] If the right to restitution is confined to a narrow field, that of taxation, then the right to interim relief is confined by its only being used within the context of Article 177 [*234*] EC references.

The Court reached the high watermark of this line of reasoning with two decisions which established more far reaching remedies. The first was the *Francovich* decision, which has been discussed earlier. The second was *Emmott* which appeared to state that limitation periods could not be invoked by a Member State where a directive which it had failed to transpose correctly was being invoked against public authorities.

---

[78]   Joined Cases C-192-218/95 *Société Comateb et al. v Directeur général des douanes et droits indirects*, [1997] ECRI-165.

[79]   Case C-213/89 *R v Secretary of State for Transport ex parte Factortame* [1990] ECR I-2433, [1990] 3 CMLR 1; Case C-465/93 *Atlanta Fruchthandelsgesellschaft GmbH et al v Bundesamt für Ernährung* [1995] ECR I-3763. See also Advocate General Elmer in Case C-334/95 *Krüger v Hauptzollamt Hamburg-Jonas*, Judgment of 17 July 1997. This case law is discussed in more detail in Chapter 8.

Case C-208/90 Emmott v Minister for Social Welfare and the Attorney General [1991] ECR I-4269, [1991] 3 CMLR 894

Mrs Emmott had been unlawfully denied full social security benefits in breach of Directive 79/7/EEC by the Irish government since 23 December 1984. In March 1987 the Court of Justice ruled that the Irish scheme was illegal.[80] Mrs Emmott claimed for the difference backdated to 23 December 1984. The Minister refused to consider her claim until the litigation in the case from the Court of Justice had been resolved. She sought judicial review of this decision. The Irish Government claimed that such a review was time barred as it must be brought within three months of when the grounds for review first arose.

18. According to the third paragraph of Article 189 of the EEC Treaty, a directive is to be binding, as to the result to be achieved, upon each Member State to which it is addressed, but is to leave to the national authorities the choice of form and methods. Although that provision leaves Member States free to choose the ways and means of ensuring that a directive is implemented, that freedom does not affect the obligation, imposed on all the Member States to which a directive is addressed, to adopt, within the framework of their national legal systems, all the measures necessary to ensure that the directive is fully effective, in accordance with the objective which it pursues (see judgment in Case 14/83 *Sabine van Colson and Elisabeth Kamann v Land Nordrhein-Westfalen* [1984] ECR 1891).

19. In this regard it must be borne in mind that the Member States are required to ensure the full application of directives in a sufficiently clear and precise manner so that, where directives are intended to create rights for individuals, they can ascertain the full extent of those rights and, where necessary, rely on them before the national courts (see, in particular, judgment in Case 363/85 *Commission v Italy* [1987] ECR 1733).

20. Only in specific circumstances, in particular where a Member State has failed to take the implementing measures required or has adopted measures which are not in conformity with a directive, has the Court recognized the right of persons affected thereby to rely, in judicial proceedings, on a directive as against a defaulting Member State. This minimum guarantee, arising from the binding nature of the obligation imposed on the Member States by the effect of directives, cannot justify a Member State absolving itself from taking in due time implementing measures appropriate to the purpose of each directive (see judgment in Case 102/79 *Commission v Belgium* [1980] ECR 1473).

---

[80]   Case 286/85 *McDermott and Cotter v Minister For Social Welfare and the Attorney General* [1987] ECR 1453.

21. So long as a directive has not been properly transposed into national law, individuals are unable to ascertain the full extent of their rights. That state of uncertainty for individuals subsists even after the Court has delivered a judgment finding that the Member State in question has not fulfilled its obligations under the directive and even if the Court has held that a particular provision or provisions of the directive are sufficiently precise and unconditional to be relied upon before a national court.

22. Only the proper transposition of the directive will bring that state of uncertainty to an end and it is only upon that transposition that the legal certainty which must exist if individuals are to be required to assert their rights is created.

23. It follows that, until such time as a directive has been properly transposed, a defaulting Member State may not rely on an individual's delay in initiating proceedings against it in order to protect rights conferred upon him by the provisions of the directive and that a period laid down by national law within which proceedings must be initiated cannot begin to run before that time.

The apparent refusal of the Court to allow Member States to protect themselves behind limitation periods undoubtedly both increased the possibilities for individual litigation and the incentives for Member States to transpose directives properly. It also exposed national authorities to a very open-ended liability, particularly as the Court was very reluctant to limit the temporal effects of its judgments. The scenario thus arose of the Court giving an interpretation of a Directive which was unexpected by the Member States and which opened them up to claims going back many years.[81] The Court has thus repeatedly limited the ambit of the *Emmott* judgment.

In *Steenhorst-Neerings* a Dutch rule limited the amount which could be retroactively claimed to one year's benefits.[82] Miss Steenhorst-Neerings claimed for 4 years' invalidity benefits which had not been paid to her in breach of Directive 79/7/EC. The Court considered the Dutch rule limiting the period for the amount for which to be claimed to be

---

[81]   It was claimed by the French Government, for example, that a French company tax declared illegal in Joined Cases C-197 & C-252/94 *Société Bautiaa* [1996] ECR I-505 exposed the French Government to a potential liability of FF 8.5 billion.

[82]   Case C-338/91 *Steenhorst-Neerings v Bestuur van de Bedrijfsvereniging voor Detailhandel, Ambachten en Huisvrouwen* [1993] ECR I-5475.

different from the law at stake in *Emmott*. For it did not, unlike the latter, prevent the applicant relying upon the directive before a national court but merely limited the amount she could claim. This form of procedural rule was a matter for the domestic legal order provided it was not less favourable than the rules governing domestic claims and was not framed so as to render virtually impossible the exercise of individual rights conferred by EC law.

The Court retreated even further in *Johnson*.[83] The situation paralleled *Steenhorst-Neerings* in that it concerned a British measure which limited the benefits claimed to those due for the 12 months before the date of the claim. The Court reaffirmed *Steenhorst-Neerings* and stated that *Emmott* should be confined to the particular circumstances of the case in which the time bar had 'the effective result of depriving the applicant of any opportunity whatever to rely on her right to equal treatment under the directive'.

In subsequent judgments the Court seemed to imply that *Emmott* was all but overruled, stating that time limits were a matter for the national legal order.[84] It thus appeared that the Court had beat a hasty retreat from its foray into national procedural remedies.[85] In a couple of judgments delivered on the same day towards the end of 1995, the Court sought to clarify the position by suggesting a new balance would be adopted. Under this *modus vivendi* national procedural autonomy would be respected but the Court would consider more closely the rationale of a particular procedural right in considering whether it might render the exercise of EC rights virtually impossible or excessively difficult.[86]

---

[83] Case C-410/92 *Johnson v Chief Adjudication Officer* [1994] ECR I-5483

[84] Case C-128/93 *Fisscher v Voorhuis Hengelo BV and Stichting Bedrijfs-pensioenfonds voor de Detailhandel* [1994] ECR I-4583; Case C-62/93 *BP Soupergas v Hellenic Republic* [1995] ECR I-1883; Joined Cases C-46/93 *Brasserie du Pêcheur SA v Federal Republic of Germany* and C-48/93 *R v Secretary of State for Transport ex parte Factortame Ltd* [1996] ECR I-1029, [1996] 1 CMLR 889.

[85] Ward, A. 'Effective Sanctions in EC Law: a Moving Boundary in the Division of Competence' (1995) 1 *ELJ* 205.

[86] De Búrca, G. 'National Procedural Rules and Remedies: The Changing Approach of the Court of Justice' in Lonbay, J. & Biondi, A. (eds.) *Remedies for Breach of EC Law* (1997, John Wiley, Chichester).

Joined Cases C-430/93 & C-431/93 Van Schijndel et al. v Stichting Pensioenfonds voor Fysiotherapeuten [1995] ECR I-4705

In the Netherlands membership of an occupational pension scheme run by the profession was compulsory for physiotherapists. Van Veen and Van Schijndel, two physiotherapists applied for, and were refused, exemption from membership of the scheme. Their respective challenges to the scheme were dismissed. They appealed to the Dutch Hoge Raad, claiming in particular that the Breda court, which had considered Van Veen's case, should have raised of its own motion certain points of EC competition law. Under the Dutch Code of Civil Procedure whilst courts were required, if necessary of their own motion, to raise points of law, there was a principle of judicial passivity which required courts not to go beyond the ambit of the dispute defined by the parties or to look at facts or circumstances other than those on which the claim is based. The Hoge Raad asked the Court of Justice whether a national court was obliged to raise a point of EC law of its own motion even if that meant abandoning the principle of judicial passivity.

17. In the absence of Community rules governing the matter, it is for the domestic legal system of each Member State to designate the courts and tribunals having jurisdiction and to lay down the detailed procedural rules governing actions for safeguarding rights which individuals derive from the direct effect of Community law. However, such rules must not be less favourable than those governing similar domestic actions nor render virtually impossible or excessively difficult the exercise of rights conferred by Community law (see, in particular, the judgments in Case 33/76 *Rewe v Landwirtschaftskammer für das Saarland* [1976] ECR 1989, paragraph 5, ...).

18. The Court has also held that a rule of national law preventing the procedure laid down in Article 177 of the Treaty from being followed must be set aside (see the judgment in Case 166/73 *Rheinmühlen v Einfuhr-und Vorratsstelle für Getreide und Futtermittel* [1974] ECR 33, paragraphs 2 and 3).

19. For the purposes of applying those principles, each case which raises the question whether a national procedural provision renders application of Community law impossible or excessively difficult must be analysed by reference to the role of that provision in the procedure, its progress and its special features, viewed as a whole, before the various national instances. In the light of that analysis the basic principles of the domestic judicial system, such as protection of the rights of the defence, the principle of legal certainty and the proper conduct of procedure, must, where appropriate, be taken into consideration.

20. In the present case, the domestic law principle that in civil proceedings a court must or may raise points of its own motion is limited by its obligation to keep to the subject-matter of the dispute and to base its decision on the facts put before it.

21. That limitation is justified by the principle that, in a civil suit, it is for the parties to take the initiative, the court being able to act of its own motion only in exceptional cases where the public interest requires its intervention. That principle reflects conceptions prevailing in most of the Member States as to the relations between the State and the individual; it safeguards the rights of the defence; and it ensures proper conduct of proceedings by, in particular, protecting them from the delays inherent in examination of new pleas.

22. In those circumstances, the answer to the second question must be that Community law does not require national courts to raise of their own motion an issue concerning the breach of provisions of Community law where examination of that issue would oblige them to abandon the passive role assigned to them by going beyond the ambit of the dispute defined by the parties themselves and relying on facts and circumstances other than those on which the party with an interest in application of those provisions bases his claim.

Case C-312/93 Peterbroeck, Van Campenhout & Cie SCS v Belgian State [1995] ECR I-4599

Peterbroeck, the Belgian legal representative of a Dutch company, Continentale & Britse trust, lodged a complaint about the rate of tax levied on the latter with the Regional Director of Direct Contributions. When this was rejected by the latter, it appealed to the Cour d'Appel, claiming, for the first time, that the method of assessment breached Article 52 [*43*] EC, on the freedom of establishment. This had not been lodged within the limitation period prescribed by Belgian law for new pleas, which required that they be made within 60 days of the lodging by the Director of a certified true copy of the contested decision. The Cour d'Appel asked the Court whether it was required to ignore this limitation period to consider the case of its own motion.

14. ..., each case which raises the question whether a national procedural provision renders application of Community law impossible or excessively difficult must be analysed by reference to the role of that provision in the procedure, its progress and its special features, viewed as a whole, before the various national instances. In the light of that analysis the basic principles of the domestic judicial system, such as protection of the rights of the defence, the principle of legal certainty and the proper conduct of procedure, must, where appropriate, be taken into consideration.

15. In the present case, according to domestic law, a litigant may no longer raise before the Cour d'Appel a new plea based on Community law once the 60-day period with effect from the lodging by the Director of a certified true copy of the contested decision has elapsed.

16. Whilst a period of 60 days so imposed on a litigant is not objectionable *per se*, the special features of the procedure in question must be emphasized.

17. First of all, the Cour d'Appel is the first court which can make a reference to the Court of Justice since the Director before whom the first-instance proceedings are conducted is a member of the fiscal authorities and, consequently, is not a court or tribunal within the meaning of Article 177 of the Treaty (see, to this effect, the judgment in Case C-24/92 *Corbiau* [1993] ECR I-1277).

18. Secondly, the limitation period whose expiry prevented the Cour d'Appel from examining of its own motion the compatibility of a measure of domestic law with Community law started to run from the time when the Director lodged a certified true copy of the contested decision. That meant, in this case, that the period during which new pleas could be raised by the appellant had expired by the time the Cour d'Appel held its hearing so that the Cour d'Appel was denied the possibility of considering the question of compatibility.

19. Thirdly, it seems that no other national court or tribunal in subsequent proceedings may of its own motion consider the question of the compatibility of a national measure with Community law.

20. Finally, the impossibility for national courts or tribunals to raise points of Community law of their own motion does not appear to be reasonably justifiable by principles such as the requirement of legal certainty or the proper conduct of procedure.

21. The answer to be given to the question submitted by the Cour d' Appel, Brussels, must therefore be that Community law precludes application of a domestic procedural rule whose effect, in procedural circumstances such as those in question in the main proceedings, is to prevent the national court, seised of a matter falling within its jurisdiction, from considering of its own motion whether a measure of domestic law is compatible with a provision of Community law when the latter provision has not been invoked by the litigant within a certain period.

Some commentators have hailed the balance struck as a clever and sensible compromise.[87] Considerable uncertainty is likely to continue, however, because of the idiosyncratic nature of national procedural rules which result in its being difficult to predict when they will be considered to render the exercise of EC rights virtually impossible or excessively difficult.[88] There is also uncertainty about the status of *Emmott*. In *Palmisani* the Court considered a time bar introduced by the Italian legislature in 1992 which required all claims for compensation as a result of the Italian Government's failure to implement Directive 80/897/EEC, protecting workers in the case of insolvency, to be brought within 12 months.[89] The Court held that the time bars were lawful on the grounds that they protected the fundamental principle of legal certainty. It, furthermore, considered that a 12 month bar did not render it excessively difficult to invoke one's EC rights.

This does not mean *Emmott* has been completely overruled, merely that it operates within a confined space. In *Denkavit* Advocate General Jacobs suggested that *Emmott* had a number of features which differentiated it from other cases.[90] He noted that Ireland had failed to implement the Directive in good faith; Mrs Emmott was denied any effective opportunity to rely on the directive for the period in question, and that she was in the particularly unprotected position of an individual dependent on social welfare. If this is so, it might be that a reserved status exists for *Emmott*, either as an action to punish particularly egregious conduct by Member States or as a device to facilitate assertion of legal rights by the most disenfranchised in society.

---

[87]   Hoskins, M. 'Tilting the Balance: Supremacy and National Procedural Rules' (1996) 21 *ELRev* 365.

[88]   On the relationship between French procedural rules and EC law see Szyszczak, E. & Delicostopoulos, J. 'Intrusions into National Procedural Autonomy: The French Paradigm' (1997) 22 *ELRev* 147.

[89]   Case C-261/95 *Palmisani v INPS*, Judgment of 10 July 1997.

[90]   Case C-2/94 *Denkavit International BV and Others v Kamer van Koophandel en Fabrieken voor Midden-Gelderland and Others* [1996] ECR I- 2827.

Further Reading

Caranta, R. 'Judicial Protection against Member States: a New Jus Commune Takes Shape' (1995) 32 *Common Market Law Review* 703

Coppel, J. 'Rights, Duties and the End of Marshall' (1994) 57 *Modern Law Review* 859

Craig, P. 'Francovich, Remedies and the Scope of Damages Liability' (1993) 109 *Law Quarterly Review* 595

-----'Once more Unto the Breach: The Community, The State and Damages Liability' (1997) 113 *Law Quarterly Review* 67

Curtin, D. & Mortelmans, K. 'Application and Enforcement of Community Law by the Member States: Actors in Search of a Third Generation Script' in Curtin, D. & Heukels, T. (eds.) *Institutional Dynamics of European Integration* (1994, Martijnus Nijhoff, Dordrecht)

Mancini, F. & Keeling, D. 'Language, Culture and Politics in the Life of the European Court of Justice' (1995) 1 *Columbia Journal of European Law* 397

Prechal, S. *Directives in EC Law. a Study on EC Directives and their Enforcement by National Courts* (1995, OUP, Oxford)

Ross, M. 'Beyond Francovich' (1992) 56 *Modern Law Review* 55

Steiner, J. 'From direct effects to *Francovich*: shifting means of enforcement of Community law' (1993) 18 *European Law Review* 3

Szyszczak, E. 'Making Europe More Relevant to Its Citizens: Effective Judicial Process' (1996) 21 *European Law Review* 351

----- and Delicostopoulos, J. 'Intrusions into National Procedural Autonomy: The French Paradigm' (1997) 22 *European Law Review* 141

Van Gerven, W. 'Bridging the Unbridgeable: Community and National Tort Laws after *Francovich* and *Brasserie*' (1996) 45 *International and Comparative Law Quarterly* 507

Ward, A. 'Effective Sanctions in EC Law: a Moving Boundary in the Division of Competence' (1995) 1 *European Law Journal* 205

8. Relations Between the Court of Justice and National Courts

I. Introduction

The discourse of constitutionalism developed by the Court of Justice since *Van Gend en Loos*[1] has implications not just for the relationship between the EC and the Member States. It also has infra-societal implications. The language most obviously appears to empower legal and natural persons, who can now assert protection of the rights granted to them by EC law. Yet these rights can only be asserted absolutely by those who enter the judicial domain.[2] Evidence on the number of litigants, as a proportion of potential litigants, who go either before national courts or the Court of Justice to assert their EC law rights is sadly lacking.

The other beneficiaries from this process of constitutionalisation have been courts, both the Court of Justice and national courts. This relationship should be seen as one of the central axes within the European Union, every bit as demanding of attention as the formal legislative procedures. National court influence is increased, in particular, horizontally, vis-à-vis the other arms of national government. National courts which did not have the power of judicial review previously are now granted the power to review acts of the other branches of government for their compatibility with EC law. Courts which previously had the power to review only certain measures,

---

[1]   Case 26/62 *Van Gend en Loos v Nederlandse Administratie der Belastingen* [1963] ECR 1, [1963] CMLR 105.

[2]   Judicially protected rights can also be asserted outside the courtroom in the 'shadow of the law'. In such circumstances, however, the right is deployed as merely one instrument in a negotiating process and loses its indefeasible qualities.

administrative acts for example, have had that power extended to cover other forms, such as legislation. Even courts with pre-existing full powers of review have had their power extended, for EC law gives them another ground against which to review acts of the executive and legislature.

II. Articles 177 [*234*] EC and *35 TEU* as a Structure for Relations between the Court of Justice and National Courts

National judicial influence has also increased in a vertical sense through the dependence of the Court of Justice on national courts. This is most easily illustrated via the manifestations of constitutionalism. These can be described as a series of duties imposed on national courts. National courts are thus, for example, required to apply EC law within their jurisdictions; to give it precedence over national law; to refuse to give a final declaration of invalidity on acts of EC institutions; to review Member State action for its compatibility with fundamental rights where it falls within the scope of EC law. Without national judicial acceptance of this doctrine, something which cannot be taken for granted, the pronouncements of the Court are reduced to little more than shallow rhetoric.[3] The formal contacts between the Court and courts of the Member States have traditionally been modulated in EC law through one Article, Article 177 [*234*] EC.

Article 177 [*234*] EC. The Court of Justice shall have jurisdiction to give preliminary rulings concerning:

     (a)   the interpretation of this Treaty
     (b)   the validity and interpretation of acts of the institutions of the Community and of the ECB;
     (c)   the interpretation of the statutes of bodies established by an act of the Council, where those statutes so provide.

---

[3]   *Brunner v European Union Treaty* [1994] 1 CMLR 57. See pp 19-20.

When such a question is raised before any court or tribunal of a member state, that court or tribunal may, if it considers that a decision on the question is necessary to enable it to give judgment, request the Court of Justice to give a ruling thereon.

When any such question is raised in a case pending before a court or tribunal of a Member State against whose decisions there is no judicial remedy under national law, that court or tribunal shall bring the matter before the Court of Justice.

Contacts between the Court of Justice and national courts have been established in other contexts. The Court has therefore competence to give preliminary rulings upon interpretation upon the Brussels Convention on Jurisdiction and the Enforcement of Judgments in Civil and Commercial Matters, a convention regulating private international legal relations between the Member States. Similarly a number of conventions have been signed within the context of JHA which give the Court the power to give preliminary rulings.[4] It is doubtful to what extent these conventions form part of, and are informed by principles of EU law, however. No provision existed, meanwhile, for national courts to refer matters which fell within the other two pillars, JHA and CFSP, to the Court of Justice. The Treaty of Amsterdam alters this in relation to JHA by allowing national governments to 'opt-in' their national judiciaries.[5]

Article 35 TEU. 1. The Court of Justice of the European Communities shall have jurisdiction, subject to the conditions laid down in this Article, to give preliminary rulings on the validity and interpretation of framework decisions and decisions, on the interpretation of conventions established under this Title and on the validity and interpretation of the measures implementing them.

---

[4]   Protocol on the interpretation by the Court of Justice of the European Communities on the Convention on the establishment of a European Police Office, OJ 1996, C 299/1; Protocol on the interpretation by the Court of Justice of the European Communities of the Convention on the protection of the European Communities' financial interests, OJ 1997, C 151/1; Protocol on the interpretation by the Court of Justice of the European Communities of the Convention on the use of information technology for customs purposes, OJ 1997, C 151/15.

[5]   This model was first used in relation to the Convention on the establishment of a European Police Office, supra n.4, Article 2(2).

2. By a declaration made at the time of the signing of this Treaty or any time thereafter, any Member State shall be able to accept a jurisdiction of the Court of Justice to give preliminary ruling as specified in paragraph 1.

3. Where a Member State has made a declaration pursuant to paragraph 2 of this Article:

(a) any court or tribunal of that State against whose decisions there is no judicial remedy under national law may request the Court of Justice to give a preliminary ruling on a question raised in a case pending before it and concerning the validity or interpretation of an act referred to in paragraph 1 if that court considers that a decision on the question is necessary to enable it to give judgment, or

(b) any court or tribunal of that State may request the Court of Justice to give a preliminary ruling on a question raised in a case pending before it and concerning the validity or interpretation of an act referred to in paragraph 1 if that court considers that a decision on the question is necessary to enable it to give judgment.

4. Any Member State, whether or not it has made a declaration pursuant to paragraph 2, shall be entitled to submit statements of case or written observations to the Court in cases which arise under paragraph 3.

5. The Court of Justice shall have no jurisdiction to review the validity or proportionality of operations carried out by the police or other law enforcement services of a Member State or the exercise of the responsibilities incumbent upon Member States with regard to the maintenance of law and order and the safeguarding of internal security.

Article 177 [*234*] EC and *35 TEU* confer two types of power upon the Court of Justice - a power to *interpret* EC law and a power to *review* acts of the EC institutions. Apart from the subject-matter of their respective jurisdictions, the principal distinction between the two is the optional nature of the latter, which leaves it to the national government to determine whether its courts, and if so which courts, should be able to refer matters on JHA to the Court of Justice. This discretion seems to protect neither national autonomy nor the Union interest particularly well. Judgments of the Court of Justice will presumably bind all Member States, including those which have not made a declaration. By opting-out of the system of preliminary rulings, Member States do not therefore opt out of the Court's jurisdiction. They merely place the courts of other

Member States in a privileged position in relation to their own, by allowing the former to be part of a law-making process, whilst denying it to the latter. From a Union perspective, however, this imbalance is unsatisfactory as it will result in the law not being uniformly applied, as the courts of some Member States will be able to have resort to the expertise of the Court of Justice whereas others will not.[6]

The manner in which the Court interprets *Article 35 TEU* will have to await the entry into force of the Treaty of Amsterdam. That said, it is not improbable that the Court will apply its powers of interpretation and review under this provision in an analogous manner to Article 177 [*234*] EC.

The Court has construed its interpretive powers under Article 177 EC [*234*] widely. It will give a ruling on anything which forms part of the EC legal order, even if, strictly speaking, it is neither interpreting a Treaty provision or a piece of secondary legislation. International agreements, such as the GATT were concluded by the Member States and came into force before the Community's existence and could not therefore have been concluded by an act of any of the EC institutions. The Court has ruled, however, that the Community has succeeded to them and that they therefore form part of the EC legal order.[7] It therefore considers that it can give preliminary rulings upon their interpretation to ensure the uniform interpretation of Community law.[8] Similarly it could be argued that the Court has no jurisdiction to give rulings upon general principles of law or fundamental rights, as a binding catalogue of these rights does not appear in any EC Treaty provision or piece of secondary legislation. Yet the Court has been willing to accept references on these in so far as they surround the interpretation of the

---

[6]   Framework Decisions and Decisions taken under JHA do not have direct effect, *Article 34(2) TEU*. It is possible that they could still be capable of indirect effect and of generating State liability. There is nothing to stop Conventions being ruled directly effective.

[7]   Joined Cases 21-24/72 *International Fruit Company v Produktschap voor Groenten en Fruit* [1972] ECR 1226, [1975] 2 CMLR 1.

[8]   Joined Cases 267-269/81 *Amministrazione delle Finanze dello Stato v SPI* [1983] ECR 801, [1984] 1 CMLR 354. For criticism see Hartley, T. *The Foundations of European Community Law* (1994, 3rd Ed., Clarendon, Oxford) 272-273.

EC Treaty and the interpretation and review of secondary legislation.[9]

The Court has applied its powers of interpretation widely in another direction. Whilst it has no general power to give rulings on provisions of national law,[10] it will give rulings on the latter wherever the latter refers to the contents of provisions of EC law or adopts similar solutions to those found in EC law.[11] In *Dzodzi*, a Togolese woman was challenging a decision by the Belgian authorities refusing her a residence permit following the death of her Belgian husband.[12] The situation was, in EC terms, an internal domestic one governed by Belgian law. The Belgian law stated however that the spouses of Belgian nationals should be treated in the same way as spouses of other EC nationals. Notwithstanding that the measure was governed by Belgian law, the Court ruled that it was manifestly in the Community interest that it should give a ruling, for, in order to forestall future differences of interpretation, it was necessary that the relevant provisions of EC law be given a uniform interpretation.

Similar reasoning was also used in *Federconsorzi* to give the Court jurisdiction to rule on certain terms of a contract.[13] In that instance some of AIMA's virgin olive oil had been stolen from Federconsorzi's premises. The contract between the two stated the latter would be liable for the losses for which it was responsible for the amount stipulated by the EC legislation in force. Once again the Court considered that the Community interest required it to give a uniform interpretation to forestall future differences of interpretation.

In addition to the functions of review and interpretation granted to the Court, the other feature worthy of note is the question of access to the Court under Article 177 [*234*] EC. The procedure is based upon a division of duties. Whilst it is for the Court of Justice to give a ruling on the point(s) of EC law in question, it is the national courts which are

---

[9]   e.g. Case 11/70 *Internationale Handelsgesellschaft v Einfuhr und Vorratsstelle Getreide* [1970] ECR 1125, [1972] CMLR 255

[10]   Case 75/63 *Hoekstra v Bedrijfsvereniging Detailhandel* [1964] ECR 177.

[11]   See Case C-231/89 *Galerie Gmurzynska-Bscher v Oberfinanzdirektion Köln* [1990] ECR I-4003; Case C-28/95 *Leur-Bloem v Inspecteur der Belastingsdienst*, Judgment of 17 July 1997.

[12]   Joined Cases C-297/88 & C-197/89 *Dzodzi v Belgium* [1990] ECR I-3673.

[13]   Case C-88/91 *Federconsorzi v AIMA* [1992] ECR I-4035.

responsible for questions of fact and dispute resolution.[14] The procedure is a court-to-court one with national courts acting as guardians to the gateway to the Court.[15] Private parties have therefore no direct access nor can they appeal decisions of the national courts to the Court of Justice. The Court has thus characterised Article 177 [*234*] EC as:

> 'a non-contentious procedure excluding any initiative of the parties who are merely invited to be heard in the course of this procedure.'[16]

The parties to the dispute are thus not wholly excluded from the procedure, as they may submit written observations to the Court.[17] In this, they may be joined by the Council, the Parliament or any of the Member States, all of whom may intervene. In addition, if any party insists or if the Court insists, there will be oral hearings at which each of the parties and those intervening may make oral representations up to between 15 and 30 minutes, depending upon the nature of the proceedings.

The final feature of note is the distinction made between those courts which fall under Article 177(2) [*234(2)*] EC and those, against whose decisions there is no judicial remedy, which fall within Article 177(3) [*234(3)*] EC. In principle, the latter are required to refer questions of EC law which are raised in a case before them, whereas the former have a discretion as to whether or not to refer. At first sight, it might seem rather odd that greater leeway is given to lower courts than to higher courts. Rationales for this are explored in the excerpt below,

---

14   Case 104/79 *Foglia v Novello* [1980] ECR 745, [1981] 1 CMLR 45.
15   Private parties who were not allowed to appear before the national court will not therefore be allowed to intervene before the Court of Justice, C-181/95 *Biogen v Smithkline Beecham* [1996] ECR I-717, [1997] 1 CMLR 704.
16   e.g. Case C-364/92 *SAT Fluggesellschaft v Eurocontrol* [1994] ECR I-43. See Mortelmans, K. 'Observations in Cases Governed by Article 177 of the EEC Treaty: Procedure and Practice' (1979) 16 *CMLRev* 557; Anderson, D. *References to the European Court* (1995, Sweet & Maxwell, London) 224-266.
17   Statute of the Court of Justice, Article 20.

which examines which courts are covered by Article 177(3) *[234(3)]* EC.[18]

Hartley, T. *The Foundations of European Community Law* **(1994, Clarendon Press, Oxford) 281**

Two points of view exist as to the meaning of the phrase: according to the 'abstract theory', the only courts within the scope of the provision are those whose decisions are never subject to appeal; according to the 'concrete theory', on the other hand, the important question is whether the court's decision in the case in question is subject to appeal. This distinction can be very important where, for example, there is a right of appeal only if the sum of money in issue is more than a certain amount.

The wording of Article 177(3) itself favours the abstract theory: if the authors of the Treaty had intended the decisive point to be whether there was a right of appeal in the particular case in question, they would not have put the word 'decisions' into the plural. The use of the plural suggests that the general position regarding appeals is the criterion. Another argument may be derived from considerations of national legal policy: the reasons rights of appeal are limited in certain cases is to prevent proceedings from becoming too drawn out and to keep costs within reasonable bounds. These objectives might be jeopardised if national courts were obliged to make a reference to Luxembourg even where the sum in issue was small or the case was generally of limited importance.

The policy of Community law, on the other hand, place paramount importance on maintaining uniformity of interpretation of Community provisions: this could be undermined if it were possible for a case involving Community law to run its course without a reference being made. Some of the most important judgments of the European Court's have in fact been handed down in cases involving very small sums of money.

III. The Creation of an EC Judiciary

The presence of Article 177 *[234]* EC was used by the Court in *Van Gend en Loos* as a reason for finding the EC legal order to have

---

[18]   The case law is unclear on the point. In *Costa* the Court seemed to adopt the concrete theory by implying that the magistrate making the theory fell within Article 177(3) *[234(3)]* EC, Case *6/64 Costa v ENEL* [1964] ECR 592, [1964] CMLR 425. It was subsequently stated by Advocate General Capotorti that it was not possible to 'resolve this issue beyond any possibility of doubt'. Case *107/76 Hoffmann La Roche v Centrafarm* [1977] ECR 957, 980.

sovereign qualities. The relationship has been a symbiotic one, however, for the reverse is also true. The Court has located the functions of Article 177 [*234*] EC by reference to the constitutional qualities of the EC Treaty. Its function is seen, in particular, as integral to the preservation of the autonomous nature of the EC legal order.[19]

Case 166/73 Rheinmühlen-Düsseldorf v Einfuhr- und Vorratstelle für Getreide [1974] ECR 33, [1974] 1 CMLR 523

Rheinmühlen had applied for a subsidy to export barley to third States. When he failed to make such an export, the German authorities sought to recover the subsidy granted to him. The Hesse Finance Court considered that they were entitled to recover the full subsidy. On appeal, the Federal Finance Court, whose judgments bound the Hesse court, ruled that they were entitled only to recover part of the subsidy. The matter was referred back to the Hesse court, which considered that the Federal court's ruling was not consistent with the EC Regulation on the matter. It therefore referred the Court of Justice the question whether it had a discretion to refer which was unfettered by rulings of superior domestic courts.

2. Article 177 is essential for the preservation of the Community character of the law established by the Treaty and has the object of ensuring that in all circumstances this law is the same in all States of the Community.

Whilst it thus aims to avoid divergences in the interpretation of Community law which the national courts have to apply, it likewise tends to ensure this application by making available to the national judge a means of eliminating difficulties which may be occasioned by the requirement of giving Community law its full effect within the framework of the judicial systems of the Member States.

Consequently any gap in the system so organized could undermine the effectiveness of the provisions of the Treaty and of the secondary Community law.

The provisions of Article 177, which enable every national court or tribunal without distinction to refer a case to the court for a preliminary ruling when it considers

---

[19] This was picked up early on in Buxbaum, R. 'Article 177 of the Rome Treaty as a Federalizing Device' (1969) 21 *Stanford Law Review* 1041. It has also been noted in a number of extra-judicial comments made by members of the Court e.g. Mancini, G. & Keeling, D. 'From CILFIT to ERT: the Constitutional Challenge Facing the Court' (1991) 11 *YBEL* 1, 2-3; Tesauro, G. 'The Effectiveness of Judicial Protection and Co-operation between the National Courts and the Court of Justice' (1993) 13 *YBEL* 1, 17.

that a decision on the question is necessary to enable it to give judgment, must be seen in this light.

3. The provisions of Article 177 are absolutely binding on the national judge and, in so far as the second paragraph is concerned, enable him to refer a case to the Court of Justice for a preliminary ruling on interpretation or validity.

This Article gives national courts the power and, where appropriate, imposes on them the obligation to refer a case for a preliminary ruling, as soon as the judge perceives either of his own motion or at the request of the parties that the litigation depends on a point referred to in the first paragraph of Article 177.

4. It follows that national courts have the widest discretion in referring matters to the Court of Justice if they consider that a case pending before them raises questions involving interpretation, or consideration of the validity, of provisions of Community law, necessitating a decision on their part.

It follows from these factors that a rule of national law whereby a Court is bound on points of law by the rulings of a superior court cannot deprive the inferior courts of their power to refer to the Court questions of interpretation of Community law involving such rulings.

It would be otherwise if the questions put by the inferior court were substantially the same as questions already put by the superior court.

On the other hand the inferior court must be free, if it considers that the ruling on law made by the superior court could lead it to give a judgment contrary to Community law, to refer to the court questions which concern it.

If inferior courts were bound without being able to refer matters to the Court, the jurisdiction of the latter to give preliminary rulings and the application of Community law at all levels of the judicial systems of the Member States would be compromised.

The establishment of this direct link between the Court of Justice and all courts and tribunals in the European Union sidelines existing national judicial hierarchies, and creates a flat court structure whereby all courts are treated equally, at least for the purposes of being able to make a reference. The assertion that it is important for the uniformity of EC law that all courts be able to refer matters to the Court of Justice throws up a further question - namely what is to be considered a court or tribunal for these purposes. For, throughout the Union, a variety of professional, regulatory and arbitral bodies, which are not formally designated as courts under national law, adjudicate upon EC rights. Given the diversity of national approaches upon this matter, it would be as unacceptable from the standpoint of the uniformity of EC law if some of these bodies were entitled to refer, but not others. It would give rise to the situation where, in the case of two bodies deciding identical matters in different Member States, one would be allowed to refer, but not the other.

Case 246/80 Broeckmeulen v Huisarts Registratie Commissie [1981] ECR 2311, [1982] 1 CMLR 91

Broeckmeulen, a Belgian national, had obtained his diploma in medicine from the University of Louvain in Belgium. He wished to practice in the Netherlands but the Dutch General Practitioners Registration Committee refused to register him. Under the rules of the profession he was allowed to appeal to the Appeal Committee, a body not recognised as a court, but nonetheless one which had certain quasi-judicial features. The Appeals Committee wished to know whether it could refer a question concerning a Directive on mutual recognition of post-university medical education.

9. According to the internal rules of the society, the Appeals Committee, appointed for a period of five years, is composed of three members appointed by the Netherlands medical faculties, three members appointed by the Board of the Society and three members, including the chairman (preferably a high-ranking judge), who are appointed by the ministers responsible for higher education and health respectively. It may therefore be seen that the composition of the Appeals Committee entails a significant degree of involvement on the part of the Netherlands public authorities.

10. Pursuant to those rules, the Appeals Committee determines disputes on the adversarial principle, that is to say having heard the Registration Committee and the doctor concerned, as well as his adviser or lawyer, if necessary.

11. The Netherlands Government stated that, in its opinion, the Appeals Committee cannot be considered a court or tribunal under Netherlands law. However, it pointed out that that fact is not decisive for the interpretation of Article 177 of the Treaty and suggested that the question whether a body such as the Appeals Committee is entitled to refer a case to the Court under that provision should be determined in the light of the function performed by that body within the system of remedies available to those who consider that their rights under Community law have been infringed.

12. In this regard, the order for reference mentions a Royal Decree of 1966, the decree concerning benefits ('Verstreckingenbesluit'), adopted under the sickness fund law; for the purposes of that decree the term 'general practitioner' refers exclusively to a doctor enrolled on the register of general practitioners maintained by the Society. The practice of a doctor who is not enrolled on the register would thus not be recognized by the sickness insurance schemes. Under those circumstances a doctor who is not enrolled on the register is unable to treat, as a general practitioner, patients covered by the social security system. In fact, private practice is likewise made impossible by the fact that private insurers also define the term 'general practitioner' in their policies in the same way as the provisions of the decree concerning benefits.

13. A study of the Netherlands legislation and of the statutes and internal rules of the Society shows that a doctor who intends to establish himself in the Netherlands may not in fact practise either as a specialist, or as an expert in social medicine, or as a general practitioner, without being recognized and registered by the organs of the Society. In the same way it may be seen that the system thus established is the result of close cooperation between doctors who are members of the Society, the medical faculties and the departments of State responsible for higher education and health.

14. It is thus clear that both in the sector covered by the social security system and in the field of private medicine the Netherlands system of public health operates on the basis of the status accorded to doctors by the Society and that registration as a general practitioner is essential to every doctor wishing to establish himself in the Netherlands as a general practitioner.

15. Therefore a general practitioner who avails himself of the right of establishment and the freedom to provide services conferred upon him by Community law is faced with the necessity of applying to the Registration Committee established by the Society, and, in the event of his application being refused, must appeal to the Appeals Committee. The Netherlands Government expressed the opinion that a doctor who is not a member of the Society would have the right to appeal against such a refusal to the ordinary courts, but stated that the point had never been decided by the Netherlands courts. Indeed all doctors, whether members of the society or not, whose application to be registered as a general practitioner is refused, appeal to the Appeals Committee, whose decisions to the knowledge of the Netherlands Government, have never been challenged in the ordinary courts.

16. In order to deal with the question of the applicability in the present case of Article 177 of the Treaty, it should be noted that it is incumbent upon Member States to take the necessary steps to ensure that within their own territory the provisions adopted by the Community institutions are implemented in their entirety. If, under the legal system of a Member State, the task of implementing such provisions is assigned to a professional body acting under a degree of governmental supervision, and if that body, in conjunction with the public authorities concerned, creates appeal procedures which may affect the exercise of rights granted by Community law, it is imperative, in order to ensure the proper functioning of Community law, that the Court should have an opportunity of ruling on issues of interpretation and validity arising out of such proceedings.

17. As a result of all the foregoing considerations and in the absence, in practice, of any right of appeal to the ordinary courts, the Appeals Committee, which operates with the consent of the public authorities and with their cooperation, and which, after an adversarial procedure, delivers decisions which are in fact recognized as final, must, in a matter involving the application of Community law, be considered as a court or tribunal of a Member State within the meaning of Article 177 of the Treaty. Therefore, the Court has jurisdiction to reply to the question asked.

If the Court's refusal in *Broeckmeulen* to accept national definitions of a court or tribunal was inspired by a desire to ensure 'the proper functioning of EC law' and the autonomous nature of the EC legal order, that judgment also indicates the tensions and limits of such a discourse. A truly autonomous EC legal order would grant the power to refer to a body purely on the basis of the functions it performs, namely whether it decides upon EC rights. For only that could ensure true uniformity of EC law. Yet such a wide-ranging definition would have resulted in bodies being recognised as courts which are not recognised as such by any Member State legal system. Unsurprisingly, it has not been adopted.

The Court has emphasised, first, that the body must have a public status in the sense that it must act under a degree of government supervision before it can refer. This leaves a whole host of private bodies such as arbitration panels and autonomous professional bodies outside of the definition. Yet despite prompting to adopt a wider approach, the Court has continued to refuse to do so.[20]

Secondly, the Court will look at the body's mode of operation. It has thus stated that a body will not be able to make a reference unless it possesses a number of features. These include that it be constituted by law, that it be independent, have a permanent existence, a binding jurisdiction, rules of adversarial procedure and that it apply the rule of law.[21] In *Corbiau* an administrative appeal over the amount of income tax paid by Corbiau was made to the Luxembourgeois Director of Revenue Services. The Court refused the reference on the grounds that

---

[20] Case 102/81 *Nordsee Deutsche Hochseefischerei GmbH v Reederei Mond Hochseefischerei* [1982] ECR 1095. For discussion of this issue see Bebr, G. 'Arbitration Tribunals and Article 177 of the EEC Treaty' (1985) 22 *CMLRev* 489.

[21] This was first established in Case 61/65 *Vaasen v Beambtenfonds voor het Mijnbedrijf* [1966] ECR 272, [1966] CMLR 508. See most recently Case C-393/92 *Gemeente Almelo v Energiebedrijf Ijsselmij* [1994] ECR I-1477.

the Director had a clear organisational link with the Department of Customs and Excise, and was not therefore sufficiently independent to constitute a court.[22]

Despite these limitations the effects of the organisational revolution carried out by the Court should not be underestimated. It has engineered a structure whereby a large number of bodies have the unencumbered opportunity to refer matters to it over a wide variety of topics. This has created a powerful dynamic with which to push forward the doctrinal development of EC law.

Alter, K. 'The European Court's Political Power' (1996) 19 *West European Politics* **458, 466-467**

While EC law supremacy posed a threat to the influence and authority of high courts and implied a significant compromise of national sovereignty, lower courts found few costs and numerous benefits in making their own referrals to the ECJ and in applying EC law. Being courts of first instance, lower-court judges were used to having another court hierarchically above them, and to having their judgments re-written by courts above. They also did not have to worry about how their individual actions might upset legal certainty or the smooth functioning of the legal system. Thus, they were more open to sending to the ECJ broad and provocative legal questions about the reach and effects of European law in the national legal order. There were also many benefits for lower courts in taking advantage of the ECJ and in invoking EC law. It allowed lower courts to circumvent the restrictive jurisprudence of higher courts, and to re-open legal debates which had been closed, and thus to try for legal outcomes of their preference for policy or legal reasons. For example, recourse to EC law allowed pro-women industrial tribunals to circumvent the Employment Appeals Tribunal and the Conservative government, to get legal outcomes which helped them to promote equal pay for men and women. Having an ECJ decision also magnified the influence of the lower-court decisions in the legal process, as the decision became part of established legal precedence, and it sometimes led to journal articles on decisions which otherwise would not have been publicly reported, but which were able to decisively contribute to the development of national law. Having an ECJ decision behind a lower-court decision also made its reversal by a higher court less likely. Thus, it actually bolstered the legal power and influence of the lower courts. For a lower court, the ECJ was akin to a second parent where parental approval wards of sanction. When a lower court did not like what it thought one parent (a higher national court) would say, or it did not agree with what one parent said, it would ask the other parent (the ECJ). Having the other parent's approval

---

[22]   Case C-24/92 *Corbiau v Administration des Contributions* [1993] ECR I-1277.

decreased the likelihood of sanctions for challenging legal precedence or government policy. If the lower court, however, did not think that it would like what that other parent might say, it could follow the 'don't ask and the ECJ can't tell' policy and not make a referral.

The different strategic calculations of national courts vis-à-vis the ECJ created a competition-between-courts dynamic of legal integration; this fed the process legal integration and came to shift the national legal context from under high courts. The limitations on interpretation of national law created by high courts provoked lower courts to make referrals to the ECJ. This enabled lower courts to deviate from established jurisprudence or to obtain preferred new legal outcomes. In so using EC law and the ECJ to achieve outcomes, lower courts created opportunities for the ECJ to expand its jurisdiction and jurisprudence, and, in some cases they actually goaded the ECJ to expand the legal authority of EC law even further. In this respect, one can say that lower courts were the motors of EC legal integration into the national order, and legal expansion through their referrals to the ECJ.

National governments' opposition to the manner in which lower courts have exercised their discretion manifested itself in three ways at Amsterdam. First, Member States making a declaration accepting the preliminary ruling system in *Article 35(2) TEU* are given a choice between accepting a process whereby all courts may refer and accepting one where only courts of last resort may refer. More drastically, Amsterdam also withdrew, for the first time, the power to refer provisions of the EC Treaty from certain courts. Only courts of last resort can refer questions on the new Title on Visas, Asylum and Immigration and Other Policies Related to Free Movement of Persons.

Article 68 EC.1. Article 234 shall apply to this Title under the following circumstances and conditions: where a question on the interpretation of this Title or on the validity or interpretation of acts of the institutions of the Community based on this Title is raised in a case pending before a court or a tribunal of a Member State against whose decisions there is no judicial remedy under national law, that court or tribunal shall, if it considers that a decision on the question is necessary to enable it to give judgement, request the Court of Justice to give a ruling thereon.

It will take some time to gauge the impact of this provision. The exclusion of certain courts from referring matters falling under this Title will lead to a reduction in the number of references upon this Title and a corresponding reduction of opportunity for the Court to influence this area of EC law. If Alter's analysis is right, the effects of *Article 68(1) EC* may be more far-reaching. With higher courts being more conservative in the type of references they make, less opportunities will be provided for judicial radicalism by the Court. Instead, *Article 68(1) EC* will be a far more defensive mechanism whereby questions are asked within a context of seeking autonomy for the domestic legal order rather than expansion of the EC legal order.

Finally, national courts have been robbed of their monopoly to refer matters to the Court of Justice in the Title on Visas, Asylum, Immigration and Other Policies Related to Free Movement of Persons.

Article 68 EC. 3. The Council, the Commission or a Member State may request the Court of Justice to give a ruling on a question of interpretation of this Title or acts of the institutions of the Community based on this Title. The ruling given by the Court of Justice in response to such a request shall not apply to courts or tribunals of the Member States which have become res judicata.

The exact impact of this provision is difficult to gauge. It is imponderable as to how ready Member States or the EC institutions will be to raise a question outside the context of a particular dispute. The reason for this is that the desire for a Court ruling settling a matter in one's favour is likely to be balanced by the feat that the Court might rule in an opposite direction. The only circumstance in which a reference is likely to come from this source are where the costs of legal uncertainty are so great for a Member State, the Council or the Commission that they outweigh the risk of an adverse ruling from the Court. One example might be where the Commission is willing to develop a programme of action in a particular area, but it is unsure whether it has competence. Another might be where a Member State wants to ringfence a particular area of EC intrusion.

IV. Docket-Control by the Court of Justice

There can be a variety of rationales for this - to reduce backlog, prevent vexatious litigation or simply because the subject-matter of the dispute is not something amenable to judicial decision.

There are two ways in which the Court can police which cases come before it. The most obvious way in which this can be done is through the Court's refusing to accept references on certain matters. This is also the most confrontational, as it seeks to *control* what the national court can refer. There is a softer, less confrontational manner in which the Court can limit references coming to it from national courts. This is by a process of orchestration, whereby, through a series of incentives, it induces national courts not to refer certain matters without actually refusing such a reference if it comes before it.[23]

i. Controlling Activities of the Court of Justice

a. Protecting the Court's 'Judicial Function'

The debate surrounding the Court's power to docket-control - to refuse to adjudicate on matters of EC law which had been referred to it by national courts - emerged in a salient manner at the end of the 1970s.[24]

---

[23] In social theory, a distinction is often made between processes which treat bodies as passive objects to be controlled, and power relations which view their subjects as free entities, whose choices are to be acted upon and structured. Foucault, M. 'The Subject and Power' in Dreyfus, H. & Rabinow, P. *Michel Foucault: Beyond Structuralism and Hermeneutics* (1982, Harvester, Brighton) 208, 219-224

[24] For an excellent, if somewhat outdated description of the use of this device by the Court of Justice see Rasmussen, H. *On Law and Policy in the European Court of Justice* (1986, Martijnus Nijhoff, Dordrecht) 465-497.

In *Mattheus v Doego* a contract was made for Mattheus, a German national, to complete a marketing study for Doego of certain Spanish and Portuguese agricultural products.[25] The contract contained a provision that Doego could terminate it should accession ever prove impracticable. Following a contractual dispute, the question was referred to the Court in what circumstances Spanish and Portuguese accession would prove impracticable. The Court refused to rule on the matter, stating that the conditions for accession would be determined by the Member States within the context of the existing procedures,[26] and that it was impossible to determine these conditions judicially in advance.

Rasmussen saw this judgment as the development of a 'political question' doctrine - a recognition by the Court that certain matters, in this case accession, were so sensitive that they fell outside the domain of the Court and were to be determined exclusively by the other institutions.[27] A more conservative interpretation is that the Court refused to give a ruling because it was being asked to give an interpretation relating to measures which had not yet been adopted by EC institutions.[28] It saw itself, in other words, as being asked to perform a speculative task which was not consistent with its judicial function. It returned to this question in the *Foglia* saga.

Case 104/79 Foglia v Novello [1980] ECR 745, [1981] CMLR 45

A contract was made that Foglia sell some Italian liqueur wine to Novello to be delivered to a friend of Mrs Novello in France with the proviso that Novello would reimburse Foglia any taxes incurred, unless, *inter alia*, these taxes were levied contrary to EC law. A contract for the carriage of the goods was made between Foglia and Danzas, a transporter, with a similar proviso that Foglia would not be liable for any taxes levied contrary to EC law. Foglia duly reimbursed Danzas the full sum. This included an amount for French taxes incurred. These amounted to just 148.000 Italian lire. He then sought to recover

---

25   Case 93/78 *Mattheus v Doego* [1978] ECR 2203, [1979] 1 CMLR 551.
26   At the time this was Article 237 EEC. It is now contained in Article O [49] TEU.
27   Rasmussen, H. supra n.24, 486-488.
28   This was the interpretation taken in Case C-343/90 *Lourenço Dias v Director da Alfândega do Porto* [1992] ECR I-4673.

the French taxes paid from Novello before an Italian court, who refused on the grounds that they were levied contrary to EC law.

9. In their written observations submitted to the Court of Justice the two parties to the main action have provided an essentially identical description of the tax discrimination which is a feature of the French legislation concerning the taxation of liqueur wines; the two parties consider that that legislation is incompatible with Community law. In the course of the oral procedure before the Court Foglia stated that he was participating in the procedure before the Court in view of the interest of his undertaking as such and as an undertaking belonging to a certain category of Italian traders in the outcome of the legal issues involved in the dispute.

10. It thus appears that the parties to the main action are concerned to obtain a ruling that the French tax system is invalid for liqueur wines by the expedient of proceedings before an Italian court between two private individuals who are in agreement as to the result to be attained and who have inserted a clause in their contract in order to induce the Italian court to give a ruling on the point. The artificial nature of this expedient is underlined by the fact that Danzas did not exercise its rights under French law to institute proceedings over the consumption tax although it undoubtedly had an interest in doing so in view of the clause in the contract by which it was also bound and moreover of the fact that Foglia paid without protest that undertaking's bill which included a sum paid in respect of that tax.

11. The duty of the Court of Justice under Article 177 of the EEC Treaty is to supply all courts in the Community with the information on the interpretation of Community law which is necessary to enable them to settle genuine disputes which are brought before them. A situation in which the Court was obliged by the expedient of arrangements like those described above to give rulings would jeopardize the whole system of legal remedies available to private individuals to enable them to protect themselves against tax provisions which are contrary to the Treaty.

12. This means that the questions asked by the national court, having regard to the circumstances of this case, do not fall within the framework of the duties of the Court of Justice under Article 177 of the Treaty.

The Court's refusal to entertain the reference carried a powerful subtext. By implying that the reference should never have been made, it was not only casting aspersions on the Italian judge's competence, it was also asserting a power to review how national courts carried out their task of referrals.

Case 244/80 Foglia v Novello (No.2) [1981] ECR 3045, [1982] 1 CMLR 585

The Italian court re-referred four questions to the Court of Justice of which the most important were the first and fourth ones. In the first question the Italian court asked what were the limits of the power of appraisal for the national judges and the Court of Justice respectively. In its fourth question it asked whether the degree of protection offered by the Court of Justice varied according to whether the administration whose laws formed the subject-matter of the dispute was represented and entered an appearance either before the national court or the Court of Justice.

14. With regard to the first question it should be recalled, as the Court has had occasion to emphasize in very varied contexts, that Article 177 is based on cooperation which entails a division of duties between the national courts and the Court of Justice in the interest of the proper application and uniform interpretation of Community law throughout all the Member States.

15. With this in view it is for the national court - by reason of the fact that it is seized of the substance of the dispute and that it must bear the responsibility for the decision to be taken - to assess, having regard to the facts of the case, the need to obtain a preliminary ruling to enable it to give judgment.

16. In exercising that power of appraisal the national court, in collaboration with the Court of Justice, fulfils a duty entrusted to them both of ensuring that in the interpretation and application of the Treaty the law is observed. Accordingly the problems which may be entailed in the exercise of its power of appraisal by the national court and the relations which it maintains within the framework of Article 177 with the Court of Justice are governed exclusively by the provisions of Community law.

17. In order that the Court of Justice may perform its task in accordance with the Treaty it is essential for national courts to explain, when the reasons do not emerge beyond any doubt from the file, why they consider that a reply to their questions is necessary to enable them to give judgment.

18. It must in fact be emphasized that the duty assigned to the Court by Article 177 is not that of delivering advisory opinions on general or hypothetical questions but of assisting in the administration of justice in the Member States. It accordingly does not have jurisdiction to reply to questions of interpretation which are submitted to it within the framework of procedural devices arranged by the parties in order to induce the Court to give its views on certain problems of Community law which do not correspond to an objective requirement inherent in the resolution of a dispute. A declaration by the Court that it has no jurisdiction in such circumstances does not in any way trespass upon the prerogatives of the national court but makes it possible to prevent the application of the procedure under Article 177 for purposes other than those appropriate for it.

19. Furthermore, it should be pointed out that, whilst the Court of Justice must be able to place as much reliance as possible upon the assessment by the national court of the extent to which the questions submitted are essential, it must be in a position to make any assessment inherent in the performance of its own duties in particular order to check, as all courts must, whether it has jurisdiction. Thus the Court, taking into account the repercussions of its decisions in this matter, must have regard, in exercising the jurisdiction conferred upon it by Article 177, not only to the interests of the parties to the proceedings but also to those of the Community and of the Member States. Accordingly it cannot, without disregarding the duties assigned to it, remain indifferent to the assessments made by the courts of the Member States in the exceptional cases in which such assessments may affect the proper working of the procedure laid down by Article 177.

20. Whilst the spirit of cooperation which must govern the performance of the duties assigned by Article 177 to the national courts on the one hand and the Court of Justice on the other requires the latter to have regard to the national court's proper responsibilities, it implies at the same time that the national court, in the use which it makes of the facilities provided by Article 177, should have regard to the proper function of the Court of Justice in this field.

.....

26. In answer to the [fourth] question thus raised it must be emphasized that all individuals whose rights are infringed by measures adopted by a Member State which are contrary to Community law must have the opportunity to seek the protection of a court possessed of jurisdiction and that such a court, for its part, must be free to obtain information as to the scope of the relevant provisions of Community law by means of a procedure under Article 177. In principle the degree of protection afforded by the courts therefore must not differ according to whether such a question is raised in proceedings between individuals or in an action to which the State whose legislation is challenged is a party in one form or another.

27. Nevertheless, as the Court has stated in its reply set out above to the first question it is for the Court of Justice to appraise the conditions in which a case is referred to it by a national court in order to confirm that it has jurisdiction. In that connection the question whether the proceedings are between individuals or are directed against the State whose legislation is called in question is not in all circumstances irrelevant.

28. On the one hand it must be pointed out that the court before which, in the course of proceedings between individuals, an issue concerning the compatibility with Community law of legislation of another Member State is brought is not necessarily in a position to provide for such individuals effective protection in relation to such legislation.

29. On the other hand, regard being had to the independence generally ensured for the parties by the legal systems of the Member States in the field of contract, the possibility arises that the conduct of the parties may be such as to make it impossible for the State concerned to arrange for an appropriate defence of its interests by causing the question of the invalidity of its legislation to be decided by a court of another Member State. Accordingly, in such procedural situations it is impossible to exclude the risk that the procedure under Article 177 may be diverted by the parties from the purposes for which it was laid down by the Treaty.

30. The foregoing considerations as a whole show that the Court of Justice for its part must display special vigilance when, in the course of proceedings between individuals, a question is referred to it with a view to permitting the national court to decide whether the legislation of another Member State is in accordance with Community law.

A heated debate arose over the jurisdictional merits of the *Foglia* judgments. Critics argued that Article 177 [*234*] EC was, traditionally, based upon a system of non-hierarchical cooperation between the national courts and the Court of Justice and the establishment of a clear division of duties with national courts being responsible for questions of fact and the Court of Justice for questions of EC law.

This was transgressed in two ways by *Foglia*. The power to refuse a reference, first, established a hierarchical element between the Court of Justice and the national court, for it granted a power to the Court of Justice to review the national court's decision to refer, the reasons for the reference and the relevance of the question.[29] Secondly, it was claimed that the judgment necessarily muddied the hitherto clear cut division of duties between the Court of Justice and national courts. For an inquiry into the existence of a 'genuine dispute' by the Court of Justice would necessarily require it to examine the factual background. Counter-arguments have been made, however, that the power of review

---

[29]   Barav, A. 'Preliminary Censorship? The Judgment of the European Court in Foglia v Novello' (1980) 5 *ELRev* 443, 451-452. See also Rasmussen, H. supra n.24, 490-494.

granted to the Court by *Foglia* is at best a marginal one, and was necessary to protect the Article 177 [*234*] EC mechanism from being abused by national courts. Furthermore, it has been argued, a refusal to give advisory opinions is a defining quality of courts - were the Court to accept advisory questions, it would be undermining its very existence as a court.[30]

Whatever the constitutional merits of *Foglia*, there were severe practical difficulties in applying it.[31] The finding of an absence of a genuine dispute requires the Court to take a view of the facts of the case. As it had no independent fact-finding powers of its own and was dependent upon the referring court and the intervening parties for the facts before it, it had little capacity to implement the judgment effectively. This became apparent in the subsequent methods the Court used to review national references. In *Rau*, a dispute concerning a Belgian law requiring that margarine could only be sold in cube-shaped blocks, the Court considered the fact that the parties' legal arguments were sufficiently different for it to find the existence of a genuine dispute, despite doubts about the adversarial nature of the proceedings.[32]

The ability to review the reference for the existence of a genuine dispute was made yet harder by the Court's acceptance that the national court has a discretion to refer a matter at whatever stage of the proceedings the latter considers appropriate. In *Pretore di Salo*, an Italian magistrate was carrying out preparatory inquiries into possible criminal activities which had led to the pollution of the river Chiesa.[33] The Court accepted the reference, notwithstanding that the investigation was at such an early stage that no perpetrators had been identified.

Equally, the Court seems ready to accept test cases. In *Leclerc Siplec v TF1 Publicité* Leclerc Siplec challenged a refusal by TF1, one of the major French television broadcasters, to televise an advertisement,

---

[30]   Wyatt, D. 'Foglia (No.2): The Court Denies it has Jurisdiction to Give Advisory Opinions' (1982) 7 *ELRev* 186. See also Gray, C.'Advisory Opinions and the Court of Justice' (1983) 8 *ELRev* 24.

[31]   Bebr, G. 'The Existence of a Genuine Dispute: An Indispensable Precondition for the Jurisdiction of the Court under Article 177 EC?' (1980) 17 *CMLRev* 525, 532.

[32]   Case 261/81 *Rau v De Schmedt* [1982] ECR 3961, [1983] 2 CMLR 496.

[33]   Case 14/86 *Pretore di Salo v X* [1987] ECR 2545, [1989] 1 CMLR 71.

which sought to persuade viewers to purchase petrol from the forecourts of Leclerc's chain of supermarkets.[34] The reason for this was a French legal requirement prohibiting television advertising of the distribution sector. Both parties to the dispute were in agreement about the domestic legal situation and the need for a reference. The Court accepted the reference, however. It noted that what was being sought was a declaration from the national court that the French law did not comply with EC law. The parties' agreement did not make the need for that declaration any less pressing or the dispute any less real. Whilst resolution of test cases is an important part of the judicial function, it is very difficult to distinguish them from hypothetical cases, for, in both, there is little conflict between the immediate parties to the dispute.[35]

Foglia's death knell seemed to have been sounded in *Eau de Cologne*.[36] Eau de Cologne, a cosmetics company, agreed to supply cosmetics to an Italian company, Provide. The contract contained a warranty that the cosmetics would comply with Italian law. Provide repudiated the contract on the grounds that the cosmetics did not comply with Italian labelling laws. Eau de Cologne argued that they complied with the EC Directive regulating the matter. Under a choice of forum provision in the agreement the matter was brought before a German court who referred a question on the interpretation of the Directive. The Court accepted the genuineness of the dispute despite a number of factors, notably the seemingly trivial nature of the breach and the choice of forum which allowed a German court to adjudicate upon the compatibility of Italian legislation with EC law.

The *Foglia* line of reasoning has not died however. Instead of being used by the Court to review the motives of the parties, it is being

---

[34] Case C-412/93 *Leclerc Siplec v TF1 Publicité* [1995] ECR I-179. See O'Neill, M. 'Article 177 and Limits to the Right to Refer: an End to the Confusion?' (1996) 2 *European Public Law* 375.

[35] It has been cogently argued, therefore, that *Foglia v Novello* was in reality a test case. See Craig, P. & De Bùrca, G. *EC Law: Text, Cases and Materials* (1995, OUP, Oxford) 438.

[36] Case C-150/88 *Eau de Cologne & Parfümerie Fabrik v Provide* [1989] ECR 3891, [1991] 1 CMLR 715.

used, instead, to review of the contents of the reference.[37] Increasingly, the Court will, therefore, examine whether the questions being asked of it are relevant to the dispute in hand.[38]

Case C-343/90 Lourenço Dias v Director da Alfândega do Porto [1992] ECR I-4673

Under a Portuguese Decree vehicles which had a fixed panel between the goods compartment and the passenger area were classified as 'light goods vehicles' and were exempt from duty. Without the panel they were classified as 'passenger vehicles' and were subject to tax. Automoveis Citroen, a Portuguese company, imported a vehicle with a fitted panel and duly paid no duty. The vehicle was sold and the panel removed. Lourenço Dias was fined by the police in Oporto for driving a passenger vehicle without having paid duty upon it. When he appealed against the fine, the national court asked a number of questions about the lawfulness of the Decree which were not directly related to the dispute in hand.

17. Nevertheless, in Case 244/80 *Foglia v Novello* [1981] ECR 3045, paragraph 21, the Court considered that, in order to determine whether it has jurisdiction, it is a matter for the Court of Justice to examine the conditions in which the case has been referred to it by the national court. The spirit of cooperation which must prevail in the preliminary-ruling procedure requires the national court to have regard to the function entrusted to the Court of Justice, which is to assist in the administration of justice in the Member States and not to deliver advisory opinions on general or hypothetical questions (*Foglia v Novello*, cited above, paragraphs 18 and 20, and Case 149/82 *Robards v Insurance Officer* [1983] ECR 171, paragraph 19).

18. In view of that task, the Court considers that it cannot give a preliminary ruling on a question raised in a national court where, *inter alia*, the interpretation requested relates to measures not yet adopted by the Community institutions (see Case 93/78 *Mattheus v Doego* [1978] ECR 2203, paragraph 8), the procedure before the court making the reference for a preliminary ruling has already been terminated (see Case 338/85 *Pardini*

---

[37]   Kennedy, T. 'First Steps Towards a European Certiorari' (1993) 18 *ELRev* 121; Anderson, D. 'The Admissibility of Preliminary References' (1994) 14 *YBEL* 179, 186-188.

[38]   Case C-83/91 *Meilicke v ADV* [1992] ECR I-4871; Case C-428/93 *Monin Automobiles (No.2)* [1994] ECR I-1707; Case C-297/93 *Grau-Hupka v Stadtgemeinde Bremen* [1994] ECR I-5535; Case C-143/94 *Furlanis Costruzioni Generali v ANAS* [1995] ECR I-3633.

v Ministero del Commercio con l'Estero [1988] ECR 2041, paragraph 11) or the interpretation of Community law or the examination of the validity of a rule of Community law sought by the national court bears no relation to the actual nature of the case or to the subject-matter of the main action (Case 126/80 *Salonia v Poidomani and Giglio* [1981] ECR 1563, paragraph 6. ...

19. It should also be borne in mind that, in order to enable the Court to provide a useful interpretation of Community law, it is appropriate that, before making the reference to the Court, the national court should establish the facts of the case and settle the questions of purely national law (see Joined Cases 36 and 71/80 *Irish Creamery Milk Suppliers Association v Ireland* [1981] ECR 735, paragraph 6). By the same token, it is essential for the national court to explain the reasons why it considers that a reply to its questions is necessary to enable it to give judgment (see, in the first place, *Foglia v Novello*, cited above, paragraph 17, and, most recently, Joined Cases 98, 162 and 258/85 *Bertini v Regione Lazio* [1986] ECR 1885, paragraph 6).

20. With this information in its possession, the Court is in a position to ascertain whether the interpretation of Community law which is sought is related to the actual nature and subject-matter of the main proceedings. If it should appear that the question raised is manifestly irrelevant for the purposes of deciding the case, the Court must declare that there is no need to proceed to judgment.

21. It is in the light of those guidelines that the objections alleging the absence of a connection between the questions referred to the Court for a preliminary ruling in the instant case and the actual dispute on which the national court is called upon to give judgment should be considered.

22. Three matters should be taken into consideration in this regard. In the first place, it appears from the documents provided by the national court itself and from a document annexed to the observations of the public prosecutor that the vehicle whose conversion gave rise to the proceedings was new, having been manufactured and purchased in 1989, and had a cubic capacity of 1,360 cc. Secondly, as regards national law, the Portuguese Government informed the Court at the hearing that, since the separation panel in question had been replaced shortly after it was found to have been removed, motor-vehicle tax is not due and all the national court has to do is to determine the amount of any fine payable, the legal basis for which is to be found in other legal provisions and not in the Decree-Law. Thirdly, the national court expresses its doubts about the compatibility with Community law of certain provisions of the Decree-Law, but has omitted to inform the Court how those provisions are to be applied in the context of the proceedings before it.

The depth of review has become increasingly rigorous, giving rise to an ancillary ground on which the Court will refuse jurisdiction, namely that the national court has failed to define sufficiently the factual and legal context to the dispute. In *Telemarsicabruzzo* the Court therefore refused to consider the compatibility of the Italian State monopoly in broadcasting with EC law on the grounds that the file provided by the national court contained insufficient information to give a reference.[39]

The Court considers that the factual and legal background to a dispute must be defined for two reasons. It is necessary, first, to ensure that the Article 177 [*234*] EC procedure is used effectively, and, secondly, to protect the procedural rights of the Member States and the EC institutions, which must have sufficiently precise information to intervene properly.[40] The number of insufficiently defined references it was receiving has led it to issues notes for guidance on the matter.

Note For Guidance On References By National Courts For Preliminary Rulings, *Proceedings of the Court 34/96*, 9-10.

5. ... Questions concerning the interpretation or validity of Community law are frequently of general interest and the Member States and Community institutions are entitled to submit observations. It is therefore desirable that the reference should be drafted as clearly and precisely as possible.

6. The order for reference should contain a statement or reasons which is succinct but sufficiently complete to give the Court and those to whom it must be notified (the Member States, the Commission and in certain cases the Council and the European Parliament), a clear understanding of the factual and legal context of the main proceedings. In particular, it should include:
- a statement of the facts which are essential to a full understanding of the legal significance of the main proceedings;
- an exposition of the national law which may be applicable;

---

[39]   Joined Cases C-320-C-322/90 *Telemarsicabruzzo v Circostel* [1993] ECR I-393. See also Case C-157/92 *Banchero* [1993] ECR I-1085; Case C-167/94 *Gomis* [1995] ECR I-1023; Case C-297/95 *Bresle v Préfet de la Région Auvergne* [1996] ECR I-233; Case C-326/95 *Banco de Fomento e Exterior v Amândio Maurício Martins Pechin* [1996] ECR I-1385. The need for such a definition is less strong where the question asked is a precise one on a 'technical' issue, Case C-316/93 *Vaneetveld v SA Le Foyer* [1994] ECR I-763.

[40]   Case C-458/93 *Mostafa Saddik* [1995] ECR I-511; Case C-17/94 *Gervais & Others* [1995] ECR I-4353; Case C-101/96 *Testa* [1996] ECR I-3081.

- a statement of the reasons which have prompted the national court to refer the question or questions to the Court of Justice, and

- where appropriate, a summary of the arguments of the parties.

The aim should be to put the Court of Justice in a position to give the national court an answer which will be of assistance to it.

The order for reference should also be accompanied by copies of any documents needed for a proper understanding of the case, especially the text of the applicable national provisions.

There is one further ground upon which the Court will refuse to give a reference. This is where, even though the reference comes from a court or tribunal, the proceedings are not of a 'judicial character'. In *Borker*, a member of the Parisian Bar complained to its Council about the refusal of a German court to allow him to plead before it.[41] The Paris Bar Council was clearly a court for the purposes of Article 177 [*234*] EC, as it was a public body which could give decisions on admission to the Paris Bar. It only had jurisdiction however to rule on matters which related directly to the Paris Bar. It certainly had no jurisdiction to give a ruling on the behaviour of a German court. As the Paris Bar Council could do no more than make a Declaration, the Court refused to accept the reference, stating that the proceedings were not of a judicial character.

The Court repeated this reasoning in *Job Centre Coop*.[42] In Italy a company can gain legal personality through a non-contentious procedure whereby it registers its articles of association with a civil court. In the course of an application by Job Centre Coop, an undertaking which was seeking to provide manpower services, the question arose over whether the Italian public monopoly over the provision of such services breached EC law. The Court of Justice refused to entertain the reference noting that the national court was carrying out administrative functions, which could equally be carried out by other administrative bodies, and, as the proceedings were not of a judicial character, it was therefore not competent to refer.

---

[41] Case 130/80 *Borker* [1980] ECR 1975.

[42] Case C-111/94 *Job Centre Coop* [1995] ECR I-3361.

b. Securing the Court's Powers of Judicial Review

One of the functions of the preliminary reference system is to enable challenge of acts of the EC institutions. This can be most easily done by an individual challenging an implementing act of the national administration. The significance of Article 177 [*234*] EC as a route for judicial review of acts of the EC institutions was enhanced by two developments in the late 1980s.[43]

In *Rau* the Court adopted Article 177 [*234*] EC as a basis for review independently of any other EC Treaty provisions which might allow individuals to bring an action before the Court challenging either an act or failure to act of an EC institution.[44] There a group of margarine producers challenged the implementation by the German authorities of a Commission Decision providing free butter to West Berlin before a German administrative court. The Court considered that the German court should be able to consider the legality of the Commission act on which the national act was based. It considered that it therefore had jurisdiction under Article 177 [*234*] EC irrespective of whether the parties could bring the matter before it under any other provision.

This judgment was qualified by *Fotofrost* which stated that national courts could not declare any EC act invalid.[45] The combined effect of these two judgments was that Article 177 [*234*] EC came to be used as a channel for national courts to pass matters on to be reviewed by the Court. This development of Article 177 [*234*] EC posed questions, however, about the relationship between Article 177 [*234*] EC and the other EC Treaty Articles which conferred jurisdiction upon

---

[43]   Bebr, G. 'The Reinforcement of the Constitutional Review of Community Acts under the EEC Treaty' (1988) 25 *CMLRev* 667.

[44]   Joined Cases 133-136/85 *Rau et al. v Bundesanstalt für Landswirtschaftliche Marktordnung* [1987] ECR 2289.

[45]   Case 314/85 *Firma Fotofrost v HZ Lubeck Ost* [1987] ECR 4199, [1988] 3 CMLR 57. In certain circumstances, national courts may grant interim relief by suspending national measures implementing EC acts, Joined Cases C-143/88 & C-92/89 *Zuckerfabrik Suderithmarschen v Itzehoe* [1991] ECR I-415, [1993] 3 CMLR 1; Case C-465/93 *Atlanta v Bundesamt für Ernährung* [1995] ECR I-3761.

the Court. Article 173(4) *[230(4)]* EC, in particular, allows individuals to challenge acts of the EC institutions. The *locus standi* requirements are severe, however. Individuals can only challenge acts which are addressed or of direct and individual concern to them.[46] Furthermore, strict time limits are set out in Article 173(5) *[230(5)]* EC.[47] There was a danger that the policy objectives of these provisions of limiting the type of interests which could be protected by judicial review and of ensuring legal certainty could be thwarted if Article 177 *[234]* EC were to become the main avenue for judicial review.[48]

Case C-188/92 TWD Textilwerke Deggendorf v Germany [1994] ECR I-833

Between 1981 and 1983 TWD, a polyamide and polyester producer, was granted DM 6.12 million in regional aid from the German authorities. In 1986, under Article 93 (2) *[88(2)]* EC, the Commission decided that the aid had been granted in breach of the EC State aid provisions and ordered the German Government to recover the aid. The German Government forwarded a copy of the letter to TWD with a note stating that the latter could seek to challenge the matter under Article 173(4) *[230(4)]* EC if it so desired. TWD did nothing but contested attempts by the German Government to reclaim the money. TWD's initial application was dismissed, and in 1990 it appealed to the Administrative Appeal Court. The latter asked the Court if it was bound by the Commission's Decision given that TWD had not challenged it within the time limits set out in Article 173(5) *[230(5)]* EC.

13. It is settled law that a decision which has not been challenged by the addressee within the time-limit laid down by Article 173 of the Treaty becomes definitive as against him (see in the first place the judgment in Case 20/65 *Collotti v Court of Justice* [1965] ECR 847).

---

[46]   See Chapter 10.

[47]   These are that the action be brought within two months of the measure's publication, of its notification to the plaintiff or of the day on which it came to the latter's knowledge.

[48]   For greater detail on the relationship between the two see Wyatt, D. 'The Relationship between Actions for Annulment and References on Validity after TWD Deggendorf' in Lonbay, J. & Biondi, A. (eds.) *Remedies for Breach of EC Law* (1997, John Wiley, Chichester). See also Case C-178/95 *Wiljo v Belgium*, Judgment of 30 January 1997, [1997] 1 CMLR 627.

14. The undertaking in receipt of individual aid which is the subject-matter of a Commission decision adopted on the basis of Article 93 of the Treaty has the right to bring an action for annulment under the second paragraph of Article 173 of the Treaty even if the decision is addressed to a Member State (judgment in Case 730/79 *Philip Morris v Commission* [1980] ECR 2671). By virtue of the third paragraph of that article, the expiry of the time-limit laid down in that provision has the same time-barring effect vis-a-vis such an undertaking as it does vis-à-vis the Member State which is the addressee of the decision.

15. It is settled law that a Member State may no longer call in question the validity of a decision addressed to it on the basis of Article 93(2) of the Treaty once the time-limit laid down in the third paragraph of Article 173 of the Treaty has expired (see the judgments in Case 156/77 *Commission v Belgium* [1978] ECR 1881 and Case C-183/91 *Commission v Greece* [1993] ECR I-3131).

16. That case-law, according to which it is impossible for a Member State which is the addressee of a decision taken under the first paragraph of Article 93(2) of the Treaty to call in question the validity of the decision in the proceedings for non-compliance provided for in the second paragraph of that provision, is based in particular on the consideration that the periods within which applications must be lodged are intended to safeguard legal certainty by preventing Community measures which involve legal effects from being called in question indefinitely.

17. It follows from the same requirements of legal certainty that it is not possible for a recipient of aid, forming the subject-matter of a Commission decision adopted on the basis of Article 93 of the Treaty, who could have challenged that decision and who allowed the mandatory time-limit laid down in this regard by the third paragraph of Article 173 of the Treaty to expire, to call in question the lawfulness of that decision before the national courts in an action brought against the measures taken by the national authorities for implementing that decision.

18. To accept that in such circumstances the person concerned could challenge the implementation of the decision in proceedings before the national court on the ground that the decision was unlawful would in effect enable the person concerned to overcome the definitive nature which the decision assumes as against that person once the time-limit for bringing an action has expired.

19. It is true that in its judgment in Joined Cases 133 to 136/85 *Rau v BALM* [1987] ECR 2289, on which the French Government relies in its observations, the Court held that the possibility of bringing a direct action under the second paragraph of Article 173 of the EEC Treaty against a decision adopted by a Community institution did not preclude the possibility of bringing an action in a national court against a measure adopted by a national authority for the implementation of that decision, on the ground that the latter decision was unlawful.

20. However, as is clear from the Report for the Hearing in those cases, each of the plaintiffs in the main proceedings had brought an action before the Court of Justice for the annulment of the decision in question. The Court did not therefore rule, and did not have to rule, in that judgment on the time-barring effects of the expiry of time-limits. It is precisely that issue with which the question referred by the national court in this case is concerned.

21. This case is also distinguishable from Case 216/82 *Universität Hamburg v Hauptzollamt Hamburg-Kehrwieder* [1983] ECR 2771.

22. In the judgment in that case the Court held that a plaintiff whose application for duty-free admission had been rejected by a decision of a national authority taken on the basis of a decision of the Commission addressed to all the Member States had to be able to plead, in proceedings brought under national law against the rejection of his application, the illegality of the Commission's decision on which the national decision adopted in his regard was based.

23. In that judgment the Court took into account the fact that the rejection of the application by the national authority was the only measure directly addressed to the person concerned of which it had necessarily been informed in good time and which it could challenge in the courts without encountering any difficulty in demonstrating its interest in bringing proceedings. It held that in those circumstances the possibility of pleading the unlawfulness of the Commission's decision derived from a general principle of law which found its expression in Article 184 of the EEC Treaty, namely the principle which confers upon any party to proceedings the right to challenge, for the purpose of obtaining the annulment of a decision of direct and individual concern to that party, the validity of previous acts of the institutions which form the legal basis of the decision which is being attacked, if that party was not entitled under Article 173 of the Treaty to bring a direct action challenging those acts by which it was thus affected without having been in a position to ask that they be declared void (see the judgment in Case 92/78 *Simmenthal v Commission* [1979] ECR 777).

24. In the present case, it is common ground that the applicant in the main proceedings was fully aware of the Commission's decision and of the fact that it could without any doubt have challenged it under Article 173 of the Treaty.

25. It follows from the foregoing that, in factual and legal circumstances such as those of the main proceedings in this case, the definitive nature of the decision taken by the Commission pursuant to Article 93 of the Treaty *vis-à-vis* the undertaking in receipt of the aid binds the national court by virtue of the principle of legal certainty.

26. The reply to be given to the first question must therefore be that the national court is bound by a Commission decision adopted under Article 93(2) of the Treaty where, in view of the implementation of that decision by the national authorities, the recipient of the aid to which the implementation measures are addressed brings before it an action in which it pleads the unlawfulness of the Commission's decision and where that recipient of aid, although informed in writing by the Member State of the Commission's decision, did not bring an action against that decision under the second paragraph of Article 173 of the Treaty, or did not do so within the period prescribed.

ii. Orchestrating Activities of the Court of Justice

The Court has also sought to induce national courts to decide more cases themselves. A difficulty it faces is that the last paragraph of Article 177 [*234*] EC requires national courts against whose decisions there is no judicial remedy under national law to refer any matter which is raised in a case pending before it. The Court has sought to curb the effects of this paragraph through the doctrines of *acte éclairé* and *acte clair*. The former states that a court need not refer if a materially identical matter has already been decided by the Court of Justice. The latter states that a question need not be referred if the provision in question is so clear that there is no reasonable doubt about its application.[49]

Case 283/81 Srl CILFIT and Lanificio di Gavardo SpA v Ministry of Health [1982] ECR 3415, [1983] CMLR 472

A dispute between a group of textile firms and the Italian Ministry of Health on whether the former should pay some levies on wool imported from outside the Community. The former claimed that Regulation 827/68 prohibited levies being imposed on 'animal products'. The Ministry of Health claimed, on the other hand, that the Regulation only applied to products listed in an Annex, and that wool was not included on that Annex. The dispute went up to the Italian Court of Cassation, the highest civil court in Italy. The Italian Ministry of Health argued that there was no need to make a reference to the Court since the interpretation of EC law in the case was so obvious. The Italian Court decided that this point was itself an issue of EC law requiring a reference.

---

[49] Early support for the application of the doctrine in EC law can be found in Lagrange, 'The Theory of Acte Clair: a Bone of Contention or a Source of Unity?' (1971) 8 *CMLRev* 313.

12. The question submitted by the Corte di Cassazione seeks to ascertain whether, in certain circumstances, the obligation laid down by the third paragraph of Article 177 might nonetheless be subject to certain restrictions.

13. It must be remembered in this connection that in its judgment of 27 March 1963 in Joined Cases 28 to 30/62 *Da Costa v Nederlandse Belastingadministratie* [1963] ECR 31 the Court ruled that: 'Although the third paragraph of Article 177 unreservedly requires courts or tribunals of a Member State against whose decision there is no judicial remedy under national law ... to refer to the Court every question of interpretation raised before them, the authority of an interpretation under Article 177 already given by the Court may deprive the obligation of its purpose and thus empty it of its substance. Such is the case especially when the question raised is materially identical with a question which has already been the subject of a preliminary ruling in a similar case.'

14. The same effect, as regards the limits set to the obligation laid down by the third paragraph of Article 177, may be produced where previous decisions of the Court have already dealt with the point of law in question, irrespective of the nature of the proceedings which led to those decisions, even though the questions at issue are not strictly identical.

15. However, it must not be forgotten that in all such circumstances national courts and tribunals, including those referred to in paragraph (3) of Article 177, remain entirely at liberty to bring a matter before the Court of Justice if they consider it appropriate to do so.

16. Finally, the correct application of Community law may be so obvious as to leave no scope for any reasonable doubt as to the manner in which the question raised is to be resolved. Before it comes to the conclusion that such is the case, the national court or tribunal must be convinced that the matter is equally obvious to the courts of the other Member States and to the Court of Justice. Only if those conditions are satisfied may the national court or tribunal refrain from submitting the question to the Court of Justice and take upon itself the responsibility for resolving it.

17. However, the existence of such a possibility must be assessed on the basis of the characteristic feature of Community law and the particular difficulties to which its interpretation gives rise.

18. To begin with, it must be borne in mind that Community legislation is drafted in several languages and that the different language versions are equally authentic. An interpretation of a provision of Community law thus involves a comparison of the different language versions.

19. It must also be borne in mind, even where the different language versions are entirely in accord with one another, that Community law uses terminology which is peculiar to it. Furthermore, it must be emphasised that legal concepts do not necessarily have the same meaning in Community law and in the law of the various Member States.

20. Finally, every provision of Community law must be placed in its context and interpreted in the light of the provisions of Community law as a whole, regard being had to the objectives thereof and to its state of evolution at the date on which the provision in question is to be applied.

21. In the light of all those considerations, the answer to the question submitted by the Corte Suprema di Cassazione must be that the third paragraph of Article 177 of the EEC Treaty is to be interpreted as meaning that a court or tribunal against those decisions there is no judicial remedy under national law is required, where a question of Community law is raised before it, to comply with its obligation to bring the matter before the Court of Justice, unless it has established that the question raised is irrelevant or that the Community provision in question has already been interpreted by the Court or that the correct application of Community law is so obvious as to leave no scope for any reasonable doubt. The existence of such a possibility must be assessed in the light of the specific characteristics of Community law, the particular difficulties to which its interpretation gives rise and the risk of divergences in judicial decisions within the Community.

Read literally, the exception to the obligation to refer in Article 177(3) [*234(3)*] EC created by the judgment is so narrow as to be almost meaningless.[50] Few will be the national judges who have the capacity to compare the nuances and context of a provision in all eleven languages of the Community.[51] Even the Court of Justice with all the backup of its translating services has struggled to come to terms with the interpretive difficulties posed by the authenticity of all the different language versions of EC law. In *Aanemersbedrijf P.K. Kraaijeveld* it had to consider whether the EC Directive on environmental impact assessment encompassed dykes.[52] The English and Finnish versions were the narrowest as they referred merely to canalisation and flood relief

---

[50] See Rasmussen, H. 'The European Court's Acte Clair Strategy in CILFIT' (1984) 9 *ELRev* 242; Mancini, F. & Keeling, D. 'From CILFIT to ERT: The Constitutional Challenge Facing the European Court' (1991) 11 *YBEL* 1, 4.

[51] For an attempt to do so by the Northern Ireland High Court see *Cunningham v Milk Marketing Board for Northern Ireland* [1988] 3 CMLR 815.

[52] Case C-72/95 *Aanemersbedrijf P.K. Kraaijeveld BV v Gedeputeerde Staten van Zuid-Hooland* [1996] ECR I-5403.

works. The Danish and Swedish versions referred to watercourses. All the other language versions referred to canalisation and regulation of watercourses. The difficulty was, as the Dutch Government observed, that dykes differ from canals in that they do not seek to alter the usual flow of the water. The Court resolved the problem by stating that as the purpose of the Directive was the assessment of the impact of activities on the environment as a whole, a broad interpretation should be taken of the concept and all works for retaining water and preventing flooding fell within the scope of the Directive. Yet such an approach is unconvincing and compromises legal certainty. For it is significantly wider than some of the language versions to the point where it is arguably *contra legem*.

To concentrate on the formal limits of *CILFIT* may be, however, to miss its significance. For *CILFIT* sends out powerful signals. Its effects, as Arnull has observed, are, taken as a whole, to encourage national courts to decide matters of EC law for themselves.[53] It was unclear how far the formal limits of the judgment would constrain them, once this initial presumption was formed. For some, therefore, the *acte clair* doctrine seemed to undermine the system for uniform application of EC law set out in Article 177 [*234*] EC. The corollary of granting courts against whose decisions there is no judicial remedy under national law a power to refuse to grant a reference was that, in those circumstances, there would be litigants who would be denied access to the Court of Justice and would have no further redress.[54]

CILFIT must be also placed in its temporal context. It occurred at a time when there was doubt about the willingness of some higher

---

[53] Arnull, A. 'Reflections on Judicial Attitudes at the European Court' (1985) 34 *ICLQ* 168, 172. See also Arnull, A. 'The Use and Abuse of Article 177 EEC' (1989) 52 *MLR* 622, 626.

[54] See the discussion in Hartley, T. *The Foundations of European Community Law* (1994, Clarendon, Oxford) 292-293; Weatherill, S. & Beaumont, P. *EC Law: The Essential Guide to the Workings of the European Community* (1995, 2nd Ed., Penguin, Harmondsworth) 304. This argument has been followed by the Austrian Constitutional Court in a judgment of 11 December 1995 (Case B 2300/95-18) in which it stated that a failure by a court of final instance to refer breached the Austrian constitutional principle of the right to access to the appropriate judge.

national courts to apply EC law at all.[55] Moreover, the insistence on the absolute nature of the duty on courts of last resort to refer is a fairly meaningless one, given that there is no means to enforce that obligation.[56] The doctrine of *acte clair*, thus, performs a 'valve' function, by providing a means for defusing a potential source of conflict between the higher national courts and the Court of Justice. For it allows the former to decide matters exclusively by themselves without engaging in any overt act of judicial rebellion.[57]

Golub, J. 'The Politics of Judicial Discretion: Rethinking the Interaction between National Courts and the European Court of Justice' (1996) 19 *West European Politics* 360, 376-377

For the purposes of the present discussion ... national judicial discretion serves as both a sword and a shield. In essence, the opportunity to refer questions to the ECJ expands the menu of options available to national judges. Provided that the national judge has some idea how the ECJ might answer the question referred to it under Article 177, references can be used in one or two ways.

First, a national judge can seek an ECJ decision which invalidates a national practice or pushes European integration faster than desired by the national government. In short, ECJ rulings can be used as a sword to force change on a reluctant national government. When provided with references the Court has historically used its influence to foster integration. Indeed, the Court's handling of preliminary references has sometimes led to claims that it exhibits a consistent pro-integration bias and a willingness to pursue its own political agenda. The ability of the ECJ, through a series of preliminary

---

[55]   Bebr, G. 'The Rambling Ghost of "Cohn-Bendit": Acte Clair and the Court of Justice' (1983) 20 *CMLRev* 439.

[56]   In 1995, according to the Commission, 53 references were made by courts of final instance. In that year alone, courts of final instance in Belgium, the Netherlands and Spain refused to refer points of EC law which were arguably necessary to decide the case in hand, EC Commission, *Thirteenth Annual Report on the Monitoring and Application of Community Law* COM (96) 600 final, 415 & 418-421.

[57]   One example of this happening in the case of the House of Lords was *Re Sandhu, The Times* 10 May 1985. In 1994, the last time the Commission researched this, it found that in that year the Italian Court of Cassation and the German Federal Financial Court, both courts of last instance, had each decided questions on the ground of *acte clair*, despite the points of EC law appearing to be less than obvious. EC Commission, *Twelfth Annual Report on Monitoring the Application of Community Law*, COM (95) 500, 342.

rulings, to devise the doctrines of supremacy, direct effect and liability as well as to shape specific policy areas was noted earlier in this article.

National judges can also use preliminary references as a sword to foster integration or to achieve national political change by taking advantage of the ECJ's expansive interpretative methods. The existence of teleological interpretation is well known. The teleological method underpinned early ECJ decisions leading to direct effect and the primacy of EC law. More recently, similar interpretative techniques have been manifest in the Court's handling of human rights doctrine, as well as environmental policy. In each of these areas, the Court has achieved significant integrationist effects, in part by applying an expansive treaty interpretation to questions referred by national courts under Article 177.

The teleological approach endorsed by the Court appeared particularly unusual to British judges whose interpretative methods focus predominantly on close textual readings. Although British judges inevitably exercise a certain amount of discretion when interpreting a statute, they enjoy far less discretion than exists for members of the ECJ. Given these differences in interpretative method, one would expect that judicially-driven integration would be inherently greater in cases involving a preliminary reference than in cases where British judges decided issues of EC law themselves.

Alternatively, national judges can seek to shield a policy from unfavourable ECJ rulings by withholding references. Not only can specific national practices be sheltered from adverse interpretations of EC law, but the ECJ can be starved of references which might be used to expand the scope or accelerate the pace of European integration. This possibility has been recognised by EC lawyers. If national judges employ their discretion and frequently find that ECJ precedent addresses the question of Community law and therefore no reference is required, the 'total effect would be a disastrous reduction of the volume of the Court's docket; and, hence, a sizeable reduction in the Court's sole means of influence and control.'

V. Article 177 [*234*] EC as a Law-Making Dynamic

The reference procedure is also an agenda-setting process. As the overwhelming majority of cases which arrive before the Court of Justice come via Article 177 [*234*] EC ,[58] the procedure acts as the principal dynamo which propels the doctrinal development of EC law.

This provides opportunities, in the first place, for litigants. Golub

---

[58]   In 1995 215 of 415 cases, or roughly 60%, of the cases decided by the Court of Justice were decided via Article 177 [*234*] EC. EC Commission, *Thirteenth Annual Report on Monitoring the Application of Community Law* COM (96) 600, 414.

has thus examined the variables which might determine the number of references coming from differing Member States' courts. He suggests that after an initial judicial learning curve, whereby national courts familiarise themselves with EC law, a link can be established between the openness of a Member State economy and the value of intra-EC trade for that economy, on the one hand, and the number of references which flow from that State's courts. The more open the economy, the greater the number of references which stem from that State's courts.[59] This empirical evidence confirms the work of others who have argued that pressure groups and corporate actors are increasingly using the preliminary reference procedure as part of litigation strategies to bring political change through law.[60] Such strategies are normally carried out by 'repeat players'. These are actors, usually well-resourced, who will engage in a series of cases with the ambition of bringing about an eventual change in policy rather than of winning any single dispute.[61] Article 177 [*234*] EC provides a fertile arena for such strategies for a number of reasons. The first is that it offers the 'repeat actor' the possibility of 'trumping the domestic legal system' through the invocation of EC law. Secondly, Article 177 [*234*] EC undermines national judicial hierarchies by enabling lower courts to ignore national systems of precedent through exercising their discretion to refer. Finally, the repeat actor is able to exploit the relationship between the national court and the Court of Justice. As there will often be a delay before the Court gives judgment, this can be exploited to give the repeat actor a space within which to work through its seeking the grant of interim relief.

---

[59] Whilst he states that transnational economic transactions are the primary determinant, he considers transnational movement of people to be an important secondary determinant. Golub, J. *Modelling Judicial Dialogue in the European Community: The Quantitative Basis of Preliminary References to the ECJ* (EUI Working Paper, RSC No. 96/58, Florence).

[60] Harlow, C. & Rawlings, R. *Pressure Through Law* (1992, Routledge, New York) 278-289; Rawlings, R. 'The Eurolaw Game: Some Deductions from a Saga' (1993) 20 *Journal of Law & Society* 309; Mattli, W. & Slaughter, A-M. *Constructing the European Community Legal System from the Ground Up: The Role of Individual Litigants and National Courts* (EUI Working Paper, RSC No. 96/56, Florence) 12-17.

[61] Gallanter, M. 'Why the "Haves" Come Out Ahead: Speculation on the Limits of Legal Change' (1974) 9 *Law and Society Review* 95.

At the heart of the process is the national court, both as an interlocutor between litigants and the Court of Justice and as an enforcer of the Court of Justice's judgments. The centrality of national courts to the process begs a fundamental question - why should these bodies, which after all are creatures of the national constitutional settlement and are bred upon a culture of judicial self-restraint, engage actively in a process which can both undermine the political arms of government and their own judicial hierarchies?

One school of thought, the rational choice school, believes that the reason lies in judicial empowerment. National courts have engaged in such a process because it has enhanced their own position within the existing political settlement. Such analysis is prominent in the reasoning of Golub[62] and Alter.[63] It was first developed by Mattli and Slaughter.[64]

Mattli, W. & Slaughter, A-M. 'Constructing the European Community Legal System from the Ground Up: The Role of Individual Litigants and National Courts' (RSC 96/56, EUI, Florence) 18-19

First is the power of judicial review to establish the validity of national legislation, which is an increase in power with respect to national legislatures. Some national courts, notably constitutional courts, already exercise this power within their domestic legal system; others gained this power with respect to at least some subset of national statutes in partnership with the ECJ. Second is the pursuit of institutional power and prestige relative to other courts within the same national judicial system. Here we draw primarily on the work of Karen Alter, who has developed an 'inter-court competition' approach to explain European legal integration. Third is the power to promote certain substantive policies through the law. In other words, where European law and national law promote different policies or have different distributional effects with respect to a particular class of litigants, a national judge may have the opportunity to achieve the result that she favours through the application of European law.

A noteworthy aspect of this refinement of judicial interests, or preferences, is that each factor may explain resistance to as well as acceptance of EC law. Courts that already exercise the power of judicial review, for instance, are likely to perceive the

---

[62]   See pp 470-471.

[63]   See pp 447-448.

[64]   Burley, A-M. & Mattli, W. 'Europe before the Court: a Political Theory of Legal Integration' (1993) 47 *International Organisation* 41; Mattli, W. & Slaughter, A-M 'Law and Politics in the European Union' (1995) 49 *International Organisation* 183.

'parallel' exercise of that power by the ECJ regarding matters of European law as a threat. Alec Stone emphasises this tension in light of the particular incentives facing national constitutional courts, typically the only European courts entitled to engage in any form of judicial review. Similarly, the inter-court competition model posits that courts that already enjoy substantial prestige and power relative to other courts within the same national legal system are likely to object to the extension or even transfer of that power elsewhere in the system; they may thus reject EC law for the same reasons that their counterparts accept it. Finally, the congruence of EC law with a particular set of substantive legal outcomes in different issue areas can produce opposition from national courts who favour the outcomes produced by the application of national law as easily as it can marshal support from judges who would like to see a change in national law.

The notion of judicial empowerment obscures a large number of other factors which might influence national courts' reasoning - such as national legal cultures, differing constitutional relations with other arms of government and notions of judicial restraint which have not led to courts behaving in such a power-hungry manner. Others suggest that rather it is the effect of certain structures, such as shared judicial identity and a shared commitment to legal reasoning which have been the primary factors in enlisting national judicial support.

Chalmers, D. 'Judicial Preferences and the Community Legal Order' (1997) 60 *Modern Law Review* 164, 176-177

Whilst unprovable, it is possible that a shared judicial identity has fostered a receptiveness to the Court's doctrine which might have been so forthcoming if the doctrine had come from other sources. This shared identity has also pushed national courts to look sideways at the actions of their counterparts in other States. In this manner acceptance of Community law in those States where national courts are more receptive to treaties being invoked before them facilitated its acceptance elsewhere. In the current climate the argument can be expressed in reverse terms. Where there is almost universal *de facto* acceptance of Community law across the European Union, it would take a brave court to fly in the face of this consensus. Acceptance of Community law has thus become linked with judicial self-identification.

More importantly, shared judicial identity entails a common reference to legal discourse. Allegiances are therefore built by the Court's reference to common legal constructs. It uses, as Weiler states: 'the language of reasoned interpretation ... the artifacts which national courts would rely upon to enlist obedience within their own national orders'.[65] In *Süderdithmarschen*[66], for example, common terminology is used to help construct the conditions under which interim relief could be sought against national measures implementing a Community Regulation.

> 'It should ... be pointed out that the suspension of enforcement must retain the character of an interim measure. The national court to which the application for interim relief is made may therefore grant a suspension only until such time as the Court has delivered its ruling on the question of validity.'

The strength of allegiance generated depends upon shared concepts of meaning, as its roots lie in an appeal to a common consciousness. The formal language of the law can provide, however, a shared identification at only the most general level. Whilst it is unclear whether a convergence of legal systems within the European Union is taking place, Legrand and Jackson have convincingly argued that the legal systems of the Member States are marked as much by disparity as by similarity. Each legal tradition operates within the particularities of its own cultural framework,[67] and each views other traditions through constructs which it itself created.[68] This both limits the depth of allegiance felt and constrains the Court of Justice from developing a sophisticated structure of its own, for the more it develops common symbols, the more it will be confronted by the different perceptions of these symbols, and the greater the risk of a cultural clash between it and any of the national courts.

VI. Proposals for Reform of the Judicial Architecture of the European Union

An interesting and lively debate has developed about the structure of the judicial architecture within the European Union, in particular whether it contributes effectively to the integration process and the administration

---

65   Weiler, J. 'Journey to an Unknown Destination: a Retrospective and Prospective of the European Court of Justice in the Arena of Political Discourse' (1993) 31 *JCMS* 417, 424.

66   Joined Cases C-143/88 *Zuckerfabrik Süderdithmarschen v HZA Itzehoe* & C-92/89 *Zuckerfabrik Soest v HZA Paderborn* [1991] ECR I-415, [1993] 3 CMLR 1.

67   Legrand, P. 'European Legal Systems are Not Converging' (1996) 45 *ICLQ* 52, 80-81.

68   Jackson, B. '"Legal Visions of the New Europe": *Ius Gentium, Ius Commune, European Law*' in Jackson, B. & McGoldrick, D. (eds.) *Legal Visions of the New Europe* (1993, Graham & Trotman, London).

of justice. There is a fair degree of consensus that some parts of the current system are not working well.

i. Weaknesses in the Current Judicial Structure

Backlog: The point decried by almost everybody is the backlog generated by the extremely centralised nature of the system. In its Report for the Intergovernmental Conference the Court of Justice states:

> 'The Court is aware of the need to reduce further the time to deal with such questions and would stress in that connection that the recent transfer to the Court of First Instance of all direct actions brought by individuals should make it possible to obtain a significant reduction in the time taken for other types of proceedings.'[69]

This is something of a smug understatement. At the end of 1994 the average length of proceedings varied between 18 and 21.2 months depending upon the type of measure brought. Furthermore, the establishment of the CFI had not only failed to reduce the backlog, but created another logjam. At the end of 1994 the average length of proceedings before it for direct actions were 23 months.[70] The length of proceedings results not only in the problem that 'justice delayed is often justice denied', but also provides incentives for national courts not to send matters to the Court of Justice and ultimately must affect the quality of the ECJ and CFI judgments by placing them under considerable time pressures.

Workload: The problem of backlog has developed as a result of the considerable workload placed on the shoulders of the ECJ and CFI. Even if this backlog had not developed, some authors consider the workload still to be a problem. In 1994 the ECJ gave 188 judgments and

---

[69] *Report of the Court of Justice for the Intergovernmental Conference, Proceedings of the Court 15/95*, 8-9. For discussion see Craig, P. 'The road to the 1996 Intergovernmental Conference: The contribution of the Court of Justice and the Court of First Instance' (1996) *PL* 13.

[70] *Proceedings of the Court of Justice and the Court of First Instance 34/94*, 34-38.

the CFI 70 judgments. It has been questioned whether the legal community within the Union can digest and consider the implications of such a large number of judgments.[71]

Expertise: The two Courts, particularly the Court of Justice, have to adjudicate upon a tremendous range of matters. Whilst all the judges are very distinguished lawyers, as lawyers most are generalists. Most do not have the familiarity with economics or environmental science, for example, that individual cases might require. This has undoubtedly affected the Court's reputation in certain areas. There has been frequent comment on the paucity of its economic analysis in the field of competition law, for example. It has also been suggested that it does not help the Court's authority to move from, one moment, giving judgments of an important constitutional nature to, next, dealing with the minutiae of staff cases or Community customs law.[72] The CFI in its Contribution to the Intergovernmental Conference was receptive to some of these criticisms through its suggestion that specialised chambers should be set up within the Court.[73]

Legitimacy: The third problem is that for whatever reason, be through its own or others' making, the Court is currently enjoying a crisis of confidence among the citizens of Europe, and certainly does not enjoy the authority or popular awareness within society that most national courts enjoy. The judicial architecture arguably contributes to this problem. The Court is cast as the authoritative interpreter of EC law. National courts through lack of familiarity with EC law are therefore often very willing to ask the Court for questions on the interpretation of EC law. Whilst EC law is meant to penetrate domestic legal systems, the Court is, however, one step removed from these legal systems, as access to it is only through the time-consuming preliminary reference procedure. These two features contribute, first, to the Court being seen as synonymous with EC law, and perhaps too strong a link

---

[71]   Jacqué, J-P. & Weiler, J. 'On the Road to European Union - a New Judicial Architecture: An Agenda for the Intergovernmental Conference' (1990) 27 *CMLRev* 185, 189.

[72]   Ibid., 190.

[73]   *Report of the Court of First Instance for the Intergovernmental Conference, Proceedings of the Court 15/95*, 17. See also Scorey, D. 'A new model for the Communities' judicial architecture in the new Union' (1996) 21 *ELRev* 224.

being perceived between the development of EC law and the powers of that institution. Secondly, as it is the Court rather than national courts which is often responsible for major developments in EC law, a perception has developed of EC law as an external intrusive pressure on national legal systems, with the Court being seen as a personification of that pressure.

ii. A System of Regional or Specialised Courts?

In 1990 two distinguished academics, Jacqué and Weiler, suggested that some of these problems could be ameliorated, first, by limiting *direct access* to the Court of Justice to those cases where the defendant was a Member State, the applicant was either a Community institution or a Member State, or a reference was sent by the highest national courts. In addition four Community Regional Courts would be established and all other matters currently considered by the ECJ or CFI should be transferred to these courts. There should be the possibility of an appeal from these Courts to the Court of Justice and, in certain circumstances, the Commission could also intervene to request that a matter be transferred to the Court of Justice.[74]

Objections to the development of regional courts have emerged on two grounds. The first is the cost of administering of such courts. This objection is less than convincing given than the establishment has never been costed, and in any case would have to be weighed against the social cost of the excessive delays that currently exist. A more weighty objection is that the development of such courts might fracture the unitary nature of Community law.

---

[74]   Supra n.71, 192-193. For less radical alterations to the judicial architecture see Arnull, A. 'Refurbishing the Judicial Architecture of the European Community' (1994) 43 *ICLQ* 296; v. Gerven, W. 'The role of the European Judiciary now and in the future' (1996) 21 *ELRev* 211.

Court of First Instance, 'Reflections on the Future Development of the Community Judicial System' (1991) 16 *European Law Review* 175, 176-177[75]

II. The principle of the uniform interpretation of Community law must more than ever be observed.

Objective 1: to avoid the juxtaposition of more than one supreme judicial authority in the Community legal order

The Court of Justice has, for a long time, played the role of 'supreme court' and 'constitutional court' in the Community legal order. In this respect, because of its status, it has made an essential contribution to the construction of the Community according to the rule of law. That being so, there seems to be a risk that the creation of one or more new 'supreme' courts each vested with its own special jurisdiction, would be such greatly to complicate the situation by giving rise to negative and positive conflicts of jurisdiction and also to diverging lines of judicial authority.

Objective 2: to avoid the compartmentalisation of lower Community courts

A unitary and hierarchical system of courts seems to be the most appropriate way of ensuring that the principle of uniform interpretation of Community law is observed. This does not of course rule out the creation of specialised courts in highly technical fields, but it does raise doubts as to the merits of proposals for the creation of, for example, 'regional Community courts' of general jurisdiction, each of which would doubtless resolutely endeavour to affirm its own case law. The functioning, composition and cost of such courts would probably also give rise to difficult problems. These disadvantages would attach *a fortiori* to the creation of an itinerant 'regional Community court'.

Objective 3: to ensure that each Community court of non-specialised jurisdiction is so composed as to enable the various legal systems to be fairly represented

This essential principle has been one of the cornerstones of the success of the Community court whose case law derives not from the dominance of the concepts of the legal system of any one Member State but from the pooling of the riches of the different systems of the Member States, taken as a whole. Here, too, the creation of 'regional courts' would be liable eventually to destroy this harmony and endanger the unity of Community law.

---

[75]   This was the text of a discussion paper of the CFI prepared for the Treaty on European Union. It has repeated its beliefs in its submissions for the 1996 Intergovernmental Conference, supra n.73, 16.

The second proposal is that a series of specialised courts should be developed.[76] There seems to be a divergence of views on this point between the ECJ and the CFI. Whilst the possibility of either the CFI developing a series of specialised chambers or even the establishment of a new series of specialized courts is considered by the ECJ to be possibly desirable in the long term,[77] the CFI considers that the setting up of new specialised courts would entail considerable budgetary costs and would jeopardise the unity of the Community judicature and of its case law.[78]

The idea has found some favour with the Member States. The Community Trade Mark Regulation envisages a Community system of trade mark courts, as it requires Member States to designate courts within their territories which shall have exclusive jurisdiction for cases concerning the validity and infringement of the Community trade mark.[79] The Regulation is something of a half-way house as references can be made from these courts to the Court of Justice. Whilst a specialised culture might be developed locally, it is unlikely that this will serve to alleviate the Court's workload. Specialisation had been taken a step further, however, in the proposed Community Patent Convention.[80] Once again Member States must designate patent courts with exclusive jurisdiction for questions of invalidity and infringement. The Convention also sets up a Common Patents Appeals Court whose duty is to ensure some homogeneity in the decisions of the national courts. Whilst a reference can be made from this court to the ECJ, the ECJ has only a limited role as its duty is merely to ensure that the Appeal Court's interpretation of the Convention does not conflict with other areas of EC law.

---

[76]   In this respect see Kapteyn, P. 'The Court of Justice of the European Communities after the Year 2000' in Curtin, D. & Heukels, T. (eds.) *Institutional Dynamics of European Integration: Liber Amicorum Schermers, Vol 1* (1994, Martijnus Nijhoff, Dordrecht) 135, 141-145.

[77]   Supra n.69, 10.

[78]   Supra n.73, 16.

[79]   Regulation 40/94 EC, OJ 1994, L 11/1, Articles 91-101.

[80]   Decision 89/695/EEC on an Agreement relating to Community Patents, OJ 1989, L 410/1; Protocol on the Settlement of Litigation concerning the infringement and validity of Community Patents, OJ 1989, L 401/34; Protocol on the Statute of the Common Appeal Court relating to Community Patents, OJ 1989, L 401/48.

iii. More Efficient Case Management?

If it is believed that any radical overhaul of the Community judicial structure, such as the creation of regional or specialised courts, will lead to the fragmentation of the EC legal order, the only solution to the current problem is to argue that the case load be handled more efficiently. A number of solutions have been suggested. Some revolve around the internal organisation of the Court. These include increased resort to Chambers by the Court; an increase in the jurisdiction of the CFI and an expansion of the translation services at the Court.[81] It has also been suggested that more could be done to ensure that national courts use the preliminary reference procedure more efficiently. Suggestions include systematic training of national judges in EC law so that they do not perceive EC law as some separate system of law upon which they do not have sufficient expertise to adjudicate. Another proposal is that national courts submit draft answers with their references. If the Court agrees at an early stage that the draft answer is correct, it would simply state that it did not object to the suggested interpretation. The final possibility is that to allow national courts to certify certain questions as urgent. Whilst this would not reduce overall workload, it might, however, serve to prioritise the backlog.[82]

The difficulties with 'case-load management' solutions is that they suggest the problem is not in any way structural, and therefore run the danger of underestimating the scale of the problem. The Court of Justice already decides a considerable number of cases a year. There must be doubts about how far it can expand its output without affecting the quality of its judgments. Solutions focusing upon the role of the national court in the process at least adopt a more decentralised approach. Yet they recognise that reform is only possible if national judges are thoroughly familiarised with EC law. This is unlikely to happen in an era of likely enlargement, however. Moreover, there is no evidence to

---

[81]   On all these see British Institute of International and Comparative Law, *The Role and Future of the Court of Justice* (1996, BIICL, London) 126-131.

[82]   On such reforms see Strasser, S. 'The Development of a Strategy of Docket Control for the European Court of Justice and the Question of Preliminary References' (Harvard Jean Monnet Working Paper No. 95/3, Camb., Mass).

suggest that increased familiarity with EC law will result in a decreased number of references. The opposite can be convincingly argued, namely that increased knowledge of EC law will allow national courts to become further seduced by the formal logic of EC law and will result in their entering, even more enthusiastically, further allegiances with the Court of Justice.

Further Reading

Alter, K. 'Who are the "Masters of the Treaty"? European Governments and the European Court of Justice' (1998) 51 *International Organisation*

Anderson, D. *References to the European Court* (1995, Sweet & Maxwell, London)

Arnull, A. 'The Use and Abuse of Article 177 EEC' (1989) 52 *Modern Law Review* 622

Barav, A. 'Preliminary Censorship? The Judgment of the European Court in Foglia v Novello' (1980) 5 *European Law Review* 443

v. Gerven, W. 'The Role and Structure of the European Judiciary now and in the future' (1996) 21 *European Law Review* 211

Golub, J. *Modelling Judicial Dialogue in the European Community: The Quantitative Basis of Preliminary References to the ECJ* (RSC No. 96/58, EUI, Florence)

Jacqué, J-P. & Weiler, J. 'On the Road to European Union - a New Judicial Architecture: An Agenda for the Intergovernmental Conference' (1990) 27 *Common Market Law Review* 185

Maher, I. 'National Courts as European Courts' (1994) 14 *Legal Studies* 226

O'Neill, M. 'Article 177 and Limits to the Right to Refer' (1996) 2 *European Public Law* 375

Schermers, H. et al. *Article 177: Experiences and Problems* (1987, TMC Asser Instituut, The Hague)

Rawlings, R. 'The Eurolaw Game: Some Deductions from a Saga' (1993) 20 *Journal of Law and Society* 309

Scorey, D. 'A new model for the Communities' judicial architecture in the new Union' (1996) 21 *European Law Review* 224

Weiler, J. 'A Quiet Revolution: The European Court of Justice and Its Interlocutors' (1994) 26 *Comparative Political Studies* 510

9. Conditions of Legality

I. Introduction

The conditions of legality for acts of the EC Institutions are set out in Article 173 [*230*] EC.

Article 173(2) [*230(2)*] EC. It [the Court of Justice] shall have jurisdiction ... on grounds of lack of competence, infringement of an essential procedural requirement, infringement of this Treaty or any rule of law relating to its application, or misuse of powers.

Whilst, at one level, the four conditions set out in Article 173(2) [*230(2)*] EC provide the standard for judicial review, their effects extend beyond the court room. They also provide a superstructure which orientates and guides decision-making by the EC Institutions. In so doing, these conditions act as a *sine qua non* for the legitimisation of EC government, firstly by introducing a sufficient element of predictability so that individuals can plan their lives around the exercise of government, and, secondly, by articulating values, such as the expression of fundamental rights, which, for good or for bad, are associated with democratic government within Western Europe.[1]

---

[1] On the various functions of fundamental rights within the integration process see Dauses, M. 'The Protection of Fundamental Rights in the Community Legal Order' (1985) 10 *ELRev* 398, 418-419. The arguments expressed there can be applied equally to all the conditions of legality.

II. Lack of Institutional Competence

i. Original Competencies

The formal limits on EC competence and its exercise have been discussed earlier.[2] In practice, the limits of the capabilities of the EC have been decided by the legislative institutions with judicial intrusion being a rare exception. The situation is different in the case of powers of the individual Institutions. In such circumstances the Court is not concerned directly with the balance of powers between the EC and Member States but rather with the balance between the different institutions. It has therefore intervened more actively to prevent institutions arrogating power for themselves at the expense of other institutions.

In the case of overtly legislative acts these tussles take place within the context of the legal base game with Member States and institutions claiming that legal base which provides the legislative procedure which most protects their interests. In such circumstances, the Court will simply declare that the measure should have been passed under another legal base rather than ruling that there is a straightforward lack of competence.[3] It is more direct about an institution's lack of competence where the latter adopts legally binding acts it is not empowered to under the guise of its administrative powers. The context within this occurs most often is where the Commission has adopted an act which should been adopted through one of the legislative procedures.[4]

An example is *France v Commission* where the Court declared that the Commission had no competence to reach an 'understanding' with the United States of America upon the enforcement of competition law

---

[2]   See Chapter 4.

[3]   See pp 213-221.

[4]   For an example of the Parliament's adopting an act which it was not competent see Case 108/83 *Luxembourg v Parliament* [1984] ECR 1945 where it was held that Parliament was not empowered to move its Secretariat from Luxembourg.

within their respective jurisdictions.[5] The reason for this was that the 'understanding' constituted an international agreement, the appropriate procedure for which was contained in Article 228 [*300*] EC, which provided for the conclusion of the agreement by the Council after consultation with the Parliament. In similar vein the Court has declared that the Commission lacked competence to issue a Communication providing for the liberalisation of the market in pension funds.[6] For the Treaty provided only for the issue of directives by the Council in this field, acting under Article 57(2)[*47(2)*] EC, and the Commission was consequently not empowered to adopt instruments of a legally binding nature in this field.

ii. Delegated Powers

The case for delegation of powers is set out below.

Baldwin, R. *Rules and Government* (1995, OUP, Oxford) 62-63

The case for employing delegated rather than primary legislation is now familiar to public lawyers. First, it is argued that Parliament has neither the time nor the personnel to legislate on matters of detail since it could not, as presently organised, consider and debate such issues. Instead, Parliament properly focuses on questions of broad principle and the establishing of frameworks upon which ministers or agencies can be authorised to base more precise provisions. Delegated legislation is, accordingly, said to serve a valuable purpose in keeping primary legislation as clear, simple, and short as possible and in assisting Parliament to focus on essential points, policies, and principles. Second, the issue to be legislated upon may be too technical to be understood and debated properly in Parliament. It is better in such cases to allow ministers or agencies to employ or consult with experts and to produce considered rules. Third, particular constituencies may have to be consulted on matters of detail (eg trade associations, specialists, unions) and this is more effectively done by the executive than by Parliament. Fourth, unforeseen circumstances may have to be anticipated or responded to quickly. Parliament cannot lay down a blueprint that provides for all eventualities and using delegated legislation allows

---

[5]   Case C-327/91 *France v Commission* [1994] ECR I-3641, [1994] 5 CMLR 517.

[6]   Case C-57/95 *France v Commission*, Judgment of 20 March 1997.

plans for the future to be developed as events unfold (perhaps employing experimental strategies and adjusting these in a course of 'muddling through'). Delegated legislation also allows rapid responses to be made to crises and emergencies. Thus, in wartime, ministerially issued regulations can be provided for in order to maintain public order and safety. Fifth, secondary legislation offers a useful way to bring Acts of Parliament into force at the appropriate time or by stages.

All these arguments apply with equal force to the European Community. Article 155 [*211*] EC therefore allows the Council to delegate tasks to the Commission. From early in the Community's history it was accepted that the powers delegated could be extensive.[7] An example of the application of the doctrine is set out below.

Case C-478/93 Netherlands v Commission [1995] ECR I-3081

Under a 1993 Council Regulation the Commission was delegated powers to draw up detailed rules on the import of bananas into the EU, in particular concerning the issue of import licences and the minimum quantity of bananas which operators were required to market. The Commission used data on the number of bananas imported into each Member State in determining how to allocate quotas. It considered some of the data supplied to be inaccurate, and therefore revised the figures it received. This was challenged by the Dutch Government who claimed that the Commission had not been granted powers to revise the figures.

26. So far as concerns the complaint of lack of competence, the applicant submits that neither Article 155 of the EC Treaty nor Article 20 of the Council Regulation empowers the Commission unilaterally to alter the information submitted by the Member States. The latter have sole responsibility for compiling the list of operators, fixing the reference quantities, as well as for detecting and preventing inaccurate declarations by operators.

27. In reply, the Commission submits that, under Article 155 of the Treaty, it has the task of detecting quantities counted twice and deducting such quantities from the reference quantities notified to it. Like the implementing regulation, the contested regulation is based on Article 20 of the Council Regulation, which contains a non-exhaustive list of matters to be covered by detailed rules.

---

[7]   Case 9/56 *Meroni v High Authority* [1958] ECR 133.

28. In order to determine whether this complaint is well founded, it is necessary to examine the respective powers of the Commission and the Member States with regard to the management of the import quota for bananas.

29. Under the fourth indent of Article 155 of the Treaty, the Commission is required, in order to ensure the proper functioning and development of the common market, to exercise the powers conferred on it by the Council for the implementation of the rules laid down by the latter. Article 20 of the Council Regulation confers on the Commission the task of adopting the detailed rules for implementing Title IV of that regulation and gives some details of what those rules are to cover.

30. The Court has consistently held that it follows from the Treaty context in which Article 155 must be placed and also from practical requirements that the concept of implementation must be given a wide interpretation. Since only the Commission is in a position to keep track of agricultural market trends and to act quickly when necessary, the Council may confer on it wide powers in that sphere. Consequently, the limits of those powers must be determined by reference amongst other things to the essential general aims of the market organization (see Case 22/88 *Vreugdenhil and Another v Minister van Landbouw en Visserij* [1989] ECR 2049, paragraph 16 and the cases cited therein).

31. Thus, the Court has held that, in matters relating to agriculture, the Commission is authorized to adopt all the measures which are necessary or appropriate for the implementation of the basic legislation, provided that they are not contrary to such legislation or to the implementing legislation adopted by the Council (Case 121/83 *Zuckerfabrik Franken v Hauptzollamt Würzburg* [1984] ECR 2039, paragraph 13).

32. It follows that the wording of Article 20 of the Council Regulation does not preclude the Commission from adopting detailed implementing rules which, although not expressly referred to in that provision, are necessary for the functioning of the import system.

33. The need to ensure equal treatment for all economic operators in all the Member States and to guarantee the functioning of the import system on the basis of accurate information means that the Commission, which is responsible for managing the common organization of the market in bananas, may adopt measures to prevent reference quantities from being counted twice when it fixes the reduction coefficient.

There is yet to be an instance of the Council being found to have delegated too wide powers to the Commission. The position is to be contrasted with the powers which may be delegated to Member States and other organisations. These must be narrowly defined and executive in nature.[8]

Case 23/75 Rey Soda v Cassa Conguaglio Zucchero [1975] ECR 1279

To prevent disturbances in the sugar market which resulted from variations in the price, Article 37(2) of Regulation 1009/67/EC stated 'the requisite provisions to prevent the sugar market from being disturbed as a result of an alteration in price level at the change-over from one marketing year to the next may be adopted in accordance with the [management committee procedure]'. The Commission was therefore delegated powers to take intervention powers where necessary. In 1974 prices for sugar in Italy rose with the danger that producers would consequently hoard sugar. The Commission delegated to the Italian Government the power to take measures to prevent disturbances as a result of the increase. The Italian Government levied a tax on stocks of sugar. The Court ruled that the Commission had delegated too wide powers to the Italian Government.

25. ... Article 37 (2) of the basic regulation enabling the Commission to take, in accordance with the consultation procedure of the management committee, measures directly applicable in a member State, cannot be interpreted as enabling the commission to impose upon a Member State the obligation to draw up, under the guise of implementation measures, essential basic rules which would not be subject to any control by the Council.

26. Thus under the system established by Article 37 (2) of the basic regulation it is for the Commission, when it decides after consultation with the management committee to require certain holders of sugar of a member state to pay a tax on the stocks, itself to determine in a precise manner the essential basic rules.

27. Since the effects of an announcement of a tax to discourage excessive stocking of a product depends to a large extent on the rate of the tax, the announcement must show, in addition to the parties liable, the bases of the calculation of the tax.

28. Accordingly in fulfilling the obligation which is placed on it under Article 37 (2), the Commission should have fixed the basis of the calculation of the tax and the categories

---

[8]   The test for the breadth of powers which may be delegated to outside bodies is similar to that for Member States. These must be executive powers which can be 'subject to strict review in the light of objective criteria determined by the delegating authority'. See Case 9/56 *Meroni v High Authority* [1958] ECR 133.

of persons liable and submitted this decision to the management committee for its opinion.

There is a question as to why such a dichotomy should be drawn between the breadth of powers which can be delegated to the Commission, on one hand, and to Member States and other bodies on the other. The delegation of broad powers to the Commission can be justified by the argument that experience elsewhere suggests that placing severe limits on the exercise of delegated powers undermines the rationale behind the initial delegation.[9] Initial delegation may be necessary as different coalition groups within the legislature struggling to assert hegemony can also result in its becoming increasingly difficult to make consistent and credible policy. A broad remit may be necessary as first the legislature has to invest otherwise considerable resources in supervising the policy, and, secondly, in many cases the technical and unpredictable nature of the subject-matter may make it difficult to specify which action to take in the first place.[10]

Such reasoning would allow broad powers to be delegated also to outside bodies such as regulatory agencies.[11] The narrowness of the powers which may be delegated to such bodies poses severe constraints upon the future tasks which may be undertaken by the various EC regulatory agencies.[12] Thus, legal problems have already arisen over the

---

[9] The starting point for this analysis is the magisterial article by Stewart, R. 'The Reform of American Administrative Law' (1975) 88 *Harvard Law Review* 1669.

[10] On this within an EU context see Majone, G. *Temporal Consistency and Policy Credibility: Why Democracies Need Non-Majoritarian Institutions* (RSC Working Paper No. 96/57, EUI, Florence, 1996).

[11] Delegation to private bodies does raise the problem of judicial control, as a private body may not be subjected to the same series of public law controls as, say, the Commission. This is not a problem in regard to bodies which are created by EC legislation who are public in nature and upon whom appropriate safeguards can be imposed.

[12] Lenaerts, K. 'Regulating the Regulatory Process: "Delegation of Powers" in the European Community' (1993) 18 ELRev 23; Everson, M. 'Independent Agencies: Hierarchy Beaters?' (1995) 1 ELJ 180, 197; Dehousse, R. 'Regulation by Networks in the European Community: the role of European agencies' (1997) 4 *JEPP* 247, 257.

possibility, as has been pressed, of the Commission transferring its regulatory capacities in competition to an independent cartel office.[13]

The argument against allowing too wide powers to be delegated to the Member States is that it would allow for the re-nationalisation of EC policy through the backdoor.[14] Yet it may be wondered whether it is any less invidious to allow the balance struck in the legislative procedures between the various interests to be sidelined by excessive delegation to the Commission. A possible distinction is that the conception of Monnet of the Commission as an 'enlightened elite' and its expertise results in its having a culture which results in its being less likely to abuse its powers than Member States.[15] Even this view is highly problematic, in the light of other perspectives which take a less benign view of bureaucracies, characterising them as rent-seeking and self-aggrandising.[16]

Even if this were not the case, it has been observed by Shapiro that arguments of expertise and efficiency cannot sideline those of democratic legitimacy. Acts taken by the Commission, or for that matter any executive agency, are as 'political' in nature as acts taken by any legislature but are seen as lacking in legitimacy precisely because they are taken by a non-majoritarian institution.[17] Such a view militates against any delegation at all, and there is indeed a danger of a dialogue of the deaf opening up here. An intermediate view has been suggested by Baldwin who has argued that delegation can be justified where a

---

13   On the debate see McGowan, L. & Wilks, S. 'Disarming the Commission: The Debate over a European Cartel Office' (1995) 33 *JCMS* 259; Ehlermann, C-D. 'Reflections on a European Cartel Office' (1995) 32 *CMLRev* 471.

14   See Advocate General Reischl in Case 804/79 *Commission v United Kingdom* [1981] ECR 1045, 1087.

15   Featherstone, K. 'Jean Monnet and the "Democratic Deficit" in the European Union' (1994) 32 *JCMS* 149.

16   Niskanen, W. *Bureaucracy and Representative Government* (1971, Aldine, Chicago); Dunleavy, P. *Democracy, Bureaucracy and Public Choice: economic explanations of political science* (1991, Harvester, London); Dowding, K. *The Civil Service* (1995, Routledge, London).

17   Shapiro, M. 'The problems of independent agencies in the United States and the European Union' (1997) 4 *JEPP* 276, 283-287. In similar vein see Kreher, A. 'Agencies in the European Community - a step towards administrative integration' (1997) 4 *JEPP* 225, 229.

number of criteria are met. It is done through legislation; there is a degree of accountability; provision is made for due process; the area requires that expert judgments be made and applied, and the delegation will result in the objectives being achieved in either a more effective manner or in a more economically efficient one.[18]

Given that extensive delegation does take place within the EC, the values of due process and accountability become increasingly important. These have been traditionally accommodated in two ways. The first is through structuring the administrative discretion so that it be exercised within the framework of a number of generally applicable rules. Yet no matter how detailed the rules the Commission will still enjoy a discretion under powers delegated to it, so that it can favour one interest over the other. Weight is therefore put by some writers on the need for juridically enforceable rights of participation and consultation for interested parties.[19]

III. Breach of an Essential Procedural Requirement

EC law is replete with procedures. The question is rarely addressed, however, why they should be judicially enforced. Judicial enforcement, after all, allows courts to intrude into domains, by definition, in which other institutions enjoy hegemony. One rationale given is that courts are perceived at being placed at securing certain values.[20] These values underpin the use of procedures as much as any other tool of EC government.

---

[18]   Baldwin, R. *Rules and Government* (1995, OUP, Oxford) 41-46.
[19]   Stewart, R. 'The Reform of American Administrative Law' (1975) 88 *Harvard Law Review* 1667; Held, D. *Models of Democracy* (1987, OUP, Oxford) 254-264.
[20]   See pp 534-536.

Galligan, D. *Due Process and Fair Procedures* **(1996, Clarendon, Oxford) 29-30**

This idea, which I shall refer to as proceduralism, can be traced to a number of theoretical positions. In Nonet and Selznick's concept of responsive law, abstract, purposive standards are given practical content through the participation of the parties.[21] A solution emerges through participation which is responsive to the conflicting interests and values. The procedural nature of this form of social process is even more marked in the concept of reflexive law developed by Habermas and Teubner.[22] Here the general argument is that in complex contexts, groups, interests, and organisations must curb and simplify their needs and demands so that co-ordination amongst them and coherent solutions to problems can be achieved. In order to bring about those ends, carefully structured procedures are necessary. A connection can be made, moreover, between these strands of theory and ideas of strong democracy. The common principle underlying different versions of strong democracy is that participation enables the parties to arrive at a notion of the common good, a notion which is responsive to private and individual interests, but which goes beyond them. Participation is then not an instrument leading to a set outcome, but rather through participation the parties are able to see beyond their own interests in order to grasp the possibilities of acting for the common good. The act of participation both heightens the awareness of the parties and leads them to a resolution. The resolution is in a sense agreed on and consensual, but to collapse this mode of action into another form of decision through agreement would be to miss its essential qualities.

Procedures exist at a number of different levels within the EC. At the highest level there exist primary legislative procedures; procedures then exist to control the exercise of delegated powers, and finally there are each institution's own Rules of Procedure. The balance accommodated between the different values and interests varies according to the procedure used.

---

21   Nonet, P. & Selznick, A. *Law and Society in Transition* (1995, University of California Press, Berkeley, California).

22   J. Habermas' notion of communicative action is discussed in A. Brand, *The Force of Reason* (1990, Allen & Unwin, Sydney). See also Teubner, G, 'Substantive and Reflexive Elements in Modern Law' (1983) 17 *Law & Society Review* 239.

i. Primary Legislative Procedures

Primary legislative procedures most overtly secure the participatory rights of EU citizens by protecting the legislative rights of the EC majoritarian institutions, most notably the Parliament. Failure to observe a primary legislative procedure sufficiently carefully will usually result in the measure being declared illegal. The form this failure usually takes is a failure to consult a particular institution. In deciding whether this will make the measure illegal, the Court will have regard to the nature of the institution which was not consulted. The Court has therefore stated that as the function of the Economic and Social Committee is to advise on practical problems of an economic and social nature, there is only a requirement to consult it on the implementation of practical measures. A failure to consult it on preparatory measures or studies will not make the measure illegal. Thus, in *Germany v Commission* the failure by the Commission to consult the Economic and Social Committee over an information-gathering exercise on the migration policies of the Member States did not invalidate the measure.[23]

The Court sees the powers of the Parliament in slightly wider terms as a reflection of the 'fundamental democratic principle that the peoples should take part in the exercise of power through the intermediary of a representative assembly'. A failure to consult the Parliament, where this is required, will, in principle, render the act illegal,[24] as will a failure to reconsult where the text adopted by the Council departs substantially from the text on which the Parliament was consulted.[25] The right to consultation is not an unqualified one, however. It cannot be used by the Parliament to obstruct the legislative procedure.

---

[23]   Joined Cases 281, 283-5, 287/85 *Germany, France, Netherlands, Denmark & United Kingdom v Commission* [1987] ECR 3203, [1988] 1 CMLR 11.

[24]   Case 138/79 *Roquette Frères v Council* [1980] ECR 3333.

[25]   Case C-65/90 *Parliament v Council* [1992] ECR I-4593.

Case C-65/93 Parliament v Council [1995] ECR I-643

The Commission proposed to add a number of States to the list of those who benefited from the General Scheme of Preferences, a system which allowed some goods from some less developed countries to enter the Community without having to pay a tariff. In October 1992 the Council noted the Parliament that it wished to consult the latter but that, as the existing scheme entered into force on 1 January 1993, the Parliament had to treat the matter as an urgent one. Having decided initially that the matter should be treated under its expedited procedure the Parliament then referred the matter back to Committee. The final debate on the matter was scheduled for 18 January 1993. The Council adopted the Regulation on 21 December 1992 without having obtained the Parliament's opinion. The Regulation was based on Articles [37] and [133] EC, both of which provide for the consultation procedure.

21. The first point to note is that due consultation of the Parliament in the cases provided for by the Treaty constitutes an essential procedural requirement, disregard of which renders the measure concerned void. The effective participation of the Parliament in the legislative process of the Community, in accordance with the procedures laid down by the Treaty, represents an essential factor in the institutional balance intended by the Treaty. Such power reflects the fundamental democratic principle that the people should take part in the exercise of power through the intermediary of a representative assembly (see the 'Isoglucose' judgments, Case 138/79 *Roquette Frères v Council* [1980] ECR 3333, paragraph 33, and Case 139/79 *Maizena v Council* [1980] ECR 3393, paragraph 34).

22. Furthermore, observance of the consultation requirement implies that the Parliament has expressed its opinion and the requirement cannot be satisfied by the Council's simply asking for the opinion ('Isoglucose' judgments, paragraphs 34 and 35 respectively). In an emergency, it is for the Council to use all the possibilities available under the Treaty and the Parliament's Rules of Procedure in order to obtain the preliminary opinion of the Parliament ('Isoglucose' judgments, paragraphs 36 and 37 respectively).

23. However, the Court has held that inter-institutional dialogue, on which the consultation procedure in particular is based, is subject to the same mutual duties of sincere cooperation as those which govern relations between Member States and the Community institutions (see Case 204/86 *Greece v Council* [1988] ECR 5323, paragraph 16).

24. In this case, it is undisputed that the Council informed the President of the Parliament in its letter of 22 October 1992 of the need to adopt the contested regulation before the end of 1992, so as to enable it to enter into force on 1 January 1993. It is also undisputed that, having regard to the special relations between the Community and the developing

difficulties, both political and technical, which would result from an ~~adopt~~ ~~and to the~~ ~~application~~ of generalized tariff preferences, that request was justified.

25. The Parliament took those considerations fully into account, since, after referring the proposal for the regulation to the Committee on Development, it decided to deal with the matter under its procedure in cases of urgency. By placing the report of the Committee on Development on the agenda for the sitting on Friday 18 December, during its last session of 1992, the Parliament clearly intended to give its opinion in time to enable the Council to adopt the regulation before 1 January 1993.

26. However, the documents before the Court show that, notwithstanding the assurances thereby given to the Council, the Parliament decided, pursuant to Article 106 of its Rules of Procedure, to adjourn the plenary session of 18 December 1992 at the request of 14 Members, without having debated the proposal for the regulation. It appears, moreover, that that decision was based on reasons wholly unconnected with the contested regulation and did not take into account the urgency of the procedure and the need to adopt the regulation before 1 January 1993.

27. By adopting that course of action, the Parliament failed to discharge its obligation to cooperate sincerely with the Council. That is so especially since the Council was unable to avail itself of the possibility open to it under Article 139 of the Treaty, the information obtained by the Council from the President of the Parliament having made it clear that it was impossible for practical reasons to convene an extraordinary session of the Parliament before the end of 1992.

28. In those circumstances, the Parliament is not entitled to complain of the Council's failure to await its opinion before adopting the contested regulation of 21 December 1992. The essential procedural requirement of Parliamentary consultation was not complied with because of the Parliament's failure to discharge its obligation to cooperate sincerely with the Council.

ii. Secondary Procedures

Frequently, secondary legislation will set out procedures with which the Commission, in particular, must comply in the exercise of powers delegated to it. Until recently, these procedures received little academic interest. It is now being increasingly realised that the establishment of these procedures has secured the representation of values and interests in the area of delegated legislation. Thus, it has been argued, that the entrenchment of secondary procedures has paved the way for increased use of scientific expertise as a regulatory tool through obligations requiring the Commission to resort to consultation of scientific committees in situations where the complexity of the matter so requires.[26]

Case C-212/91 Angelopharm v Freie und Hansestadt Hamburg [1994] ECR I-171

The Commission had been delegated powers by Directive 76/768/EEC to determine the substances which could be used in cosmetics. In its Twelfth Cosmetics Directive, Directive 90/121/EC, the Commission banned a chemical, 11 alpha OHP. Angelopharm had been marketing intermittently since 1983 a product designed to stem hair loss, Setaderm, which contained this chemical. In proceedings before a German court Angelopharm claimed that the Twelfth Directive, as Article 8(2) of the Parent Directive required the Commission to consult the Scientific Committee on Cosmetology ('the Scientific Committee') before adopting any measure. This had not been done in this instance.

30. In order to remove the ambiguity from the wording of Article 8(2) of the Cosmetics Directive and to determine whether consultation of the Scientific Committee is mandatory, it is therefore necessary to refer to the Committee's role in the procedure for the adaptation of Annexes II to VII to the Cosmetics Directive.

31. As is emphasized in particular in the preambles to Directives 76/768, 82/368 and 90/121, the drafting and adaptation of Community rules governing cosmetic products are founded on scientific and technical assessments which must themselves be based on the results of the latest international research and which are frequently complex. This is particularly the case where it is a question of assessing whether or not a substance is injurious to human health.

---

[26]   Joerges, C. *Integrating Scientific Expertise into Regulatory Decision-Making. Scientific Expertise in Social Regulation and the European Court of Justice: Legal Frameworks for Denationalized Governance Structures* (RSC 96/10, EUI, Florence) 22-25. See also on this Hankin, R. *Integrating Scientific Expertise into Regulatory Decision-Making: The Cases of Food and Pharmaceuticals* (RSC 96/7, EUI, Florence) 15-22, and, for a critical view, Shapiro, M. *Integrating Scientific Expertise into Regulatory Decision-Making. The Frontiers of Science Doctrine: American Experiences with the Judicial Control of Science Based Decision-Making* (RSC 96/11, EUI, Florence).

32. As it has itself admitted before the Court, the Commission is not in a position to carry out assessments of this kind. Thus, it was not in a position to indicate the reasons why 11 alpha OHP was a dangerous substance which had to be prohibited or to evaluate the findings of the expert appointed by the Verwaltungsgericht Hamburg within the period set by the Court for that purpose, even though that period expired long after the prohibition of 11 alpha OHP by the Twelfth Directive and the submission of the expert's report.

33. The Committee on the Adaptation to Technical Progress of the Directives on the Removal of Technical Barriers to Trade in the Cosmetic Products Sector, which consists exclusively of representatives of the Member States and of the Commission, is similarly not in a position to make such an assessment. As the United Kingdom pointed out in its oral observations before the Court, that Committee must, in the nature of things and apart from any provision laid down to that effect, be assisted by experts on scientific and technical issues delegated by the Member States.

34. The Scientific Committee, however, has the task of assisting the Community authorities on scientific and technical issues in order to enable them to determine, from a fully informed position, which adaptation measures are necessary.

35. From the preamble to Commission Decision 78/45/EEC of 19 December 1977 establishing a Scientific Committee on Cosmetology (Official Journal 1978 L 13, p. 24) it is clear that the Scientific Committee, which consists of individuals who are highly qualified in disciplines relevant to cosmetology, such as medicine, toxicology, biology and chemistry, was created in order to provide the Commission with the assistance necessary to examine the complex scientific and technical problems entailed by the drafting and adaptation of Community rules on cosmetic products.

36. In the procedure before the Court the Commission accepted that consultation of this Committee in the procedure for the adaptation of the annexes to the Cosmetic Directive made it possible to ensure that the measures had a scientific basis, that they took account of the most recent scientific and technical research and that only prohibitions necessary on grounds of public health were imposed.

37. The Commission cannot successfully argue, as it did during the oral procedure, that consultation of the Scientific Committee is necessary only when authorization of the use of a substance in the manufacture of cosmetic products is envisaged. In the first place, no provision in the Cosmetics Directive makes a distinction according to whether the measure envisaged prohibits or authorizes the use of a substance. Secondly, the Commission may not, without breaching the provisions of the Cosmetics Directive, prohibit the use of a substance which, in the light of the results of the most recent scientific and technical research, cannot be regarded as dangerous.

38. Since the purpose of consulting the Scientific Committee is to ensure that the measures adopted at Community level are necessary and adapted to the objective, pursued by the Cosmetics Directive, of protecting human health, consultation of the Committee must be mandatory in all cases.

39. That interpretation is confirmed by the new version of Article 8(2) laid down in Council Directive 93/35/EEC of 14 June 1993 amending for the sixth time Directive 76/768/EEC on the approximation of the laws of the Member States relating to cosmetic products (Official Journal 1993 L 151, p. 32), the provisions of which are not, however, applicable to the main proceedings. In its amended version, Article 8(2) of the Cosmetics Directive simply requires consultation of the Scientific Committee so that it is clear that this formality is mandatory. There is nothing in the preamble which even suggests that the Community legislature intended to alter the scope of Article 8(2) of the Cosmetics Directive on this essential point or, in particular, that it intended to make mandatory a formality which was not previously mandatory.

40. In reply to the written questions of the Court, the Commission indicated that, although the Scientific Committee had been consulted on the measures adopted in connection with certain substances referred to in the Twelfth Directive, it had not been consulted with regard to the prohibition of 11 alpha OHP.

41. The procedure for the adoption of the Twelfth Directive was thus vitiated by a substantial defect of such kind as to render the Directive invalid in so far as it prohibits the use of 11 alpha OHP in the manufacture of cosmetic products.

Scientific committees are but one form of committee with whom the Commission might have to consult. Other committees include policy-making committees, consisting of national civil servants, and interest committees, consisting of representatives of particular interest groups.[27] Whilst scientific committees might articulate a particular form of values and a particular form of rationality, the other committees represent, more directly, a particular interest or constituency. Thus Joerges and Neyer have observed how Member States have used secondary procedures to constrain the exercise of the Commission's powers through the establishment of an extensive system of comitology. In this way, they argue, the delegation of extensive powers has not led to a significant increase in the Community's supranational powers but to a new form of 'deliberative supranationalism' in which there is a perpetual

---

[27] Vos, E. 'The Rise of Committees' (1997) 3 *ELJ* 210, 213.

mutual accommodation of national and supra-national interests.[28] In relation to the final group, interest groups, it is possible to imagine that the possibility this gives for erecting structures which allows private parties a direct input in the standards that governs might create a new form of governance which oscillates between self-regulation and public regulation.

iii. Internal Procedures

There is a tendency to overplay the unitary characteristics of each institution. In practice, however, each of the legislative institutions - the Council, the Commission and the Parliament - contains a high degree of internal differentiation. Cleavages can be drawn within the institutions based upon the internal administrative structure of the organisation, and the nationality, mother tongue or political allegiance of its employees.[29] At a formal level it is each institution's Rules of Procedure which give a level of cohesion to that institution. Initially, these Rules of Procedure was seen merely as rules of self-organisation for that institution, which could not be used to generate rights for outside parties.[30] Internal Rules of Procedure can serve another purpose. They can ensure that third parties are treated with a minimum degree of due process.

Case C-137/92P Commission v BASF [1994] ECR I-2555

The Commission adopted a Decision which found that a number of undertakings had been engaged in a cartel in the PVC sector. It directed them to bring the cartel to an end, and fined them. This Decision was challenged before the CFI who found that the draft Decision adopted by the college of Commissioners had

---

28   Joerges, C. & Neyer, C. 'From Intergovernmental Bargaining to Deliberative Political Processes: The Constitutionalisation of Comitology' (1997) 3 *ELJ* 273, 292-298.

29   For a useful discussion of the level of differentiation within the Commission see Page, E. *People Who Run Europe* (1997, OUP, Oxford) Chapter 2.

30   Case C-68/89 *Nakajima v Council* [1991] ECR I-2069.

been subsequently altered in several material ways before being notified to the parties. It also found that the Commission had adopted the contested Decision only in its English, German and French versions, leaving it to the Commissioner then responsible for competition, Mr Sutherland, to adopt the text of the decision in the other official languages of the Community. It declared the Decision to be so vitiated by illegality as to be non-existent. The Commission appealed against the judgment.

48. It should be remembered that acts of the Community institutions are in principle presumed to be lawful and accordingly produce legal effects, even if they are tainted by irregularities, until such time as they are annulled or withdrawn.

49. However, by way of exception to that principle, acts tainted by an irregularity whose gravity is so obvious that it cannot be tolerated by the Community legal order must be treated as having no legal effect, even provisional, that is to say that they must be regarded as legally non-existent. The purpose of this exception is to maintain a balance between two fundamental, but sometimes conflicting, requirements with which a legal order must comply, namely stability of legal relations and respect for legality.

50. From the gravity of the consequences attaching to a finding that an act of a Community institution is non-existent it is self-evident that, for reasons of legal certainty, such a finding is reserved for quite extreme situations.

51. In this case, the Court of First Instance did not question that at the meeting of 21 December 1988, as is shown by the relevant minutes, the Commission did decide to adopt the operative part of a decision as set out in those minutes, whatever defects may have affected that decision.

52. In any event, whether considered in isolation or even together, the irregularities of competence and form found by the Court of First Instance, which relate to the procedure for the adoption of the Commission's decision, do not appear to be of such obvious gravity that the decision must be treated as legally non-existent.

53. The Court of First Instance therefore erred in law in declaring Decision 89/190 non-existent.

54. The judgment under appeal must consequently be set aside.

55. According to the second sentence of Article 54 of the Statute (EEC) of the Court of Justice, if the decision of the Court of First Instance is set aside, the Court of Justice may itself give final judgment in the matter where the state of the proceedings so permits. The Court considers that this is the case.

.....

72. As far as the Rules of Procedure are concerned, Article 16 of the Merger Treaty (a provision which has now been replaced by Article 162(2) of the EC Treaty) requires the Commission to adopt its rules of procedure so as to ensure that both it and its services operate in accordance with the provisions of the treaties and that those rules are published.

73. It follows that the Commission has an obligation, inter alia, to take the steps necessary to enable the complete text of acts adopted by the College of Commissioners to be identified with certainty.

74. For that purpose, the first paragraph of Article 12 of the Rules of Procedure in force at the relevant time provided that: 'Acts adopted by the Commission, at a meeting or by written procedure, shall be authenticated in the language or languages in which they are binding by the signatures of the President and the Executive Secretary'.

75. Far from being, as the Commission claims, a mere formality for archival purposes, the authentication of acts provided for in the first paragraph of Article 12 of its Rules of Procedure is intended to guarantee legal certainty by ensuring that the text adopted by the college of Commissioners becomes fixed in the languages which are binding. Thus, in the event of a dispute, it can be verified that the texts notified or published correspond precisely to the text adopted by the College and so with the intention of the author.

76. Authentication of acts referred to in the first paragraph of Article 12 of the Commission's Rules of Procedure therefore constitutes an essential procedural requirement within the meaning of Article 173 of the EEC Treaty breach of which gives rise to an action for annulment.

77. In the present case, it is not disputed that, on its own admission, the Commission acted in breach of the first paragraph of Article 12 of its Rules of Procedure by failing to authenticate the contested decision in the way provided for by that article.

BASF transformed the status of internal Rules of Procedure from that of convention to a series of institutional norms, which once established generate duties for the Institution which adopted them. Given the detail of the various Rules of Procedure, the effect of this should not be understated.[31] Yet the judgment is rife with uncertainty.

---

[31]   The current Rules of Procedure of the principal institutions are European Parliament, *Rules of Procedure* (1996, 11th Edition, OOPEC, Luxembourg); Council Decision of 6 December 1993, OJ 1993, L 304/1; Commission Decision 93/492, OJ 1993, L 230/15, as amended by Decision 95/148, OJ 1995, L 97/82; Rules of Procedure of the Court of Justice, OJ 1991, L 176/1,

It is clear that only Rules which are characterised as essential procedural requirements will generate rights for third parties. The Court gives little indication, however, as to how these are to be identified or, for that matter, when a breach is so serious that an act will be declared non-existent.[32]

iv. The Duty to Give Reasons

Article 190 [*253*] EC requires that most significant EC acts state the reasons upon which they are based.

Article 190 [*253*] EC. Regulations, directives and decisions adopted jointly by the European Parliament and the Council, and such acts adopted by the Council or the Commission, shall state the reasons on which they are based and shall refer to any proposals or opinions which were required to be obtained pursuant to this Treaty.

The duty to give reasons obligation has the potential to straddle two approaches to controlling government. In its least ambitious form it is just another essential procedural requirement which structures government discretion by requiring its acts to meet certain formalities, namely the statement of reasons enabling interested parties to be aware of the broad rationality behind the adoption of the measure.[33] On a more ambitious level the duty to state reasons could require complete disclosure of all the circumstances surrounding the measure's adoption. This would include imposing on the EC institutions a duty to account as

---

as amended, OJ 1997, L 103/1; Rules of Procedure of the Court of First Instance, OJ 1991, L 136/1, as amended, OJ 1997, L 103/6.

[32] The Court has therefore ruled that amended proposals made during the legislative process need not be in writing as flexibility is required during that process, Case C-280/93 *Germany v Council* [1994] ECR I-4973.

[33] The duty to give reasons only applies to acts taken by the EC institutions. It does not apply to acts of the Member States, even when taken within the field of application of EC law, Case C-70/95 *Sodemare & others v Regione Lombardia*, Judgment of 17 June 1997.

to why they have not complied with parties' suggestions. The duty of reasons would move from merely protecting transparency to increasing interested parties' participation in the policy process. A dialogue would thereby be introduced into the decision-making process, which would require EC acts to be informed by a minimum content of participatory democracy.[34] The Court has traditionally resisted the latter approach, stating that whilst a duty to give reasons is imposed upon the EC legislator, that duty does not extend to discussing every issue of fact or law raised by parties.[35] In recent years, however, the CFI, at least, has moved towards a more interventionist approach through emphasising that the statement of reasons must be sufficiently extensive to enable parties to defend their rights before the Court.[36]

Case T-459/93 Siemens SA v Commission [1995] ECR II-1675

Between 1985 and 1988 the Brussels Regional authority gave aid to Siemens for data-processing and telecommunications. By a 1992 Decision the Commission ruled that some of the aid granted was illegal and should be repaid. Siemens challenged the Decision arguing, *inter alia*, that the Commission's findings that the aid for advertising and marketing surveys was illegal and that Siemens had artificially split up its applications for aid were inadequately reasoning. The Court found in the Commission's favour but stated:

31. As to its substance, it should be noted that, as is apparent from the relevant case-law, the obligation laid down in Article 190 of the Treaty, requiring the acts referred to in Article 189 to state the reasons on which they are based, is not a mere matter of form but is intended to give an opportunity to the parties of defending their rights, to the

---

[34] Shapiro, M.'The Giving Reasons Requirement' (1992) *University of Chicago Legal Forum* 179.

[35] e.g. Joined Cases 209-215 & 218/78 *Van Landewyck v Commission* [1980] ECR 3125, [1981] 3 CMLR 134; Joined Cases 240-2, 261-2, 268-9/82 *Stichting Sigarettenindustrie v Commission* [1985] ECR 3831, [1987] 3 CMLR 661; Case 42/84 *Remia & Nutricia v Commission* [1985] ECR 2545, [1987] 1 CMLR 1; Case T-8/89 *DSM v Commission* [1991] ECR II-1833; Case T-2/93 *Air France v Commission* [1994] ECR II-323.

[36] See also Case T-166/94 *Koyo Seiko Co. Ltd. v Council* [1994] ECR II-2129; Joined Cases T-481/93 & 484/93 *Vereniging van Exporteurs in Levende Varkers et al. v Commission* [1995] ECR II-2941.

Community judicature of exercising its powers of review and to the Member States and to all interested parties of ascertaining the circumstances in which the Commission has applied the Treaty (see, in particular, the judgment of the Court of Justice in Case 24/62 *Germany v Commission* [1963] ECR 63). However, it is equally apparent from the case-law of the Court of First Instance that, in stating the reasons for the decisions it has to take in order to ensure that the rules of competition are applied, the Commission is not obliged to adopt a position on all the arguments relied on by the parties concerned and it is sufficient if it sets out the facts and the legal considerations having decisive importance in the context of the decision. ...

v. A Right to a Hearing?

The debate about the ambit of Article 190 [*253*] EC leads to the broader question of whether there should be a more general right for individuals to participate in the process leading up to the adoption of an EC act. In the United States, for example, the 'notice and comment' procedure applies to delegated legislation, allowing interested parties to comment on proposed secondary legislation.[37] The benefits to such an approach lie, in part, in a better informed government. At a deeper level, it constitutes the essence of a view of citizenship which sees it as a form of self-rule permitting the integration of the individual into the political community through active participation in the latter's decision-making structures.[38] There are difficulties, however. Even in the United States, the procedure does not apply to all acts, only applying to acts of a legislative character. There is thus first the problem of clarifying which acts the procedures should apply to. In addition, the procedures are time-consuming and costly, and can lead to more complex legislation as each interest group tries to secure provisions which particularly address its interests.[39]

---

[37] Administrative Procedure Act 1946, section 553.

[38] On this see Habermas, J. 'Citizenship and National Identity: Some Reflections on the Future of Europe' (1992) 12 *Praxis* 1, 6-7.

[39] On the difficulties of 'notice and comment' see Hamilton, R. 'Procedures for the Adoption of Rules of General Applicability: The Need for Procedural Innovation in Administrative Rulemaking' (1972) 62 *Columbia Law Review* 1976; Williams, S. 'Hybrid Rulemaking under the Administrative Procedure Act: A Legal and Empirical Analysis' (1975) 42 *University of Chicago Law*

Within the European Union, there is a practice, made a Treaty requirement at Amsterdam, that the Commission consult widely before it proposes primary legislation.[40] Yet this requirement does not apply to delegated legislative, and the duty to consult widely does not extend as far as the Commission giving a hearing to any interested party.[41]

Case C-32/95P Commission v Lisrestal & Others [1996] ECR I-5373

The Commission granted 346 million Portuguese escudos towards a vocational training scheme to improve employment opportunities in Portugal for 687 young persons under the age of 25, with a further 283 million escudos to be provided from DAFSE (the Portuguese Social Security Budget). An advance payment of 50% was paid over to the undertakings. In an audit, however, serious financial irregularities were discovered. After having given the Portuguese Government an opportunity to submit observations, the Commission determined that 138 million escudos should be repaid. The CFI annulled the Commission's Decision on the ground that the undertakings' rights of defence could not be protected through the intermediary of the Member State.[42] The Court of Justice dismissed the Commission's appeal.

21. Observance of the right to be heard is, in all proceedings initiated against a person which are liable to culminate in a measure adversely affecting that person, a fundamental principle of Community law which must be guaranteed even in the absence of any rules governing the proceedings in question (see, inter alia, Case C-135/92 *Fiskano v Commission* [1994] ECR I-2885, paragraph 39, and Joined Cases C-48/90 and C-66/90 *Netherlands and Others v Commission* [1992] ECR I-565, paragraph 44). That principle requires that the addressees of decisions which significantly affect their interests should be placed in a position in which they may effectively make known their views.

.....

24. The procedure which led to the decision at issue was 'initiated against' the respondents for the purposes of the case-law cited in paragraph 21 of this judgment.

    Review 401.

[40]   *Protocol to the EC Treaty on the application of the principles of subsidiarity and proportionality, paragraph 9.*

[41]   Lenaerts, K. & Vanhamme, J. 'Procedural Rights of Private Parties in the Community Administrative Process' (1997) 34 *CMLRev* 531.

[42]   Case T-450/93 *Lisrestal & Others v Commission* [1994] ECR II-1177.

Despite the central role played by the Member State concerned in the system established by Regulation No 2950/83, the respondents were directly implicated in the investigation which led to the decision.

.....

31. In its second argument the Commission claims that the decision does not impose any sanction or penalty on the respondents. It is merely an administrative corollary of the decision in which the Commission authorized the financial assistance and laid down the criteria to which it was subject.

32. That argument cannot be accepted.

33. As the Court of First Instance found, the decision deprives the respondents of the whole of the assistance which had initially been granted to them. They therefore directly suffer the economic consequences of the decision, which affects their assets because they incur primary liability to repay the sums unduly paid within 15 days of receipt of the letters of 24 April 1992 and 7 May 1992 from DAFSE informing them of the adoption of the decision by the Commission.

34. It must therefore be held that the decision significantly affects the respondents' interests.

The requirement that a party's interests be directly and significantly adversely affected is quite a high test of standing. The first part of the test that a party's interests be directly affected renders it unlikely that there is a right to a hearing in the case of general legislation, as the interest will be considered to be too diffuse. The requirement also configures the nature of the right. It is a right to protect private property and thus its enfranchising potential is limited, as participation is not enjoyed *qua* citizen but as property-owner.

Wider participatory rights have been granted by the EC legislature. There is indeed every reason to think this might contain. These rights are granted in a narrowly defined context and on an *ad hoc* basis.[43] For some commentators this is not sufficient. Shapiro has

---

43   e.g. The CFI has recognised the right of regional and worker bodies affected by a concentration to a hearing before the Commission under the Merger Regulation, Regulation 4064/89/EC, OJ 1990, L 252/13, Article 18(4). Case T-96/92 *Comité Central v Commission* [1995] ECR II-1213. Notice and

observed that the EU in the 1990s is facing the same forces as did the United States at the time of the entry into force of the 'notice and comment' procedure.[44] He cites in particular the growth in constitutional judicial review and the suspicion of many in the technocracy in Brussels. One way to ameliorate these tensions is to develop wider participatory rights. These rights not only open up the decision-making processes to outside interests. By allowing the judge to concentrate on due process, they all also prevent him from becoming subsumed in the mire of the substantive issues.

IV. Infringement of the EC Treaty or any Rule of Law Relating To Its Application

The discretion of EC administrators is structured not just by procedural rules but also a number of substantial constraints. It is clearly illegal for them to do anything which is expressly prohibited by the EC Treaty. The instances of this occurring are rare. Far more frequent are breaches of the principles developed by the Court of Justice. The first of these are fundamental rights recognised by the Court of Justice. The second are general principles of law developed by the Court. The distinction between the two is that fundamental rights recognise a capacity on the part of the individual to do or possess something, such as freedom of expression or the right to respect for privacy. It is the interference with this by the administration which is egregious. The rationale for general principles of law is not respect for particular individual interests. These have been characterised rather as principles of good administration. By placing limits and structuring government, they provide certain general

---

comment procedures have also been established in certain external trade instruments, Regulation 3285/94 on common rules for imports from third countries, OJ 1994, L 349/53, Article 6.

[44] Shapiro, M. 'Codification of Administrative Law: The Us and the Union' (1996) 2 *ELJ* 26, 41-44. See also Harlow, C. 'Codification of EC Administrative Procedures? Fitting the Foot to the Shoe or the Shoe to the Foot' (1996) 2 *ELJ* 3, 17-19.

guarantees to all citizens, irrespective of their activities, about the nature and degree of government intrusion into their lives.

i. Fundamental Rights

Traditionally, a trichotomy has been developed between civil rights, political rights and social rights.[45] Civil rights focus on the autonomy of the individual. They thus included freedoms such as freedom of speech, assembly, and religion; the right to own property and to trade; the right to justice, and the right to be protected against inhuman or degrading treatment. They are to be distinguished from political rights, whose essence is the right to participate in the exercise of power e.g. the right to vote or participate in any arm of government - be it legislative, executive or judicial. Finally, there are social rights which go 'the whole range from the right to a modicum of economic welfare and security to the right to share in full in the social heritage and to live the life of a civilised being according to the standards of society'.

Whilst EC law recognises a variety of political and social rights, the doctrine of fundamental rights developed by the Court of Justice dwells exclusively upon civil rights. In principle, the doctrine is an open-ended one. Certainly, the sources from which the Court draws inspiration, the constitutional traditions of Member States and international human rights treaties, are dynamic ones which are likely to evolve over time, with the corollary potential this offers for the recognition of additional civil rights and the establishment of social rights as a measure of review.[46] The practice of the Court so far has

---

[45] Marshall T. & Bottomore T, *Citizenship and Social Class* (1992, Revised Edition, Pluto Press, London).

[46] On the possible recognition of social rights as general principles of law see Betten, L. 'The Protection of Fundamental Social Rights in the European Union - Discussion Paper' in Betten, L & MacDevitt, D. (eds.) The Protection of Fundamental Social Rights in the European Union (1996, Kluwer, The Hague); Szyszczak, E. 'Social Rights as General Principles of Law' in Neuwahl, N. & Rosas, A. (eds.) *The European Union and Human Rights* (1995, Martijnus Nijhoff, Dordrecht).

been rather conservative, and the rights it has recognised fall fairly easily into three categories.

The first are assorted civil liberties. These include the right to protect of human dignity;[47] right to respect for family and private life;[48] freedom of religion;[49] freedom of trade union activity;[50]   protection against discrimination on grounds relating to sex,[51] and freedom of expression.[52] Without exception, the jurisprudence on the content of these rights is impoverished, particularly when compared with that of the European Court of Human Rights, with the Court of Justice refusing to expand upon their content.[53] Another criticism has been that the Court has been fairly conservative in the rights which it has recognised. It has not yet recognised a right to protection against discrimination on grounds of race, despite having had the opportunity to do so.[54] It has also been criticised for not developing protection of lesbian and gay rights[55] or the protection of immigrants' rights or of those with a disability.[56]

---

[47] Case 29/69 *Stauder v City of Ulm* [1969] ECR 419, [1970] CMLR 112.

[48] Case 136/79 *National Panasonic v Commission* [1980] ECR 2033, [1980] 3 CMLR 169; Case 249/86 *Commission v Germany* [1989] ECR 1263, [1990] 3 CMLR 540; Case C-404/92P *X v Commission* [1994] ECR I-4737.

[49] Case 130/75 *Prais* [1976] ECR 1589, [1976] 2 CMLR 708.

[50] Case 175/73 *Union Syndicale v Council* [1974] ECR 917, [1975] 1 CMLR 131.

[51] Case 149/77 *DeFrenne v Sabena (No.3)* [1978] ECR 1365, [1978] 3 CMLR 312.

[52] Case 100/88 *Oyowe & Traore v Commission* [1989] 4285; Case C-260/89 *ERT V DEP* [1991] ECR I-2925, [1994] 4 CMLR 540; Case C-368/95 *Vereinigte Familiapress Zeitungsverlags- und vertriebs GmbH v Heinrich Bauer Verlag*, Judgment of 26 June 1997.

[53] Whilst there is considerable case law on the right to equal treatment for men and women in the workplace. This all takes place within the context of Directive 76/207/EEC, OJ 1976 L 39/40.

[54] Case 100/88 *Oyowe & Traore v Commission* [1989] 4285.

[55] See Waaldijk, K. & Clapham, A. (eds.) *Homosexuality: A European Community issue* (1993, Martijnus Nijhoff, Dordrecht).

[56] On this see De Búrca, G. 'The Language of Rights and European Integration' 29, 34-39 in Shaw, J. & More, G. (eds.) *New Legal Dynamics of European Union* (1995, Clarendon, Oxford).

The second set of rights are economic and property rights. There is a developed jurisprudence and the Court has recognised a variety of economic rights including the freedom to pursue a trade or profession;[57] the right to own property;[58] the right to carry out an economic activity[59] and the freedom to choose with whom to do business.[60] The Court has not taken an absolutist view of property but has required, rather, that be examined in their social context. No interference with an individual's economic rights will be illegal if it can be shown that it was necessary to attain some objective of general interest. As the next judgment illustrates, the Court has used this to give the EC Institutions considerable latitude.[61]

Case C-280/93 Germany v Council [1994] ECR I-4973

The banana market had been traditionally divided into national markets with different Member States obtaining their bananas from different sources. Germany benefited from a Protocol which allowed it to import 1.37 million bananas free of customs duty. It imported these mainly from Latin America, which produced the cheapest bananas. Meanwhile, under the fourth Lomé Convention the Community agreed to import bananas free of customs duty from the ACP States (Africa, Caribbean and Pacific States). These were more expensive and were imported into France, the United Kingdom, Italy, Spain, Portugal and Greece, who protected their markets against imports from other third countries. Regulation 404/93 attempted to establish a common regime for bananas. It established a general tariff quota of two million bananas. ACP bananas falling within this quota did not need to pay a tariff. Bananas from other sources had to pay a reduced tariff of ECU 100 per tonne. Imports of all other

---

[57]   Case 240/83 *ADBHU* [1985] ECR 531.
[58]   Case 44/79 *Hauer v Rheinland Pfalz* [1979] ECR 3727, [1980] 3 CMLR 42; Case C-44/89 *Von Deetzen v Hauptzollamt Oldenburg* [1991] ECR I-5119.
[59]   Case 230/78 *Eridania v Minister of Agriculture and Fishery* [1979] ECR 2749.
[60]   Joined Cases C-90/90 & C-91/90 *Neu v Secrétaire d'Etat à l'Agriculture et à la Viticulture* [1991] ECR I-3617.
[61]   For an economic critique of the EC banana regime see Read, R. 'The EC Internal Banana Market: The Issues and the Dilemma' (1994) 17 *World Economy* 219.

bananas were subject to a far higher tariff. The licenses for this quota were subdivided between the two classes of operator. Germany challenged the regime.

78. Both the right to property and the freedom to pursue a trade or business form part of the general principles of Community law. However, those principles are not absolute, but must be viewed in relation to their social function. Consequently, the exercise of the right to property and the freedom to pursue a trade or profession may be restricted, particularly in the context of a common organization of a market, provided that those restrictions in fact correspond to objectives of general interest pursued by the Community and do not constitute a disproportionate and intolerable interference, impairing the very substance of the rights guaranteed (Case 265/87 *Schräder v Hauptzollamt Gronau* [1989] ECR 2237, paragraph 15, ...).

79. The right to property of traders in third-country bananas is not called into question by the introduction of the Community quota and the rules for its subdivision. No economic operator can claim a right to property in a market share which he held at a time before the establishment of a common organization of a market, since such a market share constitutes only a momentary economic position exposed to the risks of changing circumstances.

.....

81. With reference to the alleged infringement of the freedom to pursue a trade or business, it must be stated that the introduction of the tariff quota and the machinery for subdividing it does indeed alter the competitive position of economic operators on the German market in particular, who were previously the only ones able to import third-country bananas free of any tariff restriction, within a quota which was adjusted annually to the needs of the market. It must still be examined whether the restrictions introduced by the Regulation correspond to objectives of general Community interest and do not impair the very substance of that right.

82. The restriction of the right to import third-country bananas imposed on the economic operators on the German market is inherent in the establishment of a common organization of the market designed to ensure that the objectives of Article 39 of the Treaty are safeguarded and that the Community's international obligations under the Lomé Convention are complied with. The abolition of the differing national systems, in particular the exceptional arrangements still enjoyed by operators on the German market and the protective regimes enjoyed by those trading in Community and traditional ACP bananas on other markets, made it necessary to limit the volume of imports of third-country bananas into the Community. A common organization of the market had to be implemented while Community and ACP bananas were not displaced from the entire common market following the disappearance of the protective barriers enabling them to be disposed of with protection from competition from third-country bananas.

83. The differing situations of banana traders in the various Member States made it necessary, in view of the objective of integrating the various national markets, to establish machinery for dividing the tariff quota among the different categories of traders concerned. That machinery is intended both to encourage operators dealing in Community and traditional ACP bananas to obtain supplies of third-country bananas and to encourage importers of third-country bananas to distribute Community and ACP bananas. It should also in the long term allow economic operators who have traditionally marketed third-country bananas to participate, at the level of the overall Community quota, in the two sub-quotas introduced.

.....

87. Accordingly, the restriction imposed by the Regulation on the freedom of traditional traders in third-country bananas to pursue their trade or business corresponds to objectives of general Community interest and does not impair the very substance of that right.

The limited protection to economic rights offered by EC law has drawn criticism from two sources. The first was liberal academics. Petersmann, in particular, claimed that the Court had allowed a regime to be put in place which not only distorted competition but also taxed consumers by forcing them to buy the more expensive ACP bananas.[62] More seriously, doubts have been implied about whether there exist sufficient guarantees by an interim order of the German Constitutional Court in November 1995 in which it required import licenses to be given to a trader, stating that the property rights of the importer must be protected if it risks going bankrupt as a result of an EC Regulation.[63]

The third form of fundamental right developed have been rights of defence. The majority of the cases which have discussed rights of

---

[62]   Petersmann, E-U. 'Proposals for a New Constitution for the European Union: Building Blocks for a Constitutional Theory and Constitutional Law of the EU' (1995) 32 *CMLRev* 1123, 1164-1172. For comment see also Everling, U. 'Will Europe Slip on Bananas? The Bananas judgment of the Court of Justice and national courts' (1996) 33 *CMLRev* 401.

[63]   Neue Juristische Wochenschrift (1995) 950. For comment see Reich, N. 'Judge-made "Europe à la carte": Some Remarks on Recent Conflicts between European and German Constitutional Law provoked by the Banana Litigation' (1996) 7 EJIL 103; Zuleeg, M. 'The European Constitution under Constitutional Constraints: The German Scenario' (1997) 22 *ELRev* 19, 33-34.

defence have been in relation to the Commission's powers in the field of competition law, and it is within this context that they have been developed most extensively. These rights of defence include the right to judicial review of any administrative action which deprives any individual of the benefit of their rights;[64] the right to legal assistance and the right to all lawyer-client communications prepared for the purpose of defending oneself to be privileged;[65] the right to be heard in one's own defence before any administrative sanction is imposed;[66] protection from self-incrimination,[67] and access to the Commission's file.[68]

The protection is fairly extensive, particularly when it is remembered that the complainants are normally large multinational enterprises who are capable of exploiting these procedural rights to maximum advantage. There has still been some criticism of the Court's approach. The most substantive point relates to the refusal of the Court to develop the point that hearings be heard within a reasonable time. To be sure, where EC institutions are under a duty to act, parties can bring an action requiring them to act.[69] Yet this possibility is undermined in two ways. The first is that the Court has not only always stated that the institutions must be given a reasonable period of time within which to act, but has also taken a very relaxed view of how long that may be.[70] It has ruled, for example, that four years is not an unreasonable period for

---

64   Case 222/86 *UNECTEF v Heylens* [1987] ECR 4097, [1989] 1 CMLR 901.

65   Case 155/79 *AM & S Europe Ltd. v Commission* [1982] ECR 1575, [1982] 2 CMLR 264.

66   Case 17/74 *Transocean Marine Paint* [1974] ECR 1063, [1974] 2 CMLR 459.

67   Case 374/87 *ORKEM* [1989] ECR 3283, [1991] 4 CMLR 502.

68   This is not an unqualified right. It is subject to the principle that confidential information supplied by third parties be respected. Furthermore, failure by the Commission to disclose information will only render any Commission Decision automatically illegal where the information was inculpatory. Exculpatory information will only render any Decision illegal if the Court considers that it effectively hindered the applicant's rights of defence, Case T-30/91 *Solvay v Commission* [1995] ECR II-1775.

69   Article 175 [*232*] EC. See pp 566-572.

70   On this in relation to competition proceedings see Montag, 'The Case for a Radical Reform of the Infringement Procedure under Regulation 17' (1996) 4 *ECLR* 430.

time for the Commission to carry out an anti-dumping investigation.[71] Secondly, even where it is considered that an unreasonable period of time has been taken, that alone will not make the act of that institution illegal. In *Isidoro Oliveira* it took the Commission 38 months to come to a decision reducing the assistance it gave from the European Social Fund to a Portuguese vocational training scheme, but the CFI did not consider that the period of time taken, unreasonable though its length was, invalidated the Commission's Decision.[72]

ii. General Principles of Law

One can point to a number of principles of good administration within the Community. The procedural requirements discussed earlier in this Chapter are one example. One can also point to developments pursued in other Chapters, such as subsidiarity and transparency, which contribute to the general standard of administration which can be expected by EU citizens. There are only three general principles of law - the principles of proportionality, non-discrimination and legal certainty. It is right to claim that not too strong a contrast should be drawn from these general principles of law and other principles of administration or fundamental rights.[73] There is a slightly different emphasis of rationale. In principle, general principles of law are not concerned with how an authority comes to a decision or the extent of its administrative power. Instead, they seek to impose a substantive rationality upon the authority. They are there to ensure that, after all the other checks, it does not exercise its power in a capricious or arbitrary manner.

---

[71]   Case 121/86 *Epicheiriseon Metalleftikon Viomichanikon Kai Naftaliakon v Council* [1989] ECR 3919.

[72]   Case T-73/95 *Estabelecimentos Isodoro Oliveira v Commission*, Judgment of 19 March 1997.

[73]   Craig, P. & De Búrca, G. *EC Law: Text, Cases and Materials* (1995, Clarendon, Oxford) 339.

a. Proportionality

The concept of proportionality has its oldest legal heritage in Germany.[74] First used in Prussia in the late nineteenth century, the rationale of the principle resides in there being a presumption in favour of private autonomy and against State intrusion.[75] The classic formulation developed in Germany therefore contained three strands. The first is that the measure must be the most suitable means of attaining the objectives of the administrator. This would only be the case if the measure was necessary to achieving those aims. The second is that, of several equally suitable measures, that measure must be chosen which imposes the least interference on individuals. The third is that the means used must not be out of proportion to the ends pursued.[76] The formula most frequently used in EC law has followed that formulation.

Case C-331/88 R v Minister for Agriculture, Fisheries and Food, ex parte FEDESA [1990] ECR 4023, [1991] 1 CMLR 507

A number of traders challenged British regulations implementing Directive 88/14/EC, which prohibited the administration of five hormones to animals. They claimed that the ban was disproportionate as it would lead to the development of a black market in these hormones; the prohibition was unnecessary as consumer anxiety could be allayed by dissemination of information, and the ban caused excessive losses for them. In ruling against them the Court had this to say on proportionality.

13. The Court has consistently held that the principle of proportionality is one of the general principles of Community law. By virtue of that principle, the lawfulness of the prohibition of an economic activity is subject to the condition that the prohibitory measures are appropriate and necessary in order to achieve the objectives legitimately pursued by the legislation in question; when there is a choice between several appropriate

---

[74] For an excellent comparison of the different formulations of the principle across Europe see Emiliou, N. *The Principle of Proportionality in European Law* (1996, Kluwer, London).

[75] Schwarze, J. *European Administrative Law* (1992, Sweet & Maxwell, OOPEC, London) 685.

[76] Emiliou, N. supra n.74, 24.

measures recourse must be had to the least onerous, and the disadvantages caused must not be disproportionate to the aims pursued.

The Court has not applied the principle mechanistically, and the intensity of the review varies according to the subject-matter reviewed.[77] In areas where the Court is more hesitant about intervening, it restricts itself to considering whether there has been a manifest error of fact on the part of the administrator[78] or whether the measure is manifestly inappropriate. These formulations more closely resemble French formulations of administrative illegality - in particular that of *erreur manifeste d'appréciation des faits*, which governs situations where there has been a blatant error on evaluation of the facts and *bilan-coût-avantages*, which requires that there be a correlation between the advantages and the disadvantages of a measure to the public.[79] These formulations are less restrictive and give greater leeway to the administrator. This approach is taken where the Community legislature enjoys broad discretionary powers.[80] In such circumstances, the greater discretion presupposes a wider freedom for the legislature. This freedom to choose between alternative measures would not only be frustrated but also the task of legislation made increasingly difficult if the Court was always to insist that the legislature adopted the legislation, which, in the Court's view, was the most suitable and least restrictive. The Court has therefore applied a weaker standard of review to all harmonisation measures, stating that leeway should be given because of the difficulties in bringing together complex, national provisions.[81] Such leeway also

---

[77]   De Búrca, G. 'The Principle of Proportionality and Its Application in EC Law' (1993) 13 *YBEL* 105.

[78]   Joined Cases C-133/93, C-300/93 & C-312/93 *Crispoltoni* [1994] ECR I-4863.

[79]   Emiliou, N. supra n.74 84-95.

[80]   In certain circumstances it is permissible for Member States to derogate from EC norms. Such action must be proportionate, however. The other situation in which the Court is willing to apply a more tolerant regime, albeit rather inconsistently is where the Community norm touches on areas of particular sensitivity to the Member States.

[81]   Case C-63/89 *Les Assurances du Crédit & Compagnie Belge d'Assurance Crédit v Council & Commission* [1991] ECR I-1799, [1991] 2 CMLR 737.

applies to any area in which the Community legislature enjoys a discretionary legislative power. In *Fedesa*, for example, the Court went on to consider the measure lawful, stating:[82]

14. However, with regard to judicial review of compliance with those conditions it must be stated that in matters concerning the common agricultural policy the Community legislature has a discretionary power which corresponds to the political responsibilities given to it by Articles 40 and 43 of the Treaty. Consequently, the legality of a measure adopted in that sphere can be affected only if the measure is manifestly inappropriate having regard to the objective which the competent institution is seeking to pursue. (See in particular the judgment in Case 265/87, *Schräder* [1989] ECR 2237, paras. 21 and 22).

The proportionality principle, on any formulation, assumes a distinction between the objectives a measure pursued and the means used to pursue those objectives. It then regulates the relationship between those means and those objectives. Majone has labelled this methodology decisionism, and considers it to have a number of limitations. The first is that the idea of the EC administration having clear fixed objectives adopts a unitary analysis of the decision-maker. It ignores both intra-institutional and inter-institutional conflicts. He also considers such analysis obscures the distinction between policies and decisions. Whilst decisions are taken in relation to a particular factual situation, policies are, however, long-range in nature as they extend beyond the immediate scenario into the future. Policies deal with scenarios where facts are uncertain and risk endemic. It may not be appropriate to subject them to the same framework as decisions. Majone's most wide-ranging criticism of decisionism is his third one.

---

[82] For a more recent example see Case C-22/94 *Irish Farmers Association and Others v Minister for Agriculture, Food and Fisheries,* Judgment of 15 April 1997.

Majone, G. *Evidence, Argument and Persuasion in the Policy Process* (1989, Yale University Press, New Haven) 17-18.

A third limitation of decisionism is its exclusive preoccupation with outcomes and lack of concern for the processes whereby the outcomes are produced. A lack of concern for process is justified in some situations. If the correctness or fairness of the outcome can be determined unambiguously, the manner in which the decision is made is often immaterial; only results count. But when the factual or value premises are moot, when there are no generally accepted criteria of rightness, the procedure of decision-making acquires special significance and cannot be treated as purely instrumental.

Even in formal decision analysis the explicit recognition of uncertainty forces a significant departure from a strict orientation toward outcomes. Under conditions of uncertainty different alternatives correspond to different probability distributions of the consequences, so that it is no longer possible to determine unambiguously what the optimal decision is. Hence, the usual criterion of rationality - according to which an action is rational if it can be explained as the choosing of the best means to achieve given objectives - is replaced by the weaker notion of consistency. The rational decision maker is no longer an optimiser, strictly speaking. All that is required now, and all that the principle of maximising expected utility guarantees, is that the choice be consistent with the decision maker's valuations of the probability and utility of the various consequences. Notice that consistency is a procedural, not a substantive, criterion.

Exclusive preoccupation with outcomes is a serious limitation of decisionism, since social processes seldom have only instrumental value for the people who engage in them. In most areas of social activity, 'the processes and rules that constitute the enterprise and define the roles of its participants matter quite apart from any identifiable "end state" that is ultimately produced. Indeed in many cases it is the process itself that matters most to those who take part in it.'

b. Legal Certainty

The principle of legal certainty is derived from two conceptions. The first premises legal validity, in part, on a stabilisation of private expectations. That is to say:

> 'established law guarantees the enforcement of legally expected behaviour and therewith the certainty of law'.[83]

---

[83]   Habermas, J. *Between Facts and Norms* (1996, Polity, Cambridge) 198. Habermas perceives this as only dimension of legal validity, the other is that the law must be legitimated through its enactment through rational law-making

On such a view the coercive powers of law have a value in that they serve to pattern and structure social life. Yet this will not occur if the legal regime itself is unpredictable and opaque to such a degree that it cannot be communicated to its subjects. The second conception of legal certainty has a liberal premise. It sees the ability to plan one's life as an integral part of individual autonomy. The law is therefore required to maintain a modicum of consistency and predictability in government behaviour, so that the private domain can be secured.[84]

The principle of legal certainty is protected in some form in all national legal orders,[85] and has been protected within the EC legal order for some time.[86] Its most striking manifestation is the prohibition against retroactivity, which requires that a measure should not take effect prior to its publication.[87] This needs further explanation. A measure will not be retroactive if it regulates the future effects of situations which arose prior to publication. It will only be retroactive if it applies to events which have already been concluded.[88]

The principle is absolute in relation to penal measures.[89] Other measures may exceptionally take effect before publication where the purpose to be achieved so demands and where the legitimate concerns of those concerned are respected.[90] In *Fedesa*, therefore, following the annulment of a Directive outlawing the use of certain hormones as a result of a breach of an essential procedural defect, the subsequent Directive, which was published on 7 March 1988, stipulated that it was

---

procedures.

[84] e.g. Streit, M. 'Economic Order, Private Law and Public Policy: The Freiburg School of Law and Economics in Perspective' (1992) 142 *Journal of Institutional and Theoretical Economics* 675, 691-694.

[85] On this see Schwarze, J. *European Administrative Law* (1992, Sweet & Maxwell, OOPEC, London) 874 *et seq*.

[86] It was first set out in Joined Cases 42 & 49/59 *SNUPAT v High Authority* [1961] ECR 109.

[87] Case 84/78 *Tomadini v Amminstrazione delle Finanze dello Stato* [1979] ECR 1801, [1980] 2 CMLR 573.

[88] Case 63/83 *R v Kirk* [1984] ECR 2689, [1984] 2 CMLR 522.

[89] Case C-331/88 *R v Ministry of Agriculture, Fisheries and Food, ex parte FEDESA* [1990] ECR I-4023, [1991] 1 CMLR 507.

[90] Case 98/78 *Racke v Hauptzollamt Mainz* [1979] ECR 69.

to take effect from the beginning of that year.[91] The reason for this was to prevent a regulatory gap developing as a result of the annulment of the earlier Directive, which would have left the market unregulated for that earlier period. The Court considered there to be no breach of the principle of the legal certainty in light of the short timespan between the annulment of the first Directive and the publication of the second.

The principle of legal certainty is more wide-ranging than a simple prohibition on non-retroactivity. It requires that individuals are given sufficient information in a sufficiently precise manner to enable them to comply with the law.

Case T-115/94 Opel Austria v Council, [1997] ECR II-39

The European Economic Area came into force on 1 January 1994, and prohibited the imposition of tariffs on trade between the EC and Austria. On 20 December 1993, eleven days before the entry into force of the Agreement, the Council adopted a Regulation which imposed a 4.9% tariff on gearboxes produced by General Motors Austria (which subsequently became Opel Austria). The Regulation was published in the Official Journal dated 31 December 1993. Opel was not notified of the Regulation until 6 January 1994 and the Regulation was not made available to the public until 11 January 1994. The Court ruled that the Regulation did not come into effect until the last date. Opel brought an action claiming the Regulation violated the principle of legal certainty.

124. According to the case law, moreover, Community legislation must be certain and its application foreseeable by individuals. The principle of legal certainty requires that every measure of the institutions having legal effects must be clear and precise and must be brought to the notice of the person concerned in such a way that he can ascertain exactly the time at which the measure comes into being and starts to have legal effects. That requirement of legal certainty must be observed all the more strictly in the case of a measure liable to have financial consequences in order that those concerned may know precisely the extent of the obligations which it imposes on them (see Case 169/80 *Administration des Douanes v Gondrand Frères and Garancini* [1981] ECR 1931, paragraph 17; Case 70/83 *Kloppenburg v Finanzsamt Leer* [1984] ECR 1075, paragraph 11; Case 325/85 *Ireland v Commission* [1987] ECR 5041, paragraph 18; Joined Cases T-18/89 and T-24/89 *Tagaras v Court of Justice* [1991] ECR II-53, paragraph 40).

---

[91]   Case C-331/88 *R v Ministry of Agriculture, Fisheries and Food, ex parte FEDESA* [1990] ECR I-4023, [1991] 1 CMLR 507.

125. By adopting the contested regulation on 20 December 1993 when it knew with certainty that the EEA Agreement would enter into force on 1 January 1994, the Council knowingly created a situation in which, with effect from January 1994, two contradictory rules of law would co-exist, namely the contested regulation, which is directly applicable in the national legal systems and re-establishes a 4.9% import duty on F-15 gearboxes produced by the applicant; and Article 10 of the EEA Agreement, which has direct effect and prohibits customs duties on imports and any charges having equivalent effect. Consequently, the contested regulation cannot be regarded as Community legislation which is certain and its operation/application cannot be regarded as foreseeable by those subject to it. It follows that the Council also infringed the principle of legal certainty.

126. Although those two infringements of general legal principles must be regarded as being in themselves sufficiently serious to warrant the annulment of the contested regulation, it should also be established whether, as the applicant alleges, the Council deliberately backdated the issue of the Official Journal in which the regulation was published.

.....

132. In acting in that way, it again infringed the principle of legal certainty, which, according to the case-law referred to in paragraph 124 of this judgment, requires that any measure of the institutions having legal effects must not only be clear and precise, but also be brought to the notice of the person concerned in such a way that he can ascertain exactly the time at which the measure comes into being and starts to have legal effects.

133. The conduct of the Council's administration must therefore be regarded as particularly serious, since it is contrary to the Council's own formal instructions to the Publications Office 'intended to ensure that the date of publication borne by each issue of the Official Journal corresponds to the date on which that issue is in fact available to the public in all the languages at the said office' (*Racke*, paragraph 15). Furthermore, as the applicant has correctly observed, the legal framework which existed on 31 December 1993 was different from that which existed after 1 January 1994, the date on which the EEA Agreement entered into force.

The principle of legitimate expectations is often linked to that of legal certainty. Yet its rationale, in EC law at least, is different. Its roots lie in the concept of good faith[92] and require that having induced an operator to take one course of action, the administration should not then renege on that, so that the individual suffers loss.

---

[92] Case T-115/94 *Opel Austria v Council*, [1997] ECR II 39, paragraph 93.

Regulation 594/91 set up a system of import quotas for ozone depleting substances. Once a quota was allocated to an undertaking under the Regulation, it then had to apply for an import licence. The applicant was granted a quota by the Commission in early 1994 of chlorofluorocarbon 11 (CFC 11) for feedstock use in the manufacture of other products. The Commission then refused a request for licences to import two consignments of CFC 11 from Russia. At the time of the refusal, two trains had already left, one bound for France with a consignment of CFC 11, the other bound for the former Soviet Union with the intention of picking up a second consignment of the same substance. The applicant claimed a breach of legitimate expectations.

31. According to consistent case-law, the principle of the protection of legitimate expectations forms part of the Community legal order (Case 112/77 *Toepfer v Commission* [1978] ECR 1019, paragraph 19). The right to rely on that principle extends to any individual who is in a situation in which it is apparent that the Community administration, by giving him precise assurances, has led him to entertain justified expectations (Case T-534/93 *Grynberg and Hall v Commission* [1994] ECR-SC II-595, paragraph 51, and Case T-571/93 *Lefebvre and Others v Commission* [1995] ECR II-2379, paragraph 72). On the other hand, if a prudent and discriminating trader could have foreseen the adoption of a Community measure likely to affect his interests, he cannot avail himself of that principle if the measure is then adopted (Case 78/77 *Lührs v Hauptzollamt Hamburg-Jonas* [1978] ECR 169, point 6, and Case 265/85 *Van den Bergh en Jurgens v Commission* [1987] ECR 1155, paragraph 44).

32. In the light of these principles, it is necessary to consider whether the applicant could, by reason of the fact that an import quota had been allocated to it, have had a reasonable expectation that the import licences applied for would subsequently be granted and whether, as a prudent and discriminating trader, it could not have foreseen the Commission's refusal to grant those licences.

33. In this regard, the Court notes at the outset that there are two stages in the administrative procedure laid down in Regulation No 594/91 for obtaining authorization to import into the Community substances that deplete the ozone layer: first, the allocation of a quota under Article 3 of Regulation No 594/91 and, second, the issue, pursuant to Article 4 thereof, of one or more import licences corresponding to the quota allocated. It follows that the right to import a substance, accorded when a quota is allocated, takes effect only once an import licence has been issued.

34. It follows from all of the foregoing that the applicant could not, in good faith, have expected that import licences would be issued to it. No expectation could be derived from the allocation to it of an import quota, since that is merely the first stage in securing an effective right to import a substance. In those circumstances, the Court takes the view that, in contrast to the applicant, a prudent and discriminating trader would not have set in motion the transport by train of the consignments ordered without awaiting the Commission's decision on the application for import licences and without taking the precautions necessary to safeguard its interests in the event of its application for licences being rejected. Furthermore, the Court of Justice has stated in its case-law that a finding that legitimate expectations have arisen cannot be made where the measure liable to give rise to such expectations has been withdrawn by the administration within a reasonable period (Case 15/85 *Consorzio Cooperative d'Abruzzo v Commission* [1987] ECR 1005, paragraphs 12 to 17). In the present case, the import quota was allocated to the applicant on 4 February 1994. The latter sent its application for the grant of licences to the Commission on 15 February 1994 and the licences were refused on 24 February 1994. The Court considers that, in those circumstances, the administration acted within a reasonable period. It follows that, by beginning to place its import orders on 17 February 1994, a mere two days after submitting those applications for import licences and without awaiting the outcome, the applicant jeopardized its position by its own actions.

35. The Court also takes the view that, as an undertaking making active use of chemical substances, in particular those coming within the scope of Regulation No 594/91, the applicant was in a position to realize that the use to which it intended putting those substances clearly did not correspond to that for which a quota had been allocated to it, that is to say 'use as feedstock in the manufacture of other chemicals'. In its quota application, the applicant designated the category 'feedstock use in the manufacture of other products' and not that of 'feedstock use in the manufacture of other chemicals', which suggests that it was already aware at that stage that the description of polyurethane foam as a chemical might be open to question. In the light of those factors, the Commission's ultimate refusal cannot be treated as unforeseeable.

36. Moreover, a legitimate expectation cannot arise from conduct on the part of the administration which is inconsistent with Community rules (Case 316/86 *Hauptzollamt Hamburg-Jonas v Krücken* [1988] ECR 2213, paragraph 23). In that regard, the Commission allocated to the applicant a quota for the importation of CFC 11 for 'use as feedstock in the manufacture of other chemicals', notwithstanding the fact that the applicant had, in both the initial and the amended versions of its application, clearly indicated that it intended to use the imported CFC 11 for the production of polyurethane foam. To describe polyurethane foam as a 'chemical' is imprecise from a scientific point of view. Moreover, pursuant to the rules and definitions agreed on by the Community at international level (see paragraph 1), polyurethane foam cannot be treated as a product in the manufacture of which CFC 11 can be described as having a 'use as feedstock in the manufacture of other chemicals' since it is not eliminated in the production process. These details were, in particular, submitted by the Commission at the hearing and were not contested by the applicant. It follows that, by allocating a quota to the applicant precisely for that category of use, when it knew or ought to have known that the applicant intended to produce polyurethane foam, the Commission misapplied the Community rules in force, in particular Article 3 of and Annex II to Regulation No 594/91, as well as its Notice of 10 July 1993. The Commission's conduct was thus inconsistent with the

Community rules and could not therefore give rise to justified expectations on the applicant's part.

It is mentioned that legitimate expectations will be generated wherever precise assurances are given by the Community administration. These assurances do not have to be individualised. They need only predict EC future action. In *Sofrimport*, for example, the Commission was delegated powers to take protective measures against imports of fruit and vegetables from third countries.[93] In taking any measure it was required to take account of goods in transit. The Court therefore found that a ban on the import of Chilean apples was illegal in that it had failed to make dispensation for a shipment of apples which was en route to Marseilles at the time of the publication of the Regulation imposing the ban.

It is not clear, furthermore, that any precise assurance need be given. The adoption of a particular course of conduct which encourages certain action may be sufficient. In *Mulder*, for example, farmers were paid to take land out of milk production by the Community to reduce milk surpluses.[94] When Mulder sought to resume milk production without paying a levy, he was refused on the ground that this possibility was only available to those who had produced milk in the preceding year. The Court ruled that the measure violated Mulder's legitimate expectations, as he had been encouraged to take his land out of production by the Community offering him premiums.

Similarly in *Opel Austria* there were no undertakings from the Community administration that it would respect the Agreement on the European Economic Area until that agreement came into force.[95] The Court ruled, however, that once the EC had deposited its instruments of approval and the date of entry into force was known, traders had a legitimate expectation that the EC would not take any measures contravening the agreement in the period leading up to its entry into

---

[93] Case C-152/88 *Sofrimport v Commission* [1990] ECR I-2477, [1990] 3 CMLR 80.

[94] Case 120/86 *Mulder v Minister van Landbouw en Visserij* [1988] ECR 2321, [1989] 2 CMLR 1.

[95] Case T-115/94 *Opel Austria v Council*, Judgment of 22 January 1997.

force. The decision to levy a tariff on Opel Austria's gearboxes therefore violated their legitimate expectations.

In both *Mulder* and *Opel Austria* there was no substantial reversal of policy. The EC was, notwithstanding the action it took, still committed, respectively, to taking land out of milk production and the establishment of the European Economic Area. In each case it was therefore an instance of action being taken which was inconsistent with the existing policy framework. The question does arise, however, as to whether a reversal of policy, *per se*, can violate legitimate expectations. Craig has argued that if the principle of legal certainty is to be taken seriously, one cannot completely rule out the possibility that a reversal in policy might breach a trader's legitimate expectations.[96] For, in his view, legal certainty includes the notion that those who have relied upon a particular policy should have a claim to protection when that policy alters. In EC law there has not been a widespread acceptance of this view. Instead, there is a presumption of a freedom to legislate, as the Court considers that prudent traders ought to be able to take into account the possibility that the law might change.[97] A reversal in policy only exceptionally gives rise to a legally valid claim in legitimate expectations.

In *CNTA* the Commission suddenly stopped granting monetary compensation amounts (MCAs) in the colza and rape seed sectors.[98] MCAs are subsidies granted to traders designed to protect them against loss from fluctuations between EC currencies. This was a clear reversal of policy, which was unusual in that it was a sudden withdrawal of a subsidy. The financial effects were therefore immediate and unexpected. The Court found that there had been a breach of legitimate expectation in this case. Whilst MCAs could not be considered a guarantee against risks on the exchange rate, nevertheless, they meant, in practice, that a prudent trader might not insure himself against the risk. In the absence

---

[96]   Craig, P. 'Substantive Legitimate Expectations in Domestic and Community Law' (1996) 55 *CLJ* 289, 299.

[97]   e.g. Case 87/77 *Lührs v HZA Hamburg-Jonas* [1978] ECR 169, [1979] 1 CMLR 657; Case 265/85 *Van den Bergh en Jurgens v Commission* [1987] ECR 1155. On this see Sharpston, E. 'Legitimate Expectations and Economic Reality' (1990) 15 *ELRev* 103, 108-115.

[98]   Case 74/74 *CNTA v Commission* [1975] ECR 533, [1977] 1 CMLR 171.

of an overriding public interest, the Court considered that the immediate withdrawal of MCAs with no provision for transitional measures breached EC law.

c. Non-Discrimination

The non-discrimination principle requires that 'like cases be treated alike', and is something of a mantra in EC law. Various provisions of EC law on gender, the economy and immigration include a prohibition on discrimination.[99] Yet the non-discrimination principle is not a mechanistic principle but is a heavily loaded concept which relies heavily upon notions of distributive justice.

Schwarze, J. *European Administrative Law* (1992, Sweet & Maxwell, London) 552-553

... distributive justice is based on the proportional or geometric type of equality. The task of this second type of justice is to regulate the treatment of different persons when it comes to the allocation of property and obligations. In particular, its aim is to ensure that every member of a community is rewarded or burdened in accordance with his merits, hence that like is treated in like manner and unlike in correspondingly unlike manner.

According to the distributive philosophy, equality - and hence justice - is to be achieved by regulating each situation in due proportion. Consequently, it is not a question of systematically treating everyone in the same way; rather, the crucial factor governing the distribution of property and obligations is the worth of the individual.

After Aristotle's time, it was chiefly the second of the two doctrines, that of distributive justice, that was taken up and extended. Eventually it was formulated classically in the principle of suum cuique tribeere, enunciated by Cicero but usually quoted from the roman jurist Ulpian. Under this principle the requirement of substantive equality before the law is limited by the demand that each person should be granted his

---

[99] The starting point is the magisterial article, Lenaerts, K. 'L'Egalité de Traitement en Droit Communautaire' (1991) 27 *CDE* 3. In English for useful analyses of the various contexts within which the non-discrimination principle operates within EC law see the essays in Parts I and II in Dine, J. & Watt, B. (eds.) *Discrimination Law: Concepts, Limitations and Justifications* (1996, Longman, London); Dashwood, A. & O'Leary, S. *The Principle of Equal Treatment in EC Law* (1997, Sweet & Maxwell, London).

due and his rights, and hence that like should be treated in like manner and unlike in unlike manner.

If there were such a thing as absolute equality, the last-mentioned maxim would determine the content of the equality principle once and for all. But because 'equality' is relative, it remains an open question, in the final analysis, how someone is to receive 'his due' in the sense of suum cuique - through equal or unequal treatment. To a certain extent this decision will always be subjective and may thus lead to considerable uncertainty about the content of the equality principle. If the equality principle is regarded as a substantive legal principle derived from the concept of justice, a certain concomitant degree of legal uncertainty will generally have to be accepted.

The ethical content of the non-discrimination principle renders it impossible to apply in the abstract. The social and ethical questions involved in deciding when cases are alike for the purposes of comparison and what constitutes not just differential but disadvantageous treatment result in the content of the principle varying according to the context in which it will be discussed. The question of non-discrimination therefore raises different questions in the context of gender from those raised in the context of market integration.[100] All this renders the use of a general non-discrimination principle as a standard of judicial review quite difficult to predict. The Court will crack down on certain forms of identifiable discrimination, such as discrimination on grounds of sex[101] or nationality.[102] As a general principle of law, the non-discrimination suggests, however, a more embracing notion of equal treatment.

---

[100] Two excellent contributions on this matter are Bernard, N. 'What are the Purposes of EC Discrimination Law' in Dine, J. & Watt, B. (eds.) *Discrimination Law: Concepts, Limitations and Justifications* (1996, Longman, London) and De Búrca, G. 'The Role of Equality in European Community Law' in Dashwood, A. & O'Leary, S. The Principle of Equal Treatment in EC Law (1997, Sweet & Maxwell, London). Notwithstanding this, the structural similarities of the non-discrimination principle in gender and commercial law have been observed in Barnard, C. 'Gender and Commercial Discrimination' in Dine, J. & Watt, B. (eds.) ibid.

[101] Case 20/71 *Sabbatini v Parliament* [1972] ECR 345.

[102] Joined Cases 75 & 117/82 *Razzouk & Beydoun v Commission* [1984] ECR 1509.

Joined Cases 117/76 & 16/77 Ruckdeschel v Council [1977] ECR 1753, [1979] 2 CMLR 445

Traditionally, the Community had given identical subsidies to producers of starch and producers of quellmehl. The reason for the subsidy to starch producers was to keep its prices competitive compared with products derived from oil. The subsidy was given to quellmehl production because of its interchangeability with starch. The subsidy was withdrawn from the quellmehl producers.

7. The second subparagraph of Article 40 (3) of the Treaty provides that the common organization of agricultural markets 'shall exclude any discrimination between producers or consumers within the Community'.

Whilst this wording undoubtedly prohibits any discrimination between producers of the same product it does not refer in such clear terms to the relationship between different industrial or trade sectors in the sphere of processed agricultural products.

This does not alter the fact that the prohibition of discrimination laid down in the aforesaid provision is merely a specific enunciation of the general principle of equality which is one of the fundamental principles of Community law.

This principle requires that similar situations shall not be treated differently unless differentiation is objectively justified.

8. It must therefore be ascertained whether quellmehl and starch are in a comparable situation, in particular in the sense that starch can be substituted for quellmehl in the specific use to which the latter product is traditionally put.

In this connexion it must first be noted that the Community Regulations were, until 1974, based on the assertion that such substitution was possible.

However, the plaintiffs in the main actions on the one hand, and the Council and the Commission on the other are not in agreement concerning the continued existence of that situation.

The plaintiffs in the main actions contend that the opportunities for substitution are the same as previously, with the result that, since the abolition of the refund for quellmehl, trade in the latter has fallen off in favour of starch.

While the Council and the commission have given detailed information on the manufacture and sale of the products in question, they have produced no new technical or economic data which appreciably change the previous assessment of the position.

It has not therefore been established that, so far as the Community system of production refunds is concerned, quellmehl and starch are no longer in comparable situations.

Consequently, these products must be treated in the same manner unless differentiation is objectively justified.

9. With regard to this latter aspect, the Council and the Commission contend that the abolition of the refund for quellmehl is justified by the fact that quellmehl has been to a great extent diverted from its specific use in food for human consumption in order to be sold as animal feed.

Although this ground, the correctness of which is moreover disputed by the plaintiffs in the main actions, is referred to in the statement which accompanied the proposal submitted by the Commission to the Council and later adopted as Regulation (EEC) No 1125/74, it does not appear in the recitals to that Regulation.

During the proceedings, the commission was requested by the Court to produce evidence to show that quellmehl had been used for animal feed but it was unable to comply with this request.

Even if adequate proof had been forthcoming that it was put to such use and that subsidized starch had not been put to similar use this could have justified the abolition of the refund only in respect of the quantities put to such use and not in respect of the quantities of the products used in food for human consumption.

10. In view in particular of the length of time during which the two products were given equality of treatment with regard to production refunds, it has not been established that there are objective circumstances which could have justified altering the previous system as was done by Regulation (EEC) No 1125/74, which put an end to this equality of treatment.

It is clear from the foregoing that the abolition, as a result of Regulation (EEC) No 1125/74, of the refund for quellmehl, while the refund was maintained for maize-based starch, amounts to a disregard of the principle of equality.

Like the proportionality principle, the intensity of review varies according to the area considered. In areas where the EC institutions enjoy a margin of discretion, notably external relations and harmonisation of laws,[103] differential treatment does not appear to be sufficient to justify a finding of discrimination. Discrimination will only be found if the conduct borders on the 'arbitrary'.[104] In these circumstances the non-discrimination principle seems to add little to the proportionality principle.[105]

In areas where EC institutions enjoy less discretion, the Court is less generous towards them. In *Schöller* the applicant had entered into a network of agreements with retailers across Germany under which

---

[103]   Case 245/81 *Edeka v Commission* [1982] ECR 2745; Case C-479/93 *Francovich v Italian Republic* [1995] ECR I-3843.

[104]   Case 245/81 *Edeka v Commission* [1982] ECR 2745.

[105]   Herdegen, M. 'The Equation between the Principles of Equality and Proportionality' (1985) 22 *CMLRev* 683.

they would exclusively purchase a range of ice cream bars from it.[106] The Commission investigated the agreement for breach of EC competition law and issued interim measures, as it was entitled to do. These required the exclusivity clause to be suspended. Schöller was also prohibited from entering into any more exclusive purchasing agreements pending a final decision. Under EC law there is a block exemption which allows such agreements provided they meet certain conditions. The CFI found that not only did the Commission not have the power to issue such a prohibition but that such a prohibition violated the principle of equality by preventing one trader to enter exclusive purchasing agreements when others were free to do so.

V. Misuse of Powers

The final ground of review, misuse of powers can be mentioned almost as a postscript, such is its relative insignificance.[107] The doctrine has its intellectual origins of the French concept of administrative law of *détournement du pouvoir*. Misuse of powers in EC law arises if it appears:

> 'on the basis of objective, relevant and consistent indications to have been adopted to achieve purposes other than those for which it was intended.'[108]

Whilst invoked frequently, the principle has rarely brought joy to applicants. The first reason for this is that the test is essentially a subjective one. It has proved very difficult for applicants to prove the necessary bad faith on the part of the institution. Secondly, the threshold is further raised by the requirement that the decision being challenged must have been guided exclusively or, at least, in the main by the

---

[106] Case T-9/93 *Schöller v Commission* [1995] ECR II-1611.

[107] On misuse of powers see Hartley, T. *The Foundations of European Community Law* (1994, 3rd Edition, Clarendon, Oxford) 433-436.

[108] Case C-323/88 *Sermes v Directeur de Service des Douanes de Strasbourg* [1990] ECR I-3027.

motivation to use the power for purposes other than for which they were conferred.[109] So far, outside two staff cases,[110] the principle has only been successfully invoked once.[111]

Further Reading

Arnull, A. *General Principles of EEC Law and the Individual* (1990, Leicester University Press/Pinter, London)

De Búrca, G. 'The Principle of Proportionality and Its Application in EC Law' (1993) 13 *Yearbook of European Law* 105

----- 'The Language of Rights and European Integration' in Shaw, J. & More, G. (eds.) *New Legal Dynamics of European Union* (1995, Clarendon, Oxford)

Craig, P. 'Substantive Legitimate Expectations in Domestic and Community Law' (1996) 55 *Cambridge Law Journal* 289

Dashwood, A. & O'Leary, S. (eds.) *The Principle of Equal Treatment in EC Law* (1997, Sweet & Maxwell, London)

Dine, J. & Watt, B. (eds.) *Discrimination Law: Concepts, Limitations and Justifications* (1996, Longman, Harlow)

Emiliou, N. *The Principle of Proportionality in European Law* (1996, Kluwer, London)

Herdegen, M. 'The Equation between the Principles of Equality and Proportionality' (1985) 22 *Common Market Law Review* 683

Neuwahl, N. and Rosas, A. *The European Union and Human Rights* (1995, Martijnus Nijhoff, The Hague)

Schwarze, *European Administrative Law* (1992, Sweet & Maxwell, OOPEC, London)

Sharpston, E. 'Legitimate Expectations and Economic Reality' (1990) 15 *European Law Review* 103

---

[109] Joined Cases C-133, C-300 & C-362/93 *Crispoltoni* [1994] ECR I-4863.

[110] Joined Cases 18 & 35/65 *Gutmann v Commission* [1966] ECR 103; Case 105/75 *Giuffrida v Council* [1976] ECR 1395.

[111] Joined Cases 351 & 360/85 *Fabrique de Fer de Charleroi v Commission* [1987] ECR 3639.

10. Judicial Control of the EC Institutions

I. Introduction

Judicial review is an institutional expression of the idea that there should be legally imposed limits on the exercise of government power. Such limits need policing, and in the late twentieth century this role has increasingly been given to courts.[1] Yet, judicial review cannot be accepted unquestioningly. It gives courts the power to veto decisions taken by other areas of governments. Courts are unelected; access to them is often difficult, and rarely do they have the expertise of other arms of government. Furthermore, increasingly intrusive use of judicial review by courts can unsettle existing constitutional settlement, as other institutions react against the circumscription and reduction of their powers brought about by judicial review. The matter is rendered more unsettled within the EU context by the lack of any tradition of transnational judicial review. Other reservations voiced, thus, include the argument that as EC legislation is subject to a more laborious process of compromise than national acts, judicial intervention is particularly destabilising in this arena.[2]

The Court of Justice sees the rationale of judicial review in the EC as being to preserve the 'rule of law'. Yet its use of the term in this context implies more than merely ensuring that the other institutions observe the 'rules of the game'. 'Law' is used here as a loaded concept

---

[1] On the development of judicial review within Europe see Cappelletti, M. *The Judicial Process in Comparative Perspective* (1989, Clarendon, Oxford).

[2] Stein, E. & Vining, J. 'Citizen Access to Judicial Review of Administrative Action in a Transnational and Federal Context' (1976) 70 *AJIL* 219, 230. For a critique of this article see Rasmussen, H. 'Why is Article 173 Interpreted against Private Plaintiffs?' (1980) 5 *ELRev* 112, 117-122.

which includes values such as protection of fundamental rights and institutional accountability.

Case 294/83 Parti Ecologiste 'Les Verts' v Parliament [1986] ECR 1339, [1987] 2 CMLR 343

The Green Party wished to challenge a Parliament decision allocating funding for the 1984 European Parliament elections which used a formula which favoured parties already represented in the Parliament. At the time, however, Article 173 EC, the relevant provision only stated that acts of the Council and the Commission could be challenged.

23. It must first be emphasized in this regard that the European Economic Community is a Community based on the rule of law, inasmuch as neither its Member States nor its institutions can avoid a review of the question whether the measures adopted by them are in conformity with the basic constitutional charter, the Treaty. In particular, in Articles 173 and 184, on the one hand, and in Article 177, on the other, the Treaty established a complete system of legal remedies and procedures designed to permit the Court of Justice to review the legality of measures adopted by the institutions. Natural and legal persons are thus protected against the application to them of general measures which they cannot contest directly before the Court by reason of the special conditions of admissibility laid down in the second paragraph of Article 173 of the Treaty. Where the Community institutions are responsible for the administrative implementation of such measures, natural or legal persons may bring a direct action before the Court against implementing measures which are addressed to them or which are of direct and individual concern to them and, in support of such an action, plead the illegality of the general measure on which they are based. Where implementation is a matter for the national authorities, such persons may plead the invalidity of general measures before the national courts and cause the latter to request the Court of Justice for a preliminary ruling.

24. It is true that, unlike Article 177 of the Treaty, which refers to acts of the institutions without further qualification, Article 173 refers only to acts of the Council and the Commission. However, the general scheme of the Treaty is to make a direct action available against 'all measures adopted by the institutions ... which are intended to have legal effects', as the court has already had occasion to emphasize in its judgment of 31 March 1971 (Case 22/70 *Commission v Council* (1971) ECR 263). The European Parliament is not expressly mentioned among the institutions whose measures may be contested because, in its original version, the EEC Treaty merely granted it powers of consultation and political control rather than the power to adopt measures intended to have legal effects *vis-à-vis* third parties. Article 38 of the ECSC Treaty shows that where the Parliament was given *ab initio* the power to adopt binding measures, as was the case under the last sentence of the fourth paragraph of Article 95 of that Treaty, measures adopted by it were not in principle immune from actions for annulment.

25. Whereas under the ECSC Treaty actions for annulment against measures adopted by the institutions are the subject of two separate provisions, they are governed under the EEC Treaty by Article 173 alone, which is therefore a provision of general application. An interpretation of Article 173 of the Treaty which excluded measures adopted by the European Parliament from those which could be contested would lead to a result contrary both to the spirit of the Treaty as expressed in Article 164 and to its system. Measures adopted by the European Parliament in the context of the EEC Treaty could encroach on the powers of the Member States or of the other institutions, or exceed the limits which have been set to the Parliament's powers, without its being possible to refer them for review by the Court. It must therefore be concluded that an action for annulment may lie against measures adopted by the European Parliament intended to have legal effects *vis-à-vis* third parties.

Viewed in such terms, judicial review is seen as contributing to the democratisation of the EC. The notion that judges are best placed to secure certain societal values is not a new one, however.

Cotterell, R. 'Judicial Review and Legal Theory' 13, 17-19 in Richardson, G. & Genn, H. (eds.) *Administrative Law and Government Action* (1994, Clarendon, Oxford)

The objective principles applied in judicial review are often traced to the character of courts not as agencies of the state, nor as servants of the parliamentary will, but as guardians and pronouncers of values anchored in society and culture, outside structures of government as such. Mauro Cappelletti writes of judicial review in its varied forms in Western societies (including review of both administrative and legislative acts) as a protection against 'the mutable whims of passing majorities', a means of protecting minorities in democracies and expressing enduring values, 'the permanent will, rather than the temporary whims, of the people'.[3] On this view judicial authority is 'deeply rooted in society's daily needs, grievances, aspirations and demands'.[4] ....

The appeal to independent judicially protected values as a basis for judicial review is especially interesting when it is used to try to solve the problem of the democratic legitimacy of judicial involvement in government. In contrast to the modest

---

[3]   Capelletti, M. *The Judicial Process in Comparative Perspective* (1989, Clarendon, Oxford) 131, 206, 210.

[4]   Ibid., 44.

underworker approach which seeks to portray the activity of judicial review as so limited that it slips by unnoticed as part of the orderly machinery of government, the appeal to judicially protected values seems to follow the strategy that attack is the best form of defence. Thus it is argued 'that democracy means more than simply majority rule, that it connotes a relationship between each individual and the majority, within which the individual is guaranteed certain protections, and that these in turn may constitute fetters upon majority rule. The argument is that the values inherent in this fuller sense of democracy might be tapped by the courts in exercising review.' According to this view courts do not merely avoid intruding on democratic processes. Nor do they meekly follow the will of the democratically empowered regime. They positively help to secure values that make democracy a worthwhile system for all citizens, and not only for those whose interests are directly promoted by those in power.

An alternative claim is that democracy requires popular participation in and access to public decision-making and courts help to provide this. Potentially, they can do this in at least two distinct ways. First, they can enforce procedures in governmental decision-making that allow popular input into decision-makers' deliberations. Secondly, they can supplement administrative processes with judicial hearings, which provide different kinds of opportunity for influence on administrative matters by citizens as litigants. Courts are relatively open to public view, accountable (through appeal systems), and in some sense participatory. They not only allow, but normally require opposing voices to be heard. Hence some writers have suggested that they actually embody democratic values or have the potential to do so.

However, the fact remains that, in centralised judicial systems staffed by state-appointed judges, neither the decision-makers, nor the processes of decision-making in courts, are democratically controlled. Equally, it is not possible to argue that participation in or access to these courts is uniformly available to all citizens. Again, it cannot be said that courts actually promote participation in administrative processes in any consistent or comprehensive way. If courts operated under different conditions from those that typically prevail and with different principles of organisation their relation to democratic practice might be transformed. But the 'democratic' argument for judicial review seems to come down to one of aspiration. The claim is not that judicial enshrines democracy or promotes it but that courts have a potential to articulate democratic principles that are immanent in the organisation of collective life and reflected imperfectly in other institutions of government. State institutions are thus to be understood in the light of fundamental democratic values of the community as a whole. Judges can express these values and impose them on governmental processes even if courts do not serve directly as conduits for democratic participation.

A feature of judicial review in the EC is that the Court of Justice has a monopoly over the judicial review of the acts and omissions of EC institutions. Only the Court of Justice can declare an act of an EC institution to be void.[5] In declaring that national courts do not have the power to declare acts of the Institutions to be invalid,[6] the Court has suggested that this monopoly exists for two reasons. The first is that only it can secure uniformity of EC law, for judgments of national courts are not binding upon the courts of other Member States. The second reason given is to protect the rights of defence of the EC institutions. They are entitled to participate in proceedings before the Court,[7] and the Court also has the power to require non-participating Member States and institutions to supply all the information it considers necessary for the case.[8] A cohesive system of judicial review would also require that a single approach be taken towards questions of standing through which private and public interests can be accommodated. The Court of Justice can be seised in a variety of ways, however.

The most salient provision is Article 173 [*230*] EC, which expressly provides for annulment of acts of EC institutions. There is also a sister provision, Article 175 [*232*] EC, which allows actions to be brought against EC institutions for a failure to act. There are a variety of actions which result in judicial review, but which do not go under that name. An action for damages against the EC institutions under Article 215(2) [*288(2)*] EC will result, if successful, in the challenged act being declared void. In addition, the possibility of indirect challenge exists in Article 184 [*241*] EC. This allows an act to be challenged, which is relevant to proceedings but is not the subject-matter of the proceedings. An example is where a Decision is challenged which was adopted under a parent Regulation. Article 184 [*241*] EC allows the legality of the Regulation to be brought into question in proceedings against the Decision. One of the most common sources of judicial review, however, is references made under Article 177 [*234*] EC, where either the act is challenged directly or national implementing measures are being challenged.

All these provisions have mechanisms to screen vexatious claims. Yet the panoply of routes available has a number of undesirable

---

5 Articles 173 [*230*] EC & 183 [*240*] EC.
6 Case 314/85 *Firma Foto-Frost v HZA Lübeck Ost* [1987] ECR 4199, [1988] 3 CMLR 57.
7 Statute of the Court of Justice, Article 20.
8 Statute of the Court of Justice, Article 21.

consequences. The system is complex and opaque with little guiding rationality as to the overall principles informing the question of standing. Procedures can be used to subvert one another. Even though the Court has taken action to prevent applicants bringing actions under either Article 177 [*234*] EC[9] or Article 184 [*241*] EC,[10] the lack of standing under one procedure can often be resolved by a party bringing an action under another procedure.[11] Conversely, the variety of procedures acts to stultify reform with critics claiming the deficiencies of one procedure are obviated by the existence of other procedures.[12]

II. Acts Subject To Review

Article 173(1)[*230(1)*] EC states:

> The Court of Justice shall review the legality of acts adopted jointly by the European Parliament and the Council, of acts of the Council, of the Commission, and of the ECB other than recommendations and opinions, and acts of the European Parliament intended to produce legal effects vis-à-vis third parties.

Only acts of the EC institutions are mentioned. The Court has therefore stated that acts of the European Council[13] and COREPER[14]

---

9 Case C-188/92 *TWD Textilwerke Deggendorf v Germany* [1994] ECR I-833.

10 Case C-135/93 *Spain v Commission* [1995] ECR I-1651.

11 e.g. Article 215(2) [*288(2)*] EC can be used as an independent route of review where the applicant does not have standing under Article 173 [*230*] EC, Joined Cases 5, 7, 13-24/66 *Kampffmeyer v Commission* [1967] ECR 245. A recent, albeit unsuccessful, attempt was made to exploit this. See Case T-195/95 *Guérin Automobiles v Commission* [1996] ECR II-171 and Case T-195/95 *Guérin Automobiles v Commission*, Judgment of 6 May 1997.

12 It has thus been argued that the narrow standing requirements of Article 173(4) [*230(4)*] EC are mitigated by the existence of Article 177 [*234*] EC. Harding, C. 'The Private Interest in Challenging Community Action' (1980) 5 *ELRev* 354, 357-358.

13 Case T-584/93 *Roujansky v European Council* [1994] ECR II-585.

14 Case C-25/94 *Commission v Council* [1996] ECR I-1469.

can not be reviewed as they are not formally EC institutions. This is notwithstanding the significant influence these bodies exert upon the policies of the Council in particular. Recommendations and Opinions are also expressly excluded from judicial review. There was also initially doubt as to whether international agreements could be reviewed given that annulment might result in breach of an international law obligation towards a third State.[15] Such a partial scope would have given the EC institutions the possibility of evading review through the label they gave to a measure. The Court has sought to prevent this by taking a functional view of the kind of measures which are subject to review.

Case 22/70 Commission v Council (ERTA) [1971] ECR 263, [1971] CMLR 335

In 1967 negotiations began to revise the European Road Transport Agreement (ERTA) within the umbrella of the United Nations Economic Commission for Europe. In 1970 the Council adopted a Resolution stating any agreement was to be signed by the Member States. The Commission brought an action claiming that the agreement fell within EC competence under Article 75 [71] EC, and should be signed by the Community, instead. It had to demonstrate, however, that the Resolution was a reviewable act.

40. The objective of this review is to ensure, as required by Article 164, observance of the law in the interpretation and application of the Treaty.

41. It would be inconsistent with this objective to interpret the conditions under which the action is admissible so restrictively as to limit the availability of this procedure merely to the categories of measures referred to by Article 189.

42. An action for annulment must therefore be available in the case of all measures adopted by the institutions, whatever their nature or form, which are intended to have legal effects.

.....

---

15   Kovar, R. 'Les Accords Liant Les Communautés Européennes et l'Ordre Juridique Communautaire: A Propos d' Une Jurisprudence Récente de la Cour de Justice' (1974) 17 *Revue de Marché Commun* 345, 358.

53. .... insofar as they concerned the objective of the negotiations as defined by the Council, the proceedings of 20 March 1970 could not have been simply the expression or the recognition of voluntary coordination, but were designed to lay down a course of action binding on both the institutions and the Member States, and destined ultimately to be reflected in the tenor of the regulation.

54. In the part of its conclusions relating to the negotiating procedure, the Council adopted provisions which were capable of derogating in certain circumstances from the procedure laid down by the Treaty regarding negotiations with third countries and the conclusion of agreements.

55. Hence the proceedings of 20 March 1970 had definite legal effects both on relations between the Community and the Member States and the relationship between institutions.

International agreements have therefore been reviewed,[16] as have Commission Communications[17] and internal Codes of Conduct.[18] As yet no Recommendation or Opinion has been reviewed, but, given that Recommendations are capable of producing legal effects,[19] it has been argued that these should not be seen as being fully exempt from review.[20] This is all the more so as one of the concerns at the increasing resort to soft law is the possible evasion of judicial control.

The formula of an act 'intended to have legal effects' is an unhelpful one. By basing reviewability upon the intention of the institution, it seems to allow institutions to escape review by pleading that they did not intend the consequences of their actions. In practice, this has not happened. From the context of the ERTA judgment, it appears that the Court was concerned at institutions that as they did not have competence to adopt a particular act, it could not have legal effects and was therefore not reviewable. The formula avoids this and is really one of whether the act has *apparent legal effects*. In particular, it will

---

16   Case C-327/91 *France v Commission* [1994] ECR I-3641.
17   Case C-135/93 *Spain v Commission* [1995] ECR I-1651; Case C-57/95 *France v Commission,* Judgment of 20 March 1997.
18   Case C-303/90 *France v Commission* [1991] ECR I-5315.
19   Case C-322/88 *Grimaldi v Fonds des Maladies Profesionnelles* [1989] ECR 4407, [1991] 2 CMLR 265.
20   Albors-Llorens, A. *Private Parties in European Community Law* (1996, OUP, Oxford) 20.

look at whether the act appears to 'produce a change in somebody's rights and obligations'.[21]

The Court takes a number of factors into account in considering this. The first factor is the wording of the act. If the wording is imperative in nature and its subject-matter does not merely clarify existing law but seeks to extend it, the act is likely to be considered to be reviewable.[22] This is often difficult to predict. In *Commission v Netherlands* the Court held that the Code of Conduct on Public Access to Documents was not a reviewable act.[23] It considered it to be no more than a voluntary coordination between the Council and the Commission to ensure their approaches did not diverge which did no more than set out general principles. This was notwithstanding that the Code is actually quite a detailed document which is not much further elaborated in either the Council or Commission Decisions implementing it.

Secondly, it will often be determinative whether the EC Institution has competence to adopt the act or not. In *Sunzest* the Commission instructed the Belgian authorities at Antwerp that they should not recognise certificates issued by the 'Turkish Federated State of Cyprus' certifying the fitness of citrus fruit from Northern Cyprus.[24] Whilst the language of the Commission's letter was mandatory in nature, the Court did not recognise it as producing legal effects. It noted that the national authorities had exclusive responsibility under the Directive to apply protective measures against fruit from third countries. The Commission, in the Court's view, could only have been expressing an opinion.

Thirdly, Court will not regard preparatory acts which do not definitively lay down an Institution's position as reviewable. In *IBM*, therefore, the Court refused to annul a Commission Decision initiating

---

21   Hartley, T. *The Foundations of European Community Law* (3rd ed, 1994, OUP, Oxford), 344.

22   Case C-57/95 *France v Commission*, Judgment of 20 March 1997.

23   Case C-58/94 *Netherlands v Commission* [1996] ECR I-2169, [1996] 2 CMLR 996.

24   Case C-50/90 *Sunzest v Commission* [1991] ECR I-2917. See, along similar lines, Case 133/79 *Sucrimex v Commission* [1980] ECR 1299; Case 217/81 *Interagra v Commission* [1982] ECR 2233.

competition proceedings as it was merely the first step in a procedure.[25] By contrast, the decision not to initiate competition proceedings is reviewable as it represents the adoption of a definitive position by the Commission.[26] Often it will be difficult to determine if the Commission has adopted a definitive position or not. In *Air France* the Commission issued an oral statement that it had no jurisdiction to consider a takeover of Dan Air by British Airways.[27] There was neither any text nor was the oral statement addressed to anybody. Furthermore, the statement did not follow any notification of the takeover by British Airways to the Commission, as is actually required by the Merger Regulation. Perhaps facilitated by the Commission's admission that it had come to a firm view on the matter, the Court considered the statement to be reviewable, claiming that the measure had legal effects by reaffirming national jurisdiction over the merger and absolving the parties of their duty to notify the takeover under the Merger Regulation.

Whilst it is possible to identify the influences, many are conflicting with the result that the case law in this area is unsettled and contradictory. The uncertainty about what is a reviewable act has even had the EC judiciary at odds. This occurred in the *Geotronics* saga, which arose within the context of the PHARE programme of aid to the countries to Central and Eastern Europe. Under the scheme the beneficiary government were responsible for issuing contracts in response to tenders. The Commission was required to check that the process was carried out in a non-discriminatory manner and that the most economically advantageous tender was accepted as a condition of EC funding. The Commission informed Geotronics that it would not endorse the latter's tender to supply tachometers to the Romanian Government as the tachometers did not meet the conditions of the PHARE programme which required that any goods be produced in either an EU or PHARE State. The CFI considered that this refusal did not produce legal effects, as there was no legal relationship between Geotronic and the Commission, as it was the Romanian Government

---

25   Case 60/81 *IBM v Commission* [1981] ECR 2639, [1981] 3 CMLR 635.
26   Case C-39/93P *SFEI v Commission* [1994] ECR I-2681.
27   Case T-3/93 *Air France v Commission* [1994] ECR II-121. On this see Greaves, R. 'The Nature and Binding Effect of Decisions under Article 189 EC' (1996) 21 *ELRev* 3, 9-10.

which had the exclusive responsibility for issuing contracts.[28] On appeal the Court of Justice overturned that decision.[29] It noted that although the contract was a national one, the refusal of the Commission to endorse Geotronics resulted in the latter losing any chance of being awarded the contract, for the award to Geotronics in such circumstances would have resulted in the Romanian Government losing EC funding.

III. Jurisdiction of the Court in an Action For Annulment

i. The Schema of Article 173 [230] EC

The central article of review remains Article 173 [230] EC. A condition which must be met by all actions brought under this Article is that they be instituted within two months of the publication of the measure; its notification to the plaintiff, or, in the absence thereof, of the day on which it came to the plaintiff's knowledge.[30] This compares most unfavourably with national regimes which usually have limitation periods of at least 3 or 6 months in the case of judicial review. Beyond that, the jurisdiction of the Court depends upon the status of the plaintiff, as Article 173 [230] EC establishes a three-fold hierarchy of privileged, semi-privileged and non-privileged plaintiffs.

ii. Privileged and Semi-Privileged Applicants

The terms of jurisdiction for privileged and semi-privileged applicants are set out in Article 173(2) and (3) [230(2) and (3)] EC:

---

28   Case T-185/94 *Geotronics v Commission* [1995] ECR II-2795.

29   Case C-395/95 *Geotronics v Commission*, Judgment of 22 April 1997.

30   Article 173(5) [230(5)] EC.

Article 173(2) [*230(2)*] EC. It [the Court of Justice] shall for this purpose have jurisdiction in actions brought by a Member State, the Council or the Commission on the grounds of lack of competence, infringement of an essential procedural requirement, infringement of this Treaty or of any rule of law relating to its application, or misuse of powers.

The Court shall have jurisdiction under the same conditions in actions brought by the European Parliament [*by the Court of Auditors*] and by the European Central Bank for the purpose of protecting their prerogatives.

The privileged applicants listed in Article 173(2) [*230(2)*] EC - the Member States, Council and the Commission - have unlimited standing to challenge acts of the EC Institution subject to the time limits. Semi-privileged applicants - the Parliament, the European Central Bank and, should Amsterdam be ratified, the Court of Auditors - cannot challenge all acts but only acts which affect their 'prerogatives'. This means that they do not possess general supervisory powers over the other EC Institutions, unlike privileged applicants, but can only challenge those acts which deprive them of the possibility of exercising a power conferred upon them by EC law.[31]

iii. Non-Privileged Applicants

The position of individuals is set out in Article 173(4) [*230(4)*] EC.

Article 173 (4) [*230(4)*] EC. Any natural or legal person may, under the same conditions, institute proceedings against a decision addressed to that person or against a decision which, although in the form of a regulation or decision addressed to another person, is of direct and individual concern to the former.

Two scenarios have to be contrasted. Individuals have full standing to challenge Decisions addressed to them. Otherwise, they have to satisfy three conditions - the act must be a Decision or a Decision in

---

[31]   On this see pp 120-126.

the form of a Regulation; it must also be of both individual and direct concern to them. One feature of Article 173(4) [*230(4)*] EC cases is that since 15 March 1994 they are all decided by the Court of First Instance.[32] Another is the narrow wording of the provision. It contrasts unfavourably with its counterpart in the ECSC Treaty, Article 33 ECSC, which allows individuals to bring proceedings against measures concerning them which are 'individual in character' or against general measures which they consider to involve a misuse of powers concerning them.[33] It has thus been argued that the Member States never intended that individuals enjoy extensive powers of judicial review against EC Institutions.[34]

a. The Legal Nature of the Act

The wording of Article 173(4) [*230(4)*] EC suggested that it was largely only Decisions which could be challenged by individuals. The possibility of allowing individuals to challenge Decisions 'in the form of a Regulation' was inserted to prevent the EC institutions attempting to escape review simply by calling a Decision a Regulation. For a long period the Court vexed, therefore, over which Regulations could be challenged. In some instances it seemed to assert that even when a Regulation was of direct and individual concern to an individual, it could not be challenged by that individual where it was legislative in nature.[35] In others, it did not consider the nature of the measure but merely whether the matter was of direct and individual concern.[36] The matter was resolved in Cordorniu where the Court considered a legislative

---

[32]   Decision 93/350 EC, OJ 1993, L 144/21 as amended by Council Decision of 7 March 1994, OJ 1994, L 66/29.

[33]   Albors-Llorens, A. supra n.20, 218.

[34]   Harding, C. 'The Private Interest in Challenging Community Action' (1980) 5 *ELRev* 354, 355.

[35]   e.g. Case 64/69 *Compagnie Française Commerciale et Financière v Commission* [1970] ECR 221, [1970] CMLR 369.

[36]   e.g. Case 123/77 *UNICME v Council* [1978] ECR 845.

measure and held that the nature of the act was irrelevant to the question of standing.[37]

Case C-309/89 Cordorniu SA v Council [1994] ECR I-1853, [1995] 1 CMLR 361

A Regulation reserved the term *'crémant'* for particular types of sparkling wine produced in France and Luxembourg. Cordorniu, a Spanish producer of sparkling wine, had marketed its wine since 1924 using the phrase cremant which formed part of its trademark. Although the measure was of general application the Court granted standing to Cordorniu because its historical and economic position made it individually concerned by the measure.

17. Under the second paragraph of Article 173 of the Treaty the institution of proceedings by a natural or legal person for a declaration that a regulation is void is subject to the condition that the provisions of the regulation at issue in the proceedings constitute in reality a decision of direct and individual concern to that person.

18. As the Court has already held, the general applicability, and thus the legislative nature, of a measure is not called in question by the fact that it is possible to determine more or less exactly the number or even the identity of the persons to whom it applies at any given time, as long as it is established that it applies to them by virtue of an objective legal or factual situation defined by the measure in question in relation to its purpose (see most recently the judgment in Case C-298/89 *Gibraltar v Council* [1993] ECR I-3605, paragraph 17).

19. Although it is true that according to the criteria in the second paragraph of Article 173 of the Treaty the contested provision is, by nature and by virtue of its sphere of application, of a legislative nature in that it applies to the traders concerned in general, that does not prevent it from being of individual concern to some of them.

The Court has therefore acknowledged that in principle not only Regulations and Decisions can be challenged by individuals, but also Directives if individuals meet the other criteria of direct and individual

---

[37]   This has been followed in Case C-87/95P *Cassa Nazionale di previdenza ed assistenza a fovare degli avvocati e dei procuratori v Council* [1996] ECR I-2003. For a discussion of the earlier case law see Greaves, R. 'Locus Standi under Article 173 EEC when seeking Annulment of a Regulation' (1986) 11 *ELRev* 119.

concern.[38] If the basis for judicial review is one discussed by Cotterill, namely to protect a set of shared values, then these values should be protected against all acts, whatever their nature. On such a basis, it seems indeed odd that there are certain acts which can be challenged by privileged and semi-privileged applicants but not by private parties. Yet the generality and abstract nature of legislative acts raises questions about the judicial function. Such acts are usually strongly 'polycentric', in that they will impinge upon a wide variety of interests. Review actions determining the validity of such acts inevitably affect the same range of interests, but it is unlikely that all interests will be sufficiently represented in what is essentially a bipartisan, adversarial process.[39] The problem is particularly pressing within the EU, as almost all Article 173(4) [230(4)] EC actions are brought by corporate actors.[40] This is partly because of expense, but also because standing rules which, as shall be seen, favour the protection of private interests over group interests.[41] Within such a context, there is clearly the danger of the agenda before the Court being captured by corporate interests, with judicial review being used primarily as an avenue to pursue corporate interests which the legislative process has refused to accommodate.

b. Direct Concern

The second criterion which must be satisfied is that the act must be of direct concern to the applicant. Direct concern is to be found where there is:

---

[38] Case C-10/95P *Asocarne v Council & Commission* [1995] ECR I-4149.

[39] On the now established debate on polycentricity see Chayes, R. 'The Role of the Judge in Public Law Litigation' (1976) 89 *Harvard Law Review* 1281; Fuller, L 'The Forms and Limits of Adjudication' (1978) 92 *Harvard Law Review* 353.

[40] There are no recent statistics on this, but any perusal of the ECR will confirm this. See Bronckers, M. 'Private Enforcement of 1992: Do Trade and Industry Stand a Chance Against the Member States?' (1989) 26 *CMLRev* 513, 520-521; Harding, C. 'Who Goes to Court in Europe? An Analysis of Litigation against the Community' (1992) 17 *ELRev* 105.

[41] Harlow, C. 'Towards a Theory of Access to the European Court of Justice' (1992) 12 *YBEL* 213.

'the existence of a relationship of causality between the decision and the damage inflicted on the applicant.'[42]

Direct concern has traditionally acted as a constraint where a Decision has been addressed to a Member State but has conferred a discretion upon the latter as to how to implement it. Third parties affected by these measures will not be able to challenge them as they will not be considered to be directly concerned.[43] Even where a Member State is given a discretion by a Community, that, *per se*, will not break the causal link. The link will only be severed where there is a degree of doubt over the manner in which the Member State will exercise its discretion.[44]

Case 11/82 Piraiki-Patraiki v Commission [1985] ECR 207, [1985] 2 CMLR 46

Under Article 130 of the Greek Act of Accession the Commission was empowered to authorise other Member States to take protective measures against imports from Greece. The French Government sought and was granted an authorisation to impose a quota on cotton imports from Greece. The Commission Decision granting the authorisation was challenged by 7 Greek exporters of cotton. It was argued that as the Decision constituted an authorisation, it could not be of direct concern to the exporters.

7. It is true that without implementing measures adopted at the national level the Commission Decision could not have affected the applicants. In this case, however, that fact does not in itself prevent the decision from being of direct concern to the applicants if other factors justify the conclusion that they have a direct interest in bringing the action.

8. In that respect it should be pointed out that, as the Commission itself admitted during the written procedure, even before being authorized to do so by the Commission the French Republic applied a very restrictive system of licences for imports of cotton yarn

---

[42]   Albors-Llorens, A. supra n.20, 220.

[43]   Case 69/69 *Alcan v Commission* [1970] ECR 385, [1970] CMLR 339; Case 222/83 *Municipality of Differdange v Commission* [1984] ECR 2889; Case T-435/93 *ASPEC v Commission* [1995] ECR II-1281.

[44]   See also Joined Cases T-480 & T-483/93 *Antillean Rice Mills v Commission* [1995] ECR II-2301.

of Greek origin. It should moreover be observed that the request for protective measures not only came from the French authorities but sought to obtain the Commission's authorization for a system of import quotas more strict than that which was finally granted.

9. In those circumstances the possibility that the French Republic might decide not to make use of the authorization granted to it by the Commission Decision was entirely theoretical, since there could be no doubt as to the intention of the French authorities to apply the Decision.

10. It must therefore be accepted that the Decision at issue was of direct concern to the applicants.

Insufficient causality will exist not merely where the chain is broken by the act of a third party, but also where the instrument affects an interest which is not recognised as legally protected by the Court.

Case T-12/93 Comité Central d' Entreprise de la Société Anonyme Vittel v Commission [1995] ECR II-1247

In 1992 the Commission approved the take-over of Perrier, the French mineral water undertaking, by Demilac, a subsidiary of Nestlé, if a number of conditions were met. One of these was that Vittel, a subsidiary of Perrier, sell its Pierval plant, which employed 119 people. Three works councils brought an action challenging the imposition of this condition, both in their own right and in their capacity as representatives of the employees.

50. ..., it must be stated that the concentration in question cannot prejudice the own rights of the representatives of the employees of the undertakings concerned. Contrary to the applicants' assertions, the fact that the sale of the Pierval plant, required by the decision authorizing the concentration, entails *inter alia* the disappearance from within Vittel of the Pierval works council, and consequently the end of the central works council, does not adversely affect the latter's own rights. The central works council has not demonstrated an interest in the preservation of its functions where by reason of a change in the structure of the undertaking concerned the conditions under which the applicable national law provides for it to be set up are no longer met. Similarly, FGA-CFDT has no interest of its own in the maintenance of the Pierval plant within Vittel, on the grounds that the sale of a substantial part of that company would entail structural and financial consequences for that trade union, as the interveners argue. The employees' representative organizations can assert rights of their own only in relation to the functions and prerogatives given to them, under the applicable legislation, in an undertaking with

549

a particular structure. They cannot claim that the structure of the undertaking should last indefinitely. In that respect, moreover, it follows essentially from Article 5 of Council Directive 77/187/EEC of 14 February 1977 on the approximation of the laws of the Member States relating to the safeguarding of employees' rights in the event of transfers of undertakings, businesses or parts of businesses (OJ 1977 L 61, p. 26) that, in the event of a transfer of an undertaking, the safeguarding of the own rights of the employees' representative organizations and the protective measures enjoyed by the employees' representatives are to be ensured in accordance with the laws, regulations and administrative provisions of the Member States. It follows from all those considerations that only a decision which may have an effect on the status of the employees' representative organizations or on the exercise of the prerogatives and duties given them by the legislation in force can affect such organizations' own interests. That cannot be the case with a decision authorizing a concentration.

.....

58. .... in the present case the transfer of the Pierval plant does not in itself entail any direct consequences for the rights which the employees derive from their contract or employment relationship. In the absence of any direct causal link between the alleged attack on those rights and the Commission's decision making authorization of the concentration subject *inter alia* to the transfer of the Pierval plant, the persons concerned must have an appropriate legal remedy available for the defence of their legitimate interests not at the stage of the review of the lawfulness of the said decision, but at the stage of the measures which are the immediate origin of the adverse effects thus alleged, and which may be adopted by the undertakings or in certain cases by the social partners concerned without any intervention by the Commission. It is at the stage of the adoption of such measures, review of which is within the jurisdiction of the national courts, that the safeguards intervene which are given to employees by the provisions of national law and of Community law such as, in particular, Directive 77/187/EEC (see also the proposal for a Council directive on the approximation of the laws of the Member States relating to the safeguarding of employees' rights in the event of transfers of undertakings, businesses or parts of businesses, submitted by the Commission on 8 September 1994 with a view to recasting that directive, OJ 1994 C 274, p. 10) and Council Directive 75/129/EEC of 17 February 1975 on the approximation of the laws of the Member States relating to collective redundancies (OJ 1975 L 48, p. 9), as amended by Council Directive 92/56/EEC of 24 June 1992 (OJ 1992 L 245, p. 3).

59. For all the above reasons, the applicants cannot be regarded as directly concerned by the contested decision, ...

This judgment shatters the suggestion that direct concern might, somehow, be ideologically neutral, as it addresses the question of which interests should be represented before the Court. It may be possible, therefore, to argue that a take-over does not affect the legal interests of a trade union, but it is surely difficult to argue that such a matter does not concern a trade union. To be sure, the question of whether a party has sufficient interest to commence an action has to be addressed in judicial review, and it is possible that it should be considered under the umbrella of direct concern. Yet if this is so, it is important that the Court is flexible in the interests it recognises. Private economic interests are well-established. If judicial review is to be available to all groups within society, it is important that a place also be found for collective interests.

c. Individual Concern

The biggest hurdle to most individual applicants has proved to be that of individual concern. The starting point remains the *Plaumann* test.

Case 25/62 Plaumann & Co v Commission [1963] ECR 95, [1964] CMLR 29

The Commission refused a German Government request that tariffs on imports of clementines from third countries be suspended. Plaumann, an importer of clementines challenged this refusal. The Court found there was no individual concern.

Persons other than those to whom a decision is addressed may only claim to be individually concerned if that decision affects them by reason of certain attributes which are peculiar to them or by reason of circumstances in which they are differentiated from all other persons and by virtue of these factors distinguishes them individually just as in the case of the person addressed. In the present case the applicant is affected by the disputed Decision as an importer of clementines, that is to say, by reason of a commercial activity which may at any time be practised by any person and is not therefore such as to distinguish the applicant in relation to the contested Decision as in the case of the addressee.

For these reasons the present action for annulment must be declared inadmissible.

The language in *Plaumann* is marvellously byzantine. In helping to understand it, commentators have made a distinction between 'open' and 'closed' categories:

> 'An open category is one the membership of which is not fixed and determined when the measure comes into force; a closed category is one the membership of which is fixed and determined.'[45]

In *Plaumann* the applicant fell within an open category, as the number of importers at the time of the Decision was not fixed and determined, in that anybody theoretically could become an importer of clementines. There was thus no individual concern. The following is an example of a closed category.

Joined Cases 106 & 107/63 Toepfer v Commission [1965] ECR 405, [1966] CMLR 111

The German authorities rejected a number of applications to import maize on 1 October 1963 when the levy set for imports of grain was zero. The Commission increased the tax on imports of grain on 2 October 1963 and confirmed the decision of the German authorities on 3 October 1963 for the period 1-4 October 1964. The importers sought to have this Decision annulled.

> It is clear from the fact that on 1 October 1963 the Commission took a decision fixing new free-at-frontier prices for maize imported into the Federal Republic as from 2 October, that the danger which the protective measures retained by the Commission were to guard against no longer existed as from this latter date.
>
> Therefore the only persons concerned by the said measures were importers who had applied for an import licence during the course of the day of 1 October 1963. The number and identity of these importers had already become fixed and ascertainable before 4 October, when the contested decision was made. The Commission was in a position to know that its decision affected the interests and the position of the said importers alone.
>
> The factual situation thus created differentiates the said importers, including the applicants from all other persons and distinguishes them individually just as in the case of the person addressed.

---

[45]   Hartley, T. *The Foundations of European Community Law* (1994, 3rd Edition, Clarendon) 367.

Therefore the objection of inadmissibility which has been raised is unfounded and the applications are admissible.

The test is extremely restrictive.[46] Craig has observed that the test of whether class is fixed and determined could be applied at three dates. The first is the date of the measure; the second is the date of the challenge, and the third is some future, undefined date. By adopting the third position, *Plaumann* makes challenge impossible except in cases, such as *Toepfer*, where the Decision applies retrospectively.[47] One can thus have the absurd situation where a measure affects only one party, but that party is held not to be individually concerned. In *Spijker*, for example, the Commission imposed a ban on the import of paint brushes from China into the BENELUX.[48] At the time there was only one undertaking which imported these into the BENELUX but the Court ruled that it was not individually concerned as the possibility was open to anyone.

Notwithstanding this, the test still applies. Its remit is not universal, however, as there are a number of circumstances in which a more liberal regime will be applied. The *Plaumann* test has been relaxed in three sets of circumstances - where the Commission has been granted wide powers, be they regulatory or quasi-legislative; where no other remedy is available, and, thirdly, where a small number of traders have suffered significant loss as a result of a Community act.

aa. Wide Commission Powers

In areas where sweeping powers are granted to non-majoritarian bureaucracies, if elected politicians abstain from intervention, they are additional reasons for judicial review standing requirements being

---

[46]   This is a constant mantra of the literature. For an early example see Barav. A. 'Direct and Individual Concern: An Almost Insurmountable Barrier to the Admissibility of Individual Appeal to the EEC Court' (1974) 11 *CMLRev* 191.

[47]   Craig, P. 'Legality, Standing and Substantive Review in Community Law' (1994) 14 *OJLS* 507, 509-510.

[48]   Case 231/82 *Spijker v Commission* [1983] ECR 2559, [1984] 2 CMLR 284.

relaxed. For here the focus of judicial review moves from placing limits on government power to that of securing interest representation.

There are two areas where the breadth of Commission powers is particularly apparent. The first are its wide regulatory powers in the field of competition and external trade. The second is where it is granted legislative or quasi-legislative powers. In the fields of competition,[49] State aids,[50] mergers[51] and external trade,[52] administrative procedures have been established conferring upon the Commission investigative powers and the powers to require States or undertakings to discontinue certain practices, and in certain circumstances to sanction those practices. Third parties are given a number of procedural rights. Most notably in the field of competition and external trade they are given the right to complain to the Commission of an illegal practice, and to require the Commission to examine the factual and legal particulars of the complaint.[53] If the *Plaumann* test of individual concern was adopted, they would not be able to challenge the Commission Decision, no matter how egregious the conduct. For, on its face, their interests are only affected *qua* consumer or competitor, both of which are open classes.

---

[49]   Regulation 17, OJ Spec Edition, 1962, 204/62, 87.

[50]   Article 93(2) & (3) [*88(2) & (3)*] EC.

[51]   Regulation 4064/89/EC, OJ 1989, L 395/1 as amended by Regulation 1310/97/EC, OJ 1997, L 180/1.

[52]   The most litigated area is anti-dumping measures. Dumping is a form of price discrimination whereby a third country exporter sells a good on the Community market at a price below that sold on the domestic market, or, if this does not provide a suitable comparison, some other third country market comparable to that of the Community. The Commission and the Council are entitled to impose duties on the goods representing the differential in prices, Regulation 384/96/EC, OJ 1996, L 56/1. The Commission also has powers to take action against subsidised goods from third countries, Regulation 3284/94/EC, OJ 1994, L 349/22 as amended by Regulation 1252/95/EC, OJ 1995, L 122/2, and against 'illicit commercial practices' carried out by third country exporters, Regulation 3286/94/EC, OJ 1994, L 349/71.

[53]   In the field of competition law see Regulation 17, supra n.49, Article 3(2)(b). In the field of external trade see Regulation 384/96/EC, supra n.51, Article 5(1); Regulation 3284/94/EC, supra n.51, Article 7(1); Regulation 3286/94/EC, supra n.51, Article 3(1). On the Commission's duties see Case T-24/90 *Automec v Commission* [1992] ECR II-2223, [1992] 5 CMLR 431.

The Court has got around this by ringfencing complainants as a privileged class.

Case 26/76 Metro-SB-Grossmärkte v Commission [1977] ECR 1875, [1978] 2 CMLR 1

Metro had been excluded from a selective distribution system in electronic goods operated by SABA and initiated a complaint. In a Decision addressed to SABA, the Commission stated that the system did not infringe EC competition law. Metro challenged this Decision.

The contested decision was adopted in particular as the result of a complaint submitted by Metro and that it relates to the provisions of SABA's distribution system, on which SABA relied and continues to rely as against Metro in order to justify its refusal to sell to the latter or to appoint it as a wholesaler, and which the applicant had for this reason impugned in its complaint.

It is in the interests of a satisfactory administration of justice and of the proper application of Articles 85 and 86 that natural or legal persons who are entitled, pursuant to Article 3(2)(b) of Regulation No 17, to request the Commission to find an infringement of Articles 85 and 86 should be able, if their request is not complied with wholly or in part, to institute proceedings in order to protect their legitimate interests.

In those circumstances the applicant must be considered to be directly and individually concerned, within the meaning of the second paragraph of Article 173, by the contested decision and the application is accordingly admissible.

There was little difficulty applying this reasoning to the field of external trade where explicit rights of complaint are also granted by the secondary legislation.[54] No explicit right to complain is provided in the fields of State aids and mergers. The position in these fields has been approximated to that in competition and external trade with complainants being able to challenge Commission Decisions if it can be shown that their submissions influenced the course of proceedings and their economic interests were substantially affected by those Decisions.[55]

---

[54] Case 264/82 *Timex Corporation v Council and Commission* [1985] ECR 849, [1985] 3 CMLR 550.

[55] See Joined Cases T-481 & T-484/93 *Vereniging van Exporteurs in Levende Varkens v Commission* [1995] ECR II-2941.

In *COFAZ* the Commission was notified of a Dutch subsidy to Dutch fertiliser producers by three French fertiliser companies.[56] The companies duly challenged the Decision by the Commission authorising the subsidy. The Court noted that the right of complainants to challenge Commission Decisions in the fields of competition and external trade stemmed from the procedural guarantees given by the Regulation to the complainants to protect their legitimate interests. It noted, however, that the fact the undertaking's complaint had led to the opening of the investigation, its views were heard during the procedure and the procedure was determined by the complainant's observations indicated that the measure was of concern to the complainant. From this, the Court stated that a complainant could challenge a Commission Decision authorising a State aid provided its position on the market was significantly affected by the aid.[57] The position of complainants is, however, qualified in the field of State aids. A complainant will not be able to challenge a Commission Decision if either the 'aid' in question is a general one which is not directed to particular undertakings or it affects the complainant's interests only indirectly.[58]

The possibility to challenge Commission Decisions has been given not just to complainants but to all those who have a 'legitimate or sufficient interest recognised in the administrative proceedings leading to the adoption of the contested Decision'.[59] In *Metro (No.2)* SABA remodelled its selective distribution agreement and resubmitted it for approval to the Commission.[60] Metro had not complained to the Commission but participated in the hearings which are required before the Commission can authorise a scheme. The Court found that as Metro was recognised as having a legitimate interest in submitting observation, it was individually concerned by the Decision.

The final parties affected by the investigation are those who are the subject-matter of the investigation. In the field of competition and

---

56   Case 169/84 *COFAZ SA v Commission* [1986] ECR 391, [1986] 3 CMLR 385.

57   For a similar approach in relation to mergers see Case T-2/93 *Air France v Commission* [1994] ECR II-323.

58   Case T-398/94 *Scheppvaart v Commission* [1996] ECR II-497.

59   Albors-Llorens, A., supra n.20, 85.

60   Case 75/84 *Metro v Commission* [1986] ECR 3021, [1987] 1 CMLR 118.

mergers this poses little problem, for, as the Decisions are addressed to these parties, they can be challenged by them. In the case of State aids, the Decision is normally addressed to the Member State granting the subsidy, but it has always been accepted that the recipient of the aid is individually concerned.[61] Dumping is more problematic. In anti-dumping proceedings the Commission, or the Council, will adopt Regulations imposing duties on imports of a good from a third country. Such a category is an open category which would fail the *Plaumann* test, as anyone, theoretically could export those goods to the Community. Yet with precious little explanation, the Court has been willing to provide an exception for this category of applicant. In *Allied Corporation* the Commission adopted a Regulation imposing anti-dumping duties on certain types of fertiliser coming from the United States following two American producers withdrawing price undertakings they had given.[62] The Court noted that whilst the measure was legislative in nature, it considered that it was of individual concern to those 'charged with practising dumping'. Any producer, exporter or importer reselling the good will be able to challenge an anti-dumping Regulation if they are identified[63] in the measure or were concerned by the Commission's preliminary investigation.

The Court has also relaxed standing requirements in areas where the Commission enjoys legislative or quasi-legislative powers. These have not been relaxed in an across the board manner, but the Court will look at the conditions attached to the grant of those powers. If these conditions require the Commission to take account of a class which is fixed and identifiable, then the Court will find individual concern even though, on its face, the measure seems to apply to an open category of undertakings.[64]

---

61   Case 730/79 *Phillip Morris v Commission* [1980] ECR 2671, [1980] 2 CMLR 321.

62   Joined Cases 239 & 275/82 *Allied Corporation v Commission* [1984] ECR 1005, [1985] 3 CMLR 572.

63   An earlier judgment had identified that those named in the Regulation should be able to challenge it, Case 113/77 *NTN v Council* [1979] ECR 1185, [1979] 2 CMLR 257.

64   See also Case C-152/88 *Sofrimport v Commission* [1990] ECR I-2477, [1990] 3 CMLR 80.

Case 11/82 Piraiki-Patraiki v Commission [1985] ECR 207, [1985] 2 CMLR 46[65]

Four of the seven undertakings had already entered into contract to export cotton to France at the time the Commission authorised the French Government to impose a quota on Greek imports. These undertakings argued that they were individually concerned by reason of the obligation in Article 130(3) of the 1981 Greek Act of Accession that in the authorisation of protective measures 'priority shall be given to such measures as will least disturb the functioning of the Common Market'.

19. ..., it must be held that the fact that, before the adoption of the decision at issue, they [these applicants] had entered into contracts which were to be carried out during the months to which the decision applied constitutes a circumstance which distinguishes them from any other person concerned by the decision, in so far as the execution of their contracts was wholly or partly prevented by the adoption of the decision.

20. The Commission, however, challenges the assertion that that circumstance is sufficient in itself for the applicants to be regarded as individually concerned. It argues that in any event when it adopted the decision it was unaware of the number of contracts already entered into for the period covered by that decision and that, in contrast to the cases considered in previous decisions of the court, it had no way of obtaining information in that regard, since the contracts in question were governed by private law and there was no obligation to declare them to Community or national authorities.

21. In that respect it must be observed that the reply to be given to the question whether and to what extent the Commission was aware, or could have made itself aware, which Greek exporters had entered into contracts covering the period of application of the contested decision depends on the interpretation given to Article 130 of the Act of Accession, and in particular on the question whether the Commission, before authorizing a protective measure under that provision, is obliged to make appropriate inquiries as to the economic effects of the decision to be taken and the undertakings which would be affected by it. Since arguments related to that problem were raised in support of the assertion that the decision at issue is unlawful, the admissibility of the application from that point of view must be considered in conjunction with the substance of the case.

.....

26. That requirement [Article 130(3)] may be explained by the fact that a provision permitting the authorization of protective measures with regard to a Member State which

---

[65]   For the facts see pp 548-549.

derogate, even temporarily and in respect of certain products only, from the rules relating to the free movement of goods must, like any provision of that nature, be interpreted strictly.

......

28. It must be observed that in order to ascertain whether the measure whose authorization is being considered meets the conditions laid down in Article 130(3) the Commission must also take into account the situation in the Member State with regard to which the protective measure is requested. In particular, in so far as the circumstances of the case permit, the Commission must inquire into the negative effects which its decision might have on the economy of that Member State as well as on the undertakings concerned. In that connection it must also consider, in so far as is possible, the contracts which those undertakings, relying on the continuation of free trade within the Community, have already entered into and whose execution will be wholly or partially prevented by the decision authorizing the protective measure.

29. In that regard the Commission objects that it would be impossible for it, during the brief period within which it must act, to make itself aware of the exact number of contracts meeting that description.

30. That argument cannot be accepted in the light of the circumstances of this case. Before adopting the contested decision the Commission had sufficient time to obtain the necessary information. As the Commission admitted at the hearing, moreover, it had arranged a meeting with representatives of the Greek Government and of the trade interests concerned, which even included certain of the applicants.

31. In those circumstances it must be concluded that the Commission was in a position to obtain sufficiently exact information on the contracts already entered into which were to be performed during the period of application of the decision at issue. It follows that the undertakings which were party to contracts meeting that description must be considered as individually concerned for the purpose of the admissibility of this action, as members of a limited class of traders identified or identifiable by the Commission and by reason of those contracts particularly affected by the decision at issue.

bb. The Existence of No Alternate Remedy

The failure to establish direct and individual concern will not always leave a party without recourse. We have seen that there are other routes available to the Court. There is one authority which suggests that if these are not available, standing rules will be relaxed.[66] The case is unusual, however, as it concerned the 1984 elections to the European Parliament. For the Court to have allowed the Decision to stand would have done immense damage to the credibility of the Community and to the democratic credentials of the Parliament. The judgment has also been interpreted within its narrow institutional context as 'safeguarding a democratic community open to all parties across the political spectrum'.[67]

Case 294/83 Parti Ecologiste 'Les Verts' v Parliament [1986] ECR 1339, [1987] 2 CMLR 343

In 1982 the European Parliament adopted a formula for the allocation of funds to political parties participating in the 1984 European Parliament. Parties were to claim the money by seeking reimbursement, in line with the formula, within 90 days of the publication of the results. The Green Party challenged the 1982 Decision on the grounds that it discriminated in favour of political parties already represented in the European Parliament. The Decision affected, however, an open category of persons, as theoretically anybody could stand for the European Parliament.

35. This action concerns a situation which has never before come before the Court. Because they had representatives in the institution, certain political groupings took part in the adoption of a decision which deals both with their own treatment and with that accorded to rival groupings which were not represented. In view of this, and in view of the fact that the contested measure concerns the allocation of public funds for the purpose of preparing for elections and it is alleged that those funds are allocated unequally, it cannot be considered that only groupings which were represented and which were therefore identifiable at the date of the adoption of the contested measure are individually concerned by it.

36. Such an interpretation would give rise to inequality in the protection afforded by the Court to the various groupings competing in the same elections. Groupings not represented could not prevent the allocation of the appropriations at issue before the beginning of the election campaign because they would be unable to plead the illegality

---

[66]   For this interpretation see Joliet, R. 'The Reimbursement of Election Expenses: a Forgotten Dispute' (1994) 19 *ELRev* 243.

[67]   Craig, P. & De Búrca, G. *EC Law: Text, Cases and Materials* (1995, Clarendon, Oxford) 471.

of the basic decision except in support of an action against the individual decisions refusing to reimburse sums greater than those provided for. It would therefore be impossible for them to bring an action for annulment before the Court prior to the decisions or to obtain an order from the Court under Article 185 of the Treaty suspending application of the contested basic decision.

37. Consequently, it must be concluded that the applicant association, which was in existence at the time when the 1982 Decision was adopted and which was able to present candidates at the 1984 elections, is individually concerned by the contested measures.

cc. A Small Number of Traders Have Suffered Significant Loss

One of the criticisms of *Plaumann* is its degree of formalism. On the one hand, it gives standing to quite large numbers of persons if they fall within a closed category. On the other hand, traditionally no matter how small the number of persons affected, if the category was open standing would be denied. There are signs in some recent judgments of a more flexible approach which takes note of the 'facts on the ground' where the number of traders affected is very small and their interests are significantly affected.

Case C-358/89 Extramet v Council [1991] ECR I-2501, [1993] 2 CMLR 619

Extramet was the largest importer of calcium in the Community. Following a complaint made on behalf of Péchiney, who was both the only producer of calcium within the Community and Extramet's principal competitor, a Council Regulation imposed anti-dumping duties on Extramet's main source of supplies from the People's Republic of China and the Soviet Union. As anybody could theoretically import calcium, Extramet appeared to fall into an open category. As it was neither directly concerned by the investigation nor involved in the procedure, it could not benefit from the more liberal regime of standing which applied to other areas of the field of dumping.

13. In order to determine whether the objection of inadmissibility raised by the Council is well founded, it must be borne in mind that, although in the light of the criteria set out in the second paragraph of Article 173 of the Treaty regulations imposing anti-dumping duties are in fact, as regards their nature and their scope, of a legislative character, inasmuch as they apply to all the traders concerned, taken as a whole, their provisions

may none the less be of individual concern to certain traders (see the judgments in Joined Cases 239 and 275/82 *Allied Corporation v Commission* [1984] ECR 1005, paragraph 11, and in Case 53/83 *Allied Corporation v Commission* [1985] ECR 1621, paragraph 4).

14. It follows that measures imposing anti-dumping duties may, without losing their character as regulations, be of individual concern in certain circumstances to certain traders who therefore have standing to bring an action for their annulment.

15. The Court has acknowledged that this was the case, in general, with regard to producers and exporters who are able to establish that they were identified in the measures adopted by the Commission or the Council or were concerned by the preliminary measures (see the judgments in *Allied Corporation v Commission*, cited above, the judgments in Joined Cases C-133 and 150/87 *Nashua Corporation v Commission and Council* [1990] ECR I-719, and in Case C-156/87 *Gestetner Holdings v Council and Commission* [1990] ECR I-781), and with regard to importers whose retail prices for the goods in question have been used as a basis for establishing the export prices (see, most recently, the judgments in Case C-304/86 *Enital v Commission and Council* [1990] ECR I-2939, Case C-305/86 *Neotype Techmashexport v Commission and Council* [1990] ECR I-2945, and Case C-157/87 *Electroimpex v Council* [1990] ECR I-3021).

16. Such recognition of the right of certain categories of traders to bring an action for the annulment of an anti-dumping regulation cannot, however, prevent other traders from also claiming to be individually concerned by such a regulation by reason of certain attributes which are peculiar to them and which differentiate them from all other persons (see the judgment in Case 25/62 *Plaumann v Commission* [1963] ECR 95).

17. The applicant has established the existence of a set of factors constituting such a situation which is peculiar to the applicant and which differentiates it, as regards the measure in question, from all other traders. The applicant is the largest importer of the product forming the subject-matter of the anti-dumping measure and, at the same time, the end-user of the product. In addition, its business activities depend to a very large extent on those imports and are seriously affected by the contested regulation in view of the limited number of manufacturers of the product concerned and of the difficulties which it encounters in obtaining supplies from the sole Community producer, which, moreover, is its main competitor for the processed product.

18. It follows that the objection of inadmissibility raised by the Council must be dismissed.

It was argued initially that the implications of *Extramet* might be confined to the context of anti-dumping proceedings.[68] This reasoning has now been expanded to other areas, however. In *Air France* the applicant, Air France, was given standing to challenge a Decision by the Commission that a takeover of Dan Air by British Airways did not fall within its jurisdiction partly because it had been deprived of its right to a hearing but also because the Court considered it to be differentiated from other parties, as it was British Airways' main competitor on air routes between the United Kingdom and France.[69] The case of ASPEC was even more explicit.[70] An Association of Sorbitol Producers challenged a Commission authorisation of an Italian subsidy to an Italian producer of sorbitol, which is a form of isoglucose. The Association had not been involved in the procedure which led up to the Decision but the CFI found standing as it noted there were only 5 producers of sorbitol within the Community; the market was suffering from overcapacity and the subsidy was likely to increase production significantly.

These cases undoubtedly soften the harshness of the *Plaumann* test. *Extramet* should not be seen, however, as the basis for a remodelling of judicial review. The conditions in which it applies appear very narrowly confined. Furthermore, by requiring that standing will only be given to a limited number of firms who can show that they are particularly affected by the Community measure, the test discriminates in favour of large multinationals at the expense of smaller companies and other parties.

dd. Possible Reforms

In the run-up to the IGC it was suggested that Article 173(4) [*230(4)*] EC might be reformed and the standing rules relaxed. Two suggestions were put forward. The widest, by Neuwahl, was that a party would be

[68] Arnull, A. 'Challenging EC Anti-Dumping Regulations: The Problem of Admissibility' (1992) 13 *ECLR* 73.

[69] Case T-3/93 *Air France v Commission* [1994] ECR II-121.

[70] Case T-435/93 *ASPEC v Commission* [1995] ECR II-1281.

individually concerned if a measure infringed its individual rights.[71] Such a proposal would have been close to relaxing standing rules altogether, and would certainly have been a lot more radical than national regimes of judicial review. More cautiously, Arnull suggested that the American test be adopted whereby individuals could sue if their interests had been 'adversely affected'.[72]

In the event no reform took place, and, given the continued repetition of the *Plaumann* formula,[73] it would a *volte-face* of seismic proportions for the Court to abandon that doctrine.

There are two further areas where reform is pushed. The first is greater recognition of group rights. Group actions are mentioned most frequently in the fields of consumer and environmental law. The arguments in favour of such actions are well-established and centre around the theme that in a pluralist society diffuse interests should be as well represented as private interests.[74] Indeed, the Commission has welcomed their development in national jurisdictions as means of securing more effective enforcement of EC consumer and environmental law.[75] To some criticism,[76] the Court has so far refused to relax standing requirements for public interest litigation.[77]

---

[71] Neuwahl, N. `Article 173 Paragraph 4 EC: Past, Present and Possible Future' (1996) 21 *ELRev* 17, 31.

[72] US Administrative Procedure Act 1946, s. 10. See Arnull, A. 'Private Applicants and the Action for Annulment under Article 173 of the EC Treaty' (1995) 32 *CMLRev* 7, 49.

[73] e.g. Case C-138/95P *Campo Ebro Industrial v Council*, Judgment of 17 April 1997.

[74] Within the EC context see Führ, M. (et al.) 'Access to Justice: Legal Standing for Environmental Associations in the European Union' in Robinson, D. & Dunkley, J. (eds.) *Public Interest Perspectives in Environmental Law* (1995, Chancery, Chichester). See also Krämer, L. 'Public Interest Litigation in Environmental Matters before European Courts' (1996) 8 *JEL* 1.

[75] EC Commission, *Action Plan on Consumer Access to Justice* COM (96) 13; EC Commission, *Implementing Community Environmental Law* COM (96) 500.

[76] Gerard, N. 'Access to Justice on Environmental Matters - A Case of Double Standards?' (1996) 8 *JEL* 139.

[77] See for other failed attempts by environmental NGOs to review EC action see Case T-461/93 *An Taisce v Commission* [1994] ECR II-733; Case T-219/95R *Danielsson et al. v Commission* [1995] ECR II-3051.

Case T-585/93 Stichting Greenpeace Council v Commission [1995] ECR II-2205

In 1991 the Commission granted Spain financial assistance from the European Regional Development Fund to contribute to the construction of two power stations on the Canary Islands. Work was started without an environmental impact assessment being carried out. Despite being informed of this, the Commission continued to grant assistance to the project. Greenpeace, two Spanish environmental organisations and some private individuals sought annulment of this Decision. Having found the claims of the private individuals to be inadmissible the Court considered the position of the associations.

59. It has consistently been held that an association formed for the protection of the collective interests of a category of persons cannot be considered to be directly and individually concerned for the purposes of the fourth paragraph of Article 173 of the Treaty by a measure affecting the general interests of that category, and is therefore not entitled to bring an action for annulment where its members may not do so individually (Joined Cases 19 to 22/62 *Fédération Nationale de la Boucherie en Gros et du Commerce en Gros des Viandes and Others v Council* [1962] ECR 49. ... Furthermore, special circumstances such as the role played by an association in a procedure which led to the adoption of an act within the meaning of Article 173 of the Treaty may justify holding admissible an action brought by an association whose members are not directly and individually concerned by the contested measure (Joined Cases 67, 38 and 70/85 *Van der Kooy and Others v Commission* [1988] ECR 219 and Case C-313/90 *CIRFS and Others v Commission* [1993] ECR I-1125).

60. The three applicant associations, Greenpeace, TEA and CIC, claim that they represent the general interest, in the matter of environmental protection, of people residing on Gran Canaria and Tenerife and that their members are affected by the contested decision; they do not, however, adduce any special circumstances to demonstrate the individual interest of their members as opposed to any other person residing in those areas. The possible effect on the legal position of the members of the applicant associations cannot, therefore, be any different from that alleged here by the applicants who are private individuals. Consequently, in so far as the applicants in the present case who are private individuals cannot, as the Court has held, be considered to be individually concerned by the contested decision, nor can the members of the applicant associations, as local residents of Gran Canaria and Tenerife.

Another proposal is that greater use be made of intervention rights for third parties.

Harlow, C. 'Towards a Theory of Access for the European Court of Justice' (1992) 12 *Yearbook of European Law* 213, 247-248

The most economical way to increase interest representation without overloading the Court is, however, undoubtedly through intervention procedure. Many modern courts feel able to allow intervention freely and interventions by interest groups are particularly a feature of constitutional courts. In the Court of Justice, in sharp contrast, group interventions are rare and Articles 37 and 20 of the Statute are largely the preserve of the privileged applicants.

The Court's distinctive inquisitorial procedures could be used to design an appropriate intervention procedure without adding to burdens on applicants in the shape of greater expense or delay. Strict time-limits can already be imposed for interventions with limited rights of contradiction and oral observations already require the Court's permission. Submissions could be limited as to length. Increased use could be made of the *juge rapporteur* if orality were thought necessary; alternatively, they could be collected and evaluated by the Advocate General, forming part of his Opinion.

At present third parties can intervene wherever they can establish a legitimate interest in the result of the case.[78] There are currently strict constraints on intervention. The first is that third parties cannot intervene in any case between EC institutions or between EC institutions and the Member States.[79] This prevents them from intervening in any case brought by a privileged or semi-privileged applicant. Secondly, third parties cannot introduce radically new argument, as their intervention must be limited to supporting the submissions of one of the parties.[80]

IV. The Action for Failure to Act

i. The Context to Article 175 [*232*] EC

In certain circumstances positive duties are placed by EC law upon the EC institutions to act. The EC institutions are under a duty to complete

---

[78]   Article 37(1), Statute of the Court of Justice.
[79]   Article 37(2), Statute of the Court of Justice.
[80]   Article 37(3), Statute of the Court of Justice.

many of the objectives of Community, such as, for example, the internal market or the common transport policy.[81] Positive duties can also be placed upon institutions by secondary legislation. The Commission is required to examine the factual and legal particulars of any complaint about a breach of EC competition which is made by a person with a legitimate interest.[82] The conditions for bringing an action against an EC institution if it fails to act in these circumstances are set out in Article 175 [*232*] EC.

Article 175 [*232*] EC. Should the European Parliament, the Council or the Commission, in infringement of this Treaty, fail to act, the Member States and the other institutions of the Community may bring an action before the Court of Justice to have the infringement established.

The action shall be admissible only if the institution concerned has first been called upon to act. If, within two months of being so called upon, the institution concerned has not defined its position the action may be brought within a further period of two months.

Any natural or legal person may, under the conditions laid down in the preceding paragraphs, complain to the Court of Justice that an institution of the Community has failed to address to that person any act other than a recommendation or an opinion.

The Court of Justice shall have jurisdiction, under the same conditions, in actions or proceedings brought by the ECB in the areas falling within the latter's field of competence and in actions or proceedings brought against the latter.

Article 175 [*232*] EC and 173 [*230*] EC were described in an early judgment as prescribing 'one and the same method of recourse',[83] and they are in many ways complementary to one another. This has two aspects. The first is that Article 175 [*232*] EC cannot be used to subvert the Article 173 EC [*230*] EC. Most famously, an individual cannot evade the standing requirements of Article 173 [*230*] EC by calling upon an EC Institution to repeal an act and then bringing an Article 175 [*232*] EC action.

---

[81]   Case 13/83 *Parliament v Council* [1985] ECR 1513, [1986] 1 CMLR 138.
[82]   Case T-24/90 *Automec v Commission* [1992] ECR II-2223, [1992] 5 CMLR 431.
[83]   Case 15/70 *Chevalley v Commission* [1970] ECR 979.

Joined Cases 10 & 18/68 Eridania v Commission [1969] ECR 459

The Commission had granted aid to certain sugar refineries in Italy. The applicants challenged the Decision, claiming that their competitive position was seriously affected by the grant of the aid. The Court found that the applicants were not individually concerned by the Decision. The applicants also brought an action under Article 175 [232] EC for failure to revoke the Decision.

16. The action provided for in Article 175 is intended to establish an illegal omission as appears from that Article, which refers to a failure to act 'in infringement of this Treaty' and from Article 176 which refers to a failure to act declared to be 'contrary to this Treaty'.

Without stating under which provision of Community law the Commission was required to annul or revoke the said decisions, the applicants have confined themselves to alleging that those decisions were adopted in infringement of the Treaty and that this fact alone would thus suffice to make the Commission's failure to act subject to the provisions of Article 175.

17. The Treaty provides, however, particularly in Article 173, other methods of recourse by which an allegedly illegal Community measure may be disputed and if necessary annulled on the application of a duly qualified party.

To admit, as the applicants wish to do, that the parties concerned could ask the institution from which the measure came to revoke it and, in the event of the Commission's failing to act, refer such failure to the Court as an illegal omission to deal with the matter would amount to providing them with a method of recourse parallel to that of Article 173, which would not be subject to the conditions laid down by the Treaty.

18. This application does not therefore satisfy the requirements of Article 175 of the Treaty and must thus be held to be inadmissible.

The second feature of the complementarity of Article 173 [230] EC and 175 [232] EC is, as one author put it:

> 'the system of remedies ... would be incomplete if Community institutions were subject to judicial control only in respect of their positive actions while they could evade the obligations imposed upon them by simply failing to act.'[84]

---

[84] Toth, A. 'The Law as It Stands on the Appeal for Failure to Act' (1975/2) *LIEI* 65, 65.

In principle, Article 175 [232] EC should therefore reflect Article 173 [230] EC, so that where an act could be challenged by a party under Article 173 [230] EC, failure on the part of the EC institution in question to adopt that act can also be challenged by the same party.

ii. The Procedure

The EC institution must first be called upon to act by the applicant. Whilst the Article places no time limit within which an action must be brought, it appears that if the institution's position on the matter is clear to the applicant, it must bring the request for action within a reasonable period. In *Netherlands v Commission*, a case which involved Article 35 ECSC, the parallel provision to Article 175 [232] EC in the ECSC Treaty, the Commission informed the Dutch Government that a French restructuring plan did not violate the Treaty provisions on State aids.[85] The Dutch Government waited a further 18 months before requesting the Commission to act. The Court, reasoning from the principle of legal certainty, stated that an applicant did not have a right to raise the matter with the Commission indefinitely and had delayed too long in this instance.

The applicant can only bring the matter to Court if the institution has not 'defined its position' within 2 months of being called to act.[86] The Court is very oblique about when institutions will be deemed to have defined their position. A Decision refusing to act will be sufficient,[87] as will a Resolution.[88] An institution may permissibly act in a different way from that in which it was called to act.[89] The principle of complementarity would require that this position be an act which is

---

[85]   Case 59/70 *Netherlands v Commission* [1971] ECR 639.

[86]   There is then a limitation period upon the applicant who must bring the action within two months of this date.

[87]   Such measures are treated as a reviewable act challengeable under Article 173 [230] EC, Case T-83/92 *Zunis Holding* [1993] ECR II-1169.

[88]   Case C-41/92 *Liberal Democrats v Parliament* [1993] ECR I-3153.

[89]   Case C-25/91 *Pesqueras Echebastar v Commission* [1993] ECR I-1719; Case T-38/96 *Guérin Automobiles v Commission*, Judgment of 10 July 1997.

capable of being reviewed under Article 173 [*230*] EC. It appears, however, that an institution can define its position without adopting a reviewable act provided that the act it adopts is a prerequisite for the adoption of a reviewable act.[90] The clearest statement of this position was by the CFI in *Guérin*.[91]

Case T-186/94 Guérin Automobiles v Commission [1995] ECR II-1753

Guérin wrote to the Commission alleging that Volvo France had breached Article 86 [*82*] EC in terminating a car dealership agreement with it. The Commission wrote back stating that there were insufficient grounds for it to proceed, but invited comments from Guérin. If comments had been received, it would have decided whether or not to reject the complaint finally. Guérin instead instigated an Article 175 [232] EC action.

25. The Court finds that on the date of this judgment there is no evidence on the file that the Commission adopted a decision within the meaning of Article 189 of the Treaty in response to the applicant's complaint. That finding is not sufficient, however, to justify the conclusion that the defendant institution has failed to act because in certain circumstances an act which itself is not open to an action for annulment may nevertheless constitute a 'definition of position' terminating the failure to act if it is the prerequisite for the next step in a procedure which is to culminate in a legal act which is itself open to an action for annulment under the conditions laid down in Article 173 of the Treaty (Case 377/87 *Parliament v Council*, cited above, paragraphs 7 and 10, and Case 302/87 *Parliament v Council*, cited above, paragraph 16). It is therefore necessary for the Court of First Instance to determine whether in the circumstances of this case there occurred an act of the Commission which, even if it was not a measure against which an action for annulment could be brought, terminated the failure to act.

---

90   See earlier Case 377/87 *Parliament v Council* [1988] ECR 4017, [1989] 3 CMLR 870; Case 302/87 *Parliament v Council* [1988] ECR 5615.

91   The CFI's decision was upheld on appeal in Case C-282/95P *Guérin Automobiles v Commission*, Judgment of 18 March 1997.

iii. Locus Standi

A distinction is once again made between privileged and non-privileged applicants. There is no category of semi-privileged applicant, however. Instead Article 175 [*232*] has a broader range of privileged applicants than Article 173 [*230*] EC. It includes all the EC institutions. No constraints are therefore placed on the standing of the Council, Commission, Parliament, and the Court of Auditors. Whilst not formally an EC institution, Article 175(4) [*232(4)*] EC also gives privileged status to the ECB.

Non-privileged applicants can complain of the failure to adopt acts, other than recommendations and opinions, which would have been addressed to them. Beyond that, the position is unclear. They certainly cannot challenge acts which, when adopted, would not directly and individually concern them.[92] The principle of complementarity would require that they be allowed, however, to challenge those acts which would be of direct and individual concern.[93] The Court has certainly held that to be the case in Article 148 EURATOM, the parallel provision in the EURATOM Treaty.[94] When called upon to settle the matter, however, the CFI was more equivocal.[95]

Case T-277/94 AITEC v Commission [1996] ECR II- 351

The Commission began investigating a subsidy granted by the Greek Government in 1989. It asked for comments, and the applicant, a representative of the majority of Italian cement producers, duly intervened. In 1990 the Commission declared the subsidy illegal. The applicant considered that the Greek Government had not complied with the Decision. It therefore asked the Commission to bring Court proceedings against the Greek Government. The

---

[92]   e.g. Joined Cases 97, 99, 193 & 215/86 *Asteris v Commission* [1988] ECR 2181.

[93]   Toth, A., supra n.84, 85.

[94]   Case C-107/91 *ENU v Commission* [1993] ECR I-599.

[95]   See however Case T-32/93 *Ladbroke v Commission* [1994] ECR II-1015, where the CFI suggests more directly that the question of direct and individual concern is relevant to the standing of private parties.

Commission refused. The CFI found that this refusal was not a reviewable act. It then examined possible standing under Article 175 [*232*] EC.

61. ... it is necessary to examine the argument that a decision to institute proceedings before the Court of Justice would be of direct and individual concern to the applicant or its members, and that they can therefore bring an action for failure to act, despite the wording of Article 175 of the Treaty.

62. Assuming that such a parallel relationship between an action for annulment under Article 173 of the Treaty and an action for failure to act under Article 175 could be recognized, and, further, that the judicial protection of individuals requires a wide interpretation of the third paragraph of Article 175 of the Treaty, such as to enable a natural or legal person to contest the failure of an institution to adopt an act which is not addressed to that person but which, if adopted, would be of direct concern to that person (see the judgment in [Case 247/87] *Star Fruit Company v Commission*, cited above, and the Opinion of the Advocate General in that case ([1989] ECR 294, point 13)), it would then be necessary to examine whether AITEC or its members is, or are, in such a position.

63. As the Court has already observed, the act sought is merely an internal preparatory measure which does not have any external effects and does not concern any individual (see paragraph 59 above). The establishment of a procedural relationship between the Commission and Greece would not affect the legal situation of the applicant or its members, particularly since the 1990 decision is final. At the hearing, the applicant itself admitted that it would not be allowed to participate in such proceedings as an intervener. Only delivery of a judgment by the Court of Justice could have any effect on its legal situation or that of its members. Furthermore, the applicant also acknowledged that during the proceedings before the Court of Justice it would have to be established '... whether or not there has been a failure to fulfil obligations, and in what circumstances'. As the applicant itself acknowledges, it is therefore possible that the Court of Justice might find that the Member State concerned had not failed to fulfil its obligations. Delivery of such a judgment would not be of direct concern to the applicant either. Consequently, in no case would the act sought be of direct concern to the applicant (see, to that effect, the judgment of the Court of First Instance in Case T-32/93 *Ladbroke v Commission* [1994] ECR II-1015, paragraph 41).

64. It follows that, even assuming the existence of a parallel relationship between an action for annulment and an action for failure to act, the applicant would not be directly concerned in the present case.

V. The Plea of Illegality

Particularly in areas where the Commission enjoys delegated powers, parties face a problem when they want to challenge those acts. The Commission measure may be addressed to or be of direct and individual concern, but the parties concerned may want to challenge the act on the basis that the enabling parent measure is illegal. They may face difficulties here because the time limits may have passed, or they may not satisfy the *locus standi* requirements in relation to the parent instrument. The plea of illegality addresses this by allowing a party in proceedings against a measure to plead the inapplicability of its parent measure.

Article 184 [*241*] EC. Notwithstanding the expiry of the period laid down in the fifth paragraph of Article 173 [*230*], any party may, in proceedings in which a regulation adopted jointly by the European Parliament and the Council, or a regulation of the Council, of the Commission or of the ECB is at issue, plead the grounds specified in the second paragraph of Article 173[*230*], in order to invoke before the Court of Justice the inapplicability of that regulation.

The nature of Article 184 [*241*] EC was explained in *Wöhrmann*.

Joined Cases 31 & 33/62 Wöhrmann v Commission [1962] ECR 506, [1963] 152

The applicants sought to challenge a Commission Decision authorising the imposition by Germany of duties upon the import of powdered milk. Since the limitation period for Article 173 [*230*] EC had elapsed the applicants attempted to use Article 184 [*241*] EC, arguing that the latter could be invoked where the matter was pending before a national court.

Because Article 184 does not specify before which court or tribunal the proceedings in which the regulation is at issue must be brought, the applicants conclude that the inapplicability of that regulation may in any event be invoked before the Court of Justice. This would mean that there would exist a method of recourse running concurrently with that available under Article 173.

This is however not the meaning of Article 184. It is clear from the wording and the general scheme of this Article that a declaration of the inapplicability of a regulation is only contemplated in proceedings brought before the Court of Justice itself under some other provision of the treaty, and then only incidentally and with limited effect.

More particularly, it is clear from the reference to the time limit laid down in Article 173 that Article 184 is applicable only in the context of proceedings brought before the Court of Justice and that it does not permit the said time limit to be avoided.

The sole object of Article 184 is thus to protect an interested party against the application of an illegal regulation, without thereby in any way calling in issue the regulation itself, which can no longer be challenged because of the expiry of the time limit laid down in Article 173.

The first point raised by *Wöhrmann*, that Article 184 [*241*] EC is a parasitic action which may only be brought within the context of other proceedings before the Court of Justice, has never since been doubted.[96] The second point, that it does not result in any Regulation being declared invalid but, merely, that it will not apply to the case in hand, is less clear cut. Formally, this is probably correct.[97] Yet the CFI has ruled that the EC institutions are under a duty to review measures in the light of a judgment.[98] Whilst the continued formal validity of the measure might act as a bar to claims which concerned events which took place before the date of the judgment, it seems inconceivable that this obligation to review on the part of an EC institution would not result in its removing the offending elements in the measure.

Two other areas of doubt have surrounded the application of Article 184 [*241*] EC. The provision states that it can only be used to declare Regulations inapplicable. The first revolves around whether, notwithstanding this, it could be used against other instruments. As in other areas, the Court has examined substance rather than form. It has therefore allowed a plea of illegality to be invoked against any measure which is general and legislative in nature. In *Simmenthal*, therefore, the Court allowed an Article 184 [*241*] EC action to be brought against some Notices of Invitation to Tender which formed the legal basis for a

---

[96]   This was reaffirmed most recently in Case T-154/94 *Comité des salines de France v Commission*, Judgment of 22 October 1996, [1997] 1 CMLR 943.

[97]   Case 92/78 *Simmenthal SpA v Commission* [1979] ECR 777, [1980] 1 CMLR 25.

[98]   Case T-227/95 *AssiDomän Kraft v Commission*, Judgment of 10 July 1997.

Commission Decision setting a minimum price for beef on the ground that these were similar to Regulations in that they were general acts which 'determined in advance and objectively the rights and obligations of traders'.[99]

The second issue of controversy was whether Article 184 [*241*] EC could be used by parties who had had an earlier opportunity to challenge the act in question. The most obvious example is privileged parties under Article 173 [*230*] EC who could have challenged the Regulation at the time of its adoption. Bebr argued that to allow this would enable Article 184 [*241*] EC to be used to subvert the time limits in Article 173 EC [*230*] EC.[100] Others considered that an Article 184 [*241*] EC action should still be available, as it was only when a measure was implemented that irregularities would become apparent, and this might be well after the two month time limit set in Article 173 [*230*] EC.[101] The Court, after some period, has adopted the former view.

Case C-135/93 Spain v Commission [1995] ECR I-1651

In 1988 the Commission drew up a framework guideline for State aid to the motor vehicle industry which entered into force on 1 January 1989 and was valid for 2 years. It extended the framework in 1990. This time the extension had no duration, but the Commission agreed to review the matter after 2 years. In January 1993 the Commission wrote to the Spanish Government, stating that it had reviewed the framework Guideline, and, as the majority of Member States were happy with it, the Guideline would continue for a number of years to come. The Spanish Government challenged this Communication and also argued that the 1990 extension was unlawful.

16. With respect to the action against the 1990 extension decision, it must be stated that in its application the Kingdom of Spain does not invoke the illegality of that decision as

---

[99] Case 92/78 *Simmenthal SpA v Commission* [1979] ECR 777, [1980] 1 CMLR 25.

[100] Bebr, G. 'Judicial Remedy of Private Parties against Normative Acts of the European Communities: The Role of the Exception of Illegality' (1966) 4 *CMLRev* 7.

[101] Barav, A. 'The Exception of Illegality in Community Law: A Critical Analysis' (1974) 11 *CMLRev* 366. See also Advocate General Roemer in Case 32/65 *Italy v Commission* [1966] ECR 389.

a ground for the annulment of the decision of 23 December 1992, but formally seeks its annulment. To be admissible, such a claim should have been made within the period of two months laid down in the third paragraph of Article 173 of the Treaty.

17. In any case, to accept that an applicant could, in an action for annulment of a decision, raise a plea of illegality against an earlier act of the same kind, annulment of which he could have sought directly, would make it possible indirectly to challenge earlier decisions which were not contested within the period for bringing proceedings prescribed in Article 173 of the Treaty, thereby circumventing that time-limit.

The principle applies to any party who had an earlier opportunity to bring the matter directly to the Court of Justice. In *TWD (No. 2)* the Commission had adopted a Decision in 1986 that a subsidy from the German Land of Bavaria to the applicant, a textile company, was illegal.[102] This was not challenged. A new plan was submitted by the Bavarian government and was authorised by the Commission on condition that aid illegally granted to the applicant under the first scheme be repaid. The applicant brought a challenge against this second Decision. It also challenged the first Decision, using Article 184 [*241*] EC, claiming that the economic effects of the first Commission Decision only became apparent following the second Decision. The CFI deemed this latter complaint to be inadmissible, noting that, as the applicant could have challenged the first Decision using Article 173 [*230*] EC, it was debarred now from bringing a challenge under Article 184 [*241*] EC.

The practical effect of this principle is to ensure that Article 184 [*241*] EC has become the preserve of 'non-privileged' applicants. As privileged applicants have unlimited standing to challenge Regulations under Article 173 [*230*] EC, so, consequently, they can have no recourse to Article 184 [*241*] EC. Semi-privileged applicants will also have no recourse to Article 184 EC [*241*] EC. For they can only challenge measures which touch upon their institutional prerogatives. Article 184

---

[102] Joined Cases T-244 & T-486/93 *TWD Textilwerke Deggendorf v Commission* [1995] ECR II-2265, [1995] 1 CMLR 332.

[*241*] EC only arises, however, in the context of challenges to implementing measures which cannot touch on the institutional prerogatives of semi-privileged applicants any more than the parent measure.

VI. Civil Liability of the EC Institutions

The civil liability of the EC Institutions in both contract and tort is set out in Article 215 [*288*] EC.

Article 215 [*288*] EC. The contractual liability of the Community shall be governed by the law applicable to the contract in question.

In the case of non-contractual liability, the Community shall, in accordance with the general principles common to the laws of the Member States, make good any damage caused by its institutions or by its servants in the performance of their duties.

The preceding paragraph shall apply under the same conditions to damage caused by the ECB or its servants in the performance of their duties.

i. Jurisdiction of the Court

a. Claims in Contract

The Court's jurisdiction over claims against the EC institutions varies according to whether a claim is being brought in contract under Article 215(1) [*288(1)*] EC or in tort under Article 215(2) [*288(2)*] EC. In the case of contractual liability the Court can be conferred jurisdiction by a 'choice of law' clause.

Article 181 [*238*] EC. The Court of Justice shall have jurisdiction to give judgment pursuant to any arbitration clause contained in a contract concluded by or on behalf of the Community, whether that contract be governed by public or private law.

It is clear from the wording of Article 181 [238] EC that the Court will rule on contracts even where the governing law is not EC law.[103] In principle, there should also be circumstances where, notwithstanding that an EC institution has concluded a contract, the Court of Justice will be precluded from considering a matter by the rules of private international law. This creates a problem as the EC does not have any conflicts of law rules which apply to this situation. Hartley observes that this has rarely been a problem as the Commission usually insists on placing choice of law clauses in its contracts.[104] One set of contracts over which the Court will consider itself to have jurisdiction are staff contracts. Article 179 EC confers exclusive jurisdiction upon the Court in any dispute between the Community and its servants. The relevant provisions are set out in the Staff Regulations or the Conditions of Employment.[105]

b. Non-Contractual Claims

By contrast with the position in contract, the EC Treaty asserts an exclusive jurisdiction for Court in non-contractual claims against the EC Institutions.[106]

Article 178 [235] EC. The Court of Justice shall have jurisdiction in disputes relating to compensation for damage provided for in the second paragraph of Article 215 [288].

---

[103]   See Case 318/81 *Commission v CO.DE.MI* [1985] ECR 3693.

[104]   Hartley, T. *The Foundations of European Community Law* (1994, 3rd Edition, Clarendon, Oxford) 462.

[105]   These contracts have been classified as public law contracts by the Court. It is thus informed by principles of administrative law rather than of private law in interpreting them, Joined Cases 45, 45 & 48/59 *Von Lachmüller v Commission* [1960] ECR 463.

[106]   It must be remembered that wherever the Court is granted jurisdiction by the EC Treaty, that jurisdiction is exclusive, Article 183 [240] EC.

An action brought against the EC institutions under Article 215 (2) [*288(2)*]) EC is an 'independent' one.[107] It is not a prerequisite, therefore, that the act must, first, have been reviewed under Article 173 [*230*] EC or that an EC Institution must have been called upon to act under Article 175 [*232*] EC. The corollary of this is that, in addition to offering damage to the applicants, Article 215(2) [*288(2)*] EC can act as a substitute for these actions.

There are two preliminary limits to the Court's jurisdiction. The first is that any action must be brought within 5 years of the occurrence of the event giving rise to the proceedings.[108] The second is more restrictive and relates to areas where there may be concurrent liability on the part of the national authority. That is to say a parallel action may lie against the national authority in national courts. There are two sets of circumstances where this may occur.[109] The first, and most common, is where a national authority is implementing or administering unlawful Community acts. One example is the transposition of a Directive. Another is the collection of agricultural levies. The second set of circumstances where concurrent liability might arise is where a decision is taken jointly by a Member State and an EC institution. A common example of this is in the field of external trade where Member States are permitted to restrict imports of third country goods, once they have obtained the permission of the Commission. The most equitable solution would be to set up a system of joint and several liability in these circumstances. The plaintiff could choose who to sue under such a system, with the defendants recovering a contribution from each other afterwards.[110] Such a scheme has not been adopted by the Court.

---

[107]   Case 4/69 *Lütticke v Commission* [1971] ECR 325.

[108]   Statute of the Court of Justice, Article 43. A statement by the defendant institution that it will not plead limitation will stop the time running from the date of the communication, Case T-554/93 *Saint v Council*, 16 April 1997. On this see Heukels, T. 'The Prescription of an Action for Damages under Article 215(2) EEC' in Schermers, H. et al. (eds.) *Non-Contractual Liability of the European Communities* (1988, Martijnus Nijhoff, Dordrecht).

[109]   See Wils, W. 'Concurrent Liability of the Community and a Member State' (1992) 17 *ELRev* 191, 194-198.

[110]   For how this could be done see Oliver, P. 'Joint Liability of the Community and the Member States' 125, 128-131 in Schermers, H. et al. (ed.) *Non-Contractual Liability of the European Communities* (1988, Martijnus Nijhoff, Dordrecht).

Joined Cases 5, 7, 13-24/66 Kampffmeyer v Commission [1967] ECR 245

On 1 October 1963 the applicants applied for import licences to import maize from the German authorities following a decision by the latter to set a zero tariff on the import of maize. The German Government suspended the grant of zero-rated licences on the same day - something it was only allowed to do if so authorised by the Commission. The Commission unlawfully and retroactively gave this authorisation for the period 1-3 October 1963 on 4 October 1963.[111] One of the categories of applicant referred to here had paid the taxes demanded by the German Government. The other had subsequently repudiated their contracts as a consequence of the German decision.

... with regard to any injury suffered by the applicants belonging to the first and second categories those applicants have informed the Court that the injury alleged is the subject of two actions for damages, one against the Federal Republic of Germany before a German court and the other against the Community before the Court of Justice. It is necessary to avoid the applicants being insufficiently or excessively compensated for the same damage by the different assessment of two different courts applying different rules of law. Before determining the damage for which the Community should be held liable, it is necessary for the national court to have the opportunity to give judgment on any liability on the part of the Federal Republic of Germany. This being the case, final judgment cannot be given before the applicants have produced the decision of the national court on this matter, which may be done independently of the evidence asked of the applicant in the first category to the effect that they have exhausted all possible methods of recovery of the amounts improperly paid by way of levy. Furthermore, if it were established that such recovery was possible, this fact might have consequences bearing upon the calculation of the damages concerning the second category. However, the decisive nature of the said evidence required does not prevent the applicants from producing the other evidence previously indicated in the meantime.

The establishment of the presumption that individuals should first exhaust remedies in domestic courts before proceedings against EC institutions results in the financial risk being shifted to Member States in cases of concurrent liability. It could be argued that this is no bad thing given the Community's limited financial resources.[112] Yet it does seem odd that the policy-maker, which is the Community, should be freed

---

[111]   This Decision was annulled in Joined Cases 106 & 107/63 *Toepfer v Commission* [1965] ECR 405, [1966] CMLR 111.

[112]   Wils, W., supra n.109, 205.

from all financial incentives to act legally. The legal position is, moreover, complicated by the doctrine of exhaustion of domestic remedies not applying where it is not considered possible for the applicant to obtain a remedy before the national courts.

Case 281/82 Unifrex v Commission [1984] ECR 1969

The applicant, a French undertaking, exported agricultural products to Italy and was paid in Italian lire. To cope with swings in the value of currencies, the Common Agricultural Policy maintained a policy of monetary compensatory amounts (MCAs). These would be paid to traders to compensate for devaluations which resulted in their obtaining a lower return in a particular export market. On 23 March 1981 the lire devalued by 6%. It was only with effect from 6 April 1981 that the MCAs were modified to take account of this. The applicant sued for just under FF 3 million compensation for the loss incurred as a result of this delay. Whilst the Court ultimately rejected its claim, it did find that the applicant was right to bring its case before the Court.

11. An established body of the case-law of the Court of Justice shows that the action for damages, pursuant to Articles 178 and 215 of the Treaty, was set up as an independent action, having its own particular place in the system of means of redress and subject to conditions for its use formulated in the light of its specific purpose. It must nevertheless be viewed in the context of the entire system established by the Treaty for the judicial protection of the individual. Where an individual considers that he has been injured by the application of a Community legislative measure that he considers illegal, he may, when the implementation of the measure is left to the national authorities, contest the validity of the measure, when it is implemented, before a national court in an action against the national authorities. That court may, or even must, as provided for in Article 177, refer the question of the validity of the Community measure in dispute to the Court of Justice. However, the existence of such a means of redress will be capable of ensuring the effective protection of the individuals concerned only if it may result in making good the alleged damage.

12. That is not so in this case. The applicant has shown, without being contradicted by the Commission, that proceedings for annulment in the national administrative courts could not, in this case, have effectively protected the applicant. Even if the disputed Community rules were declared invalid by a preliminary ruling of the Court given in the context of such proceedings and the national decision were annulled, that annulment could not have required the national authorities to pay higher monetary compensatory amounts to the applicant, without the prior intervention of the Community legislature.

The Court has considered the question of when effective redress can be obtained before national courts in quite a formalistic manner. The principal situation in which it will require applicants to go before national courts is when they are claiming liquidated loss - that is to say a fixed amount. An example of this is when an applicant is seeking restitution of a fixed sum of money which was unlawfully taken. In *Haegeman*, for example, a Belgian importer sought restitution of duties which he claimed had been unlawfully levied on wine imported from Greece.[113] The Court stated that as the collection of duties was a matter for national authorities, the matter should be brought before the national authorities.

Applicants will also be required to exhaust domestic remedies where they are seeking fixed sums of money which they should have been paid. In *Asteris* a Commission Regulation granting aid to Greek tomato concentrate producers was annulled for technical reasons.[114] The Court stated that if the applicants were seeking payment of the amounts due, the appropriate venue to pursue such a claim was in the national courts as national authorities were responsible for implementing EC law.

By contrast, there are two scenarios in which the Court will declare an action admissible. The first is that of *Unifrex*. This requires action on the part of an EC institution if the illegality is to be redressed. As national courts cannot force an institution to act, there is no need to exhaust domestic remedies. Another example of this is *De Boer Buizen*.[115] In this instance the applicant had been refused a licence to export steel tubes to the United States on the basis of the EC legislation in force. The Court considered that there was no need to exhaust domestic remedies in this instance, for whilst the national court could annul the national decision it could not give the applicant a right to export the tubes - something which could only be granted by the EC legislature.

The other scenario in which an applicant can go straight before the Court of Justice is where it is suing for damages other than a fixed

---

[113]   Case 96/71 *Haegeman v Commission* [1972] ECR 1005, [1973] CMLR 365.
        See also Case C-282/90 *Vreugdenhil v Commission* [1992] ECR I-1937.
[114]   Joined Cases 106-120/87 *Asteris v Greece* [1988] ECR 5515.
[115]   Case 81/86 *De Boer Buizen v Council & Commission* [1987] ECR 3677.

sum which it was owed. The reason for this is that it is normally a condition of a successful action in tort that national authorities be shown to be at fault.[116] This cannot be shown in instances where the national authorities are implementing EC law as the fault lies with the EC institutions. In *Krohn* the national authorities refused to grant the applicant a licence to import manioc from Thailand on the basis of the Commission veto being placed on the issue of the licence.[117] The Court considered that a national court would not possibly be able to assess the damage suffered from any wrongful refusal to issue a licence and that the application was therefore admissible. Similarly in *Vereniging van Exporteurs in Levende Varkens* the CFI declared admissible an action for damages brought by a trade association against a Commission Decision, which had been implemented by the Dutch authorities, and which placed a ban on the export of Dutch pigs on the grounds of an outbreak of a deadly and contagious disease, swine vesicular fever, in the Netherlands.[118]

The position on concurrent liability is needlessly complex and far from satisfactory. Frequently, it will require an applicant to bring a claim concerning the same factual set of circumstances in both the national courts and directly before the CFI. In *Nölle*, for example the applicant, a German importer, had been required to pay anti-dumping duties on some paint brushes from China under a Regulation which was subsequently declared to be illegal.[119] The applicant sought damages both for the bank interest paid as a result of the money he had to borrow in order to pay the duties and for the legal costs in having the Regulation annulled. The CFI considered that the first action, being an action in tort, was admissible, but that the second matter was something which should be brought before the national courts. Such double litigation involves needless expense. It also creates disharmony within the EC court structure. For Article 215(2) [*288(2)*] EC actions will go before the

---

116 Case T-167/94 *Nölle v Council* [1995] ECR II-2585.
117 Case 175/84 *Krohn v Commission* [1986] ECR 752, [1987] 1 CMLR 745.
118 Joined Cases T-481 & T-484/93 *Vereniging van Exporteurs in Levende Varkens v Commission* [1995] ECR II-2941.
119 T-167/94 *Nölle v Commission* [1995] ECR II-2585. On the earlier judgment annulling the Regulation see Case C-16/90 *Nölle v Hauptzollamt Bremen-Freihafen* [1991] ECR I-5163.

CFI.[120] On the other hand, if a matter is brought before a national court there is a possibility that it will be referred under Article 177 [*234*] EC to the Court of Justice. There is thus the danger of the two courts considering the same matter under entirely separate actions with all the possibility for confusion and contradiction this engenders.

ii. The Basis for the Non-Contractual Liability of the EC Institutions

a. The Requirement of Fault

Running like a thread through all the Court's judgments in this area is that a requirement of blameworthiness or fault must be found on the part of the EC institution before it can attract liability. This was most clearly set out in *Parise*.

Joined Cases 19, 20, 25 & 30/69 Parise & Others v Commission [1970] ECR 325

A number of officials claimed that the Commission had induced them to retire early through a mistaken interpretation it issued of their pension rights under the Staff Regulation. The Commission discovered its mistake in April 1968 but did not rectify it until the end of 1968. The Court found that they had retired for other reasons. Were it not for this, it considered that the Commission's conduct would have generated liability.

31. For the application to be well founded it must be established that the defendant is liable for a wrongful act or omission which caused the applicants a still subsisting injury.

.....

---

[120]   Shaw, J. *Law of the European Union* (1996, 2nd Edition, Macmillan, Basingstoke) 363.

36. Apart from the exceptional instance, the adoption of an incorrect interpretation does not constitute in itself a wrongful act.

37. Even the fact that the authorities request those concerned to obtain information from the competent departments does not necessarily involve those authorities in an obligation to guarantee the correctness of information supplied and does not therefore make them liable for any injury which may be occasioned by incorrect information.

38. However, whilst it may be possible to doubt the existence of a wrongful act concerning the supply of incorrect information, the same cannot be said of the departments' delay in rectifying the information.

39. Although such rectification was possible as early as April 1968 it was deferred without any justification until the end of 1968.

40. Whilst it would have been simple by means of a general announcement or an individual notice to rectify an error of interpretation which was capable of invalidating a whole group of statements, the communication issued in April 1968 gives the impression that it concerns solely possible arithmetical or similar errors, difficult to identify and which could have been due to the speed with which the separate statements were drawn up.

41. A correction made shortly before or after 16 April, that is to say, before the time when those concerned had to make their decision, would have certainly enabled the defendant to avoid all liability for the consequences of the wrong information.

42. The failure to make such a correction is, on the other hand, a matter of such a nature as to render the Communities liable.

Fault can be attributed to EC institutions in two ways. The main form is *faute de service*. This is defined in Article 40 ECSC, the counterpart in the ECSC Treaty of Article 215(2) [*288(2)*] EC as

> 'a wrongful act or omission on the part of the Community in the performance of its functions.'

EC institutions are also liable in cases of *faute personelle*, wrongful acts of their servants. They are not liable for all such acts, however, but only those acts:

'which, by virtue of an internal and direct relationship, are the necessary extension of the tasks entrusted to the institutions.'[121]

Examples of *faute personelle* are rare. The reasons for this are that *faute personelle* can only arise in the course of performance of his duties by a servant of the institution. Such wrongdoing will usually be *faute de service*, as the organisation is under a duty to verify and check the acts of its servants.[122] The only scenario in which *faute personelle* is important is where an EC institution attracts liability as a result of the actions of somebody who is an agent for it. In such circumstances, it is difficult for the institution to supervise the actions of the agent and liability can only be based on *faute personelle*. In *San Marco* the CFI therefore found that the Commission was liable for the actions of a delegate based in Somalia who refused to authorise additional spending from the European Development Fund for bridges which were being constructed there, such an authorisation being made in the performance of his duties.[123]

b. The Schöppenstedt Formula

Various commentators have noted the nebulous nature of the concept of fault and how the connotations associated with it and the duties imposed by it will vary according to the surrounding context.[124] This is apparent in the Court's treatment of EC institution liability for legislative acts,[125] where, from an applicant's perspective, a far more exacting regime has been imposed.

---

[121]   Case 9/69 *Sayag v Leduc* [1969] ECR 329.

[122]   Case T-572/93 *Odigitria v Council and Commission* [1995] ECR II-2025.

[123]   Case T-451/93 *San Marco Impex Italiana v Commission* [1994] ECR II-1061.

[124]   e.g. Craig, P. & De Búrca, G. *EC Law: Text, Cases and Materials* (1995, Clarendon, Oxford) 514-515.

[125]   Legislative acts have been deemed in this context to be any measure which is general and abstract in nature, Joined Cases T-481 & T-484/93 *Vereniging van Exporteurs in Levende Varkens v Commission* [1995] ECR II-2941.

Case 5/71 Aktien-Zuckerfabrik Schöppenstedt v Council [1971] ECR 975

The applicant challenged a Regulation setting the amounts for compensation to be paid to sugar producers, arguing that it discriminated against it.

11. In the present case the non-contractual liability of the Community presupposes at the very least the unlawful nature of the act alleged to be the cause of the damage. Where legislative action involving measures of economic policy is concerned, the Community does not incur non-contractual liability for the damage suffered by individuals as a consequence of that action, by virtue of the provisions contained in Article 215, second paragraph, of the Treaty, unless a sufficiently flagrant violation of a superior rule of law for the protection of the individual has occurred. For that reason the Court, in the present case, must first consider whether such a violation has occurred.

The Court has been relatively generous in considering which principles constitute 'superior rule[s] of law for the protection of the individual'. Breaches of general principles of law, fundamental rights and misuse of powers can all generate liability.[126] The only rules of law whose breach the Court has stated will not generate liability are the doctrine of conferred powers[127] and the duty to state reasons.[128] The formulation has still proved to be extremely restrictive because of the degree of egregiousness required. Simple illegality is a *sine qua non* of liability but will not necessarily be sufficient.[129]

Joined Cases 83 & 94/76, 4, 15 & 40/77 HNL v Council and Commission [1978] ECR 1209, [1978] 3 CMLR 566

Regulation 563/76/EEC attempted to resolve the overproduction of skimmed-milk powder within the EC by forcing animal feed producers to purchase skimmed milk-powder. The powder was considerably more expensive than the

---

[126] For a summary of the position see Joined Cases T-481 & T-484/93 *Vereniging van Exporteurs in Levende Varkens v Commission* [1995] ECR II-2941.

[127] Case 22/88 *Vreugdenhil v Minister van Landbouw en Visserij* [1989] ECR 2049.

[128] Case 106/81 *Kind* [1982] ECR 2885.

[129] Joined Cases T-481 & T-484/93 *Vereniging van Exporteurs in Levende Varkens v Commission* [1995] ECR II-2941.

usual feed, soya. The Regulation was annulled on the grounds it was discriminatory and disproportionate.[130] The applicants then brought an action for damages.

4. The finding that a legislative measure such as the regulation in question is null and void is however insufficient by itself for the Community to incur non-contractual liability for damage caused to individuals under the second paragraph of Article 215 of the EEC Treaty. The Court of Justice has consistently stated that the Community does not incur liability on account of a legislative measure which involves choices of economic policy unless a sufficiently serious breach of a superior rule of law for the protection of the individual has occurred.

5. In the present case there is no doubt that the prohibition on discrimination laid down in the second subparagraph of the third paragraph of Article 40 of the Treaty and infringed by regulation no 563/76 is in fact designed for the protection of the individual, and that it is impossible to disregard the importance of this prohibition in the system of the Treaty. To determine what conditions must be present in addition to such breach for the Community to incur liability in accordance with the criterion laid down in the case-law of the Court of Justice it is necessary to take into consideration the principles in the legal systems of the Member States governing the liability of public authorities for damage caused to individuals by legislative measures. Although these principles vary considerably from one Member State to another, it is however possible to state that the public authorities can only exceptionally and in special circumstances incur liability for legislative measures which are the result of choices of economic policy. This restrictive view is explained by the consideration that the legislative authority, even where the validity of its measures is subject to judicial review, cannot always be hindered in making its decisions by the prospect of applications for damages whenever it has occasion to adopt legislative measures in the public interest which may adversely affect the interests of individuals.

6. It follows from these considerations that individuals may be required, in the sectors coming within the economic policy of the Community, to accept within reasonable limits certain harmful effects on their economic interests as a result of a legislative measure without being able to obtain compensation from public funds even if that measure has been declared null and void. In a legislative field such as the one in question, in which one of the chief features is the exercise of a wide discretion essential for the implementation of the common agricultural policy, the Community does not therefore incur liability unless the institution concerned has manifestly and gravely disregarded the limits on the exercise of its powers.

7. This is not so in the case of a measure of economic policy such as that in the present case, in view of its special features. In this connexion it is necessary to observe first that

---

[130]   Case 114/76 *Bela-Mühle v Council* [1977] ECR 1211, [1979] 2 CMLR 83.

this measure affected very wide categories of traders, in other words all buyers of compound feeding-stuffs containing protein, so that its effects on individual undertakings were considerably lessened. Moreover, the effects of the regulation on the price of feeding-stuffs as a factor in the production costs of those buyers were only limited since that price rose by little more than 2%. This price increase was particularly small in comparison with the price increases resulting, during the period of application of the regulation, from the variations in the world market prices of feeding-stuffs containing protein, which were three or four times higher than the increase resulting from the obligation to purchase skimmed-milk powder introduced by the regulation. The effects of the regulation on the profit-earning capacity of the undertakings did not ultimately exceed the bounds of the economic risks inherent in the activities of the agricultural sectors concerned.

Liability can be generated in some jurisdictions under the 'invalidity principle'. Activities will generate liability under this principle if they are invalidly performed. Under such a principle reference is had to the nature of the norm breached. This principle seems to underpin the Court's reasoning that liability will only arise where an institution has 'manifestly and gravely disregarded the limits on its powers'. It was confirmed by subsequent case law which stated that liability for legislative acts would only occur if the EC institutions were acting in an 'arbitrary manner'.[131] On the other hand, much of the reasoning is also underpinned by risk theory.[132] This states that certain interests should be protected, irrespective of the validity of the action. In particular, risk theory would require that a small group should not bear the costs for action which benefits society at large without being compensated. Risk theory would look, as happened in *HNL*, at the size of the group affected and the size of the loss incurred.[133]

The test seemed excessively restrictive, therefore, on two counts. The first was its cumulative nature. Liability would not be incurred

---

[131] Joined Cases 116 & 124/77 *Amylum NV and Tunnel Refineries Ltd. v Council and Commission* [1979] ECR 3497. See Grabitz, E. 'Liability for Legislative Acts' in Schermers, H. et al (eds.) *Non-Contractual Liability of the European Communities* (1988, Martijnus Nijhoff, Dordrecht).

[132] On risk theory and the invalidity principle see Craig, P. 'Compensation in Public Law' (1980) 96 *LQR* 413.

[133] Joined Cases 64 & 113/76, 167 & 239/78, 27, 28 & 45/79 *Dumortier Frères v Council* [1979] ECR 3091.

unless both the invalidity principle and the risk theory were infringed. Secondly, the degree of fault required seemed to be extremely high with only the most egregious behaviour generating liability. The Court has moderated its position in recent years. The fault threshold has been lowered so that there is no longer a requirement that the conduct be verging upon the arbitrary.[134]

Joined Cases C-104/89 & C-37/90 Mulder v Council and Commission [1992] ECR I-3061

In the 1970's milk farmers were given a number of incentives under EC legislation to stop dairy production for a 5 year period. Regulation 857/84 provided, however, that farmers could not be given a 'reference quantity', a licence to commence production, unless they had delivered milk in the previous year. This Regulation was declared illegal in 1988 on the grounds that it breached the principle of legitimate expectations of those farmers who had been encouraged to suspend production in the 1970's.[135] Four Dutch farmers and a German farmer then brought an action for the loss suffered by them as a result of this Regulation.

12. The second paragraph of Article 215 of the Treaty provides that, in the case of non-contractual liability, the Community, in accordance with the general principles common to the laws of the Member States, is to make good any damage caused by its institutions in the performance of their duties. The scope of that provision has been specified in the sense that the Community does not incur liability on account of a legislative measure involving choices of economic policy unless a sufficiently serious breach of a superior rule of law for the protection of the individual has occurred (see, in particular, the judgment in Joined Cases 83 and 94/76, 4, 15 and 40/77 *HNL v Council and Commission* [1978] ECR 1209, paragraphs 4, 5 and 6). More specifically, in a legislative field such as the one in question, which is characterized by the exercise of a wide discretion essential for the implementation of the Common Agricultural Policy, the Community cannot incur liability unless the institution concerned has manifestly and gravely disregarded the limits on the exercise of its powers (see in particular the judgment in *HNL v Commission and Council*, paragraph 6).

---

134   Case C-220/91P *Stahlwerke Peine-Salzgitter v Commission* [1993] ECR I-2393.

135   Case 120/86 *Mulder v Minister van Landbouw en Visserij* [1988] ECR 2321, [1989] 2 CMLR 1; Case 170/86 *Von Deetzen v Hauptzollamt Hamburg-Jonas* [1988] ECR 2355, [1989] 2 CMLR 327.

13. The Court has also consistently held that, in order for the Community to incur non-contractual liability, the damage alleged must go beyond the bounds of the normal economic risks inherent in the activities in the sector concerned (see the judgments in Case 238/78 *Ireks-Arkady v Council and Commission* [1979] ECR 2955, paragraph 11, in Joined Cases 241, 242 and 245 to 250/78 *DGV v Council and Commission* [1979] ECR 3017, paragraph 11, in Joined Cases 261 and 262/78 *Interquell Staerke v Council and Commission* [1979] ECR 3045, paragraph 14, and in Joined Cases 64 and 113/76, 167 and 239/78, 27, 28 and 45/79 *Dumortier Frères v Council* [1979] ECR 3091, paragraph 11).

14. Those conditions are fulfilled in the case of Regulation No 857/84 as supplemented by Regulation No 1371/84.

15. In this regard, it must be recalled in the first place that, as the Court held in the judgments of 28 April 1988 in *Mulder* and *von Deetzen*, cited above, those regulations were adopted in breach of the principle of the protection of legitimate expectations, which is a general and superior principle of Community law for the protection of the individual.

16. Secondly, it must be held that, in so far as it failed completely, without invoking any higher public interest, to take account of the specific situation of a clearly defined group of economic agents, that is to say, producers who, pursuant to an undertaking given under Regulation No 1078/77, delivered no milk during the reference year, the Community legislature manifestly and gravely disregarded the limits of its discretionary power, thereby committing a sufficiently serious breach of a superior rule of law.

17. That breach is all the more obvious because the total and permanent exclusion of the producers concerned from the allocation of a reference quantity, which in fact prevented them from resuming the marketing of milk when their non-marketing or conversion undertaking expired, cannot be regarded as being foreseeable or as falling within the bounds of the normal economic risks inherent in the activities of a milk producer.

Mulder generated a legacy of uncertainty.[136] It was clearly a more lenient application of the *Schöppenstedt* formula than the 1970's caselaw. Yet simple illegality still did not seem sufficient to generate

---

[136]   See also Case C-152/88 *Sofrimport v Commission* [1990] ECR I-2477. On *Mulder* see Van Gerven, W. 'Non-Contractual Liability of Member States, Community Institutions and Individuals for Breaches of Community Law with a View to a Common Law for Europe' (1994) 1 *Maastricht Journal of European and Comparative Law* 6, 25-29.

liability.[137] The position has been clarified by the recent case law on State liability. The reasoning in *Brasserie de Pêcheur* was strongly informed by the Court's interpretation of the principles underlying Article 215(2) [*288(2)*] EC.[138] Towards the end of the judgment the Court went further, suggesting that, henceforth, there would be a single regime governing the non-contractual liability of both the EC institutions and the Member States:[139]

55. ..., as regards both Community liability under Article 215 and Member State liability for breaches of Community law, the decisive test for finding that a breach of Community law is sufficiently serious is whether the Member State or the Community Institution concerned manifestly and gravely disregarded the limits on its discretion.

56. The factors which the competent court may take into consideration include the clarity and precision of the rule breached, the measure of discretion left by the rule to the national or Community authorities, whether the infringement and the damage caused was intentional or involuntary, whether any error of law was excusable or inexcusable.

Under a unitary regime simple illegality will be insufficient. More important is the clarity and precision of the rule broken and whether the EC institution had reasonable grounds for believing that what it was doing was lawful. The convergence of the regime under Article 215(2) [*288(2)*] EC with that of State liability also has implications for the requirement that the legislative act cause loss to a sufficiently defined group of individuals. In none of the State liability cases has this seemed to be a requirement. Indeed, successful cases have been brought involving quite large numbers of plaintiffs. *Factortame*, for example, concerned 79 claimants. Moreover, there are good theoretical reasons why risk theory should be abandoned. Its purest form exists in France where the doctrine of *égalité devant les charges publics* allows compensation to be recovered by a group which is particularly adversely

---

137   Case T-167/94 *Nölle v Council and Commission* [1995] ECR II-2589.
138   Joined Cases C-46 & 48/93 *Brasserie du Pêcheur v Germany; R v Secretary of State ex parte Factortame* [1996] ECR I-1029, [1996] 1 CMLR 889.
139   This has been reiterated in Joined Cases C-178-179 & C-188-190 *Dillenkofer v Bundesrepublik Deutschland* [1996] ECR I-4845, [1996] 3 CMLR 469; Joined Cases C-283, C-291 & C-292/94 *Denkavit International v Bundesamt für Finanzen* [1996] ECR I-5063.

affected by a measure. This liability exists irrespective of the legality of the measure. Once, however, it is accepted that fault and lawfulness are a consideration in establishing liability, it seems excessively severe simply to refuse to recognise any interests which are not clearly limited in nature. It creates a situation where an individual could not recover extreme loss resulting from an arbitrary act simply because s/he belongs to too large a class.

iii. Causation and Loss

The position on the types of loss which may be recovered was most clearly set out by Advocate General Capotorti in *Ireks-Arkady*:

> 'It is well known that the legal concept of "damage" covers both a material loss stricto senso, that is to say, a reduction in the person's assets and also the loss of an increase in those assets which would have occurred if the harmful act had not taken place (these two alternatives are known respectively as damnum emergens and lucrum cessans) ...The object of compensation is to restore the assets of the victim to the condition in which they would have been apart from the unlawful act, or at least to the condition closest to that which would have been produced if the unlawful act had not taken place: the hypothetical nature of that restoration often entails a certain degree of approximation.'[140]

The Court has taken a broad view of which loss, actually sustained, may be recovered. It will include any incidental loss, such as penalties the applicant had to pay as a result of having to repudiate a contract[141] or bank interest as a result of loans taken out to pay money wrongfully levied.[142] The Court has also been ready to award compensation for non-pecuniary loss such as anxiety and hurt feelings.[143]

---

[140]   Case 238/78 *Ireks-Arkady v Council and Commission* [1979] ECR 2955, 2998-2999.
[141]   Case 74/74 *CNTA v Commission* [1975] ECR 533, [1977] 1 CMLR 171.
[142]   Case T-167/94 *Nölle v Commission and Council* [1995] ECR II-2589.
[143]   Case 110/63 *Willame v Commission* [1965] ECR 649.

As mentioned above, the 'expectation interest' will also be protected. Compensation will be awarded therefore for loss of profits.[144]

A greater bar to recovery has been the requirement that the applicant demonstrate a causal link between the illegal act and the loss sustained.

Case T-168/94 Blackspur DIY v Council and Commission [1995] ECR II-2627

In 1991 the Court of Justice declared unlawful a 1989 Council Regulation imposing anti-dumping duties upon paintbrushes from the Peoples's Republic of China.[145] Blackspur, an English DIY company had placed an order for the paintbrushes in 1988. It went into receivership in 1990. It sued the Council for damage it and its directors suffered as a result of its going into receivership, claiming that this had been caused by the illegal imposition of the anti-dumping duties. The CFI rejected this, finding there to be no direct causal link.

38. The Court notes at the outset that, according to settled case-law, the Community's non-contractual liability under the second paragraph of Article 215 of the Treaty is dependent on the coincidence of a series of conditions as regards the unlawfulness of the acts alleged against the Community institutions, the fact of damage and the existence of a causal link between the conduct of the institution concerned and the damage complained of (see the judgments of the Court of Justice in Case C-308/87 *Grifoni v EAEC* [1990] ECR I-1203, paragraph 6, in Joined Cases C-258/90 and C-259/90 *Pesquerias De Bermeo and Naviera Laida v Commission* [1992] ECR I-2901, paragraph 42, and in Case C-146/91 *KYDEP v Council and Commission* [1994] ECR I-4199, paragraph 19).

39. The Court takes the view that in this case it is necessary to begin its examination by considering whether there is a causal link between the allegedly unlawful conduct of the Community institutions and the damage pleaded by the applicants.

40. The Court notes in this regard that, according to the case-law of the Court of Justice, there is a causal link for the purposes of the second paragraph of Article 215 of the Treaty where there is a direct causal link between the fault committed by the institution concerned and the injury pleaded, the burden of proof of which rests on the applicants

---

[144] Joined Cases 56-60/74 *Kampffmeyer v Commission and Council* [1976] ECR 711; Joined Cases C-104/89 & C-37/90 *Mulder v Council and Commission* [1992] ECR I-3061.

[145] Case C-16/90 *Nölle v Hauptzollamt Bremen-Freihafen* [1991] ECR I-5163.

(see the judgments of the Court of Justice in Joined Cases 9/60 and 12/60 *Vloeberghs v High Authority* [1961] ECR 197, in Case 18/60 *Worms v High Authority* [1962] ECR 195, at 206, in Case 36/62 *Aciéries du Temple v High Authority* [1963] ECR 289, at 296, in Joined Cases 241/78, 242/78 and 245/78 to 250/78 *DGV and Others v Council and Commission* [1979] ECR 3017, at 3040 et seq., in Joined Cases C-363/88 and C-364/88 *Finsider and Others v Commission* [1992] ECR I-359, paragraph 25, and in Case C-220/91P *Commission v Stahlwerke Peine-Salzgitter* [1993] ECR I-2393).

The requirement of a direct causal link has proved a difficult test for applicants to satisfy.[146] It is not sufficient for them to prove that the loss would not have occurred but for the illegal act.[147] They must also show that there was a sufficient proximity between the illegal act and the loss suffered.[148] In practice, this has made it very difficult for applicants to claim for loss of profits as these will often be too remote or speculative. The chain of causation can also be severed by third parties, such as an independent act of a Member State.[149]

Even where a causal link is established between the loss suffered and the illegal act, the applicant might still not recover full compensation. This may be, first, as a result of the doctrine of contributory negligence, where the applicant is considered to have contributed to the damage as a result of a failure to take due care.[150] Secondly, the applicant is under a duty to mitigate any loss suffered. A failure to do so will result in compensation being reduced.[151] Finally,

---

[146] On this see Toth, A. 'The Concepts of Damage and Causality as Elements of Non-Contractual Liability' in Schermers, H. et al. (eds.) *Non-Contractual Liability of the European Communities* (1988, Martijnus Nijhoff, Dordrecht).

[147] This is, however, a *sine qua non*: Case T-478/93 *Wafer Zoo v Commission* [1995] ECR II-1479.

[148] Joined Cases 64, 113/76, 167, 239/78, 27, 28, 45/79 *Dumortier Frères v Council* [1979] ECR 3091.

[149] Case 132/77 *Société pur l'Exportation des Sucres SA v Commission* [1978] ECR 1061.

[150] Case 145/83 *Adams v Commission* [1985] ECR 3539.

[151] Joined Cases C-104/89 & C-37/90 *Mulder v Council and Commission* [1992] ECR I-3061.

compensation will be reduced if there is evidence that the applicant has, or could have, passed the loss on to somebody else.[152]

VII. The Consequences of a Finding of Invalidity

We saw earlier that, as part of the process of constitutionalising the EC Treaty, it was declared that a finding of invalidity by the Court has *erga omnes* effects by binding all national courts within the European Union.[153] In keeping with this, it appears that the Court has the same powers to rule on the effects of an invalid measure, whatever the source of its jurisdiction.[154] The effects of a finding of invalidity are set out in Article 174 [*231*] EC.

Article 174 [*231*]EC. If the action is well founded, the Court of Justice shall declare the act concerned to be void.

In the case of a Regulation, however, the Court of Justice shall, if it considers this necessary, state which of the effects of the Regulation which it has declared void shall be considered as definitive.

---

[152]   Case 238/78 *Ireks-Arkady v Council and Commission* [1979] ECR 2955. The requirement that compensation will be reduced if the loss could have been passed on is certainly more restrictive than the test EC law imposes within the domestic context, which merely allows compensation to be reduced where the loss *has* been passed on: Joined Cases C-192-218/95 *Société Comateb v Directeur Général des Douanes*, Judgment of 14 January 1997. For criticism see Toth, A. 'The Concepts of Damage and Causation as Elements of Non-Contractual Liability' 23, 29-30 in Schermers, H. et al (eds.) *Non-Contractual Liability of the European Communities* (1988, Martijnus Nijhoff, Dordrecht).

[153]   Case 66/80 *ICC v Amministrazione delle Finanze* [1981] ECR 1191, [1983] 2 CMLR 593. See pp 285-286

[154]   See Joined Cases 4, 109, 145/79 *Société Co-operative 'Providence Agricole de la Champagne' v ONIC* [1980] ECR 2823; Case 112/83 *Société de Produits de Maïs v Administration des Douanes* [1985] ECR 719.

In principle, if an EC Instrument is vitiated by particularly serious and manifest defects, it will be declared void.[155] A ruling to that effect will have the consequence of releasing all parties from any obligation to which they might have thought themselves subject under the instrument. Otherwise, the effects will vary according to the instrument declared invalid. The CFI has mitigated the effects for third parties of a finding that a Decision is invalid. In *AssiDomän Kraft Products* the CFI stated that, as it can only give judgment on the subject-matter of the dispute referred to it by the parties to the dispute, it could only annul a Decision in respect of addressees who had been successful in their actions before the court.[156] The Decision will remain valid, therefore, vis-à-vis third parties.

A Regulation declared invalid, on the other hand, is void not just between parties to the disputes but also in respect of third parties. Whilst the presumption from Article 174(1) [*288(1)*] EC is that it is void *ab initio*, a wide discretion is given to the Court by Article 174(2) [*288(2)*] EC to determine the effects of its ruling.[157] The Court will, therefore, sometimes declare that only part of an instrument is void, maintaining in place other features of the legislation.[158] Temporal limitations have also been placed upon a finding of invalidity. In such circumstances, the legislation will remain in force until new legislation is put in place.

A recent example of this was the judgment annulling Regulation 2317/95/EC, which set up a list of countries, whose nationals were required to have a visa to enter the European Union.[159] The Regulation had been introduced under the consultation procedure. It was annulled by the Court of Justice, however, as the Council had introduced a number of significant amendments without reconsulting the Parliament.

---

155   Case C-137/92P *Commission v BASF* [1994] ECR I-2555.
156   Case T-227/95 *AssiDomän Kraft Products v Commission*, Judgment of 10 July 1997.
157   Although Article 174(2) [*288(2)*] EC suggests this power applies only in respect of Regulations, the Court has applied it to other instruments citing the need for legal certainty as a ground: Case 92/78 *Simmenthal v Commission* [1979] ECR 777, [1980] 1 CMLR 25.
158   Case 17/74 *Transocean Marine Paint v Commission* [1974] ECR 1063, [1974] 2 CMLR 459.
159   Case C-392/95 *Parliament v Council*, Judgment of 10 June 1997.

The effects of the Regulation were allowed to remain in place on grounds of legal certainty and because the Court wished to avoid any discontinuity in the harmonisation of national rules on visas.

A declaration of invalidity, *per se*, will often be insufficient to redress the legal position. In the case of a finding of a failure to act, it is important, for example, that an institution be required to take positive measures to comply with the judgment. Similarly, where a temporal limitation has been placed upon a finding of invalidity, it is axiomatic that the institutions be placed under a positive duty to enact a replacement measure.

Article 176 [*233*] EC. The Institution or Institutions whose act has been declared void or whose failure to act has been declared contrary to this Treaty shall be required to take the necessary measures to comply with the judgment of the Court of Justice.

The obligation shall not affect any obligation which may result from the application of the second paragraph of Article 215 [*288*].

This Article shall also apply to the ECB.

Article 176 [*233*] EC requires EC Institutions not simply to remedy their position vis-à-vis other parties to the dispute in hand, it imposes a further obligation requiring them to examine all the legal implications of a judgment and to adjust their position accordingly. This duty does not extend as far, however, as allowing the Court to require the institution to adopt a specific course of action.

Case T-227/95 AssiDomän Kraft Products v Commission, Judgment of 10 July 1997

In 1993 in the *Wood pulp* judgment the Court annulled a Commission Decision finding that forty three wood pulp producers had engaged in a price fixing cartel.[160] The action had been brought by 26 of the producers. Nine Swedish producers, who had not participated in the original action, claimed that the Decision no longer applied to them and that they should be reimbursed the fines

---

[160] Joined Cases C-89/85, C-104/85, C-114/85, C-116/85, C-117/85 and C-125-129/85 *Ahlström Osakeyhtiö v Commission* [1993] ECR I-1307.

imposed upon them. The CFI found that the Decision did not bind third parties generally. It did consider, first, however, whether Article 176 [233] EC imposed a duty upon the Commission to re-evaluate its findings. Secondly it considered whether it could make an order requiring the Commission to refund the fines.

69.The wording of Article 176 of the Treaty does not support the conclusion that the obligation referred to in that provision is restricted solely to the legal positions of the parties to the dispute which gave rise to the judgment in question. Thus it cannot be automatically ruled out that the measures that the institution concerned must adopt may, in exceptional cases, extend beyond the specific context of the dispute which resulted in the judgment of annulment in order to eradicate the effects of the illegalities found in that judgment (see to this effect Joined Cases 97/86, 193/86, 99/86 and 215/86 *Asteris and Others v Commission* [1988] ECR 2181, paragraphs 28 to 31).

70. Such an approach has been adopted by the Court in the context of Article 34 of the ECSC Treaty, which imposes on the institution concerned obligations similar to those laid down by Article 176 of the EC Treaty. The Court stated in [Joined Cases 42/59 and 49/59 *Snupat v High Authority* [1961] ECR 53] that the High Authority was required, following a judgment in which it had been held that an administrative act granting the applicant benefits in the form of exemptions was unlawful, to re-examine its previous position with regard to the legality of those exemptions and to consider whether similar decisions adopted previously, in favour of other undertakings, could be retained having regard to the principles laid down in that judgment. Furthermore, it could in certain circumstances be required under the principle of legality to revoke those decisions. ...

71. Three findings are relevant to establishing whether that case-law can be applied in this case. First, the *Wood pulp* judgment annuls part of an act made up of a number of individual decisions which were adopted on completion of the same administrative procedure. Secondly, not only were the applicants in this case addressees of that same act, but they were fined for alleged infringements of Article 85 of the Treaty which the *Wood pulp* judgment set aside in relation to the addressees of the act who had brought an action under Article 173 of the Treaty. Thirdly, the individual decisions adopted in relation to the applicants in this case are, in their view, based on the same findings of fact and the same economic and legal analyses as those declared invalid by the judgment.

72. Accordingly, the institution concerned may be required under Article 176 of the Treaty to consider, pursuant to a request made within a reasonable period, whether it needs to take measures in relation not only to the successful parties but also to the addressees of that act who did not bring an action for annulment. Where the effect of a judgment of the Court of Justice is to set aside a finding that Article 85(1) of the Treaty was infringed, on the ground that the concerted practice complained of was not proved, it would be inconsistent with the principle of legality for the Commission not to have a duty to examine its initial decision in relation to another party to the same concerted practice based on identical facts.

.....

74. The Court of Justice has held that, in order to comply with a judgment of that kind and to implement it fully, the institution concerned is required to have regard not only to the operative part of the judgment but also to the grounds which led to the judgment and constitute its essential basis, in so far as they are necessary to determine the exact meaning of what is stated in the operative part. It is those grounds which, on the one hand, identify the precise provision held to be illegal and, on the other, disclose the specific reasons which underlie the finding of illegality contained in the operative part and which the institution concerned must take into account when replacing the measure annulled (*Asteris and Others v Commission*, paragraph 27).

.....

84. Accordingly, even if those documents might constitute the basis for establishing, as against some of the Swedish addressees, the whole or part of the findings in the operative part of the wood pulp decision (see, in that regard, the Opinion of Advocate General Darmon in the case, points 464 to 476), the fact remains that the Court rejected the main evidence relied on by the Commission against all the addressees of the decision to prove that there had been concertation on prices and, therefore, that Article 85 of the Treaty had been infringed. In this respect, the judgment clearly has the potential to affect the Commission's findings relating to the Swedish addressees.

85. The Court finds, therefore, without there being any need to consider the effect which the Court of Justice's findings in paragraph 40 et seq. of the *Wood pulp* judgment, regarding the defects in the statement of objections, may have on establishing that the Swedish addressees committed an infringement by concerting on transaction prices, that, following the applicants' request, the Commission was required 'in accordance with Article 176 of the Treaty and the principle of good administration' to review, in the light of the grounds of the *Wood pulp* judgment, the legality of the wood pulp decision in so far as it relates to the Swedish addressees and to determine on the basis of such an examination whether it was appropriate to repay the fines.

.....

88. In so far as the Commission were to conclude, on the basis of a re-examination of the wood pulp decision pursuant to Article 176 of the Treaty, that certain findings to the effect that the Swedish addressees had infringed Article 85 of the Treaty were unlawful, it is appropriate, at this stage in the Court's reasoning, to examine the Commission's arguments that it was, moreover, neither obliged, nor indeed entitled, to repay the fines.

.....

90. In that regard, it is helpful to recall the case-law regarding withdrawal of administrative acts conferring individual rights or similar benefits upon the addressee.

The Court has acknowledged that the Community institutions are entitled, subject to the principles of the protection of legitimate expectations and of legal certainty, to withdraw, on the ground that it is unlawful, a decision granting a benefit to its addressee (Joined Cases 7/56 and 3/57 to 7/57 *Algera and Others v Common Assembly* [1957] ECR 39, Case 14/81 *Alpha Steel v Commission* [1982] ECR 749 and Case 15/85 *Consorzio Cooperative d'Abruzzo v Commission* [1987] ECR 1005).

91. That case-law applies a fortiori in situations where, as in this case, the decision in question merely imposes burdens or penalties on the individual. In such cases, the Commission is not precluded from withdrawing the decision by considerations relating to the protection of the legitimate expectations and vested rights of the person to whom the decision was addressed.

92. Accordingly, if the Commission were to conclude, on the basis of a re-examination of the wood pulp decision in the light of the grounds of the *Wood pulp* judgment, that certain findings to the effect that the Swedish addressees had infringed Article 85 of the Treaty were unlawful, it would be authorized to refund the fines paid in accordance with those findings. In that case, if Article 176 were not to be deprived of all its practical effect, the Commission would also be required, in accordance with the principles of legality and of good administration, to repay those fines, as they would have no legal basis.

.....

96. In their last two heads of claim, the applicants seek an order requiring the Commission to take all the necessary measures to comply with the *Wood pulp* judgment and, in particular, to refund, together with interest, part of the fines paid by them.

97. Those heads of claim, which seek the issue of directions to the Commission, are inadmissible, since the Community judicature, when exercising the jurisdiction to annul acts conferred on it by Article 173 of the Treaty, is not entitled to issue directions to the Community institutions (see, for example *Consorzio Cooperative d'Abruzzo v Commission*, paragraph 18).

98. Article 176 of the Treaty provides for a division of powers between the judicial and administrative authorities, under which it is for the institution whose act has been declared void to determine what measures are required in order to comply with a judgment annulling an act, such as the *Wood pulp* judgment, and to exercise, subject to review by the Community judicature, the discretion which it enjoys in that regard while respecting the operative part and grounds of the judgment which it is required to comply with and the provisions of Community law (*Asteris and Others v Commission*).

99. The decision whether or not to withdraw the wood pulp decision, possibly in part, is in the first place a matter for the Commission. The Court cannot take the place of the Commission, which is required to carry out that assessment pursuant to Article 176.

Further Reading

Arnull, A. 'Private Applicants and the Action for Annulment under Article 173 of the EC Treaty' (1995) 32 *Common Market Law Review* 7.

Craig, P. 'Compensation in Public Law' (1980) 96 *Law Quarterly Review* 413

----- 'Legality, Standing and Substantive Review in Community Law' (1994) 14 *Oxford Journal of Legal Studies* 507

Greaves, R. 'The Nature and Binding Effect of Decisions Under Article 189 EC' (1996) 21 *European Law Review* 3

Harding, C. 'The Choice of Court Problem in Cases of Non-Contractual Liability under EEC Law' (1979) 16 *Common Market Law Review* 389

Hartley, T. *The Foundations of European Community Law* (1994, 3rd Edition, Clarendon, Oxford) Chapters 11-17

Hedemann-Robinson, M. 'Article 173 EC, General Community Measures and *Locus Standi* for Private Persons: Still a Cause for Individual Concern?' (1996) 2 *Public Law* 127

Heukels, T. & McDonnell, A. (eds.) *The Action for Damages in Community Law* (1997, Asser Instituut, The Hague)

Schermers, H., Heukels, T. & Mead, P. (eds.) *Non-Contractual Liability of the European Communities* (1988, Martijnus Nijhoff, Dordrecht)

Usher, J. 'Individual Concern in General Legislation - 10 years On' (1994) 19 *European Law Review* 636

Wils, W. 'Concurrent Liability of the Community and a Member State' (1992) 17 *European Law Review* 191

Index